T0178539

Lecture Notes in Computer Science 12564

FoLLI Publications on Logic, Language and Information
Subline of Lectures Notes in Computer Science

More information about this subseries at http://www.springer.com/series/7407

Dun Deng · Fenrong Liu ·
Mingming Liu · Dag Westerståhl (Eds.)

Monotonicity in Logic and Language

Second Tsinghua Interdisciplinary Workshop
on Logic, Language and Meaning, TLLM 2020
Beijing, China, December 17–20, 2020
Proceedings

 Springer

Editors
Dun Deng
Department of Chinese Languages
and Literatures
Tsinghua University
Beijing, China

Mingming Liu
Department of Foreign Languages
and Literatures
Tsinghua University
Beijing, China

Fenrong Liu 🆔
Department of Philosophy
Tsinghua University
Beijing, China

Dag Westerståhl
Department of Philosophy
Stockholm University
Stockholm, Sweden

ISSN 0302-9743   ISSN 1611-3349   (electronic)
Lecture Notes in Computer Science
ISBN 978-3-662-62842-3   ISBN 978-3-662-62843-0   (eBook)
https://doi.org/10.1007/978-3-662-62843-0

LNCS Sublibrary: SL1 – Theoretical Computer Science and General Issues

This Springer imprint is published by the registered company Springer-Verlag GmbH, DE part of
Springer Nature.
The registered company address is: Heidelberger Platz 3, 14197 Berlin, Germany

Preface

Monotonicity, in various forms, is a pervasive phenomenon in logic, linguistics, computer science, and related areas. In theoretical linguistics, monotonicity and related lattice-theoretic notions such as additivity show up as semantic properties of intra-sentential environments, which determine the syntactic distribution of a class of terms robustly attested across languages called Negative Polarity Items (NPIs), such as English *any* in (1). Monotonicity is also relevant to a large array of semantic phenomena, such as the interpretation of donkey pronouns as in (2), plural definites as in (3), plural morphemes, and so on. It also plays a role for pragmatic inferences such as scalar implicatures, illustrated by the interpretative difference of disjunction in (4).

(1) a. *Somebody bought any cookies.
    b. Nobody bought any cookies.
(2) a. Every farmer who owns a donkey beats it. (universal interpretation of *it*)
    b. No farmer who owns a donkey beats it. (existential interpretation of *it*)
(3) a. Mary has read the files on her desk. (universal interpretation of *the files*)
    b. Mary has not read the files on her desk. (existential interpretation of *the files*)
(4) a. If everything goes well, we'll hire either Mary or Sue. (exclusive interpretation of *or*)
    b. If we hire either Mary or Sue, everything will go well. (inclusive interpretation of *or*)

In logic and mathematics, a function f between pre-ordered sets is monotone or increasing (antitone or decreasing) if $x \leq y$ implies $f(x) \leq f(y)$ ($f(y) \leq f(x)$). Monotonicity guarantees the existence of fixed points (points x such that $f(x) = x$) and the well-formedness of inductive definitions, and logical languages with expressive means for talking about fixed points, such as first-order fixed point logic or the modal μ-calculus, constitute a growing area of study in logic and computer science. Also, monotonicity is closely tied to reasoning, in formal as well as natural languages. Corresponding to the semantic properties of monotonicity and antitonicity there is the syntactic property of (positive or negative) polarity. Monotonicity reasoning, which involves replacement of predicates in syntactic contexts of given polarity, is a simple yet surprisingly powerful mode of inference. Starting in the 1980s, the idea of Natural Logic, comprising algorithms for polarity marking and formal calculi for monotonicity reasoning, is still a very active research area. Likewise, much of the current study of complete systems for extended syllogistic reasoning formally exploits patterns of monotonicity.

The workshop – originally scheduled at Tsinghua University in April 2020, but, due to the current COVID-19 pandemic, moved to December 17–20, 2020, online – brings together researchers from all over the world working on monotonicity and related properties from different fields and perspectives. There were around 40 submissions of abstracts of papers, 18 of which are presented at the workshop, which in addition has 5 invited talks and 2 tutorials. 12 of the full articles made it, after a careful blind-review process (usually 3 reviews per abstract, and similarly for the full papers), into these proceedings. We would like to formally and sincerely express our gratitude to all the colleagues for their support in reviewing the submissions. Those papers cover a wide range of topics where monotonicity is discussed in the context of logic, causality, belief revision, quantification, polarity, syntax, comparatives, and various semantic phenomena in particular languages.

This was the second edition of the workshop series Interdisciplinary Workshops on Logic, Language, and Meaning held at Tsinghua since its successful debut in April 2019. It is our intention to continue the event and keep exploring fascinating aspects of the interface between logic and language. We hereby invite everyone who is interested to participate in our future events.

November 2020

Dun Deng
Fenrong Liu
Mingming Liu
Dag Westerståhl

Organization

Tutorials

Jakub Szymanik (Monotonicity in logic)	University of Amsterdam
Gennaro Chierchia (Monotonicity in language)	Harvard University

Invited Speakers

Gennaro Chierchia	Harvard University
Jo-wang Lin	Academia Sinica
Larry Moss	Indiana University Bloomington
Floris Roelofsen	University of Amsterdam
Jakub Szymanik	University of Amsterdam

Program Committee

Johan van Benthem	Stanford University and Tsinghua University
Dun Deng (Co-chair)	Tsinghua University
Thomas Icard III	Stanford University
Xuping Li	Zhejiang University
Mingming Liu (Co-chair)	Tsinghua University
Larry Moss	Indiana University Bloomington
Haihua Pan	The Chinese University of Hong Kong
Stanley Peters	Stanford University
Dylan W.-T. Tsai	National Tsinghua University
Yingying Wang	Hunan University
Dag Westerståhl (Co-chair)	Stockholm University and Tsinghua University

Organizing Committee

Fenrong Liu (Chair)	Tsinghua University
Yinlin Guan	Tsinghua University
Zhiqiang Sun	Tsinghua University
Xiaoan Wu	Tsinghua University
Jialiang Yan	Tsinghua University

Sponsors

Tsinghua University – University of Amsterdam Joint Research Center for Logic
Department of Philosophy, Tsinghua University
Department of Foreign Languages and Literatures, Tsinghua University
Department of Chinese Languages and Literatures, Tsinghua University
Department of Philosophy, Stockholm University

Contents

New Logical Perspectives
on Monotonicity

Johan van Benthem[1,2,3] and Fenrong Liu[1,3(✉)]

[1] University of Amsterdam, Amsterdam, The Netherlands
johan@stanford.edu
[2] Stanford University, Stanford, USA
[3] Tsinghua University, Beijing, China
fenrong@tsinghua.edu.cn

Abstract. Monotonicity-based inference is a fundamental notion in the logical semantics of natural language, and also in logic in general. Starting in generalized quantifier theory, we distinguish three senses of the notion, study their relations, and use these to connect monotonicity to logics of model change. At the end we return to natural language and consider monotonicity inference in linguistic settings with vocabulary for various forms of change. While we mostly raise issues in this paper, we do make a number of new observations backing up our distinctions.

Keywords: Monotonicity · Generalized quantifiers · Model change

1 Varieties of Monotonicity for Generalized Quantifiers

Basic Patterns. Monotonicity is a property that is used extensively in linguistics and logic. Many valid reasoning patterns involve monotonicity, in particular with sentences containing generalized quantifiers. Here are four possible cases with a binary generalized quantifier Q and two predicate arguments A and B:

↑MON	$Q(A, B)$ and $A \subseteq C$, then $Q(C, B)$
↓MON	$Q(A, B)$ and $C \subseteq A$, then $Q(C, B)$
MON↑	$Q(A, B)$ and $B \subseteq C$, then $Q(A, C)$
MON↓	$Q(A, B)$ and $C \subseteq B$, then $Q(A, C)$

For instance, the universal quantifier "all" is downward monotonic in its left argument and upward in its right argument, thus exemplifying the type ↓MON↑. If we want to stress possible dependence of the quantifier on a total domain of discourse D, the binary notation $Q(A, B)$ will be extended to a ternary $Q_D(A, B)$.[1]

Three Senses. While the preceding definitions seem clear, intuitive explanations of monotonicity inference in natural language sometimes appeal to slightly,

---

[1] An extensive overview of monotonicity inference with generalized quantifiers can be found in (Peters and Westerståhl 2006).

© Springer-Verlag GmbH Germany, part of Springer Nature 2020
D. Deng et al. (Eds.): TLLM 2020, LNCS 12564, pp. 1–12, 2020.
https://doi.org/10.1007/978-3-662-62843-0_1

but subtly different notions. This note identifies three possible interpretations, and then goes on to discuss these in a variety of logical settings, raising new issues in the process. We will focus on upward monotonicity in what follows, though our analysis also applies to downward monotonicity.

To introduce what we have in mind, consider the following three examples:

(1a) Some boys dance.   (1b) Some people dance.

The upward monotonic step from (1a) to (1b) may be called *Predicate Replacement* in the same domain of objects. The more specific (stronger) predicate "boys" (A) is replaced by the more general (weaker) predicate "people" (C).

Next, consider a case that feels intuitively different, where the *same* predicate changes its extension. For a long time, whales were thought of as fish, but then it was found they are mammals, and the range of "mammal" was extended.

(2a) Some mammals (excluding whales) live over a hundred years.
(2b) Some mammals (including whales) live over a hundred years.

Here, a predicate acquires more members in the same domain. Call this view of monotonicity *Extension Increase*. At this stage, however, we have a distinction without a difference. Predicate Replacement and Extension Increase are the same for quantifiers viewed as set relations. But as we will see later, the distinction starts making sense when we have both syntax and semantics.[2]

But there is yet a stronger form of monotonicity, where the domain itself can be enlarged. Suppose that we are first talking about Asians, and next about all people in the World. The following monotonicity inference is valid:

(3a) Some musicians are Chinese (in Asia).
(3b) Some musicians are Chinese (in the whole World).

Let us call this form of monotonicity *Domain Enlargement*. The predicate "musician" does not change its extension in the old Asian domain, but we now consider its full extension in the new World domain. Of course, since "some" satisfies both Extension Increase and Domain Enlargement, we can even combine the two. The resulting Enlargement Monotonicity is illustrated in the following diagram:

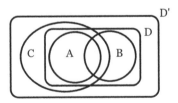

---

[2] There is also an intuitive temporal aspect to the whales example, where extensions change with the passage of time. Such more intensional aspects of monotonicity inference will be considered briefly at the end of this paper.

While the distinction between keeping the domain fixed or extending it for monotonicity seems intuitive, it, too, collapses – when we accept an assumption called *Extension* that is commonly made for generalized quantifiers:

EXT   if $A, B \subseteq D \subseteq D'$, then $Q_D(A, B)$ iff $Q_{D'}(A, B)$

Fact 1. *With EXT, upward monotonic Predicate Replacement (I) and Enlargement Monotonicity (II) are equivalent conditions on quantifiers.*

Proof. We only consider upward monotonicity in the left argument. *From (II) to (I).* Predicate replacement is clearly a special case of Enlargement Monotonicity when the domain does not change. *From (I) to (II).* Let $Q_D(A, B)$ and $A \subseteq C$, and $C, D \subseteq D'$. By EXT, we have $Q_{D'}(A, B)$, and then by (I), $Q_{D'}(C, B)$. $\square$

Shrinking domains with downward monotonic inference gives a similar result. However, EXT is crucial to all of this.

Doing Without EXT. With quantifiers whose meaning involves the domain D in an essential way, monotonicity becomes a much richer notion, where Conservativity is no longer a prominent constraint. We will only illustrate this here, since these quantifiers seem much less studied. Consider the quantifier *"many A are B"* in one plausible sense of relative proportion:

$$\frac{|A \cap B|}{|A|} > \frac{|B|}{|D|}$$

where D is the whole domain.[3] It is illustrated in the following diagram, where the numbers of objects in the different zones have been marked by x, m, k, n:

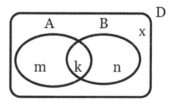

According to the above definition, we have

$$\frac{k}{m+k} > \frac{k+n}{m+n+k+x}, \quad or\ equivalently,\ kx > mn$$

Now our earlier distinction between keeping the domain fixed, or extending it makes sense. Also, the notion of monotonicity acquires new options.

Clearly, MON↑ in its standard sense can fail when we enlarge B with objects in D outside of A that increase the frequency of B in D, but not in A. However, the new setting allows for more subtle forms of monotonicity.

---

[3] In particular, with this definition, it is never true that D-relatively many A are D. We will not discuss other variants of relative "many" here.

Here is a natural candidate, keeping the A's fixed. If we enlarge B *inside of A only*, we regain MON↑. To illustrate why, just add one object of A to B, raising k to $k+1$ while lowering m to $m-1$. Then we have

$$\frac{k+1}{m-1+k+1} = \left(\frac{k}{m+k} + \frac{1}{m+k}\right) > \frac{k+1+n}{m+n+k+x}$$

Next, consider domain extension. Clearly just increasing B can make *"many A are B"* false. But we can also enlarge just $A \cap B$, putting a new B-object s in the new A. This time, *"many A are B"* remains true since it implies

$$\frac{k+1}{m+k+1} > \frac{k+1+n}{m+k+1+n+x} \quad^4$$

Merging Logic and Counting. There is no general theory of types of monotonicity in this extended setting for quantificational reasoning. Note that monotonicity as discussed here fits naturally with qualitative perspectives on numerical formulas with addition, multiplication and other elementary operations, giving us global information about how functions grow as argument values change.[5] Thus, the right format for this broader setting may be a system of 'counting logic' mixing set-theoretic and arithmetical components. This would fit with the intuitive idea that quantifiers are at heart about counting, so that actual reasoning with quantifiers may well be a mix of just this kind.[6]

Monotonicity Calculus. In practice, upward and downward monotonic inferences are equally important. Syntactically, these are triggered by *positive* and *negative* ocurrences, respectively, of the predicate replaced in the inference. And since quantifiers can occur embedded in further linguistic constructions, a calculus is needed for computing positive and negative occurrences of predicates inside complex expressions. For instance, in "every pot has a lid", "pot" is negative, supporting a downward inference, while the embedded "lid" is positive, supporting an upward inference. Taken together, it follows, e.g., that "every iron pot has a cover". A precise Monotonicity Calculus keeping track of positive and negative syntactic occurrences can be stated in terms of a categorial grammar for constructing complex expressions, cf. (van Benthem 1991). While details of this system are not relevant to us here, its existence suggests looking at logical systems that contain quantifiers to take our analysis a step further.

2   Monotonicity in First-Order Logic

Two Senses Revisited. In first-order logic, a pilot system for a mathematical theory of generalized quantifiers, truth values of formulas depend on domains of

---

[4] This inequality is equivalent to $kx + x > mn$ which is implied by the earlier $kx > mn$.

[5] A realistic concrete use of monotonicity in mathematics is the convergence test for improper integrals discussed in (Icard et al. 2017).

[6] In this combined calculus, monotonicity applies to both *set inclusion* for denotations and *greater-than* for numbers. The former is a type-lifting of the latter, and many more complex type-theoretic lifts support monotonicity reasoning (van Benthem 1991). However, beyond these, in natural language monotonicity can apply to many orderings that are sui generis: conceptual, temporal, spatial, and so on. Can the style of analysis in this paper be generalized to cover these?.

models. In other words, EXT no longer holds when first-order syntax for quantifiers is taken into account. Two notions of monotonicity may be distinguished, where again we focus on the upward case to simplify the exposition:

(Mon-inf)   From $\varphi(P)$ and $\forall x(P(x) \to Q(x))$, it follows that $\varphi(Q/P)$, where $\varphi(Q/P)$ is the result of replacing each occurrence of P in φ by Q.

(Mon-sem)   If $M, s \models \varphi(P)$ and $M \equiv_P^+ M'$ (i.e., M and M' are the same model except for the interpretation of P, and $I(P) \subseteq I'(P)$), then $M', s \models \varphi(P)$.

These correspond to the earlier Predicate Replacement and Extension Increase.

Fact 2. *Inferential monotonicity is equivalent to semantic monotonicity.*

Proof. From (Mon-sem) to (Mon-inf). Suppose, for any model M and assignment s, that $M, s \models \varphi(P)$ and $M, s \models \forall x(P(x) \to Q(x))$. Now define a new model M' which is like M except that $I'(P) = [[Q]]^M$. Clearly $M \equiv_P^+ M'$, so by Mon-sem, we have $M', s \models \varphi(P)$. By one direction of the standard Predicate Substitution Lemma for first-order logic, it then follows that $M, s \models \varphi(Q/P)$.

From (Mon-inf) to (Mon-sem). Suppose that $M, s \models \varphi(P)$ and $M \equiv_P^+ M'$. Take a new predicate letter Q not occurring in $\varphi(P)$, and set $I(Q) = I'(Q) = [[P]]^{M'}$. Then in the model M, s, the two conditions for Mon-inf are satisfied, and therefore, $\varphi(Q/P)$ is true in M, s. But this implies, by the converse direction of the Predicate Substitution Lemma, that $M', s \models \varphi(P)$.   □

The second half of this proof requires the availability of fresh predicates. We suspect that the above equivalence fails for first-order logic with a finite vocabulary while it still holds for subsystems such as monadic FOL.

For the earlier third sense of Domain Enlargement, see Sect. 3 below.

Single vs. Multiple Occurrences. In actual inferences based on Mon-inf, it is natural to focus on a single occurrence of the predicate P. Typically, this upward form is licensed when this occurrence of P is syntactically positive in φ. But note that the same P may also have negative occurrence in φ. For instance, in $P \wedge \neg(P \wedge Q)$, the first occurence of P is positive, supporting a MON↑ inference, but the second occurrence is negative, supporting a MON↓ inference.[7] However, our discussion also covers inferences with multiple replacements.

Interpolation and Monotonicity Calculus. Semantic monotonicity jumps from one model to another along the relation $\equiv_P^+$. A related general notion of transfer between models is this: φ *entails* ψ *along* R if, whenever MRN and $M \models \varphi$, then $N \models \psi$. This notion was introduced in (Barwise and van Benthem 1999), which also proves the following version of Lyndon's Theorem for FOL:

Fact 3. *The following statements are equivalent for first-order formulas φ, ψ: (a) φ entails ψ along $\equiv_P^+$, (b) there exists a formula α containing only positive syntactic occurrences of P such that $\varphi \models \alpha \models \psi$.*

---

[7] Many inferences are intuitively about single occurrences of parts of expressions. But some require comparing coordinated occurrences, like in the logical rule of Contraction, where two identical premises can be contracted to just one.

The required formulas α are generated by the grammar

$$P\mathbf{x} \mid (\neg)Q\mathbf{x}\,(Q \neq P) \mid \varphi \wedge \varphi \mid \varphi \vee \varphi \mid \exists x \varphi \mid \forall x \varphi.$$

Fact 3 can be seen as a completeness result for the monotonicity calculus of first-order logic. But to make this apply to generalized quantifier theory, one needs similar results for the logics $FOL(\mathbf{Q})$ consisting of first-order logic with added generalized quantifiers. This has been done in (Makovsky and Tulipani, 1977), using suitable extensions of the basic model-theoretic notions for FOL.[8]

Semantics that Fit Monotonicity Inference. Here is another way of phrasing the preceding completeness issue. The monotonicity calculus is a proof system for practical reasoning. Is there a natural semantics for which it is complete? Interesting answers have been given, cf. the proposals considered in (Icard et al. 2017). In addition, here is a straightforward modal perspective.

In *modal state semantics* for first-order logic, the variable assignments of Tarski semantics are viewed as abstract states, and quantifiers $\exists x$ are then interpreted using arbitrary accessibility relations R_x between states. The result of this widening of standard models is a decidable modal sublogic of FOL which blocks all valid first-order consequences except for monotonicity and aggregation of universal statements under conjunction. To block the latter, a well-known move in modal logic is a step from binary accessibility relations between states to *neighborhood models* with state-to-set neighborhood relations. A straightforward neighborhood generalization of state models for FOL will validate essentially just the monotonicity inferences. For further details, and connections to generalized quantifiers, cf. (Andréka et al. 2017).

3   Logics for Monotonicity-Related Model Change

Intuitively, the third and second sense of monotonicity in Sect. 1 involve model change. In recent years, families of logics have been studied that analyze the effects of changing models, for the purposes of information update, world change, game play, or other concrete scenarios. These logics can code our earlier reasoning about monotonicity, while at the same time, they extend practical monotonicity inference to new settings. In this section we discuss some connections.

Predicate Extension Modalities. For an illustration, take the case of upward predicate monotonicity, and add the following modality to first-order logic[9]

$$\langle \equiv_P^+ \rangle \varphi \quad \text{for:} \quad \varphi \text{ is true in some } \equiv_P^+\text{-extension of the current model.}$$

With the dual universal modality in the language, upward semantic monotonicity can now be formulated as an object-level validity of the system:

$$\varphi(P) \to [\equiv_P^+]\varphi(P)$$

---

[8] Extensions to richer type logics of relevance to natural language seem an open problem, cf. (van Benthem 1991) on the case of the Boolean Lambda Calculus.

[9] This device has not been studied yet in the literature, to the best of our knowledge, but as we shall see momentarily, it is close to second-order logic.

As another example, the fact that positive occurrence of P in φ implies upward monotonicity is expressible by a set of valid implications in this language.

The new modality is very powerful, as it can express existential second-order quantifiers. To see this, take a first-order sentence defining discrete linear orders with a beginning but no end, (i). Next, with a unary predicate P, the formula

$$\forall x \neg Px \wedge \neg \langle \equiv_P^+ \rangle (\exists x Px \wedge \forall x (Px \rightarrow \exists y (y < x \wedge Py)))$$

says there is no non-empty subset of the domain without a minimal element, (ii). The conjunction of (i) and (ii) defines the standard natural numbers, whose complete predicate logic (in a rich enough vocabulary) is non-arithmetical.

The expressive power of the monotonicity modality can be much less on fragments of FOL, representing more elementary settings for monotonicity reasoning.

Fact 4. *Adding* $\langle \equiv_P^+ \rangle$ *to monadic FOL adds no expressive power at all.*

Proof sketch. The proof is by a syntactic normal form argument in the style of (van Benthem et al. 2020). Each monadic first-order formula is equivalent to a disjunction of the following form:

(i) global state descriptions that list which of the 2^k possible true/false combinations for k unary predicates are exemplified in the model,

conjoined with (ii) local state descriptions for a finite set of variables. Prefixing a modality $\langle \equiv_P^+ \rangle$ distributes over the initial disjunction, and we are left with the modality over the described conjunctions. With this complete explicit syntactic description available, it is easy to read off what is expressed in terms of conditions that can be formulated entirely in monadic FOL.

Instead of an algorithm for deriving these conditions, we give an example:

$$\langle \equiv_P^+ \rangle (\neg \exists x (Px \wedge Qx) \wedge \exists x (Px \wedge \neg Qx) \wedge \exists x (\neg Px \wedge Qx) \wedge \neg \exists x (\neg Px \wedge \neg Qx)$$
$$\wedge Px \wedge \neg Qx) \text{ is equivalent with the monadic formula } \neg \exists x (Px \wedge Qx) \wedge$$
$$\exists x (\neg Px \wedge Qx) \wedge \exists x ((Px \wedge \neg Qx) \vee (\neg Px \wedge \neg Qx)) \wedge Px \wedge \neg Qx^{10}$$

A similar closure argument will work for monadic first-order logic with identity.

However, adding the monotonicity modality to another weak decidable fragment of FOL already yields much higher complexity. The modal 'fact change logic' of (Thompson 2020) adds a modality $\langle +p \rangle \varphi$ to basic modal logic saying that making p true in the current world makes φ true there. Under the standard translation of modal logic into first-order logic, this becomes a fragment of the language of FOL plus a special case of the modality $\langle \equiv_P^+ \rangle$. Fact change logic is still axiomatizable, but unlike the basic modal logic, it is undecidable.

Domain Enlargement. The third sense of monotonicity involved Domain Enlargement. This suggests adding a modality $\langle \subseteq \rangle \varphi$ to FOL saying that φ is true in some extension of the current model.[11] This logic encodes the usual facts such as preservation of existential first-order formulas under model extensions. But again, this system in general has very high complexity. For instance, it can

---

[10] This can be simplified to $\neg \exists x (Px \wedge Qx) \wedge \exists x (\neg Px \wedge Qx) \wedge \exists x \neg Qx \wedge Px \wedge \neg Qx$.

[11] Enlargement Monotonicity is then expressed by modal combinations like $\langle \subseteq \rangle \langle \equiv_P^+ \rangle$.

define that a first-order formula φ is satisfiable, by taking a fresh unary predicate letter P not interpreted in the current model, and stating that φ can be made true relativized to P: $\langle \subseteq \rangle (\varphi)^P$. As before, fragments are better behaved, and of particular interest are stepwise addition (or deletion) of objects in a current model, (Renardel de Lavalette 2001), in line with intuitive reasoning about diagrams with generalized quantifiers. We do not pursue this topic here.

Information Update Meets Monotonicity Inference. A final setting for model change lets inference steps meet with semantic information updates, a natural combination in practical problem solving (van Benthem 2011). For a concrete setting, in 'public announcement logic' (PAL), modalities $[!\varphi]\psi$ express that ψ will be true at the current world after original model has been updated with the information that φ is true. For details on the logic PAL, see (Baltag and Renne 2016). What upward monotonicity inferences are allowed here?

There are two places where these inferences can occur. First it is easy to see that the 'postcondition' ψ of formulas $[!\varphi]\psi$ allows for standard monotonic inference to $[!\varphi](\psi \vee \alpha)$, and similar weakenings are allowed for positive occurrences of p in ψ that are not in the scope of dynamic modalities contained in ψ.

But with p inside the announced φ, things are more complicated. $[!\varphi]\psi$ does not imply $[!(\varphi \vee \alpha)]\psi$: such a monotonic replacement may give *weaker information*, true in more worlds, changing the original update to a larger submodel where earlier effects can be blocked. For instance, for atomic facts p, the formula $[!p]Kp$ is valid in PAL: after receiving the information that p an agent will know that p. However, the formula $[!(p \vee q)]Kp$ with a weaker announcement is obviously not valid. In contrast, monotonicity in the postcondition does tell us that from stronger announced content weaker facts can become known. For instance, $[!(p \wedge q)]Kq$ is valid: we can also learn parts of what was announced.[12]

Dynamic Monotonicity. But actually, a more dynamic form of monotonicity inference may be natural in the PAL environment, triggered by a dynamic take on inclusion viewed as a relation between informational actions. Let us say that an announcement (not a proposition) $!\varphi$ *entails* an announcement $!\psi$ if

the implication $[!\varphi]\alpha \leftrightarrow [!\varphi][!\psi]\alpha$ is valid in PAL for all formulas α.

One can think of this in Gricean terms, where stating $!\psi$ after $!\varphi$ would not be appropriate, as it adds no information. Viewed as an inclusion of actions, this sort of connection can trigger inferences. The logic PAL contains information about what can be deduced from entailments between announcements.[13] This is just one way of thinking. There are other natural notions of dynamic entailment – but we must leave the study of dynamic monotonicity to another occasion.

---

[12] It is easy to see with simple concrete examples of PAL update that downward monotonicity fails as well for announced formulas: $[!\varphi]\psi$ does not imply $[!(\varphi \wedge \alpha)]\psi$.

[13] The exact information content of an announcement $!\varphi$ is that φ *was* true before the announcement (the caveat is needed since announcing an epistemic statement φ might change its truth value), and if ψ subsequently adds no new information, this means that the $!\psi$ update does not change the model. Thus, a way of taking dynamic entailment is as a valid implication $Y\varphi \rightarrow \psi$, where Y is a one-step backward-looking temporal operator beyond the language of PAL, cf. (Sack 2007).

All this leads to a question. A *Lyndon-style preservation theorem* capturing semantic monotonicity in PAL formulas in syntactic terms remains to be found. However, this is not yet a precise question. To understand what might be involved here, note that moving to a larger submodel through a weaker update does preserve some earlier postconditions ψ, namely those that are *existentially definable*. Thus, a Lyndon result in the dynamic PAL setting may have to simultaneously analyze monotonicity and preservation under model extensions. Also, since we are in an intensional setting with formulas referring to different models, the inclusion triggers for monotonicity inferences need some care. Just inclusion in an initial model need not suffice for justifying replacement in postconditions referring to updated models: we must have triggers of the right strength, or in semantic terms: inclusion of denotations in all relevant models.[14]

4   Back to Natural Language

Dynamic logics for model change are useful tools for formalizing the metatheory of monotonicity and much else besides. But they can also model concrete inferences in a setting of instructions for change. In this final section, we briefly list some possible repercussions of the preceding technical topics when we return to generalized quantifiers in natural language, the area we started with.

Linguistics Expressions of Change. Descriptions of changes in the world or instructions for achieving these changes occur explicitly in natural language. For instance, the dynamic modality of public announcement logic suggests analogies with the verb *"to learn"*, which describes a change in information state. The earlier technical observations about PAL then suggest linguistic questions about inferences that go with learning. If we view "learn that A" as a description of what the agent comes to know after the learning, A is a postcondition that allows the upward monotonic conclusion "learn that $A \vee B$". But if we take the A to be the content of the message leading to the learning, we are rather talking about an announcement $!A$ where upward inference is not allowed, or at least tricky.

Many action verbs deserve attention here, such as "change", "make", or, closer to our second and third senses of monotonicity: "add", "increase", or "remove". As an example, consider whether the following inference is valid:

(4a) All A are B.
(4b) Increasing the A's is increasing the B's.

---

[14] To make the above questions fully precise, we need to define syntactic polarity of occurrences in PAL formulas, where occurrences inside announced formulas may lack polarity. Also, given the intensional setting for PAL of a universe of many epistemic models connected through updates, the earlier semantic notion of monotonicity can be phrased in a number of ways. Finally, we need not confine ourselves to syntactic properties of single occurrences of predicates. A proper notion of monotonic inference for formulas $[!\varphi]\alpha$ might involve correlated *simultaneous* replacements of proposition letters in both φ and α. We leave these detailed issues for follow-up work. A first exploration of possible Lyndon-style theorems for PAL can be found in (Yin 2020).

Here we see an ambiguity that matches our discussion of various senses of upward monotonicity in Sect. 1. If we increase only the extension of A in some fixed domain, then B might stay the same. But if we add a new object that is A and insist on the premise, then indeed, we have also increased the number of B's.[15] So, there are options for taking proposed inferences in a dynamic setting.[16]

Also, the status of the inclusion premise needs attention. We demonstrate this with our next example. Perhaps most centrally, while classical monotonicity inference focuses on what *is* the case, the dynamic counterpart verb is *"become"*. Inferences with all of these expressions seem to involve intensional phenomena.

Monotonicity Inference and Intensionality. Consider this inference:

(5a) Prime ministers of India are male.
     Indira Gandhi became PM of India.
(5b) Indira Gandhi became male.

This is obviously incorrect. Indira Gandhi's election *falsified* the generalization expressed in the first premise. The point is that the premise is sensitive to moments in time, and can change its truth value as events happen.

We are in familiar more general territory now, monotonicity inference in intensional contexts and modal logics. These generally require modified inclusion statements, modalized to the right degree. Something that would work in all cases is a modalized "strong inclusion" true in all worlds, but the inclusion may also be more specific to the intended conclusion. If prime ministers of India were granted legal emergency powers just before Indira Gandhi's election, then we would be justified in concluding that she acquired such powers, even if that inclusion was not always the case in history. For more on monotonicity inference in the setting of modal logic, we refer to (Aloni 2005) and (Yan and Liu 2020).[17, 18]

These two brief examples may have shown how technical dynamic logics of change connect naturally with linguistic phenomena, in particular, the mono-

---

[15] (Liu and Sun 2020) discuss such inference patterns in the ancient Chinese language.

[16] With this richer linguistic vocabulary in monotonicity reasoning, the more general orderings of Footnote 7 may also come to the fore. Thomas Icard (p.c.) gives the nice example of "The tree is tall. The tree grows. Therefore, the tree is still tall.".

[17] The difference between inclusions locally true in the actual world and inclusions true also in other worlds remains somewhat hidden in common phrasings of upward monotonicity inference as a pattern "from $\varphi(P)$ to $\varphi(P \vee Q)$". The inclusion from P to $P \vee Q$ is universally valid, so usable anywhere.

[18] There are many further intensional aspect to monotonicity inference that we cannot address here. For instance, such inferences seem sensitive to *description*. In the ancient Mohist example that "Your sister is a woman. But loving your sister is not loving a woman", the issue may be under which description we are viewing the loving ('as a relative' vs. 'romantically'). This distinction is widespread. Oedipus killed a man on the road, but did not realize that the man was his father. Did he kill his father? Under one description: yes, under another: no. For many further instances of the role of description in intensional contexts, see (Aloni 2001), (Holliday and Perry 2015). Should we consider a more refined notion of monotonicity inference where inference can take place at either the level of denotations, or that of descriptions?.

tonicity inferences long studied in formal semantics. Once we take this perspective, many further connections suggest themselves. Here is a last illustration.

Monotonicity Inference as Topic Dynamics. In line with dynamic views of natural language use, we can also view drawing an inference itself as a dynamic activity (van Benthem 2011). A conclusion is often not something that just passively 'follows' (from) the premises. In addition, it can also be an active means of *changing*, or at least modifying the *topic* of discussion or investigation. In this sense, a monotonicity inference from p to $p \vee q$ is not just a 'weakening', or a form of non-relevant reasoning to be banned, but the introduction of a new topic. Indeed, topic change is again a general phenomenon for which dynamic modal logics exist, so then we have closed a circle in our considerations.

5   Conclusion

We have identified three different intuitive senses of monotonicity inference. In standard generalized quantifier theory these largely amount to the same thing. However, once we drop the usual GQT assumption of Extension, differences between the various senses emerge, including new forms of monotonicity. These came out clearly in systems that describe counting and logical inference on a par. After all, intuitively, quantifiers seem a place where logic meets quantitative reasoning. Next, when embedding quantifiers in richer languages, our three senses came apart in classical first-order logic, and yielded a number of interesting issues, including interpolation and completeness for generalized semantics. Going to less familiar settings, monotonicity also connected in interesting ways with new (modal) logics of model change, leading to an array of new questions. Finally, we have suggested that all this technical development may be taken back to natural language, suggesting a fresh look at the interplay of monotonicity inference with the rich linguistic vocabulary for expressing change.

Acknowledgments. We thank Thomas Icard, Zhiqiang Sun, Jouko Väänänen, Dag Westerståhl, Jialiang Yan, the audience of the DALI Workshop (Prague 2020), the LoLaCo audience at the ILLC Amsterdam, and the referees of successive versions of this paper for helpful comments and useful information. This research is supported by the Major Program of the National Social Science Foundation of China (NO. 17ZDA026).

References

Aloni, M.: Quantification under Conceptual Covers. Ph.D. thesis, University of Amsterdam, Amsterdam (2001)

Aloni, M.: Individual concepts in modal predicate logic. J. Philos. Logic **34**, 1–64 (2005)

Andréka, H., van Benthem, J., Németi, I.: On a new semantics for first-order predicate logic. J. Philos. Logic **46**(3), 259–267 (2017)

Baltag, A., Renne, B.: Dynamic epistemic logic. In: Edward, N.Z. (ed.) The Stanford Encyclopedia of Philosophy (2016). (Winter 2016 Edition)

Barwise, J., van Benthem, J.: Interpolation, preservation, and pebble games. J. Symbol. Logic **64**(2), 881–903 (1999) van Benthem, J., Mierzewski, K., Zaffora Blando, F.: The modal logic of stepwise removal. Rev. Symb. Log. (2020, to appear). https://doi.org/10.1017/S17550203200 00258

van Benthem, J.: Language in action: categories, lambdas and dynamic logic, Studies in Logic and the Foundations of Mathematics, North-Holland, Amsterdam, vol. 130 (1991)

van Benthem, J.: Logical Dynamics of Information and Interaction. Cambridge University Press, Cambridge (2011)

Holliday, W.H., Perry, J.: Roles, rigidity, and quantification in epistemic logic. In: Baltag, A., Smets, S. (eds.) Johan van Benthem on Logic and Information Dynamics. OCL, vol. 5, pp. 591–629. Springer, Cham (2014). https://doi.org/10.1007/978-3-319-06025-5_22

Icard, T., Moss, L.S., Tune, W.: Monotonicity calculus and its completeness. In: Proceedings of the 15th Meeting on the Mathematics of Language (2017)

Liu, F., Sun, Z.: The inference pattern Mou in Mohist logic — a monotonicity reasoning view. Roczniki Filozoficzne (Annal. Philos.) (to appear)

Peters, S., Westerståhl, D.: Quantifiers in Language and Logic. Clarendon Press, Oxford (2006)

Renardel de Lavalette, G.: A logic of modification and creation. In: Logical Perspectives on Language and Information. Stanford, CSLI Publications (2001)

Sack, J.: Adding Temporal Logic to Dynamic-Epistemic Logic. Dissertation, University of Indiana, Bloomington (2007)

Thompson, D.: Local fact change logic. In: Liu, F., Ono, H., Yu, J. (eds.) Knowledge, Proof and Dynamics. LASLL, pp. 73–96. Springer, Singapore (2020). https://doi.org/10.1007/978-981-15-2221-5_5

Yan, J., Liu, F.: Monotonic opaqueness in deontic contexts. Context, Conflict and Reasoning. LASLL, pp. 87–96. Springer, Singapore (2020). https://doi.org/10.1007/978-981-15-7134-3_7

Yin, H.: Monotonicity in public announcement logic. Manuscript. Joint Research Center for Logic, Tsinghua University, Beijing (2020)

Universal Free Choice from Concessive Copular Conditionals in Tibetan

Michael Yoshitaka Erlewine[(✉)]

National University of Singapore, Singapore, Singapore
mitcho@mitcho.com

Abstract. I describe the expression of free choice in Tibetan, which involves the combination of a *wh*-word, copula, conditional morphology, and a scalar 'even' particle. I demonstrate that the conventional semantics of these ingredients successfully combine to derive universal free choice meaning. This motivates a new approach to the compositional semantics of universal free choice, which does not prescribe its universal force. This quantificational force is parasitic on the modal/temporal operator which is restricted by the conditional; the scalar 'even' particle then ensures that the conditional restricts a necessity modal.

Keywords: Free choice · *wh* · Copula · Conditionals · *even* · Tibetan

1 Introduction

This paper has two complementary goals. The first is to report on the expression of free choice in Tibetan, based on original fieldwork.[1] Universal free choice items in Tibetan are a combination of a *wh*-word and the particle *yin.na'ang*, optionally preceded by a nominal domain.[2]

---

[1] The original data here reflect the grammars of three speakers of the Tibetan diaspora community in Dharamsala, India. One was born in Tibet and moved to India early in life; the other two were born in India. All grew up in the diaspora community with Tibetan as their first language. The data here was collected in Dharamsala in the summers of 2018 and 2019, and through some further correspondence.

[2] Abbreviations: AUX = auxiliary, COND = conditional, COP = copula, IMPF = imperfective, NEG = negation; DAT = dative, ERG = ergative, GEN = genitive. I employ Wylie romanization here, with periods indicating syllable boundaries where there is no morpheme boundary, as in Garrett 2001 (see note on p. 12).

I thank Kunga Choedon, Pema Yonden, and Tenzin Kunsang for patiently sharing their language with me. For earlier comments and discussion related to this project, I thank Maayan Abenina-Adar, Rahul Balusu, Kenyon Branan, Seth Cable, James Collins, Chris Davis, Kai von Fintel, Danny Fox, Hadas Kotek, Elin McCready, Ryan Walter Smith, two anonymous reviewers for the Workshop on Logic, Language, and Meaning, as well as audiences at NELS 50, the 2020 LSA, Triple A 7, Sinn und Bedeutung 25, and the National University of Singapore. I thank Zheng Shen and Wenkai Tay for comments on earlier drafts. This work is supported by a PYP start-up grant from the National University of Singapore.

D. Deng et al. (Eds.): TLLM 2020, LNCS 12564, pp. 13–34, 2020.
https://doi.org/10.1007/978-3-662-62843-0_2

(1)   Nor.bu [(kha.lag) **ga.re yin.na'ang**] za-gi-red.
        Norbu   food   what YIN.NA'ANG eat-IMPF-AUX
        'Norbu eats **anything / any** food.'

Example (1) describes someone who is not picky about their food. Dumplings? Norbu eats them. Frog? He eats that too. Whatever the food, Norbu eats it.

The second goal is to motivate a new compositional semantics for universal free choice based on the overt morphosyntax of these Tibetan FCIs. *Yin.na'ang* is quite transparently the combination of the copular verb *yin*,[3] conditional suffix *na*, and scalar focus particle *yang* 'even' (2). The combination may indeed appear transparently as *yin.na.yang*, but is commonly contracted to *yin.na'ang* in both writing and speech, and may further reduce to *yin.na'i* in casual speech.[4] Goldstein 2001 lists all three forms (p. 1000), but identifies *yin.na'ang* as the canonical form. I follow this convention here and report all examples with *yin.na'ang*.

(2)   **yin**   + **na**   + **yang**   =   yin.na.yang   >   yin.na'ang   >   yin.na'i
        copula   **cond**   **even**

In addition to forming *wh*-FCIs, *yin.na'ang* has two other uses, as a counterexpectational discourse particle—i.e. the translation equivalent for English 'but' and 'however'—and as a concessive scalar particle. I discuss these uses and their compositional semantics in Erlewine 2020.

Here I pursue the null hypothesis, that *yin.na'ang* in the expression of free choice indeed decomposes into the ingredients in (2). The structure in (1) is thus literally as in (3). *Wh-yin.na'ang* is a concessive conditional (i.e. *even if*; see e.g. König 1986) containing a copular description with a *wh*-word.

(3)   Norbu eats [even if {it/the food} is what].

My core analytic contribution in this paper will be to show how these ingredients in (3) together give rise to the expression's behavior as a universal FCI, without stipulating universal quantificational force. Previous work has discussed both empirical and analytic connections between universal free choice and (concessive) conditionals, as well as to *ever* free relatives and so-called unconditionals (see e.g. Gawron 2001; Rawlins 2008a,b, 2013; Szabolcsi 2019; Balusu 2019, 2020). Existing analyses which take the connection between these constructions seriously either stipulate a covert universal quantifier in these constructions (Menéndez-Benito 2005, 2010; Rawlins 2008a,b, 2013) or propose to derive universal force from a strengthening process (Chierchia 2013; Szabolcsi 2019). I argue that universal quantificational force is instead simply a necessary

---

[3] Tibetan also has another copular form, *red*, with the choice of *yin* vs *red* expressing an evidential distinction (Garrett 2001; Tournadre 2008). However, in non-root contexts where evidential distinctions are not expressed, the copula is uniformly *yin*; most importantly for our purposes, *yin* is the expected copular form in conditionals (see e.g. Garrett 2001: 254).

[4] This reduction to *yin.na'i* /yin.nɛ/ follows the common contraction of the scalar particle *yang* to *ya'i* /yɛ/, common in speech (Tournadre and Sangda Dorje 2003: 409).

consequence of the semantics of conditionals, the scalar particle 'even,' and the *wh*-phrase interpreted as a kind of indefinite, in combination.

2 An Approach to *wh*-quantification

I begin by introducing my assumptions regarding the compositional semantics of *wh*-phrases and their interaction with focus particles such as EVEN. Studies of the semantics of *wh*-questions and focus association have both motivated the idea that natural language meanings may make reference to *sets of alternative denotations* that vary in a systematic way. In a larger project in progress (see e.g. Erlewine 2019, in prep.), I pursue the hypothesis that these two forms of "alternatives" in grammar can be productively integrated, with the result being a compositional semantics for a wide range of non-interrogative uses of *wh*-words, i.e. *wh*-quantification. I present the core of this approach here, illustrating through its application to *wh*-EVEN NPIs in Tibetan (Erlewine and Kotek 2016).

I begin with a brief sketch of the compositional semantics of focus association in the framework of Alternative Semantics (Rooth 1985, 1992). Consider the interpretation of the English example (4) with the focus particle *even*.

(4)   Even Tashi came to the party.

Following Karttunen and Peters 1979, the addition of *even* here introduces a requirement that the possibility of Tashi coming to the party is somehow particularly unlikely, compared to the possibility of other people coming to the party.[5]

Let us see how this meaning can be computed compositionally. We annotate the position of focus in a sentence with ...$_F$ (Jackendoff 1972). As Jackendoff discusses, with *even* in pre-subject position in English, focus must be on the subject or a subpart thereof. We therefore take the LF structure for (4) to be as in (5a). In Alternative Semantics, each syntactic object α has two different corresponding meanings: its ordinary semantic value, $[\![\alpha]\!]^\circ$, and a set of alternative denotations of equal semantic type, $[\![\alpha]\!]^{\text{alt}}$. The alternative set (5c) is a set of propositions that includes the prejacent proposition (5b), as well as other contextually restricted alternative propositions that vary in the focused position. *Even* introduces the inference in (5d), requiring that the prejacent proposition $[\![\alpha]\!]^\circ$ (that Tashi came) be the least likely among the alternatives $[\![\alpha]\!]^{\text{alt}}$.

---

[5] This scalar requirement is frequently described as a presupposition, but Karttunen and Peters 1979 and Kay 1990 characterize it as a conventional implicature. Here I will simply refer to it as the "scalar inference" and not comment on its precise status, except that it is not at-issue. Karttunen and Peters 1979 also describes an additional, additive inference of *even*: a requirement that someone else in addition to Tashi came to the party. Here I concentrate on the scalar part of *even*.

(5)   a.   LF: EVEN $[_\alpha$ [Tashi]$_F$ came to the party $]$

        b. $\llbracket\alpha\rrbracket^\circ = {}^\wedge$Tashi came to the party

        c. $\llbracket\alpha\rrbracket^{\text{alt}} = \{{}^\wedge$Tashi came..., ${}^\wedge$Sonam came..., ${}^\wedge$Migmar came..., ...$\}$

        d. $[\text{EVEN } \alpha] \rightsquigarrow ({}^\wedge$Tashi came...$) <_{\text{likely}} ({}^\wedge$Sonam came...$) \wedge$
             $({}^\wedge$Tashi came...$) <_{\text{likely}} ({}^\wedge$Migmar came...$)$ ...

The general recipe for this scalar inference of *even* is given in (6a). *Even* simply passes up the ordinary value of its complement (6b); thus in (5), the at-issue content is the prejacent proposition, 'that Tashi came to the party.'

(6)   **The contribution of *even*:**

        a. $[\text{EVEN } \alpha] \rightsquigarrow \forall q \in \llbracket\alpha\rrbracket^{\text{alt}} [q \neq \llbracket\alpha\rrbracket^\circ \to \llbracket\alpha\rrbracket^\circ <_{\text{likely}} q]$

        b. $\llbracket\text{EVEN } \alpha\rrbracket^\circ = \llbracket\alpha\rrbracket^\circ$

        c. $\llbracket\text{EVEN } \alpha\rrbracket^{\text{alt}} = \{\llbracket\alpha\rrbracket^\circ\}$

Finally, *even* also has the function of "resetting" the alternative set to be the singleton set of the ordinary value (6c).

Let's now step back and discuss the computation of ordinary and alternative set denotations. Just as ordinary denotations of complex expressions are determined by the denotations of their subparts (7a), where $\circ$ is the appropriate mode of composition (e.g. functional application), Alternative Semantics provides a procedure for calculating the alternative set denotation for a complex expression, in (7b).

(7)   For node α with two daughters, β and γ:

        a. $\llbracket\alpha\rrbracket^\circ \equiv \llbracket\beta\rrbracket^\circ \circ \llbracket\gamma\rrbracket^\circ$

        b. $\llbracket\alpha\rrbracket^{\text{alt}} \equiv \{b \circ c \mid b \in \llbracket\beta\rrbracket^{\text{alt}}, c \in \llbracket\gamma\rrbracket^{\text{alt}}\}$

In words, for α with two daughters β and γ, each alternative denotation for β is composed with each alternative denotation for γ; the collection of such results is the alternative set denotation for α.

This method for the computation of sets of alternatives in (7b) is also useful for the interpretation of in-situ *wh*-phrases, as was proposed earlier in Hamblin 1973. *Wh*-phrases have the denotation of a set of alternatives, which then compose pointwise with other material to yield the denotation of a question as a set of alternative propositions, corresponding to possible answers. I follow Ramchand 1996, 1997, Beck 2006, and Kotek 2014, 2019, in casting this Hamblinian system of *wh*-alternatives within the Roothian two-dimensional semantic system just presented. *Wh*-phrases have an alternative set denotation corresponding to its Hamblin alternatives, but no defined ordinary semantic value. See for example the denotation of *who* in (8); its alternative set (8b) is the set of contextually-determined animate individuals which may count as short answers to *who*.

(8)   a. $\llbracket$who$\rrbracket^\circ$ undefined

        b. $\llbracket$who$\rrbracket^{\text{alt}} = \{$Tashi, Sonam, Migmar, ...$\}$

Consider now the interpretation of the Tibetan *wh*-containing clause in (9) below. This example must be interpreted as a *wh*-question, even without the final question marker *gas*. Tibetan is a *wh*-in-situ language and does not have bare *wh*-indefinites.

(9)   **Tibetan *wh*-question:**
[TP Thugs.spro-la *su*   slebs-song] (-gas?)
      party-DAT   who arrive-AUX   -Q
'Who came to the party?' / *'Someone came to the party.'

Composing 'who' (8) with the rest of the clause, we yield (10):

(10)   a. $[\![$TP$]\!]^{\circ}$ undefined

       b. $[\![$TP$]\!]^{\text{alt}} = \{^{\wedge}$Tashi came..., $^{\wedge}$Sonam came..., $^{\wedge}$Migmar came, ...$\}$

To grammatically interpret (10) as a question, the alternatives that have been calculated as an alternative set ($[\![$TP$]\!]^{\text{alt}}$) must be made the ordinary semantic value, which is the denotation that is ultimately interpreted. This is accomplished by the interrogative complementizer (Beck 2006) or by a dedicated adjoined operator, ALTSHIFT (Kotek 2019). See especially Kotek 2019 for more on the use of this framework for the interpretation of *wh*-questions.

Our interest, however, is in the non-interrogative use of *wh*-phrases, especially in concert with focus particles. In addition to *wh-yin.na'ang* FCIs, Tibetan forms NPIs through the combination of a *wh*-phrase and the scalar particle *yang* 'even' (Erlewine and Kotek 2016), as in (11):

(11)   ***Wh*-even NPI:**
Thugs.spro-la *su*-**yang**   slebs-*(**ma**)-song.
party-DAT   who-EVEN   arrive-NEG-AUX
'No one came to the party.'

Let's consider the interpretation of the grammatical (with negation) and ungrammatical (negation-less) variants of (11) in turn. Following Erlewine and Kotek 2016, I take the focus particle *yang* to correspond to a unary EVEN operator taking propositional scope at LF, as schematized in (12).[6] When we attempt to compute the EVEN in this structure, however, we run into a problem. The semantics for the scalar inference of EVEN (6a) requires that its sister have a defined ordinary value, but the sister of EVEN in (12) is a *wh*-containing clause, as in (10), and therefore does not have a defined ordinary value.

---

[6] See also Branan and Erlewine 2020 for further discussion of this approach to constituent focus particles, as well as a supporting data point from Tibetan.

(12)   <u>LF</u>: EVEN [NEG [*who* came to the party]]

To avoid this issue, I propose the adjunction of a covert operator $\exists$ (13) that defines an ordinary value that is the disjunction of its sister's alternative set, and simply passes up its sister's alternative set as its own.[7,8]

(13)   a. $[\![\exists\,\alpha]\!]^\circ = \bigvee[\![\alpha]\!]^{\text{alt}}$

        b. $[\![\exists\,\alpha]\!]^{\text{alt}} = [\![\alpha]\!]^{\text{alt}}$

The full LF for (11) is thus as follows in (14). The denotation for ① is as in (10), which has no defined ordinary value. The application of $\exists$ in ② results in (14a). Negation applies pointwise in ③ (14b). Now notice that $[\![③]\!]^\circ$ asymmetrically entails every alternative in $[\![③]\!]^{\text{alt}}$. This ensures that the scalar inference of EVEN (14c) will always be true. The end result will be equivalent to the proposition 'that no one came to the party,' as desired.

(14)   <u>LF</u>: EVEN [③ NEG [② $\exists$ [① *who* came to the party]]]

        a.   i. $[\![②]\!]^\circ = {}^\wedge$Tashi or Sonam or Migmar... came to the party
                        $= {}^\wedge$someone came to the party
              ii. $[\![②]\!]^{\text{alt}} = [\![①]\!]^{\text{alt}} = \{{}^\wedge$T came..., ${}^\wedge$S came..., ${}^\wedge$M came..., ...$\}$

        b.   i. $[\![③]\!]^\circ = $ NEG$({}^\wedge$someone came to the party$)$
                        $= {}^\wedge$no one came to the party
              ii. $[\![③]\!]^{\text{alt}} = \{{}^\wedge$T didn't come..., ${}^\wedge$S didn't come..., ${}^\wedge$M didn't..., ...$\}$

        c.   [EVEN ③] $\rightsquigarrow$ ($^\wedge$no one came...) $<_{\text{likely}}$ ($^\wedge$T didn't come...) $\wedge$
                        ($^\wedge$no one came...) $<_{\text{likely}}$ ($^\wedge$S didn't come...) $\wedge$
                        ($^\wedge$no one came...) $<_{\text{likely}}$ ($^\wedge$M didn't come...) ...   ◯

Now consider the variant of this structure without negation. (15) gives the scalar inference predicted by EVEN applying directly to ② in (14a):

(15)   [EVEN ②] $\rightsquigarrow$ ($^\wedge$someone came...) $<_{\text{likely}}$ ($^\wedge$Tashi came...) $\wedge$
                ($^\wedge$someone came...) $<_{\text{likely}}$ ($^\wedge$Sonam came...) $\wedge$
                ($^\wedge$someone came...) $<_{\text{likely}}$ ($^\wedge$Migmar came...) ...   ✕

Because the prejacent 'that someone came to the party' $[\![②]\!]^\circ$ is asymmetrically entailed by each alternative in $[\![②]\!]^{\text{alt}}$, this requirement in (15) is a contradiction. This scalar inference of EVEN can never be satisfied. Following Lahiri 1998, this

---

[7] For Erlewine and Kotek 2016, this function is served by the additive component of EVEN, in lieu of this covert $\exists$ operator. In Erlewine 2019, in prep., I argue for the use of this $\exists$ operator for *wh*-quantification in a range of languages and contexts, beyond those with additive particles.

[8] This $\exists$ operator stands in contrast to the existential closure operator of e.g. Kratzer and Shimoyama 2002, which also has the effect of collapsing or "resetting" the set of alternatives, leading to the predicted availability of bare *wh* indefinites, contrary to fact; see (9). In contrast, the $\exists$ operator defined here in (13) results in a structure that necessitates association with a higher operator which will "reset" the alternative set. See Erlewine 2019, in prep. for further discussion.

fatal requirement of EVEN in (15) leads to the ungrammaticality of the *wh*-EVEN expression without a licensing negation.[9]

In this way, the Hamblin semantics of *wh*-phrases can be productively combined with the Roothian semantics of focus, for example giving us a compositional semantics for *wh*-EVEN NPIs in Tibetan. With this background on the compositional semantics of *wh*-phrases and their interaction with focus particles in place, we are now in a position to turn to the compositional semantics of *wh-yin.na'ang* FCIs.

3   On the Syntax of *wh-yin.na'ang*

Next I address the syntax of *wh-yin.na'ang* FCIs. I first address its external syntax—how the *wh-yin.na'ang* expression relates to its containing clause—and then its internal syntax—i.e. the nature of the copular relation.

Taking its morphology at face value, *wh-yin.na'ang* is a *wh*-containing conditional clause, to which the scalar focus particle *yang* has adjoined, and I propose that it is interpreted as such. However, there is evidence that this whole FCI structure may actually occupy a nominal argument position. Consider example (16). Here the *wh-yin.na'ang* FCI hosts the dative case marker *-la*:

(16)   **Wh-yin.na'ang FCI with dative case:**
Pad.ma [(phru.gu) **su   yin.na'ang**]-la   skad.cha bshad-kyi-red.
Pema   child   who YIN.NA'ANG-DAT speech   talk-IMPF-AUX
'Pema talks to **anyone** / **any** child.'

The *wh-yin.na'ang* FCI is a clause in an argument position which describes that argument, and thus in broad strokes resembles a head-internal relative clause or a so-called *amalgam* structure (Lakoff 1974; also Kluck 2011), as in (17):

(17)   John is going to I think it's Chicago on Saturday.   (Lakoff 1974: 324)

Here I propose to follow an intuition developed by Shimoyama (1999) for the interpretation of Japanese head-internal relatives, and independently by Hirsch (2016) for English *ever* free relatives. This idea is that the embedded clause is interpreted higher at LF, as adjoined to the embedding clause, and that the argument position is then interpreted as a pronoun anaphoric to an individual described in the clause.[10] As a concrete example, then, assuming a surface structure for (16) roughly isomorphic to (18a) below, the corresponding LF for its interpretation will resemble (18b).

---

[9] Erlewine and Kotek 2016 shows that *wh*-EVEN NPIs in Tibetan must be licensed by clause-mate negation. This is explained by the interpreted LF position of EVEN needing to be in the same clause as the pronounced position of *yang*. See Erlewine and Kotek 2016: 149 for discussion.

[10] The informal coindexation in (18) will be formalized in terms of equality of nominal descriptions in Sect. 4 below.

(18)   **The structure of *wh-yin.na'ang*:**

    a. <u>Literal (16):</u> Pema talks to [even if {it/the child} is who] ⇒

    b. <u>LF:</u> [even if {it/the child}$_i's$ who], Pema talks to *them*$_i$ ⇒
        EVEN [if {it/the child}$_i's$ who, Pema talks to *them*$_i$]

I model the scalar particle *yang* as a unary EVEN operator at LF (Erlewine and Kotek 2016; see footnote 6), taking the entire conditional structure, with its consequent clause, as its complement. This is reflected in (18b) above.

Next, we turn to the internal syntax of *wh-yin.na'ang*. Again, following the overt morphology, I take the antecedent of the conditional to be a copular description involving a *wh*-phrase. I will suggest here that, within the Higgins 1973 classification of copular clauses, this is (in many cases) a specificational copular clause. Specificational copular clauses are distinguished through their information structure and use as well as in their syntax; for instance, pronominal reference to specificational subjects involve the neuter pronoun, as in (19a):

(19)   a. <u>Specificational copular clause:</u>   (Mikkelsen 2005: 72)
           The tallest girl in the class is Molly, isn't it/*she?

    b. <u>Predicational copular clause:</u>
           The tallest girl in the class is Swedish, isn't she/*it?

Mikkelsen and subsequent authors have taken such facts to reflect that the subject of a specificational copular clause is not a referential expression of type *e*. In particular, Romero 2005 proposes that (definite) specificational subjects are individual concepts (functions from worlds to individuals); see also Arregi, Francez, and Martinovic to appear for recent support. As individual concepts, (definite) specificational subjects will not impose a uniqueness requirement for the nominal restriction on the evaluation world, although they will impose a uniqueness requirement on the referent given a particular evaluation world or situation. We will return to this detail, as well as discussion of indefinite specificational subjects, in Sect. 5.3.

In cases such as (16) with explicit nominal domain *phru.gu* 'child' or (1) above with *kha.lag* 'food,' I take these nominals to be the first argument, or the "subject," of the specificational copula. In the absence of such a nominal, I posit a corresponding null nominal (*pro*) as the first argument. The second argument of the copula is the *wh*-word whose alternative set ranges over individuals of type *e*, *de re*.[11] This discussion thus motivates the informal, literal translation of the specificational copular clauses using the English '{it/the child} is who' in (18b) or '{it/the food} is what' for (1).

An alternative analysis would be for these nominals to form a constituent with the *wh*-word to form a complex *wh*-phrase. However, complex *wh*-phrases in Tibetan are headed by postnominal *ga.gi* 'which' and *wh-yin.na'ang* FCIs cannot be built from such *which*-phrases:

---

[11] I limit the discussion here to the *wh*-words *su* 'who' and *ga.re* 'what' and leave discussion of other *wh*-words in FCIs for future work.

(20)   ***Wh-yin.na'ang* does not take *which*-phrases:**

a. *[kha.lag *ga.gi*] yin.na'ang
    food   which   YIN.NA'ANG
    'any (of the) food'

b. *[phru.gu *ga.gi*] yin.na'ang
    child   which   YIN.NA'ANG
    'any child / of the children'

Therefore, I argue that the copular verb takes the noun phrase—or if absent, a corresponding null nominal—and the *wh*-word as two separate arguments.

4   Interpreting *wh-yin.na'ang*

With these preliminaries in place, we now turn to the compositional semantics of *wh-yin.na'ang*. As discussed above, *yin.na'ang* is a transparent combination of the copular verb *yin*, conditional suffix *na*, and scalar particle *yang* 'even,' in an amalgam-like argument position. In this section, I will show how these ingredients (even without considering 'even') together in the examples presented above yield a universal free choice expression. In particular, my approach does not need to stipulate the universal force for these expressions as in Menéndez-Benito 2005, 2010 or Rawlins 2008a,b, 2013, nor derive universal force from a secondary strengthening process as in Chierchia 2013 and Szabolcsi 2019.

Once we have established how universal force comes about in these grammatical examples, in Sect. 5, I show how this construction enforces universal force. There, *yang* 'even' will play a star role. Just as association with 'even' can build NPIs from indefinites (Lee and Horn 1995; Lahiri 1998), as we also saw in Tibetan in Sect. 2, the logical properties of 'even' will serve to ensure that *wh-yin.na'ang* be interpreted as a universal FCI.

Recall that Tibetan *wh-yin.na'ang* FCIs may be in argument positions.[12] I proposed in Sect. 3 above that a FCI in argument position is interpreted at LF as a conditional clause adjoined to the containing clause, with unary EVEN taking the entire conditional structure as its sister.

(21)   **The structure of *wh-yin.na'ang* in (16):**   based on (18)

a. <u>Surface stucture:</u> Pema talks to [even if {*pro*/the child} is who] ⇒

b. <u>LF:</u> EVEN [if [$_\phi$ ∃ [{*pro*/the child}$_i$ is who]],
                            [$_\psi$ IMPF [Pema talks to *pro*$_i$]]]

The ∃ operator in (21b) is the covert operator discussed in Sect. 2 above. Note that ϕ is a *wh*-containing clause, and thus without the insertion of ∃, the sister of EVEN would have no defined ordinary value (prejacent) and thus the result would be uninterpretable at LF.

As discussed in Sect. 3 above, the antecedent of the conditional ϕ is a specificational copular clause. I adopt the view that the subjects of specificational

---

[12] I suspect that they are *always* in argument positions, but in the absence of overt case markers or postpositions as in (16), it is difficult to be certain. For examples without such clues, it is possible that *wh-yin.na'ang* is overtly in its clausal adjunct position, as in (21b), with the corresponding pronoun in the consequent clause simply being null. Note that Tibetan is descriptively pro-drop.

copular clauses are individual concepts (Romero 2005). Individual concepts are functions of type $\langle s, e \rangle$ from worlds or *situations* to individuals. Situations are subparts of possible worlds, which may be thought of as limited to particular times or places (see e.g. Kratzer 1989; Heim 1990). The type s is used for all situations, including worlds, which are simply maximal situations.

Concretely, I assume that these specificational subjects as in (21b) involve a definite determiner as in (22), taken from Elbourne's work on definite descriptions in situation semantics. As Tibetan is an article-less language, I assume that THE is unpronounced. Composing THE with a nominal property such as 'child' in (23) yields the individual concept denotation in (24) of type $\langle s, e \rangle$.

(22) $[\![\text{THE}]\!] = \lambda P_{\langle e, \langle s, t \rangle \rangle}.\lambda s : \exists! x [P(x)(s)].\iota x [P(x)(s)]$ (Elbourne 2013: 35)

(23) $[\![\text{child}]\!] = \lambda x.\lambda s_s.x$ is a child in s

(24) $[\![\text{THE child}]\!] = \lambda s : \exists! x [x \text{ child in } s].\iota x [x \text{ child in } s]$

Individual concepts of this form will be undefined for world/situations where the property's extension is not unique.

In cases with no nominal restrictor, I assume a corresponding null nominal (indicated as *pro* in (21b) above) which refers to a contextually salient property P, and which we can informally describe as "THE P." Below, I will refer to this salient property as P in the general case, whether pronounced or not.

(25) $[\![\text{THE } P]\!] = \lambda s_s : \exists! x [P(x)(s)].\iota x [P(x)(s)]$

As proposed in Sect. 3, in LFs for *wh-yin.na'ang* FCIs, there is a pronoun in FCI's surface argument position which is related to the subject of the conditional clause in some way. I used co-indexation above as in "*pro*ᵢ ... *pro*ᵢ" as a notational device to highlight the link between these two nominals, but we are now in a position to specify this relationship. Specifically, I propose that these two positions refer to the same individual concept: "THE P." In the antecedent clause ϕ, "THE P" is the specificational subject. In the consequent clause ψ, "THE P" is evaluated with respect to ψ's situation or world of evaluation. We can restate the structure in (21b) in these terms as follows:

(26) **LF for (16):**   (revised from (21b))
       EVEN [if [$_\phi$ $\exists$ [THE P is who]], [$_\psi$ IMPF [Pema talks to THE P]]]

I now turn to the compositional semantics of this LF, beginning with the antecedent of the conditional, ϕ. Given the semantics for 'who' (8) and $\exists$ (13) above, we yield the following two-dimensional denotation for ϕ in (26):

(27) ϕ **in (26):**

   a. $[\![\phi]\!]^\circ = \lambda s_s : \exists! x [P(x)(s)]$
              $.\iota x [P(x)(s)] = \text{Tashi} \lor \iota x [P(x)(s)] = \text{Sonam} \lor ...$

   b. $[\![\phi]\!]^{\text{alt}} = \left\{ \begin{array}{l} \lambda s_s : \exists! x [P(x)(s)].\iota x [P(x)(s)] = \text{Tashi}, \\ \lambda s_s : \exists! x [P(x)(s)].\iota x [P(x)(s)] = \text{Sonam}, ... \end{array} \right\}$

The ordinary value of ϕ (27a) is a proposition—a predicate of situations—which presupposes that there is a unique P-individual in its argument situation s and will return true if that individual is Tashi or Sonam or Migmar, etc.; e.g. in the domain of 'who.' The individual alternatives in $[\![\phi]\!]^{\text{alt}}$ (27b) each similarly presuppose a unique P-individual in the situation, but then return true when it is a particular individual in the domain.

We now turn to the interpretation of the conditional and its consequent ψ. I adopt the now standard approach to conditionals as restricting the domain of a modal or temporal operator in the consequent clause (Lewis 1975; Kratzer 1979, 1986; von Fintel 1994). The modal/temporal operator in the consequent ψ (the overt main clause) in both examples that we have seen so far (in (1) and (16)) is the imperfective aspect with generic/habitual interpretation. Following Arregui, Rivero, and Salanova 2014 and citations there, I model the imperfective as a type of universal modal that quantifies over a particular set of situations. In particular, for generic or habitual imperfectives, in turn following Cipria and Roberts 2000, the relevant set of situations will be "normal or usual" sub-situations of the topic situation, formally described as "characteristic" (Cipria and Roberts 2000: 325). I write $s' \leq_{ch} s$ to indicate that s' is a characteristic sub-situation of s.

I spell out the interpretation of ψ with its imperfective quantification in (28). As ψ does not contain any alternative-generating (e.g. focused or wh) expression, $[\![\psi]\!]^{\text{alt}} = \{[\![\psi]\!]^{\circ}\}$.

(28) **ψ in (26):**

$$[\![\psi]\!]^{\circ} = \text{IMPF}_{habitual} \left([\![\text{Pema talks to THE } P]\!]^{\circ}\right)$$
$$= \lambda s_s.\forall s'[s' \leq_{ch} s \rightarrow \text{Pema talks to THE } P \text{ in } s']$$
$$= \lambda s_s.\forall s'[s' \leq_{ch} s \wedge \exists!x[P(x)(s')] \rightarrow \text{Pema talks to } \iota x[P(x)(s')] \text{ in } s']$$

Note that, in the third line in (28), I have unpacked the definedness requirement of "THE P" and allowed this condition to restrict the set of relevant sub-situations s'. For example, if P is 'child,' we are allowing ourselves to look at only those characteristic sub-situations where there is a unique child to refer to.[13] In all such situations, Pema talks to that child.

We now can calculate our full conditional clause, "if ϕ, ψ." Recall that the conditional clause ϕ acts as a restrictor on the modal base of the ψ's modal quantification. The two-dimensional denotation for "if ϕ, ψ" is thus as in (29). The effects of this conditional restriction are boxed here for presentation:

(29) **"If ϕ, ψ" in (26):**

$$
\text{a.} \quad [\![\text{if } \phi, \psi]\!]^{\circ} = \lambda s_s.\forall s' \left[\begin{array}{c} s' \leq_{ch} s \wedge \exists!x[P(x)(s')] \\ \boxed{\wedge\ [\![\phi]\!]^{\circ}(s')} \end{array} \rightarrow \begin{array}{c} \text{Pema talks to} \\ \iota x[P(x)(s')] \text{ in } s' \end{array} \right]
$$

$$
= \lambda s_s.\forall s' \left[\begin{array}{c} s' \leq_{ch} s \wedge \exists!x[P(x)(s')] \\ \boxed{\wedge \left(\begin{array}{c} \iota x[P(x)(s')] = \text{T} \ \vee \\ \iota x[P(x)(s')] = \text{S} \ \vee \dots \end{array} \right)} \end{array} \rightarrow \begin{array}{c} \text{Pema talks to} \\ \iota x[P(x)(s')] \text{ in } s' \end{array} \right]
$$

---

[13] A reviewer raises a concern about this presupposition in the modal prejacent affecting the set of situations that we quantify over. This can be thought of as a more general effect, where the description in the modal prejacent affects the domain of quantification chosen, as discussed by Arregui et al. (2014: 318).

b. $[\![\text{if } \phi, \psi]\!]^{\text{alt}} = \left\{ \begin{array}{l} \lambda s_s \forall s' \left[\begin{array}{c} s' \leq_{ch} s \wedge \exists! x [P(x)(s')] \\ \wedge \iota x [P(x)(s')] = \text{Tashi} \end{array} \rightarrow \begin{array}{c} \text{Pema talks to} \\ \iota x [P(x)(s')] \text{ in } s' \end{array} \right], \\ \lambda s_s \forall s' \left[\begin{array}{c} s' \leq_{ch} s \wedge \exists! x [P(x)(s')] \\ \wedge \iota x [P(x)(s')] = \text{Sonam} \end{array} \rightarrow \begin{array}{c} \text{Pema talks to} \\ \iota x [P(x)(s')] \text{in } s' \end{array} \right], \\ \dots \end{array} \right\}$

The final ingredient in the *wh-yin.na'ang* LF in (26) is EVEN. As EVEN does not change the at-issue (asserted) content, our work in interpreting example (16) is now done, in (29a). (I discuss the contribution of EVEN in the following section.) What does this result in (29a) express? It claims that, in all characteristic sub-situations s' of the topic situation s where (a) there is a unique P (e.g. 'child') in s' and (b) that unique P is Tashi or Sonam or Migmar, etc.—e.g., an individual in the domain of 'who'—Pema talks to that unique P.

Let's restate this again in slightly more informal terms, to build an intuition for the claim. Concretely, let our salient property P be 'child,' and assume that all individuals that satisfy 'child' are in the domain of 'who.' Then, (29a) conveys the following:

(30)   In any and all "normal or usual" sub-parts of the current situation/world with a unique child, Pema talks to that child.

Note that (30) does not require Pema to have actually spoken with any or all of these children. Instead, it uses the modal semantics of the imperfective to allow ourselves to consider different "characteristic" situations with different children present. What about a situation with Tashi? Pema talks to him. How about Sonam? Pema talks to her too. Pema talks to any child. We have successfully derived the expression of universal free choice.

How did we do this? In particular, where did the universal force of the FCI come from? The universal quantificational force of *wh-yin.na'ang* in this example is that of the imperfective modal/temporal operator, whose modal base was restricted by the conditional. The imperfective introduces universal quantification over situations (see e.g. Arregui et al. 2014), with a shared individual concept evaluated in both the conditional and its prejacent, allowing us to indirectly universally quantify over different individuals in different situations.[14] On this approach, this universal force need not be stipulated as in Menéndez-Benito 2005, 2010 or Rawlins 2008a,b, 2013, nor does it need to be derived using a strengthening procedure as in Chierchia 2013 and Szabolcsi 2019. Instead, it is simply a reflection of an ingredient that is already there: the modal/temporal operator restricted by the conditional.

---

[14] There are a number of precursors to this idea—see for example Giannakidou 2001: 665–666 and citations there—although the implementation here using situation-binding in conditionals is to my knowledge new. In addition, the idea that 'even' plays a critical role in enforcing universal force, which I develop in the next section, is also new.

5   Restricting the Distribution of *wh-yin.na'ang*

In the previous section, we saw how the *wh-yin.na'ang* FCI derives the effect of universal quantification over a set of individuals, parasitic on a universal modal/temporal quantifier in the sentence. In this section, I discuss two principled ways in which the use and interpretation of *wh-yin.na'ang* is restricted. First, I discuss the role of the scalar particle *yang* 'even' in ensuring the FCI's universal quantificational force. Second, I discuss the incompatibility of *wh-yin.na'ang* in necessity statements and episodic descriptions, and offer a new intuition for the nature of so-called *subtrigging* effects (LeGrand 1975).

5.1   Enforcing Universal Force

I begin by discussing the role of *yang* 'even' in enforcing the universal quantificational force of *wh-yin.na'ang*. First, we consider the effect of EVEN in example (16), which applies last in its LF (26). I repeat the two-dimensional denotation of EVEN's sister, "if ϕ, ψ," here blurring out the material that is common to all propositions, so we can more easily see their interrelationships.

(31)   **"If ϕ, ψ" from (29), schematically:**

a. $[\![\text{if } \phi,\ \psi]\!]^{\circ} = \lambda s_s.\forall s' \left[\dots \wedge \left(\begin{array}{l} \iota x[P(x)(s')] = \text{Tashi} \ \vee \\ \iota x[P(x)(s')] = \text{Sonam} \ \vee \dots \end{array} \right) \rightarrow \ \dots \right]$

b. $[\![\text{if } \phi,\ \psi]\!]^{\text{alt}} = \left\{ \begin{array}{l} \lambda s_s.\forall s' [\dots \wedge \iota x[P(x)(s')] = \text{Tashi} \rightarrow \ \dots], \\ \lambda s_s.\forall s' [\dots \wedge \iota x[P(x)(s')] = \text{Sonam} \rightarrow \ \dots], \ \dots \end{array} \right\}$

We observe that the ordinary value $[\![\text{if } \phi,\ \psi]\!]^{\circ}$ (31a) asymmetrically entails each of the alternatives in $[\![\text{if } \phi,\ \psi]\!]^{\text{alt}}$ (31b): If "in every situation where the unique P is Tashi or Sonam or ..., blah is true," then it follows that "in every situation where the unique P is Tashi, blah," and "in every situation where the unique P is Sonam, blah," etc., but not vice versa. The prejacent proposition of EVEN is necessarily less likely than all of its alternatives, so the scalar inference of [EVEN [if ϕ, ψ]] will always be true. The addition of EVEN is felicitous here.[15]

What happens if the conditional instead restricts an existential modal/temporal quantifier, e.g. a possibility modal, instead of the universal imperfective operator of the examples above? Schematically again, we can expect to yield denotations for "if ϕ, ψ" of the form in (32). The salient change from (31) is boxed.

---

[15] This appears to make the addition of *yang* in *wh-yin.na'ang* systematically vacuous. In Erlewine 2019, in prep., I suggest that this is not entirely so: The addition of an overt focus particle necessitates its sister to have a defined ordinary value, which licenses insertion of the $\exists$ operator (13), whose insertion is otherwise marked.

(32)   **"If ϕ, ψ" with ϕ restricting a possibility modal in ψ:**

   a. $[\![\text{if } \phi, \psi]\!]^{\circ} = \lambda s_s. \boxed{\exists s'} \left[\ldots \wedge \left(\begin{array}{l} \iota x[P(x)(s')] = \text{Tashi} \vee \\ \iota x[P(x)(s')] = \text{Sonam} \ \vee \ldots \end{array} \right) \wedge \ldots \right]$

   b. $[\![\text{if } \phi, \psi]\!]^{\text{alt}} = \left\{ \begin{array}{l} \lambda s_s. \boxed{\exists s'} [\ldots \wedge \iota x[P(x)(s')] = \text{Tashi} \ \wedge \ldots], \\ \lambda s_s. \boxed{\exists s'} [\ldots \wedge \iota x[P(x)(s')] = \text{Sonam} \ \wedge \ldots], \ldots \end{array} \right\}$

Here, with existential quantification over situations, the entailment relationships between the prejacent and its alternatives have reversed. Each alternative in $[\![\text{if } \phi, \psi]\!]^{\text{alt}}$ (32b) now asymmetrically entails the prejacent $[\![\text{if } \phi, \psi]\!]^{\circ}$ (32a): If any proposition of the form "there is a situation where the unique P is Tashi, and blah is true" or "there is a situation where the unique P is Sonam, and blah is true" etc. is true, it follows that "there is a situation where the unique P is Tashi or Sonam or... and blah is true" will necessarily be true. In this case, the prejacent is logically weaker than its alternatives. EVEN applied to "if ϕ, ψ" with a possibility modal will thus lead to a systematically unsatisfiable scalar inference, resulting in ungrammaticality.

The scalar particle *yang* 'even' in Tibetan *wh-yin.na'ang* FCIs thus plays a crucial role in ensuring that *wh-yin.na'ang* always expresses universal free choice, just as it may serve a crucial role in explaining the distribution of NPIs (see e.g. Lee and Horn 1995; Lahiri 1998; Erlewine and Kotek 2016). The logical requirements of EVEN—quantifying over the prejacent and its alternatives using the independently motivated semantics of *wh*-alternatives and their disjunction by $\exists$, introduced in Sect. 2—ensures that the conditional clause of *wh-yin.na'ang* restricts a universal modal/temporal operator, and therefore that *wh-yin.na'ang* itself will always have universal force.

Practically, *wh-yin.na'ang* does cooccur with possibility modals, as in example (33) below. The verb form in this example differs from (1) in the addition of the deontic possibility modal *chog*, and is also grammatical. The interpretation of *wh-yin.na'ang* here is again a universal FCI.

(33)   ***Wh-yin.na'ang* FCI with deontic possibility modal:**
        Nga-'i   khyi [(kha.lag) ga.re yin.na'ang] za-**chog**-gi-red.
        1sg-GEN dog   food   what YIN.NA'ANG eat-ALLOWED-IMPF-AUX
        'My dog is allowed to eat anything / any food.'

In such examples, there is in principle a choice as to which modal/temporal operator the conditional clause restricts. If the conditional of *wh-yin.na'ang* restricts the ability modal, we yield prejacent and alternative set denotations of the form in (32), leading to ungrammaticality due to an unsatisfiable scalar inference of EVEN. Instead, the conditional clause must be construed as restricting the modal base of the higher imperfective operator, leading to the attested meaning where universal free choice takes scope over the possibility modal.

5.2   On the Granularity of Modal Quantification

The approach to universal free choice presented here may at first glance lead us to predict the availability of *wh-yin.na'ang* FCIs in sentences with any universal modal/temporal operator, whereas in reality its distribution is further restricted. For example, the use of *wh-yin.na'ang* with the deontic necessity modal *dgos* is judged as highly marked, just as its intended translation in English is as well.

(34)   **Wh-yin.na'ang unavailable in necessity statements:**
       ??Khyed.rang [sman   ga.re yin.na'ang]   za-**dgos**-red.
       2sg   medicine what YIN.NA'ANG eat-must-AUX
       Intended: ≈ 'You must take any medicine.'

Following the presentation in Sect. 4 above, we predict (34) to have an LF representation as in (35) below. In every deontically best accessible world, where the unique medicine is x, you take x.

(35)   **LF for (34):**
       EVEN [if [∃ [THE medicine is what]], MUST [you eat THE medicine]]

The problem with (34/35), I suggest, is a conflict between the granularity of the modal quantification and the uniqueness requirement of the definite individual concept "THE medicine." Specifically, I take the modal MUST here to quantify over possible *worlds* that are best according to an ordering source. The ordering source introduces considerations of what ought to be done in particular cases, but it does not change facts of the world, such as the uniqueness of medicine. In each world of evaluation, the uniqueness requirement is not satisfied, and thus the sentence cannot be evaluated.[16] In contrast, in the grammatical examples above, the conditional in *wh-yin.na'ang* restricted the domain of quantification over a set of *situations* which could be granular enough to be restricted to situations with unique *P*-individuals.

A similar analysis applies to episodic descriptions, which is another context where *wh-yin.na'ang* FCIs are unavailable. See example (36) and a grammatical, FCI-less baseline in (37).

(36)   **Wh-yin.na'ang ungrammatical in episodic descriptions:**
       *bKra.shis da.lta [(kha.lag) ga.re yin.na'ang]   bzas-tshar-song.
       Tashi   now   food   what YIN.NA'ANG eat-finish-AUX
       Intended: ≈ 'Tashi finished eating any food now.'

(37)   bKra.shis da.lta (kha.lag) bzas-tshar-song.
       Tashi   now   food   eat-finish-AUX
       'Tashi just finished eating right now.'

Episodic descriptions simply claim the existence of a particular type of event: here, (37) asserts that there was a completion of an eating event, in the past,[17]

---

[16] Alternatively, if worlds where the uniqueness requirement is not met are filtered out of the base of modal quantification, as discussed above in footnote 13 above, the modal quantification becomes vacuous.

[17] The auxiliary *song* expresses both past tense and direct evidentiality (Garrett 2001).

in the halo of the speech time 'now.' There is no overt modal/temporal operator. Let us assume, following Kratzer 1986, that the conditional in *wh-yin.na'ang* in such a case will restrict the modal base of a high, covert epistemic necessity modal.[18] Assuming that such a covert epistemic necessity modal quantifies over doxastically accessible worlds, we will again run into problems satisfying the uniqueness requirement of the specificational subject.

5.3   Subtrigging

As with FCIs in other languages, though, the restrictions on the distribution of *wh-yin.na'ang* may not be absolute bans. Specifically, the restriction due to issues with the granularity of modal quantification just introduced above only holds in so far as the subject of the specificational clause is definite; see (35). Instead, if the content of the conditional clause in *wh-yin.na'ang* takes an indefinite specificational subject, as schematized in (38), this problem could be avoided.[19]

(38)   **Alternative LF for (34) with *indefinite* specificational subject:**
         EVEN [if [∃ [A medicine is what]], [MUST [you eat IT]]]

In particular, the structure of the form in (38) will not require the worlds (or situations) that are quantified over to have a unique individual that satisfies the property 'medicine,' which I claim led to the unavailability of the *wh-yin.na'ang* FCI in example (34). In reality, example (34) *is* judged as unacceptable, so this alternate parse in (38) with an indefinite specificational subject must not be available in example (34), if it is indeed ever available.

I propose that parses for *wh-yin.na'ang* with indefinite specificational subjects, as sketched in (38) above, *are* in principle available, and that this option holds the key to understanding another aspect of the distribution of FCIs. Specifically, I predict that the availability of the indefinite subject parse as in (38)—which predicts the availability of the FCI without quantification over granular situations, and thus in a wider range of contexts—*should only be as good as the general availability of specificational copular clauses with indefinite subjects.*

It has been independently observed that subjects of specificational copular clauses are generally definite, but tolerate certain exceptions:

---

[18] Alternatively, there simply is no universal modal/temporal operator in (36) for the conditional to restrict. Under this approach, there is no way for the scalar inference of *wh-yin.na'ang*'s EVEN to be satisfied.

[19] Here I use a pronoun *it* in the consequent clause, in the position corresponding to the surface position of *wh-yin.na'ang*. It cannot be a (simple) definite description ("THE *P*") as in (35) above, as the relevant individual (concept) is not unique in the antecedent clause situation, which is also the situation of evaluation for the consequent clause. What is needed here instead is a donkey pronoun or similar, which will pick out the particular individual (concept) witness of the indefinite in the conditional antecedent.

(39)   **Indefinite specificational subjects improve with modification:**

    a. * A doctor is John.   (Heycock and Kroch 1999: 379)

    b. ✓ One person <u>who might help you</u> is Mary.   (Higgins 1973: 270)

In particular, modification—especially by relative clauses—seems to lead to acceptability. See e.g. See e.g. Mikkelsen 2005: ch. 8, Heycock 2012, Comorovski 2007, and more recently Milway 2020 for discussion.

    I suggest that this restricted acceptability of indefinite specificational subjects and its amelioration as in (39) is in turn responsible for the similar amelioration of FCIs in some environments when modified, dubbed "subtrigging" by LeGrand (1975). Tibetan exhibits this subtrigging effect as well: Example (40) differs from the unacceptable (34) in the addition of a relative clause on the nominal domain and is judged as perfectly acceptable.

(40)   ***Wh-yin.na'ang* in (34) improves with modification:**
    [[RC Sman.pa sprad-pa-'i]   sman   ga.re yin.na'ang] za-**dgos**-red.
    doctor   give-REL-GEN medicine what YIN.NA'ANG eat-must-AUX
    '[You] must take any medicine [RC that the doctor gives [you]].'

Again, taking the morphology of the FCI seriously—in this case, that *wh-yin.na'ang* involves a copular description—led to this novel connection between the behavior of FCIs and specificational copular clauses. I will leave a further understanding of the nature of this effect itself for future work.

    Finally, we should also wonder whether the explanation for FCI subtrigging effects that I suggest here can or should be extended to account for apparently parallel subtrigging contrasts in languages such as English (41), where FCIs do not obviously reflect the involvement of a specificational copula. I will also leave the exploration of this question for future work.

(41)   **Parallel subtrigging with English *any*:**

    a. ?? You must take any medicine.

    b. ✓ You must take any medicine <u>that the doctor gives you</u>.

6   Summary and Outlook

This paper develops a new compositional semantics for universal free choice, from the predictable interactions of a number of ingredients. A specificational copular conditional clause describes an individual concept which the consequent then makes reference to. The conditional restricts the modal base of a modal/temporal operator in the sentence. And finally, the scalar particle EVEN associating with a *wh*-indefinite, enforces that the modified modal/temporal operator be a universal quantifier over situations. This leads indirectly to a kind of universal quantification over individuals in the domain of the FCI. The end result is a new approach to the universal force of universal FCIs, without directly prescribing or deriving this force. Furthermore, we have seen that this approach offers a new analytic possibility for reducing so-called "subtrigging" effects to an independently observed constraint on indefinite subjects in specificational copular clauses.

Most importantly, this proposal is not a hypothetical proof-of-concept. The expression of universal free choice in Tibetan, documented here, transparently involves these ingredients: a concessive conditional clause (*even if*) with a copular description, ranging over different possible individual referents in the domain of a *wh*-word.

If this analytic approach for universal free choice is truly successful, we might imagine that other languages would also express universal free choice claims in this way. There is recent work suggesting exactly this. For example, Rahul Balusu (2019; 2020) has investigated different uses of concessive conditional expressions in a range of Dravidian languages; one such use is the formation of FCIs with exactly the same surface morphological makeup as in Tibetan: a *wh*-word with a copula and concessive conditional ending. Balusu also describes these copular descriptions as specificational.

(42)   **Morphologically parallel FCIs in Dravidian languages:**

    a. **Een-aad-ar-uu**   tinnutteene.
        what-COP-COND-EVEN eat.will
        'I'll eat anything.'   Kannada (Balusu 2020)

    b. Ravi **eed-ai-naa**   tinTaaDu.
        Ravi what-COP-COND.EVEN eat.will
        'Ravi will eat anything / something or other.'
                                Telugu (Balusu 2019: 46)

There are, however, some subtle differences in these constructions amongst different Dravidian languages, and between them and Tibetan. For example, Telugu *wh-ai-naa* FCIs allow both universal 'anything' as well as existential 'something or other' readings, although Kannada and Tibetan do not have such existential readings. See Balusu 2019, 2020 for discussion.

Additional evidence comes from the form of universal FCIs in Japanese, which appear to be formed of a *wh*-phrase with a particle *demo*, as in (43a). On the identity of this particle *demo*, Nakanishi (2006: 141) states, "-*Demo* can be morphologically decomposed into the copular verb -*de* followed by -*mo* [*even*]. However, it is not clear whether this decomposition is necessary." In recent work, however, Hiraiwa and Nakanishi (to appear) push the decompositional hypothesis a step further, specifically proposing that Japanese *wh-demo* FCIs have the underlying structure in (43b), with a type of ellipsis obscuring the conditional morphology.[20]

---

[20] The copula in Japanese involves the copular marker *de* as well as the existential verb *ar-*, making *de ar-te* in (43) the expected verb form for a copular conditional. See e.g. Nishiyama 1999.

(43)   **Morphologically similar FCI in Japanese:**

    a.   **Nan-demo** tabemasu.   →   b.   nan(i) de   ~~ar-te~~   mo
        what-DEMO eat.will   what COP EXIST-COND EVEN
        'I will eat anything.'   (Hiraiwa and Nakanishi, to appear)

Whether expressions with *demo* indeed always reflect the structure in (43b) in the synchronic grammar of Japanese—or if the hypothesized structure in (43b) is better thought of as the diachronic source for what is now a single grammaticalized particle, *demo*—in my opinion warrants further debate. Still, the parallel as in (43) is additional fodder for the broad cross-linguistic viability of the decompositional approach to universal free choice developed here. See also Haspelmath 1997: 135–140 for discussion of indefinite expressions in many other languages which also exhibit morphological traces of copulas and concessive conditional morphology, some of which are still clearly FCIs, whereas others have extended to other indefinite types (pp. 149–150).

Furthermore, each of these concessive copular conditional expressions in both Dravidian languages and Japanese have a number of additional uses, which in fact largely overlap with the range of uses for Tibetan *yin.na'ang* (Erlewine 2020). The clear parallels in both the morphosyntactic composition and interpretational range of these expressions, across these genetically unrelated languages, further strengthens the motivation to take the decompositional approach to these expressions seriously, as well as to better document and understand the microvariation observed in their fine-grained behavior.

References

Arregi, K., Francez, I., Martinović, M.: Three arguments for an individual concept analysis of specificational sentences. Nat. Lang. Linguist. Theory, to appear

Arregui, A., Rivero, M.L., Salanova, A.: Cross-linguistic variation in imperfectivity. Nat. Lang. Linguist. Theory **32**, 307–362 (2014)

Balusu, R.: The anatomy of the Dravidian unconditional. In: Cho, S.-Y. (ed.) Proceedings of GLOW in Asia XII, pp. 40–59. The Korean Generative Grammar Circle (2019)

Balusu, R.: Unconditional-FCIs of Dravidian. Presented at FASAL 10 (2020)

Beck, S.: Intervention effects follow from focus interpretation. Nat. Lang. Semant. **14**, 1–56 (2006)

Branan, K., Erlewine, M.Y.: Anti-pied-piping. National University of Singapore (2020, manuscript)

Chierchia, G.: Logic in Grammar: Polarity, Free Choice, and Intervention. Oxford University Press (2013)

Cipria, A., Roberts, C.: Spanish imperfecto and pretérito: truth conditions and aktionsart effects in a situation semantics. Nat. Lang. Semant. **8**, 297–347 (2000)

Comorovski, I.: Constituent questions and the copula of specification. In: Comorovski, I., von Heusinger, K. (eds.) Existence: Semantics and Syntax. SLAP, vol. 84, pp. 49–77. Springer, Dordrecht (2008). https://doi.org/10.1007/978-1-4020-6197-4_2

Elbourne, P.: Definite Descriptions. Oxford University Press (2013)

Erlewine, M.Y.: Wh-quantification in alternative semantics. Presented at GLOW in Asia XII, Dongguk University, Seoul (2019)

Erlewine, M.Y.: Counterexpectation, concession, and free choice in Tibetan. In: Whitmal, A., Asatryan, M., Song, Y. (eds.) Proceedings of NELS 50, vol. 1, pp. 227–236 (2020)

Erlewine, M.Y.: Wh-quantification in Alternative Semantics. National University of Singapore, in prep, manuscript

Erlewine, M.Y., Kotek, H.: Even-NPIs in Dharamsala Tibetan. Linguist. Anal. **40**, 129–165 (2016)

von Fintel, K.: Restrictions on quantifier domains. Doctoral dissertation, University of Massachusetts (1994)

Garrett, E.J.: Evidentiality and assertion in Tibetan. Doctoral dissertation, University of California at Los Angeles (2001)

Gawron, J.M.: Universal concessive conditionals and alternative NPs in English. In: Condoravdi, C., de Lavalette, G.R. (eds.) Logical Perspectives on Language and Information, pp. 73–106. CSLI Publications (2001)

Giannakidou, A.: The meaning of free choice. Linguist. Philos. **24**, 659–735 (2001)

Goldstein, M.C. (ed.): The New Tibetan-English Dictionary of Modern Tibetan. University of California Press (2001)

Hamblin, C.: Questions in Montague English. Found. Lang. **10**, 41–53 (1973)

Haspelmath, M.: Indefinite Pronouns. Oxford (1997)

Heim, I.: E-type pronouns and donkey anaphora. Linguist. Philos. **13**, 137–177 (1990)

Heycock, C.: Specification, equation, and agreement in copular clauses. Can. J. Linguist. **57**, 209–240 (2012)

Heycock, C., Kroch, A.: Pseudocleft connectedness: implications for the LF interface level. Linguist. Inquiry **30**, 365–397 (1999)

Higgins, F.R.: The pseudo-cleft construction in English. Doctoral dissertation, Massachusetts Institute of Technology (1973)

Hiraiwa, K., Nakanishi, K.: Free choice and existential indeterminates as hidden clauses. In: Sinitsyna, J., Tatevosov, S. (eds.) Proceedings of WAFL 15, to appear

Hirsch, A.: A compositional semantics for wh-ever free relatives. In: Proceedings of Sinn und Bedeutung 20, pp. 341–358 (2016)

Jackendoff, R.: Semantic Interpretation in Generative Grammar. MIT Press (1972)

Karttunen, L., Peters, S.: Conventional implicature. In: Oh, C.-K., Dinneen, D.A. (eds.) Syntax and Semantics: Presupposition, vol. 11, pp. 1–56. Academic Press (1979)

Kay, P.: Even. Linguist. Philos. **13**, 59–111 (1990)

Kluck, M.: Sentence amalgamation. Doctoral dissertation, University of Groningen (2011)

Kotek, H.: Composing questions. Doctoral dissertation, Massachusetts Institute of Technology (2014)

Kotek, H.: Composing Questions. MIT Press (2019)

Kratzer, A.: Conditional necessity and possibility. In: Bäuerle, R., Egli, U., von Stechow, A. (eds.) Semantics from Different Points of View, pp. 117–147. Springer, Heidelberg (1979). https://doi.org/10.1007/978-3-642-67458-7_9

Kratzer, A.: Conditionals. In: Papers from the Parasession on Pragmatics and Grammatical Theory, pp. 115–135. Chicago Linguistic Society (1986)

Kratzer, A.: An investigation into the lumps of thought. Linguist. Philos. **12**, 607–653 (1989)

Kratzer, A., Shimoyama, J.: Indeterminate pronouns: the view from Japanese. In: Otsuka, Y. (ed.) The Proceedings of the Third Tokyo Conference on Psycholinguistics (TCP 2002), pp. 1–25. Hitsuji Syobo, Tokyo (2002)

König, E.: Conditionals, concessive conditionals, and concessives: areas of contrast, overlap, and neutralization. In: Traugott, E.C., ter Meulen, A., Reilly, J.S., Ferguson, C.A. (eds.) On Conditionals, pp. 229–246. Cambridge University Press (1986)

Lahiri, U.: Focus and negative polarity in Hindi. Nat. Lang. Semant. **6**, 57–123 (1998)

Lakoff, G.: Syntactic amalgams. In: Proceedings of CLS 10, pp. 321–344 (1974)

Lee, Y.-S., Horn, L.: Any as indefinite plus even. Yale University (1995, manuscript)

LeGrand, J.: Or and any: the syntax and semantics of two logical operators. Doctoral dissertation, University of Chicago (1975)

Lewis, D.: Adverbs of quantification. In: Keenan E.L. (ed.) Formal Semantics of Natural Language, pp. 3–15. Cambridge University Press (1975)

Menéndez-Benito, P.: The grammar of choice. Doctoral dissertation, University of Massachusetts Amherst (2005)

Menéndez-Benito, P.: On universal free choice items. Nat. Lang. Semant. **18**, 33–64 (2010)

Mikkelsen, L.: Copular Clauses: Specification, Predication, and Equation. Benjamins (2005)

Milway, D.: The contrastive topic requirement on specificational subjects. Can. J. Linguist./Revue canadienne de linguistique **65**, 181–215 (2020)

Nakanishi, K.: Even, only, and negative polarity in Japanese. In: Proceedings of SALT 16, pp. 138–155 (2006)

Nishiyama, K.: Adjectives and the copulas in Japanese. J. East Asian Linguist. **8**, 183–222 (1999)

Ramchand, G.C.: Questions, Polarity and Alternative Semantics. Oxford University (1996, Manuscript)

Ramchand, G.C.: Questions, polarity and alternative semantics. In: Proceedings of NELS 27, pp. 383–396. GLSA (1997)

Rawlins, K.: (Un)conditionals: an investigation in the syntax and semantics of conditional structures. Doctoral dissertation, University of California Santa Cruz (2008a)

Rawlins, K.: Unifying if-conditionals and unconditionals. In: Friedman, T., Ito, S. (eds.) Proceedings of SALT 18, pp. 583–600 (2008b)

Rawlins, K.: (Un)conditionals. Nat. Lang. Semant. **21**, 111–178 (2013)

Romero, M.: Concealed questions and specificational subjects. Linguist. Philos. **28**, 687–737 (2005)

Rooth, M.: Association with focus. Doctoral dissertation, University of Massachusetts, Amherst (1985)

Rooth, M.: A theory of focus interpretation. Nat. Lang. Semant. **1**, 75–116 (1992)

Shimoyama, J.: Internally headed relative clauses in Japanese and E-type anaphora. J. East Asian Linguist. **8**, 147–182 (1999)

Szabolcsi, A.: Unconditionals and free choice unified. In: Proceedings of SALT 29, pp. 320–340 (2019)

Tournadre, N.: Arguments against the concept of 'conjunct'/'disjunct' in Tibetan. In: Chomolangma, Demawend und Kasbek, Festschrift für Roland Bielmeier, pp 281–308 (2008)

Tournadre, N., Dorje, S.: Manual of Standard Tibetan: Language and civilization. Snow Lion Publications (2003)

Monotonicity in Syntax

Thomas Graf[(✉)]

Stony Brook University, Stony Brook, NY 11794, USA
mail@thomasgraf.net

Abstract. Extending previous work on monotonicity in morphology
and morphosyntax, I argue that some of the most important constraints
in syntax can be analyzed in terms of monotonic functions that map specific kinds of syntactic representations to fixed, universal hierarchies. I
cover the Ban Against Improper Movement, the Williams Cycle, the Ban
Against Improper Case, and omnivorous number. The general method
of analysis is remarkably similar across all phenomena, which suggests
that monotonicity provides a unified perspective on a wide range of phenomena in syntax as well as morphology and morphosyntax. I also argue
that syntax, thanks to extensive work in computational syntax, provides
a unique opportunity to probe whether the prevalence of monotonicity
principles in natural language is due to computational complexity considerations. Not only, then, is it possible to extend the purview of monotonicity from semantics to syntax, doing so might yield new insights into
monotonicity that would not be obtainable otherwise.

Keywords: Monotonicity · Syntax · Typology · Ban against improper
movement · Dependent case · Omnivorous number

There has been plenty of research on monotonicity in semantics, but much less
on its role in phonology, morphology, and syntax. One could construe this as
strong evidence that monotonicity is mostly a semantic phenomenon, but in this
paper I will argue for the very opposite position: not only are there syntactic
phenomena that can be insightfully analyzed in terms of monotonicity, syntax
may be the key to understanding why monotonicity should have any role to play
in language, be it in semantics or any other subdomain.

I will investigate a number of phenomena that have been discussed in the
generative literature: the Ban Against Improper Movement, the Williams Cycle
[36,37], the Ban Against Improper Case [28], and omnivorous number [25]. While
these phenomena are widely regarded as unrelated, I show that they can all be
unified under the umbrella of a single monotonicity requirement. I do so building on an approach first presented in [11] for morphology and morphosyntax. In
this approach, universal grammar is assumed to furnish specific linguistic hierarchies, e.g. for person or number. Linguistic phenomena are analyzed as mappings
operating on these linguistic hierarchies, and the typologically attested patterns
turn out to be exactly those that can be represented as monotonically increasing

© Springer-Verlag GmbH Germany, part of Springer Nature 2020
D. Deng et al. (Eds.): TLLM 2020, LNCS 12564, pp. 35–53, 2020.
https://doi.org/10.1007/978-3-662-62843-0_3

mappings between two structures. The very same idea can be applied to syntax, given suitable partial orders and linguistic hierarchies.

The paper thus makes several contributions. First, it unifies a number of seemingly unrelated syntactic phenomena. Second, it connects these phenomena to others in morphology and morphosyntax that have been previously analyzed in terms of monotonicity. Finally, the paper shows that there is merit to pushing the study of monotonicity beyond semantics. Moreover, the fact that the computational properties of syntax are better understood than those of semantics means that syntax is a better choice for exploring the connections between monotonicity and computation.

I will proceed as follows: I start out with a general description of monotonicity and how it is applied to morphology and morphosyntax in [11]. Section 2 then discusses one of the most robust constraints on syntactic movement, namely the *Ban Against Improper Movement*. This section also derives a *Ban Against Improper Selection*, another constraint that is widely attested but to the best of my knowledge does not have a standardized name. It also discusses the Williams Cycle, a generalized version of the Ban Against Improper Movement, and the recently proposed Ban Against Improper Case [28]. After that, in Sect. 3, I turn to a very different phenomenon known as *omnivorous number*, and I show that it, too, is an instance of monotonicity in syntax. Finally, Sect. 4 addresses the question why syntax should be sensitive to monotonicity. While I cannot offer a conclusive answer at this point, I argue that this is just a special case of a more general issue: why should any aspect of language care about monotonicity? This is a fundamental question that all research on monotonicity has to tackle, and I conjecture that there might be a link between monotonicity and computation. If this is the case, then syntax is better suited to exploring this connection because the computational properties of semantics are not as well-understood as those of syntax.

1 Background and Prior Work

In [11], a specific approach is presented for explaining typological gaps in morphology and morphosyntax in terms of mappings from underlying algebras to surface forms. It is this approach that will form the conceptual backbone of this paper.

Let us look at adjectival gradation as a concrete example. Each adjective has three forms: positive, comparative, and superlative. In many cases all three forms share the same stem, e.g. *hard-harder-hardest*. But there is also *good-better-best*, and its Latin counterpart *bonus-melior-optimus*. In the former, only the comparative and the superlative have similar stems, while in the latter each form uses a distinct stem. Abstracting away from these specific adjectives, we may refer to these three patterns as AAA, ABB, and ABC. Curiously absent is the pattern ABA, which would correspond to something like *good-better-goodest*. This gap exists across a variety of paradigms beyond adjectival gradation, suggesting a general ban against ABA patterns [3].

As shown in [11], this ban against ABA patterns can be construed as an instance of monotonicity. Consider once more the case of adjectival gradation. The three adjectival forms can be arranged according to their denotational semantics, yielding the adjectival gradation hierarchy

$$positive < comparative < superlative$$

Now assume that we take A, B, and C as arbitrary placeholders for surface forms and put them in an arbitrary order. For the sake of exposition, let's say that this order is

$$A < B < C$$

Patterns AAA and ABC can be viewed as mappings from the adjectival gradation hierarchy into this hierarchy of output forms. For instance, AAA arises when $f(\text{positive}) = f(\text{comparative}) = f(\text{superlative}) = A$ (note that AAA, BBB, and CCC all describe the same pattern as the important issue is which forms share stems, not whether we denote this stem as A, B, or C). The mappings corresponding to AAA, ABB, ABC, and ABA are depicted in Fig. 1. Since we are dealing with two linear orders, we may also view them as axes of a diagram in which we plot each pattern (Fig. 2).

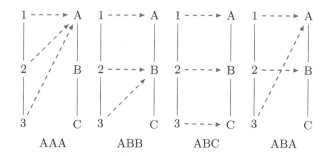

Fig. 1. Pictorial representation of mappings yielding AAA, ABB, ABC, and ABA

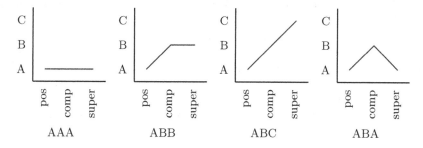

Fig. 2. Diagrammatic representation of the mappings for AAA, ABB, ABC, and ABA

Notice how the unattested ABA pattern differs from the attested ones in that I) it involves two crossing branches in Fig. 1, and II) it is the only pattern to change direction in Fig. 2. Hence we can explain the absence of ABA patterns in terms of some principle that does not allow functions to behave this way. That is exactly what one gets from the familiar notion of monotonicity.

Definition 1. *Let* $\mathcal{A} := \langle A, \leq_A \rangle$ *and* $\mathcal{B} := \langle B, \leq_B \rangle$ *be two partially ordered sets. Then a mapping f from $\mathcal{A}$ to $\mathcal{B}$ is*

- monotonically increasing *iff* $x \leq_A y$ *implies* $f(x) \leq_B f(y)$,
- monotonically decreasing *iff* $x \leq_A y$ *implies* $f(y) \leq_B f(x)$.

Throughout the paper, I will use the terms *monotonic* and *monotonically increasing* interchangeably. According to the definition above, the ABA pattern for adjectival gradation is not monotonic because we have $f(\text{positive}) = f(\text{superlative}) = A < B = f(\text{comparative})$, yet comparative < superlative. Hence the ban against ABA patterns follows from the assumption that mappings must be monotonic and the adjectival gradation forms are ordered such that positive < comparative < superlative.

In isolation, this is not particularly remarkable. But as shown in [11], the idea can be extended to a large number of phenomena in morphology and morphosyntax: personal pronoun syncretism, case allomorphy, noun stem allomorphy, the Person Case Constraint, and the Gender Case Constraint. In some cases, the linguistic hierarchy is not a linear order but a partial one, so that some elements are unordered with respect to each other. Monotonicity generalizes immediately to these partial orders, too, and thus it provides a uniform explanation for a large number of seemingly unrelated typological gaps.

As I will show in the next two sections, the same is true for syntax. I start with a discussion of the Ban Against Improper Movement, which involves hierarchies that are linear orders. In Sect. 3, I then show how the typology of omnivorous number can be explained via monotonicity over a partial order.

Before moving on, though, I have to remark on the general methodology of this approach. The line of research pursued in this paper differs from typical work on monotonicity in that the functions under discussion have fairly small domains and co-domains. Whereas work on monotonicity in semantics often assumes infinite (co-)domains, the most complex function in [11] has a domain of size 16 and a co-domain of size 2. With such small numbers, it is to be expected that most phenomena allow us to order the elements they involve in such a manner that the mapping turns out to be monotonic. This is why it is important that the posited orders be linguistically plausible. Sometimes, multiple orders could be motivated on linguistic grounds—for instance, one may posit a number hierarchy singular < dual < plural on semantic grounds, or instead go with singular < plural < dual due to the typological implication that if a language has a dual, it most likely also has a plural. In this case, there is no *a priori* reason to prefer one order over the other, and the decision is made based on whichever order offers a better fit for the available data. But once the decision has been made, the same hierarchy must be used uniformly across all relevant phenomena;

one cannot use one number hierarchy for phenomenon X and a different number hierarchy for phenomenon Y, as this would only lead to circular reasoning. This paper marks the first foray into syntax for the monotonicity approach, and thus the posited hierarchies are still limited to a few phenomena. Nonetheless, they already succeed at unifying distinct phenomena (for example, Sect. 3 ties the existence of omnivorous number directly to the existence of resolved agreement). While the findings are still limited in scope, they provide a fertile starting point.

2   Restrictions on Movement Types

Generative syntacticians make a distinction between at least three types of syntactic dependencies: selection, A-movement, and A'-movement. These dependencies are subject to a fundamental syntactic law, the Ban Against Improper Movement. These syntactic ideas will be explained in a moment. For now, the key issue is that it is still unclear why natural languages uniformly obey this law. Syntactic formalisms usually have to stipulate it instead of deriving it from independently motivated aspects of syntax. I show that the Ban Against Improper Movement can be reduced to a general monotonicity requirement. The reduction is straight-forward, but it requires us to establish a bit of linguistic background first. Readers who are already familiar with selection, A-movement, and A'-movement can skip ahead to the very last paragraph of Sect. 2.1, which covers everything that is needed to derive the Ban Against Improper Movement (Sect. 2.2). I then argue that the same idea can also account for generalized versions of this ban, such as the Williams Cycle and the Ban Against Improper Case (Sect. 2.3).

2.1   Selection, A-Movement, and A'-Movement

Selection combines a head with its arguments. It is the basic mechanism for establishing head-argument dependencies. There are many ways to handle selection in the grammar. GSPG and HPSG use subcategorization frames [7,27], Tree Adjoining Grammar encodes selectional requirements directly in its elementary trees [19,20], and Minimalist Grammars (which are inspired by Chomsky's Minimalist Program [5]) annotate each lexical item with category and selector features to control the structure-building operation Merge [33,34]. For the purposes of this paper, we can completely abstract away from these technical details. It only matters that there is a broad consensus that syntax involves combining heads with their arguments, and that this phenomenon is what we refer to as *selection*.

There is also a broad consensus that selection is maximally local. That is to say, selection cannot target a phrase that is embedded inside another phrase:

(1)   a.   John cut [_DP the carrot].

      b.   * John cut [_VP bought [_DP the carrot]].

While the verb *cut* can select the DP *the carrot* in (1a) , it cannot do so in (1b) where *the carrot* is embedded inside a VP.

An anonymous reviewer points out that this claim is at odds with the fact that *John greeted [[_DP whoever] Mary invited]* is well-formed, whereas the minimally different *John greeted [[_DP whatever] Mary invited]* is not. This suggests that the verb selects for the wh-phrase inside the complement clause. There are many ways this could be addressed. One might say that the second sentence is in fact syntactically well-formed and that its reduced acceptability is due to semantics. Other analyses allow the features that distinguish *whoever* from *whatever* to pass from the DP onto the head of the clausal complement, maintaining the locality of selection. The monotonicity approach can remain agnostic about this—the precise degree of locality of selection is immaterial as long as selection is less local than A-movement and A′-movement, which are discussed next.

A-movement and A′-movement both establish long-distance dependencies between a phrase and some other position in the sentence. *A-movement*, which is short for *argument movement*, targets positions that are in some way tied to a fixed grammatical function (the precise definition of A-movement is hotly debated, see [29] for an accessible overview). For instance, the promotion of an object to subject position in a passive sentence is commonly regarded as an instance of A-movement, and so is subject raising. Both are illustrated below, with *t* indicating the position that the phrase *John* is related to via A-movement.

(2)   a.   John was attacked *t*.   *Passive*

      b.   John seems *t* to have cut the carrot.   *Subject raising*

In (2a), *John* appears in the subject position but is interpreted as the object of *attacked*. In (2b), *John* is pronounced in the subject position of the matrix clause but is interpreted as the subject of the embedded verb *cut*. In both (2a) and (2b), we are dealing with A-movement because *John* appears in an argument position—a subject position, in this case—but the sentence is interpreted as if *John* resided in some other position.

Some readers may be puzzled that I describe A-movement as a dependency between positions and not as an operation. Admittedly the term originates from Transformational Grammar, where movement is construed as an operation that targets a phrase and puts it in a different position in the phrase structure tree. But just like selection can be implemented in many different ways, there are numerous ways of handling A-movement, many of which do not involve any kind of displacement. In fact, it is even possible to have a dedicated movement operation yet do not use it for A-movement [22]. Just as with selection, the pertinent point here is that syntax involves a cluster of phenomena that is subsumed under *A-movement*, not what specific mechanisms are the driving force behind these phenomena.

This leaves us with *A′-movement*, or *non-argument movement*. As the full name indicates, A′-movement establishes a dependency between positions that are not targeted by A-movement. This includes question formation and topicalization, among others. Neither construction involves a position that is tied to a specific grammatical function like subject or object.

(3) a. Who did Mary attack *t*.   *Question formation*

b. John, Mary attacked *t*.   *Topicalization*

A-movement and A′-movement differ in several respects, e.g. how they interact with semantic scope. But once again these details are largely immaterial for this paper, except that A-movement is more local than A′-movement; for example, only the latter can operate across finite clauses.

(4) a. * John said that Mary attacked *t*.   *A-movement of object*

b. * John seems that *t* attacked Mary.   *A-movement of subject*

c. John seems to have *t* attacked Mary.   *infinitival A-movement*

d. Who did John say that Mary attacked *t*.   *A′-movement*

Here (4a) is illicit under the intended reading that John said that Mary attacked him. We cannot establish an A-movement dependency between *John* and the object position of *attacked* because this dependency would span across the boundary of a finite clause. Similarly, (4b) is not well-formed as the A-movement dependency between *John* and the embedded subject would cross a finite clause boundary. Example (4c) shows that the problem is indeed the finiteness of the clause, as the same A-movement dependency can hold across an infinitival clause boundary. Finally, we see that the A′-movement dependency in (4d) is well-formed even though it holds across a finite clause boundary.

Depending on their theoretic priors, readers may object that the contrasts above can be explained on independent grounds that do not require A-movement to be more local than A′-movement (for instance the Case filter of Government-and-Binding theory). But this objection is based on construing the term "A-movement" as referring to a specific mechanism of the grammar, rather than a cluster of empirical phenomena. The claim is not that A-movement is intrinsically limited to be more local than A′-movement, but that syntax as a whole causes A-movement phenomena to be more limited than A′-movement phenomena. The source of this discrepancy and its causal mechanisms are deliberately abstracted away from, just like the monotonicity analysis in [11] posits a person hierarchy of $1 < 2 < 3$ while remaining agnostic about how (and even whether) person is represented in the grammar or what specific grammatical principles give rise to this order.

To sum up, there are three distinct types of syntactic phenomena that are commonly thought of in mechanical terms as selection, A-movement, and A′-movement. They differ in their locality, with selection as the most local option and A′-movement the least local one. I encode this fact in terms of a general locality hierarchy:

$$\text{selection} < \text{A-movement} < \text{A}′\text{-movement}$$

In the remainder of this section, I will refer to this hierarchy as the linear order $\mathcal{L} := \langle\{\text{selection, A-movement, A}'\text{-movement}\}, <\rangle$. In conjunction with monotonicity, $\mathcal{L}$ derives the Ban Against Improper Movement and several generalizations of this ban.

2.2   The Ban Against Improper Movement

The (simplified) examples in Sect. 2.1 may give the impression that a phrase participates in at most one instance of A-movement or at most one instance of A'-movement. But this is not the case. Quite often, a phrase participates in multiple instances of movement, and the manner in which it may do so is regulated by the Ban Against Improper Movement.

Let us consider a concrete example.

(5)   [Which boy] does John think t impressed everyone?

Here the phrase *which boy* originated from the subject position of the embedded clause. Depending on one's analysis, though, many movement steps are involved in this. For the sake of exposition, I will present a Minimalist analysis of (5). In Minimalism, movement is indeed interpreted as an operation that displaces subtrees, and there are a few additional movement steps that are motivated by theoretical considerations. Consider, then, the sequence of steps that results in (5): First, *which boy* is selected by the verb *impressed* and undergoes A-movement to the embedded subject position. From there, it moves to the left edge of its clause, which is an instance of A'-movement. This is followed by another instance of A'-movement to the left edge of the matrix clause. The resulting phrase structure tree is depicted on the left of Fig. 3 (which also shows the A-movement of *John* to the matrix subject position).

Now contrast the well-formed (5) against the illicit (6).

(6)   *[Which boy] does t think t impressed everyone?

The intended reading for this sentence is *which boy is such that he thinks that he impressed everyone*, but not only is this reading unavailable, the whole sentence is illicit. When we compare the phrase structure tree for (6) on the left of Fig. 3 to the one for (5) on the right, we can see that they differ in what types of movement take place.

In (6), *which boy* is once again selected by *impressed* and then undergoes A-movement to the embedded subject position and A'-movement to the left edge of the embedded clause. But then (5) and (6) diverge. Whereas (5) continues with A'-movement, (6) instead has *which boy* switch back to A-movement. Considered in isolation, this A-movement should be licit as it does not cross a clause boundary—the movement past the complementizer was an instance of A'-movement. Without further assumptions, then, there is no reason for (6) to be ill-formed.

Syntacticians have argued for a long time that the source of ill-formedness is the switch from A'-movement back to A-movement; this is what is commonly referred to as the Ban Against Improper Movement:

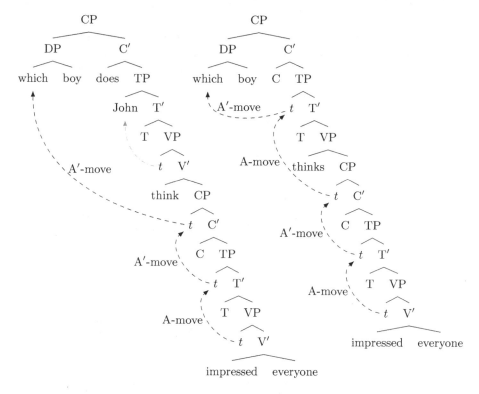

Fig. 3. Minimalist analyses of the licit (5) on the left and the illicit (6) on the right; only the latter intersperses A-movement and A′-movement.

(7) **Ban Against Improper Movement** (standard version)
A phrase that has already undergone A′-movement can no longer undergo A-movement.

Note that the Ban Against Improper Movement allows A-movement to take place after A′-movement as long as it is not the same phrase that undergoes both steps. In (5), for instance, *John* is allowed to participate in A-movement even though *which boy* has already A′-moved. In (6), on the other hand, the very same phrase *which boy* is supposed to A-move after it has already A′-moved. This violates the Ban Against Improper Movement, and hence (6) is ill-formed.

But the Ban Against Improper Movement is a stipulation, it cannot be naturally derived from other syntactic mechanisms (but see [24] for a recent attempt to do so). We can improve on this by reducing the ban to an instance of monotonicity, which is already known to be an important factor in semantics, morphology, and morphosyntax. To this end, let us consider the locality hiearchy $\mathcal{L}$, repeated here with the shorter names used in Fig. 3.

$$\text{Select} < \text{A-Move} < \text{A}'\text{-Move}$$

The Ban Against Improper Movement is, essentially, a requirement that the mapping from a phrase's sequence of operations into $\mathcal{L}$ be monotonic.

Let us look at this in detail. For any given phrase, we may record the sequence of operations it participates in. For example, *which boy* in (5) would have the sequence

$$\text{Select} < \text{A-Move} < \text{A}'\text{-Move} < \text{A}'\text{-Move}$$

while *which boy* in (6) would get the sequence

$$\text{Select} < \text{A-Move} < \text{A}'\text{-Move} < \text{A-Move} < \text{A}'\text{-Move}.$$

Note that we can also view these sequences as mappings from natural numbers into $\mathcal{L}$, where the natural number n denotes the n-th element of the sequence of operations. For example, the sequence for *which boy* in (5) above is equivalent to a mapping with $1 \mapsto \text{Select}$, $2 \mapsto \text{A-Move}$, $3 \mapsto \text{A}'\text{-Move}$, and $4 \mapsto \text{A}'\text{-Move}$. The Ban Against Improper Movement requires that the sequences, when viewed as such mappings, must obey the order of $\mathcal{L}$.

(8) **Ban Against Improper Movement** (monotonicity version)
     Given some phrase p in some syntactic structure t, let f be a function from natural numbers into $\mathcal{L}$ such that f encodes the sequence of operations that applied to p in t. Then f must be monotonically increasing.

The function f for *which boy* in the illicit (6) violates this requirement: clearly $3 < 4$, yet $f(3) = \text{A}'\text{-Move} > \text{A-Move} = f(4)$.

In fact, the monotonicity version of the Ban Against Improper Movement also makes an additional prediction: once a phrase has undergone A-movement or A'-movement, it can no longer participate in selection. This is indeed the case. A phrase that has started moving can no longer select any arguments, nor can it be selected by anything else.[1] Syntacticians treat that as yet another law of syntax, whereas the monotonicity version of the Ban Against Improper Movement already rules out this kind of *Improper Selection*. Not only then can the Ban Against Improper Movement be related to monotonicity, doing so allows us to subsume another important constraint as just another special case.

2.3 Generalized Versions of the Ban Against Improper Movement

The Ban Against Improper Movement has been modified and generalized in several ways, and these generalizations also fit under the umbrella of monotonicity.

Perhaps the best-known generalization is the *Williams Cycle* [36,37]. It starts with the assumption of some linear order of all positions that a phrase can move from or into. In Minimalist syntax, for instance, a simplified version of this hierarchy could be VP $<$ vP $<$ TP $<$ CP (the vP position was skipped

---

[1] This of course depends on how one analyzes cases such as *John greeted whoever Mary invited*, which was discussed in Sect. 2.1. In addition, there have been proposals in the Minimalist literature that a mover can undergo *Late Merge* with some of its arguments [35].

in all phrase structure trees so far, but I include it here as it will matter in the discussion of case later on). The Williams Cycle then states that a phrase p cannot move into a position that is less prominent than the position that p currently resides in. For example, if p currently resides in CP, then it cannot move into a VP- or TP-position, but it could still move into another CP position. The Williams Cycle thus derives the ungrammaticality of (6) because, as we saw in Fig. 3, the phrase *which boy* moves from a CP position into a TP position. The minimally different (5), on the other hand, is correctly predicted to be well-formed as *which boy* moves from a VP-position to a TP-position, from there to a CP-position, and from there to another CP-position. The Williams Cycle thus constitutes a more fine-grained version of the Ban Against Improper Movement.

It should be readily apparent, though, that the Williams Cycle can be analyzed in exactly the same fashion as the Ban Against Improper Movement. Once again we keep a record of the relevant syntactic steps for each phrase. But now this record is no longer a sequence that lists the relevant operation/dependency (Select, A-Move, A'-Move). Instead, it lists the kind of position that the phrase resided in (VP, TP, CP, and so on). The Williams Cycle requires that this sequence must be a monotonic mapping from natural numbers into the hierarchy VP < TP < CP (or an extended version thereof with additional types of positions). Hence the sequence VP < CP < TP < CP for (6) is forbidden because $f(2) = CP > f(3) = TP$ yet $2 < 3$. If anything, the Williams Cycle reveals the monotonic nature of the Ban Against Improper Movement even more clearly.

The Williams Cycle also provides the motivation for a recently proposed *Ban Against Improper Case* [28]. This principle starts with a specific analysis of how noun phrases receive morphological case, known as *Dependent Case Theory* (see [30] for a recent overview and a discussion of structural and lexical case in this theory). Dependent Case Theory posits that the case on one noun phrase can determine the case on another noun phrase. For example, direct objects typically receive accusative because of the nominative case on the subject, and indirect objects receive dative because of the accusative case on the direct object. Intuitively, there is a case hierarchy Nom < Acc < Dat < ⋯ and each noun phrase gets the next case that has not yet been claimed by a more prominent noun phrase. However, this kind of dependent case is not unrestricted. It is usually assumed to be clause bounded, so that the subject of the matrix clause cannot cause the subject of an embedded clause to receive accusative. The Ban Against Improper Case takes this idea and refines it in very much the same fashion that the Williams Cycle refines the Ban Against Improper Movement.

(9) **Ban Against Improper Case** (paraphrased from [28])
     Assume that there is some ordering < of syntactic positions. Then a noun phrase in position X cannot license dependent case on a noun phrase Y if there is some position Z between X and Y such that $X < Z$.

As a concrete example, consider the following sentence:

(10) [TP He [$_v$P told [VP her [CP that [TP it had been stolen]]]]].

English still displays remnants of case in its pronoun system. Here we see that the subjects *he* and *it* carry nominative, whereas the object *her* carries accusative case. The accusative case on the object *her* has to be licensed by the nominative on the subject *he*. Objects reside in VP-positions, and subjects in TP-positions. The only position between the two is *v*P. If we assume, as before, a hierarchy of the form VP < *v*P < TP < CP, then the presence of this *v*P does not violate the Ban Against Improper Case because it is not the case that *v*P > TP.

Now let us turn to the nominative case on the embedded subject *it*. Given what I said before about Dependent Case Theory, one might expect the accusative on the object *her* to cause *it* to receive dative case. That does not happen because of the Ban Against Improper Case. The subject *it* resides in a TP-position, and the object *her* in a VP-position. Between the two is a CP-position. Since TP < CP, the accusative on *her* cannot affect the case of *it* without triggering a violation of the Ban Against Improper Case. Hence the pronoun *it* appears with nominative case, effectively starting a new chain of dependent case licensing that is separate from whatever happened in the matrix clause.

The astute reader has probably figured out already how the Ban Against Improper Case reduces to monotonicity. For each phrase with licensed case, we look at the path of positions that starts right above said phrase and extends all the way up to its case licensor. When viewed as a mapping from natural numbers into the hierarchy of positions, the mapping must be monotonic. For the example above, the sequence for *her* is *v*P < TP, which is monotonically increasing. If *it* were to stand in a dependent case relation with *her*, then the corresponding sequence would be CP < VP, which is not monotonically increasing. For the same reason, *Bill* cannot stand in a case relation with *he* either, as this would yield the non-monotonic sequence CP < VP < *v*P < TP. When applied to such "case licensing paths", monotonicity does exactly the same work as the Ban Against Improper Case.

Overall, then, monotonicity can be regarded as the driving force behind the Ban Against Improper Movement/Williams Cycle, the Ban Against Improper Selection, and the Ban Against Improper Case. The treatment here is far from exhaustive. For example, I have said nothing about how head movement or sidewards movement [26] fit into this picture. Still, this is a promising start, and monotonicity can be pushed even farther.

3   Omnivorous Number

All the cases discussed so far involved a linear hierarchy. But the notion of monotonicity also applies to partial orders, and this, too, finds application in syntax. One concrete example comes from *omnivorous number* [25], to be discussed next (Sect. 3.1). The analysis of omnivorous number will also highlight some important methodological aspects of the monotonicity approach (Sect. 3.2).

3.1 Proposed Analysis

Omnivorous number is a rare phenomenon that only occurs in languages where verbal agreement is contingent on both the subject and the object. In languages with omnivorous number, a transitive verb displays plural agreement unless both its subject and its object are singular. In other words, once at least one argument of the verb is plural, the verb display plural agreement. This is illustrated by the following example from Georgian [25, p. 950].

(11) g-   xedav- t
      2NDOBJ- saw-   PL

This utterance is highly ambiguous as it could mean "I saw you.PL", "We saw you.SG", and "We saw you.PL", among other options. All of these are potential readings because each one contains at least one plural argument that could be the source of the plural agreement on the verb.

Curiously, no known language displays the opposite system where verbal agreement depends on multiple arguments yet is singular if at least one argument is singular. The absence of this pattern is striking. One major goal of syntactic theories is to allow for the vast range of cross-linguistic variation while providing an explanation as to why some logically conceivable patterns never seem to occur. Ideally, the explanation for these typological gaps is simple and not specific to just a few phenomena. Both desiderata are met by a monotonicity-based analysis of omnivorous number—the analysis is simple, and it treats omnivorous number as yet another expression of a general monotonicity principle that also drives the Ban Against Improper Movement and many other syntactic constraints. As with all the constraints seen in Sect. 2, the monotonicity account of omnivorous number will restrict the mapping from some syntactic ordering to a fixed universal hierarchy. The major innovation of omnivorous number, though, is that the syntactic ordering is no longer linear, but a partial order.

First, let us assume a universal number hierarchy such that sg < pl. This hierarchy is intuitively plausible in the sense that it replicates the ordering of quantities—a plural refers to more entities than a singular. There have been arguments in the literature that plural should be considered a semantic default from which the singular meaning is derived [31], but these do not necessarily conflict with the hierarchy above. These arguments make claims about how one meaning is derived from another, whereas the hierarchy I propose orders singular and plural in terms of their semantic extension. Moreover, we will see at the end of the section that the key insight of the monotonicity account is preserved even if one uses a hierarchy of the form pl < sg.

The hierarchy sg < pl gives us one ordering for monotonicity, but we still have to define a second ordering that represents the syntactic agreement mechanism that produces omnivorous number. Omnivorous number only arises in languages where the verb V agrees with both its subject S and its object O, and we will only consider such languages here (so English, for instance, would require a different model that omits O). Crucially, the number values of V, S, and O are not completely independent of each other. The number value of V depends on its two arguments S and O, but number values of S and O do not depend on each other. We can regard this as a partial order such that $S < V$ and $O < V$, but S and O are unordered with respect to each other.

We thus arrive at the two structures depicted below.

We can now ask what kind of mapping f can be defined from the partially ordered set on the left to the linear order on the right. Under the assumption that f must be total, there are 8 options, which are listed in Table 1. There are only three unattested patterns, all of which involve the verb displaying singular agreement even though at least one of its arguments is plural. These are exactly the cases that are ruled out if the mapping f must be monotonically increasing. Consider, for example, the case where $f(S) = f(V) = sg < pl = f(O)$. This contradicts $O < V$ and is hence ruled out. Minor variations of this equation show that the other unattested forms are not monotonic mappings either, whereas the attested patterns are.

Table 1. Potential agreement types in a language where verbs agree with subjects and objects in number

$f(S)$	$f(O)$	$f(V)$	Attested?
sg	sg	sg	yes (uniform agreement)
sg	sg	pl	yes (resolved agreement)
sg	pl	sg	no
sg	pl	pl	yes (omnivorous number)
pl	sg	sg	no
pl	sg	pl	yes (omnivorous number)
pl	pl	sg	no
pl	pl	pl	yes (uniform agreement)

We see then that monotonicity—when combined with intuitively plausible hierarchies that encode, respectively, the relation of singular and plural and how the value of the verb depends on its argument—is fully sufficient to derive the attested typology of verbal agreement systems with two arguments.

3.2   Addressing a Potential Objection

The reader might object that my account relies on two stipulations: 1) the function must be monotonically increasing rather than monotonically decreasing, and II) the number hierarchy is sg < pl rather than pl < sg. It is instructive to fully explore this issue as it highlights in what ways the monotonicity approach to syntax can(not) enhance our linguistic understanding.

First, note that assumptions I and II are interlinked. If we alter both, we get exactly the same system because "monotonically increasing" is the dual of "monotonically decreasing", and sg < pl is the dual of pl < sg; the two duals cancel each other out. Suppose, then, that we alter only one of the two. No matter which one of the two assumptions we replace with its dual, we get the predictions in Table 2. These predictions do not line up with the typological landscape. Crucially, we do not just replace omnivorous number with its counterpart, we also predict that resolved agreement is impossible. Resolved agreement occurs when two singular arguments yield a single plural agreement marker, and this behavior is attested. Under the analysis proposed in Sect. 3.1, the existence of resolved agreement predicts the existence of omnivorous number (and the other way round).

Table 2. Predicted typology if either sg < pl or the mapping must be monotonically decreasing

$f(S)$	$f(O)$	$f(V)$	Attested?	Predicted to exist?
sg	sg	sg	yes (uniform agreement)	yes
sg	sg	pl	yes (resolved agreement)	no
sg	pl	sg	no	yes
sg	pl	pl	yes (omnivorous number)	no
pl	sg	sg	no	yes
pl	sg	pl	yes (omnivorous number)	no
pl	pl	sg	no	yes
pl	pl	pl	yes (uniform agreement)	yes

This kind of unification is the principal driver of the monotonicity approach, which otherwise could quickly devolve into arbitrariness. The approach relies on domain-specific hierarchies, but since hierarchies are an abstract encoding of linguistic substance, which is not nearly as well understood as linguistic form, they are necessarily tentative. Each hierarchy has to be motivated by independent considerations, e.g. locality or semantics, among others, but that is a soft constraint at best. However, one and the same hierarchy may affect many different phenomena, and thus linguistic typology acts as a much stronger constraint on the shape of hierarchies. The monotonicity perspective deliberately abstracts away from details of the grammar in order to maximize the impact of typology. If two phenomena revolve around, say, person, then they should both be describable in terms of the same person hierarchy, even if they involve vastly different mechanisms in the grammar. This way, the hierarchies can be put on a firm empirical foundation that minimizes arbitrariness.

We have seen several concrete instances of this principle throughout the paper. The analysis above combines resolved agreement and omnivorous number into a single package: if one can occur in some natural language, the other can occur in some (other) natural language. In the discussion of movement types (Sect. 2.2), the monotonicity analysis of the Ban Against Improper Movement also subsumes a Ban Against Improper Selection, and the Ban Against Improper Case uses the same hierarchy as the Williams Cycle. This is the ideal scenario: a hierarchy that is motivated by independent considerations can be combined with monotonicity to explain not just one specific phenomenon, but an array of phenomena.

4   Why Monotonicity?

By now, the reader is hopefully convinced that a number of syntactic phenomena can be insightfully analyzed in terms of monotonicity. This raises the question, though, why monotonicity should play a role in syntax.

The apparent importance of monotonicity is particularly puzzling because there seems to be no natural way to encode monotonicity in common syntactic formalisms such as Minimalism, HPSG, LFG, or TAG. This paper deliberately analyzed syntax at a high level of abstraction that completely factors out how the relevant orders and properties may be inferred by the syntactic machinery (or how said machinery could give rise to the observed orders). But this is in fact a common strategy in syntax. For example, syntactic accounts of NPI licensing frequently gloss over how syntax determines whether a phrase is an NPI-licensor. Sometimes the issue is sidestepped via lexicalization, e.g. via a specific feature, or by assuming that there is a finite list of NPI-licensors that can be queried by syntax. But this is just one specific way of syntacticizing a more abstract concept. Similarly, there is extensive work on island constraints, yet very little on how one encodes whether a specific phrase is an island or not—attempts to do so often require unusual encoding tricks (cf. [1]). Implementation details can obfuscate more than they illuminate, and syntacticians frequently do not provide formal implementations when there is reason to believe that the implementation would not yield novel insights. I have taken the same stance here with monotonicity, implicitly assuming that the issue of how monotonocity could be recast in terms of syntactic machinery would not help us understand the role of monotonicity in syntax. Seeing how some of the most fundamental aspects of syntax are rarely encoded directly in the syntactic formalism, it is not too troubling that the same holds of monotonicity and the proposed orders and hierarchies.

One should also keep in mind the following: while it is surprising for syntax to be sensitive to monotonicity, it would be even more surprising if syntax did not care about monotonicity at all. Monotonicity is already a major factor in semantics, and the work that this paper builds on suggests that monotonicity matters in morphology, too [11]. In addition, linguists have often noted the importance of structure-preservation principles, which can be regarded as an instance of monotonicity. And finally, work on grammatical inference points towards monotonicity greatly simplifying the learning problem (see [17]). Monotonicity has a role to play in many aspects of language, and it would be surprising for syntax to be exempt from that.

In the future, it will be interesting to see if broadening the scope of research on monotonicity from semantics to all linguistic domains yields a unifying cause for the prevalence of monotonicity in language. The answer may lie in learnability and grammatical inference, but I conjecture that computational complexity is also an important factor. The work that this paper builds on [11] grew out of [9], where typological gaps are explained in terms of how specific linguistic graph structures can and cannot be rewritten if the rewriting mechanism must fit a particular notion of *subregular complexity*. Subregular linguistics is concerned with the application of very restricted subclasses of finite-state machinery to natural language. There has been a flurry of promising results in computational phonology, morphology, syntax, and even semantics (see, among others, [2,4,6, 10,12–16,18,23,32]). Monotonicity might be an elegant approximation of a more fine-grained, but also less intuitive notion of subregular complexity.

Syntax is the ideal candidate for probing the connection between monotonicity and computation. Monotonicity has been studied most extensively with respect to semantics, but this paper and related work show that morphology and syntax also seem to be exquisitely sensitive to monotonicity. Between morphology and syntax, the latter has seen a lot more work on its subregular complexity. Consequently, syntax is the only area of language right now that provides a fertile ground for both monotonicity and subregular complexity. If there is some connection between monotonicity and subregular complexity, some computational driver towards monotonicity, it should be easier to find in syntax than in phonology, morphology, or semantics.

5   Conclusion

I have presented several syntactic phenomena that can be analyzed in terms of monotonicity: the Ban Against Improper Movement, the Williams Cycle, the Ban Against Improper Case, and omnivorous number. Due to space constraints, many others had to be omitted, such as the Keenan-Comrie hierarchy [21]. There is also a plethora of work on 3/4-splits in typology, where only 3 out of 4 conceivable options ever show up in natural language. These can be regarded as monotonic maps from an order with two elements into another order with two elements. In addition, existing work such as the algebraic account of adjunct islands in [8] implicitly use monotonicity. A large number of seemingly unrelated phenomena thus fall under the purview of the same universal principle. They all can be explained in terms of monotonic mappings from some kind of abstract syntactic representation to a universal hierarchy.

That said, the work reported here is but a starting point. The posited hierarchies require a more rigorous and insightful motivation, and it will be important to also identify phenomena that do not obey monotonicity. This will give us a deeper understanding of the place of monotonicity in natural language, and may ultimately answer the question why any aspect of language, be it semantics, syntax, or something else, should care about monotonicity in the first place.

Acknowledgments. The work reported in this paper was supported by the National Science Foundation under Grant No. BCS-1845344. The paper benefited tremendously from discussion with Aniello De Santo, Alëna Aksënova, Ayla Karakas, Sedigheh Moradi, and Nazila Shafiei, as well as the detailed feedback of two anonymous reviewers.

References

1. Abels, K.: Successive cyclicity, anti-locality, and adposition stranding. Ph.D. thesis, University of Connecticut (2003)
2. Aksënova, A., Graf, T., Moradi, S.: Morphotactics as tier-based strictly local dependencies. In: Proceedings of the 14th SIGMORPHON Workshop on Computational Research in Phonetics, Phonology, and Morphology, pp. 121–130 (2016). https://www.aclweb.org/anthology/W/W16/W16-2019.pdf
3. Bobaljik, J.D.: Universals in Comparative Morphology: Suppletion, Superlatives, and the Structure of Words. MIT Press, Cambridge (2012)
4. Chandlee, J., Heinz, J.: Strict locality and phonological maps. Linguistic Inquiry **49**, 23–60 (2018)
5. Chomsky, N.: The Minimalist Program. MIT Press, Cambridge (1995)
6. De Santo, A., Graf, T.: Structure sensitive tier projection: applications and formal properties. In: Bernardi, R., Kobele, G., Pogodalla, S. (eds.) Formal Grammar, pp. 35–50. Springer, Heidelberg (2019). https://doi.org/10.1007/978-3-662-59648-7_3
7. Gazdar, G., Klein, E., Pullum, G.K., Sag, I.A.: Generalized Phrase Structure Grammar. Blackwell, Oxford (1985)
8. Graf, T.: The syntactic algebra of adjuncts. In: Proceedings of CLS 49 (2013, to appear)
9. Graf, T.: Graph transductions and typological gaps in morphological paradigms. In: Proceedings of the 15th Meeting on the Mathematics of Language (MOL 2017), pp. 114–126 (2017). http://www.aclweb.org/anthology/W17-3411
10. Graf, T.: Why movement comes for free once you have adjunction. In: Edmiston, D., et al. (eds.) Proceedings of CLS 53, pp. 117–136 (2018)
11. Graf, T.: Monotonicity as an effective theory of morphosyntactic variation. J. Lang. Modelling **7**, 3–47 (2019)
12. Graf, T.: A subregular bound on the complexity of lexical quantifiers. In: Schlöder, J.J., McHugh, D., Roelofsen, F. (eds.) Proceedings of the 22nd Amsterdam Colloquium, pp. 455–464 (2019)
13. Graf, T.: Curbing feature coding: strictly local feature assignment. Proc. Soc. Comput. Linguist. (SCiL) **2020**, 362–371 (2020)
14. Graf, T., De Santo, A.: Sensing tree automata as a model of syntactic dependencies. In: Proceedings of the 16th Meeting on the Mathematics of Language, pp. 12–26. Association for Computational Linguistics, Toronto, Canada (2019). https://www.aclweb.org/anthology/W19-5702
15. Heinz, J.: The computational nature of phonological generalizations. In: Hyman, L., Plank, F. (eds.) Phonological Typology, Chap. 5, pp. 126–195. Phonetics and Phonology, Mouton De Gruyter (2018)
16. Heinz, J., Idsardi, W.: What complexity differences reveal about domains in language. Topics Cogn. Sci. **5**(1), 111–131 (2013)
17. Heinz, J., Kasprzik, A., Kötzing, T.: Learning in the limit with lattice-structured hypothesis spaces. Theoret. Comput. Sci. **457**, 111–127 (2012). https://doi.org/10.1016/j.tcs.2012.07.017

18. Jardine, A.: Computationally, tone is different. Phonology **33**, 247–283 (2016). https://doi.org/10.1017/S0952675716000129
19. Joshi, A.: Tree-adjoining grammars: How much context sensitivity is required to provide reasonable structural descriptions? In: Dowty, D., Karttunen, L., Zwicky, A. (eds.) Natural Language Parsing, pp. 206–250. Cambridge University Press, Cambridge (1985)
20. Joshi, A., Schabes, Y.: Tree-adjoining grammars. In: Rosenberg, G., Salomaa, A. (eds.) Handbook of Formal Languages, pp. 69–123. Springer, Berlin (1997). https://doi.org/10.1007/978-3-642-59126-6_2
21. Keenan, E.L., Comrie, B.: Noun phrase accessiblity and universal grammar. Linguistic Inquiry **8**, 63–99 (1977)
22. Kobele, G.M.: A formal foundation for A and A-bar movement. In: Ebert, C., Jäger, G., Michaelis, J. (eds.) The Mathematics of Language. Lecture Notes in Computer Science, vol. 6149, pp. 145–159. Springer, Heidelberg (2010). https://doi.org/10.1007/978-3-642-14322-9_12
23. McMullin, K.: Tier-based locality in long-distance phonotactics: learnability and typology. Ph.D. thesis, University of British Columbia (2016)
24. Müller, G.: A local reformulation of the Williams cycle. In: Heck, F., Assmann, A. (eds.) Rule Interaction in Grammar, Linguistische Arbeitsberichte, vol. 90, pp. 247–299 (2013)
25. Nevins, A.: Multiple agree with clitics: person complementarity vs. omnivorous number. Nat. Lang. Linguistic Theory **28**, 939–971 (2011). https://doi.org/10.1007/s11049-006-9017-2
26. Nunes, J.: Linearization of Chains and Sideward Movement. MIT Press, Cambridge (2004)
27. Pollard, C., Sag, I.: Head-Driven Phrase Structure Grammar. CSLI and The University of Chicago Press, Stanford and Chicago (1994)
28. Poole, E.: Improper case (2020). https://ling.auf.net/lingbuzz/004148
29. Preminger, O.: Phi features, binding, and A-positions (2018). https://facultyoflanguage.blogspot.com/2018/01/phi-features-binding-and-positions.html, blog post on Faculty of Language
30. Puškar, Z., Müller, G.: Unifying structural and lexical case assignment in dependent case theory. In: Lenertová, D., Meyer, R., Šimík, R., Szucsich, L. (eds.) Advances in Formal Slavic Linguistic 2016, pp. 357–379 (2018)
31. Sauerland, U.: A new semantics for number. In: Youn, R.B., Zhou, Y. (eds.) SALT 13. CLC Publications, Ithaca (2003)
32. Shafiei, N., Graf, T.: The subregular complexity of syntactic islands. Proc. Soc. Comput. Linguist. (SCiL) **2020**, 272–281 (2020)
33. Stabler, E.P.: Derivational Minimalism. In: Retoré, C. (ed.) Logical Aspects of Computational Linguistics, Lecture Notes in Computer Science, vol. 1328, pp. 68–95. Springer, Berlin (1997). https://doi.org/10.1007/BFb0052152
34. Stabler, E.P.: Computational perspectives on Minimalism. In: Boeckx, C. (ed.) Oxford Handbook of Linguistic Minimalism, pp. 617–643. Oxford University Press, Oxford (2011)
35. Takahashi, S., Hulsey, S.: Wholesale late merger: beyond the $A/\overline{A}$ distinction. Linguistc Inquiry **40**, 387–426 (2009)
36. Williams, E.: Rule ordering in syntax. Ph.D. thesis, MIT, Cambridge (1974)
37. Williams, E.: Representation Theory. MIT Press, Cambridge (2003)

Attributive Measure Phrases in Mandarin: Monotonicity and Distributivity

Xuping Li[✉]

Department of Chinese, Zhejiang University, Hangzhou, China
xupingli@zju.edu.cn

Abstract. This paper investigates the interpretation of measure phrases (MPs) in attributive constructions in Mandarin. Contra Schwarzschild [1], we argue that the attributive position is not bound to a non-monotonic reading for MPs, and that Mandarin attributive MPs are subject to both monotonic and non-monotonic readings, which are to be recast as a contrast between object-level and kind-level readings. The alleged non-monotonic reading for attributive MPs is argued to be a result of the distributivity effect [2, 3]. It is observed in Mandarin that attributive MPs always have a distributive reading on monotonic and non-monotonic readings, which originate from two different sources. We propose that on the monotonic reading, the attributive MP distributes over the predicate Classifier-Noun, which denotes a set of non-overlapping individuals, and that the apparent non-monotonic reading is a consequence of the (sub)kind reading, such that the property expressed by MP is distributive over the instantiation set of the relevant (sub)kind. As far as their semantics is concerned, we claim that attributive MPs on the non-monotonic reading are intersective adjectives, which compose with NPs via Heim and Kratzer's [4] rule of Predicate Modification, but attributive MPs on the monotonic reading compose with NPs with functional application, as induced by the predicativizer *de*, whereby they denote degrees serving to saturate the degree argument associated with the semantics of dimensional adjectives, which is at type <d, et>.

Keywords: Measure phrase · Monotonicity · Attributive constructions · (Sub)kind · Distributivity

This study is supported by the Fundamental Research Funds for the Central Universities (Project NO.: 2020QNA107). This paper is a substantially revised version of my 2019 paper written in Chinese [10], in which the issue of distributivity was not touched at all. Among other things, the current version makes two major changes/improvements. First, we tease apart the relation between monotonicity and distributivity. Second, monotonic and non-monotonic MPs are argued to be composed in two different ways, either by the rule of Predicate Modification or Functional Application. I would like to express my gratitude to the anonymous reviewers, whose critical comments help to improve the readability of the paper. I am solely responsible for the errors.

D. Deng et al. (Eds.): TLLM 2020, LNCS 12564, pp. 54–80, 2020.
https://doi.org/10.1007/978-3-662-62843-0_4

1 The Issue: The Syntactic Dependence of Measure Predicates on Monotonicity

Measure predicates (MPs hereafter), consisting of a numeral followed by a measure word like *meter*, denote degrees of entities along a certain dimension associated with the measure word. MPs are available in a wide range of syntactic contexts, and two of such contexts are pseudopartitives and attributive constructions, as exemplified by (1) and (2) respectively [1, 5, 6]. In pseudopartitives, the MP is realized as a part of the extended functional projection above NP, such as the QP or NumP; in attributive constructions, the MP functions as an attributive modifier to the head noun.

(1)　a. two inches of cable　　(pseudopartitives)

　　　b. three pounds of beef

　　　c. six ounces of gold

(2)　a. two-inch cable　　(attributive constructions)

　　　b. 100 degree water

　　　c. 18 carat gold

According to Schwarzschild [1], monotonicity plays a crucial role in nominal syntax with MPs. It is argued that syntactic positions of MPs determine their interpretations with respect to (non-)monotonicity. Specifically, pseudopartitives are syntactically projected into a Monotonic Phrase (MonP), where the preposition *of* is realized as the head Mon^0 and the MP is surfaced as its specifier. MPs in attributive constructions are realized below the MonP and become part of noun compounds. According to Schwarzschild [1], MPs in pseudopartitives are interpreted with a monotonic reading, whereas those in attributives are read with a non-monotonic reading only. The structural ambiguity of the MP *two inch(es)* is illustrated by the syntactic trees in (3).

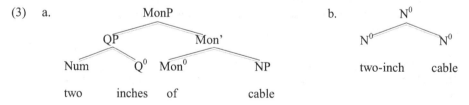

The notions of monotonic and non-monotonic predicates can be defined as in (4) and (5) in a simplified way [1, 2, 7, 8]. Accordingly, the MP *two inches* in the pseudopartitive construction *two inches of cable* measures the length of the cable, which tracks a part-whole relation of entities denoted by NP, so two inches of cable plus two inches of cable would be four inches in total. In contrast, the MP *two-inch* in the expression *two-inch cable* specifies the diameter of the cable, which remains constant and non-monotonic.

(4)　If $Meas_{DIM}$ is monotonic, then:

　　$\forall x \forall y \forall z [x = y \sqcup z \land \neg OVERLAP(y,z) \rightarrow Meas_{DIM}(x) = Meas_{DIM}(y) + Meas_{DIM}(z)]$

　　"If $Meas_{DIM}$ is extensive, then if x is the sum of y and z, and y and z do not overlap, the measure of x is the result of adding the measures of y and z."

(5)   If Meas$_{DIM}$ is non-monotonic, then: $\forall x \forall y[\ x \sqsubseteq y \rightarrow$ Meas$_{DIM}$(x) = Meas$_{DIM}$(y)]

"If Meas$_{DIM}$ is non-monotonic, then if x is part of y, x and y have the same measure."

One of the advantages of this account is that it successfully captures that measure words like *inch, meter* and *kilo* are different from those like *carat* for purity and *degree* for temperature. The former are called 'extensive' measures and the latter 'non-extensive' measures [8]. For Schwarzschild, extensive measures are subject to both monotonic and non-monotonic readings, but non-extensive ones can only have a non-monotonic reading. As shown in (6), extensive measures like *inch* are available in both pseudopartitives and attributive constructions, but non-extensive measures like *degree* and *carat* are only permitted in attributives but not in pseudopartitives.

(6)   a. two inches of cable   a'. two-inch cable
       b.* fifty degrees of water   b'. fifty-degree water
       c.*18 carats of gold   c'. 18-carat gold

Nevertheless, it is highly controversial whether monotonicity is the decisive factor responsible for the above contrast. The first issue arising is concerned with whether attributive MPs are allowed for a non-monotonic reading only. This problem is particularly prominent for extensive measure words. Can extensive MPs retain their default monotonic function in attributive positions? For instance, Kennedy [9] points out that attributive MPs do not seem to require non-monotonicity in all the cases. The MP *60 min* in the attributive position in (7b) has a similar monotonic reading as the one in (7a), both of which denote the actual duration of the analysis.

(7)   a. 60 minutes of analysis
       b. a 60 minute (long) analysis

Second, what is the correlation between non-monotonicity and distributivity for attributive MPs, if there is any? It is noted in Schwarzschild [1] that the property expressed an attributive MP is always distributive, such that it distributes either over atomic entities consisting the relevant plural entity or over the parts of an entity denoted by a mass noun (recall the examples in the second column in (6)). To rule out the monotonic reading for attributive MPs, Schwarzschild [1] claims that non-monotonic MPs entails distributivity but monotonic MPs fail to pass the test of distributivity. In contrast, Rothstein [10], McKinney-Bock and Pancheva [3] both argue for the opposite position that non-monotonicity for attributive MPs is independently determined by distributivity of such predicates.

This study addresses these two controversies by focusing on the usages of MPs in attributive constructions in Mandarin. We confine ourselves to the expression "Numeral-Classifier-MP-*de*-Noun", in which the MP followed by the modification marker *de* occupies the adnominal position and then is preceded by a true numeral and a true classifier, as illustrated in (8).

(8) a. ta   ji-le   yi   tong   1.5-sheng   de   niunai.
     he   squeeze-PFV one CL$_{bucket}$ 1.5 liter   Mod milk
     'He milked a bucket of milk, which measures 1.5 liters.'   (Non-monotonic)

     b. ta   mai-le   yi   ping   1.5   sheng   de   niunai.
     he   buy-PFV   one   CL$_{bottle}$ 1.5   liter   Mod milk
     'I bought a 1.5-liter bottle of milk.'   (Non-monotonic)

As will be argued, attributive MPs, such as *1.5-sheng* '1.5-liter' in (8), are potentially ambiguous between monotonic and non-monotonic readings. Hence, our answer to the first question is opposed to Schwarzschild's syntactically motivated proposal. We claim that the syntactic position of MPs does not always decide their readings to be monotonic or non-monotonic, and that the attributive position is not reserved for non-monotonic MPs.

Concerning the second question, we argue that the apparent ambiguity between monotonic and non-monotonic readings for MPs should be recast as the distinction between object-level and kind-level readings in Mandarin. In these two contexts, the effect of distributivity on attributive MPs has its roots in two sources: the apparent non-monotonic reading is a consequence of the (sub)kind reading in that the property expressed by MPs is distributive over the instantiation set of the relevant subkind, and on the monotonic reading, the attributive MPs distributes over the predicate Classifier-Noun, which denotes a set of non-overlapping individuals.

The remainder of the article is organized as follows. Section 2 offers a brief review on two semantic accounts of (non-)monotoicity of MPs in attributive constructions, namely, Rothstein [2] and McKinney-Bock and Pancheva [3]. In Sect. 3, we examine the usages of MPs in attributive constructions in Mandarin, which are shown to be subject to both monotonic and non-monotonic readings. The semantics of monotonic and non-monotonic MPs in attributives are worked out in Sects. 4 and 5 respectively. The article is wrapped up in Sect. 6 by summarizing the main arguments made in the paper.

2 Two Semantic Accounts for (Non-)Monotonicity of MPs

This section reviews two existing accounts which challenge the non-monotonicity restriction of MPs in attributive constructions. Contra Schwarzschild [1], Rothstein [2] argues that the projection of the so-called MonP is not syntactically but semantically determined by the availability of 'extensive' measure function for measure words [8]. One of the consequences is that it is actually possible for attributive MPs to receive both a monotonic reading and a non-monotonic reading. McKinney-Bock and Pancheva [3] also argue that attributive position is not reserved for non-monotonic readings by examining behaviors of various types of adjectives. It is concluded that non-monotonicity of attributive MPs follows from the effect of distributivity, but not vice versa.

2.1 (Non-)extensive Measure Functions

According to Schwarzschild [1], as indicated by the structure (3a), it is the head *of* in Monotonic Phrases that is responsible for assigning the quantity property expressed by the MP to individuals in the denotation of nouns. This syntactically motivated approach to monotonicity tried to account for the following two relevant facts. First, measures like *karat* and *degree* fail to be licensed in pseudopartitives, and they are restricted in attributive constructions; second, measures like *inch* or *kilo* exhibit the same non-monotonicity property as *karat* and *degree*, when they are used as attributive modifiers. The two facts are exemplified by (9) and (10) respectively.

(9) a. 18-karat gold   a   '.* 18-karat of gold

  b. 20 C° degree water   b   '.* 20 C° degree of water

(10) a. two inches of wire   a'. the two-inch wire

   b. three pounds of cherries   b'. the three-pound cherries

It is assumed that the dimension associated with the measure *karat* is not monotonic with the stuff gold, because the PURITY of any proper part of it will always remain the same. The unacceptability of (9b') also reflects the fact that temperature is not monotonic with respect to water. If the 5 ounces of water in the bottle measures 20°, then its subparts will also measure 20°. Similarly, the measure *inch* in the pseudopartitive construction tracks the monotonic dimension of length, as in (10a), but it measures the diameter of wire in the attributive construction in (10a'), where it does not track a part-whole relation to wire. The properties denoted by non-monotonic MPs are distributive over parts of entities in the NP denotation. For plural entities, each singular atom consisting the plural entity shares the same property denoted by the MP, and for mass nouns, the property holds of any subpart of the relevant entity. For Schwarzschild, the distributivity effect observed is due to the monotonic interpretation of the MPs.

However, Champollion [11] showed that the same measure word *degree* for temperature is fairly acceptable in pseudopartitives as in the example (11), where the relevant measure function, e.g. *temperature-increasing*, maps any warming event to the number of degrees of warming that it causes. Nouns like *global warming* can be categorized as 'scalar nominals' in the sense of Kennedy [9], which are compatible with the alleged 'lexically' non-monotonic MPs.

(11) a. The scientists from Princeton and Harvard universities say just *two degrees Celsius of global warming*, which is widely expected to occur in coming decades, could be enough to inundate the planet.   [11]

  b. 6 degrees of separation   [9]

We learn from the examples in (11) that the alleged intrinsically non-monotonic measure words can, in fact, be licensed in monotonic constructions, when some contexts are construed in an appropriate way. This suggests that the monotonic or non-monotonic measure function cannot be lexically determined by the measure words themselves. It is less likely to be syntactically determined either. If it were the case, some independent mechanism is still called for to explain how the same measure word *degree* is analyzed with different syntactic status in these two situations. As far as the monotonic reading is concerned, Ladusaw [12] suggests that the partitive *of*, as in 'some of the students', denotes the function from a divisible entity, i.e. an entity that has part structure, to a property that is true of parts of that entity, as formalized in (12). However, Schwarzschild assumes that the monotonic *of* in pseudopartitives is distinct from the partitive *of*. It is thus ruled out the possibility that it is the preposition *of* that is responsible for assigning a part-whole structure onto the noun denotation in pseudopartitives.

(12) *of* in partitives: $\lambda y \lambda x.\ x \leq y$

The strict mapping of attributive MPs onto a non-monotonic reading was criticized in Rothstein [2], who suggested that it is the semantics of the MP that determines its property of being monotonic or non-monotonic. It is proposed that it is the availability of extensive measure function of measure words that makes them possible in pseudopartitives. The contrast between *inch* and *degree* is suggested to be a distinction between extensive and non-extensive measure functions in the sense of Krifka [8]. The measure word *inch* denotes an extensive measure operation, and *length*, the dimension on which inch operates, is extensive, whereas *degree* which maps an entity onto a degree of heat is not extensive, and *temperature* is a non-extensive dimension. Accordingly, non-extensive measure words in (9a-b) are disallowed in pseudopatitives due to the lack of extensive measure functions. However, as shown in (11), it is possible for the alleged non-monotonic measures like *degree* to be used in monotonic constructions. The measure word *degree* in examples of (11) is assumed to denote an extensive measure function then. This further supports that the monotonicity function is neither lexically nor syntactically specified but semantically dependent.

Rothstein [2] argues against the syntactic account that (non-)monotonicity of measure predicates is determined by their syntactic positions, and propose that non-monotonicity is a consequence of the distributive interpretation of MPs. We already know that the MP *two pound* in *two-pound apples* distributes over atomic apples and has a *two-pound-per-apple* reading. But in this case, "non-monotonicity is met trivially, since atoms in the denotations of count nouns are assumed to have no parts" (ibid: 12). The difference of MPs like *two pound(s)* in pseudopartitives and attributives is more illustrative in cumulative contexts, where they differ in cumulative entailments.

(13) a. If a and b are in the denotation of the predicate *(exactly) two pounds of apples*, then a⊔b is not in the denotation of the predicate *two pounds of apples*.

b. If a and b are in the denotation of the predicate *(exactly) two-pound apples*, then a⊔b is also in the denotation of the predicate *(exactly) two-pound of apples*.

The MP *two pounds of apples* denotes the set of pluralities of apples in the denotation of apples which weigh two pounds, as in (14a). Obviously two such quantities cannot together weigh two pounds, thus the cumulative entailment in (13a) holds. In (13b), the attributive MP *two-pound* distributes over atomic apples in the denotation of the count noun apples and gives us the set of atomic apples which each weigh two pounds, as in (14b).[1] Therefore, it is not surprising that the increasing of the quantity of apples in the denotation of two-pound apples does not affect the measure value of each apple in the set.

---

[1] The semantics in (14b) was simplified by getting rid of the derivation from the root meaning of nouns to a set of atomic individuals.

(14) a. {x$_{pl}$: x$_{pl}$ ∈ APPLES}∩{x$_{pl}$: MEAS(x) =<2, POUND>}, it denotes the intersection of the set of pluralities of apples and the set of entities which weigh 2 lbs.
    b. {x: x ∈ APPLES ∧ MEAS (x) = <2, POUND>}, it denotes the set of atomic individuals which are (each) apples and which (each) weigh 2 lbs.

The account of (non-)extensive measure function predicts that the monotonic interpretation is not ruled out at all in attributive constructions. The monotonic reading of attributive MPs in English is supported by the evidence given below (adapted from Rothstein 2019).

First, additive attributive measures decrease incrementally. If the attributive were a non-monotonic predicate, (15) would be unexpected.

(15) If A is a two-pound apple, then half of A weighs one pound.

Second, we can see the effects of monotonicity in attributive predicates in accumulation entailments. Accumulation entailments are entailments of the form in (16).

(16) a. Three two-pound apples is six pounds of apples.   TRUE
    b. Three 500 meters skeins yarn is 1500 meters of yarn.   TRUE
    c. Three ten dollar tanks of gas is thirty dollars-worth of gas.   TRUE

Attributive MPs discussed here are clearly monotonic, because they contribute the measures though which the measure of the overall quantity is computed. Non-monotonic MPs do not show any of these effects.

2.2 Deriving Non-monotonicity from Distributivity

McKinney-Bock and Pancheva [3] also cast doubt onto the non-monotonicity constraint of MPs in attributive constructions. By examining the behaviors of adjectives, they reach the same conclusion that attributive modifiers are not bound to having the non-monotonic reading and its apparent non-monotonicity is attributed to distributivity.

Schwarzschild [1] suggests that when a MP combines with a substance noun in attributives, they express (possibly complex) non-monotonic dimensions, which are understood as properties distributive over atomic individuals, such as weight or price per (standard) unit, as exemplified by (17).

(17) a. 3 pound cherries: WEIGHT PER CHHEEY
    b. 20 pound paper: WEIGHT PER STANDARD UNIT
    c. $72 oil: PRICE PER STANDARD UNIT

For Schwarzschild [1], the non-monotonic reading of attributive MPs entails the distributivity effect, but McKinney-Bock and Pancheva [3] suggest that non-monotonicity follows from the independently determined distributivity of the relevant predicates. But McKinney-Bock and Pancheva's [3] arguments are mainly built upon the properties of adnominal adjectives in attributive constructions.

When the dimensional adjective *heavy* is used in the predicate position (18a), it has either a collective reading or a distributive reading, which means that the boxes are heavy as a group or each box is heavy. But, in the case of (18b), the attributive *heavy* passes the non-monotonicity requirement: the weight of individual boxes does not track the part-whole relation among boxes. The attributive *heavy* is obligatorily interpreted with a distributive reading. It is called a 'stubbornly distributive' adjective in Schwarzschild [1].

(18) a. The boxes are *heavy*.   [collective or distributive]

b. The *heavy* boxes sat in a corner.   [distributive]

McKinney-Bock and Pancheva [3] propose that the distributive reading and the collective reading of gradable adjectives can be differentiated by different comparison classes to be chosen in the context. On the distributive reading, (19) has the meaning that 'boxes that are heavy for a prototypical box', which can be represented as a covert pronominal element C, as sketched in (19b). In addition to the distributive reading (20b), the predicative *heavy* also has the collective reading, which is understood as 'the weight of the pile of boxes is compared to contextually relevant prototypical entities', as illustrated by (20c).

(19) the heavy boxes

a. $\|\text{heavy}\| = \lambda D_{<d,\triangleright} \lambda x.\ x\text{'s weight} \in D$, where D represents degree intervals.

b. $[_{DP}$ the $[_{NP}$ [POS C] $[_{NP}$ D-heavy boxes]]], where the variable C stands for the comparison class, Pos in combination with C introduces standard of comparison.

c. $\|C\| = \lambda x.\exists D[x \text{ is a D-heavy prototypical box}]$

(20) The boxes are heavy.

a. the boxes are $[_{AP}$ [POS C] $[_{NP}$ D-heavy]]

b. $\|C\| = \lambda x.\exists D[x \text{ is a D-heavy prototypical box}]$

c. $\|C\| = \lambda x.\exists D[x \text{ is a D-heavy prototypical entity}]$

If the property of (non-)monotonicity is determined syntactically, it is expected that adjectives or other forms of predicates are expected to have a non-monotonic reading only when occurring in attributive constructions. This prediction is falsified by the following facts (adapted from McKinney-Bock and Pancheva [3]).

First, when the adjective *heavy* modifies collective mass nouns like *traffic* and *jewelry*, it is interpreted collectively. *Heavy* in (21a) measures the density of vehicles, and the most prominent reading of (21b) is that the overall quantity of jewelry is heavy. These examples clearly pose a problem for the link between attributive syntax and the semantics of non-monotonicity.

(21) a. The *heavy* traffic was unbearable.

b. The *heavy* jewelry weighed down the bride.

Second, in addition to the distributive adjective *heavy*, collective adjectives like *numerous, plentiful*, and *sparse*, can also be used attributively. The semantics of *numerous* requires a plurality measured along a cardinality dimension that is not necessarily precise. The example (20) only requires the cardinality of protesters to be large enough, but it is not expected to know the exact number of protesters.

(22) The *numerous* protesters overwhelmed the counter-protesters.

Unfortunately, McKinney-Bock and Pancheva [3] only discussed (non)monotonicity of adjectives, and left untouched the property of MPs in attributive constructions. It is dubious whether these two types of phrases, i.e. attributive APs and MPs, are supposed to have the same behavior with respect to monotonicity. At least, as far as attributive QAs (Quantity Adjectives) are concerned, such as *many* and *much*, they are monotonic in a way that does not seem tied to their syntax [13].[2] We will explore in the following sections whether attributive MPs are constantly distributive.

In sum, this section offers an overview of Rothstein's [2] and McKinney-Bock and Pancheva's [3] accounts on (non-)monotonicity of attributive modifiers, which examine the behaviors of MPs and adnominal adjectives respectively. According to Rothstein [2], the monotonic reading of MPs is determined by the extensive function denoted by measures, which is available both in pseudopartitives and attributive constructions. The crucial argument made in McKinney-Bock and Pancheva [3] is that non-monotonicity of attributive adjectives like *heavy* follows as a consequence of distributivity. Both accounts are in favor of the view that modifiers in the attributive position receive a monotonic reading or a non-monotonic reading: the former depends on the measure function to be extensive or non-extensive, and the latter on the adjective to be distributive or collective.

3 (Non-)Monotonic MPs in Mandarin: the Facts

This section first shows how pseudopartitives and attributive constructions are realized in a classifier language like Mandarin. It will then be followed by the discussion on the ambiguity of attributive MPs with respect to monotonicity in this language. A caution is in place here that we will be focusing only on the use of extensive measure words like *meter* and *pound* in attributive positions in this study.

3.1 MP-*de*-N as Pseudopartitives or Attributive Constructions

In Mandarin, measure predicates can directly merge with a noun to generate pseudopartitive constructions, such as MP-N in (23). Besides, the modification marker *de* can also intervene between MP and N, which results in the expression MP-*de*-N.[3] The phrase MP-*de*-N is structurally ambiguous between pseudopartitives and attributive constructions, as exemplified by (24) [14–16].

(23) ta   mai-le   liang   bang   rou.
      she   buy-PFV   two   pound   meat
      'She bought two pounds of meat.'   [pseudopartitive construction]

---

[2] Schwarzschild (2006) treats such QAs as *many* and *much* to be realized high in some functional projection, e.g. at or above MonP.

[3] The modification marker *de* is able to turn any phrasal elements into attributive modifiers, which is schematized as "XP-*de*-NP".

(24) ta   mai-le   liang   bang   de   rou.
      she   buy-PFV   two   pound   Mod   meat
      a. 'She bought two pounds of meat.'   [pseudopartitive construction]
      b. 'She bought some two-pound meat.'   [attributive construction]

Under the pseudopartitive reading, the MP *liang-bang* in (23) and (24a) measures the overall weight of meat to be two pounds, regardless of whether *de* is present or absent. On the attributive reading, in (24b) *liang bang* specifies the meat to be the one that comes in the unit of two pounds, or "the meat that is sorted in accordance with two pounds" in Tang's [14] terms.

According to Tang [14] and Jiang [15], MP-*de*-N in (25) is associated with two distinct syntactic structures under pseudopartitive and attributive readings: the former has the structure of [MeasP Num-Meas (*de*) [NP N]] and the latter [NP [MeasP Num-Meas *de*] N]. This structural difference predicts that MP-*de*-N can be embedded in a canonical classifier phrase, i.e. Num-Cl-MP-*de*-N, only when the MP is interpreted with an attributive reading. The presence of Num-Cl before the MP impedes the availability of the monotonic reading for MP-*de*. It follows that MPs *sanbang-de* in (25a) and *wubang-de* in (25b) are attributive modifiers and are interpreted non-monotonically.

(25) a. liu   ge   san-bang   de   yingtao   [15]
         six   CL   three-pound   Mod   cherry
         'six cherries, each of which weigh three pounds'
      b. ta   mai-le liang bao   wu-bang   de   rou.   [14]
         she buy-PFV two CL_parcel five-pound   Mod   meat
         'She bought two parcels of meat that were sorted in accordance with five pounds.'

According to Tang [14] and Jiang [15], when the MP is used as an attributive modifier, it behaves like a 'classifying' adjective, which expresses properties that are able to establish subtypes of entities. Jiang [15] suggests that *san bang de yingtao* 'three-pound cherry' in (25a) refers to 'a complex kind or concept', but, unfortunately, this was not reflected in the English translation. Example (25a) is supposed to mean 'the three-pound cherry'. The term used by Tang 'sorted in accordance with' has the same effect as Jiang's [15] 'complex kind or concept' in that (25b) refers to a certain type of meat available on the market.

In this study, we will leave aside the pseudopartitive construction and focus solely on the attributive use of measure phrases, i.e. the MP in the construction "Num-Cl-MP-*de*-N". We refer readers to Li and Rothstein [17] for the discussions on the pseudopartitive expression "MP-*de*-N" in detail. We will address the following two questions concerning attributive MPs in Mandarin: (i) how can we relate the subkind reading discussed in Tang [14] and Jiang [15] to the non-monotonic reading proposed in Schwarzschild [1]? (ii) is it possible for the MP in MP-*de*-N to have a monotonic reading? If the answer is positive, how are the two monotonic readings in attributives and pseudopartitives distinguished from each other?

3.2 Ambiguity of Attributive MPs in Mandarin

In this subsection, we defend the view that the attributive position is not reserved for non-monotonic MPs in Mandarin. As will be shown, attributive MPs, as the one in [Num-Cl-[[MP-*de*]N]], are ambiguous between monotonic and non-monotonic readings. We propose that the ambiguity of attributive MPs between monotonic and non-monotonic readings should be recast a contrast between object-level and subkind-level readings in Mandarin. As a result, the apparent 'non-monotonic' reading is a consequence of the kind reading in Mandarin, whereas monotonic MPs in attributives express properties distributive over the atomic set denoted by Cl-N.

In English, attributive MPs can optionally co-occur with dimensional adjectives, such as *two meter (tall)* in (26a). This suggests that attributive MPs are not adjectives, but they are rather the degree arguments of (possibly implicit) adjectival or measure functional heads [9]. It is also suggested that attributive MPs, along with the dimensional adjective followed, have the same analysis they would have in predicative positions, where they denote properties of individuals, as in (26b).

> (26) a. a *two-meter (tall)* man
>   b. ||two-meter tall|| = $\lambda x.$ tall $(x)=2m$

If this analysis in (26) is on the right track, there is no reason to believe that attributive MPs are required to be interpreted with a non-monotonic reading. As shown in (27), the MP *60* min can be used for the noun analysis either on its mass use or its count use, which leads to pseudopartitives and attributive constructions [9]. What's important here is that the same MP receives a monotonic reading in both constructions, which means that the duration of analysis lasts 60 min.

> (27) a. 60 minutes of analysis
>   b. a 60-minute (long) analysis   [9]

We now show that monotonic and non-monotonic readings are equally available for attributive MPs in Mandarin. The example (28) with the MP *100 haosheng* '100 ml' in an attributive position has two possible readings. On the monotonic reading in (28a), it means that the actual volume of milk that was drunk amounts to 100 mls, and this sentence is true only when the whole glass of milk is finished up. On the non-monotonic reading in (28b), it means that the milk that he drank was poured out of the 100-ml bottled ones, where the property denoted by the MP '100 ml' does not track a part-whole relation over the quantity of milk.

(28) ta   he-le   yi   bei   [[yibai-haosheng   de]   niunai].
      he   drink-PFV   one   Cl$_{glass}$ 100-ml   Mod   milk
      a. 'He drank a glass of milk, which measures to be 100 mls.'   [Monotonic]
      b. 'He drank a glass of the 100-ml milk.'   [Non-monotonic]

It is more difficult for attributive MPs to obtain a monotonic reading than a non-monotonic one in some cases. But the monotonic reading becomes available, once the contexts are appropriately construed. Two extra examples are provided in (29) to show the availability of the monotonic reading in attributive constructions, but the non-monotonic reading is not excluded here.

(29) a. Tian laohan jianshang   bei-zhe   yi   dai 30 gongjin de   dami.
      Old Tian   shoulder.on   carry-Dur one Cl$_{sack}$ 30 KG   Mod   rice
      'Old Tian carried a sack of 30-KG rice on his shoulders.'
      Literal: 'Old Tian carried a sack of rice on his shoulder, which was 30 KGs.'
   b. tamen zao-le   yi dong   sanbai   mi   de   dalou.
      they build-PFV one CL   three hundred meter Mod building
      'They built a 300-meter (tall) building.'
      Literal: 'They built a building, which was 300 meters tall.'

We hypothesize that the contrast of attributive MPs between monotonic and non-monotonic readings should be recast as the distinction between object-level and kind-level predicates in Mandarin. The semantics of MPs under these two readings can be tentatively sketched in (30a–b). We suggest that the attributive MP in (30a) expresses a property of weight that is predicated of entities denoted by the noun, and that the MP in (30b) does not express a measure function of milk but a property that helps to establish a subtype of milk, e.g. the 100-ml type of milk (also see [14, 15]). In this case, the MP does not express the actual amount of milk to be taken.

(30) a. $[[100\ \text{haosheng de niunai}]] = \lambda x.\ \text{milk}(x) \wedge \mu_{\text{weight}}(x) = 100\ \text{ml}$
      b. $[[100\ \text{haosheng de niunai}]] = \lambda k.\ \text{milk}(k) \wedge 100\text{-ml}(k)$
         $= {}^{\cap}(\lambda x.\text{milk}(x) \wedge 100\text{-ml}(x))$

The posited object/kind-level ambiguity, which underscores the monotonic and non-monotonic readings associated with attributive MPs, can be justified in the following contexts in Mandarin.

First, the object-level/kind-level readings of the attributive MP affect the truth conditions of sentences. Consider the examples in (31).

(31) ta   mai-le   wu   zhi [si-liang   de   pangxie],
     he   buy-Asp five   CL   200-gram   Mod   crab
     zong   zhongliang   liang jin   budao   yidianr.
     total   weight   two pound   less.than   a bit
     'She bought five 200-gram crabs, but the overall weight is a bit less than 2 pounds.'

Under both monotonic and non-monotonic readings, attributive MPs without any approximators is expected to express exact measurement of entities in the case of English (recall Rothstein's examples from (13) to (16)). However, in Mandarin, it is possible for attributives to have inexact measurements. As shown in (31), it only requires each crab to be close enough to 200 g. We suggest that the statement of (31) is judged to be true only when the MP is interpreted with a kind reading. If the sentence is interpreted with an object reading or the so-called monotonic reading, each crab has to weigh exactly 200 g and the overall weight should be two pounds in an exact sense. In this context, the sentence (31) is then judged to be false. But if '200 g crab' is a general name of crabs of a certain subtype, in which the MP *200*-g denotes a classifying property to classify crabs, then the approximate interpretation is expected. It is a common practice in the Yangtze Delta area that crabs are sorted into the 100 g type, the 200 g type etc., and the larger they are, the more expensive they become. In this context, it only requires the actual weight of each crab to be close enough to 200 g to instantiate the relevant kind, so the overall weight can be around 2 pounds. Thus the same sentence (31) becomes true in this context. As for the question of how close it is to 200 g, it depends on how fine/coarse-grained the scale it is. We take this evidence in support of the claim that the apparent non-monotonic reading of attributive MPs should be treated as a (sub)kind reading.

The second context to distinguish between the object-level reading and the kind-level reading is concerned with the availability of dimensional adjectives after MPs. The expression "Num-Cl-MP-*de*-N" is ambiguous between an object-level reading and a kind reading, but 'Num-Cl-MP-Adj-*de*-N' has an unambiguous object-level reading and the kind reading is suppressed, when the MP is followed by a dimensional adjective, such as *chang* 'long', *kuan* 'wide', *gao* 'high', *zhong* 'heavy' and *shen* 'deep'.

(32) Scenario A:

Xiaowang	mai-le	yi	kuai	[[liang-mi	chang	de]	hongbu]
Xiaowang	buy-PFV	one	CL$_{piece}$	two meter	long	Mod	red cloth
he yi	kuai	[[san	mi	chang	de]	baibu].	
and one	CL$_{piece}$	three	meter	long	Mod	white cloth	

'Xiaowang bought an item of 2-meter long red cloth and another item of 3-meter long white cloth.'

(33) Scenario B:

Xiaowang	mai-le	yi	kuai	[[liang-mi	de]	hongbu]
Xiaowang	buy-PFV	one	CL$_{piece}$	two meter	Mod	red cloth
he yi	kuai	[[san-mi	de]	baibu].		
and one	CL$_{piece}$	three-meter	Mod	white cloth		

'Xiaowang bought an item of 2-meter red cloth and another item of 3-meter white cloth.'

The MPs in (32) are followed by the dimensional adjective *chang* 'long', but those in (33) are not. In the context depicted by (32), the overall length of cloth that was bought is 5 m, a sum of 2 m and 3 m. In contrast, in the context of (33), the overall length of cloth is either five meters or uncertain. The length of cloth becomes uncertain when the MPs are kind-level predicates, since in this context they simply specify which type of cloth and give no information on the actual length that was bought.

The insertion of dimensional adjectives after MPs in Mandarin is different from what's observed in English. As shown in (26) and (27), the insertion of adjectives after MPs does not result in any interpretational differences of the MP in English. For Kennedy [9], they are "much synonymous". Some more examples are provided in (34).

(34) a. a three-meter (long) rope

b. two 1.8 meter (tall) students

Third, object-level MPs in attributive positions differ from kind-level ones in that they allow adverbial modification, such as *duo* 'more', *budao* 'less than' and *ganghao* 'just'.

MPs with approximative modifiers in (35) can only be interpreted with a monotonic reading.

(35) a. yi   gen [[san   mi   duo   de]   dianxian]
         one   CL   three   meter   more   Mod   wire
         Possible reading: 'a stretch of wire, which is more than three meters'
         Impossible reading: a kind of wire, which is more than three meters'

      b. yi   gen [[san   mi   budao   de]   dianxian]
         one   CL   three   meter   less Mod   wire
         Possible reading: 'a stretch of wire, which is less than three meters'
         Impossible reading: a kind of wire, which is less than three meters'

      c. yi   gen [[ganghao san   mi   de]   dianxian]
         one   CL   just   three   meter   Mod   wire
         Possible reading: 'a stretch of wire, which is exactly three meters'
         Impossible reading: a kind of wire, which is exactly three meters'

Last but not least, these two types of attributive MPs are confined to some word order restriction. They must co-occur in the order of "MP$_{Object level}$ - MP$_{Kind level}$ -NP", not the other way round. Example (36) means that the watermelon belongs to the five-kilo type and that the overall quantity of each sack measures fifty kilos.

(36) ta   mai-le   liang madai [wushi gongjin de]$_{Monotonic}$[wu gongjin de]$_{Nonmonotonic}$ xigua.
      she buy-PFV two CL$_{sack}$ fifty   kilo Mod   five kilo Mod   watermelon
      'She bought two fifty-kilo sacks of five-kilo type watermelons.'

Adopting our second diagnostic that dimensional adjectives can only follow the object-level MPs, it follows that only the first MP that follows the classifier can be followed by dimensional adjectives, and the one immediately preceding the noun cannot.

(37) a. ta   mai-le   liang madai [wushi gongjin zhong de] [wu gongjin de] xigua.
         she buy-PFV two CL$_{sack}$ fifty   kilo heavy Mod five kilo   Mod watermelon
         'She bought two fifty-kilo sacks of five-kilo type watermelons.'

      b.?ta mai-le   liang madai [wushi gongjin de] [wu gongjin zhong de]   xigua.
         she buy-PFV two CL$_{sack}$ fifty   kilo   Mod five kilo   heavy Mod watermelon
         'She bought two fifty-kilo sacks of five-kilo type watermelons.'

      c.*ta mai-le   liang madai [wushi gongjin de   zhong] [wu gongjin zhong de] xigua.
         she buy-PFV two CL$_{sack}$ fifty   kilo   Mod heavy five kilo   heavy Mod watermelon
         'She bought two fifty-kilo sacks of five-kilo type watermelons.'

The co-occurrence of the two types of attributive MPs in Mandarin suggests that they are possibly realized in two distinct syntactic positions. We assume that the MP close to NP functions as adnominal adjectives and the one close to the classifier act as "pre-classifier" modifiers in terms of the scope of modification. The underlying structural relation of these two MPs in classifier phrases can be represented as: [$_{NumP}$ Num [$_{ClP}$ MP1 [$_{ClP}$ CL [$_{NP}$ MP2 [$_{NP}$ N]]]]], where MP1 and MP2 act as ClP adjunct and NP adjunct respectively. The reason why MP1 follows the classifier but does not precede it is probably due to phonological reasons. It was discussed in Li [18] that only a limited set of dimensional adjectives are allowed to appear between numeral and classifier, which are required to be used in bare forms, namely, neither degree modifiers nor the modification marker *de* is allowed. Compared with those bare adjectives, MPs are structurally more complex and phonologically heavier. This might well be the reason for their right dislocation.

The scopal difference between these two types of attributive MPs is also illustrated by the English translation, where monotonic attributive MPs modify the classifier, and non-monotonic ones modify the noun. A similar pattern is also observed in English in Rothstein [2]. But it should be noted that the adnominal MP does not have a kind reading at least in the context of (38).

> (38) a. I bought a *two-kilo* bag of flour.
>
> b. I bought two *two-kilo* crates of *two-kilo* watermelons.

To sum up, in contrast with Schwarzschild [1], we claim that the attributive position is not reserved for non-monotonic readings for MPs. Relying on the four diagnostics shown above, we suggest that attributive MPs can be interpreted either with an object-level reading or a kind level reading, which appears parallel to a monotonic or a non-monotonic reading in a loose sense. What is more important is that subkind-level and object-level MPs appear to take two distinct syntactic positions, although in Mandarin they appear linearly in the sequence of Num-Cl-MP-*de*-N. As will be argued later, monotonic and subkind-level MPs at the attributive position modify two types of nominal phrases, namely, NP or ClP/NumP. They are either adnominal modifiers or pre-classifier modifiers.

4   Deriving the Monotonic Reading of Attributive MPs

The task of this section is to work out the compositional semantics of the object-level reading of MPs in attributive positions, i.e. being monotonic. We propose that on the object-level reading, MPs are projected as part of the functional phrase DegP, distinct from its projection into AP on the kind-level reading. This is empirically motivated by the fact that the presence of dimensional adjectives after MPs triggers an unambiguous object-level reading. The relevant examples are repeated in (39).

(39)	a. yi	kuai	san-mi	de	bu		
	one	CL	three-meter	Mod	cloth		
	'a piece of three-meter cloth'					[kind-level: non-monotonic]	
	OR 'a piece of cloth, which measures three meters'					[object-level: monotonic]	
	b. yi	kuai	san-mi	chang	de	bu	
	one	CL	three-meter	long	Mod	cloth	
	'a piece of cloth, which measures three meters'					[object-level: monotonic]	

In the post-Abenian generative syntax, it has become a standard assumption that there is the functional projection DegP above the lexical projection of Adjective Phrases [19–21]. This articulated structure can accommodate the fact that either degree words or

MPs can appear before adjectives. As shown in (40), degree words are realized as Deg^0, and MPs fall in the specifier position of DegP [21].

(40) a. John is [$_{DegP}$ [$_{Deg}$ quite [$_{AP}$ tall]]].
     b. John is [$_{DegP}$ [$_{MP}$ 1.80 meters] [$_{Deg}$ [$_{AP}$ tall]]].

Following the degree-based analysis of adjectives pioneered in Cresswell [22], adjectives are argued to denote the function from degrees to properties. They are of the semantic type <d, et>. The expression MP-Adj is suggested to denote a degree predicate, which relates an individual x to x's degree along a certain dimension (see Kennedy 1997 for the "measure function" account as an alternative). As a first approximation, the semantics of degree phrase "MP-Adj" can be represented in (41).

(41) a. $\|tall\|_{<d, et>}$: $\lambda d\lambda x$. HEIGHT(x) $\geq$ d
     b. $\|1.8\ meters\ tall\| = \|tall\|$ ($\|1.8\ meters\|$) = λx. HEIGH(x) $\geq$1.8 meters

Next we extend the semantics of the degree phrase in (41) to attributive MPs on the monotonic reading. We suggest that the degree phrase MP-Adj at the predicate position can be converted into an attributive modifier by the modification marker *de*, which denotes the function from properties to property modifiers. As will be argued later on, in the shifting process, the effect of distributivity can be captured by assuming that the property denoted by attributive modifiers intersects with the comparison class provided in the context, i.e. a set of atomic individuals denoted by Classifier-Noun in our case.

Monotonic MPs can be composed in complex ways by introducing various range adverbials or approximatives, such as *duo* 'more', *budao* 'less', *ganghao* 'exactly' and *zuoyou* 'approximately'. Note that such modifiers either precede or follow the MP linearly, and their positional difference does not concern us too much.

(42) a. yi   kuai   **ganghao/budao**   san   mi   chang   de   bu.
         one   CL   exactly/less than   three meter   long   Mod   cloth
         'a piece of cloth, which measures exactly/less than three meters'
     b. yi   kuai   san   mi   **duo/zuoyou**   chang   de   bu.
         one   CL   three meter   more/approximately long   Mod   cloth
         'a piece of cloth, which measures more than/about three meters.'

Landman [23] argues that numeral expressions like the *n* noun can be represented as the *r n* noun in its complete form, where *n* is a number expression and *r* is an expression denoting numeral relations like *more than, less than, at least* etc. On Barwise and Cooper's [24] analysis, the *r n* is analyzed as a partial determiner (of generalized quantifier type). In contrast, Landman [23] suggests that the constituent structure of the *r n* noun should be [[$_{Det}$ the][$_{NP}$ *r n* noun]], and not [[$_{Det}$ the *r n*][$_{NP}$ noun]], where the numeral expression *n* is analyzed as an intersective adjective. And the relation between *r* and *n* can be represented as follows:

(43) *r n* → λx. $|x|$ r n , of type <e, t> ,
     the set of sums whose cardinality stands in relation r to number *n*.

the set of sums whose cardinality stands in relation r to number *n*.

We, following Landman [23], propose that attributive MPs denote properties of degrees equal to the value specified by MP on the monotonic reading, and that approximatives denote a degree relation like $=, >, <, \approx$. Complex MPs like those in (42) are of the type $<d, t>$ as well, if we consider approximatives or hedges as predicate modifiers.

(44) a. $\|san\text{-}mi\| = \lambda d.\ d=3$ meters

 b. $\|san\text{-}mi\ duo\| = \lambda d.\ d>3$ meters

 c. $\|san\text{-}mi\ zuoyou\| = \lambda d.\ d\approx3$ meters

We take the predicative meaning of MPs as its default, whereby they denote a set of degrees along a certain dimension. Following Partee's [25] type-shifting principles, we suggest that the predicative reading of MPs can be mapped onto arguments either by lifting them into GQs, i.e. at type $<<d,t>, t>$ or lowering them into degree terms at type d. The implementation of the shifting of MP from $<d,t>$ to type d is suggested in Kotek [26] and Grosu and Landman [27], who suggest that a maximality operator, such as the definite article *the*, is able to pick out the unique degree from the degree set in the relevant context.

(45) a. $\|\text{the}\|_{<<d,t>,d>} = \lambda f_{<d,t>}$: there is exactly one contextually salient d: f(d)=1, the unique d in the context such that f(d)=1

 b. $\|\text{the 9kg that your bag weighs}\|=$ the unique d in the context such that weigh (your bag, d) $\geq$ d $\wedge$ d=9kg

In the case of attributive MPs on a monotonic reading, we suggest that the MP be interpreted as a name for a degree at type d, such that it serves to saturate the degree argument of the adjective and turns it into a predicate of individuals. It is thus proposed that a nominalization operator NOM, as notated ^, is employed to shift the degree predicate to a degree name, as in (46). This operator is comparable to Chierchia's [28] DOWN operator $\cap$.

(46) **Step 1: Nominalization**

 a. $\|san\text{-}mi\|= \lambda d.\ d=3$ meters

 b. $d=\text{NOM}\ (\lambda d.\ d=3 \text{ meters}) =^{\wedge}\lambda d.\ d=3$ meters

  $= 3$ meters

 c. $\|san\text{-}mi\ chang\| = \|chang\|\ (\|san\text{-}mi\|)$

  $=\lambda d\lambda x.\ \text{length}\ (x)=d\ (d=3 \text{ meters})$

  $=\lambda x.\ \text{length}\ (x)= 3$ meters

The second step is to turn the measure predicate into a predicate modifier, which is achieved obligatorily by the modification marker *de*. Heim and Kratzer [4] propose that noun phrases modified by restrictive modifiers are composed by the rule of 'Predicate Modification', which intersects the properties denoted by the modifier and the head noun. However, when attributive MPs are interpreted with a monotonic/object-level reading, they compose with nouns by the rule of functional application. We suggest that the marker *de* undertakes the role of being a type-shifter coercing properties into a function of properties. This implies that attributive MPs are derived from their predicative uses, when they are interpreted with an object-level reading or a monotonic reading.

(47) **Step 2: Shifting from predicate to predicate modifier**

a. $\|de\| = \lambda P \lambda Q \lambda x. P(x) \wedge Q(x)$

b. $\|san\text{-}mi\ chang\ de\| = \|de\|\ (\|san\text{-}mi\ chang\|$

$= \lambda Q \lambda x.\ \text{length}\ (x) = 3\ \text{meters} \wedge Q(x)$

According to Schwarzschild [1], attributive MPs are interpreted with a non-monotonic reading only, which gives rise to the distributive reading of the nominal phrase. However, the distributivity constraint is also observed for attributive MPs on the monotonic reading. It will be argued that the effect of distributivity is derived by two independent mechanisms in these two contexts. As argued earlier, attributive MPs precede the head noun at the surface structure on both monotonic and non-monotonic readings, they are realized in syntactically different ways. Attributive MPs are adnominal modifiers on the non-monotonic reading, but they are pre-classifier modifiers on the monotonic reading. In the latter case, attributive MPs scope over Cl-N but not over NP, which denotes a set of entities that do not overlap with each other. This is exactly the source of distributivity for attributive MPs on the monotonic reading.

It is suggested that attributive MPs express measure properties over atomic entities in the denotation of Cl-N on the monotonic reading. This is evidenced by the examples in (48). When the attributive MP is embedded in a standard classifier phrase headed by the classifier *madai* 'sack' (48a) or *ke* 'classifier for plants' (48b), the properties denoted by the monotonic MPs, such as 'fifty kilo' and '30 meter' are predicated of the constituent Cl-N. This guarantees the distributive reading of the MP, such that members in the set of atomic individuals denoted by *madai xigua* 'sack of watermelon' or *ke shu* 'Cl tree' are supposed to have the property of being 50 kilos and 30 m respectively.

(48) a. ta   mai-le   liang   madai   [wushi gongjin de]   xigua.

      she   buy-PFV   two   CL$_{sack}$ fifty   kilo   Mod   watermelon

      'She bought two sacks of watermelons, each sack of which weighs fifty kilos.'

      b. menkou   you   liang   ke   [sanshi-mi   gao de]   shu.

      door front   have   two   CL   30 meter   tall   Mod   tree

      'There are two 30-meter tall trees in front of the door.'

The reason why Mandarin resorts to classifiers to derive an atomic set is suggested to be due to its noun semantics. Mandarin nouns are different from English counterparts in that the former has mass denotations and the latter makes a mass/count distinction. Following Chierchia [28], we assume that classifiers are argued to be type-shifters from kind denotations to sets of atomic individuals, where the atomic structure of entities is spelled out explicitly by classifiers, as in (49b). As a consequence, the property expressed by MP-Adj-*de* is predicated of Cl-N, which denotes a set of entities intersecting with atomic units, as in (49c).

(49) **Step 3: Applying the property to an atomic set**

a. $\|shu\|_k: \text{TREE}_k = {}^{\cap}\lambda x.\ \text{tree}(x)$

b. $\|ke\ shu\|_{<e\ t>} = \|ke\|_{<k,<e,t>>}\ (\|shu\|_k) = \lambda x.\ \text{ATOM}_{plant}(x) \wedge \text{Instantiation}\ (x, \text{TREE}_k)$

c. $\|ke\ san\ mi\ gao\ de\ shu\ \| = \|san\ mi\ chang\ de\|\ (\|ke\ shu\|)$

$= \lambda x.\ \text{ATOM}_{plant}\ (x) \wedge \text{Instantiation}\ (x, \text{TREE}_k) \wedge \text{length}\ (x) = 3\ \text{meters}$

The denotation of Cl-N in Mandarin is analogous to count nouns in English, both of which denote sets of atomic individuals. Borer [29] proposes that Mandarin classifiers are realized in the same syntactic position as the plural marker -*s* in English, both of which are realized as the Dividing head. It thus follows that the properties denoted by MPs operate below the projection of NumP, e.g. below the number morphology in English.

(50) a. two [tall student]s
      b. two [1.8 meter student]s

Li [18] proposes that classifiers either denote the function of counting or measuring entities, and they are associated with two distinct syntactic structures. It is suggested that counting classifiers have a counting structure: [NumP [ClP [NP]]], where they stand in a head-complement relation cyclically, whereas measuring classifiers have the measure structure: [Num-Meas [NP]], where the numeral and the measure word forms a constituent first, before merging with the noun. Our semantics in (49) correctly predicts that the monotonic reading is not available for attributive MPs when they are embedded in a true measure phrase (distinct from true classifier phrases in structures). It goes for the structure: [[Num-Meas [MP-NP]], where the classifier forms a constituent with the numeral, and the measure word in Num-Meas is resistant to being scoped over the MP. This prediction is born out by the example in (51), where the classifier position is filled in by measure words like *kilo*, and MPs are restricted to a non-monotonic reading. We suggest that measure words are not endowed with an individuation function and they do not denote sets of atoms in any case and there are no atomic entities available, to which the attributive MP can apply, to yield a monotonic reading at the object level.

(51) ta   mai le   liang gongjin [wu   gongjin de]   xigua.
      he   buy PFV two kilo   five kilo   Mod   watermelon
      a. 'He bought two kilos of the five-kilo type watermelon.'
      b. Impossible: 'He bought two kilos of watermelon, which measures five kilos.'

To wrap up, in Mandarin, MPs appearing in adnominal positions can have a monotonic reading, which is seen as an object-level interpretation in a more precise sense. Although MPs appear before nouns, they scope over the constituent of Cl-N in terms of their modification relation, which results in the effect of distributivity. It is suggested that attributive MPs on the monotonic reading are part of the DegP and they serve to saturate the degree argument associated with the semantics of dimensional adjectives, which is at type $<d, et>$.

5 Non-monotonic Reading of Attributive MPs as a Subkind Reading

Non-monotonic MPs are adnominal modifiers, which directly modify the noun that follows. The crucial question to be asked is whether the non-monotonic reading can be treated as a subkind reading. Our answer is that Mandarin and English show parametric differences in that the alleged monotonic reading should be considered as a subkind reading in Mandarin but not in English, which underscores the difference of their noun semantics. In other words, we argue that the contrast between monotonic and non-monotonic readings should be recast as an ambiguity between object-level and kind-level denotations in Mandarin.

5.1 Non-monotonic MPs as Classifying Adjectives

Adjectival modification comes into two types in Mandarin. It is either the case that adjectives can be juxtaposed to the head noun, i.e. 'Adj-N' or that the modification marker *de* intervenes between the adjective and the head noun, as in the form of Adj-*de*-N, as shown in (52) [30].

(52)	a. baiyun	a'. jiebai-de	yun	
	cloud	white-Mod	cloud	'white cloud'
	b. xiaomao	b'. xiao-de	mao	
	kitten	small-Mod	cat	'small cats'

It has been assumed by many [31–33] that the *de*-less Adj-N expressions are compounds and Adj-*de*-N are analyzed as phrases or relative clauses. If *de* insertion can be taken as diagnostic for the phrasehood of the nominal expression, then MP-*de*-N is definitely a phrase but not a compound.

One of the evidence in support of the phrasal status of MP-*de*-NP is concerned with NP ellipsis. As shown in (53), MP-*de*-NP always allows NP ellipsis, regardless of whether the MP is interpreted monotonically or non-monotonically. This suggests that the head noun has to be a maximal projection, e.g. being NP in our case [34].

(53) Pangxie, ta mai-le   liang zhi [si-liang   de]   he   yi   zhi   [liu-liang   de]].
     crab   he buy-PFV two CL 200-gram Mod   and   one   CL   300-gram Mod
     'As for crabs, she bought two 200-gram ones and a 300-gram one.'
OR 'As for carbs, she bought two weighing 200 grams each and one weighing 300 grams.'

OR 'As for carbs, she bought two weighing 200 g each and one weighing 300 g.'
Landman [23] suggests that numerals like *three* can have an adjective use, under which it expresses the cardinality property of being three. Being a numerical adjective, *three* can alternate its position with other adjectives, as exemplified in (54).

(54)   a. *Fifty* ferocious lions were shipped to Artis.

        b. Ferocious *fifty* lions were shipped to Artis.

As shown in (55), non-monotonic MPs can also flip-flop its positions with other attributive modifiers. We thus assume that MPs can be treated as an adjectival modifier in a similar way as the English *three*, which denote properties true of the individuals in the denotation of the head noun.

(55) a. yi   bu   64G-de   xinkuan   shouji
        one   CL   64G-Mod   new   cellphone
     b. yi   bu   xinkuan 64G-de   shouji
        one   CL   new   64G-Mod   cellphone

The facts exhibited by (53) and (55) suggest that attributive MPs on a non-monotonic reading are syntactically analogous to attributive adjectives. In contrast with monotonic attributive MPs, we claim that non-monotonic attributive MPs are subject to a sub-kind reading but not to an object-level reading. In other words, the distinction of attributive MPs between monotonic and non-monotonic readings is constrained by the sortal distinction between kinds and objects in the denotation of Ns.

It has been claimed since Zhu [35] that there are two different *de*'s involved in the sequence of Modifier-*de*-Modifiee, namely, the predicativizer *de* and the nominalizer *de* (also see [36] for a recent account). According to Huang [37], the former only marks expressions of type <e, t> and the latter denotes the function from an expression of type <e, t> to an individual-denoting expression at type *e*. We suggest that the particle *de* following attributive MPs, as in MP-*de*-NP, are of different status under the monotonic and non-monotonic readings. Specifically, the marker *de* following the monotonic MP is a predicativizer, as defined in Sect. 4, and the one following the non-monotonic MP is a nominalizer.

It is not our primary task to offer a detailed syntactic analysis to tease apart these two *de*'s in the expression MP-*de*-NP. We simply show that monotonic and non-monotonic MPs show different requirements on the presence of *de* in their predicative uses, if we assume that the attributive uses of MPs are derived from their predicative uses in both cases. In the monotonic context of (56), the marker *de* is needed only in attributives and it is not allowed in predicative positions; in the non-monotonic context of (57), the marker *de* is needed obligatorily both in predicative positions and attributive constructions.

(56) a. yi   kuai   <u>san</u>   <u>mi</u>   <u>chang</u> *(de) bu.
        one   CL   three   meter   long   DE   cloth
        'a three-meter piece of cloth wire.'   [attributive MP: monotonic]
     b. zhe   kuai   bu   you <u>san mi</u>   <u>chang (*de)</u>.
        this   CL   cloth   have three meter   long   DE
        'This piece of cloth reaches three meters long.'   [predicative MP: monotonic]

(57) a. zhe   kun   <u>san-haomi</u>   *(de)   <u>dianxian</u> shi wo-de.
        this   Cl$_{roll}$ 3-millimeter   DE   wire   be   mine
        'This roll of 3-mm wire is mine.'   [attributive MP: non-monotonic]
     b. zhe   kun   dianxian shi   <u>san-haomi</u>   *(de)<u></u>.
        this   Cl$_{roll}$ wire   be   3-millimeter   DE
        'This roll of wire is of 3-mm.'   [predicative MP: non-monotonic]

According to Zhu [38] and Huang [37], it is the signature property for the nominalizer *de* to appear in both predicative and attributive positions. Non-monotonic MPs behave in the same way as non-gradable adjectives, such as *golden, male, true* regarding the obligatory presence of *de*. Compare (57) with (58).

(58) a. na   ge   <u>xingzhe-de/nan-de</u>   haizi   milu le.
      that   CL   awake-DE/male-DE   child   lost PRF
      'That child awake/ the male student got lost.'

      b. na   ge   haizi   shi   <u>xingzhe-de/nan-de</u> .
      that   CL   child   be   awake-DE/male-DE
      'That child is awake/ is male.'

The contrast between (56) and (57) strongly suggests that for monotonic MPs, the marker *de* comes into play only when the MP is required to be shifted as an attributive modifier, but the one after non-monotonic MPs is persistently present, regardless of its syntactic positions. This difference is sufficient for us to treating these two *de*'s differently. In view of its similarity with non-gradable adjectives, we propose that non-monotonic MPs in predicative positions denote functions from individuals to truth values, and they have the semantics of intersective adjectives in attributive constructions, where they intersect with nouns (see Landman's 2004 semantics of numerals).

It was argued earlier that on the monotonic reading, attributive MPs are composed with the head noun by the rule of functional application, where the marker *de* is claimed to be the functor of type <et, <et,et>>. As for non-monotonic MPs, we suggest that they compose with the head noun by Heim and Kratzer's [4] rule of Predicate Modification by conjoining two entities of the type e (or k for kinds). In particular, we adopt Huang's [37] proposal that nominal modification is a case of conjunction/intersection, which requires sameness of types, which is generalized to the conjunction of nominalized properties: if the head noun (the modifiee) is of type e, the modifier must also be of type e. Its definition is illustrated by (59).

(59)   Definition of nominal modification [37]
       a. $x \wedge y = \text{nom} (\lambda z[\text{pred}(x)(z) \wedge \text{pred}(y)(z)])$
       b. xin shu → xin ∧ shu 'new book'

One of main motivations for Huang [37] to treat both attributive modifiers and the head noun to be of type e is attributed to Chierchia's [28] claim that bare nouns in Mandarin are kind terms. We, following Huang [37], suggest that the semantics of attributive MPs on a non-monotonic reading be tentatively represented in (61), where non-monotonic MPs in attributives are assumed to be classifying modifiers operating at the kind level. The details will be worked out in Sect. 5.2.

(60) a. yi   kuan   san-haomi de   dianxian
      one CL_{roll} 3-mm   DE wire
      'a roll of 3-mm wire'
      b. $\|\text{san-haomi-de dianxian}\| = {}^{\cap}(\lambda x. \, 3\text{mm}(x) \wedge \text{wire}(x))$

5.2 Non-intersective MPs as Kind Modifiers

This subsection attempts to justify non-monotonic MPs in attributives to be a kind modifier in Mandarin. We will also discuss the parametric differences between Mandarin and English. We claim that NPs with non-monotonic MPs are kind terms in Mandarin, and the counterparts in English are property-denoting, unless its bare nouns are in plural forms.

Schwarzschild [1] argues that attributive MPs cannot be interpreted as picking out a kind. At least, this is claimed to be the case in English. Schwarzschild claims that "if by 'kind' we mean 'natural kind' then *200 lb polar bear* should be unacceptable, since this is no such species. If on the other hand, we mean by 'kind' something more general, something akin to 'property', then it's hard to understand why *20 lb honey* cannot pick out portions of honey that have the property of weighing 20 pounds."

It is suggested in Chierchia [28] that "kinds are generally seen as regularities that occur in nature". The tern 'kinds' not only refers to biological ones and well-established ones, but also to artifacts and complex things, as long as we can "impute to them a sufficiently regular behavior" (ibid). We argue that in English, attributive MPs do not express natural kinds or well-established kinds, but they can express ad hoc kinds. This is reminiscent of the contrast between *the coke bottle* and *the blue bottle* made in Krifka [39]. In appropriate contexts depicted in (61), complex NPs with attributive MPs can be construed as kind expressions, which are expressed by the syntactic forms of bare plurals or definite singulars.

(61) a. 200 lb polar bears have a lower risk of heart attack.

   b. The 20 lb honey sells better than the 10 lb one.

On the basis of the intuition in (60), we propose that non-monotonic attributive MPs in Mandarin express classifying properties that help to establish subkinds. Recall the examples in (25). Jiang [15] suggests that *san bang de yingtao* 'three-pound cherry' in (25a) refers to "a complex kind or concept", which is expressed as "sorted in accordance with…" in Tang's [14] terms. The same MP-*de*-N can be preceded either by the demonstrative phrase *na zhong* 'that kind' (62a) or *na-gen* 'that individual' (62b). In the former, the MP *san haomi* '3 mm' specifies the property that defines a subkind of wire, which most naturally refers non-monotonically to the diameter of the wire to be 3 mm; in the latter, the same MP describes the property of the that particular stretch of wire, which is intended to refer to its length in a monotonic sense.

(62) a. na   zhong   san haomi   de   dianxian
         that   kind   three-millimeter   Mod wire
         'that 3-mm kind of wire'
      b. na   gen   san haomi   de   dianxian
         that   CL   three-millimeter   Mod   wire
         'that 3-mm wire'

Paul (2005, 2010) argues that a modifier without the subordinator *de* is interpreted as a defining property, whereas a modifier with *de* expresses an accessory property. According to Paul [40], "with the *de*-less modification structure, a new subcategory is established, which must present a natural, plausible class in the sense of Bolinger [41]." In the modification structure with *de*, a property is encoded as an accessory one, in the sense that this property is presented as not instrumental in establishing a new subcategory of N.

We propose that both *de*-less and *de*-marked adjectives can help to establish kinds, but two different sorts of kind entities are involved: *de*-less adjectives help to establish well-established kinds and it happens at the N^0 level, whereas *de*-marked adjectives can establish *ad hoc* kinds (or not so well-established kinds), namely, kinds based on contextually given properties and it happens at the NP level.

In Mandarin, well-established kinds and *ad hoc* kinds can be distinguished by different question types employed. Carlson [42] suggests that *what N* asks for the identity of subkind entities and it serves as the same function as *which kind of N*. However, in Mandarin, *which kind of N* can be answered by both well-established and ad hoc kinds, but *what N* can be answered by well-established kinds only.

(63) A: ni mai-le nazhong pingguo?   B: Fushi pingguo /zuotian de pingguo.
     you buy-PFV which kind apple   Fuji apple   /yesterday Mod apple
     'Which kind of apple did you buy?'   'Fuji apples'.   / 'Yesterday's apples.'

(64) A: ni   mai-le   shenme pingguo?   B: Fushi pingguo /#zuotian de pingguo.
     you buy-PFV what   apple   Fuji apple   /#yesterday Mod apple
     What apples did you buy?'   'Fuji apples.   /'#Yesterday's apples.'

As shown in (65), MP-*de*-N can only serve an answer to the question imposed by *na zhong* 'which kind' but not by *shenme* 'what'.

(65) A: ni   mai-le   *na zhong / #shenme* pingguo? B: er-liang de pingguo.
     you   buy-PFV which kind/ what   apple   100-gram Mod apple
     'Which kind of apple do you buy?'   'The 100-gram apple.'

The Mandarin expression MP-*de*-N is analogous to *the big bottle* discussed in Krifka [39]. We thus suggest that MP-*de*-N denote *ad hoc* kinds, but not well-established kinds. "What counts as kind is not set by grammar, but by the shared knowledge of a community of speakers" [28]. Roughly, we suggest that *ad hoc* kinds can be modeled as a set of entities in the intersection of nouns and attributive modifiers, which are characterized with "a sufficiently regular behavior" in the relevant context (ibid).

An extra piece of evidence in support of the correlation of the presence/absence of *de* with the distinction between well-established and *ad hoc* kinds is substantiated by the following fact exemplified by (66). The marker de after the MP can sometimes be omitted under a non-monotonic reading, which would possible lead to a compound, but the omission of *de* after the MP is never possible under a monotonic reading. In other words, *ad hoc* kinds can well be turned into established kinds, which are accompanied by the omission of the marker *de* after the MP at the syntactic level.

(66) a. 32G   (de)   neicun-ka
          32 G   Mod   memory card
          '32G memory cards'
      b. 400 mi   (de)   paodao
          400 meter   Mod   athletic track
          '400-meter athletic tracks'
      c. shuangren   (de)   chuang
          double:person Mod   bed
          'double beds'

Before working out the semantics of non-monotonic MPs, we adopt Chierchia's [28] semantics on Mandarin nouns. He claims that Mandarin is an argumental language and its bare nouns are born as arguments by making reference to kinds, and that the corresponding predicative meaning can be derived from the kind term, i.e. a process of predicativization. The kind reading and the predicative reading of the bare noun *dianxian* 'wire' can be represented as in (68).

(67) a. Bare nouns as kind terms: $\|dianxian\|_k = WIRE_k = {}^{\cap}\lambda x.\ wire(x)$
      b. Predicativization: $\|dianxian\|_{<e,t>} = {}^{\cup}WIRE_k = {}^{\cup \cap}\lambda x.\ wire(x)$

We now propose that attributive MPs can directly modify such NPs by ascribing kind-level properties to the kind entity, from which we derive a set of subkind entities. In particular, we adopt Huang's [37] 'conjunctive composition' on complex NPs in Chinese (Heim and Angelika 1998: predicate modification).

(68) a. **Step 1:** MP denotes a measure property of individuals
          $\|san\ haomi\| = \lambda x.MEAS^{diameter}(x) = 3\ mms$
      b. **Step 2:** a measure predicate is turned into an argument by the nominalizer *de*
          $\|san\text{-}haomi\ de\| = \|de\|\ (\|san\ haomi\|) = \lambda P[{}^{\cap}\lambda x.P(x)]\ (\lambda x.MEAS^{diameter}(x) = 3\ mms\ )$
          $= {}^{\cap}\lambda x.MEAS^{diameter}(x) = 3\ mms$
      c. **Step 3:** the subkind entity is derived by "conjunctive composition" [4]
          $\|san\ haomi\ de\ dianxian\| = \|san\ haomi\ de\| \wedge \|dianxian\|$
          $= {}^{\cap}\lambda x.\ MEAS^{diameter}(x) = 3\ mms\ \&\ {}^{\cap}\lambda x.\ wire(x))$

6   Conclusions

This paper challenges Schwarzschild's [1] claim that the attributive position is reserved for non-monotonic readings of measure predicates. It was shown that attributive MPs in Mandarin are potentially ambiguous between monotonic and non-monotonic readings. We propose that the apparent monotonic and non-monotonic readings in Mandarin should be recast a distinction between object and kind readings in Mandarin, but such a correlation cannot be established in English. In the case of Mandarin, attributive MPs modify ClPs on the monotonic reading but modify NPs on the non-monotonic reading, which serve as different sources for the distributivity effect observed in these two contexts. This suggests that distributivity and (non-)monotonicity are independent of each other. It is also suggested that attributive MPs on the monotonic reading denote degrees, and they are part of a DegP, but those on the non-monotonic reading are attributive adjectives and they compose with NPs via Heim and Kratzer's [4] rule of PM [37].

References

1. Schwarzschild, R.: The role of dimensions in the syntax of noun phrases. Syntax **9**, 67–110 (2006). https://doi.org/10.1111/j.1467-9612.2006.00083.x
2. Rothstein, S.: Semantics for Counting and Measuring. Cambridge University Press, Cambridge (2019)
3. McKinney-Bock, K., Pancheva, R.: Why is attributive "heavy" distributive? In: Altshuler, D., Rett, J. (eds.) The Semantics of Plurals, Focus, Degrees, and Times, pp. 81–110. Springer, Cham (2019). https://doi.org/10.1007/978-3-030-04438-1_5
4. Heim, I., Angelika, K.: Semantics in Generative Grammar. Blackwell Publishing, Malden (1998)
5. Jackendoff, R.: X-bar Syntax: A Study of Phrase Structure. MIT Press, Cambridge (1977)
6. Schwarzschild, R.: The grammar of measurement. In: Jackson, B. (ed.) Proceedings of SALTXII, pp. 225–245. Cornell University Press, Ithaca, N.Y. (2002)
7. Krifka, M.: Nominal reference, temporal constitution and quantification in event semantics. In: Bartsch, R., van Benthem, J., van Boas, E.P. (eds.) Semantics and Contextual Expressions, pp. 75–111. Foris Press, Dordrecht (1989)
8. Krifka, M.: Thematic relations as links between nominal reference and temporal constitution. In: Sag, I., Scabolcsi, A. (eds.) Lexical Matters, pp. 29–54. CSLI Publications, Stanford (1992)
9. Kennedy, C.: Measurement in NP: Schwarzschild's "Grammar of Measurement". Northwestern University, Evanston, IL (2003)
10. Li, X.P., Yang, R.: On (non-)monotonicity of attributive measure phrases. J. Foreign Lang. **42**, 60–71 (2019)
11. Champollion, L.: Parts of a Whole: Distributivity as Bridge Between Aspect and Measurement. Oxford University Press, Oxford (2010)
12. Ladusaw, W.: Semantic constraints on the English partitive construction. In: Proceedings of WCCFL, pp. 231–242 (1982)
13. Rett, J.: The polysemy of measurement. Lingua **143**, 242–266 (2014). https://doi.org/10.1016/j.lingua.2014.02.001
14. Tang, C.-T.J.: Nouns or classifiers: a non-movement analysis of classifiers in Chinese. Lang. Linguist. **6**, 431–472 (2005)
15. Jiang, L.J.: Monotonicity and measure phrases in Chinese. In: Proceedings of the Chicago Linguistics Society (2013)
16. Tang, C.-T.J.: Chinese Phrase Structure and the Extended X'-theory. Cornell University dissertation, Ithaca, N.Y. (1990)
17. Li, X.P., Rothstein, S.: Measure readings of Mandarin classifier phrases and the particle de. Lang. Linguist. **13**, 693–741 (2012)
18. Li, X.P.: Numeral Classifiers in Chinese: The Syntax-Semantics Interface. Mouton de Gruyter, Berlin (2013)
19. Corver, N.: The internal syntax of the dutch extended adjectival projection. Nat. Lang. Linguist. Theory **15**, 289–368 (1997). https://doi.org/10.1023/A:1005846812956
20. Kennedy, C.: The Syntax and Semantics of Gradability and Comparison (1997)

21. Zamparelli, R.: Pre-nominal modifiers, degree phrases and the structure of AP. In: Dolci, R. and Giusti, G. (eds.) University of Venice Papers in Linguistics, pp. 138–163 (1993)
22. Cresswell, M.J.: The semantics of degree. In: Partee, B. (ed.) Montague Grammar, pp. 261–292. Academic Press, New York (1976)
23. Landman, F.: Indefinites and the Type of Sets. Blackwell Publishing, Malden (2004)
24. Barwise, J., Cooper, R.: Generalized quantifiers and natural language. Form. Semant. Essent. Readings **4**, 75–126 (2008). https://doi.org/10.1002/9780470758335.ch3
25. Partee, B.: Noun phrase interpretation and type-shifting principles. In: Groenendijk, J., de Jongh, D., Stokhof, M. (eds.) Studies in Discourse Representation Theory and the Theory of Generalized Quantifiers, pp. 115–143. Foris Press, Dordrecht (1987)
26. Kotek, H.: Degree relatives, definiteness and shifted reference. In: Kan, S., Moor-Cantwell, C., Staubs, R. (eds.) Proceedings of NELS. GLSA Publications, Amherst, MA (2011)
27. Grosu, Alexander, Landman, Fred: Strange relatives of the third kind. Nat. Lang. Semant. **6**(2), 125–170 (1998). https://doi.org/10.1023/A:1008268401837
28. Chierchia, G.: Reference to kinds across languages. Nat. Lang. Semant. **6**, 339–405 (1998). https://doi.org/10.1023/A:1008324218506
29. Borer, H.: In Name Only. Oxford University Press, Oxford (2005)
30. Zhu, D.X.: Yufa Jiangyi [Lecture Notes on Grammar]. Commercial Press, Beijing (1982)
31. Duanmu, S.: Wordhood in Chinese. In: Packard, J. (ed.) New Approaches to Chinese Word Formation: Morphology, Phonology and the Lexicon in Modern and Ancient Chinese, pp. 135–196. Mouton de Gruyter, New York & Berlin (1998)
32. Paul, W.: Adjectival modification in Mandarin Chinese and related issues. Linguistics **43**, 757–793 (2005). https://doi.org/10.1515/ling.2005.43.4.757
33. Sproat, R., Shih, C.: Prenominal adjectival ordering in English and Mandarin. Proc. NELS **18**, 465–489 (1988)
34. Lobeck, A.: Ellipsis: Functional Heads, Licensing and Ellipsis. Oxford University Press, New York (1995)
35. Zhu, D.X.: Shuo 'de' [On 'de']. ZhongguoYuwen, pp. 1–15 (1961)
36. Li, Y.-H.A.: Mandarin noun phrases with de from the perspective of Taiwan Southern Min. In: Studies of the Particle de in Chinese, pp. 181–196. Beijing University Press, Beijing (2017)
37. Huang, S.Z.: Property theory, adjectives, and modification in Chinese. J. East Asian Ling. **15**, 343–369 (2006). https://doi.org/10.1007/s10831-006-9002-0
38. Zhu, D.X.: Cong Fangyan he Lishi Kan Zhuangtai Xingrongci [Investigation of adjectives that describe temporary properties from a dialectal and diachronic perspective]. Fangyan, pp. 81–100 (1993)
39. Krifka, M., et al.: Genericity: an introduction. In: Carlson, G.N., Pelletier, F.J. (eds.) The Generic Book. University of Chicago Press, Chicago (1995)
40. Paul, W.: Adjectives in Mandarin Chinese: the rehabilitation of a much ostracized category. In: Hofherr, P., Matushansky, O. (eds.) Adjectives: Formal Analyses in Syntax and Semantics. John Benjamins Publishing Company, Amsterdam (2010)
41. Bolinger, D.: Adjectives in English: attribution and predication. Lingua **18**, 1–34 (1967). https://doi.org/10.1016/0024-3841(67)90018-6
42. Carlson, G.N.: A unified analysis of the English bare plural. Form. Semant. Essent. Readings **1**, 35–74 (2008). https://doi.org/10.1002/9780470758335.ch2

Universal Quantification in Mandarin

Mingming Liu$^{(\boxtimes)}$

Tsinghua University, Beijing, China
markliu@scarletmail.rutgers.edu

Abstract. Mandarin universal terms such as *mei*-NPs in preverbal positions usually require the presence of *dou* 'all/even'. This motivates the widely accepted idea from Lin (1998) that Mandarin does not have genuine (distributive) universal quantifiers, and *mei*-NPs are disguised plural definites, which thus need *dou* – a distributive operator (or an adverbial universal quantifier in Lee 1986, Pan 2006) – to form a universal statement. This paper defends the opposite view that *mei*-NPs are true universal quantifiers while *dou* is not. *Dou* is truth-conditionally vacuous but carries a presupposition that its prejacent is the strongest among its alternatives (Liu 2017). The extra presupposition triggers Maximize Presupposition (Heim 1991), which dictates that [*dou* S] blocks [S] whenever *dou*'s presupposition is satisfied. This explains the *mei-dou* co-occurrence, if *mei*-NPs are universal quantifiers normally triggering individual alternatives (thus stronger than all the other alternatives). The proposal finally predicts a more nuanced distribution of obligatory-*dou*, sensitive to discourse contexts.

Keywords: Universal quantifiers · Alternatives · EVEN

1 The Puzzle and Lin's Decompositional Solution

Mandarin universal terms such as *mei/suoyou*-NPs in preverbal positions have to co-occur with the famous multi-functional adverb *dou*, usually glossed as 'all' in this context, as in (1a). This is puzzling, since if *mei/suoyou*-NPs are ∀-quantifiers like English *every/all*-NPs, it is unclear why an additional "*all*" is required (or even possible); after all, English *every/all*-NPs are not compatible with another *all*, as in (1b)[1].

---

[1] Two notes on glossing. First, when *mei* takes a NP complement, a classifier is required between the two such as the *ge* in (1a). This paper discusses the meaning of *mei*-NP as a whole and thus largely ignores its internal composition and the role of classifiers. Correspondingly, *mei.ge xuesheng* 'every CL student' is written and glossed as *mei.ge xuesheng* 'every student'. Second, a numeral *yi* 'one' is also possible between *mei* and the classifier; that is, *mei.ge xuesheng* can also be written as *mei.yi.ge xuesheng*.

I thank Haoze Li, Jowang Lin and the reviewers of this paper for their helpful comments. Support from the National Social Science Foundation of China (17CYY062) is acknowledged.

D. Deng et al. (Eds.): TLLM 2020, LNCS 12564, pp. 81–106, 2020.
https://doi.org/10.1007/978-3-662-62843-0_5

(1) a. Mei.ge/Suoyou san.nianji xuesheng *(dou) lai.le.   Obligatory-*dou*
         every/all   third.grade student   DOU   come

         "Every/all third-grade student(s) came".
     b. Every/all third-grade student(s) (*all) came.   No additional *all*

A well-known solution proposed in Lin (1998) and recently advocated by
Zhang and Pan (2019) denies the status of *mei/suoyou*-NPs as genuine distributive universal quantifiers (of type $\langle et, t\rangle$), and takes them to be referential (of
type e), synonymous with plural definites. Concretely, *mei.ge san.nianji xuesheng*[2] according to Lin (1998) denotes $\bigoplus$ THIRD.GRADE.STUDENT—the maximal
mereological sum of all entities in the THIRD.GRADE.STUDENT set, and *mei* is
essentially a (generalized) sum operator. To illustrate, in context c_1 with exactly
three third-grade students Zhangsan, Lisi and Wangwu, *mei.ge san.nianji xuesheng* and the plural definite *zhexie san.nianji xuesheng* 'these third-year students'
have the same denotation, both referring to ZS $\oplus$ LS $\oplus$ WW.

(2) a. ⟦mei.ge san.nianji xuesheng⟧ $= \bigoplus$ THIRD.GRADE.STUDENT
     b. ⟦mei⟧ $= \bigoplus$
     c. ⟦mei.ge san.nianji xuesheng⟧^{c_1}=⟦zhexie san.nianji xuesheng⟧^{c_1}=ZS $\oplus$
         LS $\oplus$ WW

Next, Lin (1998) takes *dou* to be a distributive operator (3), similar to English
each, citing (4) as evidence where *dou* forces a distributive reading.

(3) ⟦dou$_{Lin}$⟧ $= \lambda P \lambda x \forall y[y \leq_{ATOM} x \rightarrow P(y)]$ (cf. 1987)

(4) Zhangsan he   Lisi dou hua.le   liang.fu hua. (*dou* forces dist-reading)
     Zhangsan and Lisi dou draw.ASP two.CL   pictures

     "Zhangsan and Lisi each drew two pictures".

When combined with a *mei*-NP, *dou* thus universally quantifies over the
atomic parts of the maximal sum referred to by the former, and together they
deliver (5) as the meaning of (1a). The result is equivalent to a universal
statement.

(5) $\forall y[y \leq_{ATOM} \bigoplus$ THIRD.GRADE.STUDENT $\rightarrow$ CAME$(y)]$ (Meaning of (1a))
     $\equiv \forall y[$THIRD.GRADE.STUDENT$(y) \rightarrow$ CAME$(y)]$

Since *mei*-NP's are non-quantificational, they need the aid of *dou* – a quantificational element – to express a quantificational meaning, and hence the two
are compatible and their co-occurrence expected.

---

[2] The current paper focuses on *mei*-NPs, and a detailed discussion of *suoyou*-NPs
(similar to English *all*-NPs) and a comparison between *mei* and *suoyou* is left to
another occasion.

Lin's (1998) analysis is decompositional, in the sense that universal quantification is decomposed into maximization over the NP and distributivity over the VP. However, since there is no inherent connection between the two operations, assigning *mei*-NPs a plural definite semantics (maximization) does not really explain why *dou* (distributivity) is needed: there is no principled semantic reason why $\bigoplus$ THIRD.GRADE.STUDENT (of type e) cannot combine with $\lambda x.$CAME(x) (a et predicate). Lin (1998) is aware of this problem and offers a syntactic solution. Following Beghelli and Stowell (1997), he proposes that *dou* syntactically is the overt head of a Distributive Phrase (DistP), and universal DPs such as *mei*-NPs *must* move to the specifier position of DistP. The syntactic requirement accounts for the obligatory *mei-dou* co-occurrence.

This paper (focusing on *mei*-NPs) discusses two types of problems for this line of analysis. First, there is ample evidence that *mei*-NPs are genuine distributive universal quantifiers (some of which is discussed in Liu 2017) and thus cannot be treated as plural definites. Second, explaining the *mei-dou* co-occurrence as a syntactic-semantic requirement of *mei*-NPs is both too strong and too weak. It is too strong since many occurrences of *mei*-NPs in preverbal positions do not need (or even cannot have) *dou* (Huang 1996, Liu 2019), suggesting that the co-occurrence might not be due to a strict grammatical requirement. It is also too weak because the phenomenon of obligatory-*dou* goes beyond *mei*-NPs: if the context is right, conjunctions of proper names also require the obligatory presence of *dou*. Crucially, this shows that obligatory-*dou* is sensitive to discourse contexts, a fact overlooked in the previous literature.

The rest of the paper is structured as follows. Section 2 offers evidence that *mei*-NPs are true universal quantifiers. This has the implication that *dou* is better not to be treated as a quantificational element (cf. the *double quantification/requantification* problem discussed in Yuan 2012, Xu 2014, Wu 2019). Section 3 discusses the non-quantificational analysis of *dou* in Liu (2017). Section 4 first introduces Maximize Presupposition and demonstrates how it can be used to capture a large of array of *obligatory presupposition* effects, including the obligatory requirement of *dou* with *mei*-NPs. It then shows how the explanation leads to the prediction that obligatory-*dou* is not limited to *mei*-NPs and sensitive to discourse contexts. Finally, Sect. 5 concludes.

2   *Mei*-NPs are Quantificational

The section compares *mei*-NPs with plural definites. It shows that whether *dou* is present or not (e.g. no *dou* for post-verbal *mei*-NPs), the two are significantly different.

2.1   *Mei*-NPs Without *dou* in Post-verbal Positions

Non-homogeneous and Maximal. First, post-verbal *mei*-NPs do not need *dou*, for the syntactic reason that *dou* is a VP-external adverb that associates only to its left (see Sect. 4.3 for a more detailed discussion). The fact can be used to test whether *mei*-NPs indeed have a plural-definite semantics as Lin (1998) proposes, by comparing *mei*-NPs and real plural definties in post-verbal positions. Since *dou* is absent in both cases, if the two show divergences, they must be attributed to inherent difference between the two, perhaps suggesting *mei*-NPs cannot be reduced to plural definites.

Consider (6). (6a) shows a *mei*-NP without *dou* under negation retains its universal force, and thus the most salient reading (and the only reading for most speakers) of (6a) is $\neg > \forall$. By contrast, plural definites such as the demonstrative phrase in (6b) are interpreted existentially under negation, due to a well-known property of plural definites—*homogeneity* (Löbner 2000, a.o.). In other words, (6a) is true as long as there was one third-grade student to whom the speaker did not tell the news, while (6b) can only be true when the news was told to *none* ($\approx$ *not any, any* being existential) of the students.

(6) a. Wo <u>meiyou</u> ba zhe.jian.shi gaosu <u>mei.yi.ge</u> san.nianji   xuesheng.
         I   not   BA this.thing tell   every   third.grade student
         "I did<u>n't</u> tell this to <u>every</u> third-grade student". $\neg > \forall$

     b. Wo <u>meiyou</u> ba zhe.jian.shi gaosu <u>zhe.xie</u> san.nianji   xuesheng.
         I   not   BA this.thing tell   these   third.grade student
         "I didn't tell this to these third-grade students".
         $\approx$ I did<u>n't</u> tell this to <u>any</u> of these third-grade students. $\neg > \exists$

The contrast clearly shows that *mei*-NPs are not plural definites, as they do not exhibit homogeneity and behave like English *every*-NPs even without *dou*, suggesting they are universal quantifiers by themselves.

This contrast is fully general. (7) shows it under *nobody*. In a context where everyone will invite some but not all third-grade students, (7a) is true while (7b) false.

(7) a. <u>Meiyou.ren</u> hui qing <u>mei.yi.ge</u> san.nianji xuesheng.
         no.body   will invite every   third.grade student
         "<u>Nobody</u> will invite <u>every</u> third-grade student".   NOBODY $> \forall$

     b. <u>Meiyou.ren</u> hui qing   <u>zhe.xie</u> san.nianji xuesheng.
         no.body   will invite these   third.grade student
         "Nobody will invite these third-grade students".
         $\approx$ Nobody will invite <u>any</u> of these third-grade students. NOBODY $> \exists$

Next, non-maximality is another property of predication with plural definites (Brisson 1998, Malamud 2012, Križ 2016). In a context where the speaker is pointing at all the third-grade students and uses *zhe.xie san.nianjie xuesheng* 'these third-grade students' to refer to them, (8b) can still be true if some of the students being referred to were not invited by Lisi. That is, predication with plural definties allow for exceptions. This is impossible for the *mei*-NP in (8a). For (8a) to be true, Lisi had to invite every third-grade student, without exceptions.

(8) a. Lisi qing.le   mei.yi.ge san.nianji   xuesheng.
       Lisi invite.ASP every   third.grade student

    "Lisi invited every third-grade student(s)".   (Maximal only)

   b. Lisi qing.le   zhe.xie san.nianji   xuesheng.
      Lisi invite.ASP these   third.grade student

    "Lisi invited these third-grade students".   (Non-maximal allowed)

To summarize the empirical picture presented so far, a comparison between *mei*-NPs and plural definties in post-verbal positions, where *dou* is absent, suggests the two are very different. *mei*-NPs do not exhibit homogeneity and non-maximality, two well-known properties of plural definties across many languages, and they always retain their maximal universal quantificational force, in both positive and negative contexts, just like their English counterparts *every*-NPs.

Quantifier-Sensitive Expressions. There are quantifier-sensitive expressions that require the presence of a quantificational element in their host sentence, for instance exceptives *but/except* (von Fintel 1993) and approximatives *almost* (Penka 2006), both of which have been used as tests for quantificational status of DPs (Carlson 1981 Kadmon 1993). In (9), an English *every*-NP is compatible with *but* and *almost*, while a plural definite is not, precisely because the former is quantificational while the latter not.

(9) a. I invited {every boy/#the boys} but John.
    b. I invited almost {every boy/#the boys}.

Returning to Mandarin, (10) shows that post-verbal *mei*-NPs without *dou* are compatible with exceptive *chule* 'except/but' and approximative *jihu* 'almost', both of which nevertheless reject plural definites, illustrated in (11). A plausible explanation is that *chule* and *jihu* are sensitive to the presence of universal quantifiers as their English counterparts do, and *mei*-NPs are universal quantifiers even without *dou*, while plural definties without *dou* are not.

(10) *Mei*-NPs without *dou* are compatible with Q-sensitive expressions

   a. Chule Lisi, wo qing.le   mei.ge san.nianji   xuesheng.
      Except Lisi, I   invite.ASP every third.grade student

    "I invited every third-grade student but Lisi".

   b. Lisi jihu   qing.le   mei.ge san.nianji   xuesheng.
      Lisi almost invite.ASP every   third.grade student

    "Lisi invited almost every third-grade student".

(11)   Plural definites without *dou* are incompatible with Q-sensitive expressions

    a.   #<u>Chule</u> Lisi, wo qing.le   <u>zhe.xie</u> san.nianji xuesheng.

       Except Lisi, I   invite.ASP these   third.grade student

       "#I invited <u>these</u> third-grade students <u>but</u> Lisi".

    b.   #Lisi <u>jihu</u>   qing.le   <u>zhe.xie</u> san.nianji xuesheng.

       Lisi   almost invite.ASP these   third.grade student

       "#Lisi invited <u>almost</u> <u>these</u> third-grade student(s)".

2.2   *Mei*-NPs with *dou*

Section 2.1 deals with *mei*-NPs without *dou*, and shows that they are significantly different from the corresponding plural definites, unexpected under the line of analysis where the two are treated on a par. This subsection turns to *mei*-NPs with *dou*, which as we will see again exhibit properties distinct from their plural difinite counterparts[3].

Partitives and Scope. Since plural definites are referential (denoting the maximal plural individual that satisfies the NP denotation), it makes sense to use a partitive construction to predicate over only a sub-part of the maximal individual. (12) shows that English plural definites are compatible with partitives, while *every*-NPs are not. An obvious explanation is that *every*-NPs are universal quantifiers, and do not denote plural individuals that are needed for partitives.

(12)   a.   Many of the boxes were stolen.

    b.   *Many of every box were stolen.

    Turning now to Mandarin, (13) shows that partitives are compatible with plural definites such as demonstrative phrases and plural pronouns in (13a)[4], but not with *mei*-NPs in (13b). The contrast reveals that plural definites but not *mei*-NPs are referential sum-denoting expressions, suggesting the latter are in fact quantificaitonal elements.

---

[3] There has been discussion on the difference between *mei*-NPs and plural definites concerning whether they allow for non-atomic distributive interpretations (Lin 1998, Feng and Pan 2017, Zhang and Pan 2019). This subsection offers additional differences between the two.

[4] While *Daduo* and *henduo* are taken to be quantificational adverbs in Liu (2017), they are treated as partitives here. A detailed analysis of these items is beyond the scope of the paper. But in either way, the contrast between (13a) and (13b) demonstrates that *mei*-NPs are different from plural definties, presumably because they are genuine ∀-quantifiers.

(13)   Plural definites are compatible with partitives while *every*-NPs are not

    a.   {Zhexie.xuesheng/Tamen} {daduo/henduo} dou xihuan Jin.Yong.
        {these.students/they}   {most/many}   DOU like   Jin.Yong

        "Most/Many of these students/them like Jin Yong".

    b. *Mei.ge xuesheng {daduo/henduo} dou xihuan Jin.Yong.
        every   student   {most/many}   DOU like   Jin.Yong

        "*Most/many of these students like Jin Yong".

Next, we turn to the scope facts discussed in Liu (2017). Liu reports that in the case of *mei*-NPs, it is the surface position of the *mei*-NP that determines the scope of the underlying semantic universal ($\forall$), and thus it must be the *mei*-NP that contributes the $\forall$. The relevant facts are in (14). (14a) shows that in the case of *mei*-NPs with negation, to obtain a wide scope negation over universal ($\neg > \forall$) construe, the negation needs to appear *before* the *mei*-NP, not just before *dou* as in (14b).

(14)   a.   <u>Bingfei</u> mei.ge san.nianji. xuesheng dou xihuan Jin.Yong.
        not   every third.grade student   DOU like   Jin.Yong

        "Not every third-grade student likes Jin Yong".

    b. *Mei.ge san.nianji. xuesheng <u>bingfei</u> dou xihuan Jin.Yong.
        every third.grade student   not   DOU like   Jin.Yong

        Intended: "Not every third-grade student likes Jin Yong".

Conversely, for plural definites with *dou*, the same reading can only be obtained by putting negation *after* the plural definite, right before *dou*.

(15)   a. *<u>Bingfei</u> {zhe.xie san.nianji. xuesheng /tamen} dou xihuan Jin.Yong.
        not   {these   third.grade student   /they} DOU like   Jin.Yong

        Indended: "It's not the case that these third-grade students/they all like J.Y".

    b.   {Zhe.xie san.nianji. xuesheng /tamen} <u>bingfei</u> dou xihuan Jin.Yong.
        {these   third.grade student   /they} not   DOU like   Jin.Yong

        "It is not the case that these third-grade students/they all like Jin Yong".

The contrast can be explained by assuming that while plural definties are not inherently quantificational[5], *mei*-NPs are real scope-bearing universal quantifiers and thus determine scope. Since Mandarin is a highly scope-isomorphic language (Huang 1982), it is the surface position of the *mei*-NP that determines its semantic scope.

---

[5] See Liu (2017) on how plural definites receive additional quantificaitonal force (from a covert distributive operator) in the presence of *dou*, compatible with the scope facts and the claim that *dou* is not a quantificational element over individuals.

Pair-List Phenomena. It has been reported that only true distributive universals allow for certain pair-list phenomena (in the sense of Bumford 2015). Here we focus on two facts: licensing of sentence-internal singular *different* and pair-list answers with singular *wh* in matrix questions. We show that *every*-NPs with *dou* license both while plural definites with *dou* neither, and hence the former but not the latter amount to true distributive universals; since *dou* is present in both cases and yet a difference observed, it must be the case that *mei*-NPs (but not *dou*) contribute the true distributive universal force.

First, (17) shows that *every*-NPs in English license the sentence-internal use of singular *different*, in which the books that are being compared are all present in the sentence (in this case introduced by different boys)[6]. In contrast to *every*-NPs, plural definites do not license sentence-internal singular *different*, as in (17b). The crucial distinction is that *every*-NPs are genuine distributive universal quantifiers but plural definties are not (see Bumford 2015 for a full account). To get the sentence-internal reading of *different*, the NP that combines with *different* has to be plural, as in (17c).

(17)   Only distributive universals license singular internal *different*

    a.   Every boy read a different book.   Beghelli and Stowell (1997):(20)

    b.   # The boys read a different book.   Moltmann 1992 (1992):(88)

    c.   The boys read different books.

The same contrast exists in Mandarin, with *mei*-NPs and plural definties (demonstrative phrases and plural pronouns). (18a) shows that *mei*-NPs with *dou* license singular internal *different*, while (18b) shows the corresponding plural definites do not. To get the internal reading of *different* with plural definties, a bare *different*-NP has to be used, as in (18c). The contrast between (18a) and (18b) indicates that *every*-NPs with *dou* are genuine distributive universals. Since *dou* alone does not have this licensing effect (or (18b) would be good), it is the *every*-NP that is the true universal.

(18)

    a.   Mei.ge xuesheng dou mai.le   yi.ben butong   de shu.
             Every   student   DOU buy.ASP one   different DE book

          "Every student bought a different book".

    b.   #{Zhe.xie.xuesheng /tamen} dou mai.le   yi.ben butong   de shu.
             these.student   /they   DOU buy.ASP one   different DE book

          "#{These students/they} bought a different book". (cf. (17b))

---

[6] Compare (17a) with (i) below, which involves a sentence-external *different*.

(16)   John read *The Raven*. Then, Bill read a different poem.

Licensing of sentence-internal *different* discussed in (17)–(18) is a pair-list phenomenon, in the sense that different *student-book* pairs have to be listed and compared.

c. {Zhe.xie.xuesheng /tamen} dou mai.le   butong de shu.
    these   .   student DOU buy.ASP differnt DE book

"These students/they bought different books".

A similar pair-list phenomenon is the availability of pair-list answers in questions. Krifka (1992) and Dayal (1992) report that while questions with singular *wh*'s that contain distributive universals allow for pair-list answers—that is, they can be felicitously answered by specifying a list of witnessing pairs, the corresponding questions with plural definites do not, as (19)–(20) below illustrate. Again, the explanation of the contrast relies crucially on the distinction between true universal quantifiers and plural definites (see Bumford 2015 for a recent proposal couched in dynamic semantics), as the title of Krifka's (1992) paper 'Definite NPs aren't Quantifiers' clearly indicates.

(19) Which movie did every boy rent least night?

   a. (Every boy rented) Z.
   b. Al rented A, Bill rented B, and Carl rented C.

(20) Which movie did the boys rent least night?

   a. (Every boy rented) Z.
   b. # Al rented A, Bill rented B, and Carl rented C.

Again we find the same contrast between Mandarin *mei*-NPs and plural definites. (21) shows questions with *mei*-NPs admit pair-list answers, while (22) the opposite with plural definites, confirming our previous conclusion that *mei*-NPs are true $\forall$[7].

(21) a. Mei.ge xuesheng dou mai.le   yi.ben shenme shu?
          every   student DOU buy.ASP one.CL what   book

          "Which book did every student buy?"
      b. (Every boy bought) Z.
      c. Al bought A, Bill bought B, and Carl bought C.

(22) a. {Zhe.xie.xuesheng /tamen} dou mai.le   yi.ben shenme shu?
          these.students   /they DOU buy.ASP one.CL what   book

          "Which book did {these students/them} buy?"
      b. (Every boy bought) Z.
      c. # Al bought A, Bill bought B, and Carl bought C.

---

[7] (22c) is allowed as an answer if the *yi.ben* 'one.CL' in (22a) is removed (cf. (18c)). In such a case, (22c) is not a real pair-list answer, but an elaboration of a cumulative answer *Al, Bill and Carl bought A, B, C*. See Krifka (1992) and Dayal (1992).

2.3 Summary

A large array of empirical facts have been discussed in the section (summarized in (23)) all pointing to the conclusion that Mandarin *mei*-NPs are true universal quantifiers.

(23) Evidence for the quantificational status of *mei*-NPs

    a. Even without *dou*, *mei*-NPs still lack *homogeneity* and *non-maximality*—two distinctive properties exhibited by plural definites without *dou*, and retain their maximal universal force in both positive and negative contexts, similar to English *every*-NPs.

    b. Even without *dou*, *mei*-NPs are still compatible with Q-sensitive expressions, similar to English *every*-NPs, but different from their plural definite counterparts.

    c. *Mei*-NPs are incompatible with partitive constructions, similar to English *every*-NPs, but different from the corresponding plural definites.

    d. Even with *dou*, *mei*-NPs still determine the scope of the underlying $\forall$, unlike plural definites with *dou*.

    e. Unlike plural definites with *dou*, *mei*-NPs license pair-list phenomena, a property that only true distributive universals have.

If *mei*-NPs are quantificational[8], a non-quantificational story of *dou* is needed *double quantification/requantification* (Yuan 2012, Xu 2014, Wu 2019). The next section introduces such a non-quantificational analysis of *dou*, based on Liu (2017).

3 Non-quantificational *dou*

Mandarin *dou* receives a lot of attention in the literature (Lee 1986, Cheng 1995, Shyu 1995, Huang 1996, Lin 1998, Hole 2004, Pan 2006, Xiang 2008, Liao 2011, Yuan 2012, Xu 2014, Liu 2017, Wu 2019, Xiang 2020). The paper adopts a particular view on *dou*, which takes it to be an alternative sensitive operator (Liao 2011, Liu 2017, Xiang 2020). Concretely, *dou* is a strongest-prejacent operator as in (24), which is truth-conditionally vacuous but carries a presupposition that its prejacent is the strongest among its contextually relevant alternatives (the C in (24); cf. the analysis of English *even* in Karttunen and Peters 1979 and the idea of *intensifier* in Xu 2014, Wu 2019). Different 'uses' of *dou* are then analyzed by conceptualizing strength (the $\prec$ in (24)) in different ways: *even-dou* corresponds

---

[8] Two reviewers suggest that differences between *mei*-NPs and plural definites do not necessarily mean that the former are $\forall$-quantifiers. While this is true, notice in all of the contrasts discussed, *mei* pattern with English *every*, which I take to be evidence for the $\forall$-quantificational status of the former. If the reader finds the evidence not decisive, she can read the paper as an existence proof that a pragmatic analysis of the *mei-dou* co-occurrence is sensible and testable.

to being the strongest in terms of likelihood ($\prec_{likely}$), while distributive-*dou* in terms of entailment ($\subset$). In the former case, *dou* presupposes that its prejacent is the most unlikely one in the context, while in the latter case, *dou* requires its prejacent entail all the relevant alternatives.

(24) $[\![\text{dou}_C\ S]\!]$ is defined only if $\forall q \in C[[\![S]\!] \neq q \rightarrow [\![S]\!] \prec q]$
  if defined, $[\![\text{dou}\ S]\!] = [\![S]\!]$ (*Dou* as a strongest-prejacent operator)

To see how the analysis works, consider two widely discussed uses of *dou*: its *even*-use in (25a), and its use as a distributivity operator (similar to English *each*) in (25b). The two uses correspond to the above-mentioned two ways of understanding strength between propositions: *(un)likelihood* vs. *entailment*. In (25a) with prosodic focus on *Lisi*, *dou* presupposes that the prejacent *that Lisi bought five books* is unlikely than all the other alternatives such as *that Zhangsan bought five books*, *that John bought five books*, and thus we have the observed *even*-flavor. In (25b) (under the relevant reading, see footnote 9), *dou* presupposes that its prejacent entails all the other alternatives. Assume that the alternatives to the prejacent are *that Zhangsan bought five books* and *that Lisi bought five books*; the requirement can be satisfied only if the prejacent is understood distributively (*that Zhangsan and Lisi each bought five books* $\subset$ *that Zhangsan/Lisi bought five books*). In other words, entailment-based *dou* forces distributive readings of plural predication, giving rise to the appearance that *dou* is a distributivity operator[9] (cf. Szabolcsi's (2015: 181–182) explanation of the distributivity effect associated with MO-style particles).

(25) a. LISI <u>dou</u> mai.le wu.ben shu.
      Lisi DOU buy.ASP five.CL book

      'Even Lisi bought five books.'   *Even-dou* ←Likelihood

   b. Zhangsan he Lisi <u>DOU</u> mai.le   wu.ben shu.
      Zhangsan and Lisi DOU buy.ASP five.CL books

      'Zhangsan and Lisi each bought five books.'   Distributive-
      dou←Entailment

---

[9] To be clear, (25b) is ambiguous. It also has a reading which can be paraphsed as 'even Zhangsan and Lisi as a group bought five books'. This reading is captured by taking strength to be likelihood and comparing the prejacent *that Zhangsan and Lisi (as a group) bought five books* with alternatives like *that Zhangsan, Lisi and John (as a group) bought a five books*, with *dou* conveying that the prejacent is the most unlikely one. A similar ambiguity also exists for (26) below (with the additional reading being 'a group of three students bought 5 books, which is unlikely') and the same remarks apply there. Finally, it is worth noting that stress disambiguates. Under entailment-related readings (the relavant readings under (25b) and (26) discussed in the main text) *dou* is generally stressed, while for *even*-uses of *dou* the stress falls on *dou*'s associates (the *Lisi* in (25b)). The prosodic pattern has been observed for a long time and yet no concrete proposal is currently available. I have to leave this issue of stress open.

Besides offering a conceptually simple way of understanding *dou*'s various uses, the unified analysis brings together two prominent accounts of *dou* proposed in the literature: the distributivity approach that takes *dou* to be a distributivity operator similar to English *each* (Lin 1998, Chen 2008), and the maximality approach that analyzes *dou* as ι (or σ as in Shavy 1980, Link 1983) that encodes maximality/uniqueness, similar to English *the* (Giannakidou and Cheng 2006, Xiang 2008). Consider (26) (with stress on *dou*, see footnote 9), in which *dou* displays both maximality and distributivity. Specifically, in (26) the bare numeral subject associated with *dou* is interpreted as a definite (*the three students*), and the VP following *dou* is construed distributively, indicated by the *each* in the gloss. However, it is not difficult to see that neither the distributivity approach (capturing only *each*) nor the maximality approach (capturing only *the*) accounts for the two effects exhibited by *dou* in (26) at the same time.

(26) San.ge   xuesheng <u>DOU</u> mai.le   wu.ben shu.
      three.CL student   DOU   buy.ASP five.CL book

'<u>The</u> three students <u>each</u> bought five books.'

Taking *dou* as an operator that evaluates the strength of the entire prejacent (based on entailment in this case) predicts both of its effects in (26). As an entailment-based strongest-prejacent operator, *dou* presupposes that its prejacent (*that 3 students bought five books*, 3 being *at least 3*) entails all the other alternatives, with plausible candidates for the alternatives being *that 2 students bought five books, that 1 student bought five books* and so on (recall that *dou* associates to its left and thus the alternative trigger is *san* 'three', to the left of *dou*). The entailment from the prejacent to the alternatives goes through only if the VP is interpreted distributively (*that 3 students each bought five books* $\subset$ *that 2 students each bought five books*), but not collectively/cumulatively. This explain the distributivity effect, in parallel with the explanation of (25b) above.

Furthermore, for the prejacent of (26) to entail *all* the other alternatives under consideration, there have to be exactly three students in the context. This can be illustrated by a comparison of (27) and (28). With exactly three students in the context, propositions of the form *that n students each bought five books* with $n > 3$ are not in the alternative set in the first place (for it makes no sense to consider a proposition like *that 4 students each bought five books* if we already know there could only be three students), and thus the prejacent indeed entails all the other alternatives, as in (27). (28) is different. In this case, there are more than 3 students (say 4) in the context and thus there is a proposition (*that 4 students each bought five books*) in the alternative set (asymmetrically) entailing the prejacent; as a result, *dou*'s strongest-prejacent presupposition cannot be satisfied and the sentence is infelicitous in such a context. In other words, the analysis of *dou* in (24) as a strongest-prejacent operator predicts (26) to carry a presupposition that there are exactly three students in the context, and this is exactly the maximality/definiteness effect.

(27) $Alt_{=3}$:
$$\left\{\begin{array}{l} \text{3 students each bought five books } (=\pi), \\ \text{2 students each bought five books,} \\ \text{1 students (each) bought a books,} \end{array}\right\}$$

(28) $Alt_{>3}$:
$$\left\{\begin{array}{l} \text{4 students each bought five books,} \\ \text{3 students each bought five books } (=\pi), \\ \text{2 students each bought five books,} \\ \text{1 students (each) bought a books,} \end{array}\right\}$$

In sum, taking *dou* to be a strongest-prejacent operator (based on likelihood or entailment, and in this particular case entailment) accounts for both distributivity and maximality of *dou*: the former is required to ensure entailment among alternatives while the latter is needed so that the prejacent could entail *all* the other alternatives (in schematic words, strongest = distributivity + maximality). In this sense, the current analysis inherits insights from both the distributivity analysis (Lin 1998, Chen 2008) and the maximality analysis (Giannakidou and Cheng 2006, Xiang 2008).

The paper adopts this strongest-prejacent-operator treatment of *dou*, which is a non-quantificational analysis of *dou* and thus is compatible with the facts presented in Sect. 2 that suggest *mei*-NPs are genuine universal quantifiers.

Before ending the discussion on *dou*, I would like to emphasize that the requirement of *dou* that its prejacent is the strongest among the alternatives is a presupposition, since presuppositions turn out to be crucial in the explanation of the *mei-dou* co-occurrence.

Presuppositions project. The examples below show that the strongest-prejacent requirement of *dou* projects across polar questions, possibility modals, negation and conditional antecedents. Specifically, all the sentences in (29) (stress on *LISI*) conveys that Lisi buying 5 books is unlikely, while all the sentences in (30) (stress on *dou*) convey that there are exactly 3 students in the context. So the requirement is a presupposition.

(29)   a.   LISI dou mai.le   wu.ben shu   ma?
           Lisi DOU buy.ASP five.CL book Q

           "Did even Lisi buy five books?"

       b.   Haoxiang LISI dou mai.le   wu.ben shu.
           seem   Lisi DOU buy.ASP five.CL book

           "It seems that even Lisi bought five books".

       c.   Wo bu juede LISI dou mai.le   wu.ben shu.
           I   not think Lisi DOU buy.ASP five.CL book

           "I do not think that even Lisi bought five books".

       d.   Ruguo LISI dou mai.le   wu.ben shu,   na...
           If   Lisi DOU buy.ASP five.CL book, then...

           "If even Lisi bought five books, then..."

(30) a. San.ge   xuesheng DOU mai.le   wu.ben shu   ma?
        three.CL students DOU buy.ASP five.CL book Q

    "Did the three students all buy five books?"

   b. Haoxiang san.ge   xuesheng DOU mai.le   wu.ben shu.
      seem   three.CL students DOU buy.ASP five.CL book

    "It seems that the three students all bought five books".

   c. Wo bu juede san.ge   xuesheng DOU mai.le   wu.ben shu.
      I not think three.CL students DOU buy.ASP five.CL book

    "I do not think that the three students all bought five books".

   d. Ruguo san.ge   xuesheng DOU mai.le   wu.ben shu, na...
      If   three.CL students DOU buy.ASP five.CL book, then...

    "If the three students all bought five books, then..."

In sum, *dou* is truth-conditionally vacuous but carries a presupposition that its prejacent is the strongest among its contextually relevant alternatives. With this independently motivated semantics of *dou*, we turn to the *mei-dou* co-occurrence.

4   Obligatory *dou* as Obligatory Presupposition

Taking *dou* to be a presupposition trigger allows us to reduce obligatory *dou* with *mei* to the general phenomena of *obligatory presupposition*, attested independently for a class of presupposition triggers cross many languages.

4.1   Obligatory Presupposition and Maximize Presupposition

In brief, the effects of obligatory presupposition refer to the pragmatic phenomena where a class of presupposition triggers gives rise to obligatory presence when their presupposition is satisfied. Relevant examples discussed in the literature are offered below from (31) to (36) (Kaplan 1984, Heim 1991, Krifka 1999, Chemla 2008, Amsili 2009, Bade 2016, Aravind 2017). The relevant presupposition triggers are underlined.

(31) a. John went to the party. Bill went to the party, too.
   b. #John went to the party. Bill went to the party.

(32) a. Mary went swimming yesterday. She went swimming again today.
   b. #Mary went swimming yesterday. She went swimming today.

(33) a. Sam was in New York yesterday. He is still there today.
   b. # Sam was in New York yesterday. He is there today.

(34) {<u>The</u>/#A} sun is shining.

(35) I washed {<u>both</u>/#All} of my hands.

(36) Sam {<u>knows</u>/#thinks} that Paris is in France.

To illustrate, consider (32). The relevant presupposition trigger is *again*, which presupposes that the event described by the VP that *again* attaches to happened at a previous time. In (32), *again* presupposes that the event of swimming by Mary today happened before, and the requirement is locally satisfied by the first clause in (32), and hence *again* is obligatory. To take another example, consider (34). Since *the* carries an extra uniqueness presupposition which is always satisfied by the world knowledge that there is one and exactly one sun, the presupposition trigger *the* is obligatory, and blocks the version of the sentence with *a*. Similar, *both* blocks *all* in (35) by its duality presupposition satisfied by the NP *hands*, and *know* blocks *believe* when its complement is already known to be true, by its factive presupposition in (36).

Parallel effects are observed in Mandarin, illustrated below from (37a) to (37f). The relevant presupposition triggers are underlined again, and the above remarks apply to the Mandarin examples as well[10].

(37) Obligatory presupposition in Mandarin

  a. Zhangsan canjia.le   juhui, Lisi ??(<u>ye</u>) canjia.le   juhui.
      Zhangsan attemd.ASP party, Lisi also   attend.ASP party

      "Zhangsan attended the party, Lisi ??(also) attended the party".

  b. Zhangsan zuotian   qu youyong, jintian #(<u>ye</u>) qu youyong.
      Zhangsan yesterday go swimming, today   again go swimming

      "Zhangsan went swimming yesterday. She went swimming #(again) today".

  c. Zhangsan zuotian   (jiu)   zai Beijing, jintian #(<u>hai</u>) zai.
      Zhangsan yesterday (already) in Beijing, today   still   in

      "Zhangsan was in Beijing yesterday. He is #(still) there today".

  d. Wo liang.zhi shou #(<u>dou</u>) xi.le.
      I two.CL   hands DOU   wash.ASP

      "I washed both of my hands".

  e. Lisi {<u>zhidao</u> /#xiangxin} Bali zai Faguo.
      Lisi {know   /#believe} Paris in France

      "Lisi {knows/#thinks} that Paris is in France".

---

[10] See the discussion of (26) on how *dou* gives rise to a definiteness presupposition as in (37d). As for (37f), since Mandarin *chule* is ambiguous between *except* and *in addition to*, when *chule* means *in addition to*, the additive presupposition of *ye* in the matrix clause is satisfied, and thus *ye* is obligatory.

  f.   Chule   Lisi, Zhangsan #(ye) lai.le
       In.addition.to Lisi Zhangsan also   pass.ASP
       'In addition to Lisi, Zhangsan also passed.'

Obligatory presupposition can be explained by the pragmatic principle Maximize Presupposition in (38), proposed in Heim (1991).

(38)   Maximize Presupposition
       Make your contribution presuppose as much as possible.

Maximize Presupposition mandates that a speaker choose among sentences (or LFs) with identical assertive information the one that has more/stronger presuppositions, when the presuppositions are satisfied[11]. To see how it works, consider (31) again. Here *too* is truth-conditionally vacuous but carries an additive presupposition that an alternative proposition to its prejacent is also true; the presupposition is satisfied in its local context (the second clause in (31)); thus Maximize Presupposition favors [*Bill went to the party too*] over [*Bill went to the party*] since the two have the same assertion but the former has an extra presupposition, and *too* is obligatory.

Let us return to the puzzle of obligatory *dou* with *mei*. I propose that obligatory *dou* is an instance of obligatory presupposition regulated by Maximize Presupposition. Consider (39a). We have established in Sect. 2 that mei-NPs are true universal quantifiers, so the prejacent of *dou* is already a universal statement, (39b). Next, *dou* is truth-conditionally vacuous but presupposes that its prejacent is stronger than all the other contextually relevant alterrnatives. Suppuse the alternatives to a universal statement are its individual instantiations, such as the ones in (39c). *Dou*'s prejacent hence entails all its alternatives and its presupposition automatically satisfied. Maximize Presupposition is then triggered and requires [*mei.ge* student *dou* came] block its *dou*-less version [*mei.ge* student came], and *dou* is obligatory with *mei* as a result.

(39)   Explaining obligatory *dou* via obligatory presupposition

  a.   Mei.ge xuesheng *(dou) lai.le.   Obligatory-*dou*
       every   student   DOU   come
       "Every third-grade student came".

  b. $\forall x[\text{STUDENT}(x) \rightarrow \text{CAME}(x)]$ Prejacent of *dou*

  c. $\left\{\begin{array}{l} \text{student A came,} \\ \text{student B came,} \\ \text{student C came,} \\ \ldots \end{array}\right\}$ Alternatives

---

[11] When the presupposition not satisfied, the speaker will not use the trigger in the first place, so this part comes from the felicity condition on presupposition use. See Stalnaker (1973; 1978).

d. *Dou*'s prejacent entails all the alternatives and its presupposition satisfied

and thus[mei.ge xuesheng dou lai.le]

blocks #[mei.ge xuesheng lai.le] via MP

In the above explanation, an important assumption is made that universal quantifiers activate their individual alternatives. We turn to this assumption in the next subsection.

4.2   Universal Quantifiers and Their Alternatives

The individual alternatives we have proposed for *mei*-NPs belong to the type of *domain alternatives* of generalized quantifiers — alternative quantifiers with their domain of quantification different from (usually smaller than) the one in the prejacent[12]. (40) spells out the domain alternatives of *mei/every* and the corresponding propositional alternatives for the sentence in (39a). It is clear that $\forall x[x \in \{A\} \to \text{CAME}(x)]$ is just *student A came* in (39c). (39c) is identical to (40c) if the former contains propositions involving plural individuals ($\forall x[x \in \{A,B\} \to \text{CAME}(x)]$ is *student a and b came*).

(40)

a. $[\![\text{mei}_D]\!] = \lambda P \lambda Q \forall x[[x \in D \land P(x)] \to Q(x)]$

b.   Domain alternatives of $[\![\text{mei}_D]\!]$
     $= \{\lambda P \lambda Q \forall x[[x \in D' \land P(x)] \to Q(x)] \mid D' \subseteq D'\}$

c.   Domain alternatives of (39a)
$$\left\{ \begin{array}{l} \forall x[x \in \{A\} \to \text{CAME}(x)], \\ \forall x[x \in \{B\} \to \text{CAME}(x)], \\ \forall x[x \in \{C\} \to \text{CAME}(x)], \\ \forall x[x \in \{A,B\} \to \text{CAME}(x)], \\ \forall x[x \in \{A,B,C\} \to \text{CAME}(x)], \\ \dots \end{array} \right\}$$ In a context where A,B,C are students

To further illustrate the idea of domain alternatives and its application to linguistic phenomena, let us briefly turn to an influential line of thinking that crucially uses domain alternatives to explain behaviors of Negative Polarity Items (NPIs). Comparing (41a) and (41b), we see that English *any* as a NPI is only

---

[12] Scalar alternatives on the Horn scale ⟨*yixie, mei*⟩ "⟨*some, every*⟩" will also work for the analysis sketched in (39), for *every student came* entails *some students came* (assuming the universal carries an existential import), and *dou*'s presupposition satisfied. I leave an exploration of this theoretical chocie to another occasion. In addition, domain alternatives with smaller domains are called subdomain alternatives. For the purposes of this study, it is unecessary to limit alternatives to subdomain ones, since the domain of a universal statement always seems to be the largest contextually salient one. *Every student came* cannot mean *every math student came* via covert domain restriction in a context with both math and non-math students.

grammatical in downward entailing contexts such as under the scope of negation. This restricted distribution is explained in Krifka (1995), Chierchia (2013)
by first assuming that *any* is an existential quantifier that obligatorily triggers domain alternatives[13], as in (41c) and (41d). Next, these alternatives when
project to the sentence level (via pointwise composition in Rooth 1992) will be
exhautified by a covert *only*—the O in (41e). O affirms its prejacent and negates
all the alternatives (determined in this case by the alternatives of *any* specified
in (41d)) not entailed by the prejacent. Finally, applying O to (41a) returns
a contradiction, for all the alternatives with a smaller domain D' (*John read
a book in D'*) asymmetrically entails the prejacent (*John read a book in D*)
and are thus negated by O, the conjunction of these negations and the prejacent being a condtradiction (*John read a book in D but didn't read any book in
subdomains of D*). This contradiction explains the ungrammaticality of *any* in
positive contexts, under the assumption that logically determined contradiction
can give rise to ungrammaticality (Gajewski 2002). On the other hand, applying
O above negation in (41b) is vacuous, since all the alternatives of the prejacent
in this case are entailed by the prejacent (due to the fact that negation reverses
the direction of entailment) and thus no negation happens. This explains why
any can be used under negation and in other downward entailing contexts in
general. The account is schematically illustrated in (41).

(41) Explaining NPIs via domain alternatives

  a. *John read any book.

  b. John didn't read any book.

  c. $[\![\text{any}_D \text{ book}]\!] = \lambda P \exists x[x \in D \land \text{BOOK}(x) \land P(x)]$

  d. Alternaitves of $[\![\text{any}_D \text{ book}]\!]$: $\{\lambda P \exists x[x \in D' \land \text{BOOK}(x) \land P(x)] \mid D' \subseteq D\}$

  e. $[\![O_C \ S]\!] = [\![S]\!] \land \forall q \in C[[\![S]\!] \not\subseteq q \to \neg q]$

  f. $[\![O_C \ (41a)]\!]$
      $= \exists x[x \in D \land \text{BOOK}(x) \land \text{READ}(x, \text{J})]$ Prejacent
      $\land \forall D' \subset D[\neg \exists x[x \in D' \land \text{BOOK}(x) \land \text{READ}(x, \text{J})]]$ Negation of Alts
      $= \bot$

  g. $[\![O_C \ (41b)]\!]$
      $= \neg \exists x[x \in D \land \text{BOOK}(x) \land \text{READ}(x, \text{J})]$ Vacuous exhaustification
      $= [\![(41b)]\!]$

Given existential quantifiers can trigger domain alternatives, it is natural to
assume that (at least some) universal quantifiers also trigger domain alternatives.
Indeed, Zeijlstra (2017), based on certain positive polarity properties of Dutch
iedereen 'everybody' (it can show up under negation, but cannot reconstruct
below negation once it appears above it at the surface, unlike English *every-*

---

[13] *Any* according to Chierchia (2013) also triggers scalar alternatives, which can be
safely ignored in the current paper. Furthermore, *any* has free choice uses, and
several recent accounts of free choice *any* also make use of its domain alternatives
(Dayal 2013, Crnič 2019, Crnič 2019).

body), argues that it is a universal quantifier that obligatorily triggers domain alternatives.

The idea that universal quantifiers trigger domain alternatives is in fact hard to avoid in the structure-based theory of alternatives developed in Katzir (2007) and Fox and Katzir (2011). In this theory, alternatives of an expressions can be formally defined as in (42). Assuming the domain argument D is a syntactic variable at the LF (von Fintel 1994), whose interpretation depends on the index of the variable, the domain alternatives of a quantifier are simply transformed from the quantifier by replacing the index of the domain variable by other indices.

(42)   Formal Alternatives   Katzir (2007)
       ALT(ϕ) = {ϕ can be transformed into ϕ' by a finite series of deletions, contractions, and replacements of constituents in ϕ with constituents of the same category taken from the lexicon.}

I adopt Katzir's (2007) general view of how formal alternatives are generated. Next, to capture the fact that alternatives are also contextually constrained, I assume following Fox and Katzir (2011) and Katzir (2014) that the set of alternatives eventually operated by an alternative sensitive operator such as *dou* is the intersection of both the set of formally determined alternatives ALT(ϕ) and a second set of alternatives C that represents contextual relevance (cf. Rooth 1992). This is explicitly stated for *dou* in (43)[14].

(43) $[\![\text{dou}_C\ S]\!]$ is defined only if $\forall q \in \text{ALT}([\![S]\!]) \cap C[\![S]\!] \neq q \rightarrow [\![S]\!] \prec q]$
       if defined, $[\![\text{dou}\ S]\!] = [\![S]\!]$

In this setting, for cases of *mei*-NPs requiring the presence of *dou*, the individual alternatives need be both formally defined (in ALT(S)) and contextually relevant (in C). This seems natural given that contextually relevant alternatives are usually taken to represent the current Question Under Discussion (QUD, Roberts 2012, Büring 2003) and an immediate QUD for a $\forall$-statement is whether the universal statement is true (the *least subject matter* in Lewis 1988), which in turn is reduced to the question of whether each individual instantiation is true. Intuitively, to evaluate the truth of a universal statement such as the one in (39), each individual alternative needs to be checked. It is in this sense that the individual alternatives of (39) are relevant (and thus in C).

To summarize, we have shown that the individual alternatives we posit for *mei*-NPs belong to the domain alternatives of generalized quantifiers and are commonly assumed for various purposes in the alternative-&-exhaustification framework. Building on Katzir (2007), we distinguish formal alternatives and contextually relevant ones, and propose that *dou* makes reference to their intersection. The distinction is useful, since it predicts that when the individual alternatives triggered by the *mei*-NP are not relevant, *dou* is not needed (for

---

[14] Strictly speaking, writing ALT($[\![S]\!]$) in (43) is incorrect: ALT according to (42) applies to expressions, not to denotations. ALT($[\![S]\!]$) should in fact be {$[\![S']\!]$ | $S \in$ ALT(S)}. I abuse the notation in (43) for the purpose of exposition.

the intersection would be empty and there would be no alternatives for *dou* to operate on). Section 4.3 shows that this is a correct prediction.

4.3   A More Nuanced Characterization of Obligatory-*dou*

Irrelevance of Individual Alternatives and *dou*'s Absence. *Mei*-NPs sometimes do not need *dou*, and this could happen when the individual alternatives formally generated by the *mei*-NP are not contextually relevant. Consider the discourse in (44) (the corresponding Mandarin sentences are given in (45)). We find a sharp contrast between the two occurrences of the same *mei*-sentence. When *mei.ben mai $10* 'every.classifier sells.for $10' is first uttered in (45a), *dou* is not needed (and cannot appear), while in its second occurrence (45c) *dou* is obligatory. The contrast shows that the co-occurrence between *mei* and *dou* is sensitive to discourse contexts—an aspect of the phenomenon that the previous literature overlooks. Take Huang (1996) for instance. Huang's generalization is that when the sentence has a indefinite noun phrase as the syntactic object, a pre-verbal *mei*-NP does not need *dou*. The generalization is not accurate in view of (44): the same *mei.ben mai $10* CANNOT take *dou* in (45a) but REQUIRES it in (45c). What determines the presence of *dou* is the relevant context, in particular, the QUD that determines the shape of C needed for the interpretation of *dou*.

(44)   [At a secondhand bookstore]
       The owner: We are now on sale! | *Mei.ben* sells.for $10 |.   (45a)
       John: What about this comic book? It seems brand new!   (45b)
       The owner: | *Mei.ben dou* sells.for $10 |.   (45c)

(45)   a.   Ben dian da.jianjia, mei.ben mai   SHI yuan!   (from the owner)
            our store big.sale, every   sell.for ten dollar   (stress on *shi*)
            'Our store is on big sale. Every book is 10 dollars!'

       b.   Zhe.ben manhua.shu zheme xin, ye   mai   shi yuan?   (from John)
            this.CL comic.book so   new, also sell.for ten dollar
            'This comic book seems brand new. Is it also 10 dollars? '

       c.   MEI.ben dou mai   shi yuan!   (from the owner)
            every   DOU sell.for ten dollar   (Stress on *mei*)
            'EVERY book is 10 dollars!'

More concretely, when the owner first uttered *mei.ben mai $10*, her focus was on *$10* (indicated by the prosodic prominence perceived on *shi* in (45a)) and it is naturally understood that she (as the owner) was assuming that every book was sold at the same price and the QUD is *how much IS a book?*. In such a context, individual books are not relevant to the QUD, and thus are not in the C that is needed for the interpretation of *dou*. As a result, the set of contextually relevant alternatives associated with *dou* (the intersection of the set of individual alternatives of *mei*-NP and *C*) is the empty set. Assuming that *dou*, like other alternative sensitive operators, needs to be associated with a non-empty set of alternatives (cf. the presupposition of $\sim$ in Rooth 1992), the absence of *dou* is correctly predicted for (45a).

By asking about a particular comic book, John shifted the QUD to *which books are $10?*. In this new context, individual books are clearly relevant (*this comic book sells for $10* is a member of the Hamblin denotation of the new QUD) and they get into the *C* of *dou*. As a result, the intersection of the formal alternatives activated by *mei*-NP and *C* is just the set of individual alternatives of the universal statement. Since all the alternatives in this set are entailed by the universal prejacent, *dou*'s presupposition is satisfied and its obligatory presence is required by Maximize Presupposition.

The claim that irrelevance of the individual alternatives (formally triggered by *mei*-NPs) could give rise to the absence of *dou* is supported by the observation reported in Liu (2019) that *mei*-NPs with a classifier that describes a standard unit of measurement (e.g. *mi* 'meter', *sheng* 'litter', ...)[15] usually do not occur with *dou*. Relevant examples are given in (46). In these examples, the individual alternatives are not relevant (in typical scenarios where rice is sold in big bags, a particular 500 g of rice is no different from another 500 in terms of its price), and thus the set of alternative operated by *dou* is the empty set, *dou*'s presupposition is not met and it cannot be present.

(46) No *dou* for *mei*-NPs with standard measures

a. Shengyin zai sheshi ling.du.de   kongqi.zhong,
Sound   in Celsius zero.degree.DE air.in,
mei.miao   chuanbo san.bai.sanshi mi.
every.CL$_{second}$ transmit 3.hundred.30 meter

'At 0°C, sound travels 330 meters every second.'

b. Mei.jin   dami san.kuai.qi.
Every.CL$_{500.gram}$ rice 3.CL.7

'Every 500 gram of rice costs ¥3.7 (in RMB).'

Alternatives Evaluated by Other Focus Sensitive Operators and *dou*'s Absence. Another type of examples where *dou* is absent are cases where there is another focus sensitive operator in the sentence that evaluates alternatives triggered by the *mei*-NP. Consider (47) and (48)[16]. Both (47a) and (47b) require *dou*, but adding a focus sensitive operator – *only* in (47b) and a cleft-like particle *shi* in (48b) – obviates the requirement.

(47) a. Mei.ge zuo.le   zuoye   de xuesheng *(dou) de.le   gao.fen.
every do.PERF homework DE student   DOU   get.PERF high.score

'Every student who did the homework got a high score (in the exam).'

---

[15] They belong to the Type-6 classifiers in Chao (1968), called *standard measures*.

[16] Thanks to Yenan Sun for sharing (48) with me.

b. Zhiyou mei.ge zuo.le ZUOYE de xuesheng de.le gao.fen.
   Only every do.PERF homework DE student get.PERF high.score

   'Only every student [who did the homework]$_F$ got a high score (in the exam).'

(48) a. Zuotian mei.ge lingdao *(dou) ma.le Lisi.
        yesterday every leader DOU scold.PERF Lisi

        'Every leader scolded Lisi yesterday.'

   b. Zuotian shi mei.ge LINGDAO mai.le lisi, bushi mei.ge kuaiji.
      yesterday SHI every leader scold.PERF Lisi, not every account

      'It was every leader$_F$ that scolded Lisi yesterday, not every accountant.'

These examples are expected under our proposal. The additional focus particles indicate contextually salient alternatives other than the individual ones formally generated by *mei*-NPs. These alternatives (strictly speaking their intersection with the formal alternatives of *mei*-NPs) do not necessarily satisfy *dou*'s presupposition and thus *dou* is not required. In (47b) for instance, the focus associated with *only* (hinted by stress) is the modifier *who did the homework*, indicating a contextually salient set of alternatives {every student who did the homework got a high score, every student who didn't do the homework got a high score}. *Dou*'s presupposition clearly is not satisfied with this set.

Mei-NPs in Object Positions and *dou*'s Absence. As discussed in Sect. 2, *mei*-NPs in object positions do not need *dou*. This is compatible with our proposal. For syntactic reasons, *dou* only associates with items to its left and thus (49b) is ungrammatical. Consequently, (49b) cannot block (49a) via maximize presupposition, even if the *every*-NP in (49a) could trigger individual alternatives.

(49) a. Wo qing.le mei.yi.ge san.nianji xuesheng.
        I invite.PERF every third.grade student

        "I invited every third-grade student".

   b. *Wo dou qing.le mei.yi.ge san.nianji xuesheng.
      I DOU invite.PERF every third.grade student

Obligatory *dou* with Conjunction. We also predict that obligatory *dou* is not limited to *mei*-NPs. This is because obligatory *dou* in our proposal is not explained merely by some unique properties of Mandarin universal noun phrases, but via satisfaction of *dou*'s presupposition and the general pragmatic principle Maximize Presupposition. As long as the relevant set of alternatives satisfies the *dou*'s presupposition, Maximize Presupposition will enforce the presence of *dou*.

Consider (50). Since the question indicates that there are only two alternatives, a conjunction that entails the two obligatorily selects for *dou*, and we have an instance of obligatory *dou* with conjunction. More specifically, the question in (50a) explicitly establishes that the relevant alternatives are *Zhangsan came* and *Lisi came*, since *Zhangsan and Lisi came* entails both, the presupposition of *dou* is satisfied; Maximize Presupposition then requires the obligatory presence of *dou* in this context, as in (50c).

(50) a. Zhangsan he Lisi shei lai.le?   (Question with two alternatives)
          Zhangsan and Lisi who come.ASP

          'Who among Zhangsan and Lisi came?'

      b. #Zhangsan he Lisi lai.le.   (Infelicitous answer without *dou*)
          Zhangsan   and Lisi come.ASP

          '#Zhangsan and Lisi came.'

      c. Zhangsan he Lisi dou lai.le.   (Felicitous answer with obligatory *dou*)
          Zhangsan and Lisi DOU come.ASP

          'Both Zhangsan and Lisi came'

Interestingly, if the question in (50) is changed into *who among Zhangsan, Lisi and Wangwu came?* with three relevant individuals, then (50b) becomes felicitous. This is expected under our proposal, since in the new context with three alternatives, *Zhangsan and Lisi came* does not entail all the alternatives, *dou*'s presupposition not satisfied, and hence Maximize Presupposition does not apply and the blocking effect not observed[17].

To summarize, we have shown in this subsection that obligatory *dou* has a complex distribution that is compatible with the current proposal but unexpected under previous analyses. Crucially, the distribution is sensitive to discourse contexts and presence of other focus particles, and not limited to universals, suggesting an analysis that is based on general pragmatic principles (such as the present one) might be on the right track.

5 Conclusions

This paper defends the view that *mei*-NPs are true universal quantifiers while *dou* is not. *Dou* is truth-conditionally vacuous but carries a presupposition that its prejacent is the strongest among its alternatives. A pragmatic explanation of the *mei-dou* co-occurrence is offered: in default contexts where *mei*-NPs are used, the universal prejacent entails all the other alternatives and thus *dou*'s strongest-prejacent-presupposition is satisfied; Maximize Presupposition then mandates that a speaker choose *mei-dou* instead of *mei* without *dou*, for the former carries more presuppositions. As we have seen, the proposal predicts a more nuanced distribution of obligatory-*dou*, sensitive to discourse contexts.

---

[17] (50b) is OK as an answer to *who among Zhangsan, Lisi and Wangwu came?* for some speakers I consulted. This must be due to the fact these speakers are implicitly accommodating new sub-questions such as *who among Zhangsan and Lisi came?*. See Büring (2003).

References

Amsili, P., Beyssade, C.: Obligatory presuppositions in discourse. In: Kuehnlein, P., Benz, A., Sidner, C. (eds.) Constraints in Discourse 2: Pragmatics and Beyond. John Benjamins (2009)

Aravind, A., Hackl, M.: Against a unified treatment of obligatory presupposition trigger effects. In: Proceedings of Semantics and Linguistic Theory (SALT), vol. 27, pp. 173–190 (2017)

Bade, N.: Obligatory presupposition triggers in discourse-empirical foundations of the theories maximize presupposition and obligatory implicatures. Ph.D. thesis, Universitat Tubingen (2016)

Beghelli, F., Stowell, T.: Distributivity and negation: the syntax of each and every. In: Szabolcsi, A. (ed.) Ways of Scope Taking, vol. 65, pp. 71–107. Kluwer, Dordrecht (1997)

Brisson, C.: Distributivity, maximality and floating quantifiers. Ph.D. thesis, Rutgers University, New Brunswick (1998)

Bumford, D.: Incremental quantification and the dynamics of pair-list phenomena. Semant. Pragmat. 8(9), 1–70 (2015)

Büring, D.: On D-trees, beans, and B-accents. Linguist. Philos. 26(5), 511–545 (2003)

Carlson, G.N.: Distribution of free-choice any. Chicago Linguist. Soc. 17, 8–23 (1981)

Chao, Y.R.: A Grammar of Spoken Chinese. University of California Press, Berkeley (1968)

Chemla, E.: An epistemic step for anti-presuppositions. J. Semant. 35(2), 141–173 (2008)

Chen, L.: Dou: distributivity and beyond. Ph.D. thesis, Rutgers University (2008)

Cheng, L.L.S.: On dou-quantification. J. East Asian Linguis. 4(3), 197–234 (1995)

Cheng, L.L.S.: On every type of quantificational expression in Chinese. In: Rather, M., Giannakidou, A. (eds.) Quantification, Definiteness, and Nominalization, pp. 53–75. Oxford University Press, Oxford (2009)

Cheng, L.L.S., Sybesma, R.: Bare and not-so-bare nouns and the structure of the NP. Linguist. Inquiry 30(4), 509–542 (1999)

Chierchia, G.: Logic in Grammar. Oxford University Press, Oxford (2013)

Constant, N., Gu, C.C.: Mandarin 'even', 'all' and the trigger of focus movement. In: U. Penn Working Papers in Linguistics, vol. 16, pp. 21–30 (2010)

Crnič, L.: Any: logic, likelihood, and context (Pt. 1). Lang. Linguist. Compass 13(11), e12354 (2019)

Crnič, L.: Any: Logic, likelihood, and context (Pt. 2). Lang. Linguist. Compass 13(11), e12353 (2019)

Dayal, V.: Two types of universal terms in questions. In: NELS, vol. 22, pp. 443–457 (1992)

Dayal, V.: A viability constraint on alternatives for free choice. In: Alternatives in Semantics. Palgrave Macmillan (2013)

Feng, Y., Pan, H.: Is the notion of cover necessary: another look at the application of cover in semantic studies and its potential problems. Contemp. Linguist. 19(3), 379–395 (2017)

von Fintel, K.: Exceptive constructions. Nat. Lang. Seman. 1, 123–148 (1993)

von Fintel, K.: Restrictions on quantifier domains. Ph.D. thesis, University of Massachusetts, Amherst (1994)

Fox, D., Katzir, R.: On the characterization of alternatives. Nat. Lang. Seman. 19, 87–107 (2011)

Gajewski, J.: L-analyticity and natural language (2002). Manuscript, MIT

Giannakidou, A., Cheng, L.L.S.: (In)definiteness, polarity, and the role of wh-morphology in free choice. J. Semant. **23**(2), 135–183 (2006)

Heim, I.: Artikel und definitheit. In: Semantik: Ein internationales Handbuch der zeitgenssischen Forschung, pp. 487–535. de Gruyter, Berlin (1991)

Hole, D.: Focus and Background Marking in Mandarin Chinese. RoutledgeCurzon, London and New York (2004)

Huang, C.T.J.: Logical Relations in Chinese and the theory of grammar. Ph.D. thesis, MIT, Cambridge (1982)

Huang, S.: Quantification and predication in mandarin Chinese: a case study of dou. Ph.D. thesis, University of Pennsylvania (1996)

Kadmon, N., Landman, F.: Any. Linguist. Philos. **16**(4), 353–422 (1993)

Kaplan, J.: Obligatory too in English. Language **60**, 510–518 (1984)

Karttunen, L., Peters, S.: Conventional implicature. In: Syntax and Semantics 11: Presupposition, pp. 1–56. Academic Press, New York (1979)

Katzir, R.: Structurally-defined alternatives. Linguist. Philos. **30**(6), 669–690 (2007)

Katzir, R.: On the roles of markedness and contradiction in the use of alternatives. In: Pragmatics, semantics and the case of scalar implicatures. Palgrave Macmillan, London (2014)

Krifka, M.: Definite NPs aren't quantifiers. Linguist. Inquiry **23**, 156–163 (1992)

Krifka, M.: The semantics and pragmatics of polarity items. Linguist. Anal. **25**, 209–257 (1995)

Krifka, M.: Additive particles under stress. In: Semantics and Linguistic Theory (SALT), vol. 8 (1999)

Križ, M.: Homogeneity, non-maximality, and all. J. Semant. **33**(3), 493–539 (2016)

Lee, T.H.T.: Studies on quantification in Chinese. Ph.D. thesis, UCLA (1986)

Lewis, D.: Relevant implication. Theoria **54**(3), 161–174 (1988)

Liao, H.C.: Alternatives and exhaustification: non-interrogative uses of Chinese Wh-words. Ph.D. thesis, Harvard University, Cambridge (2011)

Lin, J.W.: Distributivity in Chinese and its implications. Nat. Lang. Semant. **6**, 201–243 (1998)

Link, G.: The logical analysis of plurals and mass terms: a lattice-theoretic approach. In: Meaning, Use, and Interpretation of Language, pp. 302–323. de Gruyter, Berlin (1983)

Link, G.: Generalized quantifiers and plurals. In: Gärdenfors, P. (ed.) Generalized Quantifiers, vol. 31, pp. 151–180. Springer, Berlin, Germany (1987). https://doi.org/10.1007/978-94-009-3381-1_6

Liu, L.: On the co-ocurence of 'mei p' and dou. Chin. Teach. World **33**(4), 468–480 (2019)

Liu, M.: Varieties of alternatives: mandarin focus particles. Linguist. Philos. **40**(1), 61–95 (2017)

Löbner, S.: Polarity in natural language: predication, quantification and negation in particular and characterizing sentences. Linguist. Philos. **23**(3), 213–308 (2000)

Malamud, S.A.: The meaning of plural definites: a decision-theoretic approach. Semant. Pragmat. **5**(3), 1–58 (2012)

Moltmann, F.: Reciprocals and same/different: towards a semantic analysis. Linguist. Philos. **15**(4), 411–462 (1992)

Pan, H.: Focus, tripartite and the interpretation of dou. In: Yufa, Y., Yu, T. (eds.) Grammatical Study and Research, vol. 13, pp. 163–184. The Commercial Press (2006)

Penka, D.: Almost there: the meaning of almost. In: Proceedings of Sinn und Bedeutung, vol. 10, pp. 275–286 (2006)

Roberts, C.: Information structure in discourse: towards an integrated formal theory of pragmatics. Semant. Pragmat. **5**(6), 1–69 (2012)

Rooth, M.: A theory of focus interpretation. Nat. Lang. Semant. **1**(1), 75–116 (1992)

Sharvy, R.: A more general theory of definite descriptions. Philos. Rev. **89**, 607–624 (1980)

Shyu, S.I.: The syntax of focus and topic in Mandarin Chinese. Ph.D. thesis, University of Southern California (1995)

Stalnaker, R.: Presuppositions. J. Philos. Log. **2**(4), 447–457 (1973)

Stalnaker, R.: Assertion. In: Syntax and Semantics, vol. 9. Academic Press (1978)

Szabolcsi, A.: What do quantifier particles do? Linguist. Philos. **38**(2), 159–204 (2015)

Wu, Y., Zhou, Y.: Towards a unified account of dou in Mandarin Chinese: implicit and explicit domains. Contemp. Linguist. **2**, 159–180 (2019)

Xiang, M.: Plurality, maximality and scalar inferences: a case study of mandarin dou. J. East Asian Linguis. **17**, 227–245 (2008)

Xiang, Y.: Function alternations of the Mandarin particle dou: distributor, free choice licensor, and 'even'. J. Semant. **37**(2), 171–217 (2020)

Xu, L.: Is dou a universal quantifier? Zhongguo Yuwen [Stud. Chin. Lang.] (6) (2014)

Yuan, Y.: Hanyu juzi de jiaodian jiegou he yuyi jieshi [Focus structure and semantic interpretation of Chinese sentences]. The Commercial Press (2012)

Zeijlstra, H.: Universal quantifier PPIs. Glossa: J. Gener. Linguist. **2**(1) (2017)

Zhang, L., Pan, H.: A reanalysis of the semantics of mei 'every'. Contemp. Linguist. **21**(4), 492–514 (2019)

Monotonicity in Intuitionistic Minimal Change Semantics Given Gärdenfors' Triviality Result

Xinghan Liu[✉]

Technical University of Munich, Munich, Germany
kennarsliu@gmail.com

Abstract. Monotonicity is desirable for many cognitive, computational and pragmatical reasons, even to non-monotonic logics. This paper is inspired by the role a monotonicity principle (M) plays in Gärdenfors' [5] triviality result. It is found similar to another monotonicity principle in the semantics of IVC logic [4]. Hence I give an intuitionistic minimal belief change account, or IAGM, which is immune to triviality, along with a representation theorem. Moreover, the investigation of IAGM semantics sheds new light on understanding the behavior of rational monotonicity in various non-monotonic logics (NMLs).

Keywords: Rational monotonicity · IVC · Non-monotonic logics · IAGM · Minimal change

1 Introduction

In logic monotonicity of inference refers to a property that a valid argument cannot turn to be invalid by adding new premises, namely if $\Gamma \models \varphi$, then $\Gamma \cup \{\psi\} \models \varphi$. It is a desirable property for its cognitive, computational and pragmatical reasons. But many researchers argue that non-monotonicity captures the nature of practical reasoning, for in everyday life we can find numerous counterexamples to monotonicity. A number of non-monotonic logics therefore come into being. In this paper we are going to investigate three kinds of non-monotonic logics (NMLs), which are developed in different fields but proven deeply connected in light of their semantics.

The first one is the field of conditional logics, which studies "if, then" sentences, particularly in subjunctive mood. One may read $\varphi > \psi$ as "if it were the case that φ, then it would be the case that ψ". In the literature monotonicity is rejected with respect to a counterfactual fallacy called the *Strengthening of Antecedents*. Consider the two sentences below, where the latter sounds problematic but not the former.

$$\text{If I had stuck this match, it would have lit.} \quad (1a)$$

$$\text{*If I had stuck this match and done so in a room without oxygen, it would have lit.} \quad (1b)$$

© Springer-Verlag GmbH Germany, part of Springer Nature 2020
D. Deng et al. (Eds.): TLLM 2020, LNCS 12564, pp. 107–124, 2020.
https://doi.org/10.1007/978-3-662-62843-0_6

Another approach is non-monotonic reasoning in the field of AI. In contrast with conditional logic which focuses on implication, it studies non-monotonic entailment. The conditional assertion $\varphi \mathrel{\mid\!\sim} \psi$ could be read as "if φ, *normally* ψ", or ψ is a *plausible consequence* of φ". This plausible consequence is defeasible, which means one may withdraw the previous conclusion when adding new premises. A classical example in this field is the following.

$$\text{If Tweety is a bird, then normally Tweety can fly.} \qquad (2a)$$

$$\text{If Tweety is a penguin, then Tweety is a bird.} \qquad (2b)$$

$$\text{*If Tweety is a penguin and Tweety is a bird, then normally Tweety can fly.} \qquad (2c)$$

The last and perhaps most remarkable one is the theory of belief change in formal epistemology and knowledge representation. It describes how the agent changes her belief or knowledge with respect to the increase and decrease of her belief set or knowledge base. The initial and most thoroughly studied system of belief change is the so-called AGM belief revision. Belief revision refers to an operation of adding some new belief, which may or may not be inconsistent with the agent's old ones. Belief revision is particularly remarkable here, for although it does not specifically target at logical monotonicity, AGM has a deep problem with monotonicity in light of Gärdenfors' triviality result [5], which we will discuss through the paper.

Nevertheless, monotonicity is still somehow desired in virtue of its simplicity, normativity ("you shall reason so") and rationality ("a rational agent reasons so"). Therefore, all the three fields make attempt to keep monotonicity as much as possible, even though not in its full-blown form. The strongest version expresses the following thought:

An argument is monotone as long as the added premise is not *found to contradict the old ones.*

In conditional logic the thought is captured by, e.g. CV (see Sect. 5 below). In belief revision it is crystallized as K8 (Subexpansion). In non-monotonic reasoning it is called Rational Monotonicity. Borrowing the term from non-monotonic reasoning I will use "rational monotonicity" (in small letters) as the umbrella term, and RM for the rule in non-monotonic reasoning exclusively.

Now let us focus on three most influential systems from the three approaches respectively, namely Lewis's VC [12], AGM theory [1,6] and preferential reasoning [8,10]. They all have some minimal change semantics, and consider rational monotonicity in their respective proof systems. At first glance minimal change and rational monotonicity form a natural pair. After all, they both aim at "minimizing the updating we have to do when learning new information" [10, p. 33]. The outcomes are however different. In conditional logic axioms like CV never cause technical difficulties for soundness and completeness results. AGM theory takes K8 at the price of restricted expressiveness in light of triviality result. As for preferential reasoning the case is even more complex.

So far it is just a story in classical logic. Why turn to intuitionistic logic, or in other words, loosen the restriction of classicality? Besides some philosophical and linguistic reasons discussed in [4], there are two more reasons why intuitionistic logic fits belief revision and non-monotonic reasoning.

1) In classical logic we deal with *complete* theories, namely $\Gamma \vdash \neg\varphi$ if $\varphi \notin \Gamma$. But a belief theory K in AGM is allowed to be incomplete, such that it could be possible that Γ is consistent with φ. That is to say, $\varphi \notin K$ but φ could be "added" into K, formalized in AGM as $K + \varphi$. In this case, one shall not conclude the negation of φ simply from the absence of φ, and in this sense the law of excluded middle does not apply. This observation naturally leads us to intuitionistic logic.

A similar issue occurs in database theory, a field where non-monotonic reasoning finds its application, as well. Quite often one needs to deal with some database which is not known to be complete or not. The most popular solution to this situation is the so-called *Closed World Assumption*: it is enough to derive the negation of φ in a database whenever the database fails to derive φ. Nonetheless, it seems contentious to make such a strong stipulation. In contrast, an rival of CWA is called *Open World Assumption*, which holds the view that the lack of φ is not enough for the negation of φ. Clearly intuitionistic logic could shed new lights on OWA.

2) Intuitionistic logic highlights the distinction between *absence* and *negation*, which further relates to meta- vs. objective language. For most axioms, rules and postulates in NMLs, the distinction does not play a role since they use affirmative sentences. However, rational monotonicity has to take the form of negation and/or absence. Axioms in conditional logics work totally within object language. K8 has an absence as a premise. RM is "from the absence of certain assertions in the relation, we deduce the absence of some other assertion" [8, p. 31]. The different formalizations, which may be equivalent in classical logic, are sensitive to this distinction in an intuitionistic setting.

As for the plan of the paper, in Sect. 2 we will analyze Gärdenfors' triviality result in detail, and mention a seeming similarity to IVC. Section 3 serves as a preliminary by introducing the logic and semantics of IVC. Section 4 will give an intuitionistic version of belief change theory, which I call IAGM here, and a representation theorem. In Sect. 5 we bring the topic to a broader context, and explain why AGM and preferential reasoning have certain troubles with rational monotonicity from a semantic viewpoint. It is ascribed to the different levels/types of their semantic conditions: on possible worlds, sets of worlds (states) or even the whole model. In Conclusion I will mention some possible further directions of research.

2   Incentive: Monotonicity in Gärdenfors' Triviality Result

At first glimpse, monotonicity has nothing to do with belief revision theory. However, the most classical belief revision theory, i.e. AGM [1], would share a property of monotonicity, if there were no Gärdenfors' triviality result. To see why that does not happen, let us start with the axiomatization of AGM defined as follows.

Definition 1 (AGM, the version in [6], notations modified). *Let K be any theory, i.e. a set of formulae closed under deduction of some (compact) logic, let K_φ be any theory revising K by φ satisfying these postulates:*

K1 For any theory K and formula φ, $K_\varphi = Cn(K_\varphi)$
K2 $\varphi \in K_\varphi$
K3 $K_\varphi \subseteq K + \varphi$
K4 if $\neg\varphi \notin K$, then $K + \varphi \subseteq K_\varphi$
K5 $K_\varphi = K_\perp$ iff φ is inconsistent
K6 if $\vdash \varphi \leftrightarrow \psi$, then $K_\varphi = K_\psi$
K7 $K_{\varphi \wedge \psi} \subseteq K_\varphi + \psi$
K8 if $\neg\psi \notin K_\varphi$, then $K_\varphi + \psi \subseteq K_{\varphi \wedge \psi}$

Cn stands for logical consequence and $Cn(K)$ is the deductive closure of K, $\{\psi : \vdash \varphi \rightarrow \psi$ for some $\varphi \in K\}$. $K + \varphi$ is the result of expanding K by adding φ then deductively closing it, i.e. $\{\psi : \varphi \rightarrow \psi \in K\}$. $\perp$ denotes falsum which is supposed to be in the language.

The AGM belief revision theory has gained a huge success, in the sense that it gets along well with other AGM operators, i.e. expansion $(+)$ and contraction $(\div)$. Additionally, there was a quite attractive postulate which seemed to be easily added into the axiomatization system to make it even more expressive. It is the revision-theoretic version of Ramsey test:

$$\text{Ramsey Test (RT): } \varphi > \psi \in K \iff \psi \in K_\varphi.$$

This dream, however, was defeated by the triviality result of Gärdenfors [5]. Interestingly, the proof is conducted not by directly targeting the Ramsey Test, but a monotonicity principle it derives:

$$\text{Monotonicity (M): } K \subseteq K' \text{ implies } K_\varphi \subseteq K'_\varphi.$$

Observation 1. *(RT) entails (M).*

Proof. For any $\psi \in K_\varphi$, by (RT) $\varphi > \psi \in K$. Since $K \subseteq K', \varphi > \psi \in K'$, by (RT) then $\psi \in K'_\varphi$. □

Quite simple as the proof is, it signifies the inseparability between (RT) and (M). Since not any particular feature of the conditional $>$ is mentioned, the proof applies universally to any kind of conditional. Consequently, any defeat of (M) inevitably leads to the defeat of (RT).

Theorem 1 (Main theorem in [5]). *Given any belief revision theory which satisfies K1, Preservation, K5 and Ramsey Test, there is no non-trivial belief revision model, where non-trivial means that there are at least three pairwise disjoint propositions.*

Proof (Sketch). We start with a theory K contains none of φ, ψ, χ but is consistent with all of them. They three are pairwise disjoint, namely mutually contradictory. The proof is conducted by contradiction.

1. $\psi \vee \chi \in (K_\varphi)_{\psi \vee \chi}$ by K2
2. $\neg \chi \notin (K_\varphi)_{\psi \vee \chi}$ w.l.o.g. assume
3. $K + (\varphi \vee \psi) \subseteq K + \varphi$
4. $K + \varphi \subseteq K_\varphi$ by K4, since $\neg \varphi \notin K$
5. $K + (\varphi \vee \psi) \subseteq K_\varphi$ by transitivity
6. $(K + (\varphi \vee \psi))_{\psi \vee \chi} \subseteq (K_\varphi)_{\psi \vee \chi}$ by (M)
7. $\neg \chi \notin (K + \varphi \vee \psi)_{\psi \vee \chi}$ by set theory

8. $\neg(\psi \vee \chi) \notin K + \varphi \vee \psi$ by derivation
9. $(K + \varphi \vee \psi) + \psi \vee \chi \subseteq (K + \varphi \vee \psi)_{\psi \vee \chi}$ by K4
10. $(K + \varphi \vee \psi) + (\psi \vee \chi) = K + \psi$
11. $K + \psi \subseteq (K + (\varphi \vee \psi))_{\psi \vee \chi}$ by transitivity
12. $\psi \in K + \psi$ by K4 and K2
13. $\neg \chi \in K + \psi \subseteq (K + \varphi \vee \psi)_{\psi \vee \chi}$ by derivation
14. contradiction between 7. and 13.

$\square$

As we can see, the key part is to investigate what happens in $(K + \varphi \wedge \psi)_{\psi \vee \chi}$. Postulates at stake are K2, K4 and (M). Gärdenfors holds K2 to be most natural, and weighs K4 over (M). Since (M) is inevitably derived from (RT) regardless of how one defines the conditional, consequently we have to abandon (RT) as well.

By contrast, for those who still consider (RT) attractive, to replace (K4) seems the best, even the only choice. And actually they have good reason to do so, for (K4) is such a strong postulate that intuitively it takes too many propositions in the old set on board when confronted with revision. A more modest postulate is weakening it as *if $\varphi \in K$, then $K = K_\varphi$*. Call it K4*.

There are several attempts, e.g. [9,13] starting from this point. But they all result in systems that appear a bit complex, not as simple and elegant as AGM. The obstacle to simplicity, from a technical point of view, rests on K8. It can be proved that the undesired $K4$ comes back if we simply remove it without any other change.

Observation 2. *$K4$ is derivable from $K4^*$, $K6$ and $K8$.*

Proof. First notice that $\top \in K$ since K is a theory. Hence, $K = K_\top$ according to K4*. On the other hand, by K6 $K_{\varphi \wedge \top} = K_\varphi$ since $\vdash \varphi \wedge \top \leftrightarrow \varphi$. Finally considering a special kind of K8: if $\neg \varphi \notin K_\top$, then $K + \varphi = K_\top + \varphi \subseteq K_{\varphi \wedge \top} = K_\varphi$, namely K4. $\square$

The proof indicates that rescuing (RT) is a systematic project rather than a fine tuning. Indeed, K4 is a special case of K8 in the presence of K2. As long as one wants to keep K8, adding (RT) always results in triviality.

Interestingly enough, the related field of intuitionistic conditional logics (ICLs) [4], the principle at stake here, (M), finds a natural correspondent. In many ICLs, the following semantic property is needed:

$$\text{if } w \leq w', \text{ then } f_\varphi(w') \subseteq f_\varphi(w).$$

A full definition will be given in the next section. Intuitively it states that if w' is a successor of w, then any proposition ψ made true in image of the selection function of w by assuming φ, shall also be made true in the image of the selection function of w'. It can be easily observed that if one interprets w as a set of formulae, as in canonical Kripke models, $f_\varphi(w)$ as the set of possible world whose member are supersets of K_φ, this is exactly what (M) says. And as we will see, the seeming similarity is more genuine than it seems in light of a representation theorem—and also more tricky, since the similarity conceals a crucial difference which explains the different performances of rational monotonicity in different NMLs.

3   Preliminary: Logic of IVC and Its Canonical Model $\mathfrak{M}$

In this section the logic and models of IVC are introduced as a preliminary for the representation theorem. The reader is supposed to have some acquaintance with the basic intuitionistic propositional logic (IPL), conditional logics and their Kripke semantics. However, lack of detailed knowledge should not be an obstacle. Essentially the logic coincides with the postulates in the next section, and only semantic constraints of IVC and its canonical model $\mathfrak{M}$ will be used.

3.1   The Logic of IVC

Let us start with a language $\mathcal{L}^>$, extended from the IPL language $\mathcal{L}$, given by the following BNF definition:

$$\varphi ::= p \mid \bot \mid \varphi \land \varphi \mid \varphi \lor \varphi \mid \varphi \to \varphi \mid \varphi > \varphi$$

The counterfactual $\varphi > \psi$ is read as "if it were φ, then would be ψ". As usual in intuitionistic logic, negation, the biconditional and verum are defined as:

$$\neg\varphi := \varphi \to \bot \qquad \varphi \leftrightarrow \psi := (\varphi \to \psi) \land (\psi \to \varphi) \qquad \top := \bot \to \bot$$

The Hilbert-style system for IVC presented below consists of four parts: three groups of axioms—axioms for intuitionistic propositional logic (IPL), axioms pertaining selection function semantics in general, and axioms characterizing minimal change conditions—and a group of inference rules.

Definition 2 (Proof system of IVC)

1. *Intuitionistic schemata:*
   - $\varphi \to (\psi \to \varphi)$
   - $(\varphi \to (\psi \to \chi)) \to ((\varphi \to \psi) \to (\varphi \to \chi))$
   - $\varphi \to (\psi \to \varphi \land \psi)$
   - $\varphi \land \psi \to \varphi, \ \varphi \land \psi \to \psi$
   - $\varphi \to \varphi \lor \psi, \ \psi \to \varphi \lor \psi$
   - $(\varphi \to \chi) \to ((\psi \to \chi) \to (\varphi \lor \psi \to \chi))$
   - $\bot \to \varphi$
2. *Selection function schemata:*
   - $(\varphi > \psi \land \chi) \leftrightarrow (\varphi > \psi) \land (\varphi > \chi)$
3. *Minimal change schemata:*
   - $\varphi > \varphi$
   - $(\varphi > \psi) \to (\varphi \to \psi)$

- $(\varphi \wedge \psi) \rightarrow (\varphi > \psi)$
- $(\varphi > \bot) \rightarrow (\varphi \wedge \psi > \bot)$
- $(\varphi > (\psi \rightarrow \chi)) \leftrightarrow (\varphi > \neg\psi) \vee ((\varphi \wedge \psi) > \chi)$

4. *Inference rules:*
   - *Modus ponens:*

$$\frac{\varphi \quad \varphi \rightarrow \psi}{\psi} \ (MP)$$

   - *Replacement of equivalent antecedents:*

$$\frac{\varphi \leftrightarrow \psi}{(\varphi > \chi) \leftrightarrow (\psi > \chi)} \ (RCEA)$$

   - *Replacement of equivalent consequents:*

$$\frac{\varphi \leftrightarrow \psi}{(\chi > \varphi) \leftrightarrow (\chi > \psi)} \ (RCEC)$$

Notice that the proof theory system appears nearly the same as the classical VC. However, one needs to take care that some classically equivalent formulae are no longer interchangeable here.

3.2   Models of IVC

In this section we will begin with a general notion called intuitionistic selection model, then add extra semantic constraints to obtain IVC models, and end up with canonical IVC models.

Definition 3 (Intuitionistic selection model). *An intuitionistic selection model on a language $\mathcal{L}^>$ is a tuple $M = \langle W, \leq, f, V \rangle$ s.t.*

- *W is a set whose elements are called worlds.*
- *$\leq$ is a partial order on W; the set of $\leq$ −successors of a world w is denoted as $w^\uparrow := \{w' \in W : w \leq w'\}$.*
- *$f : W \times \mathcal{L}^> \rightarrow \wp(W)$ is a family of selection functions which assigns to each world and formula a set of worlds $f_\varphi(w)$,[1] which has following constraints:*
  - *(Counterfactual) Monotonicity: $w \leq w'$ implies $f_\varphi(w') \subseteq f_\varphi(w)$*
  - *Closure: $v \in f_\varphi(w)$ implies $v^\uparrow \subseteq f_\varphi(w)$*
- *V is a valuation function which assigns to each atom p a set of worlds.*

The truth condition are defined as follows.

---

[1] A safer way is to index f by propositions as in [3,14]. To that end we need to add an algebra $\mathcal{A}$ under which propositions are closed. However, in our setting the algebraic structure is more complex with respect to intuitionistic persistency/heredity. The interested reader may see [4]. Since it will make the preliminary unnecessarily intricate, in this paper f is indexed by formulae. Nonetheless, in the presence of RCEA eventually either propositional or sentential indexing fulfills the job, as Chellas [3] discusses.

Definition 4 (Semantics for ICLs)

1. $M, w \models p \iff w \in V(p)$
2. $M, w \not\models \bot$
3. $M, w \models \varphi \wedge \psi \iff M, w \models \varphi$ and $M, w \models \psi$
4. $M, w \models \varphi \vee \psi \iff M, w \models \varphi$ or $M, w \models \psi$
5. $M, w \models \varphi \rightarrow \psi \iff \forall v \in w^{\uparrow} : M, v \models \varphi$ implies $M, v \models \psi$
6. $M, w \models \varphi > \psi \iff \forall v \in f_{\varphi}(w) : M, v \models \psi$

It is convenient to have a convention that $|\varphi| = \{w \in W : w \models \varphi\}$, and for any $X, Y \subseteq W, X \between Y := X \cap Y \neq \varnothing$. Now we are in the position to present the IVC model. For sake of convenience two aforementioned constraints also appear.

Definition 5 (IVC (selection) model). *An IVC model $M_{IVC} = \langle W, \leq, f, V \rangle$ is an intuitionistic selection model satisfying all the following constraints on f*

- *Success:* $f_{\varphi}(w) \subseteq |\varphi|$
- *Centering:* $w \in |\varphi|$ *implies* $f_{\varphi}(w) = w^{\uparrow}$
- *Trans-empty:* $f_{\varphi}(w) = \varnothing$ *implies* $f_{\varphi \wedge \psi}(w) = \varnothing$
- *Minimal Change:* $f_{\varphi}(w) \between |\psi|$ *implies* $f_{\varphi}(w) \cap |\psi| = f_{\varphi \wedge \psi}(w)$
- *(Counterfactual) Monotonicity:* $w \leq w'$ *implies* $f_{\varphi}(w') \subseteq f_{\varphi}(w)$
- *(Upwards-)Closure:* $v \in f_{\varphi}(w)$ *implies* $v^{\uparrow} \subseteq f_{\varphi}(w)$

Remark 1. For the reader familiar with VC, it is easily recognized that the first four constraints are nearly the same as Lewis's constraints in [12]—except Centering. The technical concern is the persistency property, a monotonicity principle in intuitionistic logics. Similar concerns are partially responsible for Monotonicity and Closure. Nonetheless, this stipulation is indeed the intuitionistic counterpart of semantics for VC, when $\leq$ is the identity relation, the whole structure collapses to classical setting, and we obtain the classical Centering, namely $\{w\}$ as a singleton again.

Remark 2. Besides, from a philosophical viewpoint these constraints are also intuitive and natural. We may use $\mathfrak{M}$ to model the process of gathering information, where a world w is a (partial) stage of information, $\leq$ stands for the process of information increase, and $f_{\varphi}(w)$ gives rise to a *hypothetical context*, a set of information stages, generated in w by assuming knowing φ. Centering therefore says that if φ is already obtained in the stage w, then the hypothetical context is nothing more than w itself and its expansion. Monotonicity says that the larger information stage we have, the less space for hypothesis is, i.e. the stage is more determinate. Closure says that if v is in the hypothetical context of w (with respect to φ), then any stage larger than v shall also be considered in w's hypothesis. This interpretation agrees well with the basic thought of belief theory change, when we understand propositions in the belief set as cumulative data.

It is easily noticed that f-constraints are nearly the semantic counterpart of K-postulates. For instance, Success and Minimal Change correspond to K2 and K7 + K8 respectively. The impression is enhanced by the next observation, which seems to derive the semantic counterpart of K3 + K4.

Observation 3. *If $w^\uparrow \, \emptyset \, |\varphi|$, then $f_\varphi(w) = w^\uparrow \cap |\varphi|$.*

Proof. First notice that since $w \models \top$, $f_\top(w) = w^\uparrow$. Then apply Minimal Change, since $f_\top(w) \, \emptyset \, |\varphi|$, we have $w^\uparrow \cap |\varphi| = f_\top(w) \cap |\varphi| = f_{\varphi \wedge \top}(w) = f_\varphi(w)$. $\qquad \square$

Finally we come to the canonical model part, which will play a central role in the representation theorem. Define for any theory T, $Cm_\varphi(T) := \{\psi \in \mathcal{L}^> : \varphi > \psi \in T\}$, namely the set of consequences of counterfactuals in T whose antecedent is φ.

Definition 6. *The canonical IVC model on a language $\mathcal{L}^>$ is a tuple $\mathfrak{M}^c_{IVC} = \langle W, \leq, \{f_\varphi(\cdot) : \varphi \in \mathcal{L}^>\}, V\rangle$ s.t.*

- W *is the set of all consistent IVC theories with the disjunction property*[2]
- $w \leq w'$ *iff $w \subseteq w'$*
- $f_\varphi(w) = \{v \in W : Cm_\varphi(w) \subseteq v\}$
- $w \in V(p)$ *iff $p \in w$, for any proposition letter $p \in \mathcal{L}^>$*

We abbreviate $\mathfrak{M}^c_{IVC}$ as $\mathfrak{M}$, since this is the working model of the paper. By virtue of the soundness and completeness result, we are ensured that $\mathfrak{M}$ is indeed an IVC model, and hence shares the semantic constraints of f.

At the end of this section, let me state the truth condition in $\mathfrak{M}$, which will be convenient for the representation theorem proof in the next section.

Observation 4. *For any formula $\varphi \in \mathcal{L}^>$ and $w \in \mathfrak{M}$,*

$$w \in |\varphi| \Longleftrightarrow w \models \varphi \Longleftrightarrow w \vdash \varphi \Longleftrightarrow \varphi \in w.$$

4 Intuitionistic Minimal Belief Change

In this section I will first give the intuitionistic AGM style belief change theory, which will be called IAGM here[3], and talk about some of its syntactic features. Then a representation theorem will be given making use of the canonical IVC model $\mathfrak{M}$.

Definition 7 (IAGM)

K1 For any theory K and formula φ, $K_\varphi = Cn(K_\varphi)$
K2 $\varphi \in K_\varphi$
K3 $K_\varphi \subseteq K + \varphi$

---

[2] A theory has the disjunction property, if $\varphi \vee \psi \in \Gamma$, either $\varphi \in \Gamma$ or $\psi \in \Gamma$.
[3] However, considering the distinction between *belief revision* and *knowledge update*, see e.g. [9], it seems from a semantic perspective that the system here is more like the latter than the former, though syntactically speaking it is quite alike AGM. Hence the selection function f may depict "objective similarity" rather than "subjective similarity" in the words of [11]. Anyhow the distinction is not at stake in this paper. We will leave it for another discussion.

$K4^*$ if $\varphi \in K$, then $K = K_\varphi$
$K5^*$ $K_\varphi = K_\bot$, if φ is inconsistent
$K6$ if $\vdash_{IVC} \varphi \leftrightarrow \psi$, then $K_\varphi = K_\psi$
$K7$ $K_{\varphi \wedge \psi} \subseteq K_\varphi + \psi$
$K8^*$ if $\neg\neg\psi \in K_\varphi$, then $K_\varphi + \psi \subseteq K_{\varphi \wedge \psi}$
RT $\varphi > \psi \in K$ iff $\psi \in K_\varphi$

Here are some observations which are going to be used in following sections.

Observation 5. *K6 is derivable from K1, K2, K7 and K8*.*

Proof. Since $\vdash \varphi \leftrightarrow \psi$, by K2 we have $\varphi \in K_\psi$, then according to K1 $K_\psi + \varphi = K_\psi$. By IPL reasoning $\neg\neg\varphi \in K_\psi$. Using K7 and K8* we have $K_\psi + \varphi = K_{\varphi \wedge \psi}$. Hence $K_\psi = K_{\varphi \wedge \psi}$. Similarly on the other hand $K_\varphi = K_{\varphi \wedge \psi}$. Therefore $K_\varphi = K_\psi$.

However, to follow the traditional enumeration in AGM literature we keep K6 in the axiomatization system. Still it is good news that some effort could be spared in the representation theorem.

Observation 6. *By K4*, K6 and K8* it is derivable that if $\neg\neg\varphi \in K$, then $K + \varphi \subseteq K_\varphi$*

Proof. By K8*, if $\neg\neg\varphi \in K_\top$, then $K_\top + \varphi \subseteq K_{\varphi \wedge \psi}$. Since $\top \in K$, by K4* $K = K_\top$. On the other hand, by K6 $K_{\varphi \wedge \top} = K_\varphi$. Hence, $K + \varphi \subseteq K_\varphi$.   □

Theorem 2. *Any belief theory K satisfying the IAGM postulates can be extended to an IVC theory.*

Proof. We need prove that all IVC axioms and rules are admissible from the IAGM postulates. Since the underlying logic is IPL, all intuitionistic schemata are obviously satisfied. For the selection function schemata, we show $(\varphi > \psi \wedge \chi) \rightarrow ((\varphi > \psi) \wedge (\varphi > \chi))$. Suppose it is not admissible, then there is some $K, \varphi > (\psi \wedge \chi) \in K$, but $(\varphi > \psi) \wedge (\varphi > \chi) \notin K$. According to (RT) the antecedent means $\psi \wedge \chi \in K_\varphi$, however according to the consequent $\psi \notin K_\varphi$ or $\chi \notin K_\varphi$, by K1 a contradiction. The other direction is similar.

For the minimal change schemata, most cases are similar to the above. For $(\varphi > \bot) \rightarrow (\varphi \wedge \psi > \bot)$, suppose it is not admissible for K, then it might be the case $\varphi > \bot \in K$, but $(\varphi \wedge \psi) > \bot \notin K$. By (RT) from the antecedent $\bot \in K_\varphi$, and from the consequent $\bot \in K_{\varphi \wedge \psi}$. However, since $\bot \in K_\varphi$, and $\bot \rightarrow \psi \in K_\varphi$, we have $\psi \in K_\varphi$. By K7 and K8*, $K_{\varphi \wedge \psi} = K_\varphi + \psi = K_\varphi \ni \bot$, which contradicts the consequent.

The only non-straightforward case is $(\varphi > (\psi \rightarrow \chi)) \rightarrow ((\varphi > \neg\psi) \vee (\varphi \wedge \psi) > \chi)$. Suppose it is not admissible in K, then there can be such a K and a θ, s.t. $\varphi > (\psi \rightarrow \theta) \in K$, while $\varphi > \neg\psi \notin K$ and $(\varphi \wedge \psi) > \theta \notin K$; and in addition let $\neg\neg\psi \in K_\varphi$. But in this case $K_\varphi + \psi \not\subseteq K_{\varphi \wedge \psi}$, which contradicts K8*. (Or more constructively, expand K_φ with $\neg\neg\psi$, then $\theta \in K_\varphi + \neg\neg\psi + \psi = (K_\varphi + \neg\neg\psi)_\varphi + \psi \not\subseteq (K_\varphi + \neg\neg\psi)_{\varphi \wedge \psi} \not\ni \theta$.)

For the inference rules, MP and RCEC are from deductive closure. RCEA is guaranteed by K6.   □

Now we are in the position of proving the representation theorem between IAGM and the canonical IVC selection model.

Theorem 3. *Given a canonical IVC model $\mathfrak{M}$ and a set of theories $\mathbf{K}$ closed under revision and addition on the same language, if one defines $K_\varphi = Cm_\varphi(K)$, then all the IAGM postulates are satisfied.*

Proof. Since in $\mathfrak{M}$, W denotes the set of all consistent IVC theories with the disjunction property, for any consistent K, there exists always some w s.t. $K \subseteq w$. Hence let $|K| = \{w : w \in \mathfrak{M}, K \subseteq w\}$ stand for all the "K"-worlds. Particularly, it is proven in e.g. Lemma 2 of [4] that $Cm_\varphi(T)$ is also an IVC theory whenever T is, thus $|Cm_\varphi(K)|$ is also a subset of W, namely the union of all $f_\varphi(w)$, where $w \in |K|$. Therefore $|K_\varphi| = |Cm_\varphi(K)| = \bigcup_{w \in |K|} f_\varphi(w)$. Notice that when K is inconsistent, $|K_\varphi| = \varnothing$ since $\forall w \in W, K \not\subseteq w$. It is helpful to observe some further facts about $\mathfrak{M}$ for K:

- $\varphi \in K$ iff $|K| \subseteq |\varphi|$
- $K \subseteq K'$ iff $|K'| \subseteq |K|$
- $|K + \varphi| = |K| \cap |\varphi|$

Now we check all the postulates.

RT is automatically satisfied by definition of Cm_φ.

K1. It is proven, e.g., in Lemma 2 of [4] that for any IVC theory T, $Cn_\varphi(T)$ is also an IVC theory. Hence $Cm_\varphi(K) = Cn(Cm_\varphi(K))$.

K2 through K7 are all straightforward in light of the IVC axioms and rules.

The non-trivial postulate is K8*. We must show $|K_{\varphi \wedge \psi}| \subseteq |K_\varphi| \cap |\psi|$, which is to show $\bigcup_{w \in |K|} f_{\varphi \wedge \psi}(w) \subseteq \bigcup_{w \in |K|} f_\varphi(w) \cap |\psi|$, given $\bigcup_{w \in |K|} f_\varphi(w) \subseteq |\neg\neg\psi|$. For any $w \in |K|$, if $f_\varphi(w) = \varnothing$, by Trans-empty of f, $f_{\varphi \wedge \psi}(w) = \varnothing \subseteq f_\varphi(w)$. If $f_\varphi(w) \neq \varnothing$, since $f_\varphi(w) \subseteq |\neg\neg\psi|$, then $\forall v \in f_\varphi(w), \exists v' \in v^\uparrow, v' \models \psi$. By Closure of f, $v' \in f_\varphi(w)$, which means that $f_\varphi(w) \between |\psi|$. Hence $f_\varphi(w) \cap |\psi| = f_{\varphi \wedge \psi}(w)$. Since this works for any w, it works a fortiori for their union.   □

Theorem 4. *Given a set of theories $\mathbf{K}$ closed under revision and addition satisfying all IAGM postulates, an IVC model can be induced, s.t. all the constraints on selection functions are satisfied.*

Proof. We construct such a model. Let $W \subseteq \mathbf{K}$ be the set of all IVC theories which are consistent and have the disjunction property. Theorem 2 ensures the existence of W. The intuitionistic accessibility and valuation functions are defined exactly as for the canonical IVC model. Define for any $w, v \in W \subseteq \mathbf{K}$, $v \in f_\varphi(w)$ iff $w_\varphi \subseteq v$. We will show that this is indeed an IVC model, in the sense that f satisfies all the constraints in Definition 5.

Closure. We show $v \in f_\varphi(w)$ implies $v^\uparrow \subseteq f_\varphi(w)$, which means that $\forall v', v \subseteq v', v' \in f_\varphi(w)$. According to the antecedent $w_\varphi \subseteq v \subseteq v'$, by transitivity of $\subseteq$, $w_\varphi \subseteq v'$, i.e. $v' \in f_\varphi(w)$.

Monotonicity. Directly from (M) with the help of (RT).

Success. Directly from K2.

Centering. Directly from K4*.

Trans-empty. Directly from K5* and K8*.

Minimal Change. We must show that $f_\varphi(w) \cap |\psi| \neq \varnothing$ implies $f_\varphi(w) \cap |\psi| = f_{\varphi \wedge \psi}(v)$. The easier direction directly follows from K7. We show the hard direction, i.e. $f_\varphi(w) \cap |\psi| \neq \varnothing$ implies $f_\varphi(w) \cap |\psi| \subseteq f_{\varphi \wedge \psi}(v)$. Assume not, then there is some χ, s.t. $\varphi > \neg\psi \notin w$ and $(\varphi > (\psi \to \chi)) \to ((\varphi \wedge \psi) > \chi) \notin w$. Since w obeys K8* and has the disjunction property, either $\neg\psi \in w_\varphi$ or $(\varphi > (\psi \to \chi)) \to ((\varphi \wedge \psi) > \chi) \in w$. However, this contradicts the assumption. $\qquad\square$

Remark. It is somehow expected that mostly the proof runs smoothly, since $\mathfrak{M}$ is the canonical IVC model and all IVC theories thanks to Theorem 2, are some K theories; and by virtue of the completeness proof of IVC, the bridge between K-postulates and f-constraints has already been established. To a considerable extent we can say that this intuitionistic minimal belief change, or IAGM, has an IVC semantics. Actually the semantic counterparts of K-postulates can be seen as constraints on, not possibles worlds as f-constraints do, but sets of possible worlds, or more precisely, upsets of $\mathfrak{M}$.

Now we can explain why certain K-postulates are modified in light of the semantics. The reason for rejecting K4 and K8 will be discussed in the next section. Before doing that, let me briefly mention K5, whose modification has little to do with the main topic here. There is a reason why we leave the only if direction aside tentatively. K5 expresses some property of "universality" in terms of its counterpart in Lewis's V-logics, namely any world should have a counterfactual relation to some worlds. However, sometimes we need to describe an inquiry which "stays local". That is to say, the agent may have some *blind spot*, *deep faith* or *common sense* that she refuses to revise even if the new belief does not lead to logical contradiction.

Nevertheless, we could add more axioms and semantic conditions to take K5 on board. The resulting logic will not be IVC, but intuitionistic VCU, just like what Grahne[7] did for the KM theory [9] in the classical case. The semantic condition for that is

- Universality: if $|\varphi| \neq \varnothing$, then for any w, $f_\varphi(w) \neq \varnothing$.

5   Discussion: Rational Monotonicity in NMLs

The representation theorem grounds the similarity between f-constraints and K-postulates. It also reveals, nonetheless, a crucial distinction between the two: f applies to possible worlds, while K-postulates are represented as constraints on sets of possible worlds. For most postulates the distinction does not matter: a set of possible worlds is such and such iff *any* of its members is such and such. But K4 and K8 are different, for they apply when a set of possible worlds is *not* such and such. And we know that for that it is necessary and sufficient to show that *some* member of the set is not such and such. In order to make sure that every member of $|K|$ fulfills the premise of Minimal Change of f, we have to give a stronger constraint on K, i.e. the double negation one.

Let us take the following toy model in Fig. 1 to instantiate the idea concretely.

Example 1. *Suppose* $|K| = \{u_1, u_2\}$, $|K_p| = f_p(u_1) \cup f_p(u_2) = \{u_1, u_2\}$, *and* $|K_{p \wedge q}| = f_{p \wedge q}(u_1) \cup f_{p \wedge q}(u_2) = \{u_1, u_3\}$. *Hence, it is clear that* $|K_p + q| = |K_p| \cap |q| = \{u_1\} \neq \{u_1, u_3\} = |K_{p \wedge q}|$. *Notice that since* $|K_p| = |K|$, *in the presence of K2 this counterexample applies to both K8 and K4 as the special case of the former.*

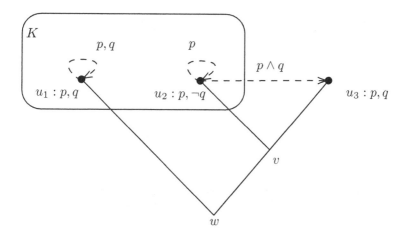

Fig. 1. Counterexample for K4 and K8

The crucial point thus appears intuitively: $\neg \psi \notin K_\varphi$ is generally too coarse-grained to delineate what happens within the set of possible worlds $|K|$. Since the absence of $p > \neg q$ in u_1 is already sufficient to satisfy the premise of K8, the situation in u_2 is unfortunately underrepresented, which in turn causes the collapse of K8.

Notice however that not all belief theories invalidate K8 in the IAGM model. Consider another belief theory K' such that $|K'| = v^\uparrow$. It is easy to check that $|K'_P| \, \lozenge \, |q|$ and $|K'_p| \cap |q| = |K'_{p \wedge q}| = \{u_3\}$. What makes the difference? The answer is that $|K'|$ is a rooted set, namely $v^\uparrow$, while $|K|$ is not. Recall Observation 3 that for any rooted set $w^\uparrow$, $f_\varphi(w) = w^\uparrow \cap |\varphi|$ if $w^\uparrow \, \lozenge \, |\varphi|$. Then by Monotonicity of f, we have $\bigcup \{f_\varphi(w') : w \leq w'\} = f_\varphi(w)$. Hence we have the following observation.

Observation 7. *If $|K|$ is a rooted set in the IAGM model, then K4 and K8 are satisfied.*

As a result, only when a belief theory K can be represented as some $w^\uparrow$ are we able to keep track of the rational monotonic revision in accordance to Monotonicity. Remember the construction of the canonical intuitionistic Kripke model, where all theories on board must have the disjunction property. Then we may make the following observation.

Observation 8. *If K has the disjunction property, then K4 and K8 are satisfied in IAGM model.*

Now the syntactic explanation of rejecting K8, in light of the semantic model, becomes clear. A belief theory K usually does not need to have disjunction property. Therefore, when it is revised by some disjunction, it is possible that neither of the disjuncts is taken on board, which renders the revised set contrary to the constructiveness of intuitionistic logics. The vital role disjunction plays here echos the fact that many triviality results, including Gärdenfors', are obtained by taking advantage of disjunctive sentences.

It is not a coincidence that K8 causes a lot of trouble in our endeavor to rescue (RT) through maintaining (M). In the literature on non-monotonic reasoning, there exists a property associated with K8, called *Rational Monotonicity* (in the form in [8, 10]):

$$\frac{\varphi \wedge \psi \not\hspace{-2pt}\sim \chi \qquad \varphi \not\hspace{-2pt}\sim \neg\psi}{\varphi \not\hspace{-2pt}\sim \chi} \text{ (RM)}$$

which is also somehow troublesome.

In a seminal paper of this field, Kraus et al. [8] investigate several logic systems, among which the most attractive one is the preferential reasoning. The name comes from its semantic model.

Definition 8 (Preferential model). *A preferential model is a triple $\langle S, l, \sqsubset \rangle$ s.t. S a set of states (sets of possible worlds) based on a set of possible worlds W, $l : S \to W$ is a labeling function assigning to each state a world, and $\sqsubset$ is a strict partial order (i.e. irreflexive, asymmetric and transitive) on S satisfying the* smoothness *condition defined below.*

Definition 9 (Smoothness condition). *A preferential model satisfies the* smoothness *condition, if for any formula φ in its language, the set of states $\widehat{\varphi} = \{s : s \in S, s \models \varphi\}$ is smooth, where $s \models \varphi$ iff $l(s) \models \varphi$, and $\models$ is the classical notion of logical consequence. A set $P \subseteq S$ is smooth, if $\forall s \in P$, either there is a minimal $s \in P$ s.t. $s \sqsubset t$ or t is itself minimal in P.*

Definition 10 (Preferential entailment). *For any preferential model $\mathfrak{P}$, $\varphi \hspace{-1pt}\sim\hspace{-1pt} \psi$ is true in $\mathfrak{P}$ iff for all s minimal in $\widehat{\varphi}$, $s \models \psi$.*

Though the semantics are quite distinct, the axiomatization of preferential reasoning almost mirrors some conditional logics by simply replacing the connective $>$ with the consequence symbol $\hspace{-1pt}\sim\hspace{-1pt}$ in the meta-language. Its axiomatization contains the following six primary axiom and rules.

$$\varphi \mathrel{\vdash\mkern-7mu\sim} \varphi \text{ Reflexivity;} \qquad \frac{\models \varphi \to \psi \quad \varphi \mathrel{\vdash\mkern-7mu\sim} \chi}{\psi \mathrel{\vdash\mkern-7mu\sim} \chi} \text{ Left Logical Equivalence;} \qquad \frac{\varphi \mathrel{\vdash\mkern-7mu\sim} \chi \quad \psi \mathrel{\vdash\mkern-7mu\sim} \chi}{\varphi \vee \psi \mathrel{\vdash\mkern-7mu\sim} \chi} \text{ Or;}$$

$$\frac{\varphi \mathrel{\vdash\mkern-7mu\sim} \psi \quad \varphi \mathrel{\vdash\mkern-7mu\sim} \chi}{\varphi \mathrel{\vdash\mkern-7mu\sim} \psi \wedge \chi} \text{ And;} \qquad \frac{\models \varphi \to \psi \quad \chi \mathrel{\vdash\mkern-7mu\sim} \varphi}{\chi \mathrel{\vdash\mkern-7mu\sim} \psi} \text{ Right Weakening;} \qquad \frac{\varphi \mathrel{\vdash\mkern-7mu\sim} \chi \quad \psi \mathrel{\vdash\mkern-7mu\sim} \chi}{\varphi \wedge \psi \mathrel{\vdash\mkern-7mu\sim} \chi} \text{ Cautious Monotonicity.}$$

Actually the resulting system is quite like Lewis' V with only one substantive difference: the lack of a counterpart to the axiom $(\varphi > (\psi \to \chi)) \to (\varphi > \neg\psi) \vee ((\varphi \wedge \psi) > \chi)$. This axiom can derive another one called CV, whose similarity to RM is already noted in [10]. It becomes clearer if we take another formalization of RM as in [2].[4]

$$((\varphi > \chi) \wedge \neg(\varphi > \neg\psi)) \to ((\varphi \wedge \psi) > \chi) \quad \text{(CV)}$$

$$\frac{\neg(\varphi \mathrel{\vdash\mkern-7mu\sim} \neg\psi) \quad \varphi \mathrel{\vdash\mkern-7mu\sim} \chi}{\varphi \wedge \psi \mathrel{\vdash\mkern-7mu\sim} \chi} \quad \text{(RM')}$$

Preferential reasoning, unfortunately, cannot derive RM. In order to make RM true, preferential models have to be restricted to ranked models. A preferential model is ranked, if $\sqsubset$ enjoys additionally *negative transitivity*.

Definition 11 (Negative Transitivity). *A relation $\sqsubset$ on S is negative transitive, if $\forall s, t, u \in S, s \sqsubset t$ implies $s \sqsubset u$ or $u \sqsubset t$.*

Nevertheless, it is still impossible to achieve a non-monotonic reasoning version of theory change. Lehmann and Magidor [10] show a negative result that in spite of having different models, ranked entailment is exactly preferential entailment, which fails to obtain a knowledge base closed under RM. Having no space here for a detailed study, we can still take a first step toward elucidation in light of the analysis for IAGM.

What parallels AGM is that ranked entailment intends (and fails) to achieve the so-called *rational extension*, namely taking all the assertions entailed by RM besides the preferential ones. This thesis is as ambitious as Gärdenfors' (RT). Consider the following theorem, which plays an important role in Lehmann and Magidor's negative result.

Theorem 5 (Theorem 3 in [10]). *Let K be a knowledge base and $\varphi \mathrel{\vdash\mkern-7mu\sim} \psi$ an assertion* not *preferentially entailed by K. The formulae inconsistent for the preferential closure of $K \cup \{\varphi \mathrel{\vdash\mkern-7mu\sim} \neg\psi\}$ are those inconsistent for the preferential closure of K.*

The theorem is both interesting and alarming, for "a direct proof using only proof-theoretic arguments seems difficult" [10, p. 10]. The proof is therefore conducted via the semantic model. However, the proof uses a technique of turning

---

[4] The formalization is a bit informal, since $\mathrel{\vdash\mkern-7mu\sim}$ should be part of the meta-language and not be negated in the language. This is an example of mixing absence/failure and negation in the classical setting.

the original model into a new one, where all items remain the same except a new relation $\sqsubset_\varphi^t$ where t becomes *the* only minimal. In such a way we move from the absence of ψ to its negation. This technique in an intuitionistic setting, nevertheless, may encounter the same situation as in Example 1, where $\widehat{\varphi}$ is not rooted, hence there is no single minimum but rather a draw.

Let us illuminate the issue in our model. Actually the ranked model is almost the same as Lewis' sphere system model, where smoothness corresponds to a limit assumption, and $\sqsubset$ ensures that states in S are nested. So it is not surprising that some selection model can be induced from the former.

Observation 9. *A ranked model $\langle S, l, \sqsubset \rangle$ induces an* **IV** *(***IVC** *without Centering) selection function model $\langle W, \leq, f, V \rangle$ such that*

- *W is the set of possible worlds on which S is based.*
- *$w \leq v \iff l^{-1}(w) = l^{-1}(v)$*
- *$v \in f_\varphi(w) \iff \exists v' \in v^\uparrow, \text{ s.t. } l^{-1}(v') = min\{s \in S : \exists w' \in w^\uparrow, l(s) = w' \ \& \ s \in \widehat{\varphi}\}$, abbreviate it as $c_w(\varphi)$*
- *$V(\varphi) = \{w : \exists w' \in w^\uparrow, l^{-1}(w') \models \varphi\}$*

Proof. It is easy to check that the model defined is indeed a selection function model. Success and Upwards-Closure are obvious by definition. Trans-empty is shown by the smoothness condition.

Counterfactual Monotonicity is trivially satisfied. If $w \leq w'$, then by definition of $\leq$ above we also have $w' \leq w$. Here $\leq$ is an equivalence relation. Hence $w^\uparrow = w'^\uparrow$.

For Minimal Change it is enough to show if $c_w(\varphi) \notin \widehat{\neg\psi}$, then $c_w(\varphi \wedge \psi) = c_w(\varphi)$. Obviously $c_w(\varphi) \sqsubset c_w(\varphi \wedge \psi)$ by definition of $c_w(\varphi)$. For the other direction, by antecedent $c_w(\varphi) \notin \widehat{\neg\psi}$, which means that $l(c_w(\varphi)) \nvDash \neg\psi$. According to intuitionistic truth condition it means $\exists v, l(c_w(\varphi)) \leq v$ and $v \models \psi$. But since $\leq$ is an equivalence relation, $v \leq l(c_w(\varphi))$ and by persistency $l(c_w(\varphi)) \models \psi$. Hence, $c_w(\varphi) \in \widehat{\varphi \wedge \psi}$, and $c_w(\varphi \wedge \psi) \sqsubset c_w(\varphi)$ by definition of $c_w(\varphi \wedge \psi)$. $\square$

Notice first that negative transitivity, which is supposed to play an essential role for the hard direction of Minimal Change of f, is not even used. That is to say, any preferential model can induce a model as defined above. We can add some state, which is *not* minimal for any $c_w(\varphi)$, to transform the model from ranked to preferential, while keeping the same selection function model. In fact Lewis already discovered that sphere system models and the derived selection function models are not one-to-one—"systems of spheres sometimes carry more information about comparative similarity than is needed to determine the truth values at all worlds of all counterfactuals" [12, p. 59]. This provides a hint why preferential and ranked entailments, though having different sphere system models, share the same syntactical closure.

What is essential to the proof is that this model "happens" to behave classically, for $\leq$ is an equivalence relation as Remark 1 of Definition 5 explains. The pivotal point occurs when $l(c_w(\varphi))$ goes from the failure of making $\neg\psi$ true to the negation of $\neg\psi$, which is equivalent to ψ. We ascribe the vital difference to the fact that the label function l assigns each state a single world, which is not the case in the intuitionistic setting. In light of Example 1 again, we reason that in the disjunctive case the state shall have more than one representative. So, for the intuitionistic preferential model the label function shall output a set of worlds instead of one. Interestingly, recall that the cumulative model [8, p. 16], which serves for preferential reasoning minus Or, does have a label function outputting sets of worlds. The two approaches are exactly reversed: from classical to intuitionistic conditional logics we lift from worlds to sets of worlds; while from cumulative to preferential reasoning Kraus et al. move from sets of worlds to worlds.

6   Conclusion and Further Research

I investigated the tension between (logical) monotonicity and rational monotonicity from an intuitionistic viewpoint. Through the lens of the intuitionistic minimal change semantics for IAGM, Gärdenfors' triviality result was diagnosed. The key point is that the IAGM semantics applies to sets of worlds, rather than to worlds in IVC. For affirmative postulates there is no difference. But for K8, intuitionistic logic makes a sharp distinction between absence and negation. The premise $\neg\psi \notin K_\varphi$ is not fine-grained enough to enforce $\forall w \in |K_\varphi|, \neg\psi \notin w_\varphi$. This semantic finding relates to the disjunction property of intuitionistic logic. A similar analysis could be applied to preferential reasoning, for both its semantic constraints and truth condition are not down to the worlds.

There are several possible further directions of research. It is necessary to study the sphere system model for IVC in general. A key point is that the model defined in Observation 9 is S5 style, where $\leq$ happens to be an equivalence relation. Otherwise Counterfactual Monotonicity of f is not trivially satisfied. The most intriguing case is when we have a $\bigwedge$ like frame, namely $w \leq w', v \leq w'$ but w and v are incomparable. The construction of spheres in this case is still unclear.

It is helpful to bring the study here to the broader tradition of modal logic. Techniques and insights from modal logic could make a contribution. In particular, belief revision has been thoroughly studied in dynamic epistemic logics (DELs), see e.g. [15]. Gärdenfors' triviality result has been explained and dealt with from many perspectives. It would be helpful to compare various explanations from the literature.

Besides the belief revision of AGM, there is another influential framework for belief change, i.e. the knowledge update of KM or KGM [7,9]. The framework I present here shares many common features with KGM: taking care of disjunction, representing K_φ as the union of sets of possible worlds etc. It would be interesting to check whether the framework in this paper is IAGM or IKGM, or in the intuitionistic setting the distinction between revision and update no longer stands.

Acknowledgment. Without the numerous discussions the author had with Hannes Leitgeb, this paper would not have been possible. The author also wish to thank Dag Westerståhl and three anonymous reviewers for their thorough comments and feedback, which greatly improved the paper.

References

1. Alchourrón, C., Gärdenfors, P., Makinson, D.: On the logic of theory change: partial meet contraction and revision functions. J. Symb. Logic **50**(02), 510–530 (1985)
2. Arló-Costa, H., Parikh, R.: Conditional probability and defeasible inference. J. Philos. Logic **34**(1), 97–119 (2005). https://doi.org/10.1007/s10992-004-5553-6
3. Chellas, B.F.: Basic conditional logic. J. Philos. Logic **4**(2), 133–153 (1975). https://doi.org/10.1007/BF00693270
4. Ciardelli, I., Liu, X.: Intuitionistic conditional logics. J. Philos. Logic **49**, 1–26 (2019). https://doi.org/10.1007/s10992-019-09538-4
5. Gärdenfors, P.: Belief revisions and the Ramsey test for conditionals. Philos. Rev. **95**(1), 81–93 (1986)
6. Gardenfors, P.: Belief Revision. Cambridge University Press, Cambridge (1992)
7. Grahne, G.: Updates and counterfactuals. In: KR, pp. 269–276 (1991)
8. Kraus, S., Lehmann, D., Magidor, M.: Nonmonotonic reasoning, preferential models and cumulative logics. Artif. Intell. **44**(1–2), 167–207 (1990)
9. Kutsuno, H., Mendelzon, A.: On the difference between updating a belief base and revise it. In: Belief Revision. Cambridge University Press (1992)
10. Lehmann, D., Magidor, M.: What does a conditional knowledge base entail? Artif. Intell. **55**(1), 1–60 (1992)
11. Leitgeb, H., Segerberg, K.: Dynamic doxastic logic: why, how, and where to? Synthese **155**(2), 167–190 (2007). https://doi.org/10.1007/s11229-006-9143-8
12. Lewis, D.K.: Counterfactuals. Blackwell, Oxford (1973)
13. Rott, H.: Conditionals and theory change: revisions, expansions, and additions. Synthese **81**(1), 91–113 (1989). https://doi.org/10.1007/BF00869346
14. Segerberg, K.: Notes on conditional logic. Studia Logica **48**, 157–168 (1989). https://doi.org/10.1007/BF02770509
15. van Benthem, J., Smets, S.: Dynamic logics of belief change. In: Halpern, J., van der Hoek, W., Kooi, B. (eds.) Handbook of Logics for Knowledge and Belief, Chap. 7, pp. 299–368. College Publications (2015)

Are Causes Ever Too Strong? Downward Monotonicity in the Causal Domain

Dean McHugh[(✉)]

Institute for Logic, Language and Computation, University of Amsterdam,
Amsterdam, The Netherlands
d.m.mchugh@uva.nl

Abstract. Is the truth of a causal claim always preserved by strengthening the cause? For instance, does "Alice flicking the switch caused the light to turn on" entail "Alice flicking the switch and it raining in New Zealand caused the light to turn on"? We argue for this entailment, proposing that causal claims are downward monotone in their cause: if C^+ entails C then (C *caused* E) entails (C^+ *caused* E). In other words, causes are never too strong. We argue for this by presenting examples of causal claims that are assertable even though the cause is stronger than required for the claim to be true (Sect. 2). These data challenge accounts (the most prominent of which is Halpern, *Actual Causality* 2016) that predict such sentences to be false. Instead, we trace differences in their acceptability to their scalar implicatures (Sect. 3). Finally, we show that Halpern's semantics of causal claims can be easily adapted to account for the data we consider; namely, by dropping his 'minimality' condition (Sect. 4).

1 Introduction

Monotonicity offers an insightful window into the logical properties of natural language expressions. This is especially true of causal expressions. Taking entailment as the relevant order, two-place functions (such as determiners and, in the case of causation, binary relations) can be investigated, in the terminology of Barwise and Cooper (1981), in terms of downward and upward monotonicity in their left and right arguments.

In this paper we investigate whether actual causal claims are downward monotone in their cause argument (DMC). That is, we study whether the truth of a causal claim is preserved under strengthening the cause, where strength is understood as logical entailment. The answer to this question is not immediately obvious. On the one hand, there are apparent counterexamples; for example, it is not at all clear whether (1a) entails (1b):

I am grateful to my supervisor Katrin Schulz for her guidance, to Milica Denić and two anonymous reviewers for remarkably helpful comments, and to Simon Rey, with whom I first discussed the topic of this paper. Special thanks also go to the organizers of the TLLM workshop for persevering despite the coronavirus pandemic.

© Springer-Verlag GmbH Germany, part of Springer Nature 2020
D. Deng et al. (Eds.): TLLM 2020, LNCS 12564, pp. 125–146, 2020.
https://doi.org/10.1007/978-3-662-62843-0_7

(1)   a.   Alice flicking the switch caused the light to turn on.
       b.   # Alice flicking the switch and it raining in New Zealand caused the light to turn on.

A first guess why (1b) is unacceptable could be that the sentence is false, which would result, for example, if the semantics of *cause* does not allow causes to be stronger than strictly required for the causal claim to be true. However, sometimes the cause is stronger than required but the causal claim is still acceptable:

(2)   Reyna was born at Royal Bolton Hospital but received a Danish passport because her mother was born in Copenhagen.[1]

Having a mother born in Copenhagen is not necessary for one to acquire a Danish passport. When it comes to receiving a Danish passport, there is nothing special about Copenhagen compared to anywhere else in Denmark.

   In this paper we propose that causes are never too strong. In other words, causal claims are downward monotonic in their cause argument. Thus (1a) entails (1b), but this is not a counterexample to DMC because, while (1b) is true whenever (1a) is, in such cases (1b) is unassertable because it triggers the scalar implicature that (1a) is false (as argued for in Sect. 3.2 below).

   In this paper we concentrate on English causal claims, where we understand "causal claims" to be either of the form "C caused E" or "E because of C". In what follows we will consider both constructions, putting aside some evidence that there might be subtle differences in meaning between them.[2]

   It is worth investigating the monotonicity properties of causal claims for two reasons. The first is that while there is a great deal of research on the monotonicity properties of quantifiers (beginning with the influential work of Barwise and Cooper 1981, van Benthem 1984 and Keenan and Stavi 1986), comparatively little has been written about the monotonicity properties of natural language connectives. It might be objected that the monotonicity properties of connectives are so straightforward that there is nothing much to say (e.g. clearly negation is downward entailing, and conjunction and disjunction are upward monotone in their left and right arguments). However, the connective *because* presents a particularly complex case study to test whether generalizations claimed to hold for determiners—e.g. that all simple determiners are monotone (Barwise and Cooper 1981)—also hold for connectives.

   The second reason to investigate the monotonicity properties of causal claims is that they can teach us about the semantics of causal claims more generally. Any semantics of causal claims should be able to say something about problematic

---

[1] *The Bolton News*, 12 February 2020. https://www.theboltonnews.co.uk/news/18226923.bolton-born-woman-receives-british-passport-six-year-fight/.
[2] Copley and Wolff (2014: 55) offer the following example.
   (i) a. Lance Armstrong won seven Tours de France because of drugs.
        b. Drugs caused Lance Armstrong to win seven Tours de France.
   According to Copley and Wolff (2014), (ia) is true but (ib) is false. We will not attempt to theorize any difference in meaning between (ia) and (ib) here, and will consider both constructions with *cause* and with *because* below.

cases such as (1b) where the cause is stronger than required for the claim to be true. Resolving the status of such sentences is important for the semantics of causal claims in general.

The structure of the paper is as follows. In Sect. 2 we present data for and against DMC in causal claims. Section 3 shows that the data is readily accounted for in terms of the pragmatics of causal claims; in particular, by attending to their scalar implicatures. In Sect. 4 we investigate DMC in the semantics of actual causal claims proposed by Halpern (2016). We show that the validity of DMC depends on how Halpern structures the variables in his modeling framework, that of structural causal models (Pearl 2000). We end by showing that there is reason for Halpern to modify his framework to support the proposal that causal claims are always DMC, by dropping a condition he calls 'minimality'.

Before we proceed, we must define exactly what it means for one causal claim to entail another. This might seem straightforward, but the task is complicated by the presuppositions of causal claims. Let us turn to those presuppositions now.

1.1   Taking the Soft Presuppositions of Causal Claims into Account

Causal claims appear to presuppose that their propositional arguments are true. For example, the sentences in (3) presuppose that the mentioned causes and effects actually occurred (e.g. that Joe Kennedy advanced, had legal skills and that his bosses were starstruck).

(3)   a.   Did Joe Kennedy advance because of his legal skills or because his bosses were starstruck?[3]
       b.   The parents of Oscar Knox have said their son didn't die because he had cancer but because they ran out of options to treat it.[4]
       c.   Did hospital readmissions fall because per capita admission rates fell?[5]

However, causal claims are still felicitous when the common ground does not establish that the stated cause or effect occurred, as shown in (4). For instance, (4b) does not imply that Putin had a stroke, and (4d) does not imply that the death rate dropped in Chicago.

(4)   a.   The outcry which followed *Morgan* was not because the House of Lords had changed the law but because the public mistakenly thought it had done so.[6]

---

[3] *Boston Magazine*, 13 May 2020. https://www.bostonmagazine.com/news/2020/05/13/joe-kennedy-iii-profile/.

[4] *Irish News*, 9 September 2017. https://www.irishnews.com/news/2017/09/09/news/family-of-oscar-knox-establish-charity-in-son-s-memory-1132115/.

[5] *Health Affairs*, November 2019. https://www.healthaffairs.org/doi/abs/10.1377/hlt haff.2019.00411.

[6] Jennifer Temkin, *Rape and the Legal Process*. Oxford University Press, 2002.

    b.   Did a stroke cause Putin's awkward English?[7]

    c.   If a mechanical failure caused my injury, can I still sue?[8]

    d.   No, the coronavirus did not cause the death rate to drop in Chicago... Overall, deaths don't appear to be declining.[9]

    e.   Did NJ bail reform cause a surge in crime? ... Concerns about a possible spike in crime did not materialize.[10]

    f.   Dogs do not have ears because they have anything we don't. They have ears because they have ears.[11]

The data in (4) suggest that causal claims 'softly' presuppose in the sense of Abusch (2002; 2010) that their propositional arguments are true, where soft triggers are "presupposition triggers where the presuppositional behavior is weak and easily suspendable" Abusch (2002). Romoli (2011; 2015) proposes in particular that *because* softly presupposes that its propositional arguments are true. Moreover, many authors have concluded that soft presuppositions are pragmatically derived (e.g. Simons 2001, Abusch 2002; 2010, Abbott 2006, Chemla 2009, Romoli 2015). For example, Abrusán (2016) explains the 'soft–hard' distinction using general principles governing the interaction of information structure and context.

While soft presuppositions are pragmatically derived, monotonicity properties are traditionally understood as part of an expression's literal meaning, independent of pragmatic reasoning. For example, we say *every* is downward monotone in its restrictor: *every P is Q* implies *every P′ is Q* whenever $P' \subseteq P$. This is despite the fact that from an utterance of *every P′ is Q*, one would typically infer that *some P′ is Q*. (5a) entails (5b), even though there are contexts where (5a) is assertable but (5b) is not (e.g. when no students are over 70).

(5)   a.   Every student passed the test.

        b. $\Rightarrow$ Every student over the age of 70 passed the test.

In defining the monotonicity properties of causal claims, we will take into account the inference that their propositional arguments are true. The definition of monotonicity properties for causal claims we adopt in this paper is given below.

---

[7] *The Atlantic*, 12 June 2013. https://www.theatlantic.com/international/archive/2013/06/did-a-stroke-cause-putins-awkward-english/276824/.

[8] https://galliganlaw.com/2018/08/29/mechanical-failure-caused-injury/.

[9] https://www.politifact.com/factchecks/2020/apr/03/facebook-posts/no-coronavirus-did-not-cause-death-rate-drop-chica/.

[10] https://eu.northjersey.com/story/news/new-jersey/2019/04/02/nj-bail-reform-no-crime-surge-pretrial-release/3336423002/.

[11] (4f) shows that the presupposition of *because* can be suspended in a more subtle way than the other examples in (4). Chierchia (2013: 378) argues that the negative polarity item *any* in (4f) is acceptable in contexts where the presupposition/implicature of *because*—that dogs have something we don't—does not arise. If did, *any* would find itself in a non-downward entailing context and would therefore not be licensed according to Chierchia's theory and the Fauconnier–Ladusaw hypothesis.

Definition 1 (Downward monotonicity in the cause (DMC)). *We define that* cause *(respectively,* because*) is downward monotone in its cause if and only if the following holds for any propositions* C, C^+ *and* E *such that* C^+ *entails* C.

If C cause E *(respectively,* E because C*) is true* <u>*and* C^+ *is true*</u>, *then* C^+ cause E *(respectively,* E because C^+*) is also true.*

Since the inference that C^+ is true is likely pragmatically derived, this perspective represents a departure from how the monotonicity properties of natural language expressions are traditionally understood.[12] However, the move it is necessary to avoid trivializing the question whether *cause* and *because* are downward monotone in their causes. Triviality would result because without the underlined clause in Definition 1, we could find counterexamples to downward monotonicity simply by picking a false C^+. For instance, the entailment from (1a) to (1b) (repeated below) would fail simply because there are cases where it is not raining in New Zealand.

(1) a. Alice flicking the switch caused the light to turn on.
     b. Alice flicking the switch and it raining in New Zealand caused the light to turn on.

2 Data on DMC in Causal Claims

If causal claims are not downward monotone in their cause, it is because in some cases, the truth of a causal claim is not preserved under strengthening the cause. That is, DMC fails just in case there are causal claims where the cause is too strong for the causal claim to the true.

Are there cases whether the cause is stronger than required for the claim to be true, but the causal claim is still assertable? We already saw an example of such an assertion in (2), repeated as (6a) below with further examples:

(6) a. Reyna was born at Royal Bolton Hospital but received a Danish passport because her mother was born in Copenhagen.   =(2)
     b. He has an American passport because he was born in Boston.[13]

---

[12] Note that the underlined clause in Definition 1 would not result from redefining monotonicity using Strawson entailment; that is, by redefining *cause* to be downward monotone in its cause iff C *cause* E Strawson entails C^+ *cause* E whenever C^+ entails C (where p Strawson entails q just in case whenever p is true *and* q *is defined*, q is true; see von Fintel 1999: 104). This is because C^+ *cause* E can be defined even when C^+ is false; e.g. given (4a), *The outcry was because the House of Lords had changed the law* is false—hence defined—even though the law did not in fact change. Thanks to Milica Denić for raising the issue of Strawson entailment.

[13] https://rupaulsdragrace.fandom.com/wiki/Charlie_Hides.

c. Naama Issachar ... could spend up to seven-and-a-half years in a Russian prison because 9.5 grams of cannabis were found in her possession during a routine security check.[14]

d. A 90-day study in 8 adults found that supplementing a standard diet with 1.3 cups (100 grams) of fresh coconut daily caused significant weight loss.[15]

For example, (6c) is acceptable even though presumably, Naama Issachar would still have gone to prison if she had been caught with, say, 9 grams of cannabis.

To take a more extreme example, the causes in (7) are far stronger (in the sense of logical entailment) than required to make the effect occur, yet the causal claims are still assertable.

(7)   a. Computers do an awful lot of deliberation, and yet their every decision is wholly caused by the state of the universe plus the laws of nature.[16]

b. If anything is happening at this moment in time, it is completely dependent on, or caused by, the state of the universe, as the most complete description, at the previous moment.[17]

c. If you keep asking "why" questions about what happens in the universe, you ultimately reach the answer "because of the state of the universe and the laws of nature."[18]

If causal claims were not DMC, it would mean there are contexts where C *cause* E is true but C^+ *cause* E is false for some C and C^+ where C^+ entails C. In other words, we would expect some true causal claim to become false by making the cause too strong. Though in (7) we find causal claims where C^+ is as strong as it can possibly be, but the claim is still assertable. Assuming that the speakers are following Grice's maxim of quality (Grice 1975), the speakers of these sentences take them to not only be assertable, but also true.

Now, the sentences in (6) and (7) do not provide conclusive evidence that causal claims are DMC. One could reply that we have missed the cases where a true causal claim is made false by strengthening the cause. Nonetheless, the data in (6) and (7) pose a challenge: one who believes that some causal claims are made false by strengthening the cause, and seeks to explain why, must ensure that their explanation does not also predict the falsity of the examples above.

---

[14] *The Jerusalem Post*, 24 November 2019. https://www.jpost.com/israel-news/will-putin-release-issachar-before-he-visits-israel-in-january-analysis-608884.

[15] https://www.healthline.com/nutrition/coconut-meat.

[16] http://commonsenseatheism.com/?p=899.

[17] George Ortega, *Exploring the Illusion of Free Will*, 2013. http://causalconsciousness.com/Second%20Edition%20Chapters/14.%20%20Why%20Both%20Causality%20and%20Randomness%20Make%20Free%20Will%20Impossible.htm.

[18] https://www.edge.org/response-detail/10164.

3   Explaining Apparent Failures of DMC

3.1   A Possible Explanation of the Failure of DMC

In (1) we saw initial evidence that actual causal claims are not always downward monotone in their cause arguments. Let us consider again the contrast observed in (1), repeated below.

(1)   a.   Alice flicking the switch caused the light to turn on.
       b.   Alice flicking the switch and it raining in New Zealand caused the light to turn on.

If causal claims are indeed not DMC, one might seek to explain this property in terms of counterfactual dependence. Beginning with Hume (1748: section VII) and taken up again by Lewis (1973), counterfactual dependence analyses of causation seek to analyse causal claims in terms of the counterfactual, *if the cause had not occurred, the effect would not have occurred* (though this view is plagued by a host of counterexamples, see e.g. Paul 1998, Schaffer 2000, Hall and Paul 2003: and many more).

In much recent work on counterfactuals, counterfactual antecedents can raise multiple scenarios, and a counterfactual is true just in case the consequent holds in *every* scenario raised by the antecedent (Kratzer 1986, Alonso-Ovalle 2006, von Fintel 2001, Ciardelli 2016 as well as many others, though see Stalnaker 1981 for an alternative view). Under this assumption, counterfactual dependence analyses of the semantics of causal claims make the following prediction:

(8)   (1b) is true iff in **all** scenarios raised by the antecedent
       $\neg$(Alice flick switch $\wedge$ rain in NZ), the light turns on.

With this apparatus, one could explain that (1b) is unassertable because it is false, and that it is false because, if it had not been that Alice flicked the switch and it was raining in New Zealand, there are multiple scenarios to consider. In particular, in one scenario raised by the antecedent, where it does not rain in New Zealand but Alice still flicks the switch, the light still turns on. (1b) would therefore be predicted to be false because the counterfactual dependence claim fails: in some scenario raised by the antecedent, *If the cause had not occurred,* the effect still occurs.

However, this explanation makes the wrong prediction for the sentences in Sect. 2. It wrongly predicts the sentences in (6) and (7) to be false. For example, if Renya's mother hadn't been born in Copenhagen, Renya might have still received a Danish passport, say, if her mother had been born in Aarhus instead. And (7b) would be false because, taking anything that is happening at this moment in time (e.g. the bird flying outside my window), if the state of the universe at the previous moment had been different, there are many possibilities to consider. Presumably in some of these, the bird is still flying outside my window.

Since the above explanation in terms of counterfactual dependence cannot account for the fact that the sentences in (6) and (7) are assertable but (1b) is not, let us examine an alternative approach. This account will attend to differences in the sentences' implicatures.

3.2 Pragmatic Deviance via False Implicature

While (1) purports to show that causal claims are not DMC, an alternative response is that (1b) is true but unassertable because it has a false implicature. Without appealing to DMC, one could seek to explain that (1b) falsely implicates the existence of a causal relationship between New Zealand's weather and the light. For, under standard assumptions about the calculation of alternatives (e.g. via deletion, see Katzir 2007), (1a) is a competing alternative utterance to (1b). So after an utterance of (1b), a listener would naturally attempt to construct a reason for mentioning the weather in New Zealand; for example, that there is in fact a causal relationship between the weather in weather and the light. The pragmatic deviance of (1b) makes it hard to conclude from examples like (1) that causal claims violate DMC. Indeed, against expectations, examples like (1) may even provide evidence that causal claims are DMC after all. We pursue this idea next.

The above pragmatic explanation of the unassertability of (1b) was admittedly rather vague. We did not provide a precise account of how (1b) implicates that the weather in New Zealand is 'causally relevant' to the light, nor what notion of 'causal relevance' is at work in the pragmatic calculation. Such an explanation could appeal to the maxim of relevance, though it is unclear how exactly the explanation would proceed. In contrast, if causal claims are DMC, it is easy to derive exactly why (1b) is unassertable: it has a false scalar implicature. Given that (1a) is an alternative utterance to (1b) (created by deleting material from (1b)), if causal claims are DMC then (1a) entails (1b), in which case a speaker who opts for (1b) is using a weaker utterance when a stronger alternative, (1a), is available. If a listener believes that a speaker of (1b) is obeying the maxim of quantity, the listener would infer that the speaker believes (1a) to be false.

Thus what turned out to be an apparent counterexample to DMC can actually be construed an argument in its favor. If *cause* is DMC, then C *cause* E entails $(C \wedge D)$ *cause* E. The explanation of (1b)'s unassertability thus becomes exactly parallel to the explanation why (9a) is unassertable when it is common ground that all students passed the test; namely, both sentences are literally true but have a false scalar implicature.

(9)   a.   Some students passed the test.
       b.   **Implicates:** Not all students passed the test.

(10)   a.   Alice flicking the switch and it raining in New Zealand caused the light to turn on.   =(1b)
       b.   **Implicates:** ¬(Alice flicking the switch caused the light to turn on).

While it may be possible to derive the infelicity of (1b) without assuming that causal claims are DMC (for example, by appealing to the maxim of relevance) the assumption of DMC allows us to derive the infelicity of (1b) 'out of the box', so to speak, from the familiar mechanism of scalar implicature calculation.[19]

Now that we have a proposed explanation for the unassertability of examples like (1b), let us put that theory to the test. We do so in the following two sections.

3.3 Sensitivity to Alternatives

An utterance's pragmatically enriched meaning, unlike its at-issue contribution, is calculated by taking into account what the speaker could have said instead— the utterance's *alternatives*. If causal claims where the cause is stronger than strictly required for the claim to hold such as (1b) are true, but unassertable due to a false scalar implicature, we would expect it to be assertable in contexts where the alternatives are such that no false implicature arises.

This prediction is borne out. We find evidence in the examples from Sect. 2. Consider (2), repeated below (though note that the remarks in this section could apply equally well to any of the sentences in (6) or (7)):

(2)   Reyna was born at Royal Bolton Hospital but received a Danish passport because her mother was born in Copenhagen.

If *Denmark* were an alternative to *Copenhagen* in (2), then assuming DMC, we would expect (2) to trigger the scalar implicature that it is false that Renya received a Danish passport because her mother was born in Denmark. This is because under DMC we have the entailment:

(11)   a.   Renya received a Danish passport because her mother was born in Denmark.   *E because C*

        b. $\Rightarrow$ Renya received a Danish passport because her mother was born in Copenhagen.   *E because C^+*

We can account for the assertability of (2) by assuming that *Denmark* is not an alternative to *Copenhagen* in (2) and therefore does not trigger a false implicature. To put this explanation to the test, we can alter the sentence to force

---

[19] For this explanation to work, the scalar implicature calculation must be *obligatory* and *blind to contextual information* (in the sense of Magri 2009). The implicature must be obligatory because if it could be canceled—say, because the truth of (1a) is already in the common ground, which is inconsistent with the implicature—we would expect (1b) to be assertable, contrary to observation (assuming (1b) is not unassertable for some other reason). And the implicature calculation must be blind to contextual information for the following reason. Assuming (1a) is in the common ground, then by DMC, (1b) is too. So (1a) and (1b) are contextually equivalent— true in all the same worlds compatible with the common ground. But then if scalar implicatures were calculated with respect to contextual entailment, (1a) would not be a strictly more informative alternative to (1b), no false implicature would be generated, and we would instead expect (1b) to be assertable (again, assuming (1b) is not unassertable for some other reason).

Denmark to be an alternative to *Copenhagen* and check whether the scalar implicature is triggered as predicted. Following the theory of alternative calculation from Fox and Katzir (2011), we can make *Denmark* an alternative by making it contextually salient and focusing *Copenhagen*, as in the following dialogue, where subscript F indicates focus marking:

(12) a. A: I have a Danish passport because my father was born in Denmark. Why do you have one?
      b. B: ??Because my mother was born in [Copenhagen]$_F$.

In this context, (12b) indeed triggers the implicature that Copenhagen is somehow special when it comes to receiving Danish passports; in other words, that it is not true that B has a Danish passport because their mother was born in Denmark. This is correctly predicted by the entailment in (11), an entailment guaranteed by DMC.

Note that while (2) optionally triggers a false scalar implicature, (1b) does so obligatorily:

(1b) # Alice flicking the switch and it raining in New Zealand caused the light to turn on.

As we saw in 3.2, we can account for this by assuming DMC and that *Alice flicking the switch* is obligatorily an alternative to *Alice flicking the switch and it raining in New Zealand*.[20]

Thus DMC allows us to explain why the sentences in (6) and (7) are assertable while (1b) is not. The difference lies in how their alternatives are derived. (6) and (7) are assertable provided that no weaker cause is an alternative to the cause appearing in the sentence, in which case no false implicature is triggered, while (1b) is obligatorily unassertable when (1a) is true because C is obligatorily an alternative to $C \wedge D$ (e.g. via deletion; see Katzir 2007), meaning $(C \wedge D)$ *cause E* obligatorily triggers the scalar implicature $\neg(D$ *cause E*$)$, that (1a) is false.

3.4 Behavior in Downward Entailing Environments

One of the most straightforward ways to test whether sentence (1b) is false, or true but unassertable, is to put it in a downward entailing environment. Examples are shown in (13).

(13) a. ?? I doubt that the light turned on because Alice flicked the switch and it was raining in New Zealand.
      b. ?? No one thinks that Alice flicking the switch and it raining in New Zealand caused the light to turn on.

In this subsection we argue that sentences in (12) provide evidence against the hypothesis that the embedded causal claim (1b) is false, and in favor of the hypothesis that (1b) is true but unassertable due to a false scalar implicature.

---

[20] For further discussion of the obligatory nature of this implicature, see footnote 19.

The crucial observation is that the sentences in (13) are improved with prosodic focus on *and it (was) raining in New Zealand*. This is unexpected according to a theory where (1b) is literally false, and so the sentences in (13) should be straightforwardly true. However, this is expected if (1b) is false but can be rescued by metalinguistic negation targeting a scalar implicature triggered by the focused material. We develop this proposal below.

Examples of metalinguistic negation are shown in (14):

(14)   a.   He didn't eat [some]$_F$ of the cookies. He ate [all]$_F$ of them.
        b.   I don't [like]$_F$ scallops. I [love]$_F$ them.

Metalinguistic negation is used to target an utterance's non-at-issue content. In (14), metaliguistic negation targets the scalar implicatures triggered by the focused material, with *some* implicating *not all* and *like* implicating *don't love*.

Let us consider some more clear-cut examples of metalinguistic negation in causal claims. In (14) and (15) alike, the focus marking is obligatory for the sentences to be felicitous.

(15)   a.   I refuse to eat it, not because it's a [pineapple]$_F$ pizza, but because it's [pizza]$_F$. I hate pizza.
        b.   I am not upset because you lost my wedding ring [and my phone]$_F$. I'm upset because you lost [my wedding ring]$_F$.
        c.   The fact that the meeting [happened]$_F$ caused my surprise. It wasn't the fact that the meeting happened [on a Sunday]$_F$.

According to Horn (1985; 1989) and Burton-Roberts (1989), metalinguistic negation only applies after the hearer realizes the sentence cannot be interpreted using truth-functional, descriptive negation. A straightforward explanation why descriptive negation cannot apply in (14) and (15) is that the negated claim is entailed by the clause following it. For if the entailment relations in (16) hold, applying descriptive negation to the stronger claim would result in a contradictory meaning.

(16)   a.   He ate all of the cookies. ⇒ He ate some of the cookies.
        b.   I love scallops. ⇒ I like scallops.

Similarly, assuming DMC the following entailments hold:

(17)   a.   The light turned on because Alice flicked the switch. ⇒ The light turned on because Alice flicked the switch and it was raining in New Zealand.
        b.   I am upset because you lost my wedding ring. ⇒ I am upset because you lost my wedding ring and my phone.
        c.   I refuse to eat it because it's pizza. ⇒ I refuse to eat it because it's pineapple pizza.
        d.   The fact that the meeting happened caused my surprise. ⇒ The fact that the meeting happened on Sunday caused my surprise.

An alternative perspective on metalinguistic negation proposes that there is only one kind of negation, but it can target an utterance's pragmatically enriched meaning (Carston 1996; 2002, Noh 1998; 2000 Moeschler 2019). If causal claims are DMC—and so the entailment relations in (17) hold—one can apply the scalar implicature calculation proposed in Sect. 3.2 to predict the following implicatures.

(18)   a.   The light turned on because Alice flicked the switch and it was raining in New Zealand.
               Scalar implicature: ¬(The light turned on because Alice flicked the switch.)
        b.   I refuse to eat it because it's pineapple pizza.
               Scalar implicature: ¬(I refuse to eat it because it's pizza)
        c.   I am upset because you lost my wedding ring and my phone.
               Scalar implicature: ¬(I am upset because you lost my wedding ring)
        d.   The fact that the meeting happened on Sunday caused my surprise.
               Scalar implicature: ¬(The fact that the meeting happened did not cause my surprise)

Adopting the theory of metalinguistic negation of Carston (1996; 2002), Noh (1998; 2000), Moeschler (2019), we can explain the data in (15) as a case where the negation targets the causal claims' scalar implicatures.

Thus, regardless of which perspective on metalinguistic negation we take, we are able to explain the observation that the sentences in (13) and (15) require focus marking to be felicitous, following the pattern of more familiar examples of metalinguistic negation such as (14). Crucially, this explanation requires assuming that the entailment relations in (17) hold—a consequence of DMC. The fact that (13) and (15) pattern with other examples of metalinguistic negation therefore provides further support for DMC.

4   Truth Conditions for Causal Claims: Halpern (2016)

The data in Sect. 2 provided evidence that causal claims are DMC. In this section we show that a recent influential analysis of the truth conditions of causal claims, due to Halpern (2016), does not account for this fact. However, we show that Halpern's semantics of causal claims can be easily adapted to account for the data we consider; namely, by dropping his 'minimality' condition.

4.1 Halpern's Semantics for Causal Claims

Halpern (2016) defines his truth conditions for causal claims in terms of structural causal models (Pearl 2000).[21] Let us briefly review this framework. We let V be a set of variables of arbitrary arity, and where X is a variable, let $\mathcal{R}(X)$ denote the *range* of X, that is, the set of values X may take. A structural causal model is then defined as follows.

Definition 2 (Structural causal model). *A* *structural causal model is a triple* $M = (V, E, F)$ *where* V *is a set of variables,* (V, E) *is a directed acyclic graph, and* F *is a set of functions of the form*

$$F_X : \mathcal{R}(pa_X) \to \mathcal{R}(X),$$

one for each endogenous variable $X \in V$ *(X is endogenous iff X has a parent in the graph), where* $pa_X := \{Y \in V \mid (Y, X) \in E\}$ *is the set of parents of X in the graph* (V, E).

Where $\boldsymbol{U}$ *is the set of exogenous (i.e. parentless) variables in* (V, E)*, and* $\boldsymbol{u} \in \mathcal{R}(\boldsymbol{U})$*, we call* $\boldsymbol{u}$ *a* setting *of* M.

In the structural causal modeling framework, the semantics of causal claims is understood in terms of interventions. An intervention is an operation that sets the value of a variable X by manually changing its function F_X. This is given in Definition 3.

Definition 3 (Truth conditions for interventions). *Where* $M = (V, E, F)$ *is a structural causal model,* $M_{X=x}$ *is the model* (V, E, F') *that results by setting, every variable* $Y \in \boldsymbol{X}$*,* $F'_Y(\boldsymbol{z}) = y$ *for every value* $\boldsymbol{z}$ *of the parents of y.*

We write $(M, u) \models \boldsymbol{X} = \boldsymbol{x}$ *just in case* $\boldsymbol{X}$ *has value* $\boldsymbol{x}$ *according to the equations in F, and write*

$$(M, \boldsymbol{u}) \models [\boldsymbol{X} \leftarrow \boldsymbol{x}]Y = y \text{ iff } (M_{\boldsymbol{X}=\boldsymbol{x}}, \boldsymbol{u}) \models Y = y.$$

With a treatment of interventions at hand, Halpern proposes the following truth conditions for causal claims.[22]

---

[21] A reviewer rightly asks how causal network models fit with natural language semantics, and in particular how the network is supposed to be derived from natural language utterances (e.g. Does the network come from explicit text? From implicit context?). In Sect. 4.2 we will address one issue affecting the construction of the network: the choice of variables; in particular, how fine-grained we should take the variables to be. Unfortunately a larger assessment of the adequacy of causal networks in natural language semantics is beyond the scope of this paper. Though since much recent work in natural language semantics adopts causal networks as a model—especially in the semantics of conditionals (e.g. Schulz 2011, Briggs 2012, Ciardelli et al. 2018, Santorio 2019)—the question of their adequacy in natural language semantics arises for a number of authors.

[22] Halpern actually proposes three separate versions of AC2: an 'original' definition, an 'updated', and a 'modified' definition. The modified version is what appears above. Halpern acknowledges that the original version is subject to counterexamples (Halpern 2016: example 2.8.1), and states that his "current preference" is for the modified definition. For this reason we only consider the modified definition.

Definition 4 (Halpern's truth conditions for actual causal claims). *Let $M = (V, E, F)$ be a structural causal model, u a context for M, and X a vector of variables. $X = x$ is an* actual cause *of φ in the causal setting (M, u) iff*

AC1 $(M, u) \models X = x$ *and* $(M, u) \models \varphi$.
AC2 *There is a vector W of variables and a value x' of X such that*

$$(M, u) \models W = w \text{ and } (M, u) \models [X \leftarrow x', W \leftarrow w] \neg \varphi.^{23}$$

AC3 X *is minimal; there is no strict subset X' of X such that $X' = x'$ satisfies conditions AC1 and AC2, where x' is the restriction of x to the variables in X'.*

In essence, the three conditions state the following.

1. The cause and the effect actually occurred.
2. Fixing some variables to their actual values, if the cause had a different value, the effect would not have occurred.
3. If the cause were any weaker (in the sense of logical entailment) it would not satisfy AC2.

While Halpern's definition is phrased in terms of $X = x$ being "an actual cause" of φ, we will apply his analysis to the constructions considered in this paper: the verb *cause* and the connective *because*. One reason why it is worth examining how Halpern's analysis fares with such constructions is that they occur much more frequently than either *a cause of* or *the cause of*.[24]

4.2   An Obstacle in the Way of Representing Monotonicity in Structural Causal Models

There is one theory-internal obstacle getting in the way using structural causal models to test the monotonicity of properties of causal claims. The problem is

---

[23] Strictly speaking, the condition AC2 above is not the condition proposed by Halpern (2016: 25). The condition above uses a conjunction, whereas Halpern's own condition uses a conditional, requiring that there is a set W of variables and a setting x' of the variables in X such that *if* $(M, u) \models W = w$ *then* $(M, u) \models [X \leftarrow x', W \leftarrow w] \neg \varphi$. The problem with the *if–then* formulation is that its predicts AC2 to always be true. Halpern's formulation of AC2 is true whenever the antecedent is false, that is, whenever there is a set of variables and an assignment that is false in the actual context u. But the actual context u always makes some assignment of values to variables false, so Halpern predicts AC2 to be always true. I think Halpern simply miswrote the formula, and intended to write AC2 with a conjunction instead. I have therefore taken the liberty to rewrite his definition as it appears above.

[24] Searches of the British National Corpus (BNC) and Corpus of Contemporary American English (CCAE) reveal that for every occurrence of either *a cause* or *the cause* there are approximately 3 occurrences of *caused* (in both the BNC and CCAE) and 36 (BNC) and 62 (CCAE) occurrences, respectively, of *because*. Frequency of *a cause*: 609 (BNC), 4852 (CCAE); *the cause*: 2161 (BNC), 16586 (CCAE); *caused*: 9243 (BNC), 62527 (CCAE); *because*: 99496 (BNC), 1346051 (CCAE). Corpora accessed at https://www.english-corpora.org/bnc/ and https://www.english-corpora.org/coca/ on 5 October 2020.

that the variables in structural causal models are taken to be *logically indepen-dent*, in the sense that every assignment of values to variables is consistent.[25] One reason for the assumption of logical independence is that SCMs are typically employed to represent the effects of interventions (see Pearl 2000). Logical independence in the sense above is required for the effect of every intervention on an SCM to be defined.[26] The assumption of logical independence implies that (19a) and (19b) cannot both be analyzed in the same SCM; for if they could, it would be possible to intervene to have John born in Boston but not in the United States, contradicting the fact that Boston is in the United States.

(19)   a.   John has an American passport because he was born in the United States.

        b.   John has an American passport because he was born in Boston.

There are many ways one might propose to get around the problem of contradictory interventions. One way would be to take variables to be maximally fine-grained. For example, instead of a binary variable representing *Was John born in Boston?* we could use a variable with a much more fine-grained range representing *Where was John born?*. By packaging logically dependent values inside the same variable, one avoids the problem of contradictory interventions because one cannot intervene to set the same variable to two different values.

Taking the variables to be fine-grained is one way to solve the problem of contradictory interventions. Though if we adopt fine-grained variables, we must make a slight technical modification to Definition 4 to adequately represent the sentences discussed in 2 in Halpern's framework. The reason is that Halpern's definition takes a cause to be an assignment of a *single* value to a variable (or vector of variables). Even if the variables are maximally specific, our ordinary causal talk often is not. The solution is straightforward enough: allow causes in Halpern's definition to be sets of values, rather than a single value. For instance, if X represents where John was born, we might take $\mathcal{R}(X)$ to be a set of locations and let *Boston* and *United States* be the appropriate subsets of $\mathcal{R}(X)$. We can then expresses causes of varying specificity, for example, that $X \in Boston$ caused John to have a US passport, or that $X \in United\ States$ did. The changes to Definition 4 are given below.

---

[25] By 'consistency' here we mean consistency with logic and with analytic relations given by world knowledge—e.g. that Copenhagen is in Denmark—while allowing for inconsistency with the causal laws, represented by structural equations (Pearl 2000).

[26] Though see Beckers and Halpern (2018) for a proposal to restrict interventions to 'allowable interventions'.

Definition 5 (Allowing weaker causes in Halpern's framework). *Where* X *is a vector of variables and* $A \subseteq \mathcal{R}(X)$, *we say* $\underline{X \in A}$ *is an* actual cause *of* φ *in the causal setting* (M, u) *iff*

AC1' $(M, u) \models X = x$ *for some* $x \in A$ *and* $(M, u) \models \varphi$.
AC2' *There is a set* W *of variables and a setting* x' *of the variables in* X *such that* $\underline{x' \notin A}$, $(M, u) \models W = w$ *and* $(M, u) \models [X \leftarrow x', W \leftarrow w]\neg\varphi$.
AC3' *No subset* X' *of* X *also satisfies AC1' and AC2'.*

According to Definition 5, causal claims are DMC with respect to causes that share the same variables. More exactly, we have the following, which is a straightforward consequence of the fact that if $A^+ \subseteq A$ and $x' \notin A$, then $x' \notin A^+$.

Fact 1. *For any causal model* M *and setting* u, *according to Definition 5, if* $X \in A$ *is an actual cause of* φ *in* (M, u) *and* $A^+ \subseteq A$, *then* $X \in A^+$ *is also an actual cause of* φ *in* (M, u).

By Fact 1, (19b) entails (19b), provided that *John was born in the United States* is represented by the same variable as *John was born in Boston*.

(19)   a.   John has an American passport because he was born in the United States.
   b.   ⇒ John has an American passport because he was born in Boston.

4.3   Failures of DMC in Halpern's Framework: Minimality

While Halpern predicts that causal claims are DMC for causes that are represented by the same variables, in turns out the opposite holds for the causes that are not represented by the same variables.

Fact 2. *For any causal model* M *and setting* u, *according to Definition 5, if* $X \in A$ *is an actual cause of* φ *in* (M, u) *and* $X \subsetneq Y$, *then for no* $B \subseteq \mathcal{R}(Y)$ *is* $Y \in B$ *an actual cause of* φ *in* (M, u).

Fact 2 holds because of Halpern's minimality condition. If X and Y were both actual causes of φ and $X \subsetneq Y$, then Y would violate minimality (AC3'). Indeed, Halpern states that he added his minimality condition precisely to rule out such cases.

> AC3 is a minimality condition, which ensures that only those elements of the conjunction $X = x$ that are essential are considered part of a cause; inessential elements are pruned. Without AC3, if dropping a lit match qualified as a cause of the forest fire, then dropping a match and sneezing would also pass the tests of AC1 and AC2. AC3 serves here to strip "sneezing" and other irrelevant, over-specific details from the cause. (Halpern 2003: 23)

Halpern's theory predicts that such "irrelevant, over-specific details" only make a truth conditional difference when they are represented by a separate variable. Overly specific causes do not render a causal claim false, provided the overly specific detail is still represented by the same variable as a weaker cause satisfying AC1–3. There is reason to think, however, that minimality should not be part of the truth conditions of causal claims after all. We explore a counterexample to minimality in the next section.

4.4   Against Minimality

If we take Halpern's definition of actual causality as an analysis of the verb *cause* or the connective *because*, his minimality condition leads to some surprising results. Consider the following scenario.[27] A committee is tasked with approving new company policies. The committee has two members: the Chairperson and the CEO. A policy is approved just in case both committee members approve it. Recently, a new proposal came before the committee. Independently, the Chairperson and CEO each liked the proposal, and so each voted in favor of adopting it.

(20)   a.   The fact that the Chairperson voted 'Yes' and CEO voted 'Yes' caused the proposal to pass.

          b.   The proposal passed because the Chairperson voted 'Yes' and the CEO voted 'Yes'.

Fig. 1. A simple model of the voting scenario in (20)

We represent the sentences in (20) in Halpern's framework as (21), 'Agent = 1' holds just in case the agent voted 'Yes', and 'Result = 1' holds just in case the policy was approved (Fig. 1).

(21)   (Chair, CEO) = (1, 1) is an actual cause of Result = 1.

(21) clearly satisfies AC1. It satisfies AC2 because, taking W to be empty, there is another setting x' of X = (Chair, CEO) such that $(M, u) \models [X \leftarrow x']$Result $\neq$

---

[27] An anonymous reviewer points out that the following example is isomorphic to the conjunctive forest fire scenario considered by Halpern (2016: example 2.3.1). We find the following committee example slightly more natural than Halpern's, in which a forest will not burn if struck by lightning or if a lit match is dropped, but will burn if both happen. Of course, since the two examples have the same causal structure, Halpern's example could be used here without affecting the conclusions we draw in this section.

1; indeed, any setting of (Chair, CEO) besides $(1,1)$—namely, $(1,0)$, $(0,1)$ or $(0,0)$—would suffice.

Nonetheless, (21) is false according to Halpern's definition because it violates minimality (AC3). Taking $X' = $ Chair or $X' = $ CEO, we have that $X' = 1$ also satisfies AC1 and AC2. This example does not seem to fit Halpern's motivation for adopting minimality; namely, to strip "irrelevant, over-specific details from the cause" (Halpern 2016: 23). Since (21) seems perfectly acceptable, but violates the minimality condition (AC3), one might recommend abandoning the minimality condition altogether.

4.5   Partial Causes to the Rescue?

The previous section showed that, in virtue of minimality, Halpern makes the wrong prediction for conjunctive causes, predicting that the conjunction *The Chairperson voting 'Yes' and the CEO voting 'Yes'* is not a cause of the motion passing, against intuitions. However, one might reply that we have simply mistranslated natural language into Halpern's formal system.[28] In particular, one might argue that we have overlooked *partial causes.* Halpern (2016: 25) defines that whenever $X = x$ is a cause of φ in context (M, u), each conjunct of $X = x$ is *part* of a cause of φ in (M, u). Halpern then offers the following remarks on the relationship between his definition and natural language:

> What we think of as causes in natural language correspond to parts of causes, especially with the modified HP definition [Definition 4 above]. Indeed, it may be better to use a term such as "complete cause" for what I have been calling cause and then reserve "cause" for what I have called "part of a cause". (Halpern 2016: 25)

Under this formalization of natural language, Halpern predicts that the CEO voting 'Yes' and the Chairperson voting 'Yes' are each, on their own, complete causes of the motion passing. Besides the fact that this is a strange use of the word 'complete', the fact remains that Halpern makes the wrong predictions for the conjunction $(\text{CEO} = 1) \wedge (\text{Chair} = 1)$, classifying it as neither a complete nor partial cause of the motion passing.

Thus, even when we take into account Halpern's suggestions above about how to formalize natural language in his framework, his definition of actual causality is still unsuitable as an analysis of the verb *cause* or the connective *because.* This is because his definition yields the wrong results for conjunctive causes, as in (20). It predicts the sentences in (20) to be false—regardless whether we interpret *caused* in (20a) as 'partially caused' or 'completely caused', and regardless whether we interpret *because* in (20b) as 'partially because' or 'completely because'.

The example in Sect. 4.4 therefore further supports dropping the minimality condition from Halpern's definition of actual causality. We end by quickly proving that dropping minimality indeed has the desired effect, resulting in truth

---

[28] Thanks to an anonymous reviewer for encouraging me to include a discussion of partial causes.

conditions for actual causal claims that are downward monotone in their cause argument.

4.6   Without Minimality: DMC Restored

Without AC3, Halpern predicts that causal claims are always downward monotone in their cause. We have already shown this in the case when one uses the same variables to represent the stronger and weaker cause (Fact 1). Below we show this in cases where the stronger cause is not represented by the same variables as the weaker cause.

Fact 3 (Downward monotonicity of AC1∧ AC2). *If $X = x$ satisfies AC1 and AC2 with respect to φ and (M, u), then for any variables Y such that $(M, u) \models Y = y$, the conjunction $X = x \wedge Y = y$ satisfies AC1 and AC2 with respect to φ and (M, u).*

Proof. AC1 follows from the assumption that $(M, u) \models Y = y$. For if $X = x$ satisfies AC1 and $(M, u) \models Y = y$, then $(M, u) \models X = x \wedge Y = y$.

And if $X = x$ satisfies AC2, then there is a setting x' of X such that $(M, u) \models [X \leftarrow x', W \leftarrow w]\neg\varphi$ for some set of variables W such that $(M, u) \models W = w$.

Let y' be the value of Y under the intervention setting X to x' and W to w. That is, let $y' \in \mathcal{R}(Y)$ be such that $(M, u) \models X \leftarrow x', W \leftarrow w]Y = y'$. Now, all structural causal models validate the following principle (which Pearl calls 'consistency', see Pearl 2000: Corollary 7.3.2):

$$\text{if } (M, u) \models A = a \wedge B = b \text{ then } (M, u) \models [A \leftarrow a]B = b.$$

Consistency says that intervening to set a variable to its actual value does not change the value of any variable. In particular, since $(M_{X \leftarrow x', W \leftarrow w}, u) \models Y = y' \wedge \neg\varphi$, by consistency, $(M_{X \leftarrow x', W \leftarrow w}, u) \models [Y \leftarrow y']\neg\varphi$, which by Definition 3 is equivalent to

$$(M, u) \models [(X, Y) \leftarrow (x', y'), W \leftarrow w]\neg\varphi.$$

Hence $(X, Y) = (x, y)$ satisfies AC2 with respect to φ and (M, u).

Thus, without minimality, Halpern's theory predicts that causal claims are always DMC.

5   Conclusion

While initial evidence suggests that causal claims are not DMC, the data can be explained by assuming that causal claims are in fact DMC. Assuming so allows us to explain the infelicity of the causal claims with a stronger cause as a case of false scalar implicature (Sect. 3.2). We also saw though the phenomenon of metalinguistic negation in Sect. 3.4 a parallel between paradigmatic entailments (e.g. *all* entails *some*, *love* entails *like*) and entailment relations between causal claims (*C cause E* entails C^+ *cause E* whenever C^+ entails C).

Turning to Halpern's semantics of causal claims, we showed what whether causal claims are DMC according to Halpern (2016) depends on how the variables are structured, though by making a slight modification to Halpern's theory— abandoning minimality—Halpern predicts that causal claims are always DMC. The modification improves Halpern's truth conditions for actual causal claims by allowing him to make the right predictions for claims with conjunctive causes (Sect. 4.4), a benefit that cannot be achieved by interpreting the causal relation in question as either partial or complete (Sect. 4.5).

While dropping minimality and validating DMC improves Halpern's semantics of causal claims, the question remains whether the resulting theory yields a convincing formal theory of causation.[29] Recent work by Beckers and Vennekens (2018) suggests that there are more fundamental problems with Halpern's analysis, problems that cannot be solved by dropping minimality. Nonetheless, while we have taken Halpern's framework as an influential case study, the data presented above suggest that every semantics of causal claims should validate DMC. We leave it to future work to determine whether other analyses—such as Yablo (2002), Beckers and Vennekens (2018), Loew (2019), and Andreas and Günther (2020)—offer a satisfactory treatment of the monotonicity properties of causal claims.

References

Abbott, B.: Where have some of the presuppositions gone? Drawing the boundaries of meaning: Neo-Gricean studies in pragmatics and semantics in honor of Laurence R. Horn, vol. 80, pp. 1–20 (2006)

Abrusán, M.: Presupposition cancellation: explaining the 'soft-hard' trigger distinction. Nat. Lang. Semant. **24**(2), 165–202 (2016). https://doi.org/10.1007/s11050-016-9122-7

Abusch, D.: Lexical alternatives as a source of pragmatic presuppositions. Semant. Linguist. Theory **12**, 1–19 (2002). https://doi.org/10.3765/salt.v12i0.2867

Abusch, D.: Presupposition triggering from alternatives. J. Semant. **27**(1), 37–80 (2010). https://doi.org/10.1093/jos/ffp009

Alonso-Ovalle, L.: Disjunction in alternative semantics. Ph.D. thesis, University of Massachusetts Amherst (2006). http://people.linguistics.mcgill.ca/~luis.alonso-ovalle/papers/alonso-ovalle-diss.pdf

Andreas, H., Günther, M.: Causation in terms of production. Philos. Stud. **177**(6), 1565–1591 (2019). https://doi.org/10.1007/s11098-019-01275-3

Barwise, J., Cooper, R.: Generalized quantifiers and natural language. Linguist. Philos. **4**(2), 159–219 (1981). https://doi.org/10.1007/BF00350139. ISSN 1573-0549

Beckers, S., Halpern, J.Y.: Abstracting causal models. CoRR, abs/1812.03789 (2018). http://arxiv.org/abs/1812.03789

Beckers, S., Vennekens, J.: A principled approach to defining actual causation. Synthese **195**(2), 835–862 (2016). https://doi.org/10.1007/s11229-016-1247-1

---

[29] Thanks to an anonymous reviewer for raising this issue.

Johan Benthemvan Benthem: Questions about quantifiers 1. J. Symbol. Logic **49**(2), 443–466 (1984). https://doi.org/10.2307/2274176

Briggs, R.: Interventionist counterfactuals. Philos. Stud. **160**(1), 139–166 (2012). https://doi.org/10.1007/s11098-012-9908-5

Burton-Roberts, N.: On horn's dilemma: presupposition and negation. J. Linguist. **25**(1), 95–125 (1989). https://doi.org/10.1017/S0022226700012111

Carston, R.: Metalinguistic negation and echoic use. J. Pragmat. **25**(3), 309–330 (1996). https://doi.org/10.1016/0378-2166(94)00109-X

Carston, R.: Thoughts and Utterances: The Pragmatics of Explicit Communication. Wiley, Hoboken (2002). https://doi.org/10.1002/9780470754603

Chemla, E.: Similarity: towards a unified account of scalar implicatures, free choice permission and presupposition projection. Under revision for Semantics and Pragmatics (2009)

Chierchia, G.: Logic in Grammar: Polarity, Free Choice, and Intervention. Oxford (2013). https://doi.org/10.1093/acprof:oso/9780199697977.001.0001

Ciardelli, I.: Lifting conditionals to inquisitive semantics. Semant. Linguist. Theory **26**, 732–752 (2016). https://doi.org/10.3765/salt.v26i0.3811

Ciardelli, I., Zhang, L., Champollion, L.: Two switches in the theory of counterfactuals. Linguist. Philos. **41**(6), 577–621 (2018). https://doi.org/10.1007/s10988-018-9232-4

Copley, B., Wolff, P.: Theories of causation should inform linguistic theory and vice versa. In: Causation in Grammatical Structures. Oxford University Press (2014). https://doi.org/10.1093/acprof:oso/9780199672073.003.0002

von Fintel, K.: NPI licensing, Strawson entailment, and context dependency. J. Semant. **16**(2), 97–148 (1999). https://doi.org/10.1093/jos/16.2.97

von Fintel, K.: Counterfactuals in a dynamic context. In: Kenstowicz, M. (ed.) Ken Hale: A Life in Language, vol. 36, pp. 123–152. MIT Press (2001)

Fox, D., Katzir, R.: On the characterization of alternatives. Nat. Lang. Semant. **19**(1), 87–107 (2011). https://doi.org/10.1007/s11050-010-9065-3

Grice, H.P.: Logic and conversation. In: Speech Acts, pp. 41–58, Brill (1975)

Hall, N., Paul, L.A.: Causation and preemption. Philosophy of Science Today, pp. 100–130 (2003)

Halpern, J.Y.: Actual Causality. MIT Press, Cambridge (2016)

Horn, L.R.: Metalinguistic negation and pragmatic ambiguity. Language **61**(1), 121–174 (1985). https://doi.org/10.2307/413423

Laurence, R.: A Natural History of Negation, Horn, Center for the Study of Language and Information (1989)

Hume, D.: Philosophical Essays Concerning Human Understanding. 1st edn. Andrew Millar, London (1748)

Katzir, R.: Structurally-defined alternatives. Linguist. Philos. **30**(6), 669–690 (2007). https://doi.org/10.1007/s10988-008-9029-y. ISSN 1573–0549

Keenan, E.L., Stavi, J.: A semantic characterization of natural language determiners. Linguist. Philo. **9**(3), 253–326 (1986). https://doi.org/10.1007/BF00630273

Kratzer, A.: Conditionals. Chicago Linguist. Soc. **22**(2), 1–15 (1986)

Lewis, D.: Causation. J. Philos. **70**(17), 556–567 (1973). https://doi.org/10.2307/2025310

Linebarger, M.C.: Negative polarity and grammatical representation. Linguist. Philos. **10**(3), 325–387 (1987). https://doi.org/10.1007/BF00584131

Loew, C.: Causes as difference-makers for processes. Res. **98**(1), 89–106 (2019). https://doi.org/10.1111/phpr.12424

Magri, G.: A theory of individual-level predicates based on blind mandatory scalar implicatures. Nat. Lang. Semant. **17**(3), 245–297 (2009). https://doi.org/10.1007/s11050-009-9042-x

Moeschler, J.: Representation and metarepresentation in negation. In: Scott, K., Clark, B., Carston, R. (eds.) Relevance, Pragmatics and Interpretation, pp. 80–92. Cambridge (2019). https://doi.org/10.1017/9781108290593.008

Noh, E.-J.: Echo questions: metarepresentation and pragmatic enrichment. Linguist. Philos. pp. 603–628 (1998). https://doi.org/10.1023/A:1005361528891

Noh, E.-J.: Metarepresentation: A Relevance-theory Approach, vol. 69. John Benjamins Publishing (2000). https://doi.org/10.1075/pbns.69

Paul, L.A.: Keeping track of the time: emending the counterfactual analysis of causation. Analysis **58**(3), 191–198 (1998). https://doi.org/10.1111/1467-8284.00121

Kyburg Jr., H.E.: Judea Pearl: Causality. Cambridge University Press, Cambridge (2000)

Romoli, J.: The presuppositions of soft triggers aren't presuppositions. Semant. Linguist. Theory **21**, 236–256 (2011). https://doi.org/10.3765/salt.v21i0.2619

Romoli, J.: The presuppositions of soft triggers are obligatory scalar implicatures. J. Semant. **32**(2), 173–219 (2015). https://doi.org/10.1093/jos/fft017

Santorio, P.: Interventions in premise semantics. Philosophers' Imprint (2019). http://hdl.handle.net/2027/spo.3521354.0019.001

Schaffer, J.: Trumping preemption. J. Philos. **97**(4), 165–181 (2000). https://doi.org/10.2307/2678388

Schulz, K.: If you'd wiggled A, then B would've changed. Synthese **179**(2), 239–251 (2011). https://doi.org/10.1007/s11229-010-9780-9

Simons, M.: Disjunction and alternativeness. Linguist. Philos. **24**(5), 597–619 (2001). https://doi.org/10.1023/A:1017597811833

Stalnaker, R.C.: A Defense of Conditional Excluded Middle. pp. 87–104. Springer, Cham (1981). https://doi.org/10.1007/978-94-009-9117-0_4

Yablo, S.: De facto dependence. J. Philos. **99**(3), 130–148 (2002). https://doi.org/10.2307/3655640

Morphosyntactic Patterns Follow Monotonic Mappings

Sedigheh Moradi[✉][iD]

Stony Brook University, Stony Brook, NY, USA
sedigheh.moradi@stonybrook.edu

Abstract. Apart from being a system of structures, language is a system of relations. Understanding the particular regularities underlying these relations helps us predict both possibilities and gaps in linguistic organization. This paper follows Graf's work [13] in positing monotonicity as a substantial underlying restriction on possible patterns in morphosyntactic paradigms. This approach not only extends the notion of monotonicity outside semantics, but also combines this formal explanation with extralinguistic motivations. The tense hierarchy I propose for syncretism in verbal paradigms is independently motivated by Reichenbach's tense system [22]. The gender hierarchy used for gender resolution rules is directly extracted from the organization of the linguistic data. The restriction on both types of paradigms is readily explained by the fact that they only allow monotonic mappings from a base hierarchy to output forms.

Keywords: Monotonicity · Morphosyntax · Tense syncretism · Gender resolution rules

1 Introduction

It is generally accepted that language variability is not limitless and there are common restrictions on the attestibility of patterns. Out of this view grew the notion of universals in pursuit of explanations in linguistics [10]. Chomsky [8] classifies *linguistic universals* as formal and substantive. *Substantive universals* are the building blocks of grammar. These are particular regularities that the formal rules express. A *formal universal* is the property of having a grammar meeting a certain abstract condition.

The majority of linguistic work is concerned with formal universals, and this holds in particular for work grounded in mathematics or computation. For example, recent work on subregular complexity ([1, 14–16] and references therein) shows that many aspects of language—from phonology to morphology, syntax,

The work reported in this article is supported by the National Science Foundation under Grant No. BCS-1845344. Special thanks go to Thomas Graf for his support of this project and his valuable comments on earlier versions of this work.

D. Deng et al. (Eds.): TLLM 2020, LNCS 12564, pp. 147–165, 2020.
https://doi.org/10.1007/978-3-662-62843-0_8

and even semantics—are very limited in terms of their computational complexity. These limits can be used to explain why certain intuitively plausible patterns do not seem to occur across languages. However, this perspective cannot explain why there is a process of intervocalic voicing, but not one of intervocalic devoicing, since both processes would have exactly the same complexity. Here it is the substance of the involved elements that matters, rather than the complexity of this process. The central claim of this paper is that monotonicity can close this gap as it provides a fruitful, formally rigorous perspective on linguistic substance.

Strictly speaking, monotonicity is a semantic notion. However, it has been linked to many fundamental aspects of linguistic processing, reasoning, and grammar [17]. Monotonicity, as explained in this article, is used to provide a formal basis for certain morphosyntactic patterns. I present typological data mapping the attested variation in two morphosyntactic domains: tense syncretism and resolved gender agreement. I then show that all the attested patterns follow monotonic mappings.

Graf [13] proposes monotonicity as a formal universal of morphosyntax. The general idea is based on two criteria: I) each morphosyntactic domain comes with a base hierarchy (e.g. person: $1 < 2 < 3$), and II) the mappings from a hierarchy to surface forms must be monotonic. This dual specification puts this approach at a major advantage because it combines substantive universals (linguistic hierarchies) and formal universals (monotonicity) to give a tighter characterization of natural language.

This paper proceeds as follows. Section 2 outlines a brief description of the notion of monotonicity. Section 3 provides an analysis of tense syncretism based on verb paradigms. The interest in verb stem syncretism is three-fold: a) it is problematic for the more restrictive *ABA generalization of Bobaljik [3], based on which two forms cannot be identical to the exclusion of any forms between them. b) the attested patterns all follow monotonicity. c) the observed hierarchy of morphological tense is independently motivated by the logical temporal relations of Reichenbach [22].

Section 4 presents the typology of gender resolution rules. Here combining abstract algebra and the notion of monotonicity helps us understand the restricted set of the attested patterns. This suggests that there might be external ordering principles for gender, similar to what we see with tense. The crucial finding is that even though masculine and feminine genders should be ordered with respect to each other, the hierarchy does not favor one over another. In other words, in a 3-gender system, both $m < n < f$ and $f < n < m$ can keep the system monotonic. One way to look at it is that gender is assigned along a path with two end nodes (masculine and feminine). You can equally use the nodes to assign gender. Neuter, which means 'neither' in Latin, is always negatively defined as neither feminine nor masculine.

Section 5 concludes the paper.

2   Monotonicity

Monotonicity is a mathematical property that corresponds roughly to the intuitive notion of order preservation. Suppose an ordering relation $\leq$ over a set $\{p, q, r, s, \ldots\}$ such that $p \leq r \leq s$. Then in a monotonic function, one cannot map both p and s to some A without also mapping r to A.

Let us consider an intuitive example. Suppose A is a list of ordered numbers and B is a list of names in alphabetical order. Then a function f from A to B is monotonic *iff* it preserves the relative order of elements. If f maps 1 to *Paniz* while 5 is mapped to *Armina*, f is not monotonic (this can be seen in crossing branches). However, mapping all the numbers between 1 and 5 to *Armina* and all the numbers from 5 to 10 to *Paniz* still preserves the original order and the function is monotonic.

Now consider the *ABA generalization, which was proposed by Bobaljik [3] as an explanation for the absence of certain patterns in morphological paradigms. Suppose an order of positive-comparative-superlative in an adjectival paradigm. For the paradigm of the English adjective *bad*, the first stem is A (*bad*), the second stem is B (*wors(e)*), and the third stem is again B (*wors(t)*). Using this notion of suppletion, one can abstract away from linguistic forms to see the underlying structure, where the positive and superlative cannot share a root distinct from the comparative, hence *ABA. If $\leq$ is a linear order, monotonicity corresponds exactly to the *ABA generalization.

Another linguistically familiar example of linear monotonicity is the ban against crossing branches in autosegmental phonology [12]. Autosegmental structures are usually presented in tiers, and within each tier segments are linearly ordered. The ban on crossing branches assures that all mappings from tones to segments follow the linear order of the two tiers.

But monotonicity is more general because it is also defined for partial orders. Suppose that $p \leq r \leq s$ as before, and $q \leq p$, but q is unordered with respect to r and s. Then a monotonic mapping could map p and r to A but q and s to B.

(1)   *Monotonic mappings in a partially ordered structure*

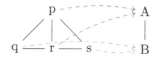

Monotonicity has already been used as an abstract condition on morphological paradigms to explain typological gaps in adjectival gradation, case syncretism, pronoun syncretism, Person Case Constraint and Gender Case Constraint [13,19]. In this paper, as we will see, the tense hierarchy is a partially ordered structure that is the same across all languages. But gender resolution rules can form both linear and partial structures depending on the number of gender values that are involved in resolution processes.

3   Tense Stem Syncretism

The *ABA generalization, introduced by Bobaljik [3], states that, given a fixed order of cells in a morphological paradigm, two cells cannot be syncretic to the exclusion of any cells between them. Bobaljik uses a specific notion of suppletion based on the form of the stems in a paradigm. In 2, I briefly explained this with an example from adjectival gradation: the positive and superlative cannot share a root distinct from the comparative. English uses the ABB pattern for the adjective *bad* (*bad - wors(e) wors(t)*), but neither English nor any other language can ever use an ABA pattern here.[1]

Bobaljik accounts for *ABA in terms of feature containment. Within the Containment Hypothesis [3], this gap is due to the fact that a superlative morpheme does not directly attach to the adjectival root because the superlative always embeds a comparative. This means that if the positive form has the feature [ADJECTIVE], then the comparative form will be [[ADJECTIVE] COMPARATIVE]] which is itself a subset of the superlative form [[[ADJECTIVE] COMPARATIVE] SUPERLATIVE].

While Bobaljik is mostly concerned with the absence of ABA patterns in adjectival gradation, he also briefly discusses tense syncretism in verb stems. He draws on Wiese's analysis [24] of ablaut in German verbs to explain German stem alternations within the same framework. Bobaljik [3] extends this presentation of verb stem alternations to English verbs. He notes that no verbs in English and German display ABA patterns if one assumes an order of present-participle-past (Table 1).

Table 1. Verb suppletion patterns in German & English

	PRS	PARTICIPLE	PAST	PATTERN
German	sprech-e	ge-sproch-en	sprach	ABC
	gieß-e	gegossen	**goß**	ABB
	geb-e	ge-**geb**-en	gab	AAB
English	sing	sung	sang	ABC
	shine	**shone**	**shone**	ABB
	come	**come**	came	AAB
	walk	**walk**ed	**walk**ed	AAA

---

[1] In adjectival paradigms AAB pattern, where positive and comparative share a root distinct from superlative, is also missing cross-linguistically [3]. The absence of this pattern does not concern us here.

Wiese and bobaljik explain the gap in the data, i.e., the unattested identicality of the present and the past to the exclusion of the participle, using the Containment Hypothesis. Given the hierarchy present < Perfect participle < past, the present tense is the default with no featural specifications ([]), the participle is contained in the past sharing the [past] feature with it; and [[] PAST] and the preterite, the highest in the hierarchy, contains the [finite] feature in addition to its [past] feature [[[] PAST] FINITE] [3].

Based on Bobaljik's approach, present and past are never syncretic to the exclusion of participle and more generally all tenses can be linearly ordered across languages so that no ABA patterns ever arise. The first assumption is compatible with the fact that there are Germanic languages which lack the past tense (preterite), which Bobaljik argues follows from its marked status. Furthermore, the participle can be used in constructions that are semantically related to the present tense. This leads us to conclude that it may share present features with the present, and past features with the preterite. "Such an intuition is particularly amenable to an analysis with overlapping decomposition [6], which could be represented schematically as [PRESENT], [PRESENT, PAST], [PAST]" [2]. In what follows, however, I show that Bobaljik's second prediction is only partially borne out once one considers a wider range of data: ABA patterns do arise if one also considers the future. This is problematic for Bobaljik's system, but can be readily explained via a partial order of morphological tenses in the monotonicity framework of Graf [13]. Crucially, this partial order is induced by the tense system of Reichenbach [22] and thus arises from third factor principles [7].

3.1   Corpus of Tense Syncretism

In order to extract the following data, I have used an opportunity sample of tense syncretism in the verbal paradigms of more than 20 languages. The languages under scrutiny represent a typologically diverse sample belonging to the following families: Altaic, Germanic, Indo-Iranian, Romance, and Slavic, among others. For simplicity, I assume that two tenses have distinct stems if the stems differ for at least one person/number cell. This may result in multiple patterns in a single language. Also keep in mind that the criterion for stem change is the specific notion of suppletion used by Bobaljik and introduced in the previous section.

The variety of ways verbal stems are paradigmatically related vary a lot, even within a language. The language sample I studied rendered the following 10 patterns of verb stem syncretism (Table 2) with an ordering of past-participle-present-future.

In order to better understand the nature of the attested patterns and anticipate the kind of hierarchy we need, let's take a look at the unattested patterns. The total number of possible patterns for a paradigm with 4 cells is 15 (Bell number of 4), from which we already have 10. The remaining 5 unattested patterns are given in Table 3.

Out of all logically possible patterns, only 5 are unattested: ABAX (where future is A, B, or C), ABBA, and ABCA. The absence of ABAX patterns shows

Table 2. Attested patterns of tense syncretism

	Pattern	Example	past	participle	present	future
(1)	AAAA	Turkish	**geldi**	**gelmiʃ**	**gelijor**	**geleçek**
(2)	AABB	Japanese	**ʃita**	**ʃiteita**	**suru**	**suru**
(3)	AABA	Serbo-Croat	**hteo sam**	**hteo**	**hoću**	**htećru**
(4)	ABCD	German	warf	geworfen	wirf	werfen
(5)	AABC	Sindhi	**wayo**	**wayo ho**	wanje tʰo	wiindo
(6)	AAAB	French	**all**	**all**	**all**	ir
(7)	ABCC	Kurdish	xward	xoria	**xweid**	**xweid**
(8)	ABCB	Spanish	fu	Øi	v	Øir
(9)	ABBB	English	went	**gone**	**go**	will **go**
(10)	ABBC	French	vin	**ven**	**ven**	viend-r

Table 3. Description of Unattested Patterns with PST-PRF-PRS-FUT order

	Pattern Description	Linear Order
(1)	past = present; participle = future	ABAB
(2)	past = future; participle = present	ABBA
(3)	past = present = future; Separate root for participle	ABAA
(4)	past = present; Distinct roots for participle and future	ABAC
(5)	past = future; Distinct roots for participle and present	ABCA

that syncretism of present and past to the exclusion of participle is not attested. The behavior of future is problematic, though. While future is never syncretic with past to the exclusion of either present or participle, AABA and ABCB violate the *ABA generalization. But if one allows for partial orders, ABA patterns with future can be accounted for in terms of the monotonicity constraint [13].

Note that there is no way of totally ordering all four tenses such that there are no ABA configurations. Consider the attested pattern where past, participle and future are syncretic to the exclusion of present, as is the case in Persian and Serbo-Croatian. This pattern will be AABA with a PST-PRF-PRS-FUT ordering and ABAA with a PST-PRS-PRF-FUT ordering, both of which violate the ABA generalization. Our linear order won't violate *ABA only if it posits present at either end of the order. But any such order will be problematic for other attested patterns leading to the violation of *ABA. Once a specific connection between semantic and morphological tenses is made, the availability of some ABA patterns is due to the fact that the semantic relations between morphological tenses only induce a partial ordering.

Suppose that present ≤ participle ≤ past, and present ≤ future, but future is unordered with respect to participle and past. Then future can be syncretic with any one of the three tenses to the exclusion of others, allowing for a limited range of what appear to be ABA patterns. This is illustrated in Fig. 1 for the attested *ABA violations AABA and ABCB. The unattested ABAX patterns do not obey monotonicity (crossing branches).

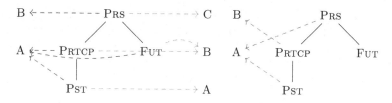

Fig. 1. Monotonic (left) and non-monotonic (right) mappings in tense syncretism

This partial hierarchy might seem obvious given that the future and the participle both are intuitively associated with the present. However, Reichenbach's tense relations [22] provides a logical framework to motivate this morphological order.

3.2   Semantic Motivation: Reichenbach's System

In Reichenbach's system [22], tense denotes a three-way relation between speech time (S), event time (E) and reference time (R). The introduction of the notion of reference time is considered Reichenbach's greatest contribution to the study of temporal relations. The position of R relative to S distinguishes the three tenses: 'past', 'present', and 'future'. The present time is the default setting in which $S = E = R$. Gradual shifts from this default point builds a partial hierarchy of temporal relations. R is located before S in the past ($R < S$) and after S in the future ($R > S$).

The position of E with respect to R distinguishes three further possibilities: 'posterior' ($R < E$, viewing the situation E from an earlier point – looking forward), 'simple' ($R = E$, used for the coincidence of R and E) and 'anterior' ($R > E$, viewing the situation E from a later point – looking backward).

In the case of perfect, E is located before R. In past perfect, R precedes S ($E < R$ and $R < S$). In present perfect, R overlaps S ($E < R$ and $R = S$). Likewise, in future perfect, both S and E precede R ($S < R$ and $E < R$).

All possible combinations involving a single time of speech (S) include three simple tenses (where $R = E$), five anterior tenses (where $E < R$), and five posterior tenses (where $R < E$). Thus, the temporal system of a language could include up to 13 tenses. The actual number of tense realizations in each language depends on the number of grammaticalized combinations [22].

Here I argue that in addition to absolute tenses (present, past, future), perfect should also be part of the hierarchy of morphological tenses. Reichenbach and Comrie agree that perfect cannot be viewed as a canonical aspect since it tells us nothing about the internal temporal organization of the situation [9]. Perfect is like tense in that it locates an eventuality relative to some reference point. In the sentence *Paniz has eaten the cake*, there is an eventuality to the act of eating: it is done in the past. This makes the present perfect very similar to the simple past. In Reichenbach's terms, the simple past expresses a temporal precedence between the speech time and the reference time, while the perfect expresses a temporal precedence between the event time and the reference time. Another point of difference between the present perfect and the simple past will be apparent once we add a past-oriented adverb to our example: *Paniz has eaten the cake yesterday.* It is unexpected for an anterior temporal relation to be incompatible with a past-oriented adverb (Klein [18] refers to this situation as the "present participle puzzle").

More in support of positioning perfect among tense relations is the fact that perfect refers to a bundle of meanings that is maintained no matter what absolute tense it is associated with. Generally, three main readings are associated with perfects: The *universal reading* asserts that an eventuality holds for an interval of time; in the *experiential reading*, the eventuality holds for a proper subset of an interval; and finally, in a *resultative reading* the result of the eventuality holds at the speech time [21]. These readings make different claims about the location of the underlying eventuality, although in some languages only a subset of them is allowed. For example, in Greek perfect participles are marked as perfective and as a result the universal reading is not possible [21].

With these facts in order, I include perfects as part of the tense system (though this should not deny their aspectual properties in some languages).[2] Once one considers only those tenses that are morphologically realized across languages, the partial hierarchy of tenses emerges clearly (Fig. 2).

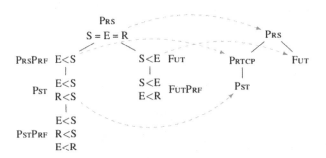

Fig. 2. The hierarchy of morphological tense motivated by Reichenbach's tense system

There are three reasons for identifying participle with present perfect. 1) The present tense refers to the default situation from which other tenses represent deviations [5]. Hence the past perfect and the future perfect follow from the semantics of the present perfect, combined with an account of the past tense and the future tense [20].

2) The claim in (1) is verifiable by comparing the frequency rates of the perfects. The future perfect seems to be the least frequent among the perfects.

---

[2] There is always a great danger resulting from terminology. It is likely that, in some descriptive traditions, the term perfect is used for an aspectual rather than a tense distinction. This is true in the Semitic tradition, for example, where perfect and imperfect are used for what is likely perfective and imperfective. The *-ive* distinction is usually aspectual.

A corpus-based study of English perfect constructions show that the present perfect is the most frequently used type of perfect in English [4].

3) The hierarchy of tense is an implicational hierarchy; if a language has a past perfect or a future perfect, it is very likely that it also has a present perfect (whereas the reverse does not necessarily hold). In this hierarchy, the present perfect has the least distance from the default point ($E = R = S$) with only one shift ($E < R, S$). The future perfect ($S < R < E$) and the past perfect ($E < R < S$) both undergo two shifts from the default. This results in the hierarchical ordering of the tenses.

In Sum, I have shown that the future tense does give rise to apparent *ABA violations in verbal paradigms. But these are expected if one combines monotonicity [13]—a more general notion of *ABA— with a partial order of tenses in the spirit of Reichenbach [22]. This establishes a strong upper bound on the range of typological variation, with the only permitted but unattested pattern being syncretism of the past and future to the exclusion of other tenses.[3]

In the next section, I will introduce the variations of gender resolution rules as yet another instance where monotonicity sets a boundary on the attestability of certain morphological patterns.

4   Gender Resolution Rules

Resolved agreement is a term used to describe the predicate agreement with a subject made up of coordinated elements. The rules that determine the forms to be used are called resolution rules. Gender resolution rules are very diverse. This is mainly because they do not always have a unified semantic justification [11]. In French for instance, if two nominal heads, one feminine and one masculine, are conjoined, the resolved form is always masculine. Thus the resolution rules in French favor masculine agreement as the default gender. This is different from Icelandic or inanimate coordination in Romanian where neuter and feminine are favored, respectively.

(2)   [le garçon et la fille]   sont compétents
      [the boy.M and the girl.F] are competent.M.PL
      'The boy and the girl are competent.'   French

(3)   [frægð-∅   og fram-i]   eru tvíeggj-uð
      [fame.F.SG and success.M.SG] are double.edged-N.PL
      'Fame and success are double-edged.'   Icelandic (Friðjónsson 1991: 90)

(4)   [uşa   şi peretele]   ele...
      [door.F.the and wall.M.the] theyF.PL...
      'The door and the wall, they...'   Romanian (Corbett 1991: 288)

---

[3] Like the absence of AAB patterns in adjectival gradation, this might be due to independent factors [7].

4.1   Possibilities and Patterns

Just like tense syncretism, resolved gender stands out for how small the number of realized systems is relative to how many logically conceivable options there. In order to fully appreciate this point, let us take a moment to look at the combinatorics of resolved gender. Given k possible genders, there are k ways for any two genders and k^{k^2} resolution systems. Assuming that the order of elements in a coordination does not matter, the number of resolution systems equals $k^{k(k+1)/2}$. This is explained below using *triangular numbers*.

Assume that (a + b) is our coordination and the number of gender values in different languages are the exponents. In each line, the binomial expansion of each expression is given. We then abstract out of the mathematical details and replace them by a dot (•).

(5)   *Triangular numbers*

$$(a+b)^0 \qquad 1 \qquad\qquad •$$
$$(a+b)^1 \qquad a \qquad b \qquad\qquad • \quad •$$
$$(a+b)^2 \qquad a^2 \quad 2ab \quad b^2 \qquad • \quad • \quad •$$
$$(a+b)^3 \quad a^3 \quad 3a^2b \quad 3ab^2 \quad b^3 \quad • \quad • \quad • \quad •$$

The number of dots in each triangular pattern is its *Triangular Number*. The first triangle, a gender-less system (g = 0) has just one dot. The second triangle (g = 1) has another row with 2 extra dots, making $1 + 2 = 3$ dots. The third triangle (g = 2) has another row with 3 extra dots, making $1 + 2 + 3 = 6$ dots. The fourth (g = 3) has $1 + 2 + 3 + 4 = 10$ dots.

The rule for calculating any triangular number is as follows. First, we rearrange the dots as below (Fig. 3):

Fig. 3. Triangular numbers are the number of dots in each triangular pattern.

Then double the number of dots, and form them into a rectangle which has the same number of rows but has one extra column (to make this clear the two triangles are shown in green and red) (Fig. 4).

Fig. 4. Doubling the number of dots in each triangular pattern to form a rectangle. (Color figure online)

Now it is easy to see that the number of dots in a rectangle is $n(n+1)$ and the number of dots in a triangle is half that, i.e., $n(n+1)/2$.

For languages with 2 genders, this yields $2^{2(2+1)/2} = 2^{6/2} = 2^3 = 8$ possibilities. Yet only two patterns are attested in our sample of seven 2-gender languages (French, Spanish, Latvian, Hindi, Panjubi, Modern Hebrew and Romanian). The same happens in 3-gender languages: out of $3^{3(3+1)/2} = 3^{6/2} = 3^6 = 729$ possibilities only 6 are realized. The space of logical possibilities quickly becomes quite large, as more and more genders are added: 8, 729, $1,048,576$ (million), $30,517,578,125$ (billion), $21,936,950,640,377,856$ (quadrillion), etc.

By definition, if A is some algebraic structure, the set of all functions X to the domain of A can be turned into an algebraic structure of the same type in an analogous way. Let us assume an underlying hierarchy of $f < n < m$ and construct a pointwise algebra to represent various gender combinations. At the top of the algebraic construction $\langle m, m \rangle$ stands for the combination of two masculine genders. At the bottom, $\langle f, f \rangle$ represents the coordination of two feminine noun phrases. All other combinations are ordered between these two nodes. Since in a coordination the order of the coordinated elements does not matter (i.e., $\langle m, n \rangle = \langle n, m \rangle$), we remove all the symmetrically repeated nodes from the previous algebra to arrive at a simplified hierarchy.

(6)   *The algebra of gender combinations*

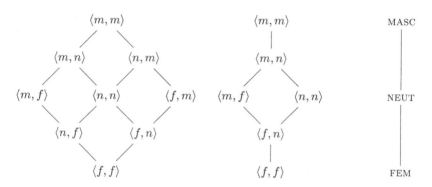

Gender assignment lacks an overall semantic justification; thus the fact that there is an overwhelming uniformity of hierarchies across the available data sample is quite impressive.

4.2   Gender Resolution Patterns

The resolution systems discussed here are primarily based on Corbett's 1991 textbook on gender, which maps out the known variation in the gender systems of the world. It includes a comprehensive survey of gender systems with data from over 200 languages, which makes for a great typological study. I have filled the gaps in data from other sources on individual languages. Here I present five representative languages: French, Slovene, Latin, Tamil and Archi. French and Slovene are representative of languages that are argued to have syntactic resolution rules. Tamil and Archi are examples of a semantic type resolution. And finally Latin is described as a mixed type system where meaning and form are both involved in the patterns of resolution [11].

French. Let us start with the simplest gender system we can consider. In French there are two genders, feminine and masculine. If in a coordination the conjuncts are of the same gender, then that gender will be used as the resolved form. If one conjunct is masculine and another is feminine, then a masculine form is used. Languages like French are quite common, e.g., Spanish, Latvian, Hindi, Italian, Panjabi, and Modern Hebrew, etc (Table 4).

Table 4. Gender values and resolution in French

SG	PL		MSC	FEM
MSC	MSC	MSC	M	M
FEM	FEM	FEM	M	F

We start by building a hierarchical algebraic construction based on an underlying hierarchy of gender. Assuming $f < m$, we construct a pointwise algebra to represent the possible gender combinations. At the top of the algebra $\langle m, m \rangle$ stands for the combination of two masculine genders. At the bottom, $\langle f, f \rangle$ represents the coordination of two feminine noun phrases. The two other combinations are ordered between these two nodes. These two sets are the same, so we remove one of them to arrive at a more simplified hierarchy.

(7)   *The gender hierarchy in French*

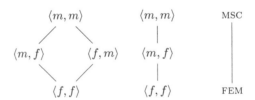

Elements of this algebraic construction are then mapped into a hierarchy of plural genders. As we can see these mappings are all monotonic. In languages with a gender structure like French, it does not matter which gender is higher in the hierarchy. If you flip this structure you get the same kinds of mappings but in the reverse order.

(8)   *Monotonic gender mappings in French*

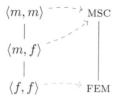

Slovene.   Slovene has three numbers and three genders. The predicate agree-ment forms are given below. In this table, *bil* is the past active participle of the verb 'be' [11]. The dual forms will result only if the two conjoined noun phrases are singular. The gender resolution works the same for both dual and plural conjunctions. The gender system in Serbo-Croatian is similar, except that there is no dual there (Table 5).

Table 5. Gender values in Slovene

	SG	DL	PL	
MSC	∅	a	i	MSC
FEM	a	i	e	FEM
NEUT	o		a	NEUT

A masculine noun conjoined with a masculine will resolve in masculine. The same way, a feminine noun conjoined with a feminine will resolve in feminine. But a masculine noun conjoined with a feminine or with a neuter resolves in a masculine predicate. If a feminine and a neuter are conjoined, you will still find the masculine agreement on the predicate.

In order to explore the hierarchical structure of Slovene, once again we start from an underlying hierarchy of $f < n < m$ to construct a pointwise algebra and represent the gender combinations. In the simplified structure, all repeated nodes are removed.

(9) *The gender hierarchy in Slovene*

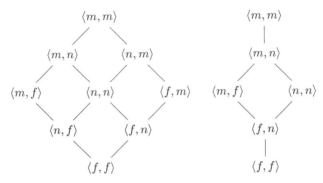

(10) *Monotonic mappings in Slovene*

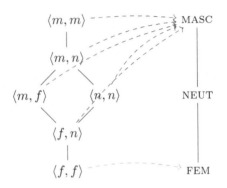

In a sense, the resolved agreement in Slovene (and similar languages like Serbo-Croatian) favors the masculine. Feminine is only used if all conjuncts are feminine, and the neuter is not used at all. Interestingly, we will have the same monotonic mappings if we flip over the structure along with the hierarchy. As long as the neuter is in the middle, all the mappings are indeed monotonic.

Latin. There are three genders in this language: masculine, feminine and neuter. Conjuncts of the same gender resolve in a form from the same gender. If conjuncts are of different genders, though, the criterion is purely semantic. Here the resolved form to be used depends on whether the nouns denote persons or not.

(11) *Resolution Rules in Latin*
      a. Masculine is used if all conjuncts are masculine;
      b. Feminine is used if all conjuncts are feminine;
      c. Masculine is used if all conjuncts are human;
      d. Otherwise, neuter is used.

The rules are ordered in this way because the masculine and the feminine genders are not semantically restricted to humans. This means that a human feminine in conjunction with a human masculine resolve in masculine rather than the default neuter (Table 6).

Table 6. Non-human and human resolution in Latin

Non-human	MSC	FEM	NEUT	Human	MSC	FEM	NEUT
MSC	M	N	N	MSC	M	M	M
FEM	N	F	N	FEM	M	F	M
NEUT	N	N	N	NEUT	M	M	M

In order to show these mappings, we divide the rules into two sets of human and non-human rules. Within each sub-system, all the mappings are monotonic.

(12) *Monotonic mappings in Latin non-human (left) and human (right)*

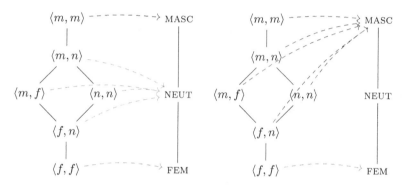

Tamil.   Dravidian languages are clear examples of semantic resolution. Tamil has three genders: masculine (for nouns denoting male rationals), feminine (for nouns denoting female rationals) and neuter (for non-rationals). The resolved forms, however, result in two forms only: rational and neuter.[4]

Table 7. Gender values in Tamil

SG	PL
MSC	RATIONAL
FEM	
NEUT	NEUT

If, in a coordination structure, all conjuncts denote rationals, the rational form is used. If all conjuncts denote neuters, the neuter form should be used.

---

[4] The resolution rules in Telugu, another Dravidian language, is the same as Tamil. This happens despite the fact that in Telugu, feminine and neuter are not distinguished in the singular.

The combination of a rational (feminine or masculine) with a neuter is generally avoided. But if ever allowed, the rational form is used (Table 7).

(13)   *Resolution Rules in Tamil*
        a. Rational is used if all conjuncts are rational;
        b. Neuter is used if all conjuncts are non-rational;
        c. Otherwise, rational is used, although an alternative construction is preferred.

Over a hierarchy that places rational (including masculine and feminine) over neuter, all the mappings from controller genders to target genders are monotonic.

(14)   *Monotonic mappings in Tamil*

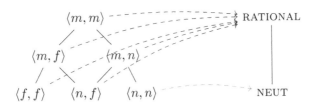

The resolution rules in Tamil are not based on formal gender values but rather follow the two semantic values, RATIONAL and NEUTER. This means that there are only two classes of nouns in the plural. Hence we can reconstruct a hierarchy that only includes those two values in a linear order. The mappings over this hierarchy are all still monotonic.

(15)   *Monotonic semantic mappings in Tamil*

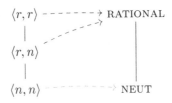

Archi.   Caucasian languages are also famous for the semantic distinctions they make. Archi is a North-East Caucasian language (Table 8).

(16)   *Archi gender system*
        I. male humans: God and other spiritual beings
        II. females
        III. most animals and some inanimate nouns
        IV. some animals and most inanimate nouns

Table 8. Gender values in Archi

	SG	PL	
MSC	w	b/ib	rational
FEM	d		
ANIMATE	b	ib	irrational
INANIMATE	t		

(17)   *Resolution Rules in Archi*
   a. I/II is used, if there is at least one rational conjunct (R);
   b. Otherwise, III/IV is used (IR).

If the rational gender (including masculine and feminine) resides higher on the hierarchy relative to the irrational, then the mappings are monotonic.

(18)   *Monotonic mappings in Archi*

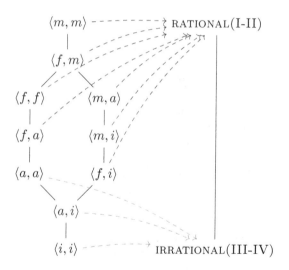

Even though this account seems to work, gender and animacy are not the defining factors in Archi resolution. If we reduce the structure of conjoined noun phrases to rational and irrational entities, then a simple pattern emerges.

(19)   *Monotonic semantic mappings in Archi*

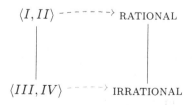

In Sum, I have shown that even though gender assignment in different languages greatly vary, the emerging gender hierarchies are substantially the same. The distinction made between the syntactic and semantic gender systems boils down to those gender values that are used in the resolved plural forms. In a syntactic system, e.g., French and Slovene, resolution rules are based on formal gender values. These systems mostly include feminine and masculine genders. As we saw, the nature of mappings remains the same as long as the feminine and masculine values reside on the two end nodes of the gender hierarchy. In a semantic system, e.g., Tamil and Archi, resolution rules are based on semantic values (RATIONAL vs IRRATIONAL), which results in a condensed hierarchy of gender that only includes those two values. Regardless of the hierarchy, in both system types, the resolution rules follow monotonic mappings from the base hierarchies to the output forms. Similarly, Latin, as a mixed gender type, combines two subsystems based on a semantic feature (the property of being human). Essentially for our account, both semantic sub-types use monotonic mappings.

5   Conclusion

In this article, we saw that the restrictions on morphosyntactic paradigms are systematically formalizable and have extralinguistic explanations. I have used a broad range of cross linguistic data to show this within two specific domains: tense syncretism in verb paradigms and resolved gender agreement. To this end, I have used the monotonicity account of Graf [13] that is based on an underlying hierarchy and the simple requirement that the mappings from these hierarchies to output forms are monotonic. I have derived the tense hierarchy from the logically rigorous framework of Reichenbach [22], while the gender hierarchy is directly motivated by typological data [11]. The findings reported in this article lend further empirical support to the idea that monotonicity is a linguistic universal that extends beyond semantics.

The major advantage of the presented account is that it combines substantive universals (linguistic hierarchies) and formal universals (monotonicity) to give a tighter characterization of morphosyntactic phenomena. Future research on this topic will be pursued with two main goals. First is to expand the range of morphosyntactic domains which requires careful treatment of typological data and motivated hierarchies. And secondly to integrate monotonicity with notions of subregular complexity in order to better understand the properties of attestable linguistic patterns.

References

1. Aksenova, A., Graf, T., Moradi, S.: Morphotactics as tier-based strictly local dependencies. In: Proceedings of the 14th Sigmorphon Workshop on Computational Research in Phonetics, Phonology, and Morphology, pp. 121–130 (2016)
2. Andersson, S.: (*)ABA in Germanic verbs. Glossa: J. General Linguist. **3**(1), 119 (2018). https://doi.org/10.5334/gjgl.733

3. Bobaljik, J.: Universals in Comparative Morphology: Suppletion, Superlatives, and the Structure of Words, vol. 50. MIT Press (2012)
4. Bowie, J., Aarts, B.: Change in the English infinitival perfect construction. The Oxford Handbook of the History of English, pp. 200–210 (2012)
5. Bybee, J., Perkins, R., Pagliuca, W.: The Evolution of Grammar: Tense, Aspect, and Modality in the Languages of the World, vol. 196. University of Chicago Press (1994)
6. Caha, P.: How (not) to derive a *ABA: the case of Blansitt's generalisation. Glossa **2**(84), 1–32 (2017). https://doi.org/10.5334/gjgl.348
7. Chomsky, N.: Three factors in language design. Linguistic Inquiry **36**, 1–22 (2005)
8. Chomsky, N.: Aspects of the Theory of Syntax. MITPress, Cambridge (1965)
9. Comrie, B.: On Reichenbach's approach to tense. In Proceedings of the 17th Meeting of the Chicago Linguistic Society (CLS), vol. 17, pp. 24–30 (1981)
10. Cooreman A., Goyvaerts D.: Universals in human language. a historical perspective. In: Revue belge de philologie et d'histoire, tome 58, fasc. 3, pp. 615–638 (1980). Langues et litteratures modernes - Moderne taalen letterkunde. https://doi.org/10.3406/rbph.1980.3295
11. Corbett, G.: Gender. Cambridge University Press, Cambridge (1991)
12. Goldsmith, J.: Autosegmental Phonology. MIT Press, London (1976)
13. Graf, T.: Monotonicity as an effective theory of morphosyntactic variation. FSMNLP/MOL special issue (2019)
14. Graf, T.: A Subregular bound on the complexity of lexical quantifiers. In: Schloder, J., McHugh, D., Roelofsen, F. (eds.) Proceedings of the 22nd Amsterdam Colloquium, pp. 455–464 (2019)
15. Graf, T.: Why movement comes for free once you have adjunction. In: Edmiston, D., et al. (eds.) Proceedings of CLS 53, pp. 117–136 (2018)
16. Heinz, J.: The computational nature of phonological generalizations. In: Hyman, L., Plank, F. (eds.) Phonological Typology, Phonetics and Phonology, chapter 5, pp. 126–195. Mouton De Gruyter (2018)
17. Icard, T.F., Moss, L.S.: Recent progress on monotonicity. In: Linguistic Issues in Language Technology (2014)
18. Klein, W.: The present perfect puzzle. Language **68**, 525–552 (1992)
19. Moradi, S.: *ABA generalizes to monotonicity. In: Baird, M., Pesetsky, J. (eds.) Proceedings of NELS 49, vol. 2. GSLA (2019)
20. Musan, R.: The present perfect in German: outline of its semantic composition. Nat. Lang. Linguistic Theory **25**, 355–401 (2001)
21. Pancheva, R.: The aspectual makeup of perfect participles and the interpretations of the Perfect. In: Perfect Explorations, vol. 2. Walter de Gruyter (2003)
22. Reichenbach, H.: Elements of Symbolic Logic. MacMillan, New York (1947)
23. Sapir, E.: Language: An Introduction to the Study of Speech. Harcourt, Brace, New York (1921)
24. Wiese, B.: Form and function of verb ablaut in contemporary standard German. In: Sackmann, R. (ed.) Studies in Integrational Linguistics. John Benjamins (2005)

Negative Polarity Additive Particles

Andreea C. Nicolae[(⊠)] [iD]

Leibniz Zentrum Allgemeine Sprachwissenschaft, Berlin, Germany
nicolae@leibniz-zas.de
https://sites.google.com/site/andreeanicolae/

Abstract. Many languages have pairs of additive markers that exhibit a common morphological core. This paper focuses on the Romanian pair *și* and *nici* and offers an analysis that derives their distribution and interpretation. The crux of the analysis is the claim that *nici* spells out the negative marker N and the additive particle ADD; N is argued to contribute the negative polarity component while ADD is assumed to make the same contribution as the positive particle, *și*.

Keywords: Additive marker · Polarity · Exhaustification · Alternatives · Coordination · Scalarity · Presupposition

1 Introduction

1.1 Data of Interest

The goal of this paper is to present a novel account of additive particles like *too* and *either*, with a special focus on their Romanian counterparts *și* and *nici*. We first begin with an overview of their distribution and interpretation when acting as additive particles. The positive additive marker *și*, like English *too*, appears predominantly in positive contexts where it makes the additive contribution that the predication holds of at least one other alternative to its associate. In the second sentence in (1), the additive component is that Maria drinks something else besides beer, namely wine.[1]

(1)   Maria bea   vin. Bea   și   bere.
       Maria drinks wine. drinks ADD beer
       'Maria drinks wine. She drinks beer too.'

---

[1] All Romanian data reported in this paper are the author's, a native speaker of Romanian, and have been checked with at least one other person for both grammaticality and acceptability judgements.

I am indebted to Gennaro Chierchia, Luka Crnič, Anamaria Fălăuș, Uli Sauerland and Yasu Sudo for their time and knowledge shared while discussing these issues with me, as well as the many anonymous reviewers who have assessed this work in its various previous forms and the editors of TLLM2020. This research was supported by the German Science Foundation (DFG) via grant NI 1850/2-1.

© Springer-Verlag GmbH Germany, part of Springer Nature 2020
D. Deng et al. (Eds.): TLLM 2020, LNCS 12564, pp. 166–182, 2020.
https://doi.org/10.1007/978-3-662-62843-0_9

Note that the use of *și* in the second sentence would not have been felicitous in the absence of an antecedent proposition such as the one provided by the first sentence specifying what else Maria drank.[2] For this reason, the additive component, which is generally argued to be a presupposition, is more specifically referred to as the antecedent requirement since the felicity conditions on the use of such additive particles is dependent on there being an antecedent in the discourse.

Și can also occur with negation, but when it does, it is usually as a negative answer in response to a possibly implicit question such as (2). This is the case regardless of the locality of negation, as shown by the lack of contrast between the two sentences in (2a-b). Note that here too, as in the case in (1), the antecedent proposition must be positive, namely that Maria wants wine.

(2)   Știu că vrea apă, dar vrea și bere?
       know that wants water, but want ADD beer?
       'I know she wants water, but does want beer too?'

   a. Nu vrea și bere.
       not wants ADD beer
       'She doesn't want beer too.'

   b. Nu cred că vrea și bere.
       not think that want ADD beer
       'I don't think she wants beer too.'

Contrast this with the negative marker *nici*, which, like the English additive *either*, must co-occur with negation and requires a negative antecedent.[3] The use of *nici* in (3) conveys that Paul drank neither beer, nor another salient alternative to beer, wine in the case below.

(3)   Paul *(nu) bea vin. *(Nu) bea nici bere.
       Paul not drinks wine. Not drinks N-ADD beer.
       'Paul doesn't drink wine. He doesn't drink beer either.'

1.2   The Goal of This Paper

In a recent analysis that aims to account for the distribution of English *too* and *either* [4], Ahn takes *too* to denote an anaphoric conjunction and *either* an anaphoric disjunction. By taking *either* to denote a disjunction, she argues that its restricted distribution can be explained by the same mechanism deriving the restricted distribution of other elements with disjunctive/existential semantics, e.g. the English negative polarity item (NPI) *any*. While this analysis captures the data, it is arguably not well suited for the Romanian data for the

---

[2] At the same time, the use of *și* seems obligatory, as has been pointed out to be the case with additive particles more generally. This issue has been investigated at length in [6,31,41] and we will return to it briefly in the analysis section.

[3] The antecedent proposition does not have to include the sentential negation, unlike the host proposition. It is enough if it's claimed that Paul dislikes wine.

following reason. The morphology of the Romanian particles suggests a common core to the positive and negative particles, and this generalization persists cross-linguistically, with other examples including Italian *anche* and *neanche* and Serbian *i* and *ni*. Given that the positive additive marker is commonly also employed as a conjunctive marker cross-linguistically, offering an additive, and thus a conjunctive semantics to both the positive and negative markers is desirable.

The goal of this paper is to present such an analysis, one which takes both markers to make the same additive contribution. I will propose that both *și* and *nici* contribute additivity, with the negative marker furthermore carrying an additional component that delivers the negative restriction; in this way I will depart from Ahn's proposal which takes only the positive particle to contribute additivity. This analysis will be shown to parallel that of other duals in the QP domain, such as positive existential quantifiers and NPIs, like *some* and *any*.

The paper is organized as follows. Section 2 lays out the analysis of the positive additive marker, accounting for its distribution and interpretation in both positive and negative contexts, as well as the antecedent requirement. Section 3 presents the analysis of the negative additive marker and shows how this analysis can account for its interpretation and its restricted distribution. Section 4 concludes with a number of open questions and directions for future research.

2   The Positive Additive Marker

2.1   Deriving the Additive Meaning

Szabolcsi in [46] claims that "*too* is a functional element whose only mission is to induce an additive presupposition." I follow her and previous authors [6,34,35] and assume that the additive marker is semantically vacuous but signals that an alternative proposition where the additive *too* is replaced by the exclusive particle *only* is not true. I will implement this intuition within an exhaustification framework by arguing that additive markers trigger obligatory exhaustification with respect to an alternative proposition containing a silent exhaustification operator. Before turning to the details of this analysis, I provide a very quick overview of how exhaustification operators work.

The exhaustification framework takes certain inferences, in particular scalar implicatures, to be derived in the grammar via silent operators [12]. Implicatures are claimed to arise as the result of a syntactic ambiguity resolution in favor of an LF which contains a covert exhaustivity operator EXH (building on work in [9, 16,25,44], among others). Scalar elements (e.g. the disjunction and conjunction particles) activate alternatives and the grammar integrates these alternatives within the meaning of the utterance by means of this exhaustification operator which is similar to overt *only* in that it negates all stronger alternatives. There are two important differences however: (i) unlike *only*, this operator also asserts its prejacent, and (ii) stronger alternatives are negated as long as no contradiction results when their negation is conjoined with the assertion.[4] These two points are encoded in its semantics below where IE(p, $Alt(p)$) is meant to pick out those alternatives which are innocently excludable, that is, whose negation does not lead to a contradiction:

(4)   EXH(p) = $p \wedge \forall q[q \in$ IE(p, Alt(p))$\rightarrow \neg q]$
       where IE(p, Alt(p)) = $\cap$ {C' $\subset Alt$(p): C' is a max subset of Alt(p) s.t.
       {$\neg q$:$q \in$C'}$\cup$\{p\} is consistent}

Let us consider how the scalar implicature associated with disjunction is generated. The first question to ask is what the alternatives to the disjunction are. Besides the conjunctive alternative, the individual disjuncts are also taken to be relevant, following Sauerland's proposal in [42]. Applying EXH delivers the strengthened exclusive interpretation that only one of the disjuncts is true by negating the one innocently excludable alternative, the conjunctive alternative. Note that negating either of the disjuncts would result in a contradiction.

(5)   LF: EXH [p$\vee$q]
   a. Alt(p$\vee$q) = {p$\vee$q, p, q, p$\wedge$q}
   b. ⟦EXH [p$\vee$q]⟧ = (p$\vee$q)$\wedge\neg$(p$\wedge$q)

Returning to the case at hand, I will argue that the alternative to *şi p* is EXH *p*, as in (6a). I assume going forward that the additive particle spells out ADD. Since the alternative EXH *p*, which amounts to *p and nothing else*, is stronger than *p* itself, it gets negated, as in (6b). The result is the expected conjunctive meaning that both the host proposition *p* and an alternative are true: *p and not only p*.[5] The intuition should be clear: the use of the additive particle is meant to mark that an exclusive interpretation was not intended. This is also entirely consistent with the observation that the use of additive markers is obligatory when the additive presupposition is satisfied [6,41].

(6)   LF: EXH [ADD p]
   a. Alt(ADD p) = {ADD p, EXH p} = {p, p$\wedge\neg$q}
   b. ⟦EXH [ADD p]⟧ = p$\wedge\neg$(p$\wedge\neg$q) = p$\wedge$q

It's been noted that additive particles have an anaphoric component by Heim and Kripke in [26,32], which amounts to the requirement that the alternative of which the predication holds needs to have been mentioned recently or be part of the "active context." In other words, a sentence like *John is having dinner right now too.* is not acceptable out of the blue even though we all know that somebody other than John is surely having dinner right now as well. One way to think of this requirement is in terms of what alternatives are relevant (or active,

---

[4] There is interesting ongoing work discussing the differences between *only* and EXH, specifically as they relate to these two points [5, among others].

[5] This does not go against a structural view of alternative selection based on complexity considerations since we are considering alternatives to ADD *p* rather than to plain *p* [17,29].

depending on your terminology) in the context. For the alternative proposition EXH p to be distinct from the prejacent, p, there needs to be an alternative proposition q relevant in the discourse. Assuming that only relevant alternatives are considered in the calculation of implicatures, this anaphoric component falls out naturally.

Why should additive markers induce obligatory exhaustification? While I cannot provide a fully satisfying answer to that question here, it is worth noting that additive particles involve association with focus [31, 40, 41]. Assuming focus activates alternatives and alternatives need to be integrated into the overall meaning, the fact that silent exhaustification is invoked is not that surprising since we see something similar at play in cases like (7a) and (7b) which appear to involve exhaustification by EXH and covert *even*, respectively, with respect to other relevant individuals.

(7)   Who came to John's party?
   a.   Mary$_F$ came!   *inference:* Only Mary came.
   b.   His ex$_F$ came!   *inference:* Even his ex came.

In his work on the topic, Krifka has argued in [31] that the prosodic stress pattern encountered with additive particles is more similar to contrastive topic association rather than to focus association. Along these lines, note that additive particles and the use of contrastive topic intonation impose a similar requirement on the context, namely that the predication hold of somebody else (taking the contribution of focused constituent in (8a) to be that of an existential quantifier).

(8)   Who ate what?
   a.   Mary$_C$ ate beans$_F$ and Sue$_C$ ate carrots$_F$.
   b.   Mary$_C$ ate beans$_F$ and Sue$_C$ ate beans too.

To what extent this parallel plays a role in the nature of the alternative (pre-exhaustified versus distinct) is going to remain an open issue here but surely one that deserves further discussion (see [28] and [39] for some recent discussion on these parallels).

2.2   The Positive Antecedent Requirement

As per the discussion in the introduction, the additive component is commonly referred to as the antecedent requirement, in light of the fact that it behaves more like a felicity condition. At first sight, this might seem to pose a problem for the current way of deriving the additive component since the semantics provided in (6) has the additivity be part of the entailed component. In her work on presupposition triggering, Abrusán has argued that any information conveyed by the sentence that is not about the main point of the sentence ends up being presupposed [1,3].[6] She uses this triggering mechanism in [2] to argue that the

---

[6] There are some caveats to this condition that are tangential to the point at hand.

additive component becomes presupposed by virtue of not being about the main point described by the sentence. One way to identify the main point(s) is by looking at the sentence's entailments and whether they are about the event time of the matrix predicate. If they are not, or they are but only accidentally so, they must not be the main point of the sentence and thus can be presupposed. To tell if an entailment is only accidentally about the main event time, one can check whether the temporal-alternatives (T-alts below) are well-formed, with such an alternative being obtained by replacing the temporal arguments of the matrix and embedded predicates with different ones. She provides the nice minimal pair in (9) to illustrate the difference between *know* and *manage* with respect to their factivity: *know* presupposes its prejacent by virtue of the well-formedness of its T-alternative, while *manage* does not.

(9) a.   John knows (at time t_1) that it was raining (at time t_1).
          T-alt: John knows (at time t_1) that it was raining (at time t_2).
    b.   John managed (at time t_1) to solve the exercise (at time t_1).
          T-alt: *John managed (at time t_1) to solve the exercise (at time t_2).

Returning to the additive component, Abrusán shows in [2] that the additive entailment is not necessarily about the main event time with the example below (her examples (20–21)). Observe that the temporal alternative where the tense in the matrix clause and the tense in the additive component differ is well-formed.

(10)   Peter invited Mary for dinner too.
          T-alt: Two days ago, John invited Mary for dinner, and yesterday Peter invited her for dinner, too.

Given the acceptability of the T-alternative, Abrusán concludes that the additive component is temporally insensitive and thus presupposed. We adopt her proposal throughout.

2.3 Positive Additives Under Negation

Recall that when *și* co-occurs with negation, as in (11), the salient interpretation is that Maria doesn't want to drink beer, and the fact that she wants something else becomes accommodated. As mentioned in the introduction, such a construction is usually employed as part of a negative answer in response to a (possibly implicit) question involving the additive particle itself.

(11) Q: Știu   că   vrea apă,   dar vrea și   bere?
         know that wants water, but want ADD beer?
         'I know she wants water, but does she want beer too?'
     A: (Nu,) nu vrea și   bere.
         (No) not want ADD beer
         '(No,) she doesn't want beer too.'

How is the additive component $q = $ *Maria wants water* derived in this example? First observe that wide scope for the additive particle, per the LF in (12), would yield the wrong interpretation, namely that Maria doesn't want either water or beer, so we can rule this out straight away. A discussion of why this LF should be ruled out is postponed to the penultimate section.

(12)   LF: EXH [ADD¬p]
   a. $Alt(\text{ADD}\neg p) = \{\text{ADD}\neg p, \text{EXH}\neg p\} = \{\neg p, \neg p \wedge q\}$
   b. $[\![\text{EXH [ADD}\neg p]]\!] = \neg p \wedge \neg(\neg p \wedge q) = \neg p \wedge (p \vee \neg q) = \neg p \wedge \neg q$

Assuming then that the additive particle takes scope under the negation, since *şi* calls for obligatory exhaustification, it follows that the exhaustification must also scope under the negation, as in (13). Here we implicitly assume a mechanism of embedded exhaustivity operators as a means to derive embedded implicatures, a result which has received substantial empirical support [8,9,42,43].

(13)   LF: ¬ EXH [ADD p]
   a. $Alt(\text{ADD } p) = \{\text{ADD } p, \text{EXH } p\} = \{p, p \wedge \neg q\}$
   b. $[\![\neg \text{ EXH [ADD } p]]\!] = \neg[p \wedge \neg(p \wedge \neg q)] = \neg(p \wedge q) = \neg p \vee \neg q$

Note that the result in (13b) does not derive q as an entailment, so how does it end up being presupposed given the mechanism put forth by Abrusán? I propose that the additive implication, which is derived below the negation, can be turned into a presupposition at that embedded level, hence its projection out of the scope of negation. It is crucial and in fact necessary to allow this triggering mechanism to apply at embedded levels. I assume this obligatoriness is governed by a principle which calls for maximizing the amount of information presupposed.

The careful reader will have noticed that the use of EXH in (13) results in weakening at the matrix level; in other words, the use of *şi* under negation does not give rise to a stronger conjunctive meaning but rather to a weaker disjunctive one. General principles of economy argue that covert operators, such as EXH, should not be used if their insertion leads to a weaker or equivalent interpretation. A more recent discussion of such an economy condition governing the distribution of EXH, particularly as it pertains to its embeddability, can be found in [18,19]. The basic idea behind the proposal is the following: an instance of EXH is considered vacuous if its overall contribution leads to weakening or an equivalent interpretation. Note that in the case above, however, the insertion of EXH is not weakening if we consider its contribution more broadly, i.e., in conjunction with the mechanism for presupposition derivation. Without the insertion of EXH no additive component would have been generated, and in turn no presupposition would have been triggered. So while the initial contribution of EXH may seem weakening, when we take the presupposition generated into account, a stronger meaning can be said to be derived.[7]

Finally, note that there is another context which would facilitate the use of *şi* under negation, namely one where *şi* contrasts with overt *only*.

(14)   Nu beau ŞI   bere, beau DOAR bere.
        not drink ADD beer, drink only   beer
        'I don't drink beer too, I drink ONLY beer.'

This interpretation can be derived if we assume the LF representation in (15). If we assume the relevant alternative is one without the additive particle, (15a), we derive the intuitively correct interpretation that *only p* is the case. This is precisely the same derivation employed to derive the "metalinguistic" use of disjunction under negation: *I didn't eat cake OR ice cream, I ate both.* in [19].

(15)   LF: EXH $[\neg [$EXH $[$ADD p$]]]$
    a. $Alt(\neg$ EXH ADD p$) = \{\neg$ EXH ADD p$, \neg$p$\}$
    b. $[\![$EXH $[\neg [$EXH $[$ADD p$]]]]\!] = \neg(p \wedge q) \wedge \neg\neg p = (\neg p \vee \neg q) \wedge p = p \wedge \neg q$

We now turn our attention to the negative additive particle *nici* which, unlike *şi*, is restricted to negative environments.

3   The Negative Additive Marker

Observe that the NPI/neg-word prefix in Romanian is *ni*, (16). We see it in *nimeni* 'nobody,' *nimic* 'nothing,' and *nicăieri* 'nowhere.'[8]

(16) a. Nu am   vorbit cu   nimeni la petrecere.
         not have talked with nobody at party
         'I didn't talk to anyone at the party.'
     b. Nu am   adus   nimic   la petrecere.
         not have brought nothing to party
         'I didn't bring anything to the party.'
     c. Nu mergem nicăieri în weekend.
         not going   nowhere in weekend
         'We're not going anywhere this weekend.'

Similarly to the negative additive particle *nici*, the neg-words in (16) are restricted to strictly negative environments, such as sentential negation and the

---

[7] Y. Sudo (pers. comm.) wonders whether this does not lead to overgenerating in the case of embedded implicatures, e.g. *Mary didn't complete some of the assignments.* In other words, if vacuous embedded exhaustification can be made available by the mechanism proposed above, what prevents it from applying to this case? I want to argue that these cases are different since in the case of scalar implicatures, the entailed negated component is necessarily about the same event time, so it does not end up being presupposed under Abrusán's system.

[8] Other neg-words in Romanian are created from *nici* and a *wh*-phrase (*niciunde* 'nowhere' and *nicidecum* 'no way') or from *nici* and an indefinite NP (*nicio fată* 'no girl'). A detailed discussion of these elements is beyond the scope of this paper.

scope of *fără* 'without,' suggesting that their restricted distribution has the same source. I propose the following analysis for *nici*:

Decompositional analysis of *nici*

- ■ *Nici* spells out the negative marker and the additive particle: N-ADD.

- ■ Each particle (N and ADD) carries an inherent focal feature indicating active alternatives which must be used up by a corresponding operator: EXH^{N} & EXH^{ADD}.

- ■ EXH^{N} & EXH^{ADD} differ in terms of what alternatives they operate on.

The analysis I present in this section will take the distribution and interpretation of the negative additive *nici* to be the result of the types of alternatives EXH^{N} and EXH^{ADD} act on and the interaction of these two exhaustification operators with other elements in the clause.

Before turning to the analysis, I will offer a brief overview of the current approaches to deriving polarity restrictions within the exhaustification framework, as proposed in [11,14,15,20,21,45] and [37,38] among many other works.

3.1 Polarity Restrictions as Constraints on Obligatory Exhaustification

There are three main lines of approaches to deriving the restriction on the distribution of negative polarity items. One line, first presented by Chierchia in [9,10], argues that the analyses of polarity phenomena and scalar implicatures should converge in light of the fact that NPIs are acceptable in precisely those contexts where an existential quantifier does not give rise to a scalar implicature, namely under negation and other logical operators which reverse the direction of entailment. To this end, he takes negative polarity items like *any* to be existential quantifiers with active sub-domain alternatives which require obligatory exhaustification. This exhaustification is performed by a covert operator **O**, which conjoins the assertion with the negation of all logically non-weaker alternatives. The meaning of **O** is similar to that of the exclusive particle *only*, and is crucially distinct from the operator EXH presented earlier in that it allows contradictions to arise. It is precisely this possibility that [10] builds on to explain why NPIs like *any* are unacceptable in upward entailing environments. Analyzing *any* as an existential quantifier means that the alternative propositions obtained by replacing the domain with each of its sub-domains are stronger than the assertion since entailments hold from subsets to supersets. Since the alternatives entail the assertion in upward entailing environments, the application of **O** will result in the negation of each of the alternatives, which will amount to a contradiction since it will express that something holds of a set but it does not hold of any of its subsets. Assuming that logical contradictions of this type always lead to ungrammaticality, following Gajewski's work in [22], the unacceptability of NPIs in upward entailing contexts falls out. As for their acceptability in downward entailing environments, [10] argues that this falls out straight away because the application of **O** is vacuous in the presence of entailment-reversing operators since the alternatives are all weaker and thus **O** has nothing to negate. Note that **O**, in the context of NPI licensing, must furthermore be immune to the restriction against vacuous exhaustification.

Another exhaustification-based account of NPIs builds on the analyses proposed by Krifka and Lahiri in [30] and [33]. Based on the morphological make-up of Hindi NPIs, which are built out of the scalar particle *bhii* 'even' and an indefinite NP, [33] argues that the distribution of such NPIs falls out straightforwardly once we assume that the contribution of *bhii*, as with *even*, is to impose on its prejacent that it be less likely than any relevant alternative. Assuming that the indefinite NP activates scalar alternatives that differ only in terms of what integer is used, the requirement imposed by *even* will only be satisfied in the presence of entailment-reversing operators since only there will the alternatives be weaker, and thus more likely (e.g., *not a/one boy came to the party* is entailed by *not two boys came to the party*). Crnič in [14,15] has extended this analysis even to NPIs which lack an overt *even* counterpart by proposing that all NPIs involve association with a covert *even*-like operator. Note that within this family of proposals, the derivation of scalar and free choice implicatures is still achieved via exhaustification via EXH.

Lastly, we turn to positive polarity elements, whose restricted distribution has been explained within the exhaustification framework as well.[9] Spector and Nicolae, in [45] and [37,38], have argued that the positive polarity character of disjunction should be analyzed as an interplay between a lexical requirement for obligatory exhaustification imposed by the polarity item and an economy condition which prevents vacuous exhaustification, following work by Fox and Spector in [18,19]. Crucially, the relevant exhaustification operator in this case is EXH, as presented earlier in the paper, which only pays attention to innocently excludable alternatives and cannot lead to contradictions. As an example, consider the complex disjunction *soit soit* in French. [45] takes this disjunction to require obligatory exhaustification with respect to an alternative proposition where the disjunction is replaced with the conjunction. In upward entailing contexts, the result of exhaustification is the strengthened exclusive interpretation. In downward entailing environments, however, the contribution of EXH is vacuous since the conjunctive alternative is weaker when negated. Since vacuous exhaustification is ruled out, the PPI-like behavior of the disjunction *soit soit* falls out. Observe that this restriction against vacuous instances of EXH is crucial to the account and in this way, stands in stark contrast with the first family of analyses proposed above, which deliver the acceptability of NPIs in downward entailing contexts precisely because the exhaustification is vacuous. A simple way to reconcile these proposals is to assume that there are indeed a number of covert exhaustification operators which perform similar tasks but are subject to different constraints, **O** and EXH.

In the following sections I will provide an analysis of the NPI status of *nici* by taking it to associate not with **O** or EVEN, but with EXH, a novel approach as far as NPI licensing is concerned.

---

[9] There are also accounts of PPIs that align better with the two analyses presented above: [27,36,47].

3.2 *Nici* in Upward Entailing Contexts

As already mentioned, I propose a decompositional analysis of *nici*:

- *Nici* spells out the negative marker and the additive particle: N-ADD.
- Each particle carries an inherent focal feature indicating active alternatives which must be used up by a corresponding operator: EXH^N & EXH^{ADD}.
- EXH^N & EXH^{ADD} differ in terms of what alternatives they operate on.

We already know what alternative EXH^{ADD} acts on, namely one where the additive particle is replaced by the exclusive particle EXH, which in turn is evaluated with respect to an alternative obtained via lexical item replacement (of p with q), repeated in (17a)[10]. The alternatives considered by EXH^N are derived via (i) lexical item replacement of p with q, and (ii) deletion, whereby constituents are replaced with their sub-constituents, e.g. *nici* p with p, as shown in (17c). Going through the composition step by step, we see that the first level of exhaustification will result in the additive meaning, (17b), while the application of EXH^N in (17d) will be vacuous since there are no stronger alternatives to negate. Assuming EXH is subject to a constraint against vacuous occurrences, the unacceptability of *nici* in UE contexts falls out.

(17)   LF: EXH^N [EXH^{ADD} [N-ADD p]]

    a. Alt(ADD p) = {ADD p, EXH p} = {p, p∧¬q}

    b. ⟦EXH^{ADD} [N-ADD p]⟧ = ⟦EXH^{ADD} [ADD p]⟧ = p∧q

    c. Alt(EXH^{ADD} N-ADD p) = $\left\{\begin{array}{c} \text{EXH}^{ADD}\ \text{N-ADD p} \\ \text{EXH}^{ADD}\ \text{N-ADD q} \\ p \\ q \end{array}\right\}$ = $\left\{\begin{array}{c} p∧q \\ p∧q \\ p \\ q \end{array}\right\}$

    d. ⟦EXH^N [EXH^{ADD} [N-ADD p]]⟧ = ⟦EXH^{ADD} [N-ADD p]⟧ = p∧q

3.3 *Nici* in Downward Entailing Contexts

For ease of presentation, I repeat the relevant example below:

(18)   Paul nu bea   vin. Nu bea   nici   bere.
        Paul not drinks wine. Not drinks N-ADD beer.
        'Paul doesn't drink wine. He doesn't drink beer either.'

We need to explain the following two facts:

- The interpretation of the sentence hosting *nici* is that of a conjunction of two negated propositions (¬p∧¬q).

---

[10] In fact, nothing prevents us from claiming that the alternative derived via deletion of ADD, namely p, is also an alternative. Given the interpretation of ADD, however, including this alternative will not add anything.

- The use of *nici* carries a negative presupposition, which amounts to the second conjunct ($\neg q$).

Given the presence of an additional operator, namely the negation, EXH^N has two possible adjunction positions. If it adjoins below the negation, the contribution of EXH^N will be vacuous as before given the nature of the alternatives.

(19) $[\neg [\text{EXH}^N [\text{EXH}^{ADD} [\text{N-ADD p}]]]] = [\neg [\text{EXH}^{ADD} [\text{N-ADD p}]]] = \neg(p \wedge q)$

If EXH^N adjoins above the negation, its prejacent will denote the disjunction of two negated propositions, so the result should be similar to what happens when EXH applies to a disjunction. Let's begin by reviewing how free choice inferences with disjunctive sentences come about within the exhaustification framework as proposed by Fox in [16]. The basic idea is that the relevant alternatives are not the disjuncts themselves, but rather their pre-exhaustified variants. One way to implement this is by assuming exhaustification can happen recursively, via two instances of the EXH operator, as in (20).[11] The first instance of EXH will be vacuous, (20b), since the alternatives are stronger but not innocently excludable, (20a). The second level of EXH will look at the pre-exhaustified alternatives in (20c) and the result will be the conjunctive interpretation in (20d). This conjunctive interpretation comes about as follows: the disjunction of A and B is possible, but it's not possible that only A is true and it's not possible that only B is true, so the conjunction itself must be possible.[12]

(20)   Jenny can invite A or B. $\rightarrow$ Jenny can invite A and she can invite B.
LF: EXH $[\text{EXH}[\Diamond[A \vee B]]]$

a. $Alt(\Diamond[A \vee B]) = \{\Diamond[A \vee B], \Diamond A, \Diamond B\}$

b. $[\![\text{EXH}[\Diamond[A \vee B]]]\!] = \Diamond[A \vee B]$

c. $Alt(\text{EXH}[\Diamond[A \vee B]]) = \left\{ \begin{array}{c} \text{EXH}[\Diamond[A \vee B]] \\ \text{EXH}[\Diamond A] \\ \text{EXH}[\Diamond B] \end{array} \right\} = \left\{ \begin{array}{c} \Diamond[A \vee B] \\ \Diamond A \wedge \neg \Diamond B \\ \Diamond B \wedge \neg \Diamond A \end{array} \right\}$

d. $[\![\text{EXH} [\text{EXH}[\Diamond[A \vee B]]]]\!] = \Diamond[A \vee B] \wedge \neg[\Diamond A \wedge \neg \Diamond B] \wedge \neg[\Diamond B \wedge \neg \Diamond A]$
      $= \Diamond[A \vee B] \wedge [\Diamond A \rightarrow \Diamond B] \wedge [\Diamond B \rightarrow \Diamond A]$
      $= \Diamond[A \wedge B]$

Carrying this over to the case at hand, invoking recursive exhaustification on the disjunction of two negated propositions will deliver precisely the right interpretation, namely the conjunction of two negated propositions. Below I go through

---

[11] More recent work does away with recursive exhaustification and instead adopts a notion of innocent inclusion of alternatives as a way to derive the conjunctive inference [7]. I believe that this new approach will be equally suitable in the case at hand but I leave it to future work to probe it further.

[12] I simplified the presentation by ignoring the conjunctive alternative since its inclusion is orthogonal to the derivation of the free choice implicature.

each step of the derivation. In (21c) I list the alternatives considered by EXH^{N}. The first application of EXH^{N} will be vacuous, (21d), as the alternatives are symmetric and neither can be negated innocently. By the second application of EXH^{N}, the result will no longer be vacuous as the alternatives in (21e) are no longer symmetric – they can both be negated without contradiction, as shown in (21f). The resulting meaning will be stronger, taking us from the disjunction of two negated propositions to their conjunction.[13,14]

(21) $[_④ \text{EXH}^{\text{N}} \ [_③ \text{EXH}^{\text{N}} \ [_② \neg \ [_① \text{EXH}^{\text{ADD}} \ [\text{N-ADD p}]]]]]$

a. $[\![①]\!] = p \wedge q$

b. $[\![②]\!] = \neg(p \wedge q) = \neg p \vee \neg q$

c. $Alt(②) = \left\{ \begin{array}{c} \neg\text{EXH}^{\text{ADD}} \ \text{N-ADD p} \\ \neg\text{EXH}^{\text{ADD}} \ \text{N-ADD q} \\ \neg p \\ \neg q \end{array} \right\} = \left\{ \begin{array}{c} \neg(p \wedge q) \\ \neg(p \wedge q) \\ \neg p \\ \neg q \end{array} \right\}$

d. $[\![③]\!] = [\![\text{EXH}]\!]^{\text{N}}([\![②]\!]) = [\![②]\!]$

e. $Alt(③) = \left\{ \begin{array}{c} \text{EXH}^{\text{N}} \neg\text{EXH}^{\text{ADD}} \ \text{N-ADD p} \\ \text{EXH}^{\text{N}} \neg\text{EXH}^{\text{ADD}} \ \text{N-ADD q} \\ \text{EXH}^{\text{N}} \ \neg p \\ \text{EXH}^{\text{N}} \ \neg q \end{array} \right\} = \left\{ \begin{array}{c} \neg(p \wedge q) \\ \neg(p \wedge q) \\ \neg p \wedge \neg\neg q \\ \neg q \wedge \neg\neg p \end{array} \right\} = \left\{ \begin{array}{c} \neg(p \wedge q) \\ \neg(p \wedge q) \\ \neg p \wedge q \\ \neg q \wedge p \end{array} \right\}$

f. $[\![④]\!] = [\![\text{EXH}^{\text{N}}]\!]([\![②]\!])$
$= \neg(p \wedge q) \wedge \neg(\neg p \wedge q) \wedge \neg(p \wedge \neg q)$
$= (\neg p \vee \neg q) \wedge (\neg p \rightarrow \neg q) \wedge (\neg q \rightarrow \neg p)$
$= \neg p \wedge \neg q$

We've thus shown why *nici* must co-occur with negation, and that is because the presence of negation allows EXH^{N} to scope above it and access stronger alternatives which can be innocently excluded. Since the overall contribution of EXH^{N} leads to a strengthened interpretation, the acceptability of *nici* in entailment-reversal environments, more generally, falls out, as does its contribution to the overall meaning, that of an additive.

---

[13] One reviewer has asked why we don't also consider alternatives without the negation, since we consider alternatives obtained via deletion. Note that if we were to consider such alternatives, then all the alternatives would be symmetric, and thus none would be excludable, resulting in the vacuous application of EXH. While this will have to remain a stipulation for now, the same stipulation regarding the non-deletion of negation has to be adopted even in the simpler cases involving indirect implicatures, i.e. cases of strong scalar items giving rise to implicatures when they occur in the scope of negation.

[14] One might wonder whether the first instance of EXH^{N} does not count as vacuous. While at the point of insertion it is, its global contribution does lead to strengthening given that its presence alters the alternatives under consideration by the higher instance of EXH.

Before we conclude, it deserves pointing out that *ni* neg-words as well as the additive *nici*, have a very restricted distribution, being allowed to appear only under negation and *without*, as well as in fragment answers, as per the distribution of neg-words in strict negative concord languages. I will not discuss how to derive this restricted distribution, but I point the interested reader to the work of Fălăuş and Nicolae in [21] for details on how to derive this distribution within an exhaustification-based framework.

3.4   The Negative Antecedent Requirement

Having shown how the additive interpretation and the restricted distribution are derived, we next turn to the antecedent requirement. Like *şi*, *nici* requires an antecedent, but unlike with *şi*, the antecedent needs to be negative. At which point does the presupposition triggering mechanism apply? There are two options, either below or above the negation. If it applies below the negation, the material presupposed, namely q, would end up contradicting the resulting interpretation in (21f). If, on the other hand, the triggering mechanism is postponed until the matrix level, the negative additive implication $\neg q$ will end up being presupposed, as desired.

3.5   Carving Out the Space of Possibilities: *şi* or *nici*?

There is one potential concern that still needs to be addressed, namely why the positive particle *şi* cannot be used with negation and have the LF in (21). I argue that this relates to the morphological point made in the beginning of this section, namely that *nici* spells out two particles, each of which associates with a distinct EXH operator. I argue that each instance of exhaustification (assuming recursive exhaustification counts as a single instance) corresponds to a focus feature on its associate. In the case of *nici*, which spells out N-ADD, there are two such features. On the other hand, *şi* can host only one focus feature, meaning that there can only be one instance of EXH associating with it.

On a separate but related note, one might wonder why *şi* cannot take wide scope with respect to negation. Recall from Sect. 2.3 that if it did, the resulting interpretation would be the same as what we derive with *nici*, yet *şi* and *nici* never overlap in their interpretation. There are languages, e.g. Japanese, where the same particle, namely *mo*, can be used in both positive and negative contexts; in fact, in Japanese *mo* is the only way to express additivity. For such particles we would surely want to argue that they have the option of scoping above the negation, unlike *şi*, thereby deriving an interpretation akin to that contributed by *nici*. This seems like a deeper problem which will have remain an open issue for now. What seems to be at play is some type of competition between the two particles, *şi* and *nici*: while in the presence of negation *şi* is ambiguous, *nici* is not, so of the two possible interpretations of *şi*, only the one not shared with *nici* can ultimately survive. How to best formalize this remains an open problem, but interestingly one we see in other cases of ambiguity resolution.

4   Summary and Open Issues

In this paper I presented a new analysis for pairs of additive particles like Romanian *și* and *nici* which, I argued, captures their additive interpretation and distribution. While Ahn's 2015 recent analysis is similarly able to capture the distribution of these particles, it is conceptually not as well suited for pairs of particles such as the Romanian ones which very clearly share a morphological and presumably semantic core with conjunctive rather than disjunctive particles; recall that her analysis takes the negative particle *either* to be a disjunction at its core. That is not to say that an analysis such as Ahn's is not viable and possibly even better suited for other additive particles, such as English *either*, which also doubles as a disjunction (*either A or B*) and free choice determiner (*either boy*), although note that her analysis cannot immediately be extended to account for these other uses.

The study of additive particles, especially in the context of polarity, is a very fertile area cross-linguistically. There is ample variation both in terms of the possible interpretations of these elements, as well as in the different roles they may play within a language. Not only has this variation not received a proper theoretical analysis, it has not even been fully mapped out yet (see for example [23] and [13]). Take for example the negative additive particle. As mentioned above, English *either* can also double as a positive disjunction and a free choice determiner. This is not the case in Romanian, where instead it can be used to form negative words by attaching to an indefinite NP (*nicio fată* 'no girl'), something we also see in, e.g., Hindi [33]. The creation of NPIs based on additive particles like *nici* and indefinite NPs is in fact cross-linguistically common. The common analyses of these elements attribute, however, a scalar semantics to the additive particles, whereby they contribute an *even*-like interpretation. This is not surprising since additive particles are cross-linguistically known to double as scalar particles. There is variation within this area as well, however. While Spanish *ni* must express a scalar meaning, Romanian *nici* can express it, while English *either* cannot.

Nici can also appear in complex coordinations, e.g. *nici A nici B* 'neither A nor B' to convey the conjunction of two negated propositions. French *ni* can also function as a negative additive particle as in Romanian, as well as a negative connective *A ni B* 'neither A nor B' and can be doubled, as in Romanian, *ni A ni B* 'neither A nor B.' The distribution and interpretation of these particles is so varied and multi-faceted that many authors have argued that a unified account is not possible for all their different uses (see e.g. recent work particularly on French *ni* by [24]). Clearly much is left to be understood.

References

1. Abrusán, M.: Predicting the presuppositions of soft triggers. Linguist. Philos. **34**, 491–535 (2011)

2. Abrusán, M.: On the focus-sensitive presupposition triggers too, again, also, even. In: Etxeberria, U., Fălăuş, A., Irurtzun, A., Leferman, B. (eds.) Sinn und Bedeutung (SuB), vol. 18, pp. 6–23. Bayonne and Vitoria-Gasteiz (2014)
3. Abrusán, M.: Presupposition cancellation: explaining the 'soft-hard' trigger distinction. Nat. Lang. Semant. **24**, 165–202 (2016)
4. Ahn, D.: The semantics of additive either. In: Csipak, E., Zeijlstra, H. (eds.) Sinn und Bedeutung 19, vol. 1, pp. 20–35 (2015)
5. Alxatib, S.: Only, or and free choice presuppositions. Nat. Lang. Seman. **28**, 395–429 (2020). https://doi.org/10.1007/s11050-020-09170-y
6. Bade, N.: Obligatory presupposition triggers in discourse. Ph.D. thesis, Universität Tübingen (2015)
7. Bar-Lev, M.E., Fox, D.: Universal free choice and innocent inclusion. In: Burgdorf, D., Collard, J., Maspong, S., Stefánsdóttir, B. (eds.) Semantics and Linguistic Theory (SALT), vol. 27, pp. 95–115. LSA, Washington (2017)
8. Chemla, E., Spector, B.: Experimental evidence for embedded scalar implicatures. J. Semant. **28**, 359–400 (2011)
9. Chierchia, G.: Scalar implicatures, polarity phenomena, and the syntax/pragmatics interface. In: Belletti, A. (ed.) Structures and Beyond, vol. 3, pp. 39–103. Oxford University Press (2004)
10. Chierchia, G.: Broaden your views: Implicatures of domain widening and the 'logicality' of language. Linguist. Inq. **37**(4), 535–590 (2006)
11. Chierchia, G.: Logic in Grammar. Oxford University Press, Oxford (2013)
12. Chierchia, G., Fox, D., Spector, B.: Scalar implicatures as a grammatical phenomenon. In: Maienborn, C., Portner, P., von Heusinger, K. (eds.) Semantics: An International Handbook of Natural Language Meaning, vol. 3, pp. 2297–2332. Mouton de Gruyter/de Gruyter edn. New York (2012)
13. Crnič, L.: Getting even. Ph.D. thesis, Massachusetts Institute of Technology, Cambridge, MA (2011)
14. Crnič, L.: Non-monotonicity in NPI licensing. Nat. Lang. Semant. **22**(2), 169–217 (2014). https://doi.org/10.1007/s11050-014-9104-6
15. Crnič, L.: Any: logic, likelihood, and context. Lang. Linguist. Compass **13**(11), e12353 (2019)
16. Fox, D.: Free choice disjunction and the theory of scalar implicatures. In: Sauerland, U., Stateva, P. (eds.) Presupposition and Implicature in Compositional Semantics, pp. 71–120. Palgrave Macmillan, New York (2007)
17. Fox, D., Katzir, R.: On the characterization of alternatives. Nat. Lang. Semant. **19**(1), 87–107 (2011)
18. Fox, D., Spector, B.: Economy and embedded exhaustification (2009). unpublished ms. (MIT and Institut Jean Nicod)
19. Fox, D., Spector, B.: Economy and embedded exhaustification. Nat. Lang. Semant. **26**(1), 1–50 (2018). https://doi.org/10.1007/s11050-017-9139-6
20. Fălăuş, A.: (Partially) free choice of alternatives. Linguist. Philos. **37**(2), 121–173 (2014)
21. Fălăuş, A., Nicolae, A.C.: Fragment answers and double negation in strict negative concord languages. In: Moroney, M., Little, C.R., Collard, J., Burgdorf, D. (eds.) Semantics and Linguistic Theory (SALT), vol. 26, pp. 584–600 (2016)
22. Gajewski, J.: L-analiticity and natural language , Ms. University of Connecticut (2002)
23. Gast, V., van der Auwera, J.: Scalar additive operators in the languages of Europe. Language **87**(1), 2–54 (2011)

24. Gonzalez, A.: Residue of universality, Harvard ms (2020)
25. Groenendijk, J., Stokhof, M.: Studies on the Semantics of Questions and the Pragmatics of Answers. Ph.D. thesis, University of Amsterdam, Amsterdam, Netherlands (1984)
26. Heim, I.: Presupposition projection. In: van der Sandt, R. (ed.) Reader for the Nijmegen Workshop on Presupposition, Lexical Meaning, and Discourse Processes (1990)
27. Iatridou, S., Zeijlstra, H.H.: Negation, polarity and deontic modals. Linguist. Inq. **44**(4), 529–568 (2013)
28. Kamali, B., Krifka, M.: Focus and contrastive topics. Theor Linguist. **46**(1–2), 1–71 (2020)
29. Katzir, R.: Structurally defined alternatives. Linguist. Philos. **30**(6), 669–690 (2007)
30. Krifka, M.: The semantics and pragmatics of polarity items. Linguist. Anal. **25**, 209–257 (1995)
31. Krifka, M.: Additive particles under stress. In: Strolovitch, D., Lawson, A. (eds.) Semantics and Linguistic Theory (SALT), vol. 8, pp. 111–128 (1998)
32. Kripke, S.A.: Presupposition and anaphora: remarks on the formulation of the projection problem. Linguist. Inq. **40**(3), 367–386 (2009)
33. Lahiri, U.: Focus and negative polarity in Hindi. Nat. Lang. Semant. **6**, 57–123 (1998)
34. Mitrović, M., Sauerland, U.: Decomposing coordination. In: Iyer, J., Kusmer, L. (eds.) North East Linguistic Society (NELS), vol. 44, pp. 39–52 (2014)
35. Mitrović, M., Sauerland, U.: Two conjunctions are better than one. Acta Linguist. Hung. **63**(4), 471–494 (2016)
36. Nicolae, A.C.: Negation-resistant polarity items. In: Piñón, C. (ed.) Empirical Issues in Syntax and Semantics, vol. 9, pp. 225–242 (2012)
37. Nicolae, A.C.: Deriving the positive polarity behavior of plain disjunction. Semant. Pragmat. **10**(5), 1–21 (2017)
38. Nicolae, A.C.: A new perspective on the shielding property of positive polarity. In: Burgdorf, D., Collard, J., Maspong, S., Stefánsdóttir, B. (eds.) Semantics and Linguistic Theory (SALT), vol. 27, pp. 266–281 (2017)
39. Nicolae, A.C.: Additional questions on contrastive topics. Theor. Linguist. **46**(1–2), 81–87 (2020)
40. Rooth, M.: Association with Focus. Ph.D. thesis, University of Massachusetts at Amherst, Amherst, MA (1985)
41. Saebo, J.K.: Conversational contrast and conventional parallel: topic implicatures and additive presuppositions. J. Semant. **2**, 199–217 (2004)
42. Sauerland, U.: Scalar implicatures in complex sentences. Linguist. Philos. **27**(3), 367–391 (2004)
43. Sauerland, U.: Intermediate scalar implicatures. In: Pistoia Reda, S. (ed.) Pragmatics, Semantics and the Case of Scalar Implicatures, pp. 72–98. Palgrave Macmillan, Basingstoke (2014)
44. Spector, B.: Aspects de la Pragmatique des Opérateurs Logiques. Ph.D. thesis, Université Paris-VII, Paris, France (2006)
45. Spector, B.: Global positive polarity items and obligatory exhaustivity. Semant. Pragmat. **7**(11), 1–61 (2014)
46. Szabolcsi, A.: Additive presuppositions are derived through activating focus alternatives. In: Cremers, A., van Gessel, T., Roelofsen, F. (eds.) Proceedings of the 21st Amsterdam Colloquium, pp. 455–464 (2017)
47. Zeijlstra, H.H.: Universal quantifier PPIs. Glossa **2**(91), 1–25 (2017)

A Causal Analysis of Modal Syllogisms

Robert van Rooij[(✉)] and Kaibo Xie

Institute for Logic, Language and Computation (ILLC), University of Amsterdam,
Science Park 107, 1098 XG Amsterdam, The Netherlands
r.a.m.vanrooij@uva.nl, xiekaibozju@gmail.com

Abstract. It is well known that in his *Prior Analysis*, Aristotle presents
the system of syllogisms. Although many commentators consider Aristotle's system of modal syllogisms almost impossible to understand from a
modern point of view or even inconsistent, many philosophers still tried
to account for these claims by looking for a consistent semantics of it. In
this paper we will argue for a causal analysis of modal categorical sentences based on the notion of *causal power*. According to Cheng (1997),
the causal power of A to produce B can be measured probabilistically.
Based on Cheng's hypothesis, we will derive a qualitative semantics for
modal categorical sentences. We will argue that our approach fits well
with Aristotle's analysis of real definition in the *Posterior Analytics*, and
that in this way we can account in a relatively straightforward way (using
just Venn diagrams) for several puzzling aspects of Aristotle's system of
modal syllogisms.

1   Introduction

In his *Prior Analytics* Aristotle (1973) made a distinction between assertoric
and modal syllogistics. The crucial difference between the two syllogistics is that
only the latter makes use of two different types of predicative relations: accidental versus essential predication. 'Animal' is essentially predicated of 'men', but
'walking' is not. Although both (a) 'Every man walks' and (b) 'Every man is an
animal' can be true, it is natural to say that the 'reasons' for their respective
truths are different. Sentence (a) is true by accident, just because every actual
man happens to (be able to) walk. The sentence (b), on the other hand, is true
because manhood necessarily involves being animate. In traditional terms it is
said that (b) is true *by definition*, although this notion of 'definition' should not
be thought of nominalistically: it is the *real* definition. A natural way to account
for accidental predication is to say that a sentence of the form 'Every S is P' is
true just in case every actual *S-individual* is also a *P-individual*. But how should
we account for essential predication? The answer to this question is important

We would like to thank the reviewers of this paper for their comments. This not only
simplified the paper, but also made it more focussed and relevant to the topic of the
workshop. The work for this paper was supported by NWO grant 'From Learning to
Meaning: A new approach to Generic Sentences and Implicit Biases' (dossiernummer
406.18.TW.007).

© Springer-Verlag GmbH Germany, part of Springer Nature 2020
D. Deng et al. (Eds.): TLLM 2020, LNCS 12564, pp. 183–206, 2020.
https://doi.org/10.1007/978-3-662-62843-0_10

for logic, because it is by now generally assumed (e.g. Malink 2013; van Rijen 1989; Thom 1991; Vecchio 2016) that Aristotle's system of modal syllogisms, which is almost impossible to understand from a modern standard modal logic point of view, should be understood in terms of the difference between accidental and essential predication.

In this paper we will argue for a *causal* analysis of essential predication. We will argue that this fits well with Aristotle's analysis of real definition in the *Posterior Analytics*, and that in this way we can account in a relatively straightforward way for several puzzling aspects of Aristotle's system of modal syllogisms presented in his *Prior Analytics*.

2   Standard and Modal Syllogistics

Syllogisms are arguments in which a categorical sentence is derived as conclusion from two categorical sentences as premises. A categorical sentence is always one of four kinds:

1. *a*-type: Universal and affirmative ('All men are mortal')
2. *i*-type: Particular and affirmative ('Some men are philosophers')
3. *e*-type: Universal and negative ('No philosophers is rich')
4. *o*-type: Particular and negative ('Some men are not philosophers').

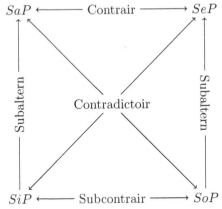

A categorical sentence always contains two *terms*. In the *a*-sentence, for instance, the terms are 'men' and 'mortal', while in the *e*-sentence they are 'philosopher' and 'rich'. Thus, the *syntax* of categorical sentences can be formulated as follows: If S and P are terms, SaP, SiP, SeP, and SoP are categorical sentences. Because a syllogism has two categorical sentences as premises and one as the conclusion, every syllogism involves only three terms, each of which appears in two of the statements. The first term of the conclusion is called the *subject term*, or *minor term*, the last term, the *predicate term*, or *major term*, and the term that does not occur in the conclusion is called the *middle term*. The premise in which the major term occurs together with the middle term is called the *major premiss*, the other one the *minor premiss*. The *quality* of a proposition is whether it is *affirmative* (in *a*- and *i*- sentences, the predicate is affirmed of the subject), or *negative* (in *e* and *o*-sentences, the predicate is denied of the subject). Thus 'every man is mortal' is affirmative, since 'mortal' is affirmed of 'man'. 'No men is immortal' is negative, since 'immortal' is denied of 'man'. The *quantity* of a proposition is whether it is *universal* (in *a*- and *e*-sentences the predicate is affirmed or denied of "the whole" of the subject) or *particular* (in *i* and *o*-sentences, the predicate is affirmed or denied of only 'part of' the subject).

Medieval logicians used the letters '*a*', '*i*', '*e*', and '*o*' for coding the various forms of syllogisms. The *mood* of a syllogism was given by a triple of letters like *aeo*. This triple, for instance, indicates that the major premiss is of type *a*, the minor premiss of type *e*, and the conclusion of type *o*. But apart from the mood, what is important as well is the *figure*. The figure of a syllogism says whether the major and minor terms occur as subject or predicate in their respective premisses. This gives rise to four possibilities, i.e., four figures:

1st	2nd	3rd	4th
MP	PM	MP	PM
SM	SM	MS	MS
SP	SP	SP	SP

A *valid* syllogism is a syllogism that cannot lead from true premisses to a false conclusion. It is well-known that by a set theoretic semantic analysis, we can account for syllogistic reasoning. For now we will interpret terms just as sets of individuals and equate for simplicity the interpretation of a term with the term itself. Then we say that SaP is true iff $S \subseteq P$, SiP is true iff $S \cap P \neq \emptyset$, SeP is true iff $S \cap P = \emptyset$, and SoP is true iff $S \not\subseteq P$.[1]

This semantic interpretation accounts for many valid syllogisms, but not all of them. In particular, not for the valid syllogisms for which it is required that SaP entails SiP. This can be easily accounted for by assuming that for the truth of SaP it is not only required that $S \subseteq P$, but also that $S \neq \emptyset$. It is well-known that with such an interpretation of categorical sentences, all and only all of the following syllogisms are predicted to be valid that Aristotle considered to be valid as well.

Barbara$_1$	Baroco$_2$	Bocardo$_3$	Camenes$_4$
Celarent$_1$	Festino$_2$	Disamis$_3$	(Fesapo$_4$)
Darii$_1$	Camestres$_2$	Ferison$_3$	Dimaris$_4$
Ferio$_1$	Cesare$_2$	Datisi$_3$	Fresison$_4$
(Barbari$_1$)	(Camestrop$_2$)	(Felapton$_3$)	(Bramantip$_4$)
(Celaront$_1$)	(Cesaro$_2$)	(Darapti$_3$)	(Camenop$_4$)

The syllogisms between brackets are only valid in case one assumes existential import, meaning that the extension of the subject term is non-empty. The above

---

[1] Warning: in the literature categorical sentences of the form XaY and XiY are read many times in the converse order as we read them and mean that all/some Y belong to X.

semantic analysis of categorical sentences is nice, because with the help of Venn-diagrams, one can now easily check the validity of any syllogistic argument.[2] For later in the paper, note that we could interpret Aristotle's standard categorical sentences probabilistically as well with equivalent predictions: SaP is true iff the conditional probability of P given S is 1, $P(P|S) = 1$, SeP is true iff $P(S \cap P) = 0$, SiP is true iff $P(S \cap P) \neq 0$ and SoP is true iff $P(P|S) \neq 1$. Notice that on this probabilistic interpretation SaP presupposes that $P(S) > 1$, which immediatelly accounts for Aristotle's subalternation inference: $SaP \models SiP$. This alternative semantics is the one we are going to use in our analysis of modal syllogisms. Therefore, we provide the following definition:

Definition 1. Truth conditions of Categorical sentences

- SaP is true iff $P(P|S) = 1$,
- SiP is true iff $P(S \cap P) \neq 0$,
- SeP is true iff $P(S \cap P) = 0$, and
- SoP is true iff $P(P|S) \neq 1$

With this definition we can give the truth definitions of categorical sentences with the following Venn diagrams (where an area has a cross when we know that it has at least one element, an area is shaded when we know it has no element, and if the area is empty we don't know whether the area has elements or not).

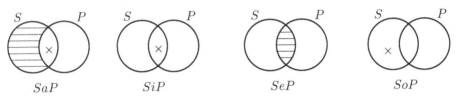

SaP $\qquad$ SiP $\qquad$ SeP $\qquad$ SoP

It is well-known that by drawing Venn diagrams one can give a *decision procedure* to determine which syllogisms are valid. Medieval logicians didn't make use of Venn diagrams, but developed another decision procedure to determine which syllogisms are valid. This procedure made crucial use of the so-called distribution-value of the terms involved. Whether a term is distributed or not is really a *semantic* question: a term is said to be distributed when it is actually applied to *all* the objects it can refer to, and undistributed when it is explicitly applied to only part of the objects to which it can refer. This formulation has been criticised by Geach (1962) and other modern logicians, but as noted by van Benthem (1973) and van Eijck (1985), it can be redefined in terms of **monotonicity**. A term occurs distributively when it occurs monotone decreasingly/negatively within a sentence, and undistributively when it occurs monotone increasingly/positively within a sentence. Denoting a distributed term by − and an undistributed term by +, the following follows at once: S^-aP^+, S^+iP^+,

---

[2] On the other hand, it is well-known that we don't need the full power of Boolean algebra to account for Syllogistic validity; semi-lattices will do.

S^-eP^-, and S^+oP^-, which we might think of now as a *syntactic* characterisation. In terms of the distribution values of terms, we can now state the laws of *quantity* or *distribution*, (R1) and (R2), and of *quality*, (R3). Together, they constitute the rules of the syllogism:[3]

(R1) The middle term must be distributed at least once.
(R2) Every term that is distributed in the conclusion is also distributed in one of the premises.
(R3) The number of negative conclusions must equal the number of negative premises.

The above rules assume existential import. Without this assumption, we have to strengthen (R2) to (R2'):

(R2') Every term that is (un)distributed in the conclusion is (un)distributed in one of the premises.

Medieval logicians and their followers standardly assumed that of all the reasoning schemas stated in syllogistic style, all and only all forms are valid that satisfy those roles. As far as we know, the first one who explicitly *proved* this was Leibniz (1966).

Let us now come back to the question what is the natural interpretation of Aristotle's *modal* syllogistics. Let us assume that $Ba^\Box C$ means that all Bs are *necessary*/essentially C. Aristotle claims that the following modal syllogisms are valid and invalid, respectively:

1. $Ba^\Box C, Aa^\Box B \therefore Aa^\Box C$ Valid   Barbara LLL
2. $Ba^\Box C, AaB \therefore Aa^\Box C$ Valid   Barbara LXL
3. $BaC, Aa^\Box B \therefore Aa^\Box C$ Invalid   Barbara XLL

Although Aristotle had intuitions about which modal syllogistic inferences are valid and which not, he did not base that on a standard semantics. As it turns out, it is already hard enough to account semantically for the intuitions concerning 1–3. But what makes the task especially challenging is that Aristotle also claims that not only conversion inference 4 is valid, but that the same holds for the modal conversion inferences 5 and 6:

4. $BeC \therefore CeB$ Valid
5. $Be^\Box C \therefore Ce^\Box B$ Valid
6. $Bi^\Box C \therefore Ci^\Box B$ Valid

Of course, it is easy to account for inferences 5 and 6 if we assume that the modal should be interpreted in a *de dicto* way. But it is equally easy to see that on such an analysis inference 2 is *not* predicted to be valid. A *de re* analysis

---

[3] Standardly, more rules are stated, but these can be derived from the rules below. One of the rules normally assumed, for instance, is that at least one of the premises must be affirmative. But this follows immediately from (R3).

of sentences like $Ba^\square C$, on the other hand, would make inference 2 valid, but such an analysis cannot account for the modal conversion inferences 5 and 6. So neither a standard *de dicto* nor a standard *de re* analysis of modal statements would work to account for Aristotle's intuitions.

Some commentators (e.g. Lukasiewicz (1966); Patzig 1968; Hintikka 1973) concluded that the combination of these statements just doesn't make any sense and that Aristotle must have been confused. Others, however, tried to account for these claims by looking for a consistent semantics of Aristotle's system (e.g. Thomason 1993; Uckelman and Johnston 2010). The most interesting of these latter accounts build on the idea that Aristotle's modal syllogistics was based on his metaphysics and philosophy of science (e.g. Rescher 1964; van Rijen 1989; Patterson 1995; Malink 2013; Vecchio 2016).[4] Unfortunately, most of these authors have difficulty making many predictions of valid modal syllogistic reasoning that correspond with Artstotle's intuitions. Recently, however, Malink (2013) has shown that it is actually possible to come up with a systematic analysis of modal syllogistic sentences such that it gives rise to predictions almost exactly in accordance with Aristotle's claims.[5] As we will see in Sect. 5, however, on his analysis the validity of Barbara LXL, for example, is reduced to the validity of Barbara LLL, which we think is unexpected. One wonders whether another analysis is not possible that interprets the second premiss of the argument not as a necessity statement. We think such an analys is possible, if we make use of a *causal* analysis of modal categorical statements.

In this paper we will argue for a *causal* analysis of Aristotle's modal claims. We will argue that this fits well with Aristotle's analysis of demonstrative inferences in the *Posterior Analytics*, and that in this way we can account in a relatively straightforward way for several puzzling aspects of Aritotle's system of modal syllogisms presented in his Prior Analytics. Although we don't see how something like the medieval distribution theory that is just based on monotonicity can be used as a decision procedure to check whether modal syllogisms are valid, to our surprise Venn diagrams can be used for this purpose, or at least for the fragment of Apodeictic syllogisms. In fact, we will see that just making use of the distribution rules, which can be thought of as a monotonicity calculus, cannot work on our causal analysis, because the rule of *right upward monotonicity* won't be valid anymore. In fact, we take this as a crucial insight behind the above problem of the three Barbara's.

---

[4] Some (van Rijen (1989)) have claimed that $Ba^\square C$ can hold only if 'B' is a substance term. This won't quite be enough (cf. Rini 1998). Malink (2013) demands on top that a substance term can only be predicated of another substance term. We take this to follow naturally from a causal view.

[5] Vecchio (2016), building on Malink (2013), even slighly improves on Malink's predictions.

3   Causal Analysis and Aristotelian Demonstrations

3.1   Causal Dependence and Causal Models

Consider the following two sentences:

(1)   a.   Aspirin causes headaches to diminish.
      b.   Aspirin relieves headaches.

Intuitively, (1-a) says that there exists a causal connexion between Aspirin and diminishing headaches: the intake of Aspirin *tends to* diminish headaches. Remarkably, (1-a) seems to express the same content as the *generic* sentence (1-b). This strongly suggests that also the generic sentence (1-b) should be given a causal analysis. Thus, not only (1-a), but also (1-b) expresses the fact that particular intakes of Aspirin *tend* to cause particular states of headache to go away, because of *what it is* to be Aspirin. Or, as we will say, because of the *causal power* of Aspirin to relieve headaches.

Causality is a kind of dependence. A number of authors have recently argued for a dependency analysis of conditionals, which is most straightforwardly done using probabilities: C depends on A iff $P(C|A) > P(C)$.[6] However, Douven (2008) has argued that dependence is not enough, 'If A, then C' is acceptable only if both $P(C|A) > P(C)$ *and* $P(C|A)$ are high.

We can implement Douven's proposal by requiring that $P(C|A) - P(C|\neg A)$ is close to $1 - P(C|\neg A)$. Since $P(C|A) > P(C)$ iff $P(C|A) > P(C|\neg A)$, we can demand that the conditional is acceptable iff $\frac{P(C|A) - P(C|\neg A)}{1 - P(C|\neg A)}$ is high. This can only be the case if both $P(C|A) - P(C|\neg A)$ and $P(C|A)$ are high, so it derives Douven's demands.

The measure $\frac{P(C|A) - P(C|\neg A)}{1 - P(C|\neg A)}$ is interesting from a causal perspective. Especially among philosophers dissatisfied with a Humean metaphysics, **causal powers** have recently become en vogue (again). Indeed, a growing number of philosophers (Harré and Madden 1975; Cartwright 1989; Shoemaker 1980; Bird 2007) have argued that causal powers, capacities or dispositions are the truth-makers of laws and other non-accidental generalities. Cheng (1997) hypothesises the existence of stable, but unobservable causal powers (Pearl (2000) calls them 'causal *mechanisms*') p_{ac} of (objects or events of kind) A to produce C. Cheng then *derives* a way how this objective but unobservable power can be estimated by an observable quantity, making use of standard probability theory and assuming certain natural independence conditions. It turns out that this quantity is exactly the above measure: $p_{ac} = \frac{P(C|A) - P(C|\neg A)}{1 - P(C|\neg A)}$. Cheng's notion has been used for the analysis of conditionals, generics and disposition statements, in van Rooij and Schulz (2019, 2020).

Dispositions and causal powers are things that (kinds of) objects have, independently of whether they show them. It is standardly assumed, though, that these (kinds of) objects *would* show them, if they *were* triggered sufficiently. Thus, there should be a relation with counterfactuals. Pearl (2000) provides a

---

[6] For a discussion of some qualitative variants, see Spohn (2013) and Rott (2019).

causal analysis of counterfactuals. He defines he 'probability of causal sufficiency of A to produce C', abbreviated by PS_A^C, as $P(C_A \mid \neg C, \neg A) = \frac{P(C_A, \neg C, \neg A)}{P(\neg C, \neg A)}$, with C_A the property that is true of an object if after making the object an A-object by intervention, the object would be a C-object.

Pearl (2000, Chap. 9) shows that under natural conditions PA_A^C reduces to Cheng's notion of causal power, $\frac{P(C|A)-P(C|\neg A)}{1-P(C|\neg A)}$. The first of these natural conditions is a **consistency assumption** used for counterfactuals,

(i) $A \Rightarrow (C_A = C)$.

This assumption is natural: if A already holds, an intervention to make A true leaves everything as is.[7] Pearl also assumes a notion of *exogeneity*, i.e., that C_A is *independent* of learning A (and thus also that $\neg C_{\neg A}$ is *independent* of $\neg A$).

(ii)   A variable A is said to be **exogenous** relative C in model M iff $P(C_A \wedge C_{\neg A}|A) = P(C_A \wedge C_{\neg A})$.

Pearl's assumption that A is exogenous to C is very similar to Cheng's (1997) assumption that the potential causes of C are *independent* of one another (the Noisy-OR assumption). It rules out that learning A influences the probability of C via an indirect way, for instance that if B is another potential cause of C, there is a common cause of A and B.

Making use of these two assumptions, Pearl (2000) shows that $PS_A^C = \frac{P(C_A \wedge \neg C_{\neg A})}{1-P(C|\neg A)}$. On the additional assumption of *monotonicity*,

(iii) C is **monotonic** relative to A iff for all u: $C_A(u) \geq C_{\neg A}(u)$,

Pearl derives that

(2) $PS_A^C = \frac{P(C|A)-P(C|\neg A)}{1-P(C/\neg A)}$.

Thus, PS_A^C can be thought of as the causal power of A to produce C, i.e., p_{ac}. Notice that if all involved causal powers have value 1, a sequence of such causal powers is **transitively closed**: if $PS_A^B = 1$ and $PS_B^C = 1$, then also $PS_A^C = 1$. Obviously, also $PS_A^A = 1$, meaning that causal power is **reflexive**, and that demanding PS to be 1 gives rise to a pre-order.

In this paper we are going to make crucial of the following interesting about the probabilistic measures $\frac{P(C|A)-P(C|\neg A)}{1-P(C|\neg A)}$ and .[8]

---

[7] If we would analyse the counterfactual $A \mathbin{\square\!\!\rightarrow} C$ by C_A, this consistency rule would validate *modus ponens* and the inference $A, C \therefore A \mathbin{\square\!\!\rightarrow} C$, also known as conjunctive sufficiency. Both inference rules are accepted by almost everyone working on counterfactuals, although, to be honest, not by everyone.

[8] Of course, the causal notions PS_A^C and p_{ac} demand this as well in case their values are 1, but in addition they demand that A is a cause of C, and not that A is uniquely caused by C. If we limit ourselves to values that are 1 or not, the probabilistic measure is antisymmetric, and thus gives rise to a partial order.

Fact 1. $\frac{P(C|A)-P(C|\neg A)}{1-P(C|\neg A)}$ *has its* _maximal value 1_ *iff* $P(C|A) = 1$ *and* $P(C|\neg A) \neq 1$.

Similarly, we predict that $PS_A^{\neg C} = 1$ and $p_{a \neg c} = 1$ holds only if $P(C|A) = 0$ and $P(C|\neg A) \neq 0$. This is due to the following fact.

Fact 2. $\frac{P(\neg C|A)-P(\neg C|\neg A)}{1-P(\neg C|\neg A)}$ *is equal to* $\frac{P(C|\neg A)-P(C|A)}{P(C|\neg A)}$ *and has its* _maximal value 1_ *just in case* $P(C|A) = 0$ *and* $P(C|\neg A) \neq 0$.

Interestingly, $p_{a \neg c}$ corresponds with Cheng's (1997) notion of *causal power* of A to *prevent* C. We propose that these notions might help us to provide a natural semantics for Aristotle's modal categorical sentences in order to illuminate Aristotle's hard to understand system of modal syllogisms.

3.2   A Causal Analysis of Aristotelian Demonstrations

Many dialogues of Plato focus on questions of the form 'What is X?', where X is typically some moral property like *virtue* or *courage*, a natural kind of thing like *human*, or *water*, or a mathematical object like *a triangle*. A good answer to this kind of question must consist of a set of features all and only all individuals of type X have. Aristotle, a pupil of Plato, was interested in the same kind of questions. But he also was more ambitious. If all (and only all) individuals or objects of type X share certain features, Aristotle also wanted to know *why*. Indeed, for Aristotle, scientific inquiry is an attempt to answer 'why' questions. A scientific explanation of a fact about the world consists of a valid syllogistic argument with some fundamental true claims as its premises and this fact as the conclusion. But not any old valid syllogism would do, for the premises must express *fundamental* true claims. A valid syllogism that satisfies this extra requirement Aristotle calls a *demonstration*. A typical Aristotelian demonstration is the following:

(3)   a.   All animals are living things.
       b.   All humans are animals.
       c.   Therefore, all humans are living things.

In this demonstration, the two premises are taken to express essential features of animals and humans, respectively. They follow from Aristotle's theory of *real definitions* of objects of type X in terms of (i) an immediately higher type Y, and a differentia Z. If X is 'human', for instance, then Y would be 'animal', and Z would be 'rational': a man is a rational animal. Thus, in 'All humans are animals', 'being animal' is essentially predicated of humans, and the second premise of the above syllogism can be expressed by $Sa^{\square}P$. However, not all true sentences of the form $Sa^{\square}P$ can be read off directly from Aristotle's theory of real definitions. Some have to be indirectly derived. This is what happens in the above syllogism. In the above syllogistic argument, the premises can be directly read off from Aristotle's theory of definition, but to reach the conclusion an additional argument is needed. This is provided by the syllogism, that can be stated as being of the form $Ba^\square C, Aa^\square B \therefore Aa^\square C$. For Aristotle, this argument *explains why* humans are living things. The argument turns a fact into a *reasoned fact*.[9]

What has this all to do with causality? Well, Aristotle had a somewhat wider notion of causality than many moderns have. For him, it is necessary for humans to be able to learn grammar. But being able to learn grammar is not an essential property of humans or of any higher kind. It just *causally follows by necessity* from being rational (according to Aristotle). Thus, even though all and only all objects of type X have feature f and g, it can be that one of the features is still only a derived feature, causally derived.

So far, it seems that scientific demonstrations must consist of two premises that are both necessary. But this is not exactly what Aristotle seems to assume. In fact, in his *Posterior Analytics* Aristotle discusses the following two valid syllogisms:

(4)   a.   All objects that are near the earth do not twinkle
     b.   All (the) planets are near the earth
     c.   Therefore, (all) the planets do not twinkle.

and

(5)   a.   All objects that do not twinkle are near the earth.
     b.   All (the) planets do not twinkle.
     c.   Therefore, (all) the planets are near the earth.

In these arguments, the premises (4-b) and (5-a) are not taken to express necessary truths. Although the second syllogism is not taken to be a scientific demonstration, Aristotle claims that the first syllogistic inference is. It leads to a 'reasoned fact', because the middle term 'being near the earth' *causally explains* the conclusion, something that is not the case for the middle term in the other inference 'objects that do not twinkle'. If we would translate the above arguments in modal syllogistic terms, they would be of the forms $Ba^\square C, AaB \therefore Aa^\square C$ and $BaC, Aa^\square B \therefore Aa^\square C$, respectively. Note that they are thus of types Barabara LXL and Barbara XLL, respectively.[10] Note also that in his *Prior Analytics*, Aristotle took only the first type of argument to be valid. So, there seems to be a close relation between what Aristotle claims in his two *Analytics*.

4   Causality and Modal Syllogisms

Causal links need not only connect propositions, they can connect properties, or features, as well. In fact, Danks (2014) argues that all prominent theories of

---

[9] For much more detailed and sophisticated analyses of Aristotelian demonstration see Crager (2015) and Vecchio (2016).

[10] According to Vecchio (2016), the argument in (9) explains why planets do not twinkle, by using a fact is which part of the nominal definition of a planet ('being near the earth'), but which is not a part of its real definition.

concepts could be represented by graphical causal models. Although not explicitly discussed, the essentialists' version is one: features of birds are connected (and thus caused) in various strengths to the essence of the kind, i.e., by what it is to be a bird.

Let us now come back to the question what the natural interpretation of Aristotle's *modal* syllogistics is. Recall that $Aa^\square B$ means that all As are *necessary/essentially* B and that Aristotle claimed that the following modal syllogisms are valid and invalid, respectively:

1. $Ba^\square C, Aa^\square B \therefore Aa^\square C$ Valid   Barbara LLL
2. $Ba^\square C, AaB \therefore Aa^\square C$ Valid   Barbara LXL
3. $BaC, Aa^\square B \therefore Aa^\square C$ Invalid   Barbara XLL

Similarly, Aristotle claims that the following modal syllogism is valid, where $Be^\square C$ means that by (*de re*) necessity no B is a C:

4. $Be^\square C, AaB \therefore Ae^\square C$ Valid   Celarent LXL

Moreover, Aristotle claims that not only conversion inference 5 is valid, but that the same holds for the modal conversion inferences 6 and 7:

5. $AeB \therefore BeA$ Valid
6. $Ae^\square B \therefore Be^\square A$ Valid
7. $Aa^\square B \therefore Bi^\square A$ Valid

We claim that Aristotle's claims make perfect sense once we understand $Aa^\square B$ as causally explaining *why* B. More in particular, we would like to say that $Aa^\square B$ just means that A has complete causal power to make B to hold, i.e., $PS_A^B = 1$ (or $p_{ab} = 1$) and that $Ae^\square B$ just means that both A or B has complete causal powers to prevent the other to hold, i.e., $PS_A^{\neg B} = 1$ and $PS_B^{\neg A} = 1$ (or $p_{a\neg b} = 1$ and $p_{b\neg a} = 1$).[11]

Definition 2. Truth conditions of universal modal sentences.

- $Aa^\square B$ is true iff $PS_A^B = 1$
- $Ae^\square B$ is true iff $PS_A^{\neg B} = 1$ and $PS_B^{\neg A} = 1$

A simple fact about probabilities is that if $P(A), P(B) \neq 0$, then $P(\neg B|A) = 1$ iff $P(B|A) = 0$ iff $P(A \wedge B) = 0$ iff $P(\neg A|B) = 1$. Because of this, and if we assume the consistency assumption for counterfactuals, exogeneity and monotonicity, and assume in addition that $P(A), P(B) \neq 0$, we can derive immediately the following facts from the above proposed analysis of modal categorical sentences:

---

[11] Aristotle's (hyperintensional) distinction between necessity and essentiality suggests that the analysis of $Aa^\square B$ as $p_{ab} = 1$ is still too coarse-grained. Notice, however, that even if A and B are necessary co-extensive, it will typically be (causally speaking) that either $p_{ab} = 1$ and $p_{ba} = 0$, or $p_{ab} = 0$ and $p_{ba} = 1$. We take the former to be the case if A is a substantive term and B an adjectival one.

Fact 3. *Facts about truth conditions of universal modal sentences.*

- $Aa^\square B$ *is true iff* $P(B|A) = 1$ *and* $P(B|\neg A) \neq 1$
  iff $P(A \wedge \neg B) = 0$ *and* $P(\neg A \wedge \neg B) \neq 0$
- $Ae^\square B$ *is true iff* $P(A \wedge B) = 0$ *and* $P(\neg A \wedge B) \neq 0$ *and* $P(\neg B \wedge A) \neq 0$

This fact shows that these truth conditions can be captured in terms of Venn diagrams. However, besides circles for A and B, we now also need to have a domain of discourse, D, to account for negation:

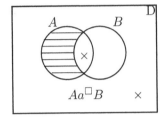   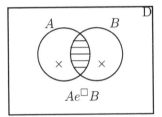

We will assume the interpretation rule for non-modal universal categorical sentences as in definition 1 repeated below

Definition 3. Truth conditions of non-modal Categorical sentences

- AaB is true iff $P(B|A) = 1$,
- AiB is true iff $P(A \cap B) \neq 0$,
- AeB is true iff $P(A \cap B) = 0$, and
- AoB is true iff $P(B|A) \neq 1$

Inference 1 is valid on this interpretation, because if the premises are true the following will hold (i) $P(C|B) = 1$, (ii) $P(C|\neg B) \neq 1$, (iii) $P(B|A) = 1$ and (iv) $P(B|\neg A) \neq 1$. Obviously, by (i) and (iii) it follows that $P(C|A) = 1$. From (ii) and (iv) it follows that (a) there are some $\neg C$s among the $\neg B$s, and (b) that there are some $\neg B$s among the $\neg A$s. By (a) and (b) this means that $P(C|\neg A) \neq 1$. Thus, $P(C|A) = 1$ and $P(C|\neg A) \neq 1$ which means that $Aa^\square C$. The validity of the inference can be checked by the following Venn diagram:

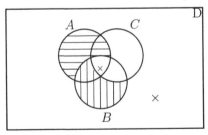

Inference 2 is also valid on this interpretation, because if the premises are true it means that the following will hold (i) $P(C|B) = 1$, (ii) $P(C|\neg B) \neq 1$ and (iii) $P(B|A) = 1$. Obviously, by (i) and (iii) it follows again that $P(C|A) = 1$. From (ii) it follows that there are some $\neg C$s among the $\neg B$s. But because AaB, it holds that all $\neg B$s are $\neg A$s, and thus there must also be some $\neg C$s among the $\neg A$s. Thus, $P(C|A) = 1$ and $P(C|\neg A) \neq 1$ which means that $Aa^\square C$. The validity of this inference follows from the same Venn diagram as the one that illustrates inference 1.

Inference 3, however, is not valid. The important thing to observe is that this is just an instance of 'right weakening',[12] or **right upward monotonicity**, an inference which should (and does) **not** hold on our causal analysis. In particular, the inference has a counterexample, in case the domain consists only of C individuals. The counterexample is illustrated by the following Venn diagram.

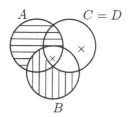

Similarly, we can account for Aristotle's intuition that inference 4 is valid. Using the above interpretation of non-modal statements, we account for inference 5. The validity of inference 6 is obvious given the truth conditions of $Ae^{\Box}B$. As for inference 7, this immediately follows from the semantic analysis of statements like $Bi^{\Box}A$ to be given in a minute.

Our predictions agree with all Aristotle's claims of (in)validities of universal modal syllogisms with modality $\Box$. For instance, we correctly predict Aristotle's claimed validity of Cesare LXL, Camestres XLL, and his claim of invalidity of Camester LXL. The latter one – $Ba^{\Box}A, CeA \not\models Be^{\Box}C$ – is particularly interesting. It is easy to see that this inference would be predicted as valid, if we analysed CeA as true iff $P(A|C) = 0$, which presupposes that $P(C) \neq 0$. However, we have analysed CeA as true iff $P(C \wedge A) = 0$, and on this interpretation Camestres LXL is *not* predicted to be valid, in accordance with Aristotle's intuitions.[13] More in particular, our analysis makes the right predictions for the modal Barbara and Celarent syllogisms of the first figure.

As for the second figure, and limiting ourselves to universal statements, we have to explain why (according to Aristotle)

(6)   a. $Ae^{\Box}B, CaB \models Ce^{\Box}A$ Cesare LXL
      b. $AeB, Ca^{\Box}B \not\models Ce^{\Box}A$ Cesare XLL

and

(7)   a. $Aa^{\Box}B, CeB \not\models Ce^{\Box}A$ Camestres LXL
      b. $AaB, Ce^{\Box}B \models Ce^{\Box}A$ Camestres XLL

---

[12] In condtional terms, right weakening means that if $A \Rightarrow B$ and $B \models C$, then also $A \Rightarrow C$.

[13] Note, though, that we would predict invalidity as well if we interpreted $Aa^{\Box}B$ as being true iff $A \subseteq B$ and $P(\neg A \cap \neg B) \neq 0$ and interpreted AeB as true iff either $P(B|A) = 0$ or $P(A|B) = 0$. Although these interpretation rules would also give us the correct predictions for inferences 1 until 5, the interpretation rule for $Aa^{\Box}B$ would, unfortunately, not give us inference 7.

As for (6-a), this follows immediately from our semantics. For (6-b) this follows because AeB is true $P(A \wedge B) = 0$. As for (7-a). This doesn't follow, because it is not guaranteed that $P(C|\neg A) \neq 0$, which makes the conclusion false.[14] Inference (7-b) is immediately verified. There are no other modal syllogisms with only universal statements of the second figure to be checked, and we don't know about Aristotle's intuitions on only 'universal' modal syllogisms of the fourth figure (Cameses$_4$). Because all valid syllogisms of the third figure involve non-universal sentences as well, we predict for all modal syllogisms that only involve universal sentence in accordance with Aristotle's intuition.

As for modal syllogisms with non-universal sentences, we first need to know what makes sentences like $Ai^{\square}B$ true. In counterfactual terms, it seems natural to propose that $Ai^{\square}B$ is true iff $\exists x : xaA, \exists D : xa^{\square}D$ and $P(B_D|\neg B, \neg D) = 1$, where xaA is the singular categorical sentence that (all) x is A, and $xa^{\square}D$ the singular categorical sentence that (all) x is necessary D. Notice that in non-counterfactual terms, our interpretation of $Ai^{\square}B$ comes down to the following: $Ai^{\square}B$ is true iff $\exists x : xaA$ & xaB and $\exists y : yeB$. But we want to account for conversion $Ai^{\square}B \models Bi^{\square}A$ as well. Therefore, we will propose a more symmetric definition: $Ai^{\square}B$ is true iff $\exists x, \exists D : xa^{\square}D$ and (i) xaA and $PS_D^B = 1$ or (ii) xaB and $PS_D^A = 1$. To simplify things, however, we won't make use of property D, but just use singular modal sentences like $xa^{\square}B$, instead. Notice that this modal sentence just reduces to the conjunction of two non-modal sentences: xaB and $\exists y : yeB$. We will do the same to give the truth conditions of the modal sentence $Ao^{\square}B$.

Definition 4. Truth conditions of non-universal modal sentences.

- $Ai^{\square}B$ is true iff $\exists x : xaA$ & xaB and $(xa^{\square}B$ or $xa^{\square}A)$
  iff $\exists x : xaA$ & xaB and $\exists y : yeB$ or yeA
- $Ao^{\square}B$ is true iff $\exists x : xaA$ & xeB and $\exists y : yeA$ & yaB

Notice that we didn't provide the simpler and perhaps more intuitive truth conditions for $Ao^{\square}B$: $Ao^{\square}B$ is true iff $\exists x : xaA$ and $xe^{\square}B$. Our truth conditions are more complicated, because we used y such that yeA instead of $\neg x$. We need these more complicated truth conditions because the simpler truth conditions can't account, for instance, for Aristotle's claimed invalidity of Baroco XLL, at least if we interpret AaB as true iff $P(B|A) = 1$.[15]

---

[14] Alternatively, we could say that AeB is true iff either $P(B|A) = 0$ or $P(A|B) = 0$. That would get those inferences right as well.

[15] To be clear, the simpler interpretation rule for $Co^{\square}B$ – which would come down to $P(\neg B|A) \neq 0$ and $P(B) \neq 0$ – is possible, if Baroco XLL were not valid. It is interesting to observe that although Aristotle claims that he found a counterexample to Baroco XLL, several commentators (e.g. Van Rijen 1989; Patterson 1995) have argued that he was mistaken. For discussion, see Malink (2013). Alternatively, we could use the simpler and more intuitive interpretation rule for $Co^{\square}B$, if we would interpret AaB as true iff $A \subseteq B$. This interpretation rule for AaB gives problems at other places, however.

Interestingly, also these non-universal modal sentences can be captured in terms of Venn diagrams, if we make one addition: if we have circles ○ in two areas, then we know that at least one of those areas must be non-empty:

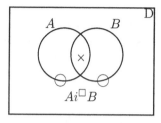

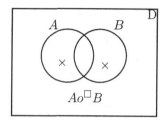

Notice that from the above interpretation rules of $Aa^\square B$ and $Ai^\square B$, inference 7, the conversion inference $Aa^\square B \therefore Bi^\square A$ is immediately predicted to be valid, in accordance with Aristotle's intuitions. Let us now see whether we can account for Aristotles' claims with respect to modal syllogisms involving also non-universal sentences. First, Aristotle claims (8-a) (of the first figure) to be valid, but (8-b) not to be so:

(8)   a. $Ba^\square A, CiB \models Ci^\square A$ Darii LXL
       b. $BaA, Ci^\square B \not\models Ci^\square A$ Darii XLL

Our interpretation rules of non-universal modal sentences indeed make Darii LXL valid. Moreover, these interpretation rule makes Darii XLL invalid, as desired. The following Venn diagram shows the counterexample to Darii XLL.

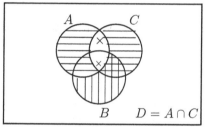

Aristotle also claims a distinction between the following syllogisms, also of the first figure:

(9)   a. $Be^\square A, CiB \models Co^\square A$ Ferio LXL
       b. $BeA, Ci^\square B \not\models Co^\square A$ Ferio XLL

Inference (9-a) follows immediately if we analyse $Co^\square A$ as true iff $\exists x : xaC, \exists D : xa^\square D$ and $P(\neg A_D | B, \neg D) = 1$. There is an easy counterexample to (9-b), again due to the fact that the conclusion $Co^\square A$ demands that there is at least one A, while premise BeA can be true without there being such an A. Notice, though, that we have not analysed $Co^\square A$ as above, but rather as in definition 4. Fortunately, the validity of Ferio LXL and the invalidity of Ferio XLL follows from this interpretation rule as well, as might be checked by a Venn diagram. We leave this to the reader.

Aristotle didn't give his opinion on every possible syllogism which involves sentences with necessity modals. In fact, he limited himself to syllogisms that (i) have a necessity modal in the conclusion, (ii) are of the first three figures and (ii) that are valid without any modal. Still, there are 6 valid syllogisms in each figure, and 3 possible combinations where at least one of the premises has a necessity modal. Of those 54 syllogisms, Aristotle expressed his opinion on 42 of those modal syllogisms.[16] 23 of those syllogisms he counted valid, and the others non-valid. He looked at 14 syllogisms where all categorical sentences involved had a necessity modal, such as Barbara LLL, and he counted all of them as valid. We can check that all such modal syllogisms are valid on our analysis as well. Let us go to one of the more challenging ones to explain: Darii LLL, $Ba^\Box A, Ci^\Box B \models Ci^\Box A$. The first premise means that $PS_B^A = 1$. According to the second premise, $\exists x : xaC, \exists D : xa^\Box D$ and $PS_D^B = 1$. Because if $PS_B^A = 1$ and $PS_D^B = 1$, it follows by transitivity that also $PS_D^A = 1$. It follows that thus $\exists x : xaC, \exists D : xa^\Box D$ and $PS_D^A = 1$, which means that conclusion $Ci^\Box A$ is true.

As for the other 30 modal syllogisms of this type that Aristotle considered, we checked them as well, and our analysis predicts in accordance with Aristotle's intuitions. Thus, our analysis makes predictions exactly in accordance with Aristotle's explicity discussed claims of (in)validity for **every** modal syllogism in which at most the modal $\Box$ occurs (a system also known as 'apodeictic syllogisms')!

Theorem 1. *Using the truth conditions of categorical sentences as given in definitions 2 until 4, all and only all <u>apodeictic</u> syllogisms are predicted to be valid that Aristotle counted as valid.*

We think this result is quite remarkable. What is perhaps even more remarkable is that validity of epodeictic syllogisms can be decided by means of Venn diagrams:

Theorem 2. *Validity of epodeictic modal syllogisms as discussed by Aristotle in his Prior Analytics can be decided by means of Venn diagrams.*

We haven't checked our predictions for *all* 16.384 modal syllogisms, though. In fact, we didn't check any syllogism that involve possibility and contingency modals that Aristotle also discussed. In this paper we did not even propose meanings of such sentences. But the smoothness of our explanation of Aritotle's intuitions concerning apodeictic syllogisms makes one optimistic that we can also account for Aristotle's intuitions on other modal syllogisms.

But there is further ground for optimism. Malink (2013) and Vecchio (2016) have recently shown how to account for most (if not all) of the Aristotle's claims about modal syllogisms making use of *essences*. $Aa^\Box B$ is true iff all As are B *in virtue of* what it is to be an A. But that is exactly how we think of our own proposal as well.

---

[16] We base ourselves here completely on appendix A of Malink (2013).

5   A Challenge: Counterexamples to Barbara LXL?

We have shown in the previous section that our causal power analysis can account for why the modal syllogism Barbara LXL, $Ba^\square C, AaB \therefore Aa^\square C$ is valid, although Barbara XLL, $BaC, Aa^\square B \therefore Aa^\square C$, is not. We have seen that this can be shown if we analyse statements like $Ba^\square C = 1$ by $\frac{P(C|B)-P(C|\neg B)}{1-P(C|\neg B)} = 1$ and $AaB = 1$ by $P(B|A) = 1$. We have also seen that the causal notions of causal power and PS_A^C come down to this probabilistic notion under certain circumstances.

Although Aristotle claimed that Barbara LXL is valid, very soon (putative) counterexamples to this modal syllogisms were offered:[17]

(10)   a.   All litererats necessarily have knowledge, all men are litarate, thus all men necessarily have knowledge.

      b. $Ba^\square C, AaB \therefore Aa^\square C$ Barbara LXL

In fact, Aristotle himself provided a (putative) counterexample to Celarent LXL himself.

(11)   a.   All ill people are necessarily not healthy, all men are ill, thus all men are necessarily not healthy.

      b. $Be^\square C, AaB \therefore Ae^\square C$ Celarent LXL

Malink (2013) and Crager (2015) argue that these counterexamples can be explained away if we take seriously Aristotle's analysis of 'genuine predication' from Aristotle's *Categories*. The idea is that terms can denote sets of different *ontological types*: some denote *substances*, while others denote *qualities*. Just as each substance has an essence, this is also the case for each quality. However, denotations of the same type can only stand in a limited number of extensional relations with each other. For instance, for any two substances A and B, it cannot be that $A \cap B \neq \emptyset$ without either $A \subset B$ or $B \subset A$. Beyond this *extensional* constraint, there lays a more important *intensional* constraint: if A and B are of the same ontological type, then, if $A \subset B$, then $Aa^\square B$. Malink (2013) and Crager (2015) argue that Aristotle took Barbara LXL and Celarent LXL to be valid because he demanded that in a demonstration with a necessary conclusion, also the seemingly nonmodal premise (in our cases, the minor premise AaB) should be a case of genuine predication.

If Malink (2013) and Crager (2015) are correct, it means that valid modal syllogisms with a necessity modal in the conclusion should, in the end, all be of the form LLL. It also suggests that our explanation in the previous section of the validity of Barbara LXL and Celarent LXL will not be correct, for otherwise the (putative) counterexamples above would likely be genuine counterexamples. If we want to stick to our causal analysis, this suggests that instead of looking at the *extensional* notion $\frac{P(C|B)-P(C|\neg B)}{1-P(C|\neg B)} = 1$ for the analysis of $Ba^\square C$ we

---

[17] For modern discussion, see van Rijen (1989), Rini (1989), Malink (2013) and Crager (2015).

should look at the *intensional* counterpart, $\frac{P(C_B)-P(C_{\neg B})}{1-P(C|\neg B)} = 1$, where intervention still plays an important role, and the counterfactual probabiltiy $P(B_A)$ is not reduced to the conditional probability $P(B|A)$. Indeed, on such an intensional analysis Barbara LXL, $Ba^\square C, AaB \therefore Aa^\square C$, would not be valid, because from $\frac{P(C_B)-P(C_{\neg B})}{1-P(C|\neg B)} = 1$ and $P(B|A) = 1$, we cannot conclude that $\frac{P(C_A)-P(C_{\neg A})}{1-P(C|\neg A)} = 1$.

We don't know, though, whether Malink's (2013) and Crager's (2015) interpretation of Aristotle is correct. For one thing, Malink (2013) himself already notes that Aristotle explicitly discusses modal syllogisms that he takes to be valid even though the nonmodal premise does not seem to involve genuine predication. But, of course, if Malink and Crager are not correct, we would have to explain away the above 'putative' counterexamples in another way. In fact, Vecchio (2016, Chap. 1) argues that Aristotle himself explained away the (putative) counterexamples to Barbara LXL and the like in a more straightforward way than was suggested by Malink (2013): by demanding that the terms are interpreted in an omnitemporal way, which makes the non-modal premise false. Vecchio (2016, Chap. 3) also argues explicitly that Aristotle used syllogisms of the form Barbara LXL in his analysis of scientific demonstrations in the *Posterior Analytics*, just as we suggested in Sect. refsec3.2. Vecchio argues that Barbara LXL can be used to turn a *nominal* definition, 'Thunder is a noise in the clouds' (of form AaB) to a *real* definition 'Thunder is (necessarily) the extinguishing of fire in the clouds' (of form $Aa^\square C$) via the essential major premise 'A noise in the clouds is (by necessity) the extinguishing of fire in the clouds' (of form $Ba^\square C$).[18] Note that if Vecchio is right, our 'extensional' causal analysis might be on the right track after all.

6   Conclusion and Outlook

In this paper we have shown that Aristotle's intuitions about apodeictic syllogisms as expressed in his *Prior Analytics* can be captured semantically by giving a causal semantics of modal categorical sentences. Moreover, we have seen that this causal semantics can be reduced to an extensional analysis just making use of probabilities, which allowed to check modal syllogisms by simple Venn diagrams. The only real complication is that whereas for standard syllogisms no domain of discourse was required, we need such a domain now, because for our analysis of modal syllogisms information about the *complement* of the denotations of terms is crucial. (Of course, we need such complications as well, once we allow negative terms to occur in standard syllogisms). Finally, we have argued that we can motivate our causal analysis by Aristotle's analysis of *demonstrative proofs* as worked out in his *Posterior Analytics*.

---

[18] There exists an interesting analogue between this and the way natural kind terms receive their content according to the causal theory of reference: first a set of superficial properties is used to identify a set of things, and later having these superficial properties is explained by some essential properties all the things in the set have in common.

Of course, we will never know whether our causal analysis fits Aristotle's semantic intuitions on modal syllogisms, because he never clearly stated these intuitions in the first place. But this leaves open the question whether our semantic analysis is plausible in the first case. One reviewer doubted the plausibility of our analysis, suggesting that the difference between AaB and $Aa^\Box B$ should not just be that $P(\neg A \wedge \neg B) \neq 0$. More in general one might doubt whether the truth conditions of modal categorical sentences could be described at all by Venn diagrams. We think that there are two points to be made here. *First* of all, our basic idea is that a sentence like $Aa^\Box B$ should be analysed causally as saying that $p_{ab} = 1$, or better perhaps that $PS_A^B = 1$. On this causal view, modality statements are really treated in an *intensional* (or even hyperintensional) manner. It is just that by making certain assumptions that $PS_A^B = 1$ holds exactly if $P(B|A) = 1$ and $P(B|\neg A) \neq 1$. Notice that if one of those assumptions is not made, the reduction of the causal notion to the purely probabilistic one would not go through. For instance, one might doubt that for causality we should really demand the *consistency assumption*, saying that if A (or $\neg A$) holds, the truth value of B_A (or $B_{\neg A}$) is the same as the truth value of B. This assumption comes down to the *strong centering* assumption known from conditional logic, and corresponds with the inference $A, B \therefore A \Rightarrow B$. Intuitively, one might argue, this inference should not hold if '$\Rightarrow$' expresses a relation of causal relevance. Indeed, A and B can both be true without there being a causal relation between them. Once the consistency condition is given up, truth conditions of modal categorical sentences could not be reduced to simple probabilistic claims that can be expressed by Venn diagrams. Something similar holds when we give up the exogeneity condition or the monotonicity condition. Importantly, however, we think that our semantics is still appropriate if we disregard the reduction to simple probabilistic claims.[19] *Second*, we don't think it is strange that the complements of the denotations of A and B *should* play a role for the semantic analysis of $Aa^\Box B$. Recall that the basic idea of our analysis is that $Aa^\Box B$ is true if A has the causal power to make B true. For A to have the causal power to make B true means that A must *make a difference* to the truth B. But if B is a necessary truth, A cannot make such a difference. So, for $Aa^\Box B$ to hold, there must be a non-B individual. But obviously, $Aa^\Box B \models AaB$, so this non-B individual cannot be an A-individual. Thus, there must be a $\neg A \wedge \neg B$-individual, meaning that $P(\neg A \wedge \neg B) \neq 0$.

Although we are surprised that our semantic analysis captures so many of Aristotle's intuitions, and in particular that this could be done by using Venn diagrams, we don't think that our analysis is, in general, unnatural. There is only one interpretation rule that we feel is really artificial: our interpretation rule for $Ao^\Box B$. This interpretation rule is artificial already because it is symmetric. This

---

[19] There is one real worry we have, though, and that is our semantic analysis of $Ao^\Box B$. We fear that our proposed analysis is not exactly natural, for one thing because it entails that $Ao^\Box B$ entails $Bo^\Box A$.

interpretation rule was given just to get the 'facts' right. These 'facts' are now Aristotle's intuitions, and we noted already in footnote 14 that his intuitions might as well be mistaken on the crucial modal syllogism (Baroco XLL) that forced us to our artificial interpretation rule.

As mentioned above, in his *Prior Analytics* Aristotle also discussed inferences concerning *possibility* and *contingency* modals. Of course, for the standard possibility modal, a natural analysis suggests itself:

$$(12) \qquad \begin{array}{ll} Aa^\Diamond B \equiv \neg(Ao^\Box B) & Ae^\Diamond B \equiv \neg(Ai^\Box B) \\ Ai^\Diamond B \equiv \neg(Ae^\Box B) & Ao^\Diamond B \equiv \neg(Aa^\Box B) \end{array}$$

We think, however, that to provide a semantic account of possibility statements we need to give up the assumption that we made in Sect. 3.1: that statements like C_A have a truth value in $\{0, 1\}$. We hypothesise that such statements have to have a value in $[0, 1]$, instead, thought of as the *chance* of C after an intervention to make A true. But it remains to be seen whether such an analysis gives rise to predictions that accord with Aristotl's intuitions. It is even less clear whether we can account for Aristotle's claims involving the contingency modal, Δ, a task that is perhaps the most challenging. Striker (1985) argues, though, that sentences like $Aa^\Delta B$ should be interpreted basically as generic sentences, where B applies *by nature*, or *for the most part*, to A. Interestingly, this suggestion would be much in line with van Rooij and Schulz's (2020) analysis of generic sentences, according to which sentences of the form 'As are B' are interpreted as having high causal power, i.e. $p_{ab} \approx 1$. But it is more natural to interpret $Aa^\Delta B$ as $\forall x \in A : \neg \exists D : xa^\Box D$ and $(Da^\Box B$ or $De^\Box B)$ and $Ai^\Delta B$ as $\neg \exists x \in A : \exists D : xa^\Box D$ and $(Da^\Box B$ or $De^\Box B)$ to account for Aristotle's claims that $Aa^\Delta B$ is equivalent with $Ae^\Delta B$ and $Ai^\Delta B$ with $Ao^\Delta B$, and that not only $Ai^\Delta B$ is equivalent with $Bi^\Delta A$, but also that $Ao^\Delta B$ is equivalent with $Bo^\Delta A$. We don't know whether with this interpretation we can account for all of Aristotle's intuitions w.r.t. modal syllogisms involving Δ.

The bulk of this paper is about modal syllogisms, involving sentences that are either true or false. As mentioned in Sect. 3, however, our approach was motivated by the *quantitative* causal analysis of conditionals and generic sentences of van Rooij and Schulz (2019, 2020). It is well-known that Adams (1965, 1966) developed a well-behaving probabilistic entailment relation $\models^p$ based on the assumption that the assertability of conditional $A \Rightarrow C$ 'goes with' the corresponding conditional probability, $P(C|A)$. This logic can be axiomatised and is now known as the basic non-monotonic logic: system **P**. A question that is still open is whether a similarly well-behaved logic can be developed that is based on the assumption of van Rooij and Schulz (2019, 2020) that conditionals and generic sentences express relations of causal relevance. The causal relevance of A for B is measured by Cheng's notion of the *causal power* of A to produce B, or (better perhaps) by Pearl's notion of the 'probability of causal sufficiency'. Because the values of these measures can be anywhere between -1 and 1, this open question is difficult to handle. The question would be easier to handle, however, when we care only whether these causal powers have values 1 or 0. Then the question becomes whether it is possible to develop a logic for conditionals that express such *qualitative* causal relevance relations. But notice that on our causal semantics of Aristotelian modal sentences we have limited ourselves to qualitative causal relevance relations. This suggests that Aristotle's system of modal syllogisms, or something very close to it, can actually be viewed as the qualitative logic that deals with causal conditionals!

A   Appendix

A.1   Table of Modal Syllogisms with Necessity Modals

See Tables 1, 2, 3 and 4.

Table 1. Conversion rules for necessity modality

Form of conversion rule	Validness
From $Aa^{\Box}B$ to $Bi^{\Box}A$	valid
From $Ai^{\Box}B$ to $Bi^{\Box}A$	valid
From $Ae^{\Box}B$ to $Be^{\Box}A$	valid

Table 2. Apodeictic syllogistic of first figure discussed by Aristotle

Name of syllogisms	Form of syllogism	Validness
Barbara LLL	From $Ba^{\Box}C$, $Aa^{\Box}B$ to $Aa^{\Box}C$	Valid
Barbara LXL	From $Ba^{\Box}C$, AaC to $Aa^{\Box}C$	Valid
Barbara XLL	From BaC, $Aa^{\Box}C$ to $Aa^{\Box}C$	Invalid
Celarent LLL	From $Be^{\Box}C$, $Aa^{\Box}B$ to $Ae^{\Box}C$	Valid
Celartent LXL	From $Be^{\Box}C$, AaC to $Ae^{\Box}C$	Valid
Celarent XLL	From BeC, $Aa^{\Box}C$ to $Ae^{\Box}C$	Invalid
Darii LLL	From $Ba^{\Box}C$, $Ai^{\Box}B$ to $Ai^{\Box}C$	Valid
Darii LXL	From $Ba^{\Box}C$, AiB to $Ai^{\Box}C$	Valid
Darii XLL	From BaC, $Ai^{\Box}B$ to $Ai^{\Box}C$	Invalid
Ferio LLL	From $Be^{\Box}C$, $Ai^{\Box}B$ to $Ao^{\Box}C$	Valid
Ferio LXL	From $Be^{\Box}C$, AiB to $Ao^{\Box}C$	Valid
Ferio XLL	From BeC, $Ai^{\Box}B$ to $Ao^{\Box}C$	Invalid

Table 3. Apodeictic syllogistic of second figure discussed by Aristotle

Name of syllogisms	Form of syllogism	Validness
Cesare LLL	From $Ce^\square B$, $Aa^\square B$ to $Ae^\square C$	Valid
Cesare LXL	From $Ce^\square B$, AaB to $Ae^\square C$	Valid
Cesare XLL	From CeB, $Aa^\square B$ to $Ae^\square C$	Invalid
Camestres LLL	From $Ca^\square B$, $Ae^\square B$ to $Ae^\square C$	Valid
Camestres LXL	From $Ca^\square B$, AeB to $Ae^\square C$	Invalid
Camestres XLL	From CaB, $Ae^\square B$ to $Ae^\square C$	Valid
Festino LLL	From $Ce^\square B$, $Ai^\square B$ to $Ao^\square C$	Valid
Festino LXL	From $Ce^\square B$, AiB to $Ao^\square C$	Valid
Festino XLL	From CeB, $Ai^\square B$ to $Ao^\square C$	Invalid
Baroco LLL	From $Ca^\square B$, $Ao^\square B$ to $Ao^\square C$	Valid
Baroco LXL	From $Ca^\square A$, AoB to $Ao^\square C$	Invalid
Baroco XLL	From CaB, $Ao^\square B$ to $Ao^\square C$	Invalid

Table 4. Apodeictic syllogistic of third figure discussed by Aristotle

Name of syllogisms	Form of syllogism	Validness
Darapti LLL	From $Ba^\square C$, $Ba^\square A$ to $Ai^\square C$	Valid
Darapti LXL	From $Ba^\square C$, BaA to $Ai^\square C$	Valid
Darapti XLL	From BaC, $Ba^\square A$ to $Ai^\square C$	Valid
Felapton LLL	From $Be^\square C$, $Ba^\square A$ to $Ao^\square C$	Valid
Felapton LXL	From $Be^\square C$, BaA to $Ao^\square C$	Valid
Felapton XLL	From BeC, $Ba^\square A$ to $Ao^\square C$	Invalid
Disamis LLL	From $Bi^\square C$, $Ba^\square A$ to $Ai^\square C$	Valid
Disamis LXL	From $Bi^\square C$, BaA to $Ai^\square C$	Invalid
Disamis XLL	From BiC, $Ba^\square A$ to $Ai^\square C$	Valid
Datisi LLL	From $Ba^\square C$, $Bi^\square A$ to $Ai^\square C$	Valid
Datisi LXL	From $Ba^\square C$, BiA to $Ai^\square C$	Valid
Datisi XLL	From BaC, $Bi^\square A$ to $Ai^\square C$	Invalid
Bocardo LLL	From $Bo^\square A$, $Ba^\square A$ to $Ao^\square C$	Valid
Bocardo LXL	From $Bo^\square A$, BaA to $Ao^\square C$	Invalid
Bocardo XLL	From BoA, $Ba^\square A$ to $Ao^\square C$	Invalid
Ferison LLL	From $Be^\square C$, $Bi^\square A$ to $Ao^\square C$	Valid
Ferison LXL	From $Be^\square C$, BiA to $Ao^\square C$	Valid
Ferison XLL	From BeC, $Bi^\square A$ to $Ao^\square C$	Invalid

References

Aristotle: Aristotle in Twenty-three Volumes. Harvard University Press (1973)

Adams, E.W.: A logic of conditionals. Inquiry **8**, 166–197 (1965)

Adams, E.: Probability and the logic of conditionals. Stud. Log. Found. Math. **43**, 265–316 (1966)

van Benthem, J.: Essays in Logical Semantics, Foris publications. D. Reidel, Dordrecht (1986a)

Bird, A.: Nature's Metaphysics Laws and Properties. Oxford University Press, Oxford (2007)

Cartwright, N.: Nature's Capacities and Their Measurement. Oxford University Press, Oxford (1989)

Cheng, P.: From covariation to causation: a causal power theory. Psychol. Rev. **104**, 367–405 (1997)

Crager, A.: Metalogic in Aristotle's epistemology. Ph.D. Dissertation, Princeton University (2015)

Danks, D.: Unifying the Mind. Cognitive Representations as Graphical Models. MIT Press, Cambridge (2014)

Douven, I.: The evidential support theory of conditionals. Synthese **164**, 19–44 (2008)

van Eijck, J.: Generalized quantifiers and traditional logic. In: van Benthem, J., ter Meulen, A. (eds.) Generalized Quantifiers and Natural Language, pp. 1–19. Foris, Dordrecht (1985)

Geach, P.: Reference and Generality. Cornell University Press (1962)

Harré, R., Madden, E.: Causal Powers: A Theory of Natural Necessity. Basic Blackwell, Oxford (1975)

Hintikka, J.: Time and Necessity: Aristotle's Theory of Modality, Oxford (1973)

Leibniz, G.: A mathematics of reason. In: Parkinson (ed.) Leibniz. Logical Papers, pp. 95–104 (1966)

Lukasiewicz, J.: Aristotle's Syllogistic from the Standpoint of Modern Formal Logic, 2d edn. Clarendon Press, Oxford (1957)

Malink, M.: Aristotle's Modal Syllogistic. Harvard University Press, Cambridge (2013)

McCall, S.: Aristotle's Modal Syllogisms. Studies in Logic and the Foundations of Mathematics. North-Holland, Amsterdam (1963)

Oaksford, M., Chater, N.: Bayesian Rationality. Oxford University Press, Oxford (2007)

Patterson, R.: Aristotle's Modal Logic. Cambridge University Press, Cambridge (1995)

Patzig, G.: Aristotle's Theory of the Syllogism. Reidel, Dordrecht (1968). Translated by J. Barnes

Pearl, J.: Causality: Models, Reasoning and Inference. Cambridge University Press, Cambridge (2000)

Rescher, N.: Aristotle's theory of modal syllogisms and its interpretation. In: Bunge, M. (ed.) The Critical Approach to Science and Philosophy, pp. 152–77 (1964)

van Rijen, J.: Aspects of Aristotle's Logic of Modalities. Synthese Historical Library, vol. 35 (1989)

Rini, A.: Is there a modal syllogistic? Notre Dame J. Formal Log. **39**, 554–572 (1998)

van Rooij, R., Schulz, K.: Conditionals, causality and conditional probability. J. Logic Lang. Inform. **28**, 55–71 (2019)

van Rooij, R., Schulz, K.: A causal power analysis of generics. Topoi (2020)

Rott, H.: Difference-making conditionals and the relevant Ramsey test. Rev. Symb. Log. 1–32 (2019)

Shoemaker, S.: Causality and poperties. In: Van Inwagen, P. (ed.) Time and Cause, pp. 109–135. D. Reidel (1980)

Spohn, W.: A ranking-theoretical approach to conditionals. Cogn. Sci. **37**, 1074–1106 (2013)

Striker, G.: Notwendigkeit mit Lücken. Neue Hefte für Philos. **24**, 146–164 (1985)

Thom, P.: The two Barbaras. Hist. Phil. Log. **12**, 135–149 (1991)

Thomason, S.K.: Semantic analysis of the modal syllogistic. J. Philos. Log. **22**, 111–128 (1993)

Uckelman, S.L., Johnston, S.: A simple semantics for Aristotelian apodeictic syllogistics. In: Beklemishev, L., Goranko, V., Shehtman, V. (eds.) Advances in modal logic, vol. 8, pp. 428–443. College Publications (2010)

Vecchio, D.J.: Essence and necessity, and the aristotelian modal syllogistic: a historical and analytical study. Ph.D. dissertation, Marquette University (2016)

Bipartite Exhaustification: Evidence from Vietnamese

Tue Trinh[(✉)] [iD]

Leibniz-Zentrum Allgemeine Sprachwissenschaft, Berlin, Germany
trinh@leibniz-zas.de

Abstract. This short note presents an empirical puzzle: the Vietnamese counterpart of **any** has two morphological variants, only one of which, namely the more complex one, is acceptable under an existential modal. The note then discusses a theory of **any** whose explanation of the acceptability of **any** under existential modals requires exhaustification. The Vietnamese fact is then shown to follow from the theory under the assumption that exhaustification has a bipartite syntax. The note ends with some open questions for further research.

Keywords: NPI · exhaustification · Vietnamese

1 An Observation About Vietnamese

Wh-phrases in Vietnamese is ambiguous between an interrogative and an NPI reading [3].

(1) Nam không đọc quyển sách nào
    Nam not   read book   which
    'which book did Nam not read?' / 'Nam did not read any book'

In this note, we will not be concerned with the interrogative reading, and will gloss **quyển sách nào** simply as ANY BOOK. Our aim is to explain an observation relating to a particular morpheme which can be prefixed to the ANY phrase, namely the word **bất kỳ**, which we will gloss as BK.

(2) Nam không đọc bất kỳ quyển sách nào
    Nam not   read BK   ANY BOOK
    'Nam did not read any book'

Unsurprisingly, both the plain NPI, henceforth ANY, and its more complex variant with BK, henceforth BK-ANY, are acceptable in standard downward

This work is supported by the ERC Advanced Grant "Speech Acts in Grammar and Discourse" (SPAGAD), ERC-2007-ADG 787929. I thank Luka Crnič for fruitful discussion and two anonymous reviewers for comments which helped improve the paper.

© Springer-Verlag GmbH Germany, part of Springer Nature 2020
D. Deng et al. (Eds.): TLLM 2020, LNCS 12564, pp. 207–216, 2020.
https://doi.org/10.1007/978-3-662-62843-0_11

entailing (DE) environments, as exemplified in (1) and (2), and unacceptable in standard upward entailing (UE) environments, as exemplified in (3) [20,21].[1]

(3)   a. *Nam đọc quyển sách nào
           Nam read ANY BOOK

       b. *Nam đọc (bất kỳ) quyển sách nào
           Nam read BK   ANY BOOK

Here is the puzzle we aim to resolve: under existential modals, ANY is deviant, while BK-ANY is acceptable and, just like English **any**, licenses the free choice inference [4].

(4)   a. *Nam được đọc quyển sách nào
           Nam may read ANY BOOK

       b. Nam được đọc bất kỳ quyển sách nào
           Nam may read BK   ANY BOOK
           'Nam is allowed to read any book'

Suppose, as the null hypothesis should be, that ANY has the same semantic and syntactic properties as **any**, a theory of **any** conducive to the explanation of the difference between ANY and BK-ANY should involve a grammatical formative X such that X is required for the well-formedness of (5a) and, at the same time, has no effect on either the well-formedness of (5b) or the deviance of (5c).

(5)   a. John is allowed to read any book
       b. John did not read any book
       c. *John read any book

This theory will enable us to simply identify the presence of BK with that of X, say by positing an Agree relationship between the two, and derive the fact, observed for Vietnamese, that ANY under existential modals requires BK (cf. (4)), ANY in DE environment allows but does not require BK (cf. (1) & (2)), and ANY in plain UE environments is deviant with or without BK (cf. (3)).

The next section presents such a theory.

2   A Theory of "any"

2.1   Licensing

What follows is essentially a modified and simplified version of the theory of **any** which has been proposed and developed by Luka Crnič in a series of recent

---

[1] The intended reading for the verb in (3) is episodic, not generic. Thus, the deviance will be clearer when the progressive aspect marker **đang** is added and the sentence is embedded under **tôi nhìn thấy** 'I saw,' as exemplified in (i) below, whose intended reading is 'I saw Nam reading a book.'

(i) *Tôi nhìn thấy Nam đang đọc (bất kỳ) quyển sách nào
     I   saw   Nam reading BK   ANY BOOK

For an explanation of the acceptability of ANY under a generic reading of the verb which is compatible with what we will say below, see [23].

papers [6–8]. I am, of course, responsible for any misrepresentation and falsehood contained in the presentation.

We assume that **any** comes with a covert domain restriction, and its lexical meaning is that of the existential quantifier [4,11]. Thus, (6) will have the meaning in (6a), which is equivalent to (6b).

(6)   John did not read any$_D$ book
       where $D \cap [\![book]\!] = \{a, b, c\}$
       a. $\neg[\exists x \in D \cap [\![book]\!]$: John read x$]$
       b. $\neg[a \vee b \vee c]$

For ease of exposition, we will often represent existentially quantified sentences as disjunctions. In a parallel fashion and for the same purpose, we will represent universally quantified sentences as conjunctions.

(7)   John read every$_D$ book
       where $D \cap [\![book]\!] = \{a, b, c\}$
       a. $\forall x \in D \cap [\![book]\!]$: John read x
       b. $a \wedge b \wedge c$

We call the intersection of D and the NP complement of **any** its "domain," and say that S and S′ are "domain alternatives" if they differ only with respect to the domain of **any**. If, furthermore, the domain of **any** in S′ is a subset of the domain of **any** in S, we call S′ a "subdomain alternative" of S. Adopting the proposal made in [6–8], we take the distribution of **any** to be constrained by the following condition.[2]

(8)   Licensing
       Any is acceptable only if it is dominated by a sentence S which entails its subdomain alternatives

The condition requires that replacing the domain of **any** with a stronger, i.e. smaller, domain should result in a weaker sentence. To see how Licensing predicts the acceptability of **any** under negation, consider (9a) and its two subdomain alternatives, (9b) and (9c). The domain of **any** is represented extensionally.[3]

(9)   a.   John did not read any $\{a, b, c\} = \neg(a \vee b \vee c)$
       b.   John did not read any $\{a, b\} = \neg(a \vee b)$
       c.   John did not read any $\emptyset = \top$

Since $\neg(a \vee b \vee c)$ is stronger than $\neg(a \vee b)$ and $\top$, Licensing is satisfied: the smaller the domain, the weaker the sentence. Now consider (10a) and its two subdomain alternatives, (10b) and (10c).

---

[2] Crnič, in [6–8], formulates this condition not in terms of entailment but in terms of Strawson entailment. We come back to this point below.

[3] $\top$ and $\bot$ represent the tautology and the contradiction, respectively.

(10)   a.   *John read any {a, b, c} = a∨b∨c
        b.   *John read any {a, b} = a∨b
        c.   *John read any ∅ = ⊥

Since a∨b∨c is weaker than a∨b and ⊥, Licensing is not satisfied: the smaller the domain, the stronger the sentence. Thus, Licensing explains the grammaticality of (5b) and the ungrammaticality of (5c).

For (5a), however, Licensing makes the wrong prediction. Specifically, it predicts (5a) to be as unacceptable as (5c), since embedding the sentences in (10) under the existential modal, henceforth symbolized as ◊, does not change entailment relations between them.

(11)   a.   John is allowed to read any {a, b, c} = ◊(a∨b∨c)
        b.   John is allowed to read any {a, b} = ◊(a∨b)
        c.   John is allowed to read any ∅ = ⊥

Since ◊(a∨b∨c) is weaker than ◊(a∨b) and ◊(⊥), Licensing is not satisfied.

The next subsection presents an auxiliary hypothesis which enables the theory to make the correct prediction about **any** under ◊.

2.2   Exhaustification

The auxiliary hypothesis is that sentences may be interpreted "exhaustively" [5,12]. We implement this hypothesis by claiming that each sentence S may be parsed as [EXH(R)(F(S))(S)] which is interpreted as follows [1].[4]

(12)   EXH(R)(F(S))(S) is true iff both (i) and (ii) hold:
        (i)   ∀S′ : S′ ∈ EXCL(S, F(S)) ∩ R   →   S′ is false
        (ii) ∀S′ : S′ ∈ INCL(S, F(S))   →   S′ is true

R is the set of "relevant" sentences, i.e. those that count as possible answers to the question under discussion. As relevance is closed under conjunction and negation, R is the Boolean closure BC(A) of some set A of sentences [14,22].

F(S) is the set of "formal alternatives" of S in the sense of [13,19,26,29]. The formal alternatives of a sentence S containing **any$_D$** are derived from S by replacing **any** with **any** or **every** and replacing **D** with any domain restriction **D′**. Thus, (13a) has (13b) as the set of its formal alternative, where E stands for the set of entities. We assume, for illustration, that a, b, c, d are all the books in the world. The existential modal is represented by ◊, so ◊a means 'John is allowed to read a,' for example.

---

[4] The background motivation for this theory is a conflict between the Gricean Maxims, especially Quality and Quantity, which seem to be truisms about linguistic communication, and the observable fact that people can convey a proposition p, for example 'John talked to Mary and not Sue,' by uttering a sentence S whose literal meaning is prima facie a proposition q which is weaker than p, for example the sentence **John talked to Mary**. Essentially, the proponents of the EXH theory resolve this conflict by denying that S is the sentence being uttered. What is uttered, they say, is really EXH(R)(F(S))(S), which in fact conveys the stronger proposition p as its literal meaning. For more discussion on this issue see [27] and references therein.

(13)   a.   S = John is allowed to read any$_D$ book

     b. $_.$F(S) = {◇(John read any$_{D', \, book}$), ◇(John read every$_D$, book) | D′
⊆ E} = {⊥, ◇a, ◇b, ◇c, ◇d, ◇(a ∨ b), ◇(a ∨ c), ◇(a ∨ d), ◇(b ∨ c),
◇(b ∨ d), ◇(c ∨ d), ◇(a ∨ b ∨ c), ◇(a ∨ b ∨ d), ◇(a ∨ c ∨ d), ◇(b ∨ c ∨ d),
◇(a ∨ b ∨ c ∨ d), ◇(a ∧ b), ◇(a ∧ c), ◇(a ∧ d), ◇(b ∧ c), ◇(b ∧ d), ◇(c ∧ d),
◇(a ∧ b ∧ c), ◇(a ∧ b ∧ d), ◇(a ∧ c ∧ d), ◇(b ∧ c ∧ d), ◇(a ∧ b ∧ c ∧ d)}

In fact, it follows from our assumption that S and its domain alternatives all
have the exact same set of formal alternatives.

    EXCL(S, F(S)) and INCL(S, F(S)) are the set of "excludable" and "includ-
able" alternatives of S in F(S), respectively. The general definition of the functions EXCL(S, A) and INCL(S, A), for any sentence S and set of sentences A,
is given in (14) [1].[5]

(14)   a.   EXCL(S, A) = ⋂{A′ | A′ is a maximal subset of A such that {S}
∪{¬S′ | S′ ∈ A′} is consistent}

     b.   INCL(S, A) = ⋂{A′ | A′ is a maximal subset of A such that {S}∪
{S′ | S′ ∈ A′} ∪ {¬S′ | S′ ∈ EXCL(S, A)} is consistent}

Now consider the sentence S_{abc} in (15a) and its two subdomain alternatives S_{ab}
and $S_∅$ in (15b) and (15c), respectively.

(15)   a. S_{abc} = John is allowed to read any$_D$ book
where D ∩ ⟦book⟧ = {a, b, c}

     (i)   F(S_{abc}) = (13b)

     (ii)   EXCL(S_{abc}, F(S_{abc})) = {⊥, ◇d, ◇(a∧b), ◇(a∧c), ◇(a∧d),
◇(b∧c), ◇(b∧d), ◇(c∧d), ◇(a∧b∧c), ◇(a∧b∧d), ◇(a∧c∧d),
◇(b∧c∧d), ◇(a∧b∧c∧d)}

     (iii) INCL(S_{abc}, F(S_{abc})) = {◇a, ◇b, ◇c, ◇(a∨b), ◇(a∨c),
◇(b∨c), ◇(a∨b∨c)}.

     b. S_{ab} = John is allowed to read any$_{D'}$ book
where D′ ∩ ⟦book⟧ = {a, b}

     (i)   F(S_{ab}) = (13b)

     (ii)   EXCL(S_{ab}, F($_{ab}$)) = {⊥, ◇c, ◇d, ◇(a∧b), ◇(a∧c), ◇(a∧d),
◇(b∧c), ◇(b∧d), ◇(c∧d), ◇(a∧b∧c), ◇(a∧b∧d), ◇(a∧c∧d),
◇(b∧c∧d), ◇(a∧b∧c∧d)}

     (iii) INCL(S_{ab}, F(S_{ab})) = {◇a, ◇b, ◇(a∨b), ◇(a∨b∨c)}

     c. $S_∅$ = John is allowed to read any$_{D''}$ book
where D″ ∩ ⟦book⟧ = ∅

     (i)   F($S_∅$) = (13b)

     (ii)   EXCL($S_∅$, F($S_∅$)) = ⋂∅

     (iii) INCL($S_∅$, F($S_∅$)) = ⋂∅

---

[5] Thus, suppose we try to conjoin S consistently with the negation of as many sentences
in A as possible. Those sentences which feature in every such trial that are not S are
the elements of EXCL(S, A). Then, suppose we try to conjoin S and the negation of
every sentence in EXCL(S, A) with as many sentences in A as possible. The sentences
which feature in every such trial that are neither S nor elements of EXCL(S, A) are
the elements of INCL(S, A).

Since $S_{abc} = \Diamond(a \lor b \lor c)$ is weaker than its subdomain alternatives $S_{ab} = \Diamond(a \lor b)$ and $S_\emptyset = \bot$, Licensing is not satisfied. Now let us ask whether Licensing is satisfied by the exhaustified variant. Specifically, let us ask (16).

(16)   Is there a parse of $\phi = \text{EXH}(R)(F(S_{abc}))(S_{abc})$ such that ϕ entails its subdomain alternatives?

Among the elements of $\text{EXH}(R)(F(S_{abc}))(S_{abc})$, only R, which denotes the set of relevant sentences, is "pronominal" in the sense that it has a contextually determined interpretation. This means that the question in (16) can be formulated more concretely as (17).

(17)   Can R be assigned a value such that (17a) entails (17b) and (17c)?
    a. $\text{EXH}(R)(F(S_{abc}))(S_{abc})$
    b. $\text{EXH}(R)(F(S_{ab}))(S_{ab})$
    c. $\text{EXH}(R)(F(S_\emptyset))(S_\emptyset)$

If the answer is affirmative, then we predict (18) to have a parse which is grammatical, which means we predict (18) to be grammatical, as observed.[6]

(18)   John is allowed to read any book

And the answer is, in fact, affirmative. Suppose we parse R as the Boolean closure of $\text{EXCL}(S_{abc}, F(S_{abc}))$, then the following holds.

(19)   Let $R = \text{BC}(\text{EXCL}(S_{abc}, F(S_{abc})))$
    a. $\text{EXH}(R)(F(S_{abc}))(S_{abc}) = \Diamond a \land \Diamond b \land \Diamond c \land \neg\Diamond d \land$
        $\neg\Diamond(a \land b) \land \neg\Diamond(a \land c) \land \neg\Diamond(b \land c)$
    b. $\text{EXH}(R)(F(S_{ab}))(S_{ab}) = \Diamond a \land \Diamond b \land \neg\Diamond d \land \neg\Diamond(a \land b)$
        $\land \neg\Diamond(a \land c) \land \neg\Diamond(b \land c)$
    c. $\text{EXH}(R)(F(S_\emptyset))(S_\emptyset) = \bot$

Since (19a) is stronger than (19b), Licensing is satisfied by these two sentences. However, (19c) is stronger than both. Thus, what we need to add to the theory is the presupposition that the domain of **any** is non-empty. Under this presupposition, and the construal of entails in (8) as 'Strawson-entails' (see footnote 2), we predict both the grammaticality of **any** under existential modals and its universal interpretation [6–8].

---

[6] We assume that a sentence is grammatical if it has one parse which is grammatical, and is ungrammatical if it has no parse which is grammatical. Crnič, in [6–8], proposes formal constraints on R to guarantee that no parse which violates the licensing condition for **any** can be generated by the grammar. As far as I can see, this is necessary only if we want the grammar to be "crash-proof." Note, also, that the account we are proposing does not concern how the value of R is determined. What it tells us is which values of R would make the sentence grammatical. In this sense it is similar to Binding Theory, which does not tell how a certain pronoun comes to carry an index in a discourse context, but does tell us which indices make the sentence grammatical.

2.3 Summary

We have seen that when **any** is embedded under an existential modal, there is an exhautified meaning of the sentence which satisfies Licensing. If the sentence is parsed without EXH, there is no meaning for it which satisfies Licensing. The reader is invited to verify for himself that exhaustification has no effect on Licensing with respect to sentences containing no existential modals. We thus have (20), where ✓ indicates satisfaction and ✗ indicates violation of Licensing.

		without EXH	with EXH
(20)	John read any book	✗	✗
	John did not read any book	✓	✓
	John is allowed to read any book	✗	✓

3 Accounting for the Observation About Vietnamese

Let us come back to the puzzle about Vietnamese presented in Sect. 1. The puzzle, to repeat, is this: BK is required for ANY under existential modals, but makes no difference when there is no modal. The situation is thus (21), where ✓ indicates acceptability and ✗ indicates unacceptability.

		without BK	with BK
(21)	John read ___ ANY BOOK	✗	✗
	John did not read ___ ANY BOOK	✓	✓
	John is allowed to read ___ ANY BOOK	✗	✓

Given the discussion in the last section, it should be clear what we can say to account for the Vietnamese facts: BK-ANY implies the presence of EXH, while simple ANY implies the absence of EXH. To implement this by familiar syntactic machineries, let us say that EXH bears a feature [F] which needs to agree with another instance of [F] in its c-command domain, and BK, which is semantically transparent, bears [F] for the whole DP headed by ANY. This situation is represented below, where ~~strikethrough~~ indicates semantic transparency.[7]

(22) [$_S$ EXH$_{[F]}$ ... [DP ~~BK~~$_{[F]}$ ANY NP]]

We note that this kind of bipartite syntax for semantic functions, where an interpreted operator at one structural position is associated with a morphological reflex at another remote structural position, is a fact about natural language which has been observed before. It has been proposed, for example, that

---

[7] An anonymous reviewer asks why not say that BK carries EXH itself. The question is justified, and my answer would be that there is no reason not to say that BK is EXH itself if semantics is all we care about. However, we also care, minimally, about phonology: we do want to take into account at least the fact that BK is pronounced inside the DP, not clause initially. Saying that BK is an agreement reflex of a clause initial EXH is just a way of saying that BK is EXH but is not pronounced where it is interpreted, a prevalent phenomenon in natural language. Alternatively, we could say that BK undergoes covert movement. Discussing the relative merits and disadvantages of these two analyses would take us beyond the scope of this note.

the quantifier **no one** is by itself an existential quantifier which agrees with a covert, structurally higher, sentential negation. Split scope phenomena such as the ambiguity of (23) have motivated such analyses [24,30].

(23)   The company needs to fire no employee
    a. $\text{NOT}_{[F]}$ [need [$\exists_x$ the company fire ~~no~~$_{[F]}$ employee$_x$]]
         = it is not necessary for the company to fire any employee
    b.   need [$\text{NOT}_{[F]}$ [$\exists_x$ the company fire ~~no~~$_{[F]}$ employee$_x$]]
         = it is necessary that the company fires no employee

Even the word **only**, which seems to be as semantically contentful as any word can be, has been analyzed as a semantically transparent element which agrees with a remote covert sentential operator which is semantically contentful [2,18]. On this view, (24a) has the analysis in (24b). [8]

(24)   a.   Mary talked to only John
        b. $\text{ONLY}_{[F]}$ [Mary talked to ~~only~~$_{[F]}$ John$_{focus}$]

Thus, the analysis we propose for BK, therefore, may not be as extraordinary as it first seems. Note that our account provides a straightforward explanation of another fact about Vietnamese: this language, just like English, does not allow ANY under universal modals.[9]

(26)   *Nam phải đọc (bất kỳ) quyển sách nào
        Nam must read (BK) ANY BOOK
        (Nam must read a book)

The readers are invited to verify for themselves that (26), with or without exhaustification, fails to satisfy Licensing.

4   Open issues

It goes without saying that this short squib leaves issues open regarding the two variants of the Vietnamese NPIs. Here are three. First, when the NP sister of ANY is modified by a numeral, the ANY phrase is in fact licensed under universal modals, provided BK is present.[10]

---

[8] In fact, a bipartite analysis for ONLY has been proposed for Vietnamese [10].

[9] Here is the English example.

(25)   *John is required to read any book

[10] English exhibits the same phenomenon, as pointed out by [8], which acknowledges it to be an unsolvable problem for the account proposed there.

(27)   John is required to read any two books

The fact that in Vietnamese the presence of BK is obligatory might be instructive as it suggests exhaustification must play a part.

(28)   Nam phải đọc *(bất kỳ) hai quyển sách nào
        Nam must read *(BK)   ANY TWO BOOK
        'Nam is required to read any two books'

Second, only BK-ANY allows the "supplementary" use [9].

(29)   Nam phải đọc một quyển sách, *(bất kỳ) quyển nào
        Nam must read a book   *(BK)   ANY BOOK
        'Nam is required to read a book, any book'

Third, while both ANY and BK-ANY allow the existential reading in neutral yes/no questions, only ANY allows this reading in biased yes/no questions.[11]

(30)   a.   Nam có   đọc (bất kỳ) quyển sách nào không?
              Nam YES read (BK)   ANY BOOK   NO
              'Does Nam read any book?' (neutral)
        b.   Nam đọc (*bất kỳ) quyển sách nào à?
              Nam read (*BK)   ANY BOOK   Q?
              'Nam read a book?' (biased)

Given our hypothesis that BK cooccurs with EXH, the question naturally arises as to how these phenomena relate to exhaustification.[12] We leave this interesting issue to future research.

References

1. Bar-Lev, M., Fox, D.: Free choice, simplification, and innocent inclusion. The Hebrew University of Jerusalem and MIT, Manuscript (2019)
2. Barbiers, S.: Syntactic doubling and deletion as a source of variation. In: Picallo, C.M. (ed.) Linguistic Variation in the Minimalist Framework. Oxford University Press (2014)
3. Bruening, B., Tran, T.: Wh-questions in Vietnamese. J. East Asian Linguist. **15**(4), 319–341 (2006)
4. Chierchia, G.: Logic in Grammar. Oxford University Press, Oxford (2013)
5. Chierchia, G., Fox, D., Spector, B.: The grammatical view of scalar implicatures and the relationship between semantics and pragmatics. In: Portner, P., Maienborn, C., von Heusinger, K. (eds.) Semantics: An International Handbook of Natural Language Meaning. De Gruyter (2012)
6. Crnič, L.: Any, alternatives, and pruning. The Hebrew University of Jerusalem, Manuscript (2019)

---

[11] The English translations of (30a) and (30b) capture rather precisely the "neutrality" of the former, which corresponds to a subject aux inversion question, and the "bias" of the latter, which corresponds to a "declarative question" in English [16,17,25]. One difference is that the biased question implies that there is contextual evidence for a 'yes' answer, while the neutral question does not have this implication.

[12] [28] proposes an account of this fact which is based on [15]. The account assumes that BK comes with a covert EVEN and that the question particle à has a semantics that is incompatible with EVEN. A unification of [28] and the account of BK-ANY under existential modals provided in this paper remains to be worked out.

7. Crnič, L.: Any: logic, likelihood, and context. Lang. Linguistic Compass **13**, 1–20 (2019)
8. Crnič, L.: Number in NPI licensing. The Hebrew University of Jerusalem, Manuscript (2020)
9. Dayal, V.: The universal force of free choice any. Linguistic Variation Yearbook **4**(1), 5–40 (2004)
10. Erlewine, M.Y.: Vietnamese focus particles and derivation by phase. J. East Asian Linguistics **26**(4), 325–349 (2017). https://doi.org/10.1007/s10831-017-9156-y
11. von Fintel, K.: Restrictions on quantifier domains. Ph.D. thesis, University of Massachussetts at Amherst (1994)
12. Fox, D.: Free choice disjunction and the theory of scalar implicatures. In: Sauerland, U., Stateva, P. (eds.) Presupposition and Implicature in Compositional Semantics, pp. 71–120. Palgrave-Macmillan (2007)
13. Fox, D., Katzir, R.: On the characterization of alternatives. Nat. Lang. Semant. **19**, 87–107 (2011)
14. Groenendijk, J., Stokhof, M.: Studies on the semantics of questions and the pragmatics of answers. Ph.D. thesis, University of Amsterdam (1984)
15. Guerzoni, E.: Even-NPIs in Yes/No questions. Nat. Lang. Semant. **12**(4), 319–343 (2004)
16. Gunlogson, C.: Declarative questions. Proc. SALT **12**, 144–163 (2002)
17. Gunlogson, C.: True to form: Rising and falling declaratives as questions in English. Routledge (2003)
18. Hirsch, A.: Only as a concord phenomenon. Minicourse taught at the Hebrew University of Jerusalem (2020)
19. Katzir, R.: Structurally-defined alternatives. Linguist. Philos. **30**, 669–690 (2007)
20. Klima, E.S.: Negation in English. In: Fodor, J.A., Katz, J.J. (eds.) The Structure of Language: Readings in the Philosophy of Language, pp. 246–323. Prentice Hall (1964)
21. Ladusaw, W.: Polarity sensitivity as inherent scope relations. Ph.D. thesis, University of Texas Austin (1979)
22. Lewis, D.: Relevant implication. Theoria **54**(3), 161–174 (1988)
23. Nickel, B.: Generically free choice. Linguist. Philos. **33**(6), 479–512 (2011). https://doi.org/10.1007/s10988-011-9087-4
24. Penka, D.: Negative Indefinites. Oxford University Press (2011)
25. Trinh, T.: How to ask the obvious - A presuppositional account of evidential bias in English yes/no questions. MIT Working Papers Linguist. **71**, 227–249 (2014)
26. Trinh, T.: Keeping it simple. Nat. Lang. Semant. **26**(2), 111–124 (2018). https://doi.org/10.1007/s11050-018-9143-5
27. Trinh, T.: Exhaustification and contextual restriction. Front. Commun. **4**, 1–7 (2019)
28. Trinh, T.: A puzzle about free choice and negative bias. Talk given the Conference on Tense and Speech Acts, 16/01/2020, Vietnam Institute of Linguistics, Hanoi (2020)
29. Trinh, T., Haida, A.: Constraining the derivation of alternatives. Nat. Lang. Semant. **23**(4), 249–270 (2015). https://doi.org/10.1007/s11050-015-9115-y
30. Zeijlstra, H.: Sentential Negation and Negative Concord. LOT, Utrecht (2004)

Comparatives Bring a Degree-Based NPI Licenser

Linmin Zhang[1,2](✉)(iD)

[1] NYU Shanghai, Shanghai, China
[2] NYU-ECNU Institute of Brain and Cognitive Science, Shanghai, China
zhanglinmin@gmail.com, linmin.zhang@nyu.edu
https://sites.google.com/site/zhanglinmin/

Abstract. Comparatives license the use of negative polarity items (NPIs) within their *than*-clause. What exactly constitutes the NPI licenser in comparatives? In this paper, I argue that it is the very status of being the standard in a comparison that constitutes the NPI licenser. Based on Zhang and Ling (2020)'s interval-subtraction-based theory on comparatives, I show that by serving as the standard in a comparison and playing the role of subtrahend in a subtraction equation, a *than*-clause is inherently downward-entailing. Moreover, it demonstrates strong negativity like the classical negation operator *not* does. Therefore, a *than*-clause licenses both weak and strong NPIs. Crucially, this NPI licenser is due to monotonicity projection based on degree semantics (implemented with intervals), not due to a set-operation-based negation operator.

Keywords: Comparatives · *Than*-clauses · Negative polarity items · Degree semantics · Interval subtraction · Subtrahend · Monotonicity · Downward-entailingness · Hierarchy of negativity · Informativeness

1 Introduction

Within the formal semantics literature on comparatives, there have been debates on whether and how *than*-clauses/phrases provide a licensing environment for negative polarity items (NPIs) (see e.g., Hoeksema 1983, von Stechow 1984, Heim 2006, Giannakidou and Yoon 2010, Alrenga and Kennedy 2014).[1]

Empirically, as shown in (1)–(5), typical **weak NPIs** (e.g., *any*), **emphatic NPIs** (or **minimizers**, e.g., *give a penny, could help*), and some **strong NPIs** (e.g., *yet, in weeks*) are licensed within *than*-clauses. Strong NPIs generally require the licensing from strongly negative-flavored expressions like *not* or *without*.

---

[1] I only focus on clausal comparatives and *than*-clauses in this paper.

This project was financially supported by the Program for Eastern Young Scholar at Shanghai Institutions of Higher Learning (to L.Z.). For judgments, discussions, and feedback, I thank Haoze Li, Mingming Liu, Michael Tabatowski, Eytan Zweig, and three anonymous reviewers. Special thanks to Dag Westerståhl. Errors are mine.

© Springer-Verlag GmbH Germany, part of Springer Nature 2020
D. Deng et al. (Eds.): TLLM 2020, LNCS 12564, pp. 217–238, 2020.
https://doi.org/10.1007/978-3-662-62843-0_12

(1)   a.   Roxy ran <u>faster than</u> **any** boy did.
      b.   (i)   Roxy di<u>dn't</u> see **any** boy.
           (ii) *Roxy saw **any** boy.

(2)   a.   John would <u>sooner</u> roast in hell <u>than</u> **give a penny** to the charity.
      b.   (i)   John left the world <u>without</u> **giving a penny** to his son.
           (ii) *John left the world with **giving a penny** to his son.

(3)   a.   My urge to steal was <u>stronger than</u> I **could help**.
      b.   (i)   I **could<u>n't</u> help** being so eager to steal.
           (ii) *I **could help** being so eager to steal.

(4)   a.   It requires <u>better</u> performance <u>than</u> I've seen **yet**.
      b.   (i)   I have<u>n't</u> read the book **yet**.
           (ii) *I have read the book **yet**.

(5)   a.   He made me feel <u>happier than</u> I felt **in years**.
      b.   (i)   He was<u>n't</u> happy **in years**.
           (ii) *He was happy **in years**.

One prevailing hypothesis is that a *than*-clause brings a silent negation operator (e.g., Alrenga and Kennedy 2014). As illustrated in (6), under the canonical 'A-not-A' analysis for comparatives (see Schwarzschild 2008 for a review), this sentence includes a hidden negation, meaning that there exists a degree d such that Mary is d-tall but John is <u>not</u> d-tall. With this proposal of a hidden negation operator for a *than*-clause, it seems a natural consequence that this negation operator constitutes the NPI licenser for licensing *than*-clause-internal NPIs.

(6)   Mary is taller than John is.
      $\exists d.[$ Mary is d-tall $\wedge\neg$ John is d-tall $]$
      $\rightsquigarrow$ There exists a degree d such that Mary's height meets or exceeds d and John's height doesn't meet d.

However, this proposal of a silent negation operator is problematic for a few reasons. First, as pointed out by Giannakidou and Yoon (2010), strong NPIs like *either* cannot be licensed within a *than*-clause, as shown in (7).

(7)   a.   *Kevin is not tall, and John is taller than Bill is **either**.
      b.   (i)   Bill is not tall, and I know that John is<u>n't</u> tall, **either**.
           (ii) *Bill is tall, and I know that John is tall, **either**.

Moreover, the presence of a hidden negation should lead to scopal ambiguity. However, as illustrated by (8), no scopal ambiguity between negation and universal quantifier *every boy* is attested.

(8)   Mary is taller than every boy is.
      a. #$\exists d[$ Mary is d-tall $\wedge\neg\forall x[$boy$(x) \rightarrow x$ is d-tall $]]$ $\neg > \forall$: unattested
      b. $\exists d[$ Mary is d-tall $\wedge\forall x[$boy$(x) \rightarrow \neg\ x$ is d-tall $]]$ $\forall > \neg$: ✓

Furthermore, whether a *than*-clause is inherently monotonic (i.e., downward- or upward-entailing) seems not fully settled, and empirical evidence seems mixed, against the prediction of those advocating a hidden negation for a *than*-clause. As noted by Larson (1988), Schwarzschild and Wilkinson (2002), and Giannakidou and Yoon (2010), though the downward-entailing (DE) pattern is observed for (9), (10) shows a clear upward-entailing (UE) pattern. It seems likely that the monotonicity hinges rather on the kind of quantifiers within a *than*-clause.

(9)   Downward entailment
    a.   X is taller than every **boy** is $\models$ X is taller than every **blond boy** is
    b.   X is taller than every **blond boy** is $\not\models$ X is taller than every **boy** is

(10)   Upward entailment
    a.   X is taller than some **boy** is $\not\models$ X is taller than some **blond boy** is
    b.   X is taller than some **blond boy** is $\models$ X is taller than some **boy** is

However, though the 'hidden negation' hypothesis is not empirically favored, this does not entirely rule out the possibility that a *than*-clause is still inherently monotonic and provides an NPI licensing environment (see also Hoeksema 1983). After all, strong NPIs like *in years* are licensed within a *than*-clause (see (5)).

In this paper, I argue that a *than*-clause indeed creates a DE environment and thus contributes an NPI licenser. Crucially, it is not a negation operator, but a degree-based one. Following Zhang and Ling (2020)'s **interval-subtraction-based** approach to comparatives, I show that it is the very status of being the **standard in a comparison**, i.e., the **subtrahend in a subtraction equation**, that makes a *than*-clause an NPI licenser. The negativity of the subtrahend is as strong as the negation operator *not*, allowing a *than*-clause to license both weak and strong NPIs (see Zwarts 1981, Hoeksema 1983).

The paper is organized as follows. Section 2 presents Zhang and Ling (2020)'s interval-subtraction-based approach to comparatives. Section 3 and 5 demonstrates, respectively, the inherent DE-ness and the strong negativity of the standard – the subtrahend – in comparatives. Between them, Sect. 4, an interlude, shows the interplay between a *than*-clause and its internal quantifiers on monotonicity projection. Then Sect. 6 explains how various NPIs are licensed within a *than*-clause. Section 7 provides a further discussion. Section 8 concludes.

2   An Interval-Subtraction-Based Analysis of Comparatives

Zhang and Ling (2020) (see also Zhang and Ling 2015) is a recent development of **interval-based** approaches to comparatives (cf. **degree-based** approaches, see Kennedy 1999, Schwarzschild 2008, and Beck 2011 for reviews; see Schwarzschild and Wilkinson 2002 and Beck 2010 for earlier development of interval-based approaches to comparatives).

According to Zhang and Ling (2020), comparatives are analyzed as a **subtraction relation** among three **definite descriptions** (see (11)): two **positions** along a scale – representing (i) the **standard** of comparison (here *β*

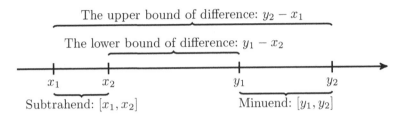

Fig. 1. The subtraction between two intervals. Here $[y_1, y_2]$ means the minuend, $[x_1, x_2]$ the subtrahend, and the difference between these two intervals is the largest range of possible differences between any two points in these two intervals, i.e., $[y_1 - x_2, y_2 - x_1]$.

o'clock) and (ii) the measurement associated with the matrix subject (here *5 o'clock*) – and the **distance** (or difference) between them (here *two hours*).

(11)   5 o'clock is two hours later than 3 o'clock is.

$$\underbrace{5 \text{ o'clock}}_{\textbf{Position 1}} - \underbrace{3 \text{ o'clock}}_{\textbf{Position 2: the standard}} = \underbrace{2 \text{ hours}}_{\textbf{the distance}} \quad \text{(along a scale of time)}$$

Crucially, within the new development of Zhang and Ling (2020), these three definite descriptions are represented in terms of **intervals** (i.e., **convex sets of degrees**),[2] and the relation among them is represented as **interval subtraction** (see (12)). The use of intervals and interval arithmetic allows for characterizing the positions and distance in a **generalized** way, supporting the expression of **potentially not-very-precise measurements** (i.e., positions) on a scale.

As illustrated in Fig. 1, here $[y_1, y_2]$ and $[x_1, x_2]$ represent two not-very-precise positions along the scale, and thus, the shortest distance between these two positions is the value of $y_1 - x_2$, while the longest distance between these two positions is the value of $y_2 - x_1$ (see Moore 1979 for details of interval arithmetic).

(12) $$\underbrace{[y_1, y_2]}_{\textbf{Position 1: minuend}} - \underbrace{[x_1, x_2]}_{\textbf{Position 2: the standard, i.e., subtrahend}} = \underbrace{[y_1 - x_2, y_2 - x_1]}_{\textbf{the distance: difference}}$$

Some examples of interval subtraction are shown in (13). In (13a), the lower bound of the difference, 2, means the minimum distance between positions $[4, 8]$

---

[2] A convex totally ordered set P is a totally ordered set such that for any two random elements a and b belonging to this set P (suppose $a \leq b$), any element x such that $a \leq x \leq b$ also belongs to this set P. For example, $\{x \mid x > 3\}$ and $\{x \mid 3 < x \leq 5\}$ are convex sets, i.e., intervals; $\{x \mid x < 3 \vee x > 5\}$ is not a convex set.

Since an interval is a convex set of degrees, an interval like $\{x \mid a \leq x < b\}$ can be written as $[a, b)$, with a **closed lower bound** '[' and an **open upper bound** ')'. Intervals like $\{x \mid x > a\}$ and $\{x \mid x \leq b\}$ are written as $(a, +\infty)$ and $(-\infty, b]$, where $+\infty$ and $-\infty$ mean positive and negative infinity.

and $[1, 2]$, while the upper bound of the difference, 7, means the maximum distance between these two positions. $[2, 7]$ stands for an interval of distance (i.e., a difference) in (13a), but an interval of position (i.e., a subtrahend) in (13b). Interval subtraction can be generalized to intervals involving open and/or unbounded end points (e.g., (13c)).

(13)　a.　$[4, 8] - [1, 2] = [2, 7]$
　　　b.　$[4, 8] - [2, 7] = [-3, 6]$ ((13a) vs. (13b): $X - Y = Z \not\equiv X - Z = Y$)
　　　c.　$(5, +\infty) - [1, 3] = (2, +\infty)$

Zhang and Ling (2020)'s interval-subtraction-based approach is particularly suitable for analyzing **clausal comparatives** that contain both *than*-clause-internal quantifiers and numerical differentials, as illustrated by (14).

(14)　The giraffe is between 3 and 5 feet taller than every tree is.
　　　⤳ The height of the giraffe falls within the interval I such that

$$\underbrace{I}_{\text{Minuend}} - \underbrace{[\![\text{than every tree is } \text{tall}]\!]}_{\text{Subtrahend}} = \underbrace{[3', 5']}_{\text{Difference}}$$

Intuitively, the standard of comparison here, i.e., $[\![\text{than every tree is}]\!]$, cannot be reduced to a single degree. However, a *than*-clause is a scope island, so that the embedded universal quantifier *every tree* cannot go through quantifier raising, disallowing the conduction of comparisons between the height of the giraffe and that of each tree (see e.g., Larson 1988, Schwarzschild and Wilkinson 2002). Under the interval-subtraction-based approach, a *than*-clause means a potentially not-very-precise position on a scale. Thus, for (14), $[\![\text{than every tree is}]\!]$ means the interval ranging from the height of the shortest to that of the tallest tree(s). Based on the formula of interval subtraction (see (12)), the sentence meaning of a comparative can be derived from the semantics of its *than*-clause and the differential. Eventually, only one comparison is performed, but both the lower and upper bounds of the comparison standard contribute to this comparison.

Specifically, gradable adjective *tall* means a relation between an interval I and an atomic entity x, meaning that the height measure of x falls at the position represented as interval I along a scale of height (see (15) – (17)). Since an interval is a convex set of degrees (of type d), the type of intervals is $\langle dt \rangle$.

(15)　$[\![\text{tall}]\!]_{\langle dt, et \rangle} \overset{\text{def}}{=} \lambda I_{\langle dt \rangle}.\lambda x.\text{HEIGHT}(x) \subseteq I$
　　　(HEIGHT is a measure function of type $\langle e, dt \rangle$, taking an atomic entity as input and returning its measurement along a scale of height, i.e., the range of markings closest to the top of x.)

(16)　**Measurement constructions**
　　　a.　My giraffe is between 19 and 20 feet tall.
　　　　　$\text{HEIGHT}(\text{my giraffe}) \subseteq [19', 20']$
　　　b.　I am 6 feet tall.　　$\text{HEIGHT}(\text{I}) \subseteq [6', 6']$, or $\text{HEIGHT}(\text{I}) \subseteq [6', +\infty)$
　　　　　(*6 feet* can have an 'at least' reading or an 'exactly' reading.)

(17)   **Positive use of adjectives** (see e.g., Bartsch and Vennemann 1972)
My giraffe is tall: HEIGHT(my giraffe) $\subseteq I^C_{\mathrm{POS}}$ (I^C_{POS}: the
context-dependent interval of being tall for a relevant comparison class)

Comparative morpheme *-er/more* denotes a positive increase, i.e., the
default, most general, positive interval $(0, +\infty)$ (see (18)). Like other additive
particles (e.g., *another*, *also*), it carries a requirement of additivity: there is a
discourse salient scalar value serving as the base of increase (i.e., standard).

(18) $[\![\text{-er/more}]\!]_{\langle dt \rangle} \overset{\text{def}}{=} (0, +\infty)$ **Requirement of additivity:**
there is a discourse-salient value serving as the base of increase.

A *than*-clause is considered a short answer to its corresponding degree question. It is derived via (i) a lambda abstraction, which generates a set of intervals,
and (ii) the application of an informativeness-based maximality operator, $[\![\text{than}]\!]$,
which picks out the most informative definite interval (see (19) and (20)).[3]

(19) $[\![\text{than every tree is } \sout{\text{tall}}]\!]$
    a.   Generating a degree question: $\lambda I. \forall x[\text{tree}(x) \rightarrow \text{HEIGHT}(x) \subseteq I]$
    b.   Deriving its most informative fragment answer:
        $\iota I[\forall x[\text{tree}(x) \rightarrow \text{HEIGHT}(x) \subseteq I]$

(20) $[\![\text{than}]\!]_{\langle\langle dt,t\rangle\rangle,dt} \overset{\text{def}}{=} \lambda p_{\langle dt,t\rangle}.\iota I[p(I) \wedge \forall I'[[p(I') \wedge I' \neq I] \rightarrow I \subset I']],$
$[\![\text{than}]\!]$ is defined when $\exists I[p(I) \wedge \forall I'[[p(I') \wedge I' \neq I] \rightarrow I \subset I']]$

Obviously, $[\![\text{than Bill is } \sout{\text{tall}}]\!]$ addresses how tall Bill is, thus amounting to the
height measurement of Bill.[4] $[\![\text{than every tree is } \sout{\text{tall}}]\!]$ addresses how tall every
tree is, thus amounting to the most informative (i.e., narrowest) interval ranging
from the height of the shortest to the tallest tree(s). Suppose there are three
trees in our context, measuring $[3', 5']$, $[6', 10']$, and $[11', 13']$, respectively. Then
$[\![\text{than every tree is } \sout{\text{tall}}]\!]$ amounts to the interval $[3', 13']$.

A silent operator is assumed to perform interval subtraction (see (21)). The
inputs are two intervals: I_{STDD} and I_{DIFF}, representing the subtrahend and the
difference. The output is a third interval, the one representing the minuend.

(21) $[\![\ominus]\!]_{\langle dt,\langle dt,dt\rangle\rangle} \overset{\text{def}}{=} \lambda I_{\mathrm{STDD}}.\lambda I_{\mathrm{DIFF}}.\iota I[I - I_{\mathrm{STDD}} = I_{\mathrm{DIFF}}]$

Thus, for a clausal comparative like (14) (repeated here in (22)), its *than*-
clause serves as the standard of comparison and plays the role of I_{STDD} (see
(22a)). A numerical differential (here *between 3 and 5 feet*) restricts the default
positive differential *-er* (see (22b)). Eventually, matrix-level semantics is derived
via interval subtraction (see (22c)). According to the formula of interval subtraction (see (12)), (22c) means that the height of my giraffe falls into an interval

---

[3] See also Zhang and Ling (2020) (especially footnote 21 in that paper) for a brief
discussion on the short-answer (or free-relative) view of *than*-clauses.
[4] Evidently, the meaning of a *than*-clause is distinct from the positive use of gradable
adjectives (see (17)). *Mary is taller than Bill is* $\sout{\text{tall}}$ does not entail that Bill is tall.

I' such that (i) the lower bound of I' minus the height of the tallest tree(s) is 3 feet, and (ii) the upper bound of I' minus the height of the shortest tree(s) is 5 feet.

(22) The giraffe is between 3 and 5 feet taller than every tree is.   (= (14))
　　　 LF of (14): The giraffe is $\underbrace{[3', 5']}_{I_{\text{DIFF}}}$ ...-er $\ominus$ $\underbrace{\text{than every tree is } \text{t̶a̶l̶l̶ } \text{tall}}_{I_{\text{STDD}}}$

a. $I_{\text{STDD}} = [\![\text{than every tree is } \text{t̶a̶l̶l̶}]\!] = \iota I[\forall x[\text{tree}(x) \rightarrow \text{HEIGHT}(x) \subseteq I]]$
　　 (Roughly, this is an interval from the height of the shortest to that of the tallest tree(s): $[\text{HEIGHT}(\text{shortest-tree}), \text{HEIGHT}(\text{tallest-tree})]$.)[5]
b. $I_{\text{DIFF}} = [3', 5'] \cap (0, +\infty) = [3', 5']$
c. $[\![(14)]\!] \Leftrightarrow \text{HEIGHT}(\text{my-giraffe}) \subseteq \iota I'[I' - I_{\text{STDD}} = I_{\text{DIFF}}]$
　　 $\Leftrightarrow \text{HGHT}(\text{grf}) \subseteq \iota I'[I' - \iota I[\forall x[\text{tree}(x) \rightarrow \text{HGHT}(x) \subseteq I]] = [3', 5']]$
　　 $\Leftrightarrow \text{HGHT}(\text{grf}) \subseteq \iota I'[I' - [\text{HGHT}(\text{shortest}), \text{HGHT}(\text{tallest})] = [3', 5']]$
　　 $\rightsquigarrow$ (i) the lower bound of I' minus the height of the tallest tree(s) is 3 feet, and (ii) the upper bound of I' minus the height of the shortest tree(s) is 5 feet (see (12)).

3   The downward-entailingness of a *than*-clause

The formula of interval subtraction (see (12), repeated in (23)) crucially underlies Zhang and Ling (2020)'s interval-subtraction-based approach to comparatives.

The three definite scalar values (in terms of intervals) in a subtraction equation constrain each other. Thus we can compute the value of the minuend from the given values of the subtrahend and the difference. In fact, this is how the matrix-level semantics of a comparative is derived (see (22)): sentence-level semantics is derived from the meaning of the *than*-clause and the differential.

Then as shown in (24), we cannot directly apply interval addition to the subtrahend and the difference to compute the value of the minuend (see Moore 1979 and the illustration in (25)).[6] Instead, we need to follow the formula of interval subtraction. Therefore, as shown in (24b), it is the **upper bound of the subtrahend** that contributes to the computation of the **lower bound of the minuend**, and it is the **lower bound of the subtrahend** that contributes to the computation of the **upper bound of the minuend**.

---

[5] To facilitate notations, I avoid writing endpoints of $\text{HEIGHT}(x)$ in this kind of cases.
[6] Applying an operation on two intervals results in a third interval that represents the largest possible range of values (see Moore 1979). Here is a general recipe for basic operations – addition, subtraction, and multiplication:

(i) $[x_1, x_2]\langle\text{op}\rangle[y_1, y_2] = [\alpha, \beta]$
　　 The lower bound of $\alpha = \text{MIN}(x_1\langle\text{op}\rangle y_1, x_1\langle\text{op}\rangle y_2, x_2\langle\text{op}\rangle y_1, x_2\langle\text{op}\rangle y_2)$
　　 The upper bound of $\alpha = \text{MAX}(x_1\langle\text{op}\rangle y_1, x_1\langle\text{op}\rangle y_2, x_2\langle\text{op}\rangle y_1, x_2\langle\text{op}\rangle y_2)$.

(23) $[y_1, y_2] - [x_1, x_2] = [y_1 - x_2, y_2 - x_1]$ **Interval subtraction** (= (12))

(24) $X - [a, b] = [c, d]$. Generally speaking, $X \neq [a + c, b + d]$
    a. X is undefined if $b + c > a + d$. (i.e., for X to be defined, the lower bound of X cannot exceed the upper bound of X.)
    b.   When defined, $X = [b + c, a + d]$.
        the **lower** bound of X = the **upper** bound of the subtrahend $[a, b]$
                + the **lower** bound of the difference $[c, d]$
        the **upper** bound of X = the **lower** bound of the subtrahend $[a, b]$
                + the **upper** bound of the difference $[c, d]$

(25)   a. $[6, 8] - [3, 4] = [2, 5]$ **Interval subtraction**
        b. $[3, 4] + [2, 5] = [5, 9]$ **Interval addition**

An interval means a range of possible values of degrees. Thus, for a given interval, it becomes less informative (i.e., including more possibilities) if we lower its lower bound or raise its upper bound, and it becomes more informative (i.e., including fewer possibilities) if we lower its upper bound or raise its lower bound.

As a consequence of (24b), raising the upper bound of the subtrahend leads to a higher lower bound for the minuend, thus decreasing the informativeness of the subtrahend but increasing the informativeness of the minuend. More generally, changing an endpoint of the subtrahend always makes the informativeness of the subtrahend and the minuend change in opposite directions. When the subtrahend becomes more informative, the minuend becomes less informative, and vice versa.

In this sense, the informativeness of a *than*-clause (i.e., a subtrahend) always projects to the matrix-level informativeness (which corresponds to the minuend) in a reverse way, demonstrating the hallmark of DE-ness (see Fauconnier 1978, Ladusaw 1979; 1980), as shown in (26) and (27):

(26)   Function f is downward-entailing iff $\forall x \forall y[x$ entails $y \rightarrow f(y)$ entails $f(x)]$.

(27)   If $I_{\text{STDD}} \subseteq I'_{\text{STDD}}$, then $\iota I'[I' - I'_{\text{STDD}} = I_{\text{DIFF}}] \subseteq \iota I[I - I_{\text{STDD}} = I_{\text{DIFF}}]$.
    (Here $f(K) = \iota I'[I' - K = I_{\text{DIFF}}]$, and I_{DIFF} means a given free variable.)

It is worth noting that this DE-ness is due to the application of interval subtraction. It is by being the **standard of a comparison** and playing the role of **subtrahend in interval subtraction** that makes a *than*-clause – the subtrahend interval I_{STDD} – inherently DE.

Another remark is that the monotonicity and the polarity of the differential (i.e., I_{DIFF}) in a comparative never interfere with the monotonicity projection from a *than*-clause to matrix-level semantics (see (27)).

According to Zhang and Ling (2020), the differential of *more-than* comparatives is positive, i.e., a subset of $(0, +\infty)$ (see (28a)–(28c)), while the differential of *less-than* comparatives is negative, i.e., a subset of $(-\infty, 0)$ (see (28d) and

(28e)). These positive and negative differentials are all definite descriptions of scalar values, i.e., similar to *the value of 4* (or *-4*). The notion of intervals is to generalize and include both precise and potentially not-very-precise values.[7]

Both I_{STDD} and I_{DIFF} are definite descriptions of intervals, each making independent contribution to the derivation of matrix-level semantics. The monotonicity projection from I_{STDD} to the minuend is entirely irrelevant to I_{DIFF} (see (27)). In particular, it is entirely irrelevant to the direction of inequalities – whether its the minuend or I_{STDD} that meets or exceeds more degrees along a scale (cf. (6)). The direction of inequalities actually amounts to the polarity of I_{DIFF} in this analysis. Thus, as illustrated in (28) and (29), the pattern of monotonicity projection is always the same for both *more-than* and *less-than* comparatives, regardless of the monotonicity or polarity of I_{DIFF}.

The contrast between (28) and (29) is due to the interplay between the subtrahend status of a *than*-clause and *than*-clause-internal quantifiers (universal vs. existential). Details of this interplay will be shown in Sect. 4.

(28)   Downward entailment for comparatives with various differentials

    a.   X is more than 2 inches taller than every **boy** is
         $\models$ X is more than 2 inches taller than every **fat boy** is
         (here $I_{\text{DIFF}} = (2, +\infty)$, a <u>positive UE differential</u>:
         more than 2 **fat boys** ran $\models$ more than 2 **boys** ran)

    b.   X is at most 3 inches taller than every **boy** is
         $\models$ X is at most 3 inches taller than every **fat boy** is
         (here $I_{\text{DIFF}} = (0, 3]$, a <u>positive DE differential</u>:
         at most 3 **boys** ran $\models$ at most 3 **fat boys** ran)

    c.   X is between 5 and 10 inches taller than every **boy** is
         $\models$ X is between 5 and 10 inches taller than every **fat boy** is
         (here $I_{\text{DIFF}} = [5', 10']$, a <u>positive non-monotonic differential</u>:
         between 5 and 10 **fat boys** ran $\not\models$ between 5 and 10 **boys** ran
         between 5 and 10 **boys** ran $\not\models$ between 5 and 10 **fat boys** ran)

    d.   X is less tall than every **boy** is
         $\models$ X is less tall than every **fat boy** is
         (here $I_{\text{DIFF}} = (-\infty, 0)$, a <u>negative differential</u>.)

    e.   X is between 5 and 10 inches less tall than every **boy** is
         $\models$ X is between 5 and 10 inches less tall than every **fat boy** is
         (here $I_{\text{DIFF}} = [-10', -5']$, a <u>negative non-monotonic differential</u>.)

(29)   Upward entailment for comparatives with various differentials

    a.   X is more than 2 inches taller than some **fat boy** is
         $\models$ X is more than 2 inches taller than some **boy** is

    b.   X is at most 3 inches taller than some **fat boy** is
         $\models$ X is at most 3 inches taller than some **boy** is

---

[7] Even for a sentence like *Sue is a few inches taller than Tom is*, *a few inches* represents **the** measurement of **the** distance between two positions on a height scale, i.e., the measurement is a **definite item** which has a **potentially not very precise** value.

c.   X is between 5 and 10 inches taller than some **fat boy** is
  $\models$ X is between 5 and 10 inches taller than some **boy** is

d.   X is less tall than some **fat boy** is
  $\models$ X is less tall than some **boy** is

e.   X is between 5 and 10 inches less tall than some **fat boy** is
  $\models$ X is between 5 and 10 inches less tall than some **boy** is

4   Monotonicity Projection Patterns from a *than*-clause

As illustrated in (30), the restrictor of universal quantifiers is DE (see (30a)), and so is the scope of *not* (see (30b)). The interplay between them leads to two reverses in monotonicity projection and eventually an UE pattern (see (30c)).

(30)   a.   every **dog** is cute $\models$ every **black dog** is cute   **DE**
     $\because \lambda x.\text{black-dog}(x) \subseteq \lambda x.\text{dog}(x)$ (i.e., [black dog] entails [dog].)
     $\therefore \lambda P.\forall x[\text{black-dog}(x) \to P(x)] \supseteq \lambda P.\forall x[\text{dog}(x) \to P(x)]$
     (i.e., **Reverse** – [every dog] entails [every black dog].)
   b.   Bill did not **run** $\models$ Bill did not **run fast**   **DE**
     $\because \lambda x.\text{run-fast}(x) \subseteq \lambda x.\text{run}(x)$ (i.e., [run fast] entails [run].)
     $\therefore \lambda x.\neg\text{run-fast}(x) \supseteq \lambda x.\neg\text{run}(x)$
     (i.e., **Reverse** – [not running] entails [not running fast].)
   c.   not every **black dog** is cute $\models$ not every **dog** is cute   **UE**
     $\lambda P.\neg\forall x[\text{black-dog}(x) \to P(x)] \subseteq \lambda P.\neg\forall x[\text{dog}(x) \to P(x)]$
     (i.e., [not every black dog] entails [not every dog].)

Similarly, the DE and UE patterns in (9) and (10) are due to the interplay between the subtrahend status of a *than*-clause and its internal quantifiers.

In (31), there is a *than*-clause-internal **universal quantifier**. Thus the monotonicity projection involves **three reverses**: (i) from the meaning of a noun phrase NP to that of *every NP*; (ii) from *every NP* to I_{STDD}, i.e., the most informative interval including the measurement of every NP; (iii) finally, from I_{STDD}, the subtrahend, to the matrix-level semantics. Eventually, these three reverses lead to the DE pattern in (9).

(31)   This tree is taller than every animal/giraffe is.
   a.   **Reverse 1**: the projection from [NP] to [every NP]
     $\because \lambda x.\text{giraffe}(x) \subseteq \lambda x.\text{animal}(x)$ (i.e., [giraffe] entails [animal].)
     $\therefore \lambda P.\forall x[\text{giraffe}(x) \to P(x)] \supseteq \lambda P.\forall x[\text{animal}(x) \to P(x)]$
     (i.e., any property P such that $\forall x[\text{animal}(x) \to P(x)]$
     also makes $\forall x[\text{giraffe}(x) \to P(x)]$ hold true.)
     (i.e., **Reverse 1** – [every animal] entails [every giraffe].)
   b.   **Reverse 2**: the projection from [every NP] to the *than*-clause
     $\because \lambda I.\forall x[\text{grf}(x) \to \text{HGHT}(x) \subseteq I] \supseteq \lambda I.\forall x[\text{anm}(x) \to \text{HGHT}(x) \subseteq I]$
     (i.e., any interval I such that $\forall x[\text{animal}(x) \to \text{HEIGHT}(x) \subseteq I]$
     also makes $\forall x[\text{giraffe}(x) \to \text{HEIGHT}(x) \subseteq I]$ hold true.)

$\therefore \iota I[\forall x[\mathsf{grf}(x) \to \mathrm{HGHT}(x) \subseteq I]] \subseteq \iota I'[\forall x[\mathsf{anm}(x) \to \mathrm{HGHT}(x) \subseteq I']]$
(i.e., the most informative interval I s.t. $\forall x[\mathsf{grf}(x) \to \mathrm{HGHT}(x) \subseteq I]$
is not less informative than the most informative interval I' s.t.
$\forall x[\mathsf{animal}(x) \to \mathrm{HEIGHT}(x) \subseteq I']$.)
(i.e., **Reverse 2** –[than every giraffe is (tall)] entails
[than every animal is (tall)].)

c.   **Reverse 3**: the projection from I_{STDD} to sentence meaning
$\because$ [than every giraffe is (tall)] $\subseteq$ [than every animal is (tall)]
$\therefore \iota I_{\mathrm{MINUEND}}[I_{\mathrm{MINUEND}} - \iota I[\forall x[\mathsf{giraffe}(x) \to \mathrm{HEIGHT}(x) \subseteq I]] = I_{\mathrm{DIFF}}] \supseteq$
$\iota I'_{\mathrm{MINUEND}}[I'_{\mathrm{MINUEND}} - \iota I'[\forall x[\mathsf{animal}(x) \to \mathrm{HEIGHT}(x) \subseteq I']] = I_{\mathrm{DIFF}}]$
(i.e., **Reverse 3** – [taller than every animal is] entails
[taller than every giraffe is].)

In (32), there is a *than*-clause-internal **existential quantifier**. The monotonicity projection from NP to *some NP* is straightforward. Then the projection
involves two reverses: (i) from *some NP* to I_{STDD}; (ii) from I_{STDD} to the matrix-
level semantics. Eventually, these two reverses lead to the UE pattern in (10).

(32)   This tree is taller than some animal/giraffe is.

a.   the projection from [NP] to [some NP]
$\because \lambda x.\mathsf{giraffe}(x) \subseteq \lambda x.\mathsf{animal}(x)$
(i.e., [giraffe] entails [animal].)
$\therefore \lambda P.\exists x[\mathsf{giraffe}(x) \wedge P(x)] \subseteq \lambda P.\exists x[\mathsf{animal}(x) \wedge P(x)]$
(i.e., any property P such that $\exists x[\mathsf{giraffe}(x) \wedge P(x)]$
also makes $\exists x[\mathsf{animal}(x) \wedge P(x)]$ hold true.)
(i.e., [some giraffe] entails [some animal].)

b.   **Reverse 1**: the projection from [some NP] to the *than*-clause
$\because \lambda P.\exists x[\mathsf{giraffe}(x) \wedge P(x)] \subseteq \lambda P.\exists x[\mathsf{animal}(x) \wedge P(x)]$
$\therefore$ for each most informative interval I s.t. $\exists x[\mathsf{grf}(x) \wedge \mathrm{HGHT}(x) \subseteq I]$,
there must exist an interval I' s.t. $\exists x[\mathsf{anm}(x) \wedge \mathrm{HGHT}(x) \subseteq I']$
and I' is not less informative than I.
(i.e., **Reverse 1** – [than some animal is (tall)] entails
[than some giraffe is (tall)].)

c.   **Reverse 2**: the projection from I_{STDD} to sentence meaning
$\because$ [than some animal is (tall)] $\subseteq$ [than some giraffe is (tall)]
$\therefore \iota I_{\mathrm{MINUEND}}[I_{\mathrm{MINUEND}} - \iota I[\exists x[\mathsf{giraffe}(x) \wedge \mathrm{HEIGHT}(x) \subseteq I]] = I_{\mathrm{DIFF}}] \subseteq$
$\iota I'_{\mathrm{MINUEND}}[I'_{\mathrm{MINUEND}} - \iota I'[\exists x[\mathsf{animal}(x) \wedge \mathrm{HEIGHT}(x) \subseteq I']] = I_{\mathrm{DIFF}}]$
(i.e., **Reverse 2** – [taller than some giraffe is] entails
[taller than some animal is].)

5   The Strong Negativity of a *than*-clause

Within the literature on NPIs, it has been widely acknowledged since Zwarts
(1981) that not all NPIs have the same requirement for their licensing environment. Zwarts (1981) (see also Zwarts 1998) classifies negative-flavored

environments into three levels – **downward-entailing, anti-additive,** and **anti-morphic** (see (33) and (34)) – and proposes that the licensing of strong NPIs (cf. weak NPIs) requires an environment that is higher on this hierarchy.

Section 3 shows that due to its subtrahend status in a subtraction equation, a *than*-clause is by nature DE. Here I show that a subtrahend also satisfies the requirements in (33) and (34). Thus a *than*-clause is anti-morphic, demonstrating strong negativity like classical negation operator *not* does.

(33)   Function f is anti-additive iff $\forall x \forall y [f(x \vee y) = f(x) \wedge f(y)]$.

(34)   Function f is anti-morphic iff it is anti-additive and anti-multiplicative. Function f is anti-multiplicative iff $\forall x \forall y [f(x \wedge y) = f(x) \vee f(y)]$.

To show that the subtrahend status of a *than*-clause is anti-additive, I follow the recipe of interval subtraction (see (12)) to prove the equivalence in (35).

(35) $\underbrace{\iota I[I - [a_1, b_1] \cup [a_2, b_2] = [c, d]]}_{f(x \vee y)} = \underbrace{\iota I[I - [a_1, b_1] = [c, d]] \cap \iota I[I - [a_2, b_2] = [c, d]]}_{f(x) \wedge f(y)}$

(Suppose all these intervals are defined, i.e., $a_1 < b_1$, $a_2 < b_2$, and $c < d$.)

I adopt Moore (1979)'s definition for the **intesection** and **union** operations on two intervals. As shown in (36), for two intervals $[a_1, b_1]$ and $[a_2, b_2]$, if their intersection interval is non-empty (i.e., not the case that $a_1 > b_2$ or $a_2 > b_1$), then their intersection is again an interval – essentially the overlap between the two input intervals. Similarly, as shown in (37), if there is overlap between two intervals, then the union of the two intervals is also an interval – essentially the entire interval including all the elements in the two input intervals. Evidently, these two operations on intervals are parallel to those defined on sets.

(36) $[a_1, b_1] \cap [a_2, b_2] = [\text{MAX}(a_1, a_2), \text{MIN}(b_1, b_2)]$ **Interval intersection**
(Defined when their intersection is non-empty.)

(37) $[a_1, b_1] \cup [a_2, b_2] = [\text{MIN}(a_1, a_2), \text{MAX}(b_1, b_2)]$ **Interval union**
(Defined when their intersection is non-empty.)

Thus, (38) and (39) show the derivation for the left and right part of (35), respectively. Together, they prove the anti-additivity of the subtrahend status.

(38) $\iota I[I - [a_1, b_1] \cup [a_2, b_2] = [c, d]]$
$= \iota I[I - [\text{MIN}(a_1, a_2), \text{MAX}(b_1, b_2)] = [c, d]]$
$= [\text{MAX}(b_1, b_2) + c, \text{MIN}(a_1, a_2) + d]$
(defined when $\text{MAX}(b_1, b_2) + c < \text{MIN}(a_1, a_2) + d$.)

(39) $\iota I[I - [a_1, b_1] = [c, d]] \cap \iota I[I - [a_2, b_2] = [c, d]]$
$= [b_1 + c, a_1 + d] \cap [b_2 + c, a_2 + d]$
$= [\text{MAX}(b_1, b_2) + c, \text{MIN}(a_1, a_2) + d]$
(defined when $\text{MAX}(b_1, b_2) + c < \text{MIN}(a_1, a_2) + d$.)[8]

To show that the subtrahend status of a *than*-clause is also anti-multiplicative (see (34)), I also use interval subtraction to prove the equivalence in (40).

(40) $\underbrace{\iota I[I - [a_1, b_1] \cap [a_2, b_2] = [c, d]]}_{f(x \wedge y)} = \underbrace{\iota I[I - [a_1, b_1] = [c, d]] \cup \iota I[I - [a_2, b_2] = [c, d]]}_{f(x) \vee f(y)}$

(41) and (42) show the derivation for the left and right part of (40), respectively. Together, they prove the anti-multiplicativity of the subtrahend status.

(41) $\iota I[I - [a_1, b_1] \cap [a_2, b_2] = [c, d]]$
$= \iota I[I - [\text{MAX}(a_1, a_2), \text{MIN}(b_1, b_2)] = [c, d]]$
$= [\text{MIN}(b_1, b_2) + c, \text{MAX}(a_1, a_2) + d]$
(defined when $\text{MIN}(b_1, b_2) + c < \text{MAX}(a_1, a_2) + d$.)

(42) $\iota I[I - [a_1, b_1] = [c, d]] \cup \iota I[I - [a_2, b_2] = [c, d]]$
$= [b_1 + c, a_1 + d] \cup [b_2 + c, a_2 + d]$
$= [\text{MIN}(b_1, b_2) + c, \text{MAX}(a_1, a_2) + d]$
(defined when $b_1 + c < a_1 + d$, and $b_2 + c < a_2 + d$.) [9]

(35) and (40) both hold true, indicating that the subtrahend in an interval subtraction equation is both anti-additive and anti-multiplicative.[10] Thus the subtrahend status is anti-morphic, demonstrating a negativity as strong as the

---

[8] Obviously, as far as $[\text{MAX}(b_1, b_2) + c, \text{MIN}(a_1, a_2) + d]$ is defined, i.e., $\text{MAX}(b_1, b_2) + c < \text{MIN}(a_1, a_2) + d$, then it must be the case that $b_1 + c < a_1 + d$, and $b_2 + c < a_2 + d$, i.e., $[b_1 + c, a_1 + d]$ and $[b_2 + c, a_2 + d]$ are defined.
   Moreover, it must be the case that $b_2 + c < a_1 + d$ and $b_1 + c < a_2 + d$, i.e., the intersection between the intervals $[b_1 + c, a_1 + d]$ and $[b_2 + c, a_2 + d]$ is non-empty.
[9] As fas as $b_1 + c < a_1 + d$ and $b_2 + c < a_2 + d$ (i.e., $[b_1 + c, a_1 + d]$ and $[b_2 + c, a_2 + d]$ are both defined), it must be the case that $\text{MIN}(b_1, b_2) + c < \text{MAX}(a_1, a_2) + d$.
[10] Here are two concrete examples illustrating (35) and (40). Suppose $[a_1, b_1] = [1, 3]$; $[a_2, b_2] = [2, 4]$; $[c, d] = [1, 7]$, then $[a_1, b_1] \cup [a_2, b_2] = [1, 4]$; $[a_1, b_1] \cap [a_2, b_2] = [2, 3]$.

(i)   For the left of (35), $\iota I[I - [a_1, b_1] \cup [a_2, b_2] = [c, d]]$. Thus the unique I is $[5, 8]$. For the right of (35), the intersection between $\iota I[I - [a_1, b_1] = [c, d]]$ and $\iota I[I - [a_2, b_2] = [c, d]]$ amounts to intersecting $[4, 8]$ and $[5, 9]$, which is also $[5, 8]$.

(ii)   For the left of (40), $\iota I[I - [a_1, b_1] \cap [a_2, b_2] = [c, d]]$. Thus the unique I is $[4, 9]$. For the right of (40), the union of $\iota I[I - [a_1, b_1] = [c, d]]$ and $\iota I[I - [a_2, b_2] = [c, d]]$ amounts to the union of $[4, 8]$ and $[5, 9]$, which is also $[4, 9]$.

classical negation operator *not*.[11] Therefore, by playing the role of subtrahend in an interval subtraction, a *than*-clause is by nature strongly negative-flavored.

Just like the inherent DE-ness of a *than*-clause is due to interval subtraction, its anti-additivity and anti-multiplicativity are also based on degree semantics implemented with interval arithmetic. The inference patterns with regard to *than*-clause-internal DPs are distinct from (35) and (40).

As shown in (43) and (44), it seems that the interpretation of comparatives is anti-additive, but not anti-multiplicative (see also Hoeksema 1983). These patterns are due to both (i) the subtrahend status of a *than*-clause and (ii) the analysis of a *than*-clause as the short answer to its corresponding degree question (see (19)). Suppose the most informative intervals standing for the heights of A and B are $[a_1, b_1]$ and $[a_2, b_2]$, respectively. As shown in (45), both *than A or B is (tall)* and *than A and B are (tall)* are analyzed as the interval $[\text{MIN}(a_1, a_2), \text{MAX}(b_1, b_2)]$.[12] For (45b), since the individual variable of a gradable adjective is an atomic entity (see (15)), I assume a distributivity operator, DIST, in deriving [than A and B are ~~tall~~]. Eventually, this analysis of *than A and B are (tall)* makes the left part of (44a) equal to 'X is taller than A is ∧ X is taller than B is' (see (43)) and thus more informative than the right part of (44a).

(43)   X is taller than A or B is ↔ X is taller than A is ∧ X is taller than B is

(44)   a.   X is taller than A and B are (↔ X is taller than A or B is)
              → X is taller than A is ∨ X is taller than B is
        b.   X is taller than A is ∨ X is taller than B is
              ↛ X is taller than A and B are

---

[11] *Not* is also anti-morphic, as illustrated by (i):

(i)   a.   Mary didn't run → Mary didn't run fast
        b.   Mary didn't sing or dance ↔ Mary didn't sing ∧ Mary didn't dance
        c.   Mary didn't sing and dance ↔ Mary didn't sing ∨ Mary didn't dance.

[12] The equivalence between [than A or B is ~~tall~~] and [than A and B are ~~tall~~] means that degree questions *how tall is A or B* and *how tall are A and B* have the same short answer. This is intuitively right, as suggested by analogous examples in (i):

(i)   Context: A ate an orange. B ate an apple. C ate a peach.
        a.   – What did A, B, or C eat?   – A piece of fruit (⤳ a range of items)
        b.   – What did (each of) A, B, and C eat?   – A piece of fruit (⤳ a range).

(45) $[\![$than A is ~~tall~~$]\!] = [a_1, b_1]$, and $[\![$than B is ~~tall~~$]\!] = [a_2, b_2]$

     a. $[\![$than A or B is ~~tall~~$]\!] = [\text{MIN}(a_1, a_2), \text{MAX}(b_1, b_2)]$

     b. $[\![$than A and B are DIST ~~tall~~$]\!] = [\text{MIN}(a_1, a_2), \text{MAX}(b_1, b_2)]$

          $(\text{DIST} \stackrel{\text{def}}{=} \lambda X_e.\lambda P_{\langle et \rangle}.\forall x[x \sqsubseteq_{\text{ATOM}} X \rightarrow P(x)])$

          $\rightsquigarrow \forall x[x \sqsubseteq_{\text{ATOM}} \textsf{A} \oplus \textsf{B} \rightarrow \text{HEIGHT}(x) \subseteq [\text{MIN}(a_1, a_2), \text{MAX}(b_1, b_2)]]$ [13]

The DE-ness and anti-additivity of clausal comparatives have previously been demonstrated by Hoeksema (1983). Here based on Zhang and Ling (2020)'s interval-subtraction-based analysis of comparatives, I further pin down the source of the DE-ness and anti-additivity in clausal comparatives: it is the sub-trahend status of their *than*-clause. Moreover, I show that the negativity of the subtrahend status is actually as strong as that of classical negation operator *not*, reaching the highest level of Zwarts' hierarchy.

6   NPI Licensing by a *Than*-Clause

How are weak and strong NPIs licensed within a *than*-clause? The brief answer is that as a subtrahend, a *than*-clause is strongly negative-flavored, naturally creating an NPI-licensing environment. NPIs are thus licensed in both *more-than* and *less-than* comparatives (see naturally occurring examples of *less-than* comparatives in (46) and (47) and *more-than* comparatives in (1)–(5)).

(46)   Millennials have <u>less</u> money <u>than</u> **any** other generation did at their age.[14]

(47)   ..., executives' views on the current global economy and expectations of future global growth are <u>less favorable than</u> they have been **in years**.[15]

Specifically, as illustrated in (48), weak NPI *any* is analyzed as a narrow-scope, non-deictic indefinite (see also Giannakidou 2011). It is distinct from a genuine deictic indefinite (e.g., *some boy*) in the sense that its narrow-scope reading is compulsory (see Barker 2018 on the scoping behavior of NPIs), so that a dynamic update with this non-deictic indefinite cannot be non-deterministic.

---

[13] With the use of this distributivity operator, DIST, evidently, for measurement con-structions and the positive use of gradable adjectives (see (16) and (17)), the follow-ing inference patterns hold, which are consistent with our intuition: (i) John and Bill are between 5.9 and 6.2 feet tall $\models$ John is between 5.9 and 6.2 feet tall; (ii) John and Bill are tall $\models$ John is tall. Nevertheless, the interval $[\![$than A is ~~tall~~$]\!]$ entails (i.e., is a subset of) the interval $[\![$than A and B are DIST ~~tall~~$]\!]$ (see (45b)).

[14] https://www.businessinsider.in/millennials-have-less-money-than-any-other-generat ion-did-at-their-age-but-youd-never-guess-it-from-the-way-theyre-flaunting-their-mo ney-on-dating-apps/articleshow/69379306.cms.

[15] https://www.mckinsey.com/business-functions/strategy-and-corporate-finance/our-insights/economic-conditions-snapshot-september-2019-mckinsey-global-survey-res ults.

Roughly, *any boy* means a **random, very vague or low informative** boy conceptualized from the contextually relevant set of individuals.[16]

Thus as shown in (48a), the *than*-clause amounts to addressing the speed of a **random** boy in the context, denoting the most informative interval I' such that the speed of a random boy (among X, Y, and Z) falls within I': i.e., the interval of speed ranging from the slowest to the fastest boy's speed, which is the interval $[6.7 \text{ m/s}, 7.8 \text{ m/s}]$. The *than*-clause serves as the standard of comparison. Then with the value of I_{DIFF} (here $[0.1 \text{ m/s}, +\infty)$), the matrix-level meaning can be thus derived via interval subtraction.

(48)   (Context: Roxy ran at a speed of 8 ± 0.1 m/s, and the boys – X, Y, and Z – ran at a speed of 6.7 m/s, 7.2 m/s, and 7.8 m/s, respectively.)
Roxy ran (at least 0.1 m/s) faster than **any** boy did.   (= (1a))
LF: Roxy ran $\underbrace{\text{at least 0.1 m/s} \ldots \text{-er} \ominus}_{I_{\text{DIFF}}} \underbrace{\text{than } \textbf{any} \text{ boy did } \cancel{\text{run fast}} \text{ fast}}_{I_{\text{STDD}}}$

    a. $I_{\text{STDD}} = [\![\text{than } \textbf{any} \text{ boy did } \cancel{\text{run fast}}]\!]$
           $= [\![\text{than } \textbf{a random boy} \text{ (among X, Y, and Z) did } \cancel{\text{run fast}}]\!]$
           i.e., the interval ranging from the slowest to the fastest boy's speed
           (see also (45a)), which is $[6.7 \text{ m/s}, 7.8 \text{ m/s}]$ under the given context.
    b. $I_{\text{DIFF}} = [0.1 \text{ m/s}, +\infty) \cap (0, +\infty) = [0.1 \text{ m/s}, +\infty)$
    c. $\text{SPEED}(\text{Roxy}) \subseteq \iota I[I - \underbrace{\iota I'[\text{SPEED}(\text{a-random-boy}) \subseteq I']}_{=[6.7 \text{ m/s}, 7.8 \text{ m/s}]} = [0.1 \text{ m/s}, +\infty)]$

                        $= [7.9 \text{ m/s}, +\infty)$ (see (12))

The licensing and interpretation of emphatic and strong NPIs are similar, as sketched below. Emphatic NPIs contribute a narrow-scope, non-deictic, scalar-related item: i.e., they can be interpreted as **a random item** conceptualized from an ordered set (of actions, times, etc). Then in interpreting a *than*-clause, an interval – a range of measures – is yielded from the use of such an NPI.

In (49), *give a penny*, a minimizer (or emphatic NPI), can be considered **a random action**, a notion abstracted from an ordered set of actions (along a contextually relevant scale such as effort amount, generosity, willingness, etc), and a (lower or upper) bound of this ordered set is *give a penny*.

In this *would sooner . . . than* sentence, the comparison is performed along a scale of willingness. Thus, the *than*-clause means a right-bounded interval, i.e., $(\ldots, \text{WILLINGNESS}(\text{give-a-penny})]$, and serves as I_{STDD} in this comparative.[17]

---

[16] In terms of dynamic semantics, we can consider *any boy* an introduced variable that (i) only exists very locally, taking narrow scope, and (ii) is vague in the sense that it only carries non-distinctive restrictions that hold true for all and each specific individual in the relevant set (e.g., here $\text{boy}(x)$ and $\text{SPEED}(x) \subseteq [6.7 \text{ m/s}, 7.8 \text{ m/s}]$).

[17] Why does *give a penny* correspond to the upper bound of an interval of willingness? I assume this is due to the meaning postulate of this idiomatic expression. This expression should also correspond to the lower bound of an interval of effort amount or generosity (e.g., *John didn't give a penny* means that John didn't even make the least effort or show the least generosity). In our world knowledge, larger effort should correlate with less willingness and more generosity.

(49)   He would sooner roast in hell than **give a penny** to others.   ($\approx$ (2a))

    a.   ⟦give a penny⟧
        ⤳ a random action abstracted from a set of actions (ordered along
        a certain scale, e.g., effort amount, generosity, willingness), 'give a
        penny' representing a (lower or upper) bound of this set
        (i.e., any action that is at least/most like 'give a penny')

    b.   ⟦than ~~he would like to~~ **give a penny** to others⟧
        = $(\dots, \text{WILLINGNESS}(\text{give-a-penny})]$

Similarly, in (50), *could help* can be considered a **random action** abstracted
from an ordered set of actions (along a scale of self-control strength, or a scale
of difficulty for resisting an urge). Eventually, the comparison here is performed
along a scale of self-control strength, and the use of *could help* leads to a right-
bounded interval in interpreting *than I could help*.[18]

(50)   My urge to steal was stronger than I **could help**.   (= (3a))

    a.   ⟦could help⟧ ⤳ a random action from a set of actions (ordered along
        a certain scale, e.g., self-control strength)

    b.   ⟦than ~~the urge~~ I **could help** ~~is strong~~⟧
        = $(\dots, \text{the largest value of my self-control strength}]$

For (51) and (52), strong NPIs *yet* and *in years* express a very vague range
of time. From the semantics of *yet*, we only know that this range of time is right-
bounded (see (51a)). From the semantics of *in years*, we only know that this
range of time is measured with the unit of years (see (52a)). Intuitively, both *yet*
and *in years* suggest a long time. The use of *yet* or *in years* presumably rules
out the existence of some deictic time point/interval. The *than*-clauses convey a
range of performance quality or happiness within these vague ranges of time.

(51)   It requires better performance than I've seen **yet**.   (= (4a))

    a.   ⟦yet⟧ ⤳ a vague range of time: $(\dots, \text{an unspecified reference time}]$

    b.   ⟦than ~~the performances~~ I've seen **yet** ~~are good~~⟧
        $\approx$ [the lowest quality of all performances I've seen,
        the highest quality of all performances I've seen]

---

[18] According to the interval-subtraction-based analysis, I_{STDD} in *more-than* comparatives needs to be right-bounded, but I_{STDD} in *less-than* comparatives needs to be
left-bounded. Therefore, for *more-than* comparatives in (49) and (50), the two I_{STDD}
(along the scales of willingness and self-control strength) should be right-bounded.
For a *less-than* comparative like *he did less than give a penny to his son*, I_{STDD} has
to be left-bounded (e.g., along a scale of effort amount).

(52)   He made me feel happier than I felt **in years**.   (= (5a))

  a.   [[in years]]
        ⤳ a vague range of time measured with the unit of years: $(\ldots, \ldots)$

  b.   [[than I felt ~~happy~~ in years]]
        ≈ [the lowest degree of my happiness over a long time,
        the highest degree of my happiness over a long time]

For the cases of NPIs licensed by classical negation operator *not* (see (53)), the low informativeness of NPIs is directly flipped by the operation of negation. As shown in (48)–(52), for the cases of *than*-clause-internal NPIs, the low informativeness of these NPIs leads to low informative intervals that serve as comparison standard, and then it is during interval subtraction that low informativeness gets flipped into high informativeness at the matrix level.

(53)   a.   Roxy didn't see **any** boy.
              ⤳ No boy was seen by Roxy.
        b.   He left the world without **giving a penny** to his son.
              ⤳ No action, not even the least effort-demanding one, accompanied his leaving the world.
        c.   I **could**n't **help** laughing.
              ⤳ Laughing was beyond my self-control.
        d.   I haven't read the book **yet**.
              ⤳ At no time have I read the book.
        e.   He wasn't happy **in years**.
              ⤳ At no time was he happy.

In sum, NPIs convey a random, low informative, non-deictic item, which can be a deficient indefinite or a very uninformative range of time (see Giannakidou 2011 on the deficiency of NPIs). NPI licensers make use of them in a way that flips informativeness, i.e., projecting the low informativeness of NPIs to sentential-level meaning and, meanwhile, flipping low informativeness into high informativeness. The subtrahend status of a *than*-clause plays exactly this role in flipping informativeness, thus licensing NPIs.

7   Discussion

The current paper is innovative in addressing the monotonicity projection resulted from the operation of interval subtraction. Thus, the subtrahend status of a *than*-clause makes it a degree-semantics-based NPI licenser. As mentioned earlier, the basic view of Hoeksema (1983) is maintained: i.e., comparatives are DE and anti-additive. The current paper further strengthens and pinpoints this view, showing that due to its subtrahend status, the negativity of the comparison standard is actually as strong as that of classical negation operator *not*.

Previously, Giannakidou and Yoon (2010) argues that comparatives do not contain a DE operator that can license NPIs. Their analysis is problematic in a few respects. First, as I have shown throughout the paper, comparatives do contain a DE operator. It is the subtrahend status of the *than*-clause. However, distinct from the classical, set-operation-based, negation operator, the subtrahend status gets its negative flavor from the operation of **interval subtraction**.

Second, according to Giannakidou and Yoon (2010), only weak NPIs, but not strong NPIs, can be licensed in a non-DE environment (such as comparatives) via a rescuing mechanism. They also analyze English minimizers like *give a penny* as weak NPIs. However, empirical data like (4), (5), and (47) (a naturally occurring example) show that English strong NPIs like *yet* and *in years* are also licensed within a *than*-clause. Thus even if weak NPIs might not rely on a DE environment for licensing, we still need to explain why some strong NPIs are nevertheless licensed within a *than*-clause.

Third, Giannakidou and Yoon (2010) suggests that *than*-clause-internal *any* is likely to be a free choice item (FCI), not an NPI, and as a consequence, *than*-clause-internal *any* does not need a DE environment for licensing. This is suspicious for two reasons (see also Aloni and Roelofsen 2014 for discussion).

(i) First, FCI *any* is ill-formed in both positive and negative episodic sentences, and FCI *any* has its own licensing environments, such as modal statements (see (54)). Then it becomes puzzling why *any* is grammatical in an embedded episodic *than*-clause, as shown in (1a) (repeated here as (55)). If, as claimed by Giannakidou and Yoon (2010), the *than*-clause is not negative-flavored, then *any* should simply be ruled out in (55), no matter it is an NPI or an FCI.

(54) a. *Anyone ate. ⤳ FCI *any*: ill-formed in positive episodic sentences
      b. *Anyone didn't eat.
                          ⤳ FCI *any*: ill-formed in negative episodic sentences
      c. Anyone can eat.   ⤳ FCI *any*: licensed in modal statements

(55) a. Roxy ran faster than any boy did (yesterday).   (= (1a))

(ii) Second, according to Giannakidou and Yoon (2010), *than*-clause-internal *any* can be modified by *almost*, suggesting that it is FCI *any*, not NPI *any* (see the contrast in (56)). However, it is questionable whether the use of *almost* is a great test for distinguishing FCI and NPI *any*, and the empirical evidence is not as clear-cut as shown in (56) (which repeat Giannakidou and Yoon 2010's (51)). On the one hand, naturally occurring examples from *Corpus of Contemporary American English* (CoCA, Davies 2008) show that NPI *any* can be compatible with the modification of *almost* (see (57)). On the other hand, Kadmon and Landman (1993) argue for a unified account for NPI and FCI *any*.

(56) a. Mary wrote more articles than **almost any** professor suggested.
      b. ??Mary didn't buy **almost any** book.

(57) a. BA and BS aren't worth **almost anything** now ...
      b. These people, they don't have **almost anything**.
      c. ...they didn't get **almost anything** that they wanted.

Taken together, these provide evidence showing that it is questionable to analyze *than*-clause-internal *any* (see (1a)/(55)) as FCI.

A further issue raised by the analysis of Giannakidou and Yoon (2010) is on *either*. According to Giannakidou and Yoon (2010), *either* is a genuine strong NPI in English, and it cannot be licensed within a *than*-clause (see (7a), repeated here as (58)). Indeed, *either* can only appear in sentences containing classical negative words like *not, no one, never*, etc. However, I tend to think that the semantics of *either* is largely different from NPIs like *any, give a penny, could help, yet, in years*, etc. Intuitively, the ungrammatical use of *either* in positive sentences (see (7b-ii), repeated here as (59)) is much more similar to the ungrammatical use of *too* in negative sentences (see (60b)) than to an unlicensed NPI. If *too* is not analyzed as a positive polarity item (PPI), why do we need to analyze *either* as an NPI? After all, the interpretation of other NPI phenomena involves monotonicity projection and downward inferences, introducing narrow-scope, non-deictic variables, or triggering strengthening implications, but the interpretation of *either* does not involve any of these.

(58)   *Kevin is not tall, and John is taller than Bill is **either**.   (= (7a))

(59)   *Bill is tall, and I know that John is tall, **either**.   (= (7b-ii))

(60)   a.   Mary came. I know that Bill came, **too**.
          b.   *Mary didn't came. I know that Bill didn't came, **too**.

The current analysis on NPI licensing in comparatives is rooted in Ladusaw's and Zwarts' theories on DE-ness and negativity: NPI phenomena mark downward inferences. The current analysis is also compatible with three other influential theories of NPI phenomena.

Specifically, my sketched analysis of NPIs as narrow-scope, low informative, non-deictic items captures the essence of Giannakidou's non-veridicality theory of NPIs (see Giannakidou 2011 for a review): NPIs are distinct from genuine indefinites in that there is no projectable existential force.

Then the communicative value of NPIs in my analysis is consistent with Kadmon and Landman (1993)'s view that NPI licensing triggers strengthening implications: NPIs convey locally low informativeness, but this low informativeness is eventually flipped into high informativeness by DE operators.

Finally, according to Barker (2018)'s scope-marking theory, NPIs signal that an indefinite is taking narrow scope, and the narrow-scope reading is more informative than a wide-scope reading. This view captures our intuition that NPIs seem to be interpreted as locally existential, but globally universal (see (61)). Therefore, Barker (2018) provides a generalized view for the universal flavor of NPIs. My analysis of *than*-clause-internal *any* as NPI *any* is thus a special case. There is no need to attribute this universal flavor to an FCI-*any* account.

(61)   Mary didn't see any cat.   (cf. $\exists x[\text{cat}(x) \wedge \neg\text{see}(\text{Mary}, x)] - \exists > \neg$)

    a. $\neg\exists x[\text{cat}(x) \wedge \text{see}(\text{Mary}, x)]$ $\neg > \exists$

    b. $\forall x[\text{cat}(x) \rightarrow \neg\text{see}(\text{Mary}, x)]$ $\forall > \neg$

Among the core issues on NPIs, compositionality has not been much addressed in the current paper. I analyze the meaning of a *than*-clause as a definite, most informative scalar value (in terms of an interval) that is the short answer to a corresponding degree question. However, I haven't gone into the compositional details of a comparative containing *than*-clause-internal NPIs. Strong NPIs cannot be used in *wh*-questions or degree questions. Thus, a plausible derivation scheme should involve a delayed evaluation mechanism in interpreting a *than*-clause that contains NPIs (see Barker and Shan 2014, Zhang 2020 for relevant discussions on the evaluation order in NPI licensing and the compositional issue of *than*-clause-internal quantifiers). This is left for future research.

Another issue worth mentioning is how the current analysis can be extended to account for NPI licensing in phrasal comparatives (e.g., phrasal comparatives in Greek/English, Japanese *yori*-comparatives, Chinese *bǐ*-comparatives). Cross-linguistically, these constructions do not necessarily demonstrate the same pattern with regard to licensing *than*-phrase-internal NPIs. Besides, I suspect that emphatic and strong NPIs like *give a penny* and *in years* simply cannot be used in phrasal comparatives, due to syntactic reasons. A full investigation is also left for another occasion.

8   Conclusion

With the use of an existing, independently motivated analysis of comparatives (i.e., Zhang and Ling 2020's interval-subtraction-based analysis), I have shown that by serving as the standard in a comparison and playing the role of subtrahend in a subtraction equation, a *than*-clause is by nature strongly negative-flavored. The subtrahend status is downward-entailing, anti-additive, and anti-morphic, flipping the informativeness of an interval standing for the subtrahend. Therefore, a *than*-clause is a natural NPI licenser.

The current analysis has profound implications for theories of NPIs and NPI licensing, especially with regard to how NPIs are composed and evaluated with other parts of a sentence. There is still much left for future research.

References

Aloni, M., Roelofsen, F.: Indefinites in comparatives. Nat. Lang. Semant. **22**(2), 145–167 (2014). https://doi.org/10.1007/s11050-013-9103-z

Alrenga, P., Kennedy, C.: *No more* shall we part: quantifiers in English comparatives. Nat. Lang. Semant. **22**(1), 1–53 (2013). https://doi.org/10.1007/s11050-013-9099-4

Barker, C., Shan, C.-C.: Continuations and Natural Language. OUP (2014)

Barker, C.: Negative polarity as scope marking. Linguist. Philos. **42**(1), 483–510 (2018). https://doi.org/10.1007/s10988-018-9234-2

Bartsch, R., Vennemann, T.: The grammar of relative adjectives and comparison. Linguistische Berichte **20**, 19–32 (1972)

Beck, S.: Quantifiers in than-clauses. Semant. Pragmat. **3**(1), 1–72 (2010). https://doi.org/10.3765/sp.3.1

Beck, S.: Comparison constructions. In: von Heusinger, Maienborn, Portner (eds.) Semantics: An International Handbook of Natural Language Meaning, vol. 2, pp. 1341–1390. de Gruyter (2011)

Davies, M.: Corpus of Contemporary American English: 450 million words, 1900 - present (2008). https://www.english-corpora.org/coca/

Fauconnier, G.: Implication reversal in a natural language. In: Guenthner, F., Schmidt, S.J. (eds.) Formal semantics and pragmatics for natural languages, pp. 289–301. Springer, Heidelberg (1978). https://doi.org/10.1007/978-94-009-9775-2_10

Giannakidou, A.: Negative and positive polarity items. In: von Heusinger, Maienborn, Portner (eds.) Semantics: An International Handbook of Natural Language Meaning, vol. 2, pp. 1660–1712. de Gruyter (2011)

Giannakidou, A., Yoon, S.: No NPI licensing in comparatives. Proc. CLS (Chicago Linguist. Soc.) **42** (2010)

Heim, I.: Remarks on comparative clauses as generalized quantifiers. MS (2006)

Hoeksema, J.: Negative polarity and the comparative. Nat. Lang. Linguist. Theory **1**, 403–434 (1983). https://doi.org/10.1007/BF00142472

Kadmon, N., Landman, F.: Any. Linguist. Philos. **16**, 354–422 (1993). https://doi.org/10.1007/BF00985272

Kennedy, C.: Projecting the Adjective: The Syntax and Semantics of Gradability and Comparison. Routledge (1999)

Ladusaw, W.: Negative polarity items as inherent scope relations. Ph.D. thesis, UT Austin (1979)

Ladusaw, W.: On the notion affective in the analysis of negative polarity items. In: Formal Semantics: The Essential Readings, pp. 457–470 (1980)

Larson, R.: Scope and comparatives. Linguist. Philos. **11**(1), 1–26 (1988). https://www.jstor.org/stable/pdf/25001296.pdf

Moore, R.: Methods and Applications of Interval Analysis. SIAM (1979)

Schwarzschild, R., Wilkinson, K.: Quantifiers in comparatives: a semantics of degree based on intervals. Nat. Lang. Semant. **10**, 1–41 (2002). https://doi.org/10.1023/A:1015545424775

Schwarzschild, R.: The semantics of comparatives and other degree constructions. Lang. Linguist. Compass. **2**(2), 308–331 (2008). https://doi.org/10.1111/j.1749-818X.2007.00049.x

von Stechow, A.: Comparing semantic theories of comparison. J. Semant. **3**, 1–77 (1984). https://doi.org/10.1093/jos/3.1-2.1

Zhang, L.: Split semantics for non-monotonic quantifiers in than-clauses. Syntax Semant. **42**, 331–362 (2020). https://doi.org/10.1163/9789004431515

Zhang, L., Ling, J.: Comparatives revisited: Downward-entailing differentials do not threaten encapsulation theories. Proc. Amsterdam Colloquium **20**, 478–487 (2015)

Zhang, L., Ling, J.: The semantics of comparatives: a difference-based approach. J. Semant. (2020). https://ling.auf.net/lingbuzz/005223

Zwarts, F.: Negatif polaire uitdrukkingen I. GLOT **4**(1), 35–133 (1981)

Zwarts, F.: Three types of polarity. In: Hamm, F., Hinrichs, E. (eds.) Plurality and Quantification, pp. 177–238. Springer, Dordrecht (1998). https://doi.org/10.1007/978-94-017-2706-8_5

Author Index

Printed in the United States
By Bookmasters

La memoria vegetal

La memoria vegetal

Umberto Eco

Traducción del italiano de
Helena Lozano

Lumen
_____

ensayo

Papel certificado por el Forest Stewardship Council®

Título original: *La memoria vegetale e altri scritti di bibliofilia*

Primera edición: abril de 2021

© 2018, La nave di Teseo Editore, Milán
© 2021, Penguin Random House Grupo Editorial, S. A. U.
Travessera de Gràcia, 47-49. 08021 Barcelona
© 2021, Helena Lozano Miralles, por la traducción

Printed in Spain – Impreso en España

ISBN: 978-84-264-0628-6
Depósito legal: B-2.594-2021

Compuesto en M. I. Maquetación, S. L.

Impreso en Egedsa
Sabadell (Barcelona)

H 4 0 6 2 8 A

Índice

Sobre la bibliofilia

La memoria vegetal[1]

Quiero empezar recordando que esta conferencia —a la que sería deseable que siguieran otras— la ha organizado el Aldus Club, en colaboración con la Biblioteca de Brera, no para bibliófilos empedernidos o para eruditos que tienen mucha, incluso excesiva, familiaridad con los libros, sino, al contrario, para un público más amplio, también joven, de ciudadanos de un país donde las estadísticas nos dicen que, junto a una multitud de personas que nunca toman un libro entre sus manos, hay otras muchísimas, demasiadas, que no se acercan a más de un libro al año. Y las estadísticas no nos dicen en cuántos de esos casos se trata tan solo de un manual de cocina o una recopilación de chistes.

No importa que luego la austeridad del lugar y la dificultad del título hayan convocado aquí a más arzobispos que catecúmenos. Propongo el mío como ejemplo de una serie de discursos que los lectores podrían dirigir, en diferentes circunstancias educativas, a quienes son un poco menos lectores.

1. Conferencia pronunciada en Milán el 23 de noviembre de 1991 en la Sala Teresiana de la Biblioteca Nazionale Braidense. Rovello la publicó en un pequeño volumen, en edición numerada (Milán, 1992).

1. Desde los tiempos de Adán, los seres humanos manifiestan dos debilidades, una física y la otra psíquica: por el lado físico, antes o después se mueren; por el psíquico, los seres humanos lamentan tener que morirse. Al no poder obviar la debilidad física, intentan encontrar compensación en el plano psíquico, preguntándose si existe una forma de supervivencia después de la muerte, pregunta a la que responden la filosofía, las religiones reveladas y varias formas de creencias míticas y mistéricas. Algunas filosofías orientales nos dicen que el flujo de la vida no se detiene, y que después de la muerte nos reencarnaremos en otra criatura. Ante esta respuesta, la pregunta que nos surge espontánea es: cuando yo sea esa otra criatura, ¿seguiré acordándome de que fui yo?, ¿y sabré fundir mis antiguos recuerdos con los nuevos que esa criatura tendrá? Si la respuesta es negativa, nos sentimos decepcionados, porque no hay ninguna diferencia entre ser alguien que no sabe que ha sido yo y desaparecer en la nada. Yo no quiero sobrevivir como alguien más, quiero sobrevivir como yo en persona. Y puesto que de mí no quedará el cuerpo, espero que sobreviva el alma; ahora bien, la respuesta que todos daríamos nos dice que identificamos nuestra alma con nuestra memoria. Como decía Valéry: «Soy yo mismo, en cada instante, un enorme hecho de memoria».

Y en efecto, nos parecen más humanas esas religiones que nos aseguran que después de la muerte lo recordaré todo de mí, e incluso el infierno no será sino un eterno recordar las razones por las que he sido castigado.

Y claro, si supiéramos que en el infierno sufriría alguien que no sabe haber sido yo, todos pecaríamos alegremente: ¿qué más me dan los sufrimientos de uno que no solo no tendrá mi cuerpo actual, sino tampoco mis recuerdos?

La memoria cumple dos funciones. Una, y es la función en la que todos piensan, es la de retener en el recuerdo los datos de nuestra experiencia previa; pero la otra es también la de filtrarlos, la de dejar caer algunos y conservar otros. Quizá muchos de ustedes conozcan ese bello cuento de Borges que se titula «Funes el memorioso». Ireneo Funes es un personaje que todo lo percibe sin filtrar nada y, sin filtrar nada, todo lo recuerda:

Nosotros, de un vistazo, percibimos tres copas en una mesa; Funes, todos los vástagos y racimos y frutos que comprende una parra. Sabía las formas de las nubes australes del amanecer del treinta de abril de mil ochocientos ochenta y dos y podía compararlas en el recuerdo con las vetas de un libro en pasta española que solo había mirado una vez y con las líneas de la espuma que un remo levantó en el Río Negro la víspera de la acción del Quebracho. Esos recuerdos no eran simples; cada imagen visual estaba ligada a sensaciones musculares, térmicas, etc. Podía reconstruir todos los sueños, todos los entresueños. Dos o tres veces había reconstruido un día entero; no había dudado nunca, pero cada reconstrucción había requerido un día entero. Me dijo: «Más recuerdos tengo yo solo que los que habrán tenido todos los hombres desde que el mundo es mundo». Y también: «Mis sueños son como la vigilia de ustedes». Y también, hacia el alba: «Mi memoria, señor, es como vaciadero de basuras». Una circunferencia en un pizarrón, un triángulo rectángulo, un rombo, son formas que podemos intuir plenamente; lo mismo le pasaba a Ireneo con las aborrascadas crines de un potro, con una punta de ganado en una cuchilla, con el fuego cambiante y con la innumerable ceniza, con las muchas caras de un muerto en un largo velorio. No sé cuántas estrellas veía en el cielo. [...]

En efecto, Funes no solo recordaba cada hoja de cada árbol de cada monte, sino cada una de las veces que la había percibido o imaginado. Resolvió reducir cada una de sus jornadas pretéritas a unos setenta mil recuerdos, que definiría luego por cifras. Lo disuadieron dos consideraciones: la conciencia de que la tarea era interminable, la conciencia de que era inútil. Pensó que en la hora de la muerte no habría acabado aún de clasificar todos los recuerdos de la niñez.

Pero recordarlo todo significa no reconocer ya nada:

Este, no lo olvidemos, era casi incapaz de ideas generales, platónicas.

No solo le costaba comprender que el símbolo genérico *perro* abarcara tantos individuos dispares de diversos tamaños y diversa forma; le molestaba que el perro de las tres y catorce (visto de perfil) tuviera el mismo nombre que el perro de las tres y cuarto (visto de frente). Su propia cara en el espejo, sus propias manos, lo sorprendían cada vez.

Refiere Swift que el emperador de Lilliput discernía el movimiento del minutero; Funes discernía continuamente los tranquilos avances de la corrupción, de las caries, de la fatiga. Notaba los progresos de la muerte, de la humedad. Era el solitario y lúcido espectador de un mundo multiforme, instantáneo y casi intolerablemente preciso.

Babilonia, Londres y Nueva York han abrumado con feroz esplendor la imaginación de los hombres; nadie, en sus torres populosas o en sus avenidas urgentes, ha sentido el calor y la presión de una realidad tan infatigable como la que día y noche convergía sobre el infeliz Ireneo, en su pobre arrabal sudamericano. Le era muy difícil dormir. Dormir es distraerse del mundo;

Funes, de espaldas en el catre, en la sombra, se figuraba cada grieta y cada moldura de las casas precisas que lo rodeaban.

[...] Había aprendido sin esfuerzo el inglés, el francés, el portugués, el latín. Sospecho, sin embargo, que no era muy capaz de pensar. Pensar es olvidar diferencias, es generalizar, abstraer. En el abarrotado mundo de Funes no había sino detalles, casi inmediatos.

¿Cómo es que logramos reconocer a una persona querida incluso algunos años después (y después de que su cara se haya modificado), o de volver a encontrar el camino de casa todos los días, aunque en los muros haya nuevos carteles, o cuando la tienda de la esquina puede haber sido decorada con colores nuevos? Porque hemos retenido solo algunos rasgos fundamentales del rostro amado y del trayecto habitual, una suerte de esquema, que permanece invariado por debajo de muchas modificaciones superficiales. De otro modo, nuestra madre con una cana más, o nuestra casa con las persianas de otro color, nos resultarían una experiencia nueva y no las reconoceríamos.

Esta memoria selectiva, tan importante para permitirnos sobrevivir como individuos, funciona también a nivel social y permite que las comunidades sobrevivan. Desde los tiempos en que la especie empezaba a emitir sus primeros sonidos significativos, las familias y las tribus han necesitado a los ancianos. Tal vez antes no sirvieran y prescindían de ellos cuando ya no eran capaces de encontrar comida. Pero, con el lenguaje, los ancianos se convirtieron en la memoria de la especie: se sentaban en la caverna, alrededor del fuego, y contaban lo que había pasado (o se decía que había pasado, de ahí la función de los mitos) antes de que los jóvenes hubieran nacido. Antes de que se empezara a cultivar esa memoria social, el hombre nacía sin experiencia, no le daba tiempo a adquirirla, y moría. Después, un joven de veinte años era como si hubiera vivido cinco mil. Los hechos acontecidos antes que él, y lo que los ancianos habían aprendido, entraban a formar parte de su memoria.

Los ancianos, que articulaban el lenguaje para entregar a cada uno las experiencias de quienes los habían precedido, seguían representando, en su nivel más evolucionado, la memoria orgánica, la que registra y administra nuestro cerebro. Ahora bien, con la invención de la escritura, asistimos al nacimiento de una memoria mineral. Digo mineral porque los primeros signos se graban en tablillas de arcilla, se esculpen en la piedra; porque forma parte de la memoria mineral también la arquitectura, dado que, desde las pirámides egipcias hasta las catedrales góticas, el templo era asimismo un registro de números sagrados, de cálculos matemáticos, y a través de sus estatuas o sus pinturas transmitía historias, enseñanzas morales; en definitiva, como se ha dicho, era una enciclopedia de piedra.

Y si los primeros ideogramas, caracteres cuneiformes, runas, letras alfabéticas tenían un soporte mineral, también tiene un soporte mineral la más actual de las memorias, la de los ordenadores, cuya materia prima es el silicio. Hoy en día, gracias a los ordenadores, disponemos de una memoria social inmensa: basta con conocer las modalidades de acceso a las bases de datos y, sobre cualquier argumento, podríamos obtener todo lo que se necesita saber; sobre un solo tema, una bibliografía de diez mil títulos. Pero no hay mayor silencio que el ruido absoluto, y la abundancia de información puede generar la absoluta ignorancia. Ante el inmenso almacén de memoria que las computadoras pueden ofrecernos, todos nosotros nos sentimos como Funes: obsesionados por millones de detalles, podemos perder cualquier criterio de selección. Saber que existen diez mil libros sobre Julio César es lo mismo que no saber nada: si me hubieran aconsejado uno, habría ido a buscarlo; ante el deber de empezar a explorar esos diez mil títulos, no sigo adelante.

Con la invención de la escritura fue naciendo poco a poco el tercer tipo de memoria, que he decidido llamar vegetal porque, aunque el pergamino estuviera hecho con piel de animales, vegetal era el papiro y, con la llegada del papel (desde el siglo XII), se producen libros con trapos de lino, cáñamo y tela; y, por último, la etimología tanto de *biblos* como de *liber* remite a la corteza del árbol.

Los libros existían ya antes de la imprenta, aunque al principio tenían la forma de un rollo y solo poco a poco fueron volviéndose cada vez más parecidos al objeto que conocemos. El libro, con cualquier forma, permitió que la escritura se personalizara: representaba una porción de memoria, incluso colectiva, pero seleccionada desde una perspectiva personal. Ante los obeliscos, las estelas, las tablas o las inscripciones en losas sepulcrales, nosotros intentamos descifrarlos; es decir, intentamos conocer el alfabeto usado y saber cuáles eran las informaciones esenciales que se transmitían: aquí está enterrado Fulano, este año se han recolectado tantas gavillas de trigo, estos y aquellos países los ha conquistado este señor. No nos preguntamos quién los redactó o grabó. En cambio, ante el libro, buscamos a una persona, una manera individual de ver las cosas. No intentamos solo descifrar, sino que intentamos interpretar también un pensamiento, una intención. Al ir a buscar una intención, se interroga un texto, del que pueden darse incluso lecturas distintas.

La lectura se convierte en un diálogo, pero un diálogo —y esta es la paradoja del libro— con alguien que no está delante de nosotros, que quizá murió hace siglos, y que está presente solo como escritura. Se da una interrogación de los libros (se llama hermenéutica), y si hay hermenéutica, hay culto del libro. Las tres grandes religiones monoteístas, hebraísmo, cristianismo e islam, se desarrollan en forma de interrogación continua de un libro sagrado. El libro se convierte hasta tal punto en un símbolo de la verdad que custodia, y que desvela al que sepa interrogarlo, que para zanjar una discusión, afirmar una tesis, derrotar a un adversario, se dice: «Está escrito aquí». Dudamos siempre de nuestra memoria animal («Me parece recordar que..., pero no estoy seguro»), y en cambio exhibimos la memoria vegetal para disipar toda duda: «El agua es de verdad H_2O, Napoleón murió de verdad en Santa Elena, lo dice la enciclopedia».

En la tribu primitiva, el anciano aseguraba: «Así sucedieron las cosas en la noche de los tiempos, lo afirma la tradición que se ha transmitido de boca en boca hasta nuestros días», y la tribu depositaba su confianza en la tradición. Hoy los libros son nuestros ancianos. Aunque sabemos que a menudo se equivocan, de todas maneras nos los tomamos en serio. Les pedimos que nos den más memoria que la que nos permitirá acumular la brevedad de nuestra vida. No nos damos cuenta, pero nuestra riqueza con respecto a los analfabetos (o a los alfabetos que no leen) es que ellos están viviendo y vivirán solo su vida mientras que nosotros, vidas, hemos vivido muchísimas. Una vez, Valentino Bompiani inventó un eslogan editorial que decía: «Un hombre que lee vale por dos». La verdad es que vale por mil. A través de la memoria vegetal del libro nosotros podemos recordar, junto a nuestros juegos de infancia, también los de Proust, nuestros sueños de adolescencia mezclados con los de Jim en busca de la isla del Tesoro; y no solo de nuestros errores extraemos lecciones, sino también de los errores de Pinocho, o de los de Aníbal en Capua; no nos hemos angustiado solo por nuestros amores, sino también por los de la Angélica de Ariosto o, si son ustedes más modestos, por los de la Angélica de los Golon; hemos asimilado algo de la sabiduría de Solón, nos hemos estremecido por ciertas noches de viento en Santa Elena y nos repetimos, junto al cuento de hadas que nos ha contado nuestra abuela, el cuento que contó Sherezade.

A alguien (por ejemplo, a Nietzsche), todo esto le daba la impresión de que, nada más nacer, ya somos insoportablemente ancianos. Pero está más decrépito el analfabeto (de origen o de retorno) que sufre arteriosclerosis desde niño y no recuerda (porque no ha leído) qué pasó en los Idus de Marzo. Naturalmente, los libros pueden inducirnos a recordar también muchas mentiras, pero tienen la virtud, al menos, de contradecirse entre ellos, y nos enseñan a valorar críticamente las informaciones que nos ofrecen. Leer ayuda también a no creer en los libros. Al no conocer las sinrazones de los demás, el analfabeto no conoce ni siquiera sus propios derechos.

El libro es un seguro de vida, un pequeño anticipo de inmortalidad. Hacia atrás (por desgracia) en lugar de hacia delante. Pero no se puede tenerlo todo y enseguida. No sabemos si conservaremos la memoria de nuestras experiencias después de nuestra muerte individual. Pero sabemos, seguro, que conservamos la memoria de las experiencias de los que nos han precedido, y que otros que nos seguirán conservarán la memoria de las nuestras. Aunque no seamos Homero, podremos permanecer en la memoria del futuro como los protagonistas, qué sé yo, de un azaroso accidente en la autopista Milán-Roma la noche del 14 de agosto. De acuerdo, sería poco, pero siempre mejor que nada. Con tal de ser recordado por la posteridad, Eróstrato incendió el templo de Diana en Éfeso y la posteridad, por desgracia, lo ha vuelto célebre al recordar su estupidez. Nada nuevo bajo el sol: uno se vuelve famoso también desempeñando el papel del tonto del pueblo en una tertulia de televisión.

2. De vez en cuando, algunos dicen que hoy se lee menos, que los jóvenes han dejado de leer, que hemos entrado, como ha dicho un crítico americano, en la edad del *Decline of Literacy*. No lo sé; es verdad que hoy en día la gente ve mucha televisión, y hay individuos de riesgo que solo ven televisión, así como hay individuos de riesgo a quienes les gusta inyectarse sustancias mortales en las venas, pero también es verdad que nunca se ha publicado más que en nuestra época, y que nunca como hoy en día están floreciendo librerías que parecen discotecas, llenas de jóvenes que, incluso cuando no compran, hojean, miran, se informan.

El problema es, más bien, incluso para los libros, la abundancia, la dificultad de elección, el peligro de no lograr ya discriminar: es natural, la difusión de la memoria vegetal tiene todos los defectos de la democracia, un régimen en el que, para permitir que todos hablen, es necesario dejar hablar también a los insensatos, e incluso a los sinvergüenzas. Se nos plantea el problema de cómo educarnos para elegir, por supuesto, entre otras cosas porque, si no aprendemos a elegir, nos exponemos al riesgo de quedarnos delante de los libros como Funes ante sus infinitas percepciones: cuando todo parece digno de ser recordado, ya nada es digno, y desearíamos olvidar.

¿Cómo educarnos para elegir? Por ejemplo, preguntándonos si el libro que vamos a tomar en nuestras manos es uno de esos que tiraremos después de haberlo leído. Me dirán que no podemos saberlo antes de haberlo leído. Pero si, después de haber leído dos o tres libros, nos damos cuenta de que no desearíamos conservarlos, quizá deberíamos revisar nuestros criterios de selección. Tirar un libro después de haberlo leído es como no desear volver a ver a una persona con la que acabamos de mantener una relación sexual. Si eso sucede, se trataba de una exigencia física, no de amor. Y sin embargo, hay que conseguir establecer relaciones de amor con los libros de nuestra vida. Si uno lo consigue, eso quiere decir que se trata de libros que se prestan a una amplia interrogación, hasta tal punto que cada relectura nos revela algo distinto. Se trata de una relación de amor porque justo en el estado del enamoramiento los enamorados descubren, con alegría, que cada vez es como si fuera la primera. Cuando descubrimos que cada vez es como si fuera la segunda, ya estamos preparados para el divorcio o, en el caso del libro, para el cubo de la basura.

Poder tirar o conservar significa que el libro es asimismo un objeto, que puede ser amado no solo por lo que dice, sino además por la forma en que se presenta. Esta conferencia ha sido organizada por un club de bibliófilos, y un bibliófilo es alguien que colecciona libros también por la belleza de su composición tipográfica, de su papel, de su encuadernación. Los bibliófilos perversos se dejan embargar a tal punto por el amor de esos componentes visuales y táctiles que no leen los libros que coleccionan y, si todavía están intonsos, no les cortan las páginas para no depreciar su valor comercial. Toda pasión genera sus formas de fetichismo. Ahora bien, es legítimo que el bibliófilo pueda desear tener tres ediciones distintas del mismo libro, y a veces la diferencia de las ediciones repercute también en la manera como nos acercamos a la lectura. Un amigo mío, que no por casualidad es un poeta, al que de vez en cuando sorprendo mientras busca antiguas ediciones de versificadores italianos, me repite que es muy distinto el placer de leer a Dante en un libro de bolsillo contemporáneo o en las bellas páginas de una edición aldina. Y muchos, cuando encuentran la primera edición de un autor contemporáneo, experimentan una emoción especial al releer esos versos en esos caracteres con que los leyeron sus primeros destinatarios. A la memoria que el libro transmite, por así decir, adrede, se añade la memoria que rezuma como cosa física, el perfume de la historia de la que está impregnado.

La bibliofilia suele considerarse una pasión cara, y está claro que si uno de nosotros quisiera poseer un ejemplar de la primera Biblia de cuarenta y dos líneas impresa por Gutenberg, debería disponer de por lo menos siete mil millones de liras. Digo por lo menos, porque por esa suma se vendió hace dos años uno de los últimos ejemplares en circulación (los otros están en bibliotecas públicas, custodiadas como tesoros) y, por tanto, quien hoy deseara cederla pediría quizá el doble. Pero, aun sin ser ricos, podemos desarrollar un amor por el coleccionismo.

Quizá no todos sepan que algunas ediciones del siglo XVI todavía pueden encontrarse a poco menos o poco más de cincuenta mil liras, que se juntan evitando dos comidas en un restaurante o renunciado a dos cartones de cigarrillos. No siempre es la antigüedad lo que cuesta, hay ediciones de aficionados impresas hace veinte años que valen un potosí, pero por el precio de un par de botas Timberland puede experimentarse el placer de tener en la propia librería un bonito volumen infolio, tocar su encuadernación de pergamino, sentir la textura de sus hojas, incluso seguir el curso del tiempo y de los agentes externos a través de las manchas, de las sombras de humedad, del trabajo de los gusanos que a veces excavan a lo largo de centenares de páginas recorridos de tan gran belleza como la de los cristales de nieve. Asimismo, un ejemplar mutilado puede contar una historia a menudo dramática: el nombre del editor borrado para escapar a los rigores de la censura, páginas censuradas por lectores o por bibliotecarios demasiado prudentes, páginas enrojecidas porque la edición se imprimió de forma clandestina con materiales baratos, marcas de tal vez una larga permanencia en los sótanos de un monasterio, firmas, anotaciones, subrayados que relatan la historia de los distintos propietarios a través de dos o tres siglos...

Pero, sin soñar con libros antiguos, puede practicarse el coleccionismo de libros de los últimos dos siglos, encontrándolos en los puestos callejeros, en las ferias del libro viejo, dando caza a las primeras ediciones, a los ejemplares intonsos. En este caso, el juego se halla al alcance de muchísimos bolsillos, y el placer no consiste solo en el entusiasmo de la *trouvaille*, sino en la búsqueda, en el seguir el propio olfato, en el rebuscar, en el encaramarse a escaleritas enclenques para descubrir qué tendrá el chamarilero en ese último estante al que lleva años sin quitarle el polvo.

El coleccionismo, incluso menor, también de objetos del siglo XX, a menudo es un acto de piedad, me gustaría decir de miramientos ecológicos, porque no tenemos que salvar solo a las ballenas, a las focas monje, a los osos de los Abruzos, sino también los libros.

3. ¿De qué tenemos que salvar a los libros? A los antiguos, del descuido, de la sepultura en lugares húmedos e impracticables, del viento y la lluvia que azotan los puestos callejeros. A los más recientes, también de un mal maligno que anida en sus células.

Los libros envejecen. Algunos envejecen bien, otros no. Depende de las condiciones en que hayan sido conservados, sin duda, pero también del material con que se produjeron. En cualquier caso, sabemos que hacia la mitad del siglo pasado aconteció un fenómeno trágico. Dejaron de producirse libros con papel de trapos porque se empezó a fabricar papel con madera. Como podrán constatar en cualquier biblioteca, el papel de trapos sobrevive a los siglos. Hay libros del siglo XV que parecen recién salidos de la imprenta, el papel todavía está blanco, fresco, cruje bajo los dedos. A partir de la segunda mitad del siglo XIX, empero, la vida media de un libro, se dice, no podrá superar los setenta años. De algunos libros que ya tienen más de cien, a pesar de su precoz amarilleo, puede decirse que se produjeron con papel de calidad y resistente. Pero las ediciones científicas o las novelas de los años cincuenta, sobre todo francesas, duran mucho menos de setenta años. Ya hoy se deshacen, como hostias, nada más cogerlas. Tenemos la certidumbre de que un libro de bolsillo producido hoy tendrá una vida de veinte o treinta años, y basta con que vayamos a buscar en nuestras librerías las ediciones de bolsillo producidas hace una década para entender que ya están al borde de la senescencia precoz.

El drama es terrible: producidos como testimonios, recopilaciones de memoria, siguiendo el modelo de los manuscritos o las construcciones arquitectónicas que habían de desafiar a los siglos, los libros no conseguirán cumplir ya con su tarea. Cada autor que no trabajara solo por dinero sino por amor hacia su propia obra sabía que encomendaba al libro un mensaje que perduraría en los siglos. Ahora sabe que su libro tan solo podrá sobrevivirle un poco. Naturalmente, el mensaje queda encomendado a las reediciones, pero las reediciones siguen el gusto de los contemporáneos, y no siempre los contemporáneos son los mejores jueces del valor de una obra. Y además, nosotros ahora somos capaces de darnos cuenta de que ha llegado el momento de releer un libro que se publicó en el siglo XVIII y que cayó injustamente en el olvido porque sus ejemplares sobreviven en las bibliotecas. Pero ¿qué le sucedería a un libro importante, no valorado hoy y que podría ser apreciado dentro de un siglo? Dentro de un siglo no quedará ni siquiera un ejemplar de él.

Hemos visto que la política de las reediciones, si se encomienda al mercado, no ofrece garantías. Pero peor aún sería que una comisión de sabios tuviera que decidir qué libros salvar reimprimiéndolos y qué libros condenar a la desaparición definitiva. Cuando se dice que los contemporáneos a menudo se equivocan al juzgar el valor de un libro, se tiene en cuenta también el error de los sabios, esto es, el error de la crítica. Si le hubiéramos hecho caso a Saverio Bettinelli, en el siglo XVIII habrían tirado a la basura a Dante Alighieri.

Para los libros futuros, muchas editoriales universitarias estadounidenses, por ejemplo, ya están adoptando políticas clarividentes mediante la producción de obras con *acid-free paper*, esto es, por decirlo de forma sencilla, con papel especial que resiste más tiempo a la disolución. Pero, aparte de que esto sucederá en el caso de las obras científicas y no en el de la obra del joven poeta, ¿qué hacer con los millones de libros ya producidos desde finales del siglo pasado hasta ayer?

Existen medios químicos para proteger los libros de las bibliotecas, página por página. Están disponibles, pero son muy caros. Bibliotecas con millones de volúmenes (y son las que cuentan) no podrán intervenir en todos sus libros. También en este caso tendrán que llevar a cabo una selección. ¿Quién elegirá? Naturalmente, existe la posibilidad de microfilmarlo todo, pero todos nosotros sabemos que a las microfichas solo pueden acceder investigadores motivados, y con buena vista. Ya no habrá la posibilidad de rebuscar entre viejos estantes, fascinados por descubrimientos casuales. Con la microficha uno busca aquello cuya existencia ya conoce. Con los modernos medios electrónicos es posible grabar a través del escáner, almacenar en la memoria de una computadora central, e imprimir las páginas que necesitamos. Excelente para consultar anualidades de periódicos (consideren que el papel de periódico se echa a perder en unos diez años), pero no para imprimirse una novela olvidada de ochocientas páginas. En cualquier caso, estas posibilidades valen para los estudiosos, no para el lector curioso. Por lo que sabemos, hoy en día no hay un medio para salvar de forma indolora todos los libros modernos reunidos en las bibliotecas públicas, y los de las bibliotecas privadas están inexorablemente condenados: dentro de un siglo ya no existirán.

Aun así, el amor del coleccionista, al defender un viejo librito del polvo, de la luz, del calor, de la humedad, de la carcoma, de la contaminación, del descuadernamiento casual, podría alargar la vida de una edición económica de los años veinte. Al menos hasta que alguien la redescubriera, revalorizara la obra y diera inicio a un proceso de reimpresión. Vean, por tanto, como también un coleccionismo modesto y no millonario puede contribuir a la conservación de un inmenso patrimonio de memoria vegetal. Tomen ejemplo de los coleccionistas de cómics que salvan viejos álbumes impresos en papel malo en fundas de plástico, construyendo un archivo de una literatura a menudo menor, a veces incluso pésima, pero que debe permanecer por lo menos como documento de las costumbres. Y también se debe al coleccionismo el que se hayan rescatado las planchas originales de muchos grandes artistas del cómic (ahora en venta a precios astronómicos: una de las primeras planchas de *Flash Gordon* de Raymond vale por lo menos cincuenta mil dólares), planchas que de otro modo, quizá, las redacciones habrían mandado a reciclar o habrían dejado pudrirse en algún almacén.

Los libros no se mueren solo por su cuenta. A veces son destruidos. En las primeras décadas de nuestro siglo se asistió a la quema en la hoguera de los libros «degenerados» encendida por los nazis en Nuremberg. Era un gesto simbólico, desde luego, porque ni siquiera los nazis hubieran querido destruir todo el patrimonio de libros de su país. Pero son símbolos que cuentan. Teman a quienes destruyen, censuran, prohíben los libros: quieren destruir o censurar nuestra memoria. Cuando se dan cuenta de que los libros son demasiados, e inasequibles, por lo que la memoria vegetal resulta amenazadora, entonces destruyen memorias animales, cerebros, cuerpos humanos. Se empieza siempre por los libros, luego se abren las cámaras de gas.

Una anotación cuando menos curiosa: el gas Zyklon que servía para asesinar a los judíos en los campos de exterminio sigue comercializándose, lo aconsejan para cámaras de desinsectación de muebles y libros amenazados por la carcoma. Probablemente funcione a la perfección y es legítimo que se use con finalidades tan pacíficas; ahora bien, cuando me lo propusieron, el nombre me dio miedo, y renuncié. Alguien luego me aconsejó una forma de mantener alejada a la carcoma sin matarla. Un gran despertador, de esos que tenían nuestras abuelas en la cocina y hacían un tictac infernal. Por la noche, cuando la carcoma se dispone a salir a la intemperie, el despertador hace que vibre la librería en que está apoyado y la carcoma, asustada, no sale. No es que la solución sea piadosamente ecológica: al no poder salir, la carcoma muere de hambre. Siempre habrá que elegir, o ellos o nosotros.

Hay otros enemigos de los libros: quienes los esconden. Hay muchas maneras de esconder los libros. Puesto que, a fin

de cuentas, cuestan dinero, cuando no se forma una red suficiente de bibliotecas ambulantes, se les esconden los libros a
aquellos que no podrían comprarlos. Cuando los accesos a las
bibliotecas se dificultan, y para pedir dos libros hay que rellenar diez fichas y esperar una hora, se sustraen los libros a sus
normales consumidores. Se esconden los libros abandonando
nuestras grandes bibliotecas históricas al deterioro. Hay que
combatir contra quienes esconden los libros, porque son tan
peligrosos como la carcoma. No usaremos el Zyklon sino las
armas políticas y civiles más apropiadas. Pero debemos saber
que son enemigos de nuestra memoria colectiva.

4. Se dice que los nuevos medios de información matarán al
libro. Se dijo que el libro mataría a los medios de información
más antiguos. En el *Fedro* de Platón se cuenta cómo reaccionó
el faraón Thamus cuando el dios Theuth, o Hermes, le presentó su ultimísima invención, la escritura:

> Pero, cuando llegaron a lo de las letras, dijo Theuth: «Este cono
> cimiento, oh rey, hará más sabios a los egipcios y más memorio
> sos, pues se ha inventado como un fármaco de la memoria y de la
> sabiduría». Pero él le dijo: «¡Oh artificiosísimo Theuth! A unos
> les es dado crear arte, a otros juzgar qué de daño o provecho
> aporta para los que pretenden hacer uso de él. Y ahora tú, preci
> samente, padre que eres de las letras, por apego a ellas, les atribu
> yes poderes contrarios a los que tienen. Porque es olvido lo que
> producirán en las almas de quienes las aprendan, al descuidar la
> memoria, ya que, fiándose de lo escrito, llegarán al recuerdo des
> de fuera, a través de caracteres ajenos, no desde dentro, desde
> ellos mismos y por sí mismos».

Ahora ya sabemos que Thamus no tenía razón. La escritura no solo no ha acabado con la memoria, sino que la ha potenciado. Ha nacido una escritura de la memoria y ha nacido la memoria de las escrituras. Nuestra memoria se fortalece al recordar los libros y al hacer que hablen entre ellos. Un libro no es una máquina para bloquear, grabándolos, los pensamientos. Es una máquina para producir interpretaciones y, por tanto, para producir nuevos pensamientos.

Hay otra página, escrita el siglo pasado, pero que recuerda cuáles pueden haber sido los sentimientos de quienes veían nacer el nuevo instrumento, el libro impreso, en la segunda mitad del siglo XV. Victor Hugo en *Notre-Dame de Paris*, cuenta una escena que se desarrolla entre el diácono Frollo y el médico del rey de Francia.

> Y abriendo [Frollo] la ventana de la celda, señaló con el dedo la inmensa iglesia de Nuestra Señora, que perfilando contra el cielo estrellado la negra silueta de sus dos torres, de sus costillas de piedra y de su monstruosa grupa, parecía una enorme esfinge de dos cabezas sentada en medio de la ciudad. El archidiácono contempló silencioso durante unos momentos el gigantesco edificio, y extendiendo con un suspiro su mano derecha en dirección del libro impreso, abierto encima de la mesa, y su mano izquierda hacia Nuestra Señora, y paseando con pena la mirada del libro a la iglesia, dijo:
>
> —¡Ay! Esto matará a aquello.*

Después de esta escena, Hugo, con su retórica habitual —la que hizo decir a Gide que Hugo era el mayor escritor francés,

---

* Traducción de Carlos R. de Dampierre, Madrid, Alianza Editorial, 2008. (*N. de la T.*)

por desgracia (*hélas*)—, dedica algunas páginas al glorioso pasado de la arquitectura sagrada, a ese templo ·de Salomón en cuyos muros concéntricos los sacerdotes podían leer el verbo traducido para los ojos, recordando cómo durante los primeros seis mil años del mundo, desde la más inmemorial de las pagodas del Indostán hasta la catedral de Colonia, la arquitectura fue la gran escritura del género humano. Ahora, en el momento en que Frollo está hablando, la forma de expresión de la humanidad se está transformando radicalmente y se produce la definitiva muda de piel de esa serpiente que, desde los días de Adán, representa a la inteligencia.

> Bajo la forma de imprenta el pensamiento es más imperecedero que nunca; es volátil e indestructible. Se mezcla con el viento. Con la arquitectura se hacía montaña y se apoderaba con gran fuerza de una época y de un lugar; ahora se convierte en bandada de pájaros, se disemina a los cuatro vientos y ocupa al mismo tiempo todos los lugares del espacio y del aire.

La arquitectura, dice Hugo (que tenía ante sus ojos mucha pésima arquitectura de principios del siglo XIX), está destinada al ocaso, se deseca, se atrofia, se desnuda, el cristal sustituye a las vidrieras. Y, en cambio, la imprenta se agranda, compone el edificio más colosal de los siglos modernos; un hormiguero de inteligencias se dedica a erigir una construcción que se amplía en espirales sin fin: «Es la segunda torre de Babel del género humano».

En su orgullo luciferino, Hugo no preveía que esa torre podría derrumbarse un día. Vislumbra perfectamente el papel que la imprenta desempeñará en el mundo moderno, se equivoca al representar un duelo mortal entre esta y la arquitectura. Sin duda, la arquitectura pierde su función enciclopédica que tenía antes, ya no transmite nociones, se convierte en símbolo, función, máquina, pero no por ello se vuelve menos bella y menos fundamental para la cultura humana.

Creo que los que lloran por el declive de la alfabetización ante los nuevos medios visuales y la información electrónica resultarán un día tan patéticos como hoy en gran parte nos parece Hugo. Desde luego, la imprenta perderá algunas funciones que tuvo en el pasado. Ya los periódicos se están convirtiendo en algo distinto de las antiguas gacetas, porque lo que hacían las gacetas, dar información fresca, ahora lo hace con un adelanto de doce horas la televisión. Quizá ya no tengamos que imprimir horarios de ferrocarriles, tan difíciles de consultar, si vamos a poder comprar en los quioscos pequeños aparatos electrónicos que podremos usar una temporada, donde al escribir Milán-Battipaglia veamos de un solo vistazo todas las posibilidades que tenemos de llevar a cabo ese recorrido.

Pero nadie puede usar un ordenador si no tiene una impresora que transforme los datos introducidos o elaborados en páginas escritas. En la pantalla del ordenador podemos leer solo datos breves y durante un tiempo breve. Si es breve, y si tenemos el módem adecuado, podemos incluso recibir y leer una carta de amor, porque no cuenta el medio, sino lo que dice esa carta y el estado de ánimo con que la leemos. Ahora bien, si la carta de amor es larga, tendremos que imprimirla, para poder releérnosla en un rincón secreto.

Hace algunos miles de años que la especie se ha adaptado a la lectura. El ojo lee y todo el cuerpo entra en acción. Leer significa también encontrar una posición correcta, es un acto que atañe al cuello, a la columna vertebral, a los glúteos. Y la forma del libro, estudiada durante siglos y configurada en los formatos ergonómicamente más apropiados, es la forma que debe tener ese objeto para que la mano pueda asirlo y colocarlo a la correcta distancia del ojo. Leer tiene que ver con nuestra fisiología.

Permítanme que acabe con una última página de otro gran libro: es el final del cuarto capítulo del *Ulises* de Joyce. A alguien la página podrá parecerle vulgar. En ese caso, que consulte a su psicoanalista, porque la página es en cambio sublime.

Leopold Bloom, de buena mañana, va al retrete y defeca. Mientras defeca, lee:

Tranquilamente leyó, conteniéndose, la primera columna, y cediendo pero resistiendo, empezó la segunda. A medio camino, rindiendo su última resistencia, permitió a sus tripas liberarse tranquilamente mientras leía; aún leyendo pacientemente, ese ligero estreñimiento de ayer ha desaparecido del todo. Espero que no sea demasiado grande no vuelvan las almorranas. No, exactamente lo conveniente. Así. ¡Ah! Estreñido, una tableta de cáscara sagrada. La vida podría ser así. No le conmovía ni afectaba pero era algo vivo y bien arreglado. Imprimen cualquier cosa ahora. Temporada estúpida. Siguió leyendo sentado en calma sobre su propio olor que subía. Bien arreglado, eso sí. *Matcham piensa a menudo en el golpe maestro con que conquistó a la risueña brujita que ahora.* Empieza y termina con moralidad. *Juntos de la mano.* Listo. Volvió a echar una ojeada a lo que había leído, y a la vez que sentía sus aguas fluir silenciosamente, envidió benévolamente al señor Beaufoy que había escrito eso y recibido pago de tres libras, trece con seis.*

---

* Traducción de José María Valverde, Barcelona, Lumen, 2000. *(N. de la T.)*

El ritmo de la lectura sigue el del cuerpo, el ritmo del cuerpo sigue el de la lectura. No se lee solo con el cerebro, se lee con todo nuestro cuerpo, y por eso con un libro lloramos, reímos, y al leer un libro de terror se nos ponen los pelos de punta. Porque, incluso cuando parece hablar solo de ideas, un libro nos habla siempre de otras emociones, y de experiencias de otros cuerpos. Y, cuando no es tan solo un libro pornográfico, cuando habla de cuerpos, sugiere ideas. Y tampoco somos insensibles a las sensaciones que la yema de los dedos perciben al tocarlo y ciertos desafortunados experimentos hechos con encuadernaciones e incluso con hojas de plástico nos dicen hasta qué punto la lectura es también una experiencia táctil.

Si la experiencia del libro aún les cohíbe, empiecen a leer, sin temor, libros en el retrete. Descubrirán que también ustedes tienen un alma.

Reflexiones sobre la bibliofilia[1]

Una cosa es hablar de bibliofilia a los bibliófilos, y otra hablar de bibliofilia a las personas, por así decir, normales. El verdadero tormento de un coleccionista de libros valiosos es que, si coleccionara cuadros del Renacimiento o porcelanas chinas, los tendría en su sala de estar y todas sus visitas se quedarían extasiadas. En cambio, el bibliófilo nunca sabe a quién enseñarle sus tesoros: los no bibliófilos les echan una mirada distraída y no entienden por qué un librejo del siglo XVII en doceavo, con las páginas oxidadas, puede ser el orgullo de aquel que es el único que ha logrado adquirir el último ejemplar que quedaba en circulación; y, a menudo, los otros bibliófilos manifiestan síndromes de envidia (también ellos quisieran tener ese libro y se irritan) o de desprecio (piensan que tienen en su biblioteca libros mucho más raros, o coleccionan un tema distinto: eso significa que un coleccionista de libros de arquitectura del Renacimiento puede permanecer insensible ante la más rica colección existente de panfletos rosacruces del siglo XVIII).

La mayor razón de desinterés por parte de las personas normales es que la bibliofilia se considera una pasión cara, que solo

1. Publicado en un pequeño volumen en edición numerada, Edizioni Rovello, 2001.

pueden cultivar personas muy ricas. Ahora bien, es verdad que hay libros antiguos que cuestan centenares de millones de liras, y que el último ejemplar en circulación de la primera edición del incunable de la *Divina comedia* se subastó por mil quinientos millones, pero el amor por el libro puede manifestarse también a través de colecciones de primeras ediciones modernas, que a menudo se encuentran a precios muy accesibles en los puestos callejeros: un alumno mío se dedicaba a mirar en todos los puestos solo guías turísticas de cualquier época y país. Rebuscando en los puestos, un joven de modesta condición económica puede encontrar pequeñas ediciones del siglo XVI que todavía cuestan como una cena en una pizzería más un cine. El amor por el libro antiguo o raro puede empezar también en estos niveles del mismo modo que muchos de nosotros coleccionábamos sellos de pequeños y no podíamos permitirnos piezas raras, pero soñábamos despiertos con tierras lejanas mirando en nuestros álbumes sellos de Madagascar o de las islas Fiyi comprados en la papelería, como era costumbre por aquel entonces, en sobrecitos con diez o treinta piezas sorpresa.

Cuenta la leyenda que Gerberto de Aurillac, es decir, el papa Silvestre II, el Papa del año 1000, consumido por su amor por los libros adquirió un día un código de la *Farsalia* de Lucano, imposible de encontrar, a cambio de una esfera armilar. Gerberto no sabía que Lucano no pudo acabar su poema porque, mientras tanto, Nerón lo había inducido a cortarse las venas. De modo que recibió el precioso manuscrito, pero lo encontró incompleto. Todo buen amador de libros, después de haber cotejado el volumen recién adquirido, si lo encuentra incompleto, lo devuelve al librero. Gerberto, para no privarse al menos de la mitad de su tesoro, decidió enviar a su correspondiente no la esfera entera, sino solo la mitad.

Esta historia me parece admirable, porque nos dice qué es la bibliofilia. Está claro que Gerberto quería leer el poema de Lucano —y eso nos dice mucho sobre el amor por la cultura clásica en aquellos siglos que nos obstinamos en considerar oscuros—, pero, si solo hubiera querido leerlo, habría pedido prestado el manuscrito. No, él quería poseer esas hojas, tocarlas, quizá olerlas a diario, y sentirlas como cosa propia. Y un bibliófilo que, después de haber tocado y olfateado, se da cuenta de que el libro está mutilado, que le falta aunque solo sea el colofón o una hoja de fe de erratas, experimenta la sensación de un *coitus interruptus*. Que el librero le devuelva el dinero (o acepte solo media esfera armilar), no alivia el dolor del bibliófilo. Podía tener la primera edición del libro amado, y con márgenes amplios y sin manchas de óxido ni agujeros de carcoma, y su sueño se esfuma: se encuentra con un libro mutilado, y ninguna indulgencia a lo políticamente correcto podrá persuadirlo a amar a esa desventurada criatura.

¿QUÉ ES LA BIBLIOFILIA?

La bibliofilia es, sin lugar a dudas, el amor por los libros, pero no necesariamente por su contenido. Es verdad que hay bibliófilos que reúnen colecciones temáticas e incluso leen los libros que acumulan. Ahora bien, para leer muchos libros, es suficiente ser un ratón de biblioteca. No, el bibliófilo, aun atento al contenido, quiere el objeto, y que posiblemente sea el primero en salir de la prensa del impresor. A tal punto que hay bibliófilos, a quienes yo no apruebo pero entiendo, que, habiendo recibido un libro intonso, no le cortan las páginas para no violentar el objeto que han conquistado. Para ellos, cortar las páginas de un libro raro sería igual que, para un coleccionista de relojes, romper la caja para ver el mecanismo.

Al amante de la lectura, o al estudioso, le encanta subrayar los libros contemporáneos, entre otras cosas porque, a distancia de años, un determinado tipo de subrayado, una señal en el margen, una variación entre rotulador negro y rotulador rojo, le recuerdan una experiencia de lectura. Yo poseo una *Philosophie au Moyen Âge* de Gilson de los años cincuenta, que me ha acompañado desde los días de mi tesis de licenciatura hasta hoy. El papel de aquella época era infame, el libro ya se me desmenuza en cuanto lo toco o intento pasar las páginas. Si para mí solo fuera una herramienta de trabajo, no tendría más que comprarme una nueva edición, que se encuentra barata. Podría incluso dedicar dos días a volver a subrayar todas las partes anotadas, reproduciendo colores y estilo de mis notas, que iban cambiando durante los años y las relecturas. Pero no puedo resignarme a perder ese ejemplar, que con su frágil vetustez me recuerda mis años de formación, y los siguientes, y que es, por consiguiente, parte de mis recuerdos.

¿Deben subrayarse, aunque solo sea en los márgenes, los libros raros? En teoría, un ejemplar perfecto, si no está intonso, ha de tener amplios márgenes, ser blanco, con las páginas que crujen bajo los dedos. Una vez adquirí un Paracelso, de escaso valor desde el punto de vista anticuario, porque se trataba de un solo volumen de la primera edición de la *opera omnia* recopilada por Huser, 1589-1591. Si la obra no está completa, ¿qué gracia tiene? Pues bien, encuadernado en media piel de época, con nervios en el lomo, medianamente oscurecido de forma uniforme, firma manuscrita en el frontispicio, todo el volumen está entretejido con subrayados rojos y negros y notas marginales de época, con títulos en versalitas rojos y florilegio latino del texto alemán. Es un objeto bellísimo de ver, las anotaciones se confunden con el texto impreso, y a menudo lo hojeo con el placer de revivir la aventura intelectual de quien lo marcó con su propio testimonio manual.

Señal, pues, de que la bibliofilia es amor por el objeto libro, pero también por su historia, como atestiguan los precios de los catálogos que privilegian ejemplares, aun no perfectos, que lleven marcas de propiedad. Todo el mundo desea un ejemplar del libro más bello que se haya imprimido jamás, la *Hypnerotomachia Poliphili*; lo desea perfecto, sin manchas de humedad ni carcoma, con amplios márgenes y, si acaso fuera posible, en pliegos sueltos todavía no encuadernados. Pero ¿qué haríamos nosotros y los anticuarios si circulara un ejemplar con densas notas al margen de James Joyce, y en gaélico?

No me agita la *hybris* demencial de ensuciar con bolígrafo mi ejemplar de la *Hypnerotomachia*, confiando en que acreciente su valor en los siglos venideros, pero admito que, si tengo que estudiar en el libro raro, me atrevo a hacer marcas a lápiz en el margen, bastante ligeras para que un día puedan borrarse con una goma, y eso me ayuda a sentir el libro como cosa mía. Soy, por tanto, un bibliófilo, no un bibliómano.

Bibliomanía

¿Cuál es la diferencia entre bibliofilia y bibliomanía? La literatura al respecto es enorme, y por extrañas razones, si en el siglo pasado los franceses escribieron cosas egregias, en este siglo la bibliografía de los «Books on Books» es una característica anglosajona. Puesto que en esta charla mía no pretendo llevar a cabo un trabajo erudito, me limitaré a citar, para la bibliomanía, *A Gentle Madness* de Nicholas A. Basbanes (Nueva York, Holt, 1995) y para un sosegado y agudo discurso sobre la bibliofilia el reciente *Collezionare libri* de Hans Tuzzi (Milán, Edizioni Sylvestre Bonnard, 2000).

Para establecer una línea divisoria entre bibliofilia y bibliomanía pondré un ejemplo. El libro más raro del mundo, en el sentido de que con toda probabilidad ya no existen más ejemplares circulando libremente en el mercado, es también el primero, esto es, la Biblia de Gutenberg. El último ejemplar en circulación se vendió en 1987 a compradores japoneses por unos siete mil millones de liras (al cambio de entonces). Si apareciera otro ejemplar, no valdría siete mil millones, sino setenta mil, o un millón de millones.

Así pues, todo coleccionista tiene un sueño recurrente. Encontrar una viejecita de noventa años que tiene en su casa un libro que intenta vender, sin saber de qué se trata, contar las líneas, ver que son cuarenta y dos y descubrir que es una Biblia de Gutenberg, calcular que a la pobrecilla le quedan solo pocos años de vida y necesita cuidados médicos, decidir alejarla de la avidez de un librero deshonesto que probablemente le daría unos cuantos millones de liras (y ella sería muy feliz), ofrecerle doscientos millones, con los que la viejecita se liberaría muy contenta de sus penurias económicas hasta la muerte, y llevarse a casa un tesoro.

Después de lo cual, ¿qué sucedería? Un bibliómano conservaría secretamente el ejemplar para sí mismo, sin mostrarlo jamás porque solo con hablar de la Biblia movilizaría a ladrones de medio mundo, por lo que debería hojearlo él solo por las noches, como el Tío Gilito cuando se baña en sus dólares. Un bibliófilo, en cambio, querría que todos vieran semejante maravilla, y supieran que es suya. Entonces escribiría al alcalde de su ciudad, le pediría que la expusiera en el salón principal de la biblioteca municipal, pagando con fondos públicos los enormes gastos del seguro y la vigilancia, y concediéndole el privilegio de ir a verla, junto a sus amigos bibliófilos, cada vez que lo deseara, y sin hacer cola. Ahora bien, ¿cuál sería el placer de poseer el objeto más raro del mundo sin poder levantarse a las tres de la madrugada para ir a hojearlo? Ese es el drama: tener la Biblia de Gutenberg sería como no tenerla. Y entonces ¿por qué soñar con esa utópica viejecita? Pues bien, el bibliófilo sueña siempre con ella, como si fuera un bibliómano.

ROBAR LIBROS

El bibliómano roba libros. Podría robarlos también el bibliófilo, llevado por la indigencia, pero el bibliófilo suele considerar que, si para poseer un libro no ha llevado a cabo un sacrificio, no experimenta el placer de la conquista (la diferencia entre tener una mujer porque la has fascinado y tenerla violentándola). Por otra parte, se cuenta de un gran anticuario que habría dicho: «Si no consigues vender un libro, en el próximo catálogo redobla su precio».

El bibliómano roba libros con gesto desenvuelto mientras habla con el librero: le indica una edición rara en el estante alto y hace desaparecer otra igual de rara bajo la chaqueta; o roba partes de libros merodeando por bibliotecas donde corta con una cuchilla de afeitar las páginas más apetecibles. Yo estoy orgulloso de poseer una *Crónica de Nuremberg* con la anhelada lámina trece de los monstruos, mientras que en una biblioteca de Cambridge he visto un ejemplar sin esa lámina, cortada por un bibliómano endemoniado.

Hay personas de buena cultura, satisfactoria condición económica, fama pública y reputación casi inmaculada que roban libros. Los roban por incontenible pasión, y gusto por el escalofrío, como los ladrones gentilhombres que roban solo joyas famosas. El ladrón bibliómano se avergonzaría de robar una pera en la frutería, pero juzga excitante y caballeresco robar libros, como si la dignidad del objeto excusara su robo. Si pudiera, robaría tantos libros que no tendría ni siquiera el tiempo de mirárselos. Le corroe el frenesí de su posesión.

El mayor ladrón de libros que la historia de la bibliomanía recuerda es un señor que, *nomen omen*, se llamaba Guglielmo Libri. Era un insigne matemático italiano del siglo pasado que se convirtió en eminente ciudadano francés (Legión de Honor, Collège de France, miembro de la Academia, inspector general de Bibliotecas). Es verdad que Libri llegó a ser benemérito porque visitó todas las bibliotecas más desvalidas de Francia, encontró y clasificó obras rarísimas que yacían abandonadas; pero quizá se comportó como esos grandes arqueólogos que dedican su vida a sacar a la luz tesoros perdidos de los países del tercer mundo y consideran una honesta recompensa a todos sus esfuerzos llevarse a casa una parte de lo que encuentran. Libri debió de exagerar: el caso es que hubo un escándalo público, perdió todos sus cargos y su reputación y acabó su vida en el exilio, perseguido por órdenes de captura. También es verdad que algunos de los mejores nombres de la cultura francesa e italiana, como Guizot, Mérimée, Lacroix, Guerrazzi, Mamiani y Gioberti, se batieron por la inocencia de un hombre tan célebre y estimado, todos ellos dispuestos a jurar que Libri había sido víctima de una persecución política. No sé realmente hasta qué punto Libri era culpable de veras, pero el caso es que había acumulado cuarenta mil textos antiguos, entre libros y manuscritos rarísimos y, desde luego, la cantidad induce a sospechar.

Libri era, sin duda alguna, un bibliófilo: creyó que esos libros estaban mejor en su casa, mimados y amados, que en cualquier biblioteca de provincias donde nunca nadie iría a buscarlos. Pero al haber amado demasiados, seguramente no pudo haberlos amado uno a uno. Sepultados en su origen, volvían a estar sepultados en la meta. Por eso era también un bibliómano. Además, sepultar los libros coincide con la biblioclasia.

BIBLIOCLASIA

Hay tres formas de biblioclasia: la biblioclasia fundamentalista, la biblioclasia por dejadez y la biblioclasia por interés. El biblioclasta fundamentalista no odia los libros como objeto: teme su contenido y no quiere que otros lo lean. Además de un criminal también es un loco, por el fanatismo que lo anima, pero la historia registra solo casos excepcionales de biblioclasia, como las hogueras de los nazis o el incendio de la biblioteca de Alejandría, que (según una leyenda que ya se considera falsa) fue incendiada por un califa siguiendo el principio de que o todos aquellos libros decían lo mismo que el Corán y entonces eran inútiles, o decían cosas distintas y entonces eran dañinos.

La biblioclasia por dejadez es la de muchas bibliotecas italianas, tan pobres y tan poco cuidadas que a menudo se convierten en lugares de destrucción del libro; porque hay una manera de destruir los libros dejando que se deterioren o haciéndolos desaparecer en reconditeces inaccesibles.

El biblioclasta por interés destruye los libros porque vendiéndolos por partes saca mucho más que vendiéndolos enteros.

Leo el catálogo reciente de una casa de subastas y encuentro: «Sebastian Münster, Civitella... Xilografía, folio entero 325 × 221 mm. Buenos márgenes. En el verso, batalla. Texto en alemán en el r. y en el v. Sin acuarelar. Vista a vuelo de pájaro sacada de una de las primeras eds. en alemán de la *Cosmographia*, Basilea *c.* 1570». Precio de salida, entre quinientas y seiscientas mil liras.

Si se presenta un aficionado, la obra se batirá incluso a un precio superior, quién sabe, las xilografías de Münster son agradables, y las páginas también son tipográficamente interesantes. Los márgenes declarados son buenos (un ejemplar más que aceptable puede tener 31 × 20,5, y el coleccionista queda satisfecho). La xilografía no está coloreada, pero qué se le va hacer. La edición no es realmente una de las «primeras», porque se empieza en 1541, y entre esa fecha y 1570 hay por lo menos dos en alemán, tres en italiano, una francesa y una bohema y no es que mis datos sean completos. De todas maneras, si el papel es fresco, al tener márgenes amplios no faltará quien esté contento de enmarcarla.

Había una vez un viejo librero de Nueva York, mister Salomon, en la esquina de la Tercera Avenida con la calle Nueve (ahora ha fallecido, y la tienda la mantiene en funciones su hija, pero creo que sigue viviendo gracias al fondo acumulado por el padre), a quien le compré por sumas que iban de uno a dos dólares páginas bellísimas de libros antiguos, excelentes para decorar la casa de campo, y por pocas decenas de dólares llené dos paredes con imágenes de caballeros, frailes y monjas de Bonanni, coloreadas *au pochoir*. El viejo librero me decía: «Yo hago vandalismo democrático; a todos aquellos que jamás podrán permitirse poseer la *Crónica de Nuremberg*, les doy una página por pocos dólares. Pero que quede claro: yo adquiero solo libros que ya están condenados a la destrucción».

Es posible. Ahora bien, ¿hasta qué punto es rentable desencuadernar un libro completo? Saquemos cuentas. No sé cuánto puede valer una Münster 1570. Sé que los ejemplares de otras fechas que han aparecido recientemente en los catálogos dan indicaciones de este tipo: Kistner 1554, piel de cerda de época con cierres, fresca en su conjunto y de márgenes amplios, veinticinco millones de liras; Hünerdorff 1559, treinta y cuatro millones; Martayan Lan 1559, sesenta millones; Reiss 1564, compósita, veintiocho millones. Otra Intersigne «Consultar Precio» (lo que quiere decir mucho). A bulto, el ejemplar desaparecido cuya página se subasta, considerando los márgenes amplios, podría haberse valorado en unos treinta millones de liras.

Pues bien, la *Cosmographia* cuenta con más de un millar de páginas, y tiene unas cuarenta vistas de ciudades a doble página, de las cuales suele haber tres plegadas más veces, suele tener catorce mapas a doble página, más unos noventa grabados en madera en el texto. En mi Basilea 1554 no he conseguido identificar una imagen de Civitella con una batalla en el reverso, pero no es nada raro, porque con el paso del tiempo el libro iba enriqueciéndose con nuevos lugares del mundo. En cualquier caso, debe de tratarse de un grabado en madera en el texto, y no de uno de los mapas dobles o triples, porque entonces no se hablaría de un solo folio.

De forma que, si se desencuadernara hoy una *Cosmographia* 1570, calculando que por lo menos cuatrocientos folios contienen bellas xilografías o en el recto o en el verso, a seiscientas mil liras por folio se podrían ganar doscientos cuarenta millones. En cambio, en el caso de las sesenta y cuatro páginas dobles (y no tomo en consideración las láminas plegadas más de una vez), aventurando en proporción por lo menos dos millones por mapa o vista, se conseguirían otros ciento veintiocho millones. En total, por muy mal que vaya, alrededor de trescientos millones de liras. Trescientos cobrados por treinta invertidos es una buena rentabilidad.

Naturalmente, el ejemplar completo que aparezca posteriormente en el mercado, habiéndose vuelto más raro, costará el doble, y el doble costarán las láminas sueltas. De este modo, de una sola vez, se destruyen obras de inconmensurable valor, se obliga a los coleccionistas a sacrificios insostenibles y se aumenta el precio de las láminas individuales. Sé que no estoy contando historias desconocidas a los coleccionistas. Es la razón por la que un Ortelius completo, por poner un ejemplo, vale lo que vale: ¿por qué conservar el libro si es más conveniente desmembrarlo?

No creo que haya medios para detener esta forma progresiva de vandalismo bastante poco democrático. Alguien propuso hace tiempo llevar a cabo una especie de resistencia pasiva: que ningún coleccionista comprara ya hojas sueltas. El problema es que el mercado de las hojas sueltas es infinitamente más vasto que el de los coleccionistas, llega incluso al público que hace que el decorador le compre volúmenes a metros. ¿Una ley que prescribiera que hay que demostrar, por cada hoja suelta, que procede de un ejemplar irremediablemente incompleto? Pero ¿quién puede controlar de dónde procede una hoja aislada que entra en el mercado? ¿Y qué significa «irremediablemente incompleto» para ciertas obras? Si mal no recuerdo, la Pierpont Morgan Library tiene dos biblias Gutenberg, y una está incompleta, pero la cuida mucho, y quienquiera que hoy desmembrara una cuarenta y dos líneas solo porque está incompleta sería como alguien que demoliera el Partenón para vender sus piedras al detalle.

Así pues, no veo soluciones, ni quiero criticar a aquellos que, habiendo adquirido una página de la *Cosmographia*, sin sentirse culpables por haberla separado con bisturí y cuchilla de un volumen original, la ponen en venta.

No quedaría sino difundir criterios de gusto: el que enmarca en casa una página de un volumen antiguo es un cateto y demuestra por eso su incultura. Para apoyar esa campaña estaría dispuesto a deshacerme de los hermosos folios coloreados que durante muchos años he colgado de mis paredes, tras encontrarlos aquí y allá. No sería imposible crear un esnobismo de masas por el que quien cuelga una página de libro en la pared es como si colgara un monito en el parabrisas posterior de su utilitario. Claro que este criterio esnob vale para quienes hoy tienen un coche de gran cilindrada, no para aquellos que en el utilitario pegan también los adhesivos del fútbol. Y además, ¿cómo pedirles a los libreros que no vendan los millares de hojas sueltas que tienen en stock, gracias a las cuales viven cuando se acercan las vacaciones navideñas?

En definitiva, no hay solución, excepto un llamamiento a la honradez. Los libros demasiado bien ilustrados están destinados a desaparecer (salvo los que se custodian en las bibliotecas; aunque también para ellos existe siempre el riesgo de la cuchilla de afeitar), o a costar más allá de las humanas posibilidades del coleccionista.

Es difícil hacer pedazos una catedral, o la capilla Sixtina, pero los libros están amenazados incluso por quienes los aman tanto (o tan poco) que quieren poseer incluso un uno por mil.

UN BIEN QUE ESTÁ AGOTÁNDOSE

El problema es que, independientemente de la biblioclasia, el libro antiguo es un objeto destinado inevitablemente a ir desapareciendo del mercado. Pongamos un ejemplo. Si ustedes heredan de su fallecido padre un mueble Luis XV, un óleo de escuela ferrarense, un diamante, pueden decidir venderlos. Así se alimenta el mercado de las antigüedades. Y lo mismo hacen si su padre ha reunido algunas decenas de libros del siglo XVIII. Eso explica por qué los decoradores pueden adquirir en los puestos *Les Aventures de Télémaque* en sus distintas ediciones. Si el bibliófilo atento, al visitar la casa de un señor de buena posición económica, ve en los estantes *Les Aventures de Télémaque* y algún tratadillo de filosofía del período ilustrado, sabe que su anfitrión es un *parvenu* que ha hecho que su arquitecto le eligiera los libros a metros.

Ahora bien, si su padre era un coleccionista verdadero, no habrá adquirido libros al azar, sino que habrá juntado una colección por tema, y cuando todavía vivía no habrá querido que desapareciera y la habrá legado en su testamento a alguna institución pública. O también, los herederos, al encontrarse ante una colección completa, no serán tan necios como para malvendérsela al librero de viejo y se la encomendarán a Christie's o a Sotheby's. Después de lo cual, la colección la adquirirá una biblioteca estadounidense o un banco japonés, y no volverá a salir nunca más de esos santuarios. Eso explica por qué el precio de los libros antiguos, sobre todo si forman una colección, crece a un ritmo superior que el de los muebles y las joyas. Llegará un día en que seguirá habiendo mercado de joyas, muebles barrocos y lienzos renacentistas, mientras que los libros se habrán convertido en objetos inalienables.

La biblioteca

El bibliófilo recopila libros para tener una biblioteca. Parece obvio, pero la biblioteca no es una suma de libros, es un organismo vivo con una vida autónoma. Una biblioteca de casa no es solo un lugar donde se recogen libros: es también el lugar que los lee por nuestra cuenta. Me explico. Creo que todos los que tienen en casa un número bastante elevado de libros han convivido por años con el remordimiento de no haber leído algunos, que nos han mirado durante años desde las estanterías para recordarnos nuestro pecado de omisión. Con mayor razón sucede con una biblioteca de libros raros, que a veces están escritos en latín o incluso en lenguas desconocidas (recuerdo que hay bibliófilos que coleccionan encuadernaciones, y a fin de tener una bella encuadernación pueden adquirir un libro en copto). Además, un hermoso libro antiguo puede ser también aburridísimo. Creo que todo aficionado quisiera tener los cuatro volúmenes del *Oedipus Aegyptiacus* de Kircher, cuyas ilustraciones son fascinantes, pero no conseguiría leer el texto, desgarradoramente complejo.

Claro que, de vez en cuando, sucede que un día tomamos uno de esos libros descuidados, empezamos a hojearlo, y nos damos cuenta de que sabíamos ya todo lo que decía. Ese fenómeno singular, que muchos pueden atestiguar, tiene solo tres explicaciones razonables. La primera es que, habiendo tocado varias veces ese libro en el curso de los años para cambiarlo de sitio, quitarle el polvo, incluso solo para apartarlo con la finalidad de tomar otro libro, algo de su sabiduría se le ha transmitido al cerebro a través de la yema de nuestros dedos y nosotros lo hemos leído táctilmente, como si estuviera escrito en alfabeto Braille. Yo soy un seguidor del CICAP, el Comité Italiano para la Investigación de Afirmaciones Pseudocientíficas, y no creo en los fenómenos paranormales, pero en este caso sí, entre otras cosas porque no considero que el fenómeno sea paranormal: es muy normal, está certificado por la experiencia cotidiana.

La segunda explicación es que no es cierto que no hayamos leído ese libro: cada vez que lo cambiábamos de sitio o le quitábamos el polvo, le echábamos una ojeada, se abría alguna página al azar, algo en el diseño gráfico, en la textura del papel, en los colores, hablaba de una época, de un ambiente. Y de este modo, poco a poco, ha ido absorbiéndose gran parte de ese libro.

La tercera explicación es que, mientras los años pasaban, leíamos otros libros en los que se hablaba también de ese, de modo que sin darnos cuenta hemos aprehendido lo que decía (ya se tratara de un libro célebre, del que todos hablaban; ya se tratara de un libro trivial, con ideas tan corrientes que las encontrábamos continuamente por doquier).

La verdad es que creo que son verdaderas las tres explicaciones. Todos esos elementos juntos «cuajan» de forma milagrosa y concurren todos ellos a hacernos familiares esas páginas que, desde un punto de vista puramente legal, nunca hemos leído.

Naturalmente, el bibliófilo, también y sobre todo el que colecciona libros contemporáneos, está expuesto a la insidia del imbécil que te entra en casa, ve todas esas estanterías, y exclama: «¡Cuántos libros! ¿Los ha leído todos?». La experiencia cotidiana nos dice que esta pregunta la hacen también personas con un cociente intelectual más que satisfactorio. Ante este ultraje existen, según mi entendimiento, tres respuestas estándar. La primera corta al visitante e interrumpe toda relación, y es: «No he leído ninguno, si no ¿para qué los tendría aquí?». Esta respuesta gratifica, sin embargo, al importuno cosquilleando su sensación de superioridad y no veo por qué hemos de hacerle semejante favor.

La segunda respuesta sume al importuno en un estado de inferioridad, y suena así: «¡Muchos más, señor, muchísimos más!».

La tercera es una variación de la segunda y la uso cuando quiero que el visitante caiga presa de un doloroso estupor. «No —le digo—, los que ya he leído los tengo en la universidad, estos son los que he de leer para la semana que viene.» Dado que mi biblioteca milanesa cuenta con treinta mil volúmenes, a partir de ese momento el infeliz intenta solo anticipar su despedida, alegando repentinos compromisos.

Lo que el infeliz no sabe es que la biblioteca no es solo el lugar de tu memoria, donde conservas lo que has leído, sino el lugar de la memoria universal, donde un día, en el momento fatal, podrás encontrar lo que otros leyeron antes que tú.

Un repositorio donde, en última instancia, todo se confunde y genera un vértigo, un cóctel de la memoria docta, pero ¿qué importa? He aquí el contenido virtual de una biblioteca: Monsieurs les anglais, je me suis couché de bonne heure. Tu quoque, alea! Licht, mehr Licht über alles. Aquí estamos construyendo Italia no pisamos sobre mojado, en ese ramal del lago de Como duermen pájaros con largas alas, oh hermanos de Italia mía el enemigo que huye va a helarte el corazón, y al arado que traza el surco puente de plata, Italia está hecha pero no se rinde, combatiremos a la sombra ocaso dorado colinas plateadas, en bosques y espesuras yo me la llevé al río y más la piedra dura fue a dar en la mar, la inconsciente azagaya bárbara a la que tendías la mano infantil, no pidas la palabra enloquecida de luz desde los Alpes hasta las Pirámides, se fue a la guerra y picó su pica en Flandes, frescas te sean mis palabras en la tarde a docena a docena de fraile, pan tierra y libertad sobre las alas doradas, adiós montañas que salís de las aguas pero mi nombre es Lucía o Elisa o Teresa vida mía, quisiera Guido una llama de amor viva, pues conocí la trémula mano roja de las armas los amores, de la musique où marchent des colombes, vuélvete paloma por donde has venido, clara y dulce es la noche y el capitán soy capitán, me ilumino de plenitud, aunque hablar sea en vano los he visto en Pontida, septiembre vamos a donde florecen los limones, quién hubiera tan ventura del Pélida Aquiles, a la pálida luz de la luna de mis soledades vengo, en principio era la tierra y todo pasa y todo queda. Condesa, ¿qué será la vida? Amor y pedagogía.

BIBLIOFILIA Y COLECCIONISMO

Esta especie de confianza en un repositorio universal del saber, que queda a tu disposición, explica por qué el bibliófilo no se afana tanto en leer como en acumular. En ese sentido, el bibliófilo corre el riesgo de convertirse en un coleccionista. Quisiera subrayar la diferencia entre coleccionistas y bibliófilos. Los coleccionistas quieren tener todo lo que se puede recopilar sobre un tema determinado y lo que les interesa no es la naturaleza de cada pieza sino lo completa que resulta la colección. Tienden a acelerar los tiempos. El bibliófilo, aunque trabaje en un argumento, espera que la colección no acabe nunca, que haya siempre y todavía algo que buscar. Y a veces puede enamorarse de un hermoso libro que nada tiene que ver con su tema.

El coleccionismo es una pasión quizá milenaria, los patricios romanos coleccionaban antigüedades griegas (incluso falsas) y los chicos de hoy coleccionan cromos. Coleccionar es una forma de apropiarnos de un pasado que se nos escapa. Pero ¿de qué pasado? Si consultamos el boletín mensual de Christie's, vemos que se hacen subastas en las que se venden a golpes de centenares de millones no solo lienzos, joyas, muebles, sino «memorabilia» como un par de calcetines que pertenecieron al duque de Windsor. Vale, los ricos están locos. ¿Y los pobres no?

Con un solo número de la revista *Collezionare* descubrí cuántas ferias y rastrillos de objetos de colección hay. Se piden y proponen (junto a libros, grabados, sellos, coches de época, muñecas, relojes, objetos masones, postales o bronces) pegatinas y tarjetas, billetes —incluidos los *miniassegni*, los minitalones de los años setenta—, llaves, botellas de Coca-Cola, cuchillas de afeitar, carnés y diplomas. Una sección está dedicada solamente a *mignonettes*, o sea, botellitas de licor o perfume, aunque estén vacías. Un tipo cambia ciento cincuenta perfumes *mignon* por sellos italianos nuevos —ustedes dirán: serán del siglo XIX, del Reino Pontificio, pero no, de 1978 a 1988—. Por último, en la sección dedicada a envoltorios y sobres, encontramos un buen anuncio: «¿Tenéis envoltorios de fruta? Busco también sobres de azúcar llenos». Otro busca los papeles de envolver las naranjas Moro Tarocco; otro, servilletas de bar. Son todas ellas pasiones respetables, por amor de Dios, pero me atenaza la angustia de ese pasado futuro que vamos descartando a nuestro alrededor, la cajita con los cacahuetes que dejo (tal vez llena) en el tren, el sobre usado de Nescafé que va a parar a la basura, con colillas, y cajetillas de cigarrillos, y carteritas de cerillas vacías y desgarradas. Me siento un vándalo, un califa que está quemando la biblioteca de Alejandría. ¿Cómo es posible dilapidar de este modo la arqueología del mañana?

A veces el bibliófilo y el coleccionista coinciden. He conocido al doctor Morris Young, ahora un encantador nonagenario que, al ganar bien como oculista, se ha pasado la vida reuniendo colecciones junto a su mujer. Ha coleccionado muchas cosas, desde materiales para prestidigitadores hasta libros sobre los códigos militares. Cuando la colección estaba completa, perdía todo gusto por el tema en cuestión, y lo vendía todo, para empezar una nueva colección. Su colección de mayor entidad y éxito fue una sobre la memoria. Por eso lo conocí: la recién nacida Universidad de San Marino quería enriquecer su biblioteca con algún fondo de insignes rarezas y había sabido a través de un librero de Nueva York que Young quería vender su colección de libros antiguos sobre las mnemotécnicas. Yo sabía de su existencia, porque quienes coleccionan *artes memoriae* conocen el catálogo Young, una mina de noticias sobre todos los libros de ese tipo. Me encontré con Young, descubrí que tenía un fondo respetable de artes de la memoria, un manuscrito, muchos incunables y las obras mayores de los siglos XVI, XVII y XVIII. Pero al mismo tiempo entendí por qué quería vender: ya no sabía dónde guardar, aun disponiendo de un segundo piso que se parecía al almacén de un chamarilero, todo lo que, junto a los libros raros, había recogido sobre la memoria.

Tenía todos los libros publicados durante los siglos XIX y XX por psicólogos, expertos en inteligencia artificial, neurólogos y filósofos. Tenía un inmenso repertorio de juegos inspirados en la memoria, y otros *memorabilia*, que comprendían incluso tacitas que llevaban escrito REMEMBER ME, más un fondo de manuscritos y cartas de estudiosos de la memoria. Auténtico Funes el Memorioso de la Memoria, Young había coleccionado todo aquello que de alguna manera podía recordar la memoria. Ya no le faltaba nada, y vendía. Como todo buen bibliófilo, vendía a un organismo cultural, de modo que su patrimonio no se dispersara y se volviera inalienable. Era tan poco bibliómano, sin embargo, que estaba dispuesto a deshacerse de su colección.

El bibliófilo y el fin del libro

Al bibliófilo no le asustan ni internet ni los CD ni los e-books. En internet encuentra ya los catálogos anticuarios; en el CD esas obras que un particular difícilmente podría tener en su casa, como los doscientos veintiún volúmenes infolio de la Patrología Latina de Migne; en un e-book estaría muy dispuesto a llevarse por el mundo bibliografías y catálogos, disponiendo así de un repertorio precioso siempre consigo, sobre todo cuando visita una feria de libros antiguos. Para todo lo demás confía en que, aunque desaparecieran los libros, su colección sencillamente redoblaría, pero ¡qué digo!, decuplicaría su valor. Por tanto, *pereat mundus!*

Ahora bien, el bibliófilo sabe también que el libro tendrá una larga vida, y lo nota mirando con ojo amoroso sus estanterías. Si toda esa información que ha acumulado hubiera sido guardada, desde los tiempos de Gutenberg, en un soporte magnético, ¿habría logrado sobrevivir doscientos, trescientos, cuatrocientos, quinientos, quinientos cincuenta años? ¿Y se habrían transmitido, junto a los contenidos de las obras, las huellas de los que la tocaron, cotejaron, anotaron, maltrataron y a menudo ensuciaron con marcas del pulgar antes de nosotros? ¿Y podríamos enamorarnos de un disquete como nos enamoramos de una página blanca y dura, que hace crac, crac bajo nuestros dedos como si acabara de salir de la prensa?

Qué hermoso un libro, que ha sido pensado para ser tomado en la mano, en la cama o una barca, también allá donde no hay enchufes eléctricos, también donde y cuando todas las baterías se ha descargado; qué hermoso un libro que soporta anotaciones y esquinas dobladas, que puede dejarse caer al suelo o abandonado y abierto sobre nuestro pecho o rodillas cuando nos acomete el sueño; un libro que cabe en un bolsillo, que se

estropea, que registra la intensidad, la asiduidad o la regulari-
dad de nuestras lecturas, que nos recuerda (si se presenta demasiado fresco o intonso) que todavía no lo hemos leído...

La forma-libro está determinada por nuestra anatomía.
Puede haber libros muy grandes, pero suelen tener la función
de documento o decorativa; el libro estándar no debe ser más
pequeño que un paquete de cigarrillos o mayor que un tabloi-
de. Depende de las dimensiones de nuestra mano, y esas —de
momento— no han cambiado, le guste o no a Bill Gates.

Es tarea del bibliófilo, más allá de la satisfacción personal de
su deseo privado, testimoniar el pasado y el porvenir del libro.
Recuerdo el primer Salón del Libro de Turín, cuando le reserva-
ron todo un largo pasillo al libro antiguo (después me parece
que esa bonita costumbre se perdió). Visitaban la exposición
chicos de los colegios, y los vi pegados a las vitrinas para descubrir por primera vez qué era un verdadero libro, no un fasciculi-
to de quiosco, un libro con todos sus atributos en el lugar adecuado. Me recordaron al bárbaro de Borges, cuando ve por vez
primera esa obra maestra del arte humano que es una ciudad.
Aquel cayó de rodillas ante Rávena y se convirtió en un romano.
Me conformaría con que los chicos de Turín se llevaran a casa
por lo menos una emoción, acaso una carcoma benéfica.

Ah, se me olvidaba, la carcoma también forma parte de la pasión del bibliófilo. No todas ellas devalúan el libro. Algunas,
cuando no afectan al texto, parecen un delicado encaje. Yo, lo
confieso, amo también las carcomas. Naturalmente, al librero
que me vende el libro le manifiesto desdén y disgusto, para que
baje el precio. Pero ya lo he dicho: por amor a un hermoso libro estamos dispuestos a cualquier bajeza.

Colaciones de un coleccionista[1]

Permítanme empezar con algunas observaciones de un gran bibliógrafo y bibliófilo, que tengo el privilegio de citar libre e impunemente, por directa aunque implícita investidura, recibida el día en que subí a un avión para ir a verlo. Me refiero al prefacio escrito por Mario Praz para el *Catálogo 15* de la Libreria della Fiera Letteraria, en 1931, pocos meses antes de mi nacimiento, y beneméritamente reimpresa en el volumen *Bibliofobia*, con docta introducción de Roberto Palazzi, Pierre Marteau Editore de Roma, diciembre de 1988, doscientos setenta ejemplares numerados del 1 al 270, más algunos ejemplares fuera de comercio punzonados HC, 24 ★ 17, 10 h. s. n., 21-125 pp. (1 h. blanca) (3 h. s. n.), numerosas reproducciones de grabados en el texto; rústica, papel de los aguafuertes de 160 g, mi ejemplar punzonado HC, barbas, numerosas anotaciones manuscritas de época a lápiz, rara Association Copy con dedicatoria a lápiz del prologuista. Ligero cerco de whisky en el margen superior izquierdo del frontis, por lo demás fresco. Obra de insigne raridad, ausente en Hain y Goff, inexplicablemente desconocido por Graesse, Cicognara y Sommervogel.

---

1. Conferencia leída en la Mostra del Libro Antico el 29 de marzo de 1990. Se publicó en *L'Esopo* (n.º 46, junio de 1990).

Todavía ningún ejemplar NUC, 270 ejemplares en la Narren-schift Bibliothek del Hortus Palatinus.

Praz observaba el placer que le producía al bibliófilo leer catálogos de antigüedades de libros, igual que se leen novelas negras. «Os aseguro —decía— que ninguna lectura ha generado jamás una acción tan rápida y emocionante como lo hace la lectura de un catálogo interesante.» A renglón seguido, Praz dejaba vislumbrar que podían hacerse lecturas rápidas y conmovidas también de catálogos no interesantes.

Nos fascina ver premiados a los autores oscuros y descubrir depreciados a aquellos que, besados por el éxito, han entregado a la posteridad tiradas vulgarmente altísimas; y satisfacen nuestro sadismo intelectual esos autores «de escaso mérito, y en absoluto considerados hoy en día, que puntualmente vuelven a presentarse en cada catálogo [...] con las mismas caras largas de gente fracasada o de poseedores de acciones que ya no cotizan en Bolsa». Praz ponía los ejemplos del *Rimario* de Ruscelli y de las *Immagini degli Dei Antichi* de Cartari (que él consideraba obra de los emblemas en sentido espurio). Yo añadiría —sin entrar en cuestiones de mérito científico o literario, sino solo de exceso editorial— las *Aventures de Télémaque*, primer recurso de cualquier decorador que ponga en escena cultura por metro cuadrado, cualquier *Sfera* de Sacrobosco, cualquier *Comte de Gabalis* que no sea la primera edición, todos los *Grand* y *Petit Albert* de los hermanos Beringos, el diccionario bíblico de Calmet, los doceavos y dieciseisavos del siglo XVI de los *Misterios* de Jámblico y, para los devotos del siglo XIX, todas las obras de Lacroix y de Figuier. Y me resulta grato recordar la ironía que un crítico de la bibliofilia reservaba al intelectual advenedizo que asombra a los burgueses afirmando que tiene en su casa numerosas *cinquecentine*. Las *cinquecentine* son aún más numerosas que las latas de Coca-Cola y a menudo valen menos que una latita de caviar, aunque en los puestos de la piazza Fontanella Borghese de Roma se las enseñen susurrando lascivos como si se tratara de un *Kamasutra* ilustrado.

Leer los catálogos significa también descubrir las presencias inesperadas y, entonces, se pasa del policíaco en que el asesino es el mayordomo Ruscelli, al policíaco inédito en que la víctima es el narrador y el lector es el ladrón gentilhombre. Me sucedió que, en el catálogo de una subasta Zisska, encontré citada la primera edición de los Manifiestos rosacruces de 1614. Ni siquiera el mayor coleccionista al respecto, el señor Rittman de la Bibliotheca Hermetica de Amsterdam, la poseía todavía. La cifra de salida era razonable y le escribí a un amigo de Munich para que pujara, pero le avisé de que, si veía merodear por aquellas salas a un tal señor Jannssen, no hiciera nada. Jannssen actúa por cuenta del señor Rittman, quien por poseer esa obra estaría dispuesto a ceder los derechos que recibe de todos los cubiertos de plástico que usamos en los aviones de cualquier aerolínea. En efecto, lo que pasó fue que Jannssen estaba (cómo no iba a estar) y compró el libro por algunas toneladas de tenedores de plástico.

Ahora bien, los días anteriores a la subasta, hojeando el mismo inmenso catálogo, en la sección «Teología» encontré un libro, con un frontispicio anónimo y con el título teológicamente inofensivo *Offenbarung göttlicher Mayestat*, Hanau 1619. Precio de salida, doscientos miserables marcos. Praz ya lo dijo, hay que leer los catálogos buscando «palabritas mágicas» y por suerte cada uno tiene las propias. Esa *Offenbarung* estimuló algunas de mis neuronas, ya en liquidación. ¿Dónde lo había oído yo? Diantres, era la obra de Aegydius Guttman, legendariamente considerado el inspirador de los manifiestos rosacruces. La obra circulaba manuscrita desde el siglo anterior, pero se publicó por vez primera justo en 1619. Gottfried Arnold, desde 1740, en su *Unpartheyische Kirchen-und-Ketzer Historien*, la consideraba inencontrable y citaba no sé ya qué landgrave que había pagado una fortuna en táleros o florines para poseer uno de los pocos ejemplares todavía en circulación.

Llamé a mi amigo de Munich y le aconsejé que hiciera pequeñas y desganadas ofertas para que Jannssen no sospechara, en el caso de que ese diablo de hombre no hubiera mirado en el sector de teología. Conseguí el libro por trescientos marcos, doscientas sesenta y cinco mil liras, sólidamente encuadernado en piel de época, ligera, casi tiernamente oxidado de manera uniforme, con maravillosas anotaciones manuscritas de época, en dos colores. Tuve la tentación de escribir a Jannssen para mofarme, en nombre de nuestra conflictiva amistad, pero luego lo dejé correr: mejor no meterle peligrosas ideas en la cabeza. Dejemos que los rosacrucianos no exploren las secciones de teología y se queden confinados en los catálogos de ocultismo, a los que al fin y al cabo tienen que dedicar mucho tiempo, dado que muchos anticuarios colocan ya bajo ese epígrafe todas las obras con títulos apetecibles, como *Sidereus Nuncius*, *Selenographia* o *Novum Organum*.

El catálogo comercial a menudo enfatiza pero, a veces, como el Oráculo de Delfos del que habla Heráclito, no dice ni oculta sino que solo insinúa. Para explicitar la información, el coleccionista se remite a las bibliografías más vulnerables y a los catálogos comerciales que ya se han vuelto históricos.

Para quienquiera que los consulte, también las bibliografías y los catálogos históricos son fuente de saber y al mismo tiempo sendas de perdición. En efecto, hay una diferencia radical entre una bibliografía como repertorio de textos que hay que consultar y una bibliografía como descripción de objetos que hay que poseer. La primera no describe ejemplares, sino clases de ejemplares, designadas por autor, título, lugar y fecha. Que el estudioso encuentre uno u otro ejemplar es indiferente, como es indiferente que poseamos, leamos o escuchemos por teléfono un libro prohibido: es el contenido lo que cuenta, no el vehículo. En cambio, la paradoja de cualquier *Trésor de livres rares et précieux* es que habla de objetos individuales en los que el vehículo físico es más o igual de precioso que el contenido.

Cuando un libro aparece, cualquier ejemplar suyo es por definición intercambiable con cualquier otro ejemplar, pero cuando empieza a desaparecer, es el ejemplar singular el que se busca por su carácter de unicidad, o de rareza. En este proceso de rarefacción, cada ejemplar se vuelve único por las alteraciones que la obra del encuadernador, del poseedor, del tiempo y de los agentes atmosféricos le ha impuesto como sello; pero, al mismo tiempo, cada ejemplar adquiere valor en la medida en que se acerca a las condiciones del ejemplar ideal.

Para los aficionados a objetos producidos industrialmente en serie (coleccionistas de automóviles de época o de lámparas Tiffany) existe un criterio de idealidad: el ejemplar tiene que adecuarse a las instrucciones facilitadas por su proyecto originario (proyecto que a menudo se conserva), y se vuelve tanto más apetecible cuantas menos marcas de deterioro presente. En el caso de los objetos de artesanía, piensen en el mueble antiguo, no existe el tipo que ha determinado una serie de ejemplares todos iguales, por lo que se extrapola de la tradición un modelo genérico, por ejemplo, de mesa frailera renacentista. En ambos casos, el aficionado, una vez establecida la adherencia del ejemplar al tipo, y evaluado su estado aparente de conservación, debe preguntarse solo si es antiguo de verdad. No es una empresa baladí, y precisamente por eso en esos sectores prosperan las mesas fraileras de Cantù y los Vuitton de los manteros.

¿Qué sucede con el libro antiguo? Para el libro no existe un tipo abstracto con el que comparar sus casos. Cada pieza salida de la imprenta es, en principio, el tipo de todas las demás. Pero dado que antaño se vendían pliegos sueltos que se encuadernaban según el capricho del cliente, que los procesos aún artesanales permitían corregir la composición incluso en el curso de la impresión, y dado que el ejemplar nos llega marcado de diferentes maneras por el tiempo y la posesión, si consideramos una edición con tirada de mil ejemplares, en teoría ningún ejemplar es igual al otro.

Y tampoco podemos decir que el problema central es verificar la efectiva antigüedad del ejemplar. El juicio de autenticidad es esencial, pero no dramático. Incluso un simple aficionado puede reconocer el ejemplar compuesto, restaurado, lavado, parcheado con folios anastáticos. Además, la falsificación perfecta es improbable porque supondría la ruina de cualquier falsificador. Si para un buen artesano (que tenga a disposición madera vieja y un fusil de caza para crear los agujeros de la carcoma) resulta conveniente falsificar una artesa del siglo XVII, producir *ex novo* un incunable, volver a fabricar el papel, imprimir una copia fotográfica de la página original, pero dándole al papel las debidas marcas de envejecimiento, sería tan caro que parece más conveniente aplicar el mismo ingenio a falsificar billetes. Quizá valdría la pena para un libro inmensamente caro, como por ejemplo la Biblia de Gutenberg, pero en ese caso su mismo precio aconsejaría a un posible cliente tales y tantas pruebas científicas que la falsificación en cualquier caso se descubriría.

El verdadero problema consiste en verificar la rareza de los ejemplares de una determinada edición (lo cual es bastante factible con la ayuda de buenos repertorios) y en decidir si el ejemplar que se examina responde a los requisitos de un ejemplar ideal. Desafortunadamente, no solo el ejemplar tipo no existe, sino que el concepto de ejemplar ideal cambia con la historia misma de los ejemplares que han sobrevivido. Si una *Hypnerotomachia Poliphili* que carece de la fe de erratas se degrada casi a ejemplar de estudio, un libro de nigromancia que haya incurrido en los rigores de la Inquisición se considera excelente, aunque una mano temerosa haya borrado el nombre del editor.

Muchos catálogos apostillan respecto a los libros del siglo XVII: «Con los fuertes y acostumbrados enrojecimientos, debidos a la calidad del papel». Pues bien, casi todos los ejemplares de la *Historia Utriusque Cosmi* de Fludd suelen estar oxidados, y mucho; y muchos otros ejemplares presentan más o menos florituras en las mismas signaturas (interesante indicio del hecho de que a determinadas partidas de papel les correspondía la misma composición química para todos los ejemplares de una misma tirada), pero he visto por lo menos un Fludd de gran frescura. Si alguien tuviera la amabilidad de destruir ese ejemplar, el Fludd ideal sería el mío, obra maestra alquímica de obra al rojo.

¿Cuál es el estándar de conservación de un ejemplar? Para saberlo, sería necesario conocer *intus et in cute* todos los ejemplares que han sobrevivido, y ya es una suerte si logramos hacerlo con la Biblia de cuarenta y dos líneas. Por consiguiente, nos remitimos a las descripciones publicadas, donde, sin embargo, los autores suelen describir como ideal el ejemplar que han tenido en su poder.

Claro que si, por casualidad, Hain y Goff han tenido a su alcance un ejemplar imperfecto, el tipo ideal al que se atienen los libreros es la descripción de un ejemplar imperfecto, o perfecto de forma anómala. En aquel librito mío que algunos de ustedes conocen sobre las peripecias de la Hanau 1609[2] se muestra cómo los criterios ideales de sucesión de las láminas dependen del ejemplar que el bibliógrafo vio o dice haber visto. Hace poco tuve la oportunidad de ver tres ejemplares de la *Crónica de Nuremberg*. Uno no cuenta, está en la Library del Queens College de Cambridge, me lo enseñaron con conmoción, pero no vale ni siquiera como ejemplar de estudio, porque le han mutilado algunas de sus más bellas láminas, entre ellas obviamente la de los monstruos. El otro, en Italia, parecía no corresponder a la descripción de Hain. Pero una inspección más cuidadosa permitió llegar a la conclusión de que la descripción de Hain se adaptaba al ejemplar en cuestión, con tal de que se aceptara que el encuadernador había colocado en otra posición cinco hojas sin paginar que presumiblemente se pueden colocar con cierta libertad. El tercer ejemplar lo vi en venta en Nueva York y tenía los márgenes ligeramente más amplios que el ejemplar italiano. Como el ejemplar estadounidense tiene una encuadernación del siglo XVIII, se trata quizá de un ejemplar encuadernado por primera vez solo posteriormente; ahora bien, el ejemplar italiano tiene una encuadernación casi de época y, por tanto, casi de época se presenta su desbarbado. ¿Cuál entre todos habrá de definirse como ejemplar ideal?

Se objetará que un catálogo fidedigno es el que no informa de un solo ejemplar, sino el que resume un trabajo pluridecenal de pacientes cotejos, y de eso nos fiamos, por lo menos, en

2. Véase en este volumen «El extraño caso de la Hanau 1609».

lo que atañe a la colación aunque tal vez no nos sirva para conocer un estado de conservación ideal. Claro que ¿existe el catálogo totalmente fidedigno? También los mejores son como las mejores enciclopedias, que pueden exhibir una excelente entrada «membranáceas» y una pésima «monocotiledóneas». El autor de tesoros de libros raros y preciosos ha visto demasiados libros, y demasiados quiere describir, para poder describirlos todos con la misma acribia. No es extraño que describa como ejemplar tipo una copia que no ha visto, cuya descripción saca de un catálogo anterior, el cual a su vez la saca de uno aún más antiguo. Por no hablar de chismosos como Dorbon o Caillet, que refieren también las habladurías de la portera, todas las veces que Graesse copia de Brunet y si Brunet habla de oídas... De este modo, un error original se transmite de catálogo en catálogo, y todos se refieren a un ejemplar tipo que nunca existió, ni siquiera como caso individual.

Hace unos meses encontré, encuadernados en un volumen y por un precio bastante modesto, el *Opus Mago Cabbalisticum et Theosophicum* y el *Tractatus Mago-cabbalistico chymicus et Theosophicus* de Georg von Welling. El catálogo del anticuario decía que el *Opus*, de 1735, era solo la primera edición de la primera parte de una obra cuya segunda parte, y en su segunda edición, era el *Tractatus*, de 1729. En efecto, como supe acto seguido por catálogos de renombre, esta segunda parte de 1729 reproducía una edición 1719, la cual desgraciadamente no se titulaba *Tractatus*, como todos habríamos esperado, sino *Opus*, como la primera edición de la primera parte (omito el hecho de que los tres títulos enteros, tan largos que ocupan una página, como es buena costumbre, son aparentemente iguales pero en realidad parcialmente distintos el uno del otro). Como pueden ver, un buen lío, que explica cómo los bibliógrafos empezaron a perder la cabeza, aun admitiendo que alguno de ellos examinara alguna vez las tres ediciones juntas. Pero esto no es todo.

Como he averiguado con arduo trabajo, y experimentando más dificultades en descifrar los catálogos que la prosa del autor, Welling, con el seudónimo de Sallwigt, publica un primer libro sobre la química de la sal en 1719 y lo llama *Opus*. Luego en 1729 vuelve a publicarlo anónimo con pequeñas diferencias y lo llama *Tractatus*. Después, en 1735, con el nombre de Welling, publica un *Opus* que incluye como primera parte el texto del *Opus* 1719 y del *Tractatus* 1729 (y los tres textos son sustancialmente idénticos en su contenido y conciernen sin la menor duda a la química de la sal), más una segunda parte sustanciosa e inédita.

El *Opus* de 1735 es la primera edición de la obra completa. Pero los dos volúmenes previos no constituyen su segunda parte, sino la primera, propuesta también en el *Opus* de 1735. Por lo tanto, yo compré no la primera y la segunda parte de una misma obra, sino dos obras distintas, y al precio de una, porque el anticuario se había fiado de los catálogos.

Nótese que Duveen, en su *Bibliotheca Alchemica et Chimica*, se había percatado de todo, y criticaba precisamente un descuido del Ferguson de la *Bibliotheca Chemica*. También Ferguson sabía cómo estaba el tema, y lo decía, pero desafortunadamente en una anotación en cuerpo menor (y ustedes saben cuántas escribía y por doquier) se confundía y llamaba segunda parte la que previamente había llamado primera. Ignorando a Duveen y leyendo mal a Ferguson, el autor del catálogo de la Colección Mellon, reputadísimo, retoma la anotación equivocada y la enfatiza, y es imitado de inmediato por el autor del catálogo de la Hall Collection. Todos los que llegan después los siguen a pies juntillas.

Pues bien, para entender quién tenía razón, comparé página por página las ediciones 1729 y 1735, y aun sin tener la 1719, verifiqué que el texto de la 1729 correspondiera a la primera parte de la 1735.[3] Sencillísimo. Pero hacía falta partir de un principio: que los libros, también los antiguos, se deben leer, por lo menos un poco.

Y esta no es una idea universalmente aceptada entre los amantes de libros raros y preciosos, incluidos sus bibliógrafos. Los cuales eran, sin duda alguna, bibliófilos pero, a menudo, también bibliómanos, cuando no eran bibliocleptómanos, como Gugliemo Libri. Un bibliómano se distingue del bibliófilo porque, con tal de poseer un libro raro e intonso, y de conservarlo como tal, renuncia a leerlo. Creo que no hay ninguna diferencia entre un bibliómano y un bibliófobo, esto es, entre conservar libros sin leerlos y destruirlos. Los libros están hechos para ser leídos.

Permítanme concluir, por tanto, estas consideraciones mías, empezadas bajo la égida de la bibliofobia, bajo la égida de esa sabia y sana bibliofilia que, en 1345, testimoniaba Richard De Bury en su *Philobiblon*:

Los libros nos encantan cuando la prosperidad nos sonríe, y consuelan cuando nos amenaza una mala racha; dan fuerza a convicciones humanas y sin ellos no se pronuncian los juicios graves.

Las artes y las ciencias residen en los libros; ningún espíritu sería capaz de sentir todo el provecho que de ellos puede sacarse. ¡Qué valor no alcanza el poder admirable de estos libros cuando gracias a ellos podemos distinguir los límites de la Tierra y dis-

3. Esto, en la época en que escribía estas anotaciones mías. Ahora poseo también la 1719 y las cuentas salen igualmente.

cernir los del tiempo y contemplar como en el espejo de la eternidad las cosas que son y las que no son!

Con los libros atravesamos las cordilleras y bajamos hasta la profundidad de los abismos observando las especies que en el aire no podrían subsistir. En los libros distinguimos las propiedades de los ríos, de las fuentes y de los diversos terrenos. De los libros extraemos el género de los metales y las piedras preciosas, así como los elementos que componen cada mineral. Examinamos a nuestro gusto la naturaleza de las hierbas, de los árboles, de las plantas y de toda la familia de Neptuno, Ceres y Plutón. Si nos agrada visitar a los moradores de los cielos, dejando bajo nuestros pies el Tauro, el Cáucaso y el Olimpo, nos transportamos al reino de Júpiter y medimos con cuerdas y círculos los siete territorios de los planetas. Por fin, llegamos al supremo firmamento, decorado con una admirable variedad de signos, grados e imágenes. Allí descubrimos el Polo Austral, que ningún ojo humano vio jamás, y admiramos con un delicioso placer el camino luminoso de la Vía Láctea y el Zodiaco pintado con animales celestes. Desde allí pasamos, siempre por medio de los libros, a las sustancias inmateriales para que nuestra inteligencia salude a esas inteligencias que se le asemejan y el ojo del espíritu vea la causa primera de todas las cosas y el inmutable motor de la virtud infinita, y se una a él para siempre. [...] Además por ellos hacemos saber a nuestros amigos y enemigos las cosas [...] porque «la voz del Autor penetra hasta la cámara del príncipe, donde, seguramente, sería rechazada, cosa que a los libros no sucede».

Si nos encontramos encadenados en una prisión, privados completamente de libertad, nos servimos de los libros como embajadores cerca de nuestros amigos; les confiamos el trámite de nuestros asuntos y se los transmitimos allí donde nuestra presencia sería para nosotros motivo de muerte.

[...] ¿Qué más queremos? Séneca nos enseña que sin ninguna duda «... la ociosidad de los libros es la muerte y la sepultura del hombre vivo». Por ello concluiremos afirmando que los libros y las letras constituyen el nervio de la vida [cap. XV].

Efectivamente, Richard De Bury nos dice qué hacer con los libros después de haberlos coleccionado y cotejado.

Historica

Sobre el libro de Lindisfarne[1]

¿Cómo hojear las páginas miniadas de los Evangelios de Lindisfarne? De forma ingenua, disfrutando de ellas por lo que son, o intentando entender el ambiente en que nacen y el gusto al que se refieren...

Tomás de Aquino sintetizó los principios de la estética medieval en una definición famosa (entre otras cosas, ya que hablaremos de Irlanda, es la que retoma el primer Joyce para fundar la propia visión del arte en *The Portrait of the Artist as a Young Man*): «Ad pulchritudinem tria requiruntur. Primo quidem integritas sive perfectio: quae enim diminuta sunt, hoc ipso turpia sunt. Et debita proportio sive consonantia. Et iterum claritas: unde quae habent colorem nitidum pulchra esse dicuntur». Lo que significa que contribuyen a la belleza tres condiciones o características: la integridad, porque decimos feo a lo que es incompleto; la proporción y la claridad o nitidez del color.

Tomás resumía las definiciones que, procedentes de la Antigüedad clásica, habían sido retomadas de formas distintas por sus predecesores a lo largo de los siglos de la Edad Media. La proporción era un criterio de origen pitagórico, aunque es interesante ver cómo, en el curso del tiempo, y aun usando siempre

1. Artículo escrito para la edición Faksimile Verlag del *Book of Lindisfarne*.

el mismo término, artistas, filósofos y teólogos tenían presentes tipos distintos de proporción. Por ejemplo, baste observar cómo, por lo que atañe a las proporciones musicales, en el siglo IX se reconocía todavía el intervalo de quinta como ejemplo de proporción imperfecta, mientras que ya se la reconoce perfecta en el siglo XII, y solo mucho más tarde se admitirá como perfecto también el intervalo de tercera.

La integridad parece ser una condición bastante intuitiva, y a menudo en los textos medievales se repite que el hombre mutilado pierde la propia belleza; ahora bien, el concepto era mucho más complejo. Por integridad se entendía que toda cosa natural había de adaptarse a los límites precisos fijados por las leyes de la especie, por lo que no era bello sino monstruoso un perro del tamaño de un elefante, o una manzana del tamaño de una calabaza; y ese criterio se aplicaba también a las obras de arte. Por lo que se refiere a la *claritas*, hablaremos de ella más adelante.

He citado los criterios de la belleza típicos de la Edad Media para sugerir que las obras de arte irlandesas y célticas en general, florecidas en las islas Británicas en los últimos siglos del primer milenio, parecen traicionar todo criterio de proporción e integridad.

En el mundo latino se había contrapuesto el estilo denominado asiano (y luego africano) al estilo ático, y alguien ha observado que se trataba ya entonces de un debate entre una estética clasicista y una estética barroca. Para Quintiliano, el estilo clásico debe tender a lo sublime pero no a lo temerario, a la grandeza pero no al énfasis, y Vitruvio había deplorado que se representaran a menudo monstruos en lugar de figuras claramente definidas. Al principio de la cultura cristiana, san Jerónimo había arremetido contra ese estilo en el que «todo se hincha y se afloja como una serpiente enferma que se parte mientras intenta enroscarse» y donde «todo se desarrolla en nudos verbales inextricables». Y, siglos después, es conocida la invectiva de san Bernardo contra los monstruos que adornaban los capiteles de las abadías cluniacenses.

Bernardo parecía oponerse (experimentando su fascinación) a esas violaciones de los principios de proporción e integridad que habían poblado el imaginario helenístico y cristiano e invadido los textos de los bestiarios, centenares de miniaturas y de *marginalia*, y que aparecían incluso en los portales de las catedrales. Se trataba —y solo la lista puede reproducir la sensación de «desproporción» que animaba el mundo de la teratología medieval— de los Acéfalos, con los ojos en los hombros y dos agujeros en el pecho a modo de nariz y boca; de los Andróginos, con un solo seno y ambos órganos genitales; de los Artabantes de Etiopía, que andan inclinados como ovejas; de los Astómatas, que tienen un solo pequeño orificio como boca y se alimentan con una pajita; de los Astomotores, que carecen completamente de boca y se alimentan únicamente de olores; de los Bicéfalos; de los Blemios, sin cabeza y con ojos en la boca y el pecho; de los Centauros; de los Unicornios; de las Quimeras, animales triformes con cabeza de león, parte posterior de dragón y la central de cabra; de los Cíclopes; de los Cinocéfalos con la cabeza de perro, mujeres con colmillos de jabalí, cabello hasta los pies y cola de vaca; de los Grifones, con el cuerpo de águila delante y de león detrás; de los Poncios, con las piernas rectas sin rodilla, el casco de caballo y el falo en el pecho; de otros seres con el labio inferior tan grande que cuando duermen se cubren la cabeza con él; de la Leucrocota, con el cuerpo de burro, el dorso de ciervo, pecho y cola de león, pies de caballo, un cuerno biforcudo, una boca cortada hasta las orejas de las que sale una voz casi humana, y en lugar de dientes un solo hueso; de la Mantícora, con tres hileras de dientes, cuerpo de león, cola de escorpión, ojos azules, tez color sangre, siseo de serpiente; de los Panocios, con orejas tan grandes que caen hasta las rodillas; de los Phitios, con los cuellos larguísimos, pies largos y brazos parecidos a sierras; de los Pigmeos, siempre en lucha contra las grullas, que miden tres palmos y viven a lo sumo siete años y se casan y tienen hijos cada seis meses; de los Sátiros, con la nariz aquilina, los cuernos y la parte inferior caprina. Y siguen serpientes con la cresta en la cabeza que caminan con piernas y tienen siempre la garganta abierta de la que gotea veneno; ratones grandes como lebreles, capturados por mastines porque los gatos no consiguen cazarlos; hombres que andan con las manos; hombres que caminan con las rodillas y tienen ocho dedos por pie; hombres con dos ojos delante y dos detrás; hombres con los testículos tan grandes que les llegan a las rodillas; Esciápodos, con una sola pierna con la que corren rapidísimos y que yerguen cuando descansan, para estar a la sombra de su grandísimo y único pie.

Así pues, al celebrar la proporción y la integridad, la Edad Media padecía la fascinación de lo inmenso y lo desproporcionado. Y este sentimiento se impone precisamente en ese estilo que florece, tanto en las artes como en la literatura, en las islas Británicas durante la segunda mitad del primer milenio, y que se ha definido como «estética hispérica».

El texto más célebre que representa la estética hispérica es la *Hisperica Famina*, una serie de composiciones poéticas (probablemente realizadas como ejercicio retórico en algún *scriptorium* monástico), que contienen descripciones de objetos, acontecimientos y fenómenos naturales. Ningún lector acostumbrado al latín clásico, e incluso al de la decadencia de los primeros

textos cristianos, podía entender ese torrente impetuoso de neo-
logismos nacidos de étimos hebreos, de raíces celtas y de quién
sabe qué otras influencias bárbaras. Baste solo algún ejemplo,
que me parece que puede evocar, si no imágenes precisas, por
lo menos la aglomeración de imágenes que se ven en los Evangelios de Lindisfarne y en manuscritos irlandeses como el *Book
ok Kells*.

Véase esta descripción del mar:[2]

> *Gemellum neptunius collocat ritum fluctus:*
> *protinus spumaticam pollet in littora adsisam*
> *refluamque prisco plicat recessam utero.*
> *Geminum solita flectit in orgium discurrimina:*
> *afroniosa luteum uelicat mallina teminum,*
> *marginosas tranat pullulamine metas*
> *uastaque tumente dodrante inundat freta,*
> *arboreos tellata flectit hornos in arua.*
> *Assiduas littoreum glomerat algas in sinum,*
> *patulas eruit a cautibus marinas,*

2. Un valiente ejemplo de traducción (inglesa) de estos textos se halla en
Michael W. Herren, *The Hisperica Famina*, Toronto, Pontifical Institute of Medieval Studies, 1974: «Neptune's flood has a double movement: / continually it
propels the foamy tide to the shore / and enfolds it within its ancient womb as it
flows backwards. / It directs its customary double motion to a double purpose: /
the foamy tide covers the muddy land, / crosses the shore's boundaries in its
burgeoning, / and floods vast channels in a swelling tidal wave. / It bends the
white ash trees toward the earthen fields, / heaps up mounds of algae on the
shore of the bay, / uproots open limpets from the rock, / tears away purple-co-
loured conchs, / spins the bodies of beasts toward the sandy harbour in great
profusion; / the billowing waters undulate toward the canyons of rock, / and the
foaming storm roars as it swells». El lector que no entiende nada de inglés se
encuentra en la misma situación de un lector de aquel entonces que hubiera sido
educado con el latín escolar.

illitas punicum euellit conchas,
belbecinas multiformi genimine harenosum euoluit
    effigies ad portum,
fluctivagaque scropheas uacillant aequora in termopilas
ac spumaticum fremet tumore bromum.

Y, para llegar a los Evangelios de Lindisfarne, aquí tienen la descripción de una tablilla de escritura:

De tabula
Haec arborea lectis plasmata est tabula fomentis,
quae ex altero climate caeream copulat lituram.
Defidas lignifero intercessu nectit colomellas,
in quis compta lusit c<a>el[l]atura.
Aliud iam latus arboreum maiusculo ductu stipat situm,
uaria scemicatur pictura,
ac comptas artat oras.[3]

Edgar De Bruyne, en su monumental historia de la estética medieval,[4] se demora mucho en el estilo hispérico de la Alta Edad Media y cita un verso de la *Hisperica Famina* donde, para describir un ímpetu de alegría se dice *Ampla pectoralem suscitat vernia cavernam*, «una amplia alegría dilata las cavernas de mi pecho». El estudioso belga vincula estas páginas con la admoni-

---

3. «This wooden tablet was made from choice pieces; / it contains rubbing wax from another region; / a wooden median joins the little divided columns, / on which lovely carving has played. / The other side has a somewhat larger area of wood; / it is fashioned with various painted designs / and has decorated borders.»

4. *Études d'esthétique médiévale*, Brujas, De Tempel, 1946 (ahora París, Albin Michel, 1998, I, pp. 132-141).

ción horaciana sobre los peligros de colocar una cabeza humana en una cerviz equina y plantea un paralelismo entre estos
ejercicios verbales y los *entrelacs* de las miniaturas irlandesas. Ve
inmediatamente esa violación de proporción e integridad en un
estilo en que el detalle se vuelve esencial y donde una riqueza
exuberante de líneas decorativas se impone no para poner de
relieve el tema del texto que comentan, sino por amor a sí mismas, y hace entender (aunque no lo dice) que aquí nos encon-
traríamos ante la única manifestación medieval del «arte por el
arte», del arabesco hecho por amor al arabesco, que a nosotros
nos parece más bien un criterio moderno.

Debemos decir que Edgar De Bruyne, que tiene evidentes
preferencias por un estilo clásico, queda perturbado y trastorna-
do, tanto como san Bernardo, por esos laberintos visuales donde
nos perdemos como en una selva (quizá la «selva oscura» en la
que se perderá siglos después Dante Alighieri), y los compara
justamente con los laberintos verbales de los textos hispéricos,
donde se multiplican los epítetos tal como en la miniatura se
acumulan las curvas sinuosas, los enroscamientos serpentinos de
los que afloran forman zoomorfas y humanoides, pájaros, gatos
casi atónitos, colas. «El enigma verbal que se oculta bajo la perí-
frasis es reproducido en miniatura por el enigma plástico que se
desarrolla en curvas interminables.» Y cita el juicio de Angelo
Mai, que al introducir la *Hisperica Famina* en la Patrologia Latina (PL 90, col. 1188) habla de «stylus autem operis tumidus,
abnormis, exorbitans, obscurus ac saepe inextricabilis».

Por último, muchos han visto en las miniaturas de las islas
Británicas no solo la desproporción, sino también la falta de
integritas. Un historiador insigne como Richard Hamann[5] ano-

5. *Geschichte der Kunst*, Berlín, 1932.

taba cómo, en la miniatura irlandesa, se sustituye el gusto de la composición orgánica con el gusto de una repetición indefinida de signos geométricos, «en lugar de construir un conjunto coherente y organizado».

Lo que llama la atención en estos juicios es que parecen olvidar que, en las miniaturas, el *entrelac* es en cambio una obra maestra de proporción. Al lector curioso que quede fascinado con los laberintos del libro de Lindisfarne le aconsejaría que buscara en internet la entrada «entrelacs»: encontrará distintos sitios donde se ofrecen instrucciones y modelos geométricos para la construcción de *entrelacs*, y verá que, por debajo de ese florecimiento de volutas aparentemente sin regla, se oculta una serie de esquemas matemáticos muy rigurosos, de modo que resulta posible componer *entrelacs* intrincadísimos incluso con el ordenador. No es por reducir la imaginación de los miniaturistas de Lindisfarne a pura informática, sino para decir (como se había sugerido) que cada época tenía su criterio de proporción y, por tanto, las miniaturas de Irlanda y de Northumbria tampoco contradecían ese criterio, sino que lo realizaban de forma propia.

Por otra parte, más allá de su rechazo debido a arraigadas preferencias de gusto, Edgar De Bruyne tampoco conseguía sustraerse al hechizo de ese «beau chaos», de ese «torrent capricieux», de ese «désordre élémentaire et pourtant rythmé comme les vagues de la mer, les souffles du vent, le fracas de la tempête». Ese mar está hecho con cristales de nieve.

¿Por qué Edgar De Bruyne veía hermoso el caos? Porque en esas miniaturas se realiza en su mayor grado el tercer criterio de la belleza, la *claritas*, o sea, la *suavitas coloris*.

La Edad Media estaba prendada de los colores sencillos, nítidos, intensos. Para Isidoro de Sevilla, los mármoles son bellos por su blancura, los metales por la luz que reflejan, y el aire mismo es bello y se denomina *aes-aeris* por el esplendor del *aurum*, es decir, del oro (y, en efecto, como el oro, en cuanto la luz lo acaricia, resplandece). Las piedras preciosas son hermosas por su color, dado que el color no es sino la luz del sol aprisionada y materia purificada. Los ojos son bellos si son luminosos, y los más bellos son los ojos glaucos. Una de las primeras cualidades de un cuerpo bello es la piel sonrosada. En los poetas, esta sensación del color brillante siempre está presente: la hierba es verde, la sangre roja, la leche cándida, una mujer bella tiene para Guinizzelli un «rostro de nieve coloreado de granada» (por no hablar, más tarde, de las claras, frescas, dulces aguas de Petrarca); las visiones místicas de Hildegarda de Bingen nos muestran llamas rutilantes, y la misma belleza del primer ángel caído está hecha de piedras refulgentes como un cielo estrellado, de modo que la innumerable turba de las chispas, resplandeciendo en el fulgor de todos sus ornamentos, aclara el mundo con su luz. La iglesia gótica, a fin de que penetre lo divino en sus naves de otro modo oscuras, está seccionada por hojas de luz que entran por los vitrales y, para dar lugar a esos corredores de luz, se ensancha el espacio de las ventanas y los rosetones, los muros casi se anulan en un juego de contrafuertes y arcos rampantes, y toda la iglesia se construye en función de la irrupción de la luz a través de un calado de estructuras.

Pues bien, las miniaturas de Lindisfarne son un triunfo del color donde los colores están en estado elemental: fulgurante es su acercarse, contrastarse, componerse en una sinfonía de rojos, azules, amarillos, blancos y verdes; el esplendor lo genera el acorde del conjunto, sin dejarse determinar por una luz que envuelve las cosas desde fuera o que hace que el color se desborde más allá de los límites de la figura. En estas páginas la luz parece irradiar de la página, y reluce como gemas que brillan en un cáliz de bronce, como las escamas de una serpiente monstruosa y terrible.

Yo creo que quien hojea este libro sin intenciones filológicas podría experimentar las mismas emociones que experimenta Des Esseintes, el protagonista de *À rebours* de Huysmans, cuando coloca sobre una alfombra suntuosa a su tortuga convertida en joya artificial. Para quienes no la conocen, o no la recuerdan, la historia es la siguiente.

Des Esseintes se había enclaustrado en su morada de campo para aislarse del mundo y concederse todo tipo de voluptuosidades decadentes, en un universo puramente artificial del cual había sido excluida la naturaleza y donde dominaba únicamente el gusto del arte por el arte. Después de haberse embriagado con el sabor corrupto del latín de la decadencia y de los primeros siglos cristianos (ignorando, por desgracia, el estilo hispérico), se apasionó por una alfombra oriental, y siguiendo el brillo de sus reflejos plateados, que emanaban de la urdimbre amarilla y violeta de la lana, se dijo que sería hermoso colocar sobre esa superficie algo que se moviera y encendiera la vivacidad de sus colores. Adquirió entonces una gran tortuga marina e hizo que le doraran el dorso.

En un primer momento se complació de ese efecto, como si hubiera visto un rutilante escudo visigodo con las escamas imbricadas por un artista bárbaro. Pero luego decidió que había que avivar aún más esa coraza y, tomando como modelo un enjambre de flores de un dibujo japonés, decidió engastarle unas piedras preciosas. Descartó inmediatamente el diamante, demasiado corriente y burgués, y por las mismas razones las esmeraldas y los rubíes, el topacio, la amatista y el zafiro. Se dedicó, pues, a buscar piedras más raras, y creo que el resultado final debe dejarse en francés, porque los nombres preciosos de esos minerales (acaso intraducibles) evocan los colores que Des Esseintes quería materializar:

Les feuilles furent serties de pierreries d'un vert accentué et précis: de chrysobéryls verts asperge; des péridots vert poireau; d'olivines vert olive; et elles se détachèrent de branches en almadine en ouwarovite d'un rouge violacé, jetant des paillettes d'un éclat sec de même que ces micas de tartre qui luisent dans l'intérieur des futailles. Pour les fleurs [...] il usa de la cendre bleue [...] Il choisit exclusivement des turquoises de l'Occident, des pierres qui ne sont, à proprement parler, qu'un ivoire fossile imprégné de substances cuivreuses et dont le bleu céladon est engorgé, opaque, sulfureux, comme jauni de bile. Cela fait, il pouvait maintenant enchâsser les pétales de ses fleurs épanouies au milieu du bouquet, de ses fleurs les plus voisines, les plus rapprochés du tronc, avec des minéraux transparents, aux lueurs vitreuses et morbides, aux jets fiévreux et aigres. Il les composa uniquement d'yeux de chat de Ceylan, de cymophanes et des saphirines. Ces trois pierres dardaient en effet, des scintillements mystérieux et pervers, douloureusement arrachés du fond glacé de leur eau trouble [...] Et la bordure de la carapace? [...] Il se décida enfin pour des minéraux dont les reflets devaient s'alterner: pour l'hyacinthe de Compostelle, rouge acajou; l'aigue marine, vert glauque; le rubis-balais, rose vinaigre; les rubis de Sudermaine, ardoise pâle...

Dejamos aquí la descripción de este exquisito trabajo de orfebrería decadente. El efecto final ya satisfacía a Des Esseintes cuando, al cabo de algunos días, la tortuga, oprimida por tanta riqueza mineral, murió. Despidámonos de Des Esseintes y no nos dejemos atrapar por sus languideces de Bajo Imperio. Una vez muerta la tortuga y desaparecida la alfombra de Huysmans, nos quedan las páginas de los Evangelios de Lindisfarne, y creo que podríamos sentirnos autorizados a hojearlas con ese mismo gusto por lo maravilloso, aunque no hayan sido imaginadas por estetas enfermos de estética, sino por monjes que tan solo anhelaban celebrar la palabra divina.

Por otra parte (y lo escribía yo en la introducción del facsímil del *Book of Kells*),[6] se podría divagar sobre estas miniaturas viéndolas como si fueran la traducción visual del *Finnegans Wake* de Joyce (que recibió inspiración de páginas como estas).

Pero quizá sea mejor volver a los países y al clima donde estas páginas fueron miniadas e intentar hallar intacta su fragancia, el gozo de la *claritas*, la sensación venturosa y no exenta de riesgos de una incontinente proporción. Se descubrirá también que en estos pergaminos se plasma, en el modo propio de la imaginación hispérica, un principio de *integritas*: el libro miniado representa una manera orgánica de alternar las imágenes casi realistas de los evangelistas con un juego solo aparentemente decorativo de motivos geométricos y fantásticos que cumple la misma función que los cálices y las patenas cuajadas de gemas, de los paramentos adamascados, de los relicarios de marfil o de plata, todos ellos formas muy medievales y monásticas de cantar las alabanzas de Dios y del texto sagrado. Orgánicamente perfecta es, por tanto, esta ceremonia casi litúrgica hecha de palabras murmuradas en plegaria y de cantos, de luces y de sagrada puesta en escena.

Y sucederá tal vez que (permítanme que, para mantener intacta la cita, transgreda las reglas de la sintaxis) *ampia pectoralem suscitat vernia cavernam*.

---

6. «Foreword», en P. Fox, *Commentary to The Book of Kells*, Lucerna, Faksimile Verlag, 1990, pp. 11-16.

Sobre las *Très Riches Heures*[1]

Me tropecé con las *Très Riches Heures du duc de Berry** cuando tenía poco más de veinte años, en una pequeña edición cartoné que contenía, naturalmente, solo las miniaturas de los meses.

Digo «naturalmente» porque el destino del aficionado no especializado es encontrar siempre ese manuscrito como si consistiera solo en esas doce famosas representaciones. A veces pueden encontrarse en algún libro de arte también otras imágenes, pero se acaba por olvidarlas. Las *Très Riches Heures* han quedado fijadas en ese cliché, como les ha pasado a Beethoven y a Chopin, que muchísimos ya conocen únicamente por la *Sonata al claro de luna* y el *Preludio de la gota*. El fetichismo alienta la pereza, y la pereza da alas al fetichismo. De ambos puede nacer la saciedad. Solo pudiendo hojear la reproducción de todo el manuscrito en la espléndida edición de la Faksimile Verlag, de Lucerna —a quienes no les sea concedida la gracia ya rarísima de tocar el original de Chantilly—, se descubre hasta qué punto son más ricas, inventivas, a veces enigmáticas las *Très Riches*

---

1. Publicado como «Introducción» a *Illuminations of Heaven and Earth. The Glories of the Très Riches Heures du Duc de Berry*, Nueva York, Abrams, 1988.
* Publicado en castellano como *Las muy ricas horas del duque de Berry*.

Heures. Y se entiende por qué los ejecutores testamentarios del duque las llamaron de este modo: «très riches».

Para mí, veinteañero, esas miniaturas fueron de todas formas una vía para acercarme a la Edad Media, que me disponía a estudiar. Es verdad que se trata de una Edad Media tardía, en la que ya vibran muchos presagios del Renacimiento: pero yo, mientras miraba las *Très Riches Heures*, leía el *Otoño de la Edad Media* de Huizinga. Vivía la gracia, la languidez de esa época en su ocaso, y en ella revivía yo los siglos que tenía a su espalda. A fin de cuentas, todos hemos conocido y tal vez entendido la civilización de los romanos a través de las ruinas que se remontaban solo al Bajo Imperio.

Mi lectura de entonces era sin duda también estetizante, neogótica, decadente. Y yo le hacía una injusticia a las *Très Riches Heures*, resaltaba solo su aspecto decorativo.

De este manuscrito se pueden ofrecer otras lecturas. Naturalmente, la del crítico e historiador del arte, que trata de datar las imágenes, busca las influencias iconográficas, evalúa la calidad de su ejecución... Aunque no es esto lo que quiero sugerir al lector apasionado, pero no especializado. Probaré otros recorridos, que sean recorridos de la imaginación más que de la filología y del rigor histórico.

Uno de esos recorridos lo exploré más tarde, cuando descubrí los estudios históricos de la escuela de los *Annales*. Las *Très Riches Heures* son un documento insustituible para comprender la vida material, las costumbres, la sociedad, los gustos de la época. Por eso son fundamentales las miniaturas de los meses, pero a partir de ahí pueden explorarse también las otras imágenes, en busca de indicios menores, a veces ocultos.

Las miniaturas de los meses son una gran reserva de información sobre la ropa y las armaduras. Nos cuentan cómo se preparaba la mesa, qué comidas y bebidas se servían; cuál era la relación con los animales domésticos, cómo se llevaban a cabo los trabajos de temporada; nos dicen cómo eran las herramientas agrícolas, cómo vivían campesinos y pastores, cuáles eran las técnicas de cultivo de los campos y la arquitectura de los jardines. Nos hablan de la forma de las colmenas, de los arreos de los caballos, del arrastre de los carros. Y también nos ofrecen una reseña de castillos, de arquitecturas religiosas, de obras de construcción en plena actividad, nos hablan de interiores de iglesias y de palacios, de estatuas, de estandartes... Los detalles son tan minuciosos y fieles que a partir de ellos algunos historiadores de arte han logrado fechar las diferentes imágenes.

Las *Très Riches Heures* son un documental cinematográfico, una máquina visual que nos cuenta la vida de una época. Ninguna película podrá igualar jamás la fidelidad, el esplendor, la conmovedora belleza de esa reconstrucción.

Segundo recorrido, la caza de lo maravilloso. Este manuscrito es pobre de *marginalia* grotescos que, en cambio, son tan evidentes en otras obras. Solo de vez en cuando encontramos a un cazador o a un pajarero, o esas representaciones del mundo del revés que en su momento Baltrusaitis nos invitó a descubrir en los márgenes de muchos manuscritos devotos. Como si los miniaturistas no hubieran osado insistir en representaciones «divertidas» para un libro destinado a la oración y a los ojos púdicos de la familia del duque. Pero se trata de prestar atención, porque el gusto medieval por los *babouins* (o *baewyn*, como los llamaban) se manifiesta en las letras capitulares. Estas son, ante todo, una galería de retratos, y, si rebuscamos bien, ahí encontramos a una criatura satírica y peluda, justo al principio de un Ave Maris Stella; allá un oso, ahí un cojo, o un perro, o un conejo, que parecen querer sorprender al duque en oración, distraerlo de la plegaria, o hacerlo reflexionar sobre algún devoto proverbio o parábola que la imagen hubiera podido traerle a la mente.

La distracción. Se trata de un tercer recorrido. El libro está destinado a la meditación, la oración y la concentración. La Edad Media fue rica en invectivas contra las imágenes de las iglesias y los claustros, que podían distraer los ojos curiosos del coloquio con Dios. Todos conocen la célebre invectiva de san Bernardo contra la escultura románica: «Quid facit illa ridicula monstruositas, mira quaedam de formis formositas ac formosa deformitas? Quid ibi immundae simiae? Quid feri leones? Quid monstruosi centauri? Quid semihomines? Quid maculosae tigrides?» (*Apologia ad Guillelmum*). Y por otro lado, añadía Bernardo, ¿por qué llegar a esas imágenes de santos y de santos demasiado bellos, a esas reliquias cubiertas de oro?

Ni que decir tiene que desde los tiempos de san Bernardo hasta los del duque de Berry habían pasado por lo menos dos siglos, y la tensión mística, el rigorismo se habían atenuado. Además, en el palacio del duque estamos en la corte y no en un convento; y, por último, el duque es un curioso, no solo un coleccionista atraído por libros espléndidos y objetos de gran valor artístico, sino también un precursor de las *Wunderkammern* barrocas: su tesoro contenía maravillas como cuernos de liocornio, dientes de ballena, nueces de coco, conchas de los siete mares y el anillo de compromiso de san José. Ese hombre sofisticado tenía ojos curiosos y golosos, y de la distracción había hecho un arte. Y por eso podemos imaginárnoslo, arrodillado en oración, mientras sus labios recitan mecánicamente un salmo, con los ojos que se demoran no tanto en el tema sagrado de la imagen, sino en los fondos, en los jardines, en las colinas, en los castillos, en los ropajes de las damas, en las florituras de los márgenes.

No olvidemos que hay algunas secuencias, por ejemplo la de la pasión, que tienen un ritmo y un dramatismo cinematográficos, con bruscos cambios de escena, de hora del día, con pasos de la luz a las tinieblas. No le faltaríamos al respeto si pensáramos en el duque de Berry mientras, en la penumbra de la iglesia, sigue ávidamente las páginas de su libro tal como hoy en día nosotros vemos la televisión. Espléndido compromiso entre misticismo y estética, deber y placer, meditación y libre juego de la imaginación, las *Très Riches Heures* nos ayudan a entender mucho de la Edad Media, una época en que las manifestaciones de pública virtud acompañaban las manifestaciones de pública lujuria con gran desenvoltura. Una época en que tal vez no se pecaba más que en la nuestra, pero a buen seguro se hacía con menos vergüenza, aun en el momento mismo en que se hacía profesión de fervor religioso y austera moralidad.

Este objeto aparentemente tan delicado y precioso, esta obra maestra de orfebrería, esta suprema manifestación del artificio culto y sofisticado, es también un documento profundamente humano porque, si sabemos leerlo, nos dice mucho de las debilidades de nuestros antepasados bajo-medievales (y de las de sus antepasados).

El hombre medieval solía encontrar dificultades en distinguir el placer de los sentidos del placer del alma. Tenía un gusto, mucho más desarrollado que el nuestro, por los colores nítidos, bien extendidos, intensos, amaba el esplendor del oro, el fulgor de las joyas, la irrupción de la luz, y su juego en el verde de los campos, en el azul del agua, en los vestidos de brocado... Y aun así, en el triunfo del color, de la luz, del oro (y tales son las *Très Riches Heures*), veía también una manifestación del poder divino. Para nosotros, el duque de Berry se distraía siguiendo la sinfonía de los rojos y los azules, acariciaba quizá con los dedos el oro que incrusta cada página de este libro. Pero al hacerlo, él, el duque, tenía la convicción de estar celebrando, y de una manera sumamente agradable, la presencia de la divinidad en el mundo. Con bellísima hipocresía se sentía virtuoso y humilde en la distracción suntuosa que se concedía.

En cuanto a los hermanos Limbourg, o a quienes trabajaron después de ellos, se aplicaban para estimular a su mecenas; y véase cómo consiguen componer, con gran sensibilidad por soluciones coloristas casi abstractas, orlas monocromáticas, caídas rojas de réprobos, asambleas doradas de beatos, cascadas azules de ángeles. Hay una miniatura donde, para obtener un efecto decorativo de loriga, de dorso escamoso de pez precioso, el miniaturista tiene el valor de representar a un tropel de santos todos ellos de espaldas, de manera que aparezcan solo, en su plena rotundidad, sus aureolas. El duque fantaseaba, y pensaba que el paraíso es una espléndida vitrina de joyas, muy parecida a su tesoro.

¿Otras lecturas? El libro está incompleto, tiene páginas sin letras miniadas, algunas blancas, marcadas solo por las rayas trazadas para alguna miniatura futura. Es un libro no homogéneo que revela manos distintas. De este modo cuenta la historia de su fabricación, hace alusión a los años de trabajo que costó, deja vislumbrar una historia de interrupciones, vueltas a empezar, correcciones; en definitiva, es la representación (una vez más casi cinematográfica) del laboratorio donde fue concebido, del largo tiempo de preparación, ejecución, cambios de idea, interpolaciones, durante el cual fue haciéndose poco a poco. Es el monumento celebrativo erigido al propio *atelier*.

Hay otras lecturas posibles. Por ejemplo, la búsqueda de todos los temas iconográficos que la Edad Media elaboró, y que aquí se encuentran como en una enciclopedia. O la maliciosa identificación de creencias y prácticas que la Iglesia oficialmente condenaba pero que la cultura de corte admitía, y pienso en la abundancia de referencias astrológicas, muy precisas, que implican una competencia elaborada, un discurso habitual, y no solo en los círculos que están encima de los meses, sino también en esa página reveladora del folio 14, el Hombre Anatómico, que hace pensar ya en las representaciones de las relaciones entre micro y macrocosmos que encontraremos en los magos del Renacimiento, en Robert Fludd o en Athanasius Kircher. Pero no olvidemos que el libro se produce pocas décadas antes del nacimiento de Marsilio Ficino, mientras están prefigurándose en la Florencia humanista las condiciones para una nueva afirmación pública de la astrología y la magia.

Tal vez sea preciso detenernos aquí. Tal vez sería poco respetuoso hacia el lector sugerir otras claves de lectura. Las *Très Riches Heures* son un objeto extraordinario precisamente porque, obra abierta, alientan mil itinerarios distintos de la imaginación. Que el lector lo abra al azar, elija la propia puerta de entrada y luego recorra él solo este *Hortus Deliciarum*.

¿Por qué Kircher?

No recuerdo cuándo me tropecé con el nombre de Athanasius Kircher por primera vez en mi vida, pero sin duda recuerdo cuándo empecé a hojear sus libros para extraer algunos de sus fantasiosos iconismos. Era hacia finales de 1959, cuando comencé a recopilar material para una *Historia figurada de las invenciones*, que luego publicó Bompiani, y para la cual no solo visité bibliotecas sino también archivos de museos de la ciencia, como el (riquísimo) archivo del Deutsches Museum de Munich.

¿Por qué recuerdo este hecho, que de por sí interesaría tan solo a una poco deseable autobiografía mía? Para decir que por aquel entonces a Kircher se lo recordaba solo como anticipador de máquinas futuribles, como la fotografía o el cine, como un Verne *ante litteram*, y para todo lo demás sus textos yacían en las bibliotecas, consultados por algún surrealista rezagado o por algún cazador de textos bizarros y obsoletos como Baltrusaitis. Si miro las bibliografías del *Athanasius Kircher S.J., Master of a Hundred Arts* de P. Conor Reilly (Wiesbaden-Roma, Edizioni del Mondo, 1974) y de Valerio Rivosecchi (*Esotismo in Roma barocca*, Roma, Bulzoni, 1982), encuentro una lista de títulos, en su mayoría artículos, que es inferior a la de las obras kircherianas. En Italia diría yo que el primer interés seriamente manifestado por Kircher —que trabajó y vivió en Roma— son las actas del congreso que se le dedicó en 1985 (*Enciclopedismo in Roma barocca*, Venecia, Marsilio, 1986), donde no es una casualidad que aparezcan, entre los prologuistas, pioneros kircherianos como Eugenio Battisti y Giulio Macchi.

Como curiosidad, cuando a principios de los años ochenta empecé a coleccionar todas las obras del fuldense, se podía conseguir un Kircher por algo así como ochocientas mil liras. Hoy, dejando aparte el *Oedipus* completo, la *China*, el *Mundus Subterraneus* o la *Musurgia*, que están alcanzando la cifra de varias decenas de millones de liras cada uno, cuestan algún que otro millón también las obras menores, sin ilustraciones, como el *Archetypon Politicum*, modestísimo desde el punto de vista de la bibliofilia.

Cito estos datos para decir que, más allá de la atención de los doctos, en los últimos veinte años se ha desencadenado hacia Kircher la atención de los aficionados y los bibliófilos. Las razones no serían extrañas, los libros de Kircher están espléndidamente ilustrados, pero los antiguos catálogos del siglo XIX los daban como poco solicitados, lo cual nos indica que también el concepto de ilustración apreciable varía con los años.

La fascinación de Kircher se debe también a la dificultad de clasificarlo. Se puede elaborar una lista de afirmaciones equivocadas que Kircher hizo en el curso de su vida, libro por libro, y reducir al pobre jesuita a un autodidacta que carecía de espíritu crítico y que nunca atinó una. En este sentido, Kircher pertenecería a esa categoría denominada en francés «les fous littéraires», que incluye también a los locos científicos, sobre los que existen catálogos y bibliotecas especializadas. Triste destino para un hombre que, poderosísimo en su orden, y estimadísimo por sus contemporáneos, incluidas personas como Leibniz, se vería relegado a ítem de esos mismos museos de teratologías naturales cuyo iniciador fue él mismo, portento apropiado solo para una *Wunderkammer*.

Por otra parte, en sus obras suelen mezclarse de forma inextricable lo que hoy llamaríamos el dato científico y la concesión a la fascinación por lo excepcional, así como a hipótesis arriesgadas y seguramente imprudentes. Véanse, por ejemplo, sus estudios de egiptología, desde el *Prodromus coptus sive aegyptiacus* (1636) y el *Obeliscus Pamphilius* (1650), a través del monumental *Oedypus Aegyptiacus* (1652-1654), hasta la *Obelisci aegyptiaci interpretatio hieroglyphica* (1666) y la *Sphynx mystagoga* (1676). Kircher estudió los obeliscos romanos y cualquier otro testimonio que pudiera encontrar en Roma, y elaboró una teoría para descifrar el lenguaje jeroglífico apasionante pero totalmente falsa. Y aun así, sin los dibujos de sus libros, Champollion nunca hubiera podido estudiar a fondo el mismo tema y encontrar (pero tenía en su poder también la estela trilingüe de Rosetta) la clave adecuada para leer todas aquellas imágenes. De modo que aún hoy en día, a Kircher se lo define como el padre de la egiptología, aunque fuera un padre demasiado fantasioso.

Podríamos ser generosos y acreditarle solo lo que atinó. En *China* (1667), gracias a los informes de sus hermanos jesuitas, recopila y documenta una extraordinaria variedad de noticias sobre ese país; al interpretarlas a su manera, muchas veces se equivoca, traicionado también por la fantasía de los grabadores (fantasía que, por otro lado, siempre contribuía a avivar). Con todo, entendió que los ideogramas chinos tenían orígenes icónicos (parece extraño, pero personajes ilustres como Bacon o Wilkins no lo sospecharon), e intuyó el futuro de una especie de antropología cultural que había de hacerse viajando por continentes remotos y desconocidos y recopilando todo tipo de documentos (Kircher fue un buen ejemplo de explorador incansable que, sin moverse de su casa, ponía a trabajar a sus hermanos).

En el *Ars magna lucis et umbrae* (1646), sobre todo en la edición de 1671, entre invenciones de teatros catóptricos y estudios esciatéricos, se queda a un paso de inventar el cine; en el *Ars magna sciendi* (1669), de inspiración luliana y repleto de análisis combinatorios, propone sugestiones que aún hoy siguen impresionando a los estudiosos de informática; aunque, a fin de cuentas, sobre ambos temas era un epígono: la cámara oscura no la inventó él y de ella ya había hablado Della Porta; en la linterna mágica había pensado ya Huygens, y la había vuelto popular Thomas Rasmussen Walgenstein; en los prodigios de la combinatoria lo había precedido Raimundo Lulio.

Lo cierto es que Kircher entendió que debe usarse el microscopio, y cómo, además de que las pestilencias se debían a microorganismos; tuvo miedo de ser galileano, pero intentó la solución intermedia propuesta por Tycho Brahe que, para aquel entonces, no era en absoluto despreciable: falsa pero ingeniosa. Por no hablar de las observaciones sobre los volcanes, que por cierto había visitado personalmente tantas veces, y, hace poco, han sido precisamente los vulcanólogos los que han vuelto a publicar un bello facsímil del *Mundus Subterraneus*.[1]

Por otra parte, en su tiempo también se tomaron muy en serio su obra aquellos que compartían muy pocas opiniones con él (Huygens decía que Kircher «había de ser apreciado más por su piedad que por su habilidad»). En cualquier caso, aún antes de que saliera el libro, Oldenburg le escribía a Boyle al respecto, Spinoza le había enviado un ejemplar a Huygens, Ste-

---

1. *Mundus Subterraneus in XII Libros digestus. Editio Tertia*, a cargo de Gian Battista Vai, Bolonia, Forni, 2004.

no lo menciona en algún sitio, el mismo Oldenburg escribe una recensión en el primer volumen de *The Philosophical Transactions of the Royal Society* y en el número siguiente imprime una sección del libro (*An experiment of a way of preparing a liquor that shall sink into a color the whole body of marble...*).[2]

Naturalmente, tampoco en esta obra se desmiente Kircher: voraz e insaciable nos habla de la luna y del sol, de las mareas, de las corrientes oceánicas, de los eclipses, de aguas y fuegos subterráneos, de ríos, lagos y manantiales del Nilo, de salinas y minas, de fósiles, metales, insectos y hierbas, de destilación, fuegos artificiales, generación espontánea y pansmermia; ahora bien, con idéntica desenvoltura nos cuenta (y nos hace ver) dragones y gigantes (y también es verdad que naturalistas ilustres, desde Aldrovandi a Johnston, no podían prescindir de los dragones: al fin y al cabo, Kircher mismo demuestra saber algo sobre las iguanas, y un naturalista que haya visto o haya oído hablar de las iguanas puede tomarse en serio también los dragones).

De todos los aspectos del *Mundus*, más allá de su interés geológico, hay uno de enorme importancia para la historia de la cultura y, me gustaría decir, para la afirmación de una mentalidad científica contra el delirio ocultista.

En el decimoprimer libro del *Mundus*, Kircher decide tratar la alquimia. Lo hace como historiador y estudioso experimental: por un lado, se relee toda la tradición alquímica, desde las fuentes antiguas (obviamente empieza por Hermes Trismegisto, pero no descuida fuentes coptas y hebreas, además de la tradición árabe) hasta el Pseudo-Lulio, Arnaldo de Vilanova, Roger Bacon, Basilius Valentinus, etcétera; por el otro, monta en su laboratorio (y nos hace ver las imágenes) varios tipos de horno, recopila recetas seculares, las experimenta, critica su vaguedad o vanidad, y está claro que para probar (y volver a probar) toda una serie de preceptos tradicionales acoge en su corte a una plétora de embusteros a fin de que le enseñen sus artilugios, y así llegar a comprender los fundamentos que hoy diríamos «racionales», es decir, explicables experimentalmente sin echar mano de ninguna hipótesis de piedra filosofal.

De este modo, Kircher distingue entre quienes creen que la transmutación alquímica es imposible (o posible solo por intervención divina o diabólica), pero persiguen igualmente las investigaciones químicas con otros objetivos y hacen metalurgia, y quienes venden imitaciones de oro y plata y comercian con sus propios embustes.

No era algo baladí para sus tiempos medirse críticamente con Paracelso y, sobre todo (en el capítulo séptimo del decimoprimer libro), arremeter contra autoridades reconocidas como Sendivogius o Robert Fludd, además de asestar sablazos casi de exorcista contra la tradición rosacruz que llevaba casi cuarenta años seduciendo a media Europa. De acuerdo, se había entablado una batalla de la cultura contrarreformista contra la tradición protestante de la que procedían los primeros libelos rosacruces pero, en definitiva, Kircher se bate por una visión más racional y experimental de la química futura, en pleno siglo XVII y cuando la tradición alquímica continuaría tranquilamente hasta los masones del siglo XIX y —a juzgar por muchos textos en circulación todavía hoy, que celebran la sabiduría de la Tradición— no acaba de morirse, al menos en sus aspectos místico-herméticos.

Podría concluirse, entonces, que en el libro maestro kircheriano (quisiera decir su Tariffa) hay un empate: mucho ha adivinado, en mucho se ha equivocado, y los malignos insinuarán que, al haberse ocupado de todo, y en decenas de millares de páginas, desde un punto de vista estadístico no podía no pasarle precisamente eso: atinar un poco sí y un poco no, como si estuviera haciendo una apuesta.

Sin embargo, sigue abierta la cuestión de por qué Kircher nos apasiona. Yo diría que nos fascina por la misma razón por la que se ha equivocado tanto. Por su voracidad, y por su bulimia científica, por su ansia enciclopédica, y por el hecho de haber servido a su propia pasión mientras se encontraba, y no era culpa suya, a medio camino entre dos épocas de la enciclopedia. La primera, la grecorromana (piénsese en Plinio) y medieval, por la cual el enciclopedista recopilaba cuanto había oído decir, sin preocuparse por verificarlo; la segunda, la de la *Encyclopédie* ilustrada, en la que el enciclopedista dirigía el trabajo de una multitud de expertos y cada uno hablaba solo de lo que conocía por experiencia directa. Kircher habla de todo, incluso de oídas, pero de todo quiere dar una prueba, una imagen, un diagrama, sus leyes de funcionamiento, sus causas y efectos. Llegado con retraso, o con adelanto, Kircher habla en tono científico de cosas sobre las que se equivoca, y nunca renuncia a hablar de todo.

Desde luego, la razón principal de nuestra fascinación por él es aquello en lo que no trabajó directamente, pero en lo que sin duda reparó: los iconismos.

Este hombre supo activar la imaginación de sus colaboradores empujándolos a inventar, junto con él, el más extraordinario de los teatros barrocos. Todo lo que hay de Kircher detrás de esa empresa nos lo indica el hecho de que, de un libro a otro, parece casi como si la misma mano hubiera dibujado siempre las imágenes. En los iconismos de Kircher la pretensión de la exactitud científica genera el más disparatado delirio de la fantasía, de modo que resulta verdaderamente imposible discernir lo verdadero de lo falso, más que en la obra escrita.

En el fondo, no es una casualidad que Kircher haya sido amado por algunos surrealistas. Surrealista es su manera de encarar el conocimiento. Es un cazador de lo maravilloso, y su poética, y la justificación de muchos de sus errores, podemos encontrarla en esa dedicatoria que le hacía al emperador Fernando III al principio del tercer libro del *Oedipus*, donde las configuraciones jeroglíficas se vuelven una suerte de dispositivo alucinatorio:

Desarrollo ante tus ojos, o Sagradísimo César, el polimorfo reino del Morfeo Jeroglífico: digo de un teatro dispuesto en inmensa variedad de monstruos, y no de desnudos monstruos de la naturaleza, sino de un teatro tan adornado por Quimeras enigmáticas de una antigua sabiduría que confió en que los ingenios sagaces pudieran localizar en él desmedidos tesoros de ciencia, no sin provecho para las letras. A este lado el Can de Bubastis, el León Saítico, el Cabrío Mendesio, el Cocodrilo espantoso por sus horrendas fauces de par en par abiertas descubren los ocultos significados de la divinidad, de la naturaleza, del espíritu de la Sabiduría Antigua, bajo el umbrátil juego de las imágenes. A este otro lado, los sitibundos Dípsodas, los Áspides virulentos, las astutas Mangostas, los crueles Hipopótamos, los monstruosos Dragones, el sapo con el vientre abultado, el caracol con la concha retorcida, el gusano peludo e innumerables espectros muestran la prodigiosa cadena ordenada que se extiende en los sagrarios de la naturaleza. Se presentan aquí mil exóticas especies de cosas en otras y otras imágenes transformadas por la metamorfosis, convertidas en figuras humanas y de nuevo restauradas en sí mismas en mutuo entrelazamiento, la ferinidad con la humanidad, y esta con la artificiosa divinidad; y por último, la divinidad que, en palabras de Porfirio, fluye por el universo entero, contrae con todos los entes un monstruoso connubio; donde ahora, sublime por el rostro variado, alzando la cerviz canina, se presentan el Cinocéfalo, y el malvado Ibis, y el Esparaván embozado en una máscara rostrada [...] y donde aún atrayendo con virginal aspecto, bajo el envoltorio del Escarabajo, se cela el acúleo del Escorpión [...] [todo esto y mucho más, enumerado en cuatro páginas] contemplamos en este pantomorfo teatro de Naturaleza, desplegado ante nuestra mirada, bajo el velo alegórico de una oculta significación.

Es difícil clasificar a Kircher, que vivió toda su existencia con un pie en su «pantomorfo» teatro, y el otro en el control *de visu* de los datos que recopilaba. Personaje barroco como pocos, Arcimboldo de la historia de la ciencia, en nuestros días ha acabado por hechizar más a los soñadores que a los científicos.

Pero, en el fondo, lo que le debemos a Kircher es la idea de que con la ciencia y la técnica se puede soñar. Algo que cada científico sabe, salvo que mas allá de cierto límite se contiene; y algo que sabe todo autor de ciencia ficción, salvo que se propone el proyecto de traspasar ese límite. También en este caso Kircher viaja a medio camino, entre la preocupación por la exactitud del científico (más allá de la cual, sin embargo, intenta siempre ir) y la fantasía del fabulador (que, empero, siempre intenta limitar).

Quizá nosotros releemos (y sobre todo re-miramos) a Kircher precisamente por esa tensión que fue felizmente incapaz de componer.

Mi Migne, y el otro[1]

Mi historia con el abate Migne empieza así. En todas las clases de bachillerato se hacen jueguecitos insensatos, para pasar el tiempo y garantizar la cohesión social. Nosotros, por razones a estas alturas imponderables, en los años del instituto nos habíamos dividido en dos grupos, cada uno de los cuales eligió una palabra mágica, y el juego consistía en ver cada mañana quién entraba en clase antes y escribía el lema en la pizarra, el *Shibbolet*, el mantra, la palabra de orden de su clan. También la elección de la palabra mágica fue casual, quién sabe cómo nacen esas cosas...

El primer grupo se había quedado fascinado con el término *Boletus satanas* (una seta venenosa) oído en la clase de ciencias; el segundo (el mío, y quién sabe por qué) había captado como extraño, misterioso, evocativo el nombre de Migne, pronunciado por el profesor de filosofía que, al hablarnos de la filosofía medieval y patrística (evidentemente estábamos en primero), nos había citado, como monumentos imprescindibles, las dos colecciones de la Patrología Griega y de la Patrología Latina de Migne. Quizá nos impresionara el número de volúmenes: 247 para las dos series de la Patrología Griega y 221 para la Patrología

---

1. Publicado como introducción a R. Howard Bloch, *Il Plagiario di Dio*, Milán, Sylvestre Bonnard, 2002.

Latina; y eso que todavía no los habíamos visto en vivo, en su majestuoso formato infolio, capaces de ocupar toda una pared de biblioteca, o toda la sala, según el tamaño de la misma.

En cualquier caso, nos abalanzábamos a la pizarra y escribíamos o Migne o Boletus. No recuerdo qué grupo consiguió la mejor puntuación (al final uno se cansa de estos juegos), pero desde luego —y lo repito, por razones imponderables— el abate Migne había entrado en mi vida. A diferencia de lo que les ocurrió a otros compañeros de clase, entró y se quedó. Tal vez era una señal del cielo: más tarde escribiría mi tesis sobre la filosofía medieval, he seguido ocupándome de la Edad Media en el curso de mi vida y la consulta del Migne se ha convertido en costumbre frecuente. Es fácil decir que muchos de los textos publicados por Migne ya han ido apareciendo en los años siguientes (es más, podemos hablar ya de un siglo y medio) en ediciones críticas más seguras. También para estos textos, para un primer contacto, el Migne sigue siendo fundamental, porque ahí se encuentra todo junto, por no hablar de los textos que todavía son localizables exclusivamente en sus páginas. Tanto es así que el editor Brepols sigue reimprimiendo el Migne y las bibliotecas lo compran.

Como coleccionista de libros antiguos, me habría gustado tener un día todo el Migne, por lo menos la Patrología Latina. Es difícil encontrar una colección completa en algún anticuario, pero si uno se pone a buscar, un volumen aquí y otro allá, sin preocuparse de que sean todos de la misma camada, se podría reunir, y la cifra final no sería completamente astronómica. La que es sideral es la cifra del nuevo apartamento, por lo menos de tres habitaciones, que el coleccionista tendría que comprarse o alquilar para guardar todos sus volúmenes.

Ahora mismo, el sueño es realizable por vía digital: por una cifra que hace años ya era de cincuenta mil dólares, se puede adquirir el Migne latino completo en cinco disquetes (o abonarse a la consulta vía internet), con texto original, prefacios, aparato crítico e índices. Con dos toques de teclado pueden encontrarse todas las veces que aparece un determinado término e imprimir los textos. Fabuloso.

Mi historia con Migne no acaba aquí. Ya estaba yo estupefacto de cómo un solo hombre, trabajando con manuscritos o antiguas ediciones de antes del siglo XIX, transcribiendo a mano, entregando luego esas hojas al impresor y, por último, corrigiendo las galeradas, había podido completar tamaña empresa. No dudaba de que se habría valido de algún colaborador (yo no sabía que eran centenares) y, aun así, admiraba a aquel humilde cura, nacido a principios del siglo XIX y fallecido setenta y cinco años después, y me conmovía pensando en sus ojos ya deteriorados, encorvado sobre sus sudados papeles consumiendo su vida a la sombra de algún claustro (porque, a nuestros oídos italianos, el *abbé* francés, que a la postre significa padre, cura seglar, reverendo, me sonaba como «abad» y, por tanto, a Migne le atribuía yo monásticas virtudes, como al aún más venerable Mabillon).

Salvo que, creciendo en edad y sabiduría (además de en habilidad de coleccionista), descubrí que en el currículum de Migne las dos Patrologías eran solo la punta del iceberg. Debajo había, solo por citar algo, un *Scripturae Sacrae Cursus Completus*, de veintiocho volúmenes, un *Theologiae Cursus Completus*, también de veintiocho volúmenes, las *Démonstrations Évangéliques*, de veinte volúmenes, la *Collection Intégrale et Universelle des Orateurs Sacrés* en dos series, nada menos que de ciento dos volúmenes, la *Summa Aurea de Laudibus Beatae Mariae Virginis*, de trece volúmenes, la *Encyclopédie Théologique*, de ciento setenta y un volúmenes, por no hablar de otras recopilaciones de escritos de santo Tomás, santa Teresa y otros. Descubrí por último que Migne, que evidentemente no se privaba de nada, había publicado también —como tomo cuarenta y ocho de la *Encyclopédie Théologique*— un *Dictionnaire des Sciences Occultes* (y ese lo tengo), que contiene en apéndice un *Traité Historique des Dieux et des Démons du Paganisme* de Benjamin Binet, y una *Réponse à l'Histoire des Oracles de M. de Fontenelle* del reverendo padre Baltus. Es verdad que aclaré que se trataba de una reedición del *Dictionnaire Infernal* de Collin de Plancy, enriquecido casi como un *collage* con artículos tomados de otras publicaciones del autor, pero incluso volver a publicar obras ajenas corregidas y actualizadas era siempre un hermoso *tour de force*.

Hasta que conocí a Howard Bloch, justo cuando él acababa de publicar el libro que se disponen a leer en traducción italiana, y del que inmediatamente me hizo amable obsequio. Una revelación. Migne no era solo un genio de la organización editorial y las finanzas, era asimismo un explotador de mano de obra intelectual y —digámoslo también— un hombre de poquísimos escrúpulos, por no definirlo como un aventurero, y quién sabe en qué se habría convertido si, en lugar de traficar con textos sagrados y pergaminos vetustos, hubiera podido trabajar con cadenas de televisión y redes de internet.

De modo que el libro de Bloch se presenta como una lectura increíble y apasionante incluso para quienes nunca hayan tenido entre sus manos un volumen de la Patrología y sean insensibles a las bellezas de ese latín medieval, corrompido y maltrecho, que se deshacía en la lengua decadente del Des Esseintes de *À rebours*.

Espero de verdad que esta extraordinaria figura de sinvergüenza genial, benefactor de las humanas letras y de sí mismo, pueda fascinar al lector tanto como me ha fascinado a mí (aun algo desengañado porque, cuando los mitos caen, nos dejan un regusto amargo en la boca).

El extraño caso de la Hanau 1609[1]

Cuando el coleccionista tiene en su poder el ejemplar de un libro raro, que lleva deseando mucho tiempo, y se prepara para alguna forma de colación, suele temblar ante la idea de una simple alternativa: o bien su ejemplar corresponde a la descripción de los catálogos más acreditados, y llega el triunfo, o bien parece que le falta algo, y llega la desesperación. En contados casos el desaliento se tiñe de una tenue esperanza, si la carencia, por ejemplo, de una lámina, permite una búsqueda para llegar a una *made-up copy* que satisfaga por lo menos los criterios de integridad, ya que no puede aspirar a los de la perfección.

Hay una tercera posibilidad: que el ejemplar huela a incompleto, pero que los catálogos no estén de acuerdo sobre los criterios de integridad, e incluso las más atrevidas colaciones den resultados distintos. En esos casos, la búsqueda se vuelve doble: por un lado, intenta encontrar el elemento o los elementos que faltan; por el otro, intenta componer las aparentes discrepancias de los catálogos. Doble intriga policíaca, que podría inclu-

1. Una primera versión se publicó con el mismo título en *L'Esopo*, n.º 40, 1988. Con el mismo título y algunas añadiduras salió en un volumen, en edición no venal, Milán, Bompiani, 1989. Esta tercera versión aporta algunos datos añadidos en lo que concierne a la colación final.

so concluirse victoriosamente en todas las circunstancias, cuando se descubriera que no existe un ejemplar estándar del libro porque, por varias peripecias, todos sus ejemplares son por definición el resultado de una fusión.

Este es el caso del *Amphitheatrum Sapientiae Aeternae* de Heinrich Khunrath, conocido por lo general en la edición Hanau 1609. Quizá mi investigación no aporte nada nuevo por lo que concierne al *Amphitheatrum* en cuanto «tipo», pero probablemente diga algo sobre algunas de sus «ocurrencias» (o ejemplares físicos). Desde luego constituye una reflexión sobre la manera como los bibliógrafos y los historiadores hablan al respecto: se tiene la impresión de que la mayor parte de ellos han revoloteado a su alrededor, como mariposas nocturnas enloquecidas, a la pálida luz de algunas descripciones previas, algunos habiendo visto con seguridad un solo ejemplar, otros ninguno. La historia de muchas doctas colaciones suele ser una mera historia de citas intertextuales en cadena: los catálogos no hablan de los libros sino de otros catálogos. Como decía Dennis Duveen al presentar la segunda edición de su *Bibliotheca Alchemica et Chemica*, expresiones como «Not in Duveen» y «Not in Ferguson» suelen significar solo que el coleccionista no tenía ni las ganas ni el dinero para hacerse con ese libro, y que, por consiguiente, la ausencia de una edición no significa que, como dicen otros catálogos, se trate de una obra «de la plus insigne rareté».

KHUNRATH

Brunet (III, p. 658) dice que el *Amphitheatrum* es «obra singular pero poco buscada». Pero un siglo antes, Lenglet du Fresnoy avisa en su bibliografía de que «malgré plusieures éditions, ce libre ne laisse paz d'être assez rare». Diría que la obra es singular, desde luego; ahora está solicitada pero no puede decirse que sea rarísima, por lo menos en la edición Hanau 1609 que aparece en varias colecciones y bibliotecas.[2] El problema, lo veremos, es cómo aparece.

Aun admitiendo que no haya estado muy solicitada hasta tiempos más recientes, voy a ofrecer algunas informaciones esenciales.

Heinrich Khunrath, a veces Kunrath, otras veces Kuhrath, Kunraht, Cunrath, Cunrad, Conrad (de modo que se lo toma por su hermano Conrad Khunrath, véase Ferguson I, pp. 462-464), nace en Leipzig en 1560, estudia medicina en Leipzig y en Basilea, donde sigue cursos de espagírica junto al místico protestante Johannes Arndt (cfr. BPH, p. 33). Alquimista, más en la vertiente simbólica que en la operativa, sobre todo en el *Amphitheatrum*.[3] Muere a los cuarenta y cinco años, en 1605. En el retrato que aparece en el *Amphitheatrum Sapientiae Aeternae*, Khunrath parece mucho más viejo, pero en aquellos tiempos se envejecía deprisa, sobre todo si se usaban los fármacos aconsejados por Paracelso.

Respecto al *Amphitheatrum*, copio la ficha que describe mi ejemplar, que debe considerarse completo.

---

2. Ocho ejemplares NUC.

3. Sobre las distintas obras de Khunrath, véase Jung (que, en *Psicología y Alquimia*, en el *Mysterium Conjunctionis* y en *Arquetipos e inconsciente colectivo*, cita preferentemente el *Von hylealischen... Chaos*, ed. de 1597). Para las referencias de Jung al *Amphitheatrum*, cfr. Mellon I, p. 210. En las otras historias de la alquimia, Khunrath aparece rara vez, excepto en el reciente Van Lennep. Naturalmente, constituye una excepción Thorndike (VII), a quien nada se le escapa. Sobre la vida de Khunrath, cfr. J. Moller, *Cimbria Literata*, Hannover, 1744; H. Kopp, *Geschichte der Chemie*, Brunswick, 1844 (cit. en Van Lennep). A Khunrath le está reservado un amplio espacio en las distintas obras sobre los rosacruces.

Amphitheatrvm Sapientia Aeternae, Solivs Verae, Christiano-Kaba-
listicvm, Divino-Magicvm, nec non Physico-Chymicvm, Tertrivn-
vm, Catholicon: instructore Henrico Khvnrath Lips: Theosophiae
amatore fideli et Medicinae utriusq. Doct: Hallelu-Iah, Hallelu-
Iah! Hallelu-Iah. Phy diabolo! E Millibvs Vix Vni...
Anno MDCII. Cvm Privilegio Caesareae Majest: Ad Decennivm;
A Prima Impressione Die. (Colophon: Hanoviae Excudebat Guiliel-
mus Antonius MDCIX. Cum S.ae Caesareae Majestatis Privilegio
ad decennium a prima impressionis die.)
Folio (30 ★ 19,5). Π^2, A-G^4, H^2, A-2E^4; pp. 60 + 222, + (2), 1 h.
s. p. Errores de numeración en la segunda parte: 62 por 42, 147
por 145, 148 por 146, 149 por 147, 150 por 148, 191 por 192,
192 por 193, 217 por 127.
Frontispicio grabado, retrato, 9 láminas dobles sueltas, 1 lámina
suelta con lechuza, dos tablas dobles sueltas (de las cuales una
está grabada). Las láminas, en el orden de encuadernación al
principio del volumen son: frontis anónimo, retrato de Johan
Diricks; cinco láminas dobles rectangulares sin nombre del gra-
bador y con varias expresiones atribuidas a la inspiración de K.
(*Adumbratio Gymnasii, Designatio Piramidum* o *Tabula Smarag-*
dina, Ypothyposis Arcis o *Ciudadela, Porta Amphitheatri, El Autor*
y sus enemigos); cuatro láminas dobles circulares firmadas por
Khunrath como *inventor* y por Van der Doort como *sculptor*; la
última firmada también por H. F. Vriese como *pictor* (*Cristo,*
Adán andrógino, Rebis, Laboratorio de K.); sello con lechuza, anónimo. Capitulares y orlas.

Las láminas se enumeran en el orden en que aparecen en mi
ejemplar. Como veremos, no he encontrado dos ejemplares que
sigan el mismo orden y la opinión de quienes han descrito su-
cesiones «ideales» no concuerdan. Como, además, varios auto-

res dan a estas láminas nombres fantasiosos, me he atenido, para las láminas rectangulares, a la expresión que aparece al principio de la leyenda (excepto para la lámina ya conocida universalmente como lámina de los enemigos) y, para las láminas circulares, a la que me parecía la vulgata más corriente. A veces la lámina con el Cristo (que aun teniendo los brazos extendidos no está en la cruz) se interpreta como lámina de la rosacruz, dado que los ocultistas ven siempre como una rosa cualquier estructura circular con una apariencia de simetría radial. Mientras no caben dudas en la identificación de la lámina del Laboratorio, respecto a las otras dos todo es muy vago. La segunda representa una figura con dos caras insertada en una estructura triangular, y suele entenderse como la lámina de Adán y Eva o del Adán andrógino. La tercera lámina representa indudablemente el Rebis, presenta en la parte baja el caso primigenio, habla de la piedra filosofal.

Por otra parte, es difícil reconocer las láminas a partir de la descripción que da Khunrath al final del volumen. En efecto, como veremos más adelante, las láminas circulares se identifican solo a partir de la edición de 1595. Y sobre esa base, podrá afirmarse que la sucesión que resulta en mi ejemplar es la que autoriza el texto.

La verdad es que todo el tono de la obra es extremadamente hermético. Se trata de un discurso de elevada temperatura mística, acompañado de invocaciones, exhortaciones, interjecciones exorcistas, a menudo con elaborada composición tipográfica, que describe siete grados de ascesis y de descubrimiento de la sabiduría. El texto avanza comentando 365 versículos bíblicos (de los Proverbios y de la Sabiduría), uno por cada día del año, propuestos en dos versiones paralelas (*Vulgata* y nueva traducción del griego o del hebreo), y se concluye con una isagoge o comentario de las cuatro láminas circulares. Abundan las referencias a la alquimia, a la cábala, a la doctrina de las signaturas y a otros temas corrientes del hermetismo renacentista y barroco, en especial se usa la parafernalia alquímica como metáfora místico-ascética (relación de analogía entre la Lapis y Cristo).

Sobre el estilo de esta obra, ha habido juicios severos desde el principio. Johann Anton Söldner en *Fegfeuer der Chymisten* dice que el *Amphitheatrum* demuestra la arrogancia y la ignorancia de su autor, que no está inspirado por el espíritu divino, sino por el demonio del orgullo. Si Fictuld (*Probier-Stein*) lo tiene en gran honor, Carbonarius, el autor con seudónimo de *Beytrag zur Geschichte de höhern Chemie*, lo ataca con ferocidad. Para Lenglet du Fresnoy, el libro es muy alegórico y está lejos del alcance de la mayoría de los lectores (*Histoire de la philosophie hermétique*, III, p. 198), porque Khunrath «par une obscurité affectée, a prétendu se faire passer pour un grand homme». Es verdad, había anotado también Lenglet, que en estos escritores la excesiva claridad se considera nociva (I, p. 382).

Waite (1924, p. 61) lamenta que Khunrath tendiera a la «disastrous literary fashion» difundida por Paracelso, mezclando el latín con el alemán, y viceversa, de modo que su lectura se convierte en una cruz para el lector que conoce solo una de esas lenguas.

Si el texto es oscuro, igual de oscuras pero decididamente fascinantes son las láminas. Se trata de complejas construcciones verbo-visuales, donde, leyendas, letreros, composiciones en forma de jeroglífico se funden con representaciones simbólicas. Las láminas rectangulares representan paisajes surrealistas, itinerarios iniciáticos, y culminan en el acceso a la Porta Amphiteatri, una especie de ascensión dantesca hacia un pasa-je mágico que, como veremos, recuerda a muchos la tumba de Christian Rosenkreutz tal como se describe en la *Fama* rosacruz. Tres de las láminas circulares son alegorías alquímicas, la cuarta representa el celebérrimo oratorio-laboratorio donde el alquimista está arrodillado en adoración, en un ambiente cargado de símbolos matemáticos, musicales, arquitectónicos y químicos. Por lo menos tres veces (Frontispicio, Hipotiposis, Enemigos), se presenta el símbolo de la Monas Hyerogliphica de John Dee.[4]

Es fácil imaginar las ilaciones, las conjeturas, las desconstrucciones interpretativas que este material figurativo ha alentado en el curso de los siglos, y en especial con referencia a la influencia que puede haber tenido en los supuestos redactores de los manifiestos rosacruces y (entre ellos) en Johann Valentin Andreae como autor de *Las bodas químicas de Christian Rosenkreutz*.

Por un lado, los textos rosacruces parecen atacar a Khunrath: la *Confessio* (1615) contiene una invitación a rechazar los «Pseudoschymicorum [...] libellos quibus vel SS. Triade ad futilia abuti lusus: vel monstruosis figuris atque aenigmatibus homines decipere jocus: vel credulorum curiositas lucrum est: quales aetas nostra plurimum produxit: unum ex iis praecipuum Amphitheatralem histrionem...» (XII).

Andreae (en *Mythologia Christiana*, V, p. 45) cuenta el apólogo de un charlatán que sale a la plaza pública a fin de atraer a la gente con el sonido de su trompeta y venderles medicinas milagrosas, y cuando la gente se huele el embuste, él contesta

4. Una buena biografía de Dee como la de French no menciona ni siquiera a Khunrath, que aun así se encontró con Dee en Praga. Las relaciones con Dee, en cambio, están subrayadas por Yates, 1972, y por Edighoffer, 1982, además de Evans, 1973 (quizá el más preciso de los historiadores en su bibliografía sobre el *Amphitheatrum*).

«Este es el secreto más secreto de todos los secretos, mi cosa es invisible para todos excepto para los adeptos de este arte, y ni siquiera uno entre mil es capaz de concebirlo». Andreae cita en latín «ex millibus uni». Y el frontispicio del *Amphitheatrum* lleva el lema «e millibus vix uni».

Además, Andreae comenta el discurso del charlatán con expresiones como «Chaos Magnesiae, Pyramis Triumphalis, bonum Macrocosmicum, Arx primaterialis, Antrum Naturae, Gymnasium Universale, Porta Sapientiae, Speculum Legis, Oratoriolaboratorium, rejectio binarii und ähnliche Orbimperipottendificuncta, undiquo-quoversum bombitarantarantia, verbocinatoria und so fort...». La alusión al *Amphitheatrum* parece explícita. Es curioso que el mismo episodio sea referido casi literalmente por Comenio en su *Laberinto del mundo* (escrito en 1623 y publicado, en checo, en 1631) y que Frances Yates (1972), al citar el paso detenidamente, ignore su ascendencia y, sobre todo, no identifique las evidentes citas de Khunrath, considerando por el contrario que se trata de referencias a Fludd.

Ahora bien, ¿cómo conciliar este ataque con la idea —fija para los rosacruces posteriores— de que Khunrath fue su inspirador? ¿Cómo conciliarlo con la afirmación de Andreae (*Mythologia Christiana*, III, p. 23), que sitúa a Khunrath entre los «insolitae eruditionis homines»?

Además, el inspirador de Andreae fue Arndt, y Arndt en varios escritos se expresa con entusiasmo respecto de Khunrath. No solo: se le atribuye (cfr. BPH, pp. 38-40) el comentario entusiasta a la primera versión del *Amphitheatrum* y a las láminas circulares (que Benedictus Figulus publica, anónimo, como apéndice a Khunrath, *De igne magorum et philosophorum*, en 1608).

Ante esta ambigüedad, las explicaciones se anulan entre ellas. Si se considera que Andreae a veces habla bien de Khunrath, eso demostraría que no es él el autor de la *Confessio*. Pero, como hemos visto, habla también mal y, por tanto, concuerda con la *Confessio*. Para acabar, el ataque a Khunrath aparece en la edición latina 1615 de la *Confessio* y desaparece en las sucesivas traducciones alemanas, excepto una; y es curioso que desaparezca también en las tres traducciones que estoy consultando (Yates, 1972; Gorceix, 1970; Wehr, 1980), evidentemente realizadas a partir de ediciones posteriores.

BPH (p. 40) sugiere que Andreae no apreciaba a Khunrath, que respetaba a Arndt, pero que creía que el *judicium* atribuido a Arndt era una manipulación de Figulus. Explicación muy retorcida, que no aclara por qué Andreae en otros pasos habla bien de Khunrath. Waite (1924, p. 63) confiesa cándidamente que tuvo noticia a través de un tal Dr. Cantor[5] de que en la *Confessio* habría un ataque a Khunrath, pero tiende a excluirlo por las siguientes razones: una persona respetable como Khunrath no podía ser acusada de charlatanería, y en la época del supuesto ataque, llevaba muerto diez años y no se entiende por qué había de ser atacado.[6]

---

5. Se trata sin duda del gran matemático Georg Cantor, de notorias propensiones para-ocultistas, hasta el punto de ser el autor de una opereta sobre la *Bacon-Shakespeare controversy* (*Die Rawley'sche Sammlung von zweiunddreissig Trauergedichten auf Francis Bacon. Ein Zeugniss zu Gusten der Bacon-Shakespeare-Theorie mit einem Vorwort herausgegeben von Georg Cantor*, Halle, Niemeyer, 1897).

6. En este tipo de literatura hay que distinguir entre devotos del hermetismo, siempre chapuceros y poco fiables, con tendencia a falsear las fuentes o a equivocarse en las citas (los mencionaré solo a título de información sensacionalista), y estudiosos serios. Waite es un devoto rosacruz, pero sigue siendo el más prudente y el menos crédulo de todos.

El debate podría prolongarse mucho tiempo si no se toman en consideración por lo menos otros tres factores. Ante todo, el tono irónico y satírico que domina en la mayor parte de las obras de Andreae: uno puede haber sido influido por un autor, pero nada impide que divise sus excesos, así como el uso desaforado que otros hacen de él, de donde el ataque, casi como un *in-joke*. En segundo lugar, el hecho de que Andreae, en un momento determinado, tenga que demostrarle a todo el mundo que no es el autor de los manifiestos rosacruces y que no pensaba, en ningún caso, que enjambres de alquimistas y de aventureros de lo oculto fueran a usarlos, le lleva a recalcar las reservas que ya estaban contenidas en la *Confessio*, como diciendo que —sí— Khunrath le había proporcionado imágenes y metáforas para sus *Bodas químicas*, pero él no estaba dispuesto a suscribir su teosofía ultravioleta. Por último, Andreae habla bien de Khunrath, y luego lanza sus dardos contra el *Amphitheatrum*. ¿Por qué? Quizá porque no sabe si es auténtico.

LAS EDICIONES DEL *AMPHITHEATRUM*

Cuando se le habla de un ejemplar del *Amphitheatrum*, lo primero que pregunta el coleccionista es si está el grabado con la lechuza (o el petrel o como quieran llamarlo); la segunda es si tiene la lámina de los enemigos.

En efecto, empezó Guaita (1899) avisando de que «le plus grand nombre des exemplaires de l'*Amphitheatrum* n'ont que 4 ou 5 de ces gravures; et la planche qui représente K. entouré de ses ennemis (déguisés en oiseaux bridés et en insectes d'enfer) —cette planche étonnante qui est un véritable Callot par anticipation manque dans presque tous les exemplaires signalés. Il en est de même pour le 2 tableaux synoptiques de Kabbale synthétisée...».[7] Más o menos lo mismo dice también Ferguson (I, p. 463).

La pregunta obvia que deberíamos plantearnos es: la lechuza y la lámina de los enemigos, ¿estaban ya en la primera edición? En efecto, alguien sugiere que la lechuza llegó después, y en cuanto a la lámina de los enemigos, es claramente distinta de las otras cuatro láminas rectangulares. Estas están sembradas de leyendas y rótulos sobre todo en latín; aquella, de leyendas y rótulos sobre todo en alemán; aquella está dominada por figuras humanas y antropomorfas, y puede evocar a Callot; estas están dominadas por estructuras arquitectónicas y paisajes. Entonces, ¿qué había en la primera edición?

Por desgracia, los problemas empiezan cuando se trata de determinar cuál fue la primera edición. Si queremos encontrar listas de ediciones, no tenemos más que elegir. Lenglet du Fresnoy citaba Magdeburgo 1608, Hamburgo 1611 y Frankfurt 1653 (pasando por alto Hanau). Ferguson (I, p. 463) describe solo Hanau 1609, enumera como «reported» Praga 1598, Magdeburgo 1602, Hanau 1604, Magdeburgo 1606, Frankfurt 1608, Lipsia 1608, Lübeck 1608, Magdeburgo 1608, Hamburgo 1611, 1648, 1651, Hanau 1653, Frankfurt 1653, Hamburgo 1710; sin embargo, admite razonablemente que puede tratarse de falsificaciones y, siguiendo a De Bure (*Bibliographie Instructive*, II, p. 248) sugiere que Hanau 1609 es la auténtica primera edición.

Es posible entender cómo pueden haber nacido estas afirmaciones con poco fundamento hojeando la Hanau 1609. Lle-

---

7. Cfr. el catálogo de Guaita y S. de Guaita, *Essais de sciences maudites, I. Au seuil du mystère*, París, 1890, pp. 57-59, 99-147.

va en el frontispicio la fecha de 1602 y en el colofón la fecha de 1609. Ojalá fuera solo eso. El privilegio está fechado en 1598 (p. 2), mientras que en la página 8 aparece una invocación a Jehová que acaba con «anno Masiach 1604». Para complicar el tema, las láminas rectangulares, que muchos juzgan muy posteriores, están fechadas en 1602, mientras que las circulares, que como veremos deberían existir desde 1595, no llevan fecha. El epílogo lleva la fecha de 1602.

Khunrath muere en 1605. En 1609, su discípulo Erasmus Wolfart publica la obra como legado del autor, afirmando haberla completado en una pequeña parte inacabada «sed non magna» (p. 10). Comparando, como haremos, con la edición de 1595, nos sentimos inducidos a darle crédito. Del texto de Wolfart se deduce que la de 1609 debería ser la primera edición que ve la luz con esa forma completa. Ahora bien, ¿cuándo se grabó el frontispicio, con su 1602?

LA 1602 FANTASMA

Esta única fecha (dice Hall) induce a Brunet (III, p. 658) a afirmar que las diez ilustraciones de esta obra fueron apareciendo por separado a partir de 1602, con un frontispicio sin fecha, el privilegio y el retrato del autor. Graesse (iv, p. 15) también señala que una primera edición que incluía solamente los grabados (pero ¿cuáles?) sin fecha y sin editor debería haber aparecido en 1602-1605.[8] Aparte de que no se entiende por qué, no llevando fecha el frontispicio de 1602, el de 1609 debe llevar

---

8. Graesse cita *Adelung. Gesch. d. menschl. Narrheit t. V.* pp. 95 ss., Baumgarten, Hall Bibl. t. VII, pp. 411 ss., y Ebert (*Allg. Bibliogr. Lexicon*, 11368).

grabado 1602, hay otro indicio que frena esta hipótesis. Una fe de erratas de la 1609 (p. 123) avisa al lector de que, por error, al final de cada *Gradus* se indica dónde introducir nada menos que siete ilustraciones, pero esas ilustraciones no existen. «Sed Amphitheatrum ipsum constat figuris, & suas habet Introductiones.» Ahora, existen cuatro isagoges finales que claramente comentan solo las láminas dobles circulares. Ninguna mención a las láminas rectangulares, por no hablar de la lechuza. Esto ha inducido a pensar que fueron introducidas después, por los encuadernadores.[9]

Mellon (1968), al no haber encontrado jamás un ejemplar de la edición de 1602, considera que se trataba de un ejemplar mútilo de la de 1609 que circuló con las láminas rectangulares, fechadas precisamente 1602. Pero entonces la de 1602 no carecería de fecha, como afirman Brunet y Graesse, a menos que no tuviera otro frontispicio. En ese caso, tendríamos una edición de 1602 sin fecha y una edición de 1609 con frontispicio fechado 1602, lo cual, francamente, parece demasiado novelesco. Alguien afirma haber visto una 1602. La *Bibliotheca Magica Pnemautica* de Rosenthal registra (ítem 481) un infolio de esa fecha a la que faltarían los folios preliminares 36 y las páginas 147-150. Salta a la vista que está refiriéndose al error de numeración que caracteriza las Hanau 1609. La poca credibilidad de la colación se debe también al hecho de que se cita un último folio con el *impressum* (sin especificar su fecha) y un

---

9. Por otra parte, sigue siendo misteriosa la causa del error (y de la fe de erratas): ¿en qué estaba pensando el editor imaginando que tenía que introducir siete imágenes, cuando las figuras o son cuatro (circulares), o cinco (rectangulares), o todas juntas nueve, es más, diez si se cuenta también la lechuza, u ocho si faltaran tanto la lámina de los enemigos como la lechuza? En definitiva, se calcule como se calcule, no se llega a siete.

segundo título (?). El catálogo Gilhofer 133 (*Alchemie und Che-mie*, 1984, ítem 213), mientras registra una Hanau completa, por lo que concierne a la 1602, refiere la noticia de Ebert, pero no aporta más pruebas.

En 1898, Chacornac publica una traducción francesa de esta obra, hecha por Grillot de Givry, y vuelve a proponerla en 1900 con un comentario de Papus y Marc Haven.[10]

Papus y Haven afirman que existe una edición de 1602 («in-connue de Fictuld») con texto alemán, frontispicio y solo las cuatro láminas circulares, grabadas por Van der Doort bajo la dirección de Khunrath. La lechuza habría sido añadida pos-teriormente. Habría, además, una primera edición latina de Magdeburgo 1608, la Hanau 1609 y Hamburgo 1611 con las mismas imágenes. En 1619, Wolfart publicaría la primera edi-ción con doce láminas, añadiendo el retrato y las cinco láminas rectangulares. Se trataría de imágenes que quizá existían en los manuscritos de Khunrath, pero en cualquier caso se añadieron después de su fallecimiento.

Estas noticias no están sustentadas por la menor prueba, es más, las pruebas a disposición las refutan: Papus y Haven, evi-dentemente, se equivocan al decir que las láminas rectangulares llegaron solo en 1619, porque todos los ejemplares descritos por los catálogos identifican las láminas también en la edición Ha-nau 1609 (cfr. para la misma objeción también Dorbon y Van Lennep). En la página i/6, en el curso de la citada invocación fechada en 1604, Khunrath presenta su Anfiteatro como «re-

10. Ahora bien, Grillot de Givry (en *Le Musée des Sorciers*, París, Librairie de France, 1929, p. 223) afirma haberla hecho en 1899. La edición Chacornac 1900 sigue la disposición tipográfica de la edición de 1609, y reproduce todas las láminas grabadas. La edición ahora está en facsímil: Milán, Arché, Col. Se-bastiani, 1975.

cens revisum [...] instructum quattuor circularibus, aliisque hieroglyphicis figuris, in aes affabre scalptis». Por tanto, si no cinco, por lo menos alguna lámina rectangular existe desde esa fecha.

¿Cómo puede haber sucedido que a Papus y Haven se les haya escapado esta frase contenida en la edición Hanau que reproducen? No es el único caso en que los dos conocidos ocultistas demuestran estar fabulando a rienda suelta. Reconocen que los cuatro comentarios (o isagoges) colocados al final del libro explican solo las imágenes circulares, pero añaden que tales comentarios aparecen solo en la edición de 1653, sin darse cuenta de que los tienen ante los ojos, en su edición Hanau (desde la p. 185 hasta la p. 214). Pero quizá no hayan visto nunca de verdad la Hanau, y publicaron la traducción de Grillot de Givry sin siquiera leerla.[11]

11. Por lo que se refiere a Givry, este comete otro desacierto, aunque más excusable. Secret 1985 (p. 250) demuestra en efecto que Khunrath en la p. 2/6 cita unos versos del *Olearius* enviados a Elhanan ben Menahem, conocido como Pablo de Praga, y Givry traduce «Quelques vers que le très illustre Jean Olearius [...] a écrit à Prague sur Saint Paul».

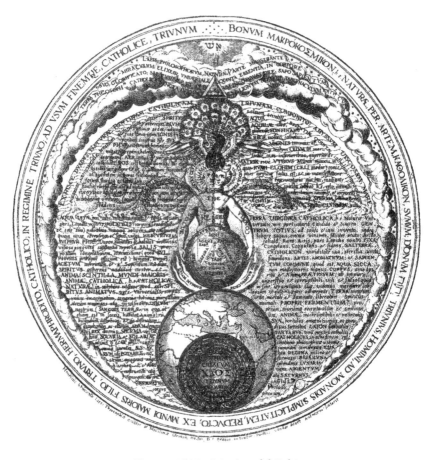

Hanau 1609. *Lámina del Rebis*

Hanau 1609. *Lámina del Laboratorio*

Hanau 1609. *Lámina del Cristo*

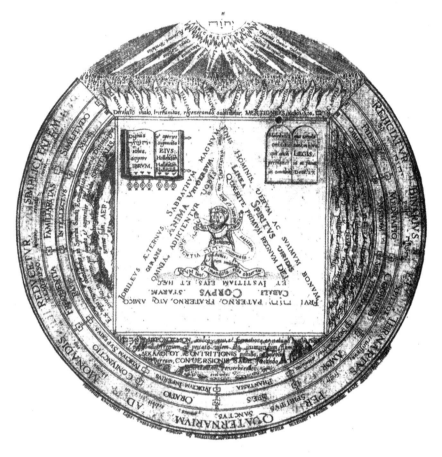

Hanau 1609. *Lámina del Adán andrógino*

Página siguiente: Hanau 1609. *Lámina de la Adumbratio Gymnasii*

CVM NVMINE LVMINE ET
IN LVMINE NVMEN.

PORTA
AMPHITHEATRI
SAPIENTIÆ ÆTERNÆ,
SOLIVS VERÆ.

f magnum, à IEHOVA ELOHIM unice sit, omnibus, uentis ac singulis liberaliter extrusti; Vbi per Cælum, Astra, Terram,
uenire aut superficie Terræ, aut sub Cælo nascuntur, IEHOVA mirabili SAPIENTIAM mirificam in libro Naturæ catholico ac
ens, SAPIENTIÆ, æternæ scintillula sapiens, naturaliter-magice manifestando uidesesto docet ac prostetsur: quod Patres &
iniusque Partes & Regiones, pro chartis, fructus inuureri pro lißern & Linguis non olim secundum longum, latum, altum atsß
nint, omnesßß studiosi Philosophiæ Theosophicæ, soliir veræ, fideles, etiameiam hodierno die, autoritate Divina & Sapien,
e ELOHIM celtus istau atsß illuminati, geartem Signaturâ Divinisve Naturæ characterismis hieroglyphicis, quibus Res
NTIÆ ÆTERNÆ, soliir veræ, in Viuerlo Mundano hoc Sapienter manifestatæ, cognitionem solidam atsß perfectam, etiam
one ac sensibus hauriret, Phynia genuini veræ, Philosophi non opinantes, sed scientes, ita fierent: quales plures hic sa,
icio Naturæ speculo, CREATOPVEM, quæ uidelic et æterna eius sit tum Potentia, tum Divinitas, Rom i, v. 20 &, quem misit
uidere nossent possimus; ideoßß semper & Vbiß orthodoxè ac Sapienter Philosophari; honestè viuere, & h\$ ac\$ mori
IVNRA sei LIPS. Theosophiæ amator subst. & MED. utriusßß Doct. Anno à MASCHIACH insso. M. DC. II.

Frontispicio de la Hanau 1609

׃ יהרה אלהים עלם אמת

TOTIQVE CELESTIS EXERCITVS SPIRITVALIS, MILITIÆ,
PROXIMO SVO FIDELI, ET SIBIMETIPSI,
NATVRÆ ATQVE ARTI,

AMPHITHEATRVM
SAPIENTIÆ ÆTERNÆ, SOLIVS VERÆ,

nec non
Virginum velut, ei à cubiculis atq; secretis, castissimarum,
quibus, in totius machinæ Mundi, non sanctiore, non præstantiores ulla,

puta

CABALÆ,   MAGEJÆ,   ALCHEMIÆ,

Dominæ suæ miraculosæ, in ORATORIO & LABORATORIO, MICRO ac MACROCOSMICE, artificio mirifico sapienter administrantium,
secundum Christianæ & Philosophicæ veritatis normam, à diabolica Sophistmatum exsecrandorum, pro veritate falsè falsò substituentium, lævis fucatis, separatarum, Catholicæ, dexteritate, ad Archetypi exemplar reformatarum, primordiálibus simplicitati rituni, Catholicæ, dignè resonantium,

CABALISTICVM,   MAGEJCVM,   PHYSICOCHEMICVM,
TERTRIVNVM.   CATHOLICON,

HOC,

OPVS, ingentiæ vix superbiæ, ex nemine, verum absolutum, cui natura figuris qvæ sunt Theosophicæ, forma Regali en as affabre sculptis, in publicam vm emittendum, ut intergratis proprietates potess diabolo obsessis, nec omnibus omnia concurrentur, cui quibus, quando, & quantum.
SAPIENTIA Christiana, Cui, Qvid, I'bi, qvædno Arxilius, Cur, Qvomodo Qvando pers possit, verè docent;
Summum HOMINIS BONVM, DEI DONVM Tertrinum, Catholicum,

videntur,

Agnitionem, Cognitionem, Cognationem, Vnionem, Fruitionem,

JEHOVÆ,   CREATVRÆ ATQVE NATVRÆ,   NOSTRIIPSIVS,

TRIVNIVS,

hoc est,

CATHOLICE   OMNIA,

unaqvam in liqvido speculo THEOSOPHICE ostendens:
QVOD, Lege certa, æqva & justa, solis debetur Disciplinæ atq; Doctrinæ filiis, SS: SAPIENTIAS hæredibus fidelibus dilectis:
laborem, sumptibus non exiguis, at, gratia DEO, propriis, plus duodecim annorum,

ANIMI GRATI, AC REVERENTIAE,
CHARITATIS ET GRATVLATIONIS,
ADMIRATIONIS, A Top HONORIS DEBITI

ergò,

Consecrat, Offert, Ponit,

HENRICVS KHVNRATH LIPS. THEOSOPHIAE AMATOR, ET MED. DOCT.
Veritatis DEO: SCRIPTVRÆ, Leta NATVRÆ, Christianæq; CONSCIENTIAE Lege,
JEHOVAH assertor, inculcatione, simul-tones in dantes, dantes, duobus, uiventem, entem.

Anno MASCHIACH juxta promissionem missi, M.D. VC. mai XXXV.
Cum Gratia & Privilegio SS: tricennali, Mai: DIVINÆ,
ad perpetuum.: NON FVTVR FACIAI

Qvod violantem

Commendo Psalmis, DEO, & Exsecratoribus ejus.

Ab-improbis & Hypocritum DEI,   O salvas Scientiæ secundo
Secundentur NATVRÆ ignaris,   ria, Amorû beato, fide de fidi
cultus, quod luodori ut: cultus   Hospibus atq Arcilier brevi,
plorasti, vituperari.   exolorem.

PAVCIS, IISq; THEOSOPHICE DOCTIS, PLACERE,
SIGNVM VERITATIS.

Halelu-Jáh: Halelu-Jáh: Halelu-Jáh:
phi Diabolus.

SOLI DEO GLORIA,
E MILLIBUS VIX VNI,
NON INTELLIGIT.
NISI CUI SPIRITUS SAPIENTIAE ADSISTIT.

Hamburgo 1595. *Frontispicio*

HAMBURGO 1595

El hecho es que el 1602 que aparece en el frontispicio no ante-
data bastante la primera fantasmal edición de nuestro libro.
Thorndike (VII, pp. 272 ss.)[12] dice que un «brief preliminary
sketch or draught» de la obra se publica en Hamburgo 1595.
Diez años antes de Thorndike, esta tesis la había explorado
Duveen. En «Notes on some alchemical books», después de
haber reconocido razonablemente que «much confusion seems
to exist as to the number of editions actually issued and as to
which was the first», afirmaba haber visto la edición infolio
oblongo de 1595: (1) 24 (1) y solo cuatro láminas. Evidentemente, Duveen pudo hacerse con un ejemplar después, que
ahora pertenece a la colección Duveen de la Universidad de
Wisconsin, y que se describe en el catálogo Duveen. De la edición de 1595 se conoce solo otro ejemplar, conservado en la
Universitätsbibliothek de Basilea, cuya microficha tengo ante
los ojos.[13] Ni siquiera Duveen se atreve a referir el frontispicio
en su totalidad, mucho más prolijo que el de la Hanau 1609
y, en cualquier caso, el que desee verlo que se remita a la lámina X del catálogo Duveen.

El infolio oblongo de Basilea corresponde sustancialmente a la descripción del ejemplar Duveen, salvo por dos detalles. Las páginas impresas son veinticinco y no veinticuatro
—como dice Duveen— y entre las ilustraciones aparece un
folio con dos grabados circulares que representan el Mundus

---

12. Citando de Maggs, *Catalogue of Strange Books and Curious Titles*, 1932,
ítem 91.

13. Aprovecho esta ocasión para darle las gracias al doctor Frank Hyeroni-
mus por su colaboración.

Archetypus y el Mundus Intelligentiarum; dado que no se puede detectar ninguna analogía estilística con las cuatro láminas circulares, yo tendería a pensar que han sido introducidas por el arbitrio del encuadernador. En efecto, en los *omissis* del frontispicio hay una indicación explícita de cuatro (y no más) láminas grabadas.

Como dice también Duveen, a pesar del número de páginas inferior, la 1595 sustancialmente corresponde a la 1609. El *Prologos* lleva en forma sinóptica la versión antigua y moderna de los textos bíblicos, aunque el número de los versículos y su orden son distintos (la 1595 es más sucinta). Igualmente, las notas que rodean los textos bíblicos se corresponden (otra vez de forma más sucinta, pero en esencia análoga) con los textos que en la 1609 ocupan las muchas páginas de los siete *Gradus* explicativos.

En la página 24 aparece un «Addo» que corresponde en sustancia al texto de las páginas 82-83 de la 1609, con la excepción de que en la segunda edición hay una invocación final. Igualmente, en la página 25, el *Epilogos* corresponde más o menos al de la 1609, pero está fechado en 1602. A estas alturas ya no hay que sorprenderse por esta última extravagancia: es probable que, tras una primera versión de 1595, Khunrath preparase una segunda versión del epílogo ya desde 1602.

Las cuatro láminas circulares son las mismas que están presentes en Hanau, con una diferencia. Dado el formato mayor de la edición 1595, los grabados están rodeados —con respecto a la edición Hanau— con una amplia orla de texto grabado. La firma con la fecha está grabada en los bordes de la circunferencia externa. En la edición Hanau, eliminado el círculo externo, se ha eliminado evidentemente también la firma, que ha sido regrabada a lo largo de la circunferencia menor, pero sin la fecha.

El análisis de las láminas del ejemplar 1595 permite resolver también otro problema. En la Hanau 1609, después de los siete *Gradus* de comentario a los versículos bíblicos, aparecen cuatro isagoges que comentan las láminas circulares, y muchos de esos comentarios se nos presentan tan oscuros que hacen difícil la referencia a la lámina de la que se ocupan. Conformémonos con una muestra de la primera isagoge.

Esta se compone de una serie de versículos, primero en hebreo y después en latín, que dicen, por ejemplo: «Qui Erat; Qui Est; Qui Erit; Pleni Sunt Celi, Plena Est Omnis Terra, Majestatis Gloriae Eius». O también: «Lavamini. Mundi Estote». Los que conjeturaran (con buenas razones) que estas explicaciones se refieren a la lámina denominada del Cristo, podrían trabajar solo aplicando el sentido común, porque el grabado del Cristo no presenta textos comparables con los de la isagoge correspondiente. Si, en cambio, se va a ver el grabado de 1595, se descubre que los textos referidos en la primera isagoge 1609 son exactamente los que están escritos en el círculo exterior, posteriormente eliminado, de la figura 1595. Y así sucede en los otros tres casos. Los textos impresos de las cuatro isagoges 1609 son los que en la 1595 aparecen grabados en el círculo exterior de las figuras; o, por lo menos, son sustancialmente los mismos, salvo diferencias menores.

Así pues, el editor de la Hanau 1609, probablemente Wolfart, teniendo que eliminar por razones técnicas los círculos externos de las imágenes de la 1595, imprimió esos mismos textos en el volumen en forma de cuatro isagoges.

OTRAS EDICIONES FANTASMA

Si la 1595 es seguramente la primera edición parcial y la existencia de la 1602 es dudosa, ¿qué diremos de otras ediciones fantasma?

Un primer fantasma aparece en el catálogo de Jouin y Descreux (1930). Este catálogo no solo se edita con los auspicios de una misteriosa revista que en los años treinta llevó a cabo campañas antisemitas y antimasónicas, sino que describe la colección A. Peeters Baertsoen, que posteriormente se dispersó. Y aquí aparece un *Amphitheatrum sapientiae cum tabulis*, Praga 1598. El título haría pensar en una anticipación del tipo de la 1595, pero la descripción del catálogo autoriza a creer que se trata ni más ni menos que de una Hanau 1609, debidamente enmascarada.

La conjetura se sostiene con lo que puede decirse de otras dos ediciones fantasma, la Magdeburgo 1608 (que Waite y otros con él mencionan, pero afirman no haber visto nunca), y la que está registrada en el catálogo impreso de la Biblioteca Nacional de París como s. l., 1605. Entre muchas ediciones fantasma, estas son las menos fantasma de todas, porque al menos existen como objetos identificables.

De la Praga 1638 conozco por lo menos dos ejemplares. Uno está en la Bibliotheca Philosphica Hermetica de Amsterdam y otro en la Biblioteca Trivulziana (pero este último ejemplar tiene solo el frontispicio y ninguna lámina).

Ahora, si se abre la edición de 1608, se encuentra un frontispicio nuevo, que lleva el mismo título que el de 1602, salvo que después de *E millibus uni* recita: «Accessit, Jam noviter, diu desiderata Explicatio Singvlaris, ejusdem Autoris P.M. qua Novem tabulae in aes incisae dilucide explicantur, & ita tractantur ut singulis diebus, una saltem periodo observata, totum opus Amphitheatri unis anni spacio absolvi, & memoriter infigi possit». Sigue la indicación del editor-librero: *Magdaeburgi Apud Levinum Brauns Bibliopolam in aureo cornu venale exponitur, Anno MDCVIII*. Después de esta página, el resto de la obra, hasta el colofón incluido, no es nada más que la edición Hanau 1609, incluidos los ya citados errores de numeración y las dos tablas.

Sin la menor duda —y BPH coincide— Magdeburgo 1608 es un libro impreso en Hanau en 1609 al que Levinus Brauns colocó un frontispicio fechado en 1608. El *Accesit* del frontispicio, contra todo desvarío de Papus y Haven, precisa que las láminas ya son nueve desde la impresión de Hanau.

Lo mismo puede decirse de la edición 1605 de la Biblioteca Nacional de París. Registrada como 1605 en el catálogo impreso (donde, quién sabe por qué, se dice que la fecha se deduce del título grabado), reaparece en el catálogo manuscrito, consultable en la misma biblioteca, como impresa en 1601. Se trata de un doble error de catalogación, que se remonta a quién sabe cuándo, dado que el ejemplar fue adquirido en el siglo XVIII. En realidad, estamos de nuevo ante una Hanau 1609, mutilada de su colofón (y sin la lechuza). Es inútil decir que los errores de numeración de las páginas son los mismos que los de la Hanau 1609, y el frontispicio es el consabido de 1602.

Igualmente, la Frankfurt, apud Tobiam Gundermannum, 1653, es una vez más una Hanau 1609 con un nuevo frontispicio (véanse Graesse, Dorbon, Rosenthal).[14]

---

14. En 2004 vi por fin un ejemplar en la Librería Malavasi de Milán. Se parece en todo a la Hanau 1609 (aunque carezca de la lámina con la lechuza) y lleva en el colofón: «Hanoviae, excudebat Guilelmus Antonius, MDCIX».

FABULACIONES

¿Por qué no podemos fiarnos de otras menciones? Porque, lo repito, allá donde la reconstrucción no era al fin y al cabo tan difícil, al menos después de Duveen, cada vez que alguien habla del *Amphitheatrum* se enreda con imprecisiones fatales.

Ya hemos visto los deslices de Papus y Haven. Antes de ellos, había dado una buena prueba de desenvoltura Eliphas Levi en su *Histoire de la Magie* de 1860. En poco menos de dos páginas consigue decir que Khunrath nació en 1502, que la obra es de 1598 y que el texto comenta «los oráculos de Salomón». Dado que Levi había estudiado en un seminario y colaborado con Migne, es curioso que no consiga reconocer los Proverbios y la Sabiduría, entre otras cosas porque el texto los menciona sin parar. Por la descripción que Levi da del libro, parece indudable que no lo había visto. Y la descripción de las nueve láminas es tan fantasiosa que resulta difícil reconocerlas. En 1913, Waite traduce la historia de Levi al inglés,[15] acompañándola con notas críticas, y saca a la luz todos sus errores. Propone también con suficiencia un orden distinto de las láminas, y acusa a Levi de haber descrito la Puerta como iluminada por siete rayos mientras que los rayos —dice Waite— son tres. En cambio, por una vez, tenía razón Levi, los rayos son siete y son del tamaño de una ventana. ¿Había visto Waite de verdad el libro? Quizá sí, pero citaba de memoria.

Tomemos ahora a un autor que ha escrito una historia de la alquimia muy rica de informaciones y llena de sensatísimas observaciones, Van Lennep (1985). En la página 170 nos dice que «además del frontispicio, la obra contiene diez ilustraciones», enu-

---

15. *The History of Magic*, Philadelphia, McKay, 1913.

mera las láminas rectangulares y circulares y la lechuza, pero no menciona el retrato. Entonces añade que «Duveen ha descrito con precisión un ejemplar hoy desaparecido». No solo no ha desaparecido, sino que —como hemos visto— hay dos (en cualquier caso, habiéndome inducido esta afirmación a la sospecha, escribí a la biblioteca de la Universidad de Wisconsin y recibí una carta de su director, en la que me aseguraba que el ejemplar existe y goza de buena salud). De las láminas de la Hamburgo 1595 dice Van Lennep que «como para la edición 1609, estaban firmadas por Paul Van der Doort de Amberes... 1595». En cambio, en Hanau las láminas no están fechadas. Siguiendo con los grabados circulares, afirma que «el editor Wolfart asegura que nunca se publicaron antes de 1609». Basta con leerse el prefacio de Wolfart, que son dos páginas, incluso en la edición Chacornac, y se ve que no lo dice en absoluto. En la página 167 da el *judicium* de Arndt como publicado en 1747 en *Chymischen Lust-Gärtlein*, mientras que sabemos que aparece en 1608.[16] En la página 168 traduce Hanau (en latín «Hanovia») como Hanovre (Hannover), error por lo demás común a los autores franceses, véase Gorceix 1970 (p. xix). Por último, recoge las afirmaciones erróneas de un tal Wittemans,[17] según el cual Spinoza habría hecho publicar en Hamburgo algunas obras suyas con el nombre de Khunrath. Además de increíble, la noticia nace de un *qui-pro-quo* que ya fue desmontado por Paul Arnold (p. 307) precisamente refiriéndose a Wittemans: en 1670,

---

16. La noticia deriva probablemente de Ferguson que, en efecto, cita solo esa edición.

17. *Histoire des Rose-Croix*, París, 1979 (pero la primera edición es París, Aydar, 1925, cfr. pp. 59-60). Sobre la lucidez de este autor, véase Edighofer, 1982 (p. 210): «Wittemans [...] reproche à Andreae d'avoir volontairement sabordé la future Franc-Maçonnerie, d'avoir porté un coup mortel à l'enfant spirituel qu'il avait le plus aidé à voir le jour».

Spinoza publica de manera anónima su *Tractatus Theologico-Politicus*, en Hamburgo «apud Heinricum Khünrath». Sencillísimo, se trata del nombre del editor. Wittemans, con tal de adscribirlo a la tradición hermética, estaría dispuesto a decir que Gide publicaba con el nombre de Mercure de France, obviamente Trimegiste.

Serge Hutin[18] habla de las «doce célebres láminas colocadas al final de libro». Debe de haber visto solo la reedición de Chacornac, porque no me consta que las láminas estén encuadernadas al final en ningún ejemplar y, en cualquier caso, por lo menos el retrato y el frontispicio deberían estar al principio (en Chacornac, en cambio, aparecen todos los grabados al final).

La devoción obceca también el sentido bibliográfico. El catálogo Hall (1986, y Manly Hall es autor de muchos libros herméticos, uno incluso de «anatomía oculta»), por ejemplo, da saltos mortales para no decir que, con toda probabilidad, su ejemplar del *Amphitheatrum* carece de lechuza. Dorbon deriva de Caillet y de Guaita, aunque con poca atención. Su ficha de Hanau 1609 es correcta, pero los problemas empiezan cuando tiene que describir las diferentes ediciones Chacornac. Aparte de la ingenuidad del comentario («Tout porte à faire croire qu'il possédait la Pierre Philosophale»), se dice que la segunda parte de la edición 1898-1900 «contiene en doble página las doce láminas extraordinarias que parecerían salidas de la imaginación de Callot», cuando a estas alturas sabemos que en doble página hay solo nueve láminas, y que la comparable con Callot es solo una.

En *A Christian Rosenkreutz Anthology*[19] se publican «once» láminas de la edición Hanau, y se anuncia pomposamente que

---

18. *Histoire des Rose-Croix*, París, Le Courrier du Livre, 1971, p. 34.

19. Ed. de Paul Allen, Nueva York, Rudolf Steiner Publications, Blauvelt, 1968, pp. 329 ss.

se publican como serie completa por primera vez, desde su aparición en 1609, según el ejemplar que perteneció a la biblioteca de Isaac Meyer, «eminent american authority on the Cabala». Es falso que las láminas aparecieran por vez primera en 1609, es falso que nunca se hubieran vuelto a publicar antes, es falso que sean solo once. En efecto, falta la lechuza, que aparece aparte, pero desde la edición 1616 del *Von hylealischen Chaos*, también de Khunrath. Así pues, la eminente autoridad sobre la cábala poseía un ejemplar incompleto.

La *Annotated Bibliography*, que figura en la página 483, cree de nuevo que el comentario de Arndt aparece por primera vez en 1747,[20] cita —evidentemente de segunda mano— la *Mythologia Christiana* de Andreae para decir que contiene elogios sobre Arndt (que apreciaba a Khunrath), pero soslaya el hecho de que, como hemos visto, contenga un ataque feroz a Khunrath.

Puntos firmes y conjeturas

A estas alturas, nuestra investigación llega a algunos puntos firmes. Existe una edición 1595, probablemente impresa en Hamburgo, que consta de veinticinco páginas de texto y de cuatro grabados circulares. De esta edición se conocen dos ejemplares.

No hay pruebas de la existencia de una edición 1602, pero si la hubiera, podría ser una recopilación como la de 1595, con cuatro láminas rectangulares más y un nuevo frontispicio. De haber existido, habría tenido un epílogo fechado en 1602. Parece que, a su muerte, Khunrath había llevado a término el texto de-

20. Véase la nota 16.

finitivo, y lo más que sabemos es que en 1604 acaba la invocación inicial.

Todas las demás ediciones citadas aquí y allá son, hasta que se demuestre lo contrario, camuflajes de la edición Hanau.

Una confirmación definitiva de la relación directa entre la edición de 1595 y la de 1609, sin otras ediciones intermedias, nos la da, entre otras cosas, el breve texto que Figulus colocaba al pie de la edición del *De igne magorum* (1608, p. 125), después del *Iudicium* sobre el *Amphitheatrum* atribuido a Arndt. ¿Qué dice Figulus? Que le había parecido útil publicar ese texto sobre el *Amphitheatrum* porque la obra se había publicado solo en una edición muy limitada, destinada a pocos elegidos y, por tanto, hasta ese momento (1608) a la mayoría no le había sido posible verla; pero que, con todo y afortunadamente, ya estaba en curso de imprenta (*sub praelo*) una edición más accesible y menos cara, con muchas láminas más. Figulus se refería evidentemente, en 1608, a la Hanau 1609, *à paraître*, salvo que la citaba como «*Hanoviae* bey Frankfurt», y francamente no entiendo qué quería decir. En cualquier caso, la indicación me parece clara: solo después de 1608 el lector puede tener entre sus manos una edición más accesible que la de 1595.

La edición Hanau 1609 es, por tanto, la primera edición de la obra completa en todas sus partes, hecha tras la muerte de su autor, e incluye las láminas rectangulares que con toda probabilidad encargó Khunrath mismo de cara a una edición 1602, que empezó a hacer imprimir en vida sin poder terminarla.

Intentemos reconstruir de forma novelesca la historia. El buen Khunrath quiere coronar su carrera con el *Amphitheatrum*. En 1595 manda ejecutar los grabados circulares, y los publica acompañándolos de un primer comentario. Luego vuelve a ponerse manos a la obra. Va a tal velocidad que en 1598 se siente casi listo y se asegura el privilegio imperial. Antes de 1602, para ganar tiempo, reescribe y fecha el epílogo y, como el tiempo apremia, manda grabar el frontispicio. Quizá en aquellos años da instrucciones para la ejecución de las láminas rectangulares. Luego, en 1605, muere.

Entra en escena Wolfart, ya sin rival, que pone a trabajar a Guillermo Antonio. Este empieza a imprimir y acaba en 1609, fecha del colofón y de la introducción de Wolfart. A esas alturas algo sucede.

Primera hipótesis: Guillermo Antonio encuaderna su edición con todas las láminas y le coloca el frontispicio de 1602, que ya existe, y es bonito, y además garantiza una autenticidad khunrathiana; quizá piensa también en introducir nuevos grabados e imprime las instrucciones para poner siete al final de cada *Gradus*; Wolfart se da cuenta del intento de manipulación, se pelea con Antonio, y en el último minuto lo obliga a poner la fe de erratas.

Entretanto, observa desde la sombra el diabólico librero de Magdeburgo, que desde hacía un año tascaba el freno, ya había mandado imprimir su frontispicio 1608 y le había encargado a Antonio un número determinado de ejemplares. Le llegan los ejemplares Hanau, les coloca su frontispicio antedatado y los pone en circulación. No olvidemos que el privilegio imperial vale diez años desde la fecha de impresión (que es 1609). Quizá quien pone en circulación ejemplares con fecha de 1608 intenta eludir la ley con torpeza, confiando en que los controladores miren el frontispicio y no el colofón.[21]

---

21. Hipótesis: el número de las láminas impresas es inferior a los ejemplares del texto, y Brauns, con gran desenvoltura, pone a la venta ejemplares sin grabados. Esto explicaría el ejemplar de 1608 conservado en la Biblioteca Trivulziana, que precisamente carece de láminas.

Segunda hipótesis: Brauns es quien de verdad hace el encargo y el sinvergüenza es otro, que usa ejemplares Hanau vendiéndolos con el frontispicio 1602, tomado quién sabe de dónde, o adquirido en pliegos sueltos desde hacía tiempo, junto a las láminas.

Quizá Khunrath intuía que pasaría lo que pasó. Muy preocupado, en el frontispicio 1595, confiaba, si no en el privilegio imperial, en el divino: «Cum gratia et privilegio SSe tremendaque Maiestatis Divinae, ad perpetuum: Non Furtum Facias».

Nadie, ni siquiera Dios, lo escuchó.

EL ORDEN DE LAS LÁMINAS

En todo caso, está claro que las láminas circulaban ya antes de 1609. Esto explicaría otro problema que he afrontado. De los diferentes ejemplares citados, ninguno encuaderna los grabados siguiendo el mismo orden. Incluso el retrato en algunos casos funciona como portadilla, en otros sigue al frontispicio.

Indiquemos las láminas como sigue: F (Frontispicio), K (Retrato de K.), G (Adumbratio Gymnasii), D (Designatio Pyramidum), H (Hypothiposis Arcis), P (Porta Amphitheatri), N (Enemigos), C (Cristo), R (Rebis), A (Adán Andrógino) L (Laboratorio), O (Lechuza). Veamos ahora en qué orden aparecen en los siguientes ejemplares: Eco, Casanatense, Bolonia, Trivulziana, Ambrosiana, París Bibliothèque Nationale (pseudo 1605), Sorbona, Matton, Bailly 1 y Bailly 2, además de los ejemplares descritos en los catálogos de Guaita, Myer, Levi, Waite, Van Lennep, Chacornac (en el caso de los ejemplares controlados directamente, la ausencia de una lámina significa que no existe, mientras que en los ejemplares descritos, queda la duda de si se trata de una carencia no denunciada explícitamente o de colación imperfecta).[22]

Resulta el siguiente esquema:

	1	2	3	4	5	6	7	8	9	10	11	12
Eco	F	K	G	D	H	P	N	C	A	R	L	O
Casanatense	F	K	D	H	P	R	–	A	C	L	G	O
Bolonia	F	K	G	D	P	C	A	R	L	N	H	–
Trivulziana	K	F	G	D	P	H	–	C	A	R	L	O
Ambrosiana	F	K	P	C	A	G	H	R	L	D	N	O
B. N. París	F	K	N	L	R	A	C	P	H	D	G	–
Guaita	F	K	O	R	L	A	C	P	H	G	D	N
Myer	K	F	P	L	G	H	D	N	R	A	C	–
Levi	–	–	D	A	G	P	C	L	H	R	N	–
Waite	–	–	L	G	A	D	P	C	H	R	N	–
Van Lennep	K	F	O	P	G	H	D	N	C	A	R	L
Chacornac	F	K	D	G	P	H	C	A	R	O	L	N
Matton	F	K	H	D	P	G	A	L	R	C	N	O
Bailly 1	F	O	K	L	C	A	R	N	H	P	G	D
Bailly 2	F	K	H	L	A	R	C	N	P	D	G	–
Sorbona	F	K	G	D	H	P	A	C	R	L	O	N

22. En las primeras versiones de este texto no se citan cuatro ejemplares (Sorbona, Matton, Bailly 1 y Bailly 2), que fueron cotejadas por Jean-Claude Bailly, editor de la edición francesa (*L'énigme de la Hanau 1609*, París, J.-C. Bailly Éditeur, 1990). El ejemplar descrito en el catálogo de la colección Verginelli Rota parece corresponder al descrito por Guaita. Hall cita «Three engraved charts in text», pero se trata evidentemente de un error. La Biblioteca Universitaria de Bolonia posee también, catalogada como ejemplar del *Amph* (A v L III 27), un volumen atlántico en el que las diez láminas, sin frontispicio y retrato, están montadas junto a otros *excerpta* de Fludd y otras obras alquímicas y cabalísticas. En la edición francesa de mi texto, Bailly cita en nota una tirada de la primera lámina plegada, con el mismo texto, pero compuesto de forma distinta, que lleva en el recto el privilegio de Rodolfo II, con fecha de 1598.

El test me parece suficiente para establecer que, a causa de la oscuridad del texto, cuyas referencias a las láminas son muy vagas, se encuadernaban los grabados al azar o como le gustara a quien asumía el encargo. Dado que las láminas habían sido publicadas y puestas en circulación antes, los distintos encuadernadores ponían solo las disponibles.

Por consiguiente, cada ejemplar de la Hanau 1609 es un ejemplar compuesto, y creo que es imposible establecer si existió de verdad un ejemplar tipo. Aun cuando se asumiera que debe haber existido (y debe haber existido) el primer ejemplar salido de los tipos de Guillermo Antonio, y que fuera encuadernado inmediatamente en la imprenta, nada nos dice que el orden de las láminas fuera el que pensó Khunrath y quiso Wolfart.

Por otra parte, ¿qué podíamos pretender? El 1 de febrero de 1625 la obra fue condenada por la Sorbona como «llena de impiedades, errores y herejías y de una constante y sacrílega profanación de los pasos de la Sagrada Escritura», capaz de llevar a sus lectores a la práctica de artes secretas y criminales.[23] Eso explica las vicisitudes de las distintas ediciones y de los mismos ejemplares individuales, que probablemente sobrevivieron a duras penas.

23. Argentré, *Collectio judiciorum de novis erroribus*, II, ii, p. 162, citado también con fecha equivocada por Mersenne, *Correspondance*, II; cfr. Thorndike, VII, p. 275.

Locos literarios (y científicos)

Varia et curiosa[1]

Leer los catálogos significa descubrir presencias inesperadas, con tal de tener la paciencia de ir a explorar esas secciones que los libreros suelen titular *Varia et curiosa*. Se descubren, entonces, libros cuyos títulos nos hacen soñar, y quisiéramos poseerlos todos, si no fuera porque son legión y su reunión completa llevaría a la ruina al más rico de los coleccionistas.

GABINETES DE CURIOSIDADES

Hace casi diez años tuve la oportunidad de reseñar, como si fuera un inédito rabelaisiano, el catálogo *Cabinet de curiosités II* de la librería parisina Intersigne y, al hojear la lista de esos quinientos treinta y cinco títulos, me encontré con exquisitas publicaciones médicas de la época positivista: análisis de la locura de Rousseau; un *Mahoma considerado un enajenado* de 1842; experimentos de trasplantes de testículos del mono al hombre; prótesis testiculares de plata; las obras del célebre Tissot sobre la masturbación (como causa de ceguera, sordera, demencia

---

1. Conferencia dictada en la Biblioteca Nacional de Nápoles el 18 de enero de 2002, luego publicada con el mismo título en *L'Esopo*, n.º 89-90, 2002.

precoz, etcétera); una obrita en la que se denuncia la peligrosidad de la sífilis como enfermedad que puede causar tuberculosis; otra de 1901 sobre la necrofagia.

Voy a limitarme, sin embargo, a títulos decididamente menos científicos. Me gustaría tener a un tal Andrieu, sobre el palillo y sus inconvenientes, 1869. Me atrae Ecochoard, sobre las diferentes técnicas de empalamiento, además de Fournel, sobre la función de los golpes de bastón (1858), donde se ofrece una lista de escritores o artistas célebres a los que les dieron bastonazos, desde Boileau hasta Voltaire y Mozart. Un tal Bérillon (indicado como ejemplo de hombre de ciencia cegado por el nacionalismo) en plena guerra mundial (1915) escribe *La polychésie de la race allemande*, donde demuestra que el alemán medio produce más materia fecal que el francés, y de olor más desagradable.

Un tal señor Chesnier-Duchene (1843) elabora un complejo sistema para traducir el francés a jeroglíficos de nuevo cuño, a fin de hacerlo comprensible a todos los pueblos. Un tal Chassaignon (y este lo tengo) escribe en 1770 cuatro volúmenes cuyo título vale la pena saborear: *Cataractes de l'imagination, déluge de la scribomanie, vomissement littéraire, hémorragie encyclopédique, monstre des monstres*. Digamos que este señor —pero ¿quién ha tenido jamás el valor de leerse todas esas mil quinientas páginas?—, que los bibliógrafos definen por unanimidad como un insensato, juega con toda la literatura universal, desde Virgilio hasta los escritorzuelos más demencialmente marginales, para arrastrarlos al torbellino de su propio delirio, sacando citas, episodios curiosos, observaciones que llenan páginas y páginas de notas, pasando por los peligros de la crítica de la modestia al elogio de la alabanza, de las profecías de Ezequiel a las raíces del regaliz.

Encontré también una obrita de 1626 sobre la Orden de los Cornudos Reformados, que describe el estatuto de sus adeptos, su ceremonia de iniciación, y remonta el origen de los cornudos a la Torre de Babel. Faltaba en ese catálogo (pero había aparecido otras veces en otros catálogos del mismo librero) un libro que tuvo innumerables ediciones desde 1714 hasta principios del siglo XIX. Se trata (también este lo tengo, pero no es un libro raro) del *Chef d'oeuvre d'un inconnu* de Saint-Hyacinthe.[2]

SOBRE LOS LOCOS LITERARIOS

¿Estaban locos todos los autores de los libros que acabo de citar? Uso con razón la palabra «locos» porque al respecto existe un género de ensayo y bibliográfico que puede definirse como historiografía de los locos literarios, y que se ocupa de autores «chiflados», no solo en el ámbito de la literatura sino también de las ciencias. Cito, por ejemplo, *L'histoire littéraire des fous* de Delepierre, 1860; obras que se ocupan de una sola área geográfica, como *Les fous littéraires du Quercy* de Louis Greil, 1866; por no hablar del célebre Quérard, *Supercheries littéraires*, 1845, que trata de locos que «se aprovechan», es decir, plagiarios, apócrifos y organizadores de burlas editoriales. Pero quizá la obra más célebre es *Les fous littéraires* de Philomneste Junior (seudónimo de Gustave Brunet), publicada en Bruselas en 1880. Ya sea por juego, ya sea por polémica, o por falta de método, nuestro Brunet no hacía una clara distinción entre obras locas y obras (in-

---

2. Véase en este mismo volumen el ensayo dedicado a Saint-Hyacinthe, «La obra maestra de un desconocido».

cluso sensatísimas) de autores que en su vida privada padecían de trastornos psiquiátricos. Está claro que Brunet consideraba que la obra de un demente era demencial y que una obra que a él le parecía demencial presuponía un autor loco.

Resulta obvio, pues, que, junto a un Attardi que en 1875 había publicado un libro sobre la posibilidad de la abolición de la muerte tanto violenta como natural, o a un Henrion que en 1718 presentó una memoria sobre la estatura de Adán, Brunet incluyera a varios místicos, visionarios, alquimistas y cabalistas, desde Paracelso hasta Fludd, desde Cyrano de Bergerac hasta Sade y Fourier. A veces, Brunet apostaba por casos sin duda singulares, como cuando presentaba a Wronski, un señor que publicó millares de páginas de matemáticas, ciencias naturales, política, escribiendo cartas al zar de Rusia y a otros regentes de estados europeos para proponer una Reforma Absoluta del Saber Humano y de la Mecánica Celeste, con la finalidad de combatir el Siniestro Desorden Revolucionario y las sociedades secretas. Un banquero llamado Arson, que aspiraba también él al saber absoluto, lo financió durante mucho tiempo, luego se produjo una ruptura violenta entre ambos y Wronski escribió páginas y más páginas contra Arson, llegó incluso a querellarse contra él, sin llegar a ganar nunca el pleito en que pedía doscientos mil francos de aquel entonces, por robo de verdades filosóficas. Nótese que Wronski de vez en cuando atinaba algunas ideas, dignas de consideración, y Jakobson, por ejemplo, lo cita con mucho respeto.[3]

Sin embargo, lo que nos hará saltar en la silla es que encontramos en esta compañía a Sócrates, Newton, Poe y Walt Whit-

---

3. Véase Roman Jakobson, *Lo sviluppo della semiotica*, Milán, Bompiani, 1978.

man, y no solo a ellos. Hay que decir que Brunet tenía su lógica: encontraba en Whitman un principio de orgullo y sublevación, la exaltación de la propia individualidad y frases como «yo vuelvo divino todo lo que toco». Y comentaba: «¿Acaso no están aquí todos los síntomas de la demencia?». Respecto a Sócrates, se preguntaba Brunet en primer lugar si había que considerarlo un escritor porque el pobrecillo jamás escribió, y abrigaba alguna duda de si clasificar entre los locos a un señor que afirmaba tener un demonio familiar. Llegaba a la conclusión de que se trataba, en cualquier caso, de monomanía. Respecto a Newton era fácil decirlo: genio inmortal sí, pero visionario que se había ocupado de cábala, de fuerzas ocultas e interpretaciones del Apocalipsis. Que, entre otras cosas, era verdad, salvo que Brunet omitía las aportaciones, sin duda menores, al estudio de la gravitación universal o al cálculo diferencial.

También Gustave Brunet, sin embargo, como todo loco literario, puede sugerir algo bueno y, es decir, que la noción de locura puede cambiar mucho según las épocas y las perspectivas filosóficas. Hace tiempo estaba hablando yo con un insigne matemático que me reveló estupefacto que Leibniz estaba loco. «¡Imagínate —me dijo— que he descubierto que este hombre, que escribió opúsculos de lógica y matemáticas verdaderamente geniales, escribió también obras marginales con fantasías delirantes sobre las mónadas y sobre la armonía preestablecida!»

Entre los herederos de Brunet, el más célebre hoy en día ha sido André Blavier, fallecido hace menos de un año, miembro activo del Oulipo y (como yo) Sátrapa Trascendente del Colegio de Patafísica, que publicó un volumen de casi mil páginas sobre *Les Fous Littéraires*. Desde que escribí *El péndulo de Foucault*, recibo decenas de cartas de aquellos que en la novela definía como los Diabólicos, que no se han dado cuenta de que mi novela era su representación grotesca, pero (al estar precisamente locos) me envían revisitaciones delirantes de la cábala, o numerologías sin pies ni cabeza. Desde que escribí *La búsqueda de la lengua perfecta* (donde argumento que no es posible construirla), recibo siempre textos de numerosos centenares de páginas donde alguien presenta un nuevo lenguaje universal. Con todo ello he juntado una biblioteca bastante modesta de unos cien títulos, mientras que los que enumera Blavier son mil quinientos más o menos. ¿Cómo lograr reunir mil quinientas obras de locos literarios? Es la tarea de una vida, y la obra de un genio.

Abriendo al azar las páginas de esa reseña de miríficos horrores podríamos citar de todo: inventores de lenguas universales, apóstoles de nuevas cosmogonías, profetas, visionarios, nuevos mesías, cuadradores del círculo, inventores de máquinas del movimiento perpetuo, filántropos que proponen palingenesias sociales, higienistas que celebran las ventajas del salto atrás, médicos que han estudiado la cantidad de «animalejos» nocivos que habitan el esperma humano, un sociólogo que propone un método para usar socialmente a los asesinos, un tal Mandrolle, que discute de la teología de los ferrocarriles, la obra de Félix Passot, *Démonstration de l'immobilité de la terre*, de 1829, la *Réfutation du système de Copernic* de Pierre Sindoco, de 1878; el trabajo de un tal Tardy, que prueba que nuestro globo gira sobre sí mismo en cuarenta y ocho horas; el *Essai d'une nouvelle hypothèse planétaire* de Van Cotte (1851), donde se demuestra que, si se acepta a Copérnico, una ciudad no podría ser bombardeada jamás porque, al quedar la bomba suspendida por lo menos algún segundo en el aire antes de caer, durante ese instante la superficie de la tierra se desplazaría.

Tierras huecas y otras astronomías delirantes

En la recopilación de Blavier, existen alusiones a los partidarios de las varias teorías sobre la Tierra Hueca, pero sus fuentes son más bien francesas, mientras que las obras principales sobre la Tierra Hueca están en inglés y alemán.

Desde 1925, en los ambientes nazis, se hacía propaganda a la teoría de un pseudocientífico austríaco, Hans Hörbiger, denominada WEL, es decir, *Welteislehre*, o teoría del hielo eterno. Esa teoría gozó de los favores de hombres como Rosenberg y Himmler. Pero con el ascenso de Hitler al poder, a Hörbiger lo tomaron en serio también en algunos ambientes científicos, por ejemplo, estudiosos como Lenard, que había descubierto los rayos X con Roentgen. La teoría del hielo eterno había sido expuesta en 1913 por Philip Fauth en su *Glacial-Kosmogonie*: el cosmos es el teatro de una lucha eterna entre hielo y fuego, que produce no una evolución sino una alternancia de ciclos, o de épocas. Antaño hubo un enorme cuerpo a alta temperatura, millones de veces mayor que el sol, que entró en colisión con una inmensa acumulación de hielo cósmico. La masa de hielo penetró en ese cuerpo incandescente, y después de haber trabajado en su interior como vapor durante centenares de millones de años, lo hizo estallar todo. Varios fragmentos se proyectaron tanto al espacio helado como a una zona intermedia, donde constituyeron el sistema solar. La Luna, Marte, Júpiter y Saturno están helados y un anillo de hielo es la Vía Láctea, allí donde la astronomía tradicional ve estrellas; pero se trata de trucos fotográficos. Las manchas solares están producidas por bloques de hielo que se separan de Júpiter.

Actualmente, la fuerza de la explosión originaria va disminuyendo y cada planeta no lleva a cabo una revolución elíptica, como cree erróneamente la ciencia oficial, sino una aproximación en espiral (imperceptible) alrededor del planeta mayor que lo atrae. Al final del ciclo en que estamos viviendo, la Luna irá aproximándose cada vez más a la Tierra, y hará que vayan elevándose las aguas de los océanos, los trópicos quedarán sumergidos y aflorarán solo las montañas más altas, los rayos cósmicos se volverán más poderosos y determinarán mutaciones genéticas. Por último, nuestro satélite estallará y se convertirá en un anillo de hielo, agua y gas, que al final caerá sobre el globo terráqueo. A causa de complejas vicisitudes debidas a la influencia de Marte, también la Tierra se transformará en un globo de hielo y al final será reabsorbida por el Sol. Luego habrá una nueva explosión y un nuevo inicio, del mismo modo que, por otra parte, en el pasado la Tierra tuvo y reabsorbió otros tres satélites.

Habrán notado que esta cosmogonía presuponía una suerte de Eterno Retorno que se remitía a mitos y epopeyas antiquísimos. Una vez más, lo que también los nazis de hoy en día denominan el saber de la Tradición se oponía al falso saber de la ciencia liberal y judía. Además, una cosmogonía glacial parecía muy nórdica y aria. En *El retorno de los brujos*, Pauwels y Bergier atribuyen a esta profunda creencia en los orígenes glaciales del cosmos la confianza, alimentada por Hitler, de que sus tropas podrían arreglárselas muy bien en el hielo del territorio ruso. Pero sostienen también que la exigencia de probar cómo reaccionaría el hielo cósmico retrasó incluso los experimentos sobre las V1. Todavía en 1952, un tal Elmar Brugg publicó un libro en honor de Hörbiger como el Copérnico del siglo XX, sosteniendo que la teoría del hielo eterno explicaba los vínculos profundos que unen los acontecimientos terrenos con las fuerzas cósmicas, y concluía que el silencio de la ciencia democrático-judía con respecto a Hörbiger era un caso típico de conspiración de los mediocres.

Que alrededor del partido nazi actuaran cultores de ciencias mágico-herméticas y neotemplarias, por ejemplo los adeptos de la *Thule Gesellschaft* fundada por Rudolf von Sebottendorf, es un fenómeno que ha sido ampliamente estudiado.[4]

En el ambiente nazi se habría dado crédito también a otra teoría, la de la Tierra Vacía. En efecto, las teorías de la Tierra Vacía son dos. Según la primera, nosotros habitamos en la corteza, pero en el interior hay otro mundo, que no conocemos, en el cual (en opinión de algunos) está el reino misterioso de Agartha, sede del rey del mundo (y véanse, por ejemplo, las fantasías de René Guénon). Según la otra, nosotros creemos que vivimos en la corteza exterior, pero en realidad vivimos en el interior (es decir, creemos que vivimos en una superficie convexa mientras que, de hecho, vivimos en una superficie cóncava).

Una de las primeras teorías de la Tierra Vacía la propuso en 1692 Edmund Halley (el de la cometa, precisamente). Fascinado por el problema del campo magnético terrestre, Halley descubrió que la dirección del campo variaba ligeramente en el curso del tiempo y sacó la conclusión de que no existía un solo campo magnético sino muchos. De ahí la idea de que la Tierra estuviera vacía y que dentro de ella existiera una segunda esfera con otro campo magnético. Por último, propuso que la Tierra estuviera compuesta por cuatro esferas, cada una encajada en la otra, como muchas matrioskas: el interior del planeta es-

---

4. Véanse, por ejemplo, Nicholas Goodrick-Clarke, *The Occult Roots of Nazism*, Wellingborough, Aquarian Press, 1985; René Alleau, *Hitler et les sociétés secrètes*, París, Grasset, 1969; Giorgio Galli, *Hitler e il nazismo magico*, Milán, Rizzoli, 2005.

taba habitado e iluminado por una especie de atmósfera ligera y las auroras boreales no eran sino fugas de ese gas luminoso a través del casquete polar.

En el siglo XVIII, el célebre matemático Euler sustituyó la teoría de las esferas múltiples con la de una sola esfera cóncava y vacía, que contenía un sol que calentaba e iluminaba una civilización avanzada. Más tarde, el matemático escocés sir John Leslie afirmó que en el interior de la Tierra había no uno sino dos soles, que llamó Plutón y Proserpina.

La teoría de la Tierra Vacía volvió a ser propuesta a principios del siglo XIX por un tal capitán J. Cleves Symmes de Ohio, que escribió a varias sociedades científicas: «A todo el mundo: yo declaro que la tierra está vacía y es habitable en su interior; que contiene cierto número de esferas sólidas, concéntricas, es decir, colocadas una dentro de la otra, y que está abierta en los dos polos por una extensión de doce o dieciséis grados». En la Academy of Natural Sciences de Filadelfia se conserva todavía la maqueta, de madera, de su universo. Una de las ideas de Symmes era que en el Polo Norte y en el Polo Sur había dos aberturas que llevan al interior del globo, y a fin de identificarlas intentó en vano recoger fondos para una expedición a las regiones polares. No logró llevar a cabo su proyecto, pero la idea la retomó un editor de periódicos, Jeremiah Reynolds. Reynolds se lo tomó a pecho y promovió la expedición a cargo del gobierno estadounidense, que invirtió trescientos mil dólares, naturalmente sin resultado alguno. En 1846 el descubrimiento de un mamut atrapado en el hielo de Siberia fue usado por Marshall Gardner como prueba de la Tierra Hueca. Gardner consideraba que el mamut se había conservado tan bien porque había muerto hacía poco y que, por tanto, otros ejemplares de esa especie debían de circular todavía en el interior de la Tierra. El mamut siberiano, con toda evidencia, había salido por el agujero del Polo Norte y había sido arrastrado, tras su muerte, hasta Siberia por algún flujo glacial.

La teoría fue retomada, en la segunda mitad del siglo, por Cyrus Reed Teed, quien especificaba que lo que nosotros creemos cielo es una masa de gas, que llena el interior del globo, con zonas de luz brillante. El Sol, la Luna y las estrellas no serían globos celestes sino efectos visuales provocados por distintos fenómenos.

Como ha sido señalado, la teoría de Teed era difícil de refutar por parte de los matemáticos del siglo XIX porque era posible proyectar la superficie convexa de la Tierra sobre una superficie cóncava sin que se notaran demasiadas discrepancias.

Tras la muerte de Teed, en 1909, poco a poco sus ideas fueron difundiéndose por Alemania y, después de la Primera Guerra Mundial, la teoría fue retomada por Peter Bender, y luego por Karl Neupert, que había fundado el movimiento de la *Hohlweltlehre*, la teoría de la Tierra Hueca.

Según algunas fuentes,[5] las altas jerarquías alemanas se tomaron en serio la teoría, y en algunos ambientes de la Marina germánica se consideraba que la teoría de la Tierra Hueca permitía establecer con mayor exactitud las posiciones de los buques ingleses porque, de usarse rayos infrarrojos, la curvatura de la Tierra no oscurecería la observación. Otra habladuría sostiene que, aún durante la Segunda Guerra Mundial, Hitler habría enviado una expedición a la isla báltica de Rugen donde

---

5. Por ejemplo, Gerard Kniper, del observatorio de Monte Palomar, en un artículo publicado en *Popular Astronomy* en 1946, y Willy Ley, que trabajó en Alemania en las V1, en su artículo «Pseudoscience in Naziland», en *Astounding Science Fiction*, n.º 39, 1947.

un tal doctor Heinz Fischer habría apuntado una cámara teles-
cópica hacia el cielo para localizar a la flota británica que estaba
navegando en el interior de la superficie convexa de la Tierra
Hueca. El experimento no produjo resultados interesantes.

Se dice incluso que algunos lanzamientos con las V1 resul-
taron erróneos precisamente porque se calculaban sus trayecto-
rias partiendo de la hipótesis de una superficie cóncava y no
convexa. Donde —si es verdad— se ve la utilidad histórica y
providencial de las astronomías delirantes.

Pero es fácil decir que los nazis estaban locos y que, salvo
Martin Bormann, del que siempre se ha supuesto que permanece escondido en alguna parte, están todos muertos. El hecho
es que si ustedes buscan en internet y le piden a cualquier bus-
cador que les encuentre sitios que se ocupan de la Hollow Earth,
es decir, de la Tierra Hueca, verán que existen todavía muchísimos seguidores de las dos versiones, aquella por la que dentro
de la Tierra vivimos nosotros y aquella por la que en el centro se
halla el reino misterioso de Agartha...

Si luego ponen «Byrd», encontrarán muchos sitios web que
parten del hecho de que en 1926 el almirante Byrd sobrevoló el
Polo Norte y en 1929 el Polo Sur sin ver agujero alguno que
permitiera el acceso al interior de la Tierra. Pues bien, sobre los
viajes de Byrd ha surgido una vasta literatura, donde varios es-
píritus extravagantes interpretan sus observaciones en el sentido estrictamente contrario, como prueba de que los agujeros de
acceso existen. Entre otras cosas porque, si se fotografían las
zonas de interés durante el día, se nota una zona oscura que es
la porción de círculo ártico que, durante los meses invernales,
el sol no ilumina nunca.

Y es inútil decir que los sitios web (y los libros a los que hacen publicidad) han sido creados por algunos sinvergüenzas

que especulan con un público de credulones y/o devotos de la New Age. El problema social y cultural no son los granujas, sino los credulones, que evidentemente siguen siendo legión.

AUTORES DE CUARTA DIMENSIÓN

En los años setenta empecé a ocuparme de los autores que denominaba de Cuarta Dimensión. La denominación dependía de haber definido como Primera Dimensión la dimensión de la obra en forma manuscrita y, como Segunda Dimensión, la de la obra publicada por un editor serio. Estableciendo como Tercera Dimensión la del éxito (dado que muchos autores, incluso buenísimos, permanecen relegados a la segunda dimensión, destinados a la destrucción o a los *remainders*), identificaba yo la Cuarta Dimensión como la de los autores a sus expensas, que suelen ser publicados por editoriales especializadas en la explotación de esos talentos justamente incomprendidos. No diré nada más sobre el fenómeno, primero porque lo traté de forma narrativa hablando de las editoriales Manuzio y Garamond en *El péndulo de Foucault* y, segundo, porque, si en aquellos tiempos la Cuarta Dimensión la gestionaban pocos editores bien conocidos, hoy se ha extendido también al maremágnum de internet y es difícil ofrecer una geografía completa.

Pero, en fin, al hacer aquella investigación, reuní una pequeña biblioteca de autores a sus expensas que, a estas alturas, dado que han pasado treinta años, tiene todos los requisitos para entrar en el mercado anticuario.

Una de mis piezas más preciosas es el *Dizionario biografico di personaggi contemporanei* («Diccionario biográfico de personajes contemporáneos») de Domenico Gugnali, Gugnali editore, Módica. Busquemos la entrada «Cesare Pavese». Es exacta y sobria: «Pavese, Cesare. Nacido en Santo Stefano Belbo el 9-9-1908. Fallecido en Turín el 27 de agosto de 1950. Traductor, escritor». Poco más adelante tenemos, en cambio, a «Paolizzi, Deodato. Hombre de pluma y hombre de letras; ese es Deodato Paolizzi. Desde su primera juventud destacaba por sus espontáneas poesías, pero sobre todo por sus escritos incisivos en los que ya se vislumbraba al abogado que llegaría a ser». Siguen notas sobre su célebre novela *Il destino in marcia* («El destino en marcha») y menciones de su actividad cívica y política.

Todavía en la «P», después de tres líneas sobre «Piovene, Guido», sigue una larga biografía de Pusineri Chiesa, Edvige, maestra de escuela de Lodi, poetisa y escritora, autora de *Mesti palpiti* («Tristes latidos»), *Alba serena* («Alba serena»), *Cantici* («Cánticos»), *Il legionario* («El legionario»), *Sussurri lievi* («Susurros leves»), *Aurei voli* («Áureos vuelos»), *Chiarori nell'ombra* («Claridades en la sombra»), *Le avventure di Fuffi* («Las aventuras de Fuffi»). Es redactora milanesa de la revista *Intervallo*, editada, una mera coincidencia, por el mismo Gugnali que publica el diccionario en cuestión. La entrada está acompañada por la foto de Pusineri Chiesa, que aparece en todo el esplendor de su opulenta madurez junto a la imagen de la «delicada poetisa de Cerdeña» Puligheddu, Michelina.

Las biografías de Gugnali nos revelan un universo literario rico y fecundo, a menudo bosquejan una personalidad de escritor en pocas pinceladas esenciales: «Cariddi, Walter. Nacido en San Pietro Vernotico, Brindisi, el 4-2-1930, donde reside (conocido)». Poeta, crítico y publicista «tiene una vocación por los estudios serios junto al compromiso de éxitos más notables». Están Gavazzi, Leonida (*Cromatogramma tridimensionale dell'esistenza*, «Cromatograma tridimensional de la existencia», y *La ragnatela dell'essere*, («La telaraña del ser»); Gargiuto, Gaetano, fundador del movimiento poético del armonismo (que envía también poesías mecanografiadas en edición numerada a los periódicos); Maira, Rosangela («participó en el concurso Guapa e Inteligente convocado entre las estudiantes sicilianas del "Progreso ítalo-americano" [...] premiada con un aparato de radio»); Montanelli Menicatti, Elena («una de las más apreciadas poetisas de nuestro tiempo»); Mignemi, Gregorio (autor de *Temi svolti*, «Redacciones hechas»); Moscucci, Cittadino («autor de muchas canciones ligeras a las que el maestro Cotogni puso música y cantó en la radio el tenor Sernicoli») y, para acabar, Scarfò, Pasquale (autor de *Il signore delle camelie*, «El caballero de las camelias»), de quien se sabe que, perito y licenciado en economía, ha preferido siempre la vida militar a la profesión de asesor fiscal; por no hablar de un Umani, Giorgio, autor no solo de *L'ineffabile orgasmo* («El inefable orgasmo»), sino también de un volumen *Umani 1937* que, como dice su biografía con cierta redundancia, «es profundo estudioso de problemas de los humanos y de los Umani».

Tengo dos volúmenes de Carlo Cetti, *Difetti e pregi dei Promessi Sposi* («Defectos y virtudes de *Los novios*») y *Rifacimento dei Promessi Sposi* («Refundición de *Los novios*»), de los que el segundo es la realización de los propósitos críticos del primero. Argumenta Cetti que bien habría hecho Manzoni en volver a escribir una vez más su novela, aligerándola con la reducción de un tercio del número de las sílabas. «"¿Por qué decir "lago de Como" y "mediodía" en lugar de "Lario" y "sur"? [...] En lugar de decir "sembrados de pueblos, de aldeas, de caseríos" es mejor decir "sembrados de pueblos, aldeas, caseríos", evitando la triple repetición de ese "de".» De este modo Cetti consigue reescribir la novela en tan solo 196 páginas (publicadas a cargo del autor, Como, 1965), desde el principio, que suena «Ese ramal del Lario...», hasta el final que dice sobriamente, tras la muerte del padre Cristóforo, «el pobre joven superado por conmoción y alegría, lloraba». Nótese que no se trata de un simple resumen sino de un auténtico calcado con extirpación de sílabas excedentes. Con *Los novios* se ensaña también Vincenzo Costanza («admitido al examen para la docencia universitaria por un caso especial de elevada ciencia») en *Il pecoronismo incantevole in Italia* («El borreguismo encantador en Italia») donde, sin embargo, la polémica abandona rápidamente a Manzoni para sostener que no se dice «Treccàni» sino «Trèccani».

Un escritor de quien poseo, creo, la *opera omnia*, es Giovanni Tummolo, de Trieste, autor de obras como *Luce sepolta* («Luz enterrada»), *Il divoratore di se stesso* («El devorador de sí mismo»), la reducción dramática del episodio que relata De Amicis en *Corazón*: *Sangue romagnolo* («Sangre de Romaña»), las *Meditazioni diaboliche* («Meditaciones diabólicas») y varios libritos en los que difunde su doctrina, el misticateísmo, como el vivaz *Come evitare la terza guerra* («Cómo evitar la tercera guerra»), rico de invectivas contra sus conciudadanos poco comprensivos u otros autores con quienes dialoga en varias revistas. De *Luce sepolta* decía un recensor ítalo-americano en la revista *Supersum* de Nueva York que «es una novela lírica y a veces superlírica [...] La literatura de Tummolo se distingue ante todo por ser humilde. Lo cual debería suscitar un movimiento de piedad en el corazón humano [...] en teoría, en la práctica casi siempre sucede lo contrario [...]. Está demostrado que casi todos los que han reseñado de manera desfavorable el libro *Luce sepolta* voluntaria o involuntariamente, a través de su síntesis narrativa, se han demostrado falsos e incapaces de comprender-lo». Los dardos del recensor apuntan aquí a aquellos recensores que se han equivocado al hacer el resumen del libro pero, se observa, «estas interpretaciones equivocadas las justifican sus responsables constatando la enorme producción literaria de Italia, tierra de genios y héroes, una producción tan gigantesca que efectivamente no deja tiempo para un análisis escrupuloso». Aunque con Tummolo podría perderse un poco de tiempo porque, anota el recensor, no solo tiene un estilo, sino un pensamiento original, mientras que Novalis era solo el cantor de la filosofía de Schelling.

Así como existe el poeta y el narrador, también existe el filósofo de Cuarta Dimensión. La figura que ha sobresalido cual gigante en este campo hacia la mitad del siglo XX ha sido la de Giulio Ser-Giacomi, de Offida (Ascoli Piceno), que sembraba el desconcierto en los congresos filosóficos y fue autor de volúmenes de gran mole. Entre ellos, es célebre el epistolario con Einstein y Pío XII, que recopilaba en centenares de páginas todas las cartas que el autor envió a Pío XII y a Einstein (naturalmente, sin obtener jamás respuesta alguna), en el que se refutaban al mismo tiempo tanto la metafísica cristiana como la relativista. En las reflexiones conclusivas del decimoséptimo congreso de filosofía (donde, como en los congresos anteriores, las intervenciones de Ser-Giacomi suscitaban legítima preocupación), el filósofo afirmaba: «Los numerosos argumentos sobre la historia, por mí planteados y resueltos en *Alea iacta est* y, por tanto, "anticipados", a nadie le ha interesado discutirlos, como tampoco los otros que expuse en *Gutta cavat lapidem*, que bien me preocupé de entregar a muchos estudiosos antes del congreso [...]. La filosofía necesita una nueva linfa, esa linfa que desde hace tiempo yo le he dado...». Ser-Giacomi concluía su intervención en el congreso lanzando una petición a fin de que lo ayudaran a encontrar un mecenas «para la reimpresión, en millares de ejemplares, de todos mis escritos».

Otro incomprendido trágicamente empeñado en una batalla contra el mundo del saber es Eulogo D'Armi, de Cagliari. En su *Teismo e monismo di fronte* («Teísmo y monismo frente a frente»), D'Armi, después de haber polemizado con el pensamiento italiano contemporáneo, cuenta cómo en el congreso de filosofía de 1958, la secretaría «bofiosa [...] aducía frívolos y mendaces pretextos para disuadirlo de cualquier intervención». Pero nuestro D'Armi se había dado cuenta de que el jefe de la delegación soviética, Mitin, superaba el tiempo que se le había asignado («¡Las ventajas de tener a sus espaldas a una gran potencia!») y se sublevaba contra el evidente atropello.

El filósofo burlado e incomprendido ve los reglamentos de los congresos como artificios pensados adrede para impedir sus intervenciones. Y no puede hablarse de manía de persecución porque efectivamente una de las primeras preocupaciones de cualquier congreso o revista filosófica es, precisamente, impedir la participación a menudo incontenible de los excéntricos.

Mi recopilación de autores de Cuarta Dimensión sigue enriqueciéndose. Hace algunos años recibí como «prueba de imprenta – muestra gratuita» (y luego veremos por qué) el libro de Romano Pizzigoni *Rivolta di un uomo tranquillo* («Rebelión de un hombre tranquilo»). El libro contiene las cartas que Pizzigoni mandó prácticamente a todo el mundo. Al editor Baraghini para discutir la relatividad y quejarse de que el *New York Times* y *Los Angeles Times*, a los que había enviado muchísimos artículos, habían retomado libremente sus ideas; a Bush (padre) para pedirle que no volviera a presentarse a las elecciones; a los diputados y senadores para protestar contra el Festival de la Canción de San Remo; a Enzo Biagi sobre la existencia de Dios; al rey de Arabia Saudí y a Sadam Husein para darles consejos sobre el equilibrio mundial; a Giorgio Bocca sobre el comunismo; a la redacción de *L'Espresso* para pedirles que dejaran de mandarle gratis el semanario (lo cual me sorprende, porque no me lo mandan ni siquiera a mí); al presidente de Random House, de cuya existencia dice haber sabido leyendo *L'Espresso*; al director de France Culture; al Instituto Pasteur sobre la investigación biológica; a la revista *Nature* sobre la desaparición de los dinosaurios; a la fundación Nobel para exhortarlos a no premiar a sinvergüenzas; a varias instituciones para acusar a Hawking de haberlo plagiado; a Guido Ceronetti sobre el nazismo; a Enzo Tortora, ya enfermo de cáncer, indicándole los medios psicológicos para no morir; a Canale 5 y con copia a Silvio Berlusconi para ofrecer su colaboración; a Norberto Bobbio sobre dictadura y democracia; a Francesco Alberoni sobre la enseñanza obligatoria; y me paro aquí por falta de espacio.

Quién es Pizzigoni nos lo decía él mismo en una página autobiográfica. Entonces tenía cincuenta y seis años y estudios de primaria, había huido de la represión de la enseñanza obligatoria, fue obrero en la fábrica de Alfa-Romeo durante dos meses, rechazó la cadena de montaje, emigró a París, trabajó en la agencia Ansa como operador de teletextos, se convirtió en fotorreportero durante diez años, después empezó otra actividad no especificada que le permitiría construirse una casa con vistas al mar, pero «los chacales al acecho, disfrazados de jueces, abogados, banqueros, lo despojarían, dejándolo casi desnudo en medio de una montaña entre poblaciones semisalvajes». Por lo cual, en protesta contra el mundo, hacía largas huelgas de hambre (pero distintas de las que hacía el político Pannella que, en cuanto la gente se daba la vuelta, «comía a dos carrillos»). Para no tener que pagar los impuestos prefería no ganar nada, logrando vivir con cinco mil liras al día (entre las cuales no sé si incluía los gastos postales).

Escribía y quizá siga escribiendo aún para expresar su indignación, y eso me lo hizo simpático. Pero no carecía de ambición, y pedía que lo nombraran dictador por un período de un año. Su programa estaba compuesto por unos sesenta puntos, entre los cuales: prohibición de emitir bonos del Tesoro durante algunos años; despido de al menos el setenta por ciento de los funcionarios del Estado; abolición del permiso de conducir; supresión de mutuas y jubilaciones, todo tipo de impuestos, consulados y embajadas (que habrían de sustituirse con contactos radiotelevisivos); libertad de comercio y exportación para los objetos de arte; clausura casi total de los hospitales y creación de un cuerpo médico que enseñara a los ciudadanos cómo no enfermar; lactancia de pecho obligatoria; escuelas diversificadas al máximo... Y estos eran los propósitos que habrían podido atraer también a nuestro nuevo gobierno. Pero parecía difícil conciliar los intereses del nuevo gobierno con estas otras decisiones: abolición del fútbol profesional; prohibición de los chicles; abolición de la caza; abolición del ochenta por cierto de los automóviles; en los momentos de crisis, obligación para las empresas de renunciar a sus ganancias; abolición de toda la publicidad televisiva; sueldo mínimo a todos los ciudadanos italianos, desde su nacimiento hasta su muerte. Por no hablar de propuestas que pondrían en apuros a cualquier grupo político, excepto a la Liga Lombarda, como la abolición de las fuerzas armadas, la expulsión de todos los extranjeros del territorio nacional, o el traslado de la capital a Merano (en medio de los Alpes).

Ahora bien, Pizzigoni no carecía del sentido de la realidad: los ejemplares piloto de sus libros contenían unos impresos con los que los lectores podían suscribir obligaciones de un millón de liras cada uno (no más de setenta en total, para cubrir los gastos de imprenta), completamente reintegrables cuando se alcanzaran los primeros cincuenta mil ejemplares vendidos. Era un riesgo para los lectores, en el desafortunado caso en que el autor consiguiera vender solo cuarenta y nueve mil ejemplares. Pero podía valer la pena, visto que el segundo apartado del contrato preveía que cada suscriptor recibiría intereses de tres millones cuando se alcanzaran los primeros cuatrocientos cincuenta mil ejemplares vendidos. Una proposición honesta, porque cuatrocientos cincuenta mil ejemplares a cinco mil liras son dos mil doscientos cincuenta millones, y tres millones por setenta son doscientos diez millones. Por lo cual estaríamos poco por debajo del diez por ciento de intereses. Claro que ¿qué habría ocurrido si Pizzigoni hubiera logrado la obra maestra de vender solo cuatrocientos noventa y nueve mil novecientos noventa y nueve ejemplares?

La Cuarta Dimensión es vasta. En ella nace de todo. Y puede prosperar también el excéntrico sobre quien pesará siempre una sospecha de originalidad, quizá de grandeza. El ejemplo más vistoso (y más ignorado) de este umbral ambiguo entre una dimensión y otra es la obra del piamontés Augusto Blotto. Blotto, que creo lleva o llevaba una vida de empleado inofensiva e integérrima, publicó en los años sesenta volúmenes lujosos con el editor Rebellato, y no me consta que se vendieran jamás en las librerías. Se mandaban, en cambio, con liberalidad a críticos y periódicos. Cada volumen está formado por entre trescientas y seiscientas páginas de poesía. Los títulos son, sin duda alguna, geniales: *Trepide di prestigio* («Trepidantes de prestigio»), *Autorevole e tanto disperso* («Reputado y muy disperso»), *Il maneggio per erti, senza sugo* («El picadero para empinados, sin salsa»); *Castelletti, regali, vedute* («Pequeños castillos, regalos, vistas»); *La forza grossa e varia* («La fuerza pesada y varia»); *I boli (i baldi)* («Los bolos, los bravos»); *Nell'insieme, nel pacco d'aria* («En su conjunto, en el paquete de aire»); *Triste, attentissimo informarsi* («Triste, atentísimo informarse»); *Svenevole a intelligenza* («Desmayable a inteligencia»); *Tranquillità e presto atroce* («Tranquilidad y presto atroz»); *Gentile dovere di congedare vaghi* («Amable deber de saludar vagos»); *Le soglie tremolanti e nette* («Los umbrales temblorosos y netos»); *Basso come umido* («Bajo como húmedo»); *L'anno d'aggiustature di morte* («El año de reparaciones de muerte»); *Il vuoto da vigore: l'agevole* («El vacío de vigor: lo practicable»); *Lo stupore nel risvegliarsi all'esempio* («El estupor al despertarse en el ejemplo).

Los versos de Blotto muestran casi siempre una desenfrenada invención verbal. La objeción de que en su mayoría sea absolutamente gratuita (lo que la distingue de Gadda) corre el riesgo de caer ante la constancia con la cual el poeta se inventa en millares de páginas un lenguaje personal de demencial protervia inventiva: «La cadera de asfalto, toda ella un tigricio, un talco — entre los escamosos prados un poco de pizarra — un céreo — separarse quizá con obnúbilo, ser bien ausentes [...] un Cristo aserelado — de agujeros de piedras, de mariposíos mantidismos de escápulas...». El léxico de Blotto está hecho de «tarde cabonieta», de «báculo de vehemencia del meridión detestador», «de malasuñas frascadas», de «pinturo tal vez gusanito de corrillo», de «estragarme a inentrarnos», de «lincustras». Los versos son duros, pedregosos, la sintaxis ardua, la comprensibilidad nula (lo cual no significa nada), la plausibilidad de difícil determinación. Pero en millares, millares y millares de versos, Blotto construye su mundo al borde de esos acantilados bífidos donde a un lado está el genio y en el otro la monomanía. Es uno de los casos, por lo menos, en los que la acumulación cuantitativa genera una sospecha de calidad incomprendida.[6]

LAS LOCURAS DE LOS EXPERTOS

Por otra parte, nosotros somos severos con los locos literarios. Ahora bien, ¿cuántos, que hoy consideramos grandísimos, no fueron considerados dementes en los tiempos de sus exordios? Como llamada de atención a un mayor respeto por los locos literarios, recordaré algunos episodios históricos, a los que se han dedicado dos obras que considero fundamentales, *Rotten Rejections* de André Bernard (Pushcart Press, 1990, y luego republicado por Robson Books, 2005) y *The Experts Speak* de Christopher Cerf y Victor Navasky.

«Es posible que yo sea algo duro de entenderas, pero no consigo comprender cómo un señor puede emplear treinta páginas para describir las vueltas y revueltas que se da en la cama antes de conciliar el sueño.» Con esta motivación, un lector del editor Ollendorf rechazó la *Recherche* de Proust.

En 1851, *Moby Dick* es rechazado en Inglaterra con el siguiente juicio: «No pensamos que pueda funcionar para el mercado de literatura juvenil. Es largo, de estilo anticuado, y nos parece que no merece la reputación de la que parece disfrutar». A Flaubert en 1856 le rechazan *Madame Bovary* con esta carta:

---

6. En los últimos años, todavía me ha llegado de Blotto *La vivente uniformità dell'animale* («La viviente uniformidad del animal», San Cesario, Manni, 2003) con el prefacio de un crítico de paladar fino como Stefano Agosti, quien recuerda también los comentarios positivos de Sergio Solmi y Giorgio Barberi-Squarotti.

«Señor, habéis enterrado vuestra novela en un cúmulo de detalles que están bien delineados pero que son completamente superfluos». A Emily Dickinson le rechazan el primer manuscrito de poesías en 1862 con: «Dudoso. Las rimas están todas equivocadas».

Por lo que atañe a nuestro siglo, aquí van algunos ejemplos. Colette, *Claudine en la escuela*, 1900: «No conseguiría vender ni siquiera diez ejemplares». Henry James, *La fuente sagrada*, 1901: «Ataca decididamente los nervios... Ilegible. La sensación de esfuerzo se vuelve exasperante en sumo grado. No hay historia». James Joyce, *Dedalus*, 1916: «Al final todo el libro se desmorona. Tanto la escritura como las ideas estallan en fragmentos pastosos, como polvo pírico mojado». Francis Scott Fitzgerald, *A este lado del paraíso*, 1920: «La historia no llega a una conclusión. Ni el carácter ni la carrera del protagonista parecen llegar a un punto que justifique el final. Resumiendo, me parece que la historia no llega a nada». Faulkner, *Santuario*, 1931: «Dios mío, Dios mío, no podemos publicarlo. Acabaríamos todos en la cárcel».

George Orwell, *Rebelión en la granja*, 1945: «Imposible vender historias de animales en Estados Unidos». Sobre *Molloy* de Beckett, 1951: «No tiene sentido pensar en publicarlo: el mal gusto del público norteamericano no coincide con el mal gusto de la vanguardia francesa». Respecto al *Diario* de Anna Frank, 1952: «Esta joven no parece tener una percepción especial, es decir, el sentimiento de cómo puede elevarse este libro por encima de un nivel de simple curiosidad». Nabokov, *Lolita*, 1955: «Debería contarse a un psicoanalista y probablemente así se ha hecho, y se ha transformado en una novela que contiene algunos pasajes de hermosa escritura, pero es excesivamente nauseabundo, incluso para el más iluminado de los freudianos

[...] recomiendo enterrarlo durante mil años». Joseph Heller, *Trampa 22*, 1961: «No consigo entender de ninguna manera qué quería hacer este hombre. Se trata de un grupo de soldados norteamericanos en Italia que se acuestan con las mujeres el uno del otro y con alguna prostituta italiana, pero sin que el asunto parezca interesante. Sin duda el autor quisiera resultar divertido, quizá hace sátira, pero no consigue divertir en ningún plano intelectual. Tiene dos ocurrencias, ambas pésimas, y vuelve a ellas sin parar [...] Un aburrimiento sin fin».

H. G. Wells, *La máquina del tiempo*, 1895: «Poco interesante para el lector normal y no lo suficientemente profundo para el lector científico». *La buena tierra* de Pearl S. Buck, 1931: «Lo siento, pero al público norteamericano no le interesa nada que concierna a China». Le Carré, *El espía que surgió del frío*, 1963: «Démosle el pasaporte. Le Carré no tiene futuro».

Para pasar de los juicios editoriales a la crítica militante, aquí tienen los que Eugène Poitou decía de Honoré de Balzac en la *Revue des Deux Mondes* de 1856: «En sus novelas no hay nada que revele especiales dotes imaginativas, ni la trama, ni los personajes. Balzac no ocupará jamás un lugar de relieve en la literatura francesa».

En cuanto a Emily Brontë: «En *Cumbres borrascosas*, los defectos de *Jane Eyre* [de su hermana Charlotte] se multiplican por mil. Bien pensado, el único consuelo que nos queda es pensar que la novela nunca llegará a ser popular» (James Lorimer, *North British Review*, 1849). Emily Dickinson: «La incoherencia y la falta de forma de sus poemitas —no sabría definirlos de otro modo— son espantosas» (Thomas Bailey Aldrich, *The Atlantic Monthly*, 1982).

Thomas Mann: «*Los Buddenbrook* no son más que dos gruesos volúmenes en los que el autor cuenta historias insignificantes de gente insignificante con un estilo insignificante» (Eduard Engel, 1901). Herman Melville: «*Moby Dick* es un libro triste, sórdido, plano, incluso ridículo [...]. Ese capitán loco, además, es de un aburrimiento mortal» (*The Southern Quarterly Review*, 1851). Walt Whitman: «Walt Whitman tiene la misma relación con el arte que un cerdo con las matemáticas» (*The London Critic*, 1855).

Pasemos a la música. Sobre Bach, Johann Adolph Scheibe afirmaba en *Der critische Musikus*, 1737: «Las composiciones de Johann Sebastian Bach carecen totalmente de belleza, de armonía y, sobre todo, de claridad». Louis Spohr reseñaba en 1808 la primera ejecución de la *Quinta* de Beethoven con: «Una orgía de estruendo y de vulgaridad». Ludwig Rallstab (*Iris im Gebiete der Tonkunst*, 1833) decía que si Chopin «hubiera sometido sus músicas al juicio de un experto, este las habría hecho pedazos [...], de todos modos, quisiera hacerlo yo». La *Gazette Musicale de Paris*, 1853, escribía que «*Rigoletto* es flojo en el plano melódico. Esta ópera no tiene ninguna posibilidad de entrar en el repertorio». Por otro lado, también *Amadeus* (obra de teatro y película) han vuelto célebre el juicio del emperador de Austria después de *Las bodas de Fígaro* de Mozart: «Hay demasiadas notas».

Respecto a las artes, Ambroise Vollard (marchante de arte célebre por su olfato), en 1907 liquidaba así *Les Demoiselles d'Avignon* de Picassso: «Es la obra de un loco». Omito a un tal Hunt que a principios del siglo XIX decía que Rembrandt no podía compararse ni de lejos con Rippingille (les aviso que están obligados a saber quién era), y un señor un poco más conocido que Hunt y Rippingille, nada menos que William Blake, afirmaba: «No veo la razón de mencionar el nombre de Tiziano y de los vénetos cuando se habla de pintura. Son unos idiotas, no unos artistas». Pero aquí entramos en el área de las incomprensiones entre genios, y bastarán pocos ejemplos. Émile Zola, con ocasión de la muerte de Baudelaire, en su necrológica decía: «Dentro de cien años *Les fleurs du mal* serán recordadas solo como una curiosidad». No contento con haber destrozado a Baudelaire, decía de Cézanne: «Habrá tenido las dotes de un gran pintor, pero le ha faltado la voluntad de convertirse en uno». En el diario de Virginia Woolf se lee: «Acabo de terminar de leer el *Ulysses* y lo considero un fracaso [...] es prolijo y desagradable. Es un texto tosco, no solo en sentido objetivo, sino también desde el punto de vista literario». Chaikovski en su diario escribía de Brahms: «He estudiado mucho la música de ese bribón. Es un bastardo que carece de toda calidad». Degas le aconsejaba a un coleccionista, a propósito de Toulouse-Lautrec: «¡Compra unos Maurins! ¡Lautrec está vinculado a una época!». Hablando de Renoir, Manet le decía a Monet: «Ese joven no tiene ningún talento».

Pasando al *show business*. Irving Thalberg, directivo de la Metro, en 1936 disuadía a alguien de que comprara los derechos de *Lo que el viento se llevó* diciendo que «ninguna película sobre la guerra civil ha dado nunca ningún dinero»; y Gary Cooper, tras rechazar el papel de Rhett Butler, comentaba: «*Lo que el viento se llevó* será el fiasco más clamoroso de la historia de Hollywood. Estoy muy contento de que sea Clark Gable quien se vea en apuros y no Gary Cooper». Por otra parte, tras una audición de Clark Gable, en 1930, Jack Warned decía: «¿Qué hago yo con un tipo con semejantes orejas?»; y también un directivo de la Metro, después de una audición de Fred Astaire, en 1928: «No sabe actuar, no sabe cantar y es calvo. Se le da un poco bien el baile». Lo que, en definitiva, bien pensado, no estaba completamente equivocado. Y con todo fue un error.

Lo que nos llama la atención en estas recopilaciones es que se trata de juicios contemporáneos, emitidos en caliente. Como para avisarnos de que las obras de arte hay que dejarlas reposar, igual que los vinos.

ELOGIO DE LA INCONGRUENCIA

Con esto no quiero insinuar que debamos revisitar todas las obras de los locos literarios para redescubrir talentos ocultos. Lo bonito de los catálogos de antigüedades, para retomar el tema, es que nos hablan de un pasado al que ya se le han aplicado muchos filtros. Lo que debe salvarse, en esta lectura de los *Varia et curiosa*, es su aire de lista incongruente, en la cual, como en una página de Rabelais, un tratado sobre la masturbación se acompaña de una disquisición sobre el sexo de los ángeles.

Una vez, en uno de mis artículos para *L'Espresso*, me concedí una lista incongruente y, no recuerdo a propósito de qué, enumeré, entre aquellos que presumiblemente no sentían interés alguno por la Accademia dei Lincei,* a tejedores, hojalateros, viticultores que usan metanol, usureros, agentes secretos, industriales de barras para hormigón, empleados de garajes en coma profundo, charcuteros, parados, habitantes de *bidonvilles*, mártires, vírgenes, confesores, sargentos mayores y algunos parlamentarios. Recibí una carta, perspicaz y educada aunque anónima, de un sargento mayor en activo, que enumeraba con mucha erudición los temas que un sargento de brigada conoce, recordando que muchos sargentos de brigada tienen una cultura universitaria. Se trataba de un buen caso de susceptibilidad de categoría.

---

* Primera academia de las ciencias de Italia, fundada en 1603. *(N. de la T.)*

Contesté precisando que en mi lista no había usado artículos determinados por lo que no afirmaba que todas las vírgenes y los confesores (y ni siquiera todos los sargentos) desconocieran la Accademia, sino solo algunos de ellos. Por último, explicaba yo que el mío era un ejemplo de lista incongruente, técnica que, por ejemplo, ilustraba Borges con esa lista suya que dividía a los animales entre los que pertenecían al emperador, los embalsamados, los amaestrados, los lechones, las sirenas, los fabulosos, los perros sueltos, los incluidos en aquella clasificación, los que tiemblan como locos, los dibujados con un pincel finísimo de pelo de camello, etcétera. La lista incongruente tiene su efecto precisamente porque es incongruente, es decir, porque pone en relación categorías que no podrían estar juntas. Su función es, a menudo, la de sustituir la expresión, «lo más variado».

Por otro lado, ninguna lista incongruente es verdaderamente incongruente, si se elige el criterio de conjunto apropiado. Pensemos en esta lista: «Un canguro, un sargento de brigada italiano, Totò, Pío XII, Cavour, mi abuela, Ana Bolena, Craxi, el Padre Pío y el monstruo de Scandicci». Parece incongruente, pero enumera una serie de personas que no estaban en Hiroshima en 1945. Otra lista: «Pequeños cuclillos, soldados de primera, chicas *au pair*, paguros, gitanos, enviados especiales, gusanos solitarios, embajadores, mafiosos confinados, misioneros, condenados a cadena perpetua». Aquí hay una serie de personas o animales que por definición no viven en su propia casa.

¿Qué tiene que ver esta reflexión mía sobre la lista incongruente con el tema de este ensayo? En teoría y según el sentido común, nada, y esto formaría parte de la técnica de la incongruencia. Pero tiene que ver porque la exploración de los *Varia et curiosa* nos invita a saborear el hechizo de la incongruencia, y hace que nuestras Glándulas Surreales palpiten.

Y a propósito de las Glándulas Surreales, ya se me ocurre que se podría escribir y publicar un excitante tratado para el próximo catálogo de *Varia et curiosa*. Le paso la idea al «loco» de turno y vuelvo, con cierta añoranza, al hastío de mi cotidiana sabiduría.

La obra maestra de un desconocido[1]

Términos como paratexto, epitexto y peritexto pertenecen al discurso semiótico contemporáneo y como tales han sido difundidos e impuestos por Gérard Genette, en *Seuils*.[2] Pero la «cosa en sí» que está detrás de estos nombres es mucho más antigua, o mejor dicho, es contemporánea al nacimiento del libro.

En palabras sencillas, si en un vehículo-libro (en cuanto objeto físico hecho de papel) aparece un texto, pongamos *Los novios*, que empieza con «Ese ramal del lago de Como» y acaba con «creed que no lo hemos hecho aposta», el paratexto es todo lo que (en general impreso, pero nada excluye que pueda manifestarse de otra manera; hoy, por ejemplo, podría ser un disquete adjunto) está antes, después y alrededor del texto.

Será peritexto todo ese material que se presenta físicamente vinculado con el vehículo-libro, como el frontispicio, el colofón, las introducciones, las dedicatorias, los pre o posfacios, las solapas, la misma encuadernación o la sobrecubierta, etcétera; y será epitexto lo que se coloca exteriormente al vehículo-libro pero se

---

1. Publicado en el *Almanacco del Bibliofilo 2005*, como una versión distinta del ensayo «Para Peri Epi, e dintorni in un falso del XVIII secolo», *Paratesto*, I, 2004.

2. París, Le Seuil, 1987.

refiere a él directamente, como los comunicados de prensa, las anticipaciones, las reseñas y, permítanme usar dos términos ingleses que me resultan más precisos, todo aquello que tiene que ver con el *advertising* (el anuncio pagado) y la *publicity*, es decir el «ruido» que el editor consigue obtener en torno al libro como, por ejemplo, las entrevistas al autor, las opiniones que se piden a terceros, las polémicas e incluso las crónicas sobre veladas de presentación y discusión de la obra.

Omito algunos interesantes problemas teóricos, como si debe considerarse paratexto el título o si forma, en cambio, parte integrante del texto, ya que, si *Ulysses* se titulase *A New Iliad*, le daríamos una lectura completamente distinta. Por otra parte, muchas intervenciones peritextuales, sobre todo las introducciones, pueden cambiar nuestra manera de entender una obra. En efecto, la finalidad de todo aparato paratextual siempre ha sido la de orientar la lectura del texto, es decir, inducir a los lectores a acercarse al texto con simpatía, interés y siendo conscientes de su valor e importancia.

Mientras en el campo epitextual pueden producirse intervenciones contrarias al texto (como las recensiones negativas), no se conocen aparatos peritextuales que avisen al lector de que el texto que acompañan es indigno de consideración, pésimo e ilegible (tanto en el sentido de que no es comprensible como en el de que no debe leerse en absoluto, y no sé si vale la pena acuñar para este último caso los términos de ilegendo o ilegituro). A lo sumo, un peritexto (pongamos que sea la introducción a una edición crítica en hebreo de *Mein Kampf*) puede dirigir al lector a leer con cautela y desconfianza, considerando el texto como típico ejemplo de delirio racista, pero nunca le dice que no debe leerlo, de lo contrario el libro no habría sido publicado.

En ese sentido el aparato paratextual siempre ha existido, incluso cuando los incunables no tenían frontispicio, porque llevaban siempre un íncipit de alguna manera explicativo, o algún tipo de introducción, por no hablar de un colofón extremadamente detallado. No solo: en los siglos pasados, gran parte de lo que hoy sería epitexto confluía directamente en el peritexto, y la obra se abría con la portadilla (que quería ser su introducción alegórica), retrato del autor, textos ajenos que lo elogiaban, frontispicios que celebraban largo y tendido las características y las virtudes de la obra.

Semejantes excesos paratextuales fueron típicos en especial de las ediciones de los siglos XVI y XVII con picos vertiginosos en el siglo XVII; al respecto existe una amplia literatura, pero vale al menos la pena citar un frontispicio por siglo, para recordar cómo concisión y modestia no eran virtudes de aquellas épocas:

Tolomeo, Claudio

La Geografia, Di Clavdio Tolomeo Alessandrino, Nouamente tradotta di Greco in Italiano, di Girolamo Rvscelli, Con Espositioni del medesimo, particolari di luogo in luogo, & universali sopra tutto il libro, et sopra tutta la Geografia, ò modo di far la descrittione di tutto il mondo. Et con nuoue et bellissime figure in istampe di rame, oue, oltre alle XXVI antiche di Tolomeo, se ne son aggiunte XXXVI altre delle moderne. Con la carta da nauigare, & col modo d'intenderla, & d'adoperarla. Aggiuntoui vn pieno discorso di M. Gioseppe Moleto Matematico. Nel quale si dichiarano tutti i termini & le regole appartenenti alla Geografia. Et con una nuoua & copiosa Tauola di nomi antichi, dichiarati coi nomi moderni, & con moltre altre cose vtilissime & necessarie, che ciascuno leggendo potrà conoscere. In Venetia, Appresso Vincenzo Valgrisi, MDLXI.

Knorr von Rosenroth, Christian

Kabbala denudata seu Dottrina Hebraeorum Transcendentalis et Metaphysica Atqve Theologica. Opus Antiquissimae Philosophiae Barbaricae variis speciminibus refertissimum, In Qvo Ante ipsam Traslationem Libri difficillimi atq; in Literatura Hebraica Summi, Commentarii nempe in Pentateuchum, & quasi totam Scripturam V.T. Cabbalistici, cui nomen Sohar, Tam Veteris, quam recentis, ejusque Tikkunim seu Supplementorum tam Veterum, quam recentiorum praemittitur Apparatus, Cujus Pars prima continet Locos Communes Cabbalisticos, secundum ordinem Alphabeticum concinnatos, qui Lexici Cabbalistici instar esse posunt: Opusculum in quo continentur I. Clavis ad Kabbalam antiquam: i.e. Explicatio et ad debitas Classes Sephiristicas fatta distributio omnium Nominum et cognominum divinorum e Libro Pardes. II. Liber Schaare Orah, seu Porta Lucis ordine Alphabetico propositus, maxime inter Hebraeos auctoritatis. III. Kabbala recentior, seu Hypothesis famigeratissimi illius Cabbalistae R. Jizchak Lorja Germani ex Manuscripto latinitate donata. IV. Index plurimarum materiarum Cabbalisticarum in ipso Libro Sohar propositarum. V. Compendium Libri Cabbalistico – Chymici, Aesch-Mezareph ditti, de Lapide Philosophico, &c. Pars secunda vero constat e Tractatibus variis, tam didacticis, quam Polemicis, post illius titulum enumeratio. Partium autem seq. tituli suis Tomis praemittentur: Adjectusque est Index Latinus, et Locorum Scripturae, insolita et rariore explicatione notabilium. Scriptus omnibus Philologis, Theologis omnium Religionum atq; Philochymicis quam utilissimum. Sulzbaci, Typis Abrahami Lichtenthaleri MDCLXXVI.

Trismosin, Salomon

Avrevm vellvs Oder Guldin Schatz und Kunst-Kammer, Darinnen der aller fürnemisten, fürtreffenlichsten, ausserlesenesten, herrlichsten und bewehrtesten Auctorum Schrifften und Bücher, auss dem gar uralten

Schatz der uberblibnen, verbognen, hinderhaltenen Reliquien und Monumenten der Aegyptiorum, Arabum, Chaldeorum & Assyriorum Küingen und Weysen. Von Dem Edlen, hocherleuchten, fürtreffenlichsten, bewehrten Philosopho Salomone Trismosino (so dess grossen Philosophi und Medici Theophrasti Paracelsi Praeceptor gewesen) in sonderbare underschiedliche Tractätlein disponiert, und in das Teutsch gebracht. Sampt anderen Philosophischen alter und newer Scribentem sonderbaren Tractätlein, alles zuvor niemalen weder erhörtnoch gesehen, wie der Catalogus gleich nach der Vorrede zuverstehen gibt. Durch einen der Kunstliebhabern mit grossen Kosten, Mühe, Arbeyt und Gefahr, die Originalia und Handschriften zusammen gebracht, und auffs trewlichest und fleissigt an Tag geben. Vormahls gedruckt zu Korschach am Bodensee, Anno MDXCVIII. und zu Basel 1604, in fünff verschiedenen Tractaten; isso aufs neuen auffgelegt und in ein Volumen gebracht. Hamburg, bey Christian Liebezeit, in der St. Joh. Kirch 1708.

Es notable que en todo *Seuils* de Genette no se mencione nunca a Thémiseul de Saint-Hyacinthe, es decir, a Hyacinthe Cordonnier, esto es, Chrysostome Matanasius o Mathanasius (1684-1746), porque su *Le chef d'oeuvre d'un inconnu* parece hecho aposta para demostrar qué son peritexto y epitexto, frontispicio y apéndices, nombre del autor, lugar, destinatarios, función, dedicatorias, dedicadores y dedicatarios, epígrafes, epigrafiadores y epigrafiatarios, avisos sobre la novedad, importancia, veracidad, indicaciones de contexto y declaraciones de intención, prefacios, posfacios, notas, coloquios, debates, autocomentarios tardíos, declaraciones de añadiduras y de eliminaciones; podríamos seguir así hasta el infinito, naturalmente en clave de parodia.

Thémiseul de Saint-Hyacinthe no ocupa un gran lugar en las historias de la literatura y del pensamiento (cuando no está completamente ausente), y por él suelen interesarse algunos especialistas, libreros, anticuarios y cazadores de obras excéntricas.[3] Fue director de un periódico, *L'Europe Savante*, desde 1718 hasta 1720; publicó un *Recueil de divers écrits sur l'amour et l'amitié* (París, Pissot, 1736); en 1720 tradujo al francés la novela *Robinson Crusoe*, con un frontispicio suficientemente detallado;[4] fue autor de una novela que todavía hoy aparece en las bibliografías de «erotica»[5] y de algún texto filosófico;[6] se le atribuyeron obras que sin lugar a dudas no eran suyas;[7] mantu-

3. Véanse, por ejemplo, A. Petzel, *Thémiseul de Saint-Hyacinthe (1684-1746): Studien zum Werke eines Frühaufklürers*, Berlín-Nueva York, Peter Lang, 1994; A. Gaillard, «Le Chef d'oeuvre d'un inconnu de Thémiseul de Saint-Hyacinthe (1714): folie raisonnante», en René Démoris y Henri Lafon (eds.), *Folies romanesques au Siècle des lumières*, París, Desjonquères, 1998, pp. 275-293; C. Lelouch, «Le péritexte au service de la formation des esprits: l'exemple du *Chef-d'oeuvre d'un inconnu* de Saint-Hyacinthe (1714)», *Littératures classiques*, n.º 37, otoño de 1999, pp. 185-199; E. Méchoulan, «Les deux vies de Saint-Hyacinthe: dans les marges du Dr Mathanasius», *Tangence*, n.º 57, mayo de 1998, pp. 23-39. Véase también A. Cioranescu, *Bibliographie de la littérature française du dixhuitième siècle*, 3 vols., París, CNRS, 1969.

4. D. Defoe, *La vie et les avantures surprenantes de Robinson Crusoe, contenant entre autres événements, le séjour qu'il a fait pendant vingt-huit ans dans une île déserte, situee sur la Côte de l'Amérique, pres l'embouchure de la grande rivière Oroonoque. – La vie et les avantures surprenantes de Robinson Crusoe. Contenant son retour dans son isle, & ses autres nouveaux voyages. – Réflexions sérieuses et importantes de Robinson Crusoe, faites pendant les avantures surprenantes de sa vie. Avec sa vision du monde Angélique*, Amsterdam, Honoré et Chatelain, 1720-1721.

5. *Histoire du Prince Titi*, Bruselas, François Foppens, 1736 (del mismo año hay también una edición parisina).

6. Por ejemplo, *Recherches philosophiques sur la nécessité de s'assurer par soi-même de la vérité*, Londres, Jean Nourse, 1743.

7. Por ejemplo, *Les Aventures de Pomponius chevalier Romain, ou l'Histoire de notre Temps*, A Rome, chez les Héritiers de Ferrante Pallavicini [Hollande, à la Sphère], 1724; obra que fue atribuida, además de al nuestro, a los benedictinos Lobineau y Lefevre, probablemente por Labadie, benedictino también él, ayudado por Prévost. Por otro lado, ya el nombre ficticio del editor, con sus connotaciones libertinas, nos hace abrigar dudas sobre todo el asunto.

vo una dura polémica con Voltaire, que durante un tiempo fue amigo suyo.[8]

La obra de la que hablamos, cuyo frontispicio de la primera edición de 1714 copio, solo podía proceder de un polígrafo tan extravagante.

> *Le chef-d'oeuvre d'un inconnu. Poème heureusement découvert & mis au jour avec des remarques savantes & recherchées, par M. le Docteur Christostome Matanasius.* The Hague (i.e. Rouen). Au dépens de la Compagnie, 1714.
>
> Dos partes en volumen 8.º (o 12.º), [26 hh. s. p. con retrato], 195 pp.; [2 hh. s. p.], 50 pp., [16 hh. s. p.]

La obra en sí sería un ejemplo de elefantiasis paratextual, porque la obra maestra que se publica es una cancioncita popular de unos cuarenta versos, de todo punto irrelevante, cuyo principio cito precisamente para mostrar su irrelevancia:

> *L'autre jour COLIN malade*
> *Dedans son Lit,*
> *D'une grosse maladie*
> *Pensant mourir,*
> *De trop songer à ses Amours*
> *Ne peut dormir;*
> *Il veut tenir celle qu'il aime*
> *Toute la nuit.*

Otro panfleto que se le atribuyó fue *Pensées secrètes et observations critiques attribuées à feu M. de Saint-Hyacinthe*, Londres, 1769 (con rumores sobre una primera edición de 1735, de la que no hay rastro).

8. Cfr. E. Carayol, «Thémiseul de Saint-Hyacinthe, 1684-1746», *Studies on Voltaire and the Eighteenth Century*, vol. 221, Oxford, 1984.

Sobre estos pocos versos el autor monta un aparato crítico inicialmente de unas doscientas páginas, con las remisiones intertextuales más dispares, afrontando la polémica de los Antiguos y los Modernos, tratando de manera grotesca su texto como si fuera una obra excelsa, sin ahorrarse ninguna exhibición erudita. Y sería ya bastante para ver en la *Chef d'oeuvre* una hermosa parodia de la crítica docta y, quisiéramos decir, de la excedencia del paratexto sobre el texto, si el texto relevante desde el punto de vista de la parodia no fuera justo el aparato crítico, texto elevado al cuadrado cuyo mero pretexto son solo esos cuarenta versos objeto del comentario. Pero no basta.

Para hojear el libro y representarlo con exactitud, me atengo a la cuarta edición de 1716 (donde resulta evidente que en dos años aparecieron otras dos ediciones de las que no tengo noticia). Esto es lo que dice el frontispicio:

> *Le chef d'oeuvre d'un inconnu. Poème heureusement découvert & mis au jour, avec des Remarques savantes & recherchées par le Docteur Chrisostome Matanasius. On trouve de plus une Dissertation sur Homère & sur Chapelain; deux Lettres sur des Antiques, & plusieurs autres choses non moins agréables qu'instructives. Quatrième édition revue, corrigée, augmentée, & diminuée.*
>
> *À La Haye: Chez Pierre Husson, Anno AE V MDCCXVI.*

12.º, 5 hh. paginadas, 3 hh. sin paginar, retrato, 25 hh. paginadas de forma irregular, lámina plegada con partitura musical, segundo retrato, 322 pp., con otra lámina plegada que representa un jarrón, 4 hh. sin paginar con la *Table des matières*.

Como se ve, en la cuarta edición (en la que colaboraron también amigos como W. J. Gravesande, A. H. de Sallengre, Prosper Marchand y Justus Van Effen), el libro ya ha pasado de 333 a 394 páginas. Pero su éxito, o la acribia del autor y de sus compañeros, no dan tregua al lector. Tras una edición de 1728, resulta que la de 1732 se presenta en dos volúmenes, con un número total de 620 páginas, la edición de 1745 tiene 619 páginas, la 1758 tiene 634 páginas, y así hasta la edición de 1807, donde se introduce también un texto de polémica con el *Chef d'oeuvre*, de un tal Anon, *L'Anti-Mathanase, ou Critique du chef d'oeuvre d'un inconnu. Le tout critiqué dans le goût moderne*, Utrecht, Aux depens de l'éditeur, 1729.

Por otro lado, en su *Supercheries littéraires* (col. 1073)[9] Quérard refiere varios ejemplos de «matanasiana», esto es, de proliferación del personaje inventado por Saint-Hyacinthe, entre los cuales quizá el caso más conocido sea la «Relation de ce qui s'est passé au sujet de la réception de Messire Christophile Mathanasius de l'Académie Françoise», que aparece en el *Dictionnaire néologique* de Desfontaines (otro buen ejemplo más de malignidad literaria y de enemistad con el consabido Voltaire).[10]

9. Para una edición moderna: *Les Supercheries littéraires dévoilées. Galerie des écrivains français de toute l'Europe qui se sont déguisés sous des anagrammes, des astéronymes, des cryptonymes, des initialismes, des noms littéraires, des pseudonymes facétieux ou bizarres...*, París, Maisonneuve & Larose, 1964, 3 vols. Véase también G. Brunet, *Supplément aux Supercheries littéraires dévoilées et au Dictionnaire des ouvrages anonymes* de J. M. Quérard y A. E. Barbier, París, Maisonneuve & Larose, 1964.

10. Desfontaines, Abbé Pierre François Guyot, *Dictionnaire néologique à l'usage des Beaux-Esprits du Siècle*, París, Lottin, 1726. La «Relation» se introduce a partir de la tercera edición, pero se publica en París, 1721 (cfr. F. Drujon, *Les livres à clef*, París, Rouveyre, 1888, col. 35) aunque, citando esa misma edición, Quérard anota «douteux».

Quérard cita también una *Chanson d'un inconnu... par le doc-teur Christophe Mathanasius, sur l'air des pendus*, Turín (Ruan), Alétophile, 1732, y un *Voyage de Mathanasius à la tour de son église*, París, Delaforest, 1828.

Pero volvamos a la edición de 1716 y me refiero a ella no porque sea la *editio princeps* sino sencillamente porque es la que yo poseo. Se empieza con un anuncio (falso) que avisa que la fe de erratas estará al final del libro, a lo que siguen tres car-tas de *Approbation*, obviamente burlescas, firmadas por muy improbables teólogos (y fechadas Calif City o Molinople). En-tonces sigue una serie de poemas de alabanza del pseudoautor Chrisosthome Matanasius, el primero en hebreo, con traduc-ción enfrentada, el segundo en griego, el tercero en latín, el cuarto en inglés, el quinto en flamenco, el sexto y el séptimo en francés.

Después del retrato de Matanasius, sigue una carta dedica-toria del mismo Matanasius a «Monsieur...», un prefacio (fe-chado el 12 de octubre de 1715, en Pédantstadt) en el que se discuten los consensos recibidos por las ediciones anteriores y se publican cartas de lectores entusiastas. Se pasa, entonces, al prefacio de la primera edición, seguido por una larga lista de libros y personajes a los que se hace referencia en el comentario que seguirá (divinidades paganas, naciones y sociedades, auto-res elogiados, otros autores evidentemente no elogiados, semi-dioses, héroes, etcétera).

Siguen una epístola en versos y una oda al doctor Matha-nasius (esta vez con H), y una serie de testimonios de cartas y reseñas, en francés y flamenco. Por último, después de la lámi-na musical, ahí está la primera estrofa de la obra maestra y el comentario, del cual, obviamente, no puede ofrecerse un resu-men, porque toda síntesis reduciría esa tumescencia que —si se me permite el oxímoron y la aliteración— constituye su quintaesencia.

El comentario va desde la página 1 hasta la página 253. Empiezan entonces los *addenda*, entre los cuales hay una disertación sobre Homero de anónimo, precedida obviamente por un «Avis au Lecteur», una carta de Mr. De la Roque, un juicio de Reverendos Padres, la respuesta a Mr. De la Roque, una carta de monsieur Chrisologos Caritides a monsieur le professeur Burmandiolus, unos «Remarques et Diverses Leons» seguidos finalmente por una amplia «Table des matières».

En la edición 1728 se añade una carta a monseigneur le Duc D. En la de 1732 aparece una «Déification de l'incomparable Docteur Aristarchus Masso» (ácido ataque a Voltaire); en la edición 1745 se introducen «Deux lettres sur des antiques; la préface de Cervantes sur l'histoire de D. Quixote de la Manche; [...] & plusieurs autres choses non moins agréables qu'instructives».[11]

¿Dónde colocar al doctor Matanasius? Las grandes bibliografías decimonónicas, como las de Brunet y Graesse, lo ignoran (solo Brunet hace una rápida alusión a la edición 1807), y es significativo que Matanasius o Cordonnier o Saint-Hyacinthe como quiera llamárselo, no aparezca en las grandes recopilaciones dedicadas a los «fous littéraires».[12]

---

11. De todas maneras, para tener una idea de los diferentes textos, véanse dos ediciones modernas, *Le Chef-d'oeuvre d'un inconnu*, texto fijado, presentado y anotado por Jean Lebois, Aviñón, Aubanel, Bibliothèque d'un Homme de Goût, 1965, y *Le chef-d'oeuvre d'un inconnu / Thémiseul de Saint-Hyacinthe*, a cargo de Henri Duranton, Lyon, Centre Régional de Publication de Lyon, 1991.

12. Cfr. *L'histoire littéraire des fous* de Delepierre, 1860; *Les fous littéraires du Quercy* de Louis Greil, 1866; *De quelques livres excentriques* de Charles Nodier, 1835; *Les fous littéraires* de Yvan Tcherpakoff, 1883; *Gens singuliers* de

¿Por qué ninguno de los bibliógrafos de la demencia y de la incontinencia cita al incontinente Saint-Hyacinthe, si —según una definición de Nodier—[13] se entiende por libro excéntrico «un livre qui est fait hors de toutes les règles communes de la composition et du style, et dont il est impossible ou très difficile de deviner le but, quand il est arrivé par hasard que l'auteur eut un but en l'écrivant»?

La razón me parece la misma por la cual nuestro autor está citado, en cambio, en las *Supercheries littéraires* de Quérard, que no se ocupa de locos inocentes sino de autores que «se aprovechan», es decir, plagiarios, apócrifos y organizadores de burlas editoriales. Así pues, si el imaginario doctor Matanasius podía considerarse un loco literario, el verdadero señor de Saint-Hyacinthe no lo era, y más bien hacía, y con mucha lucidez, crítica de la cultura, o de las modas culturales de su tiempo. En el fondo, quería demostrar que los locos literarios eran los demás.

Al hacerlo —sin saber que luego la industria editorial de los siglos sucesivos enfatizaría y elefantizaría cada vez más la dimensión epitextual—, Saint-Hyacinthe sigue arrojando todavía hoy una sombra de sospecha sobre el «susurro» artificial que

---

Lorédan Larchey, 1867; *Les cris de Paris* de Victor Fournel, 1887; *Les fous littéraires* de Philomneste Junior (seudónimo de Gustave Brunet), Bruselas, 1880; *La folie et les fous littéraires en Espagne (1500-1650)* de Martine Bigeard (París, Centre de recherches Hispaniques, 1972); *Aux confins des ténèbres. Les fous littéraires du XIXe siècle* de Raymond Queneau (París, Gallimard 2002); *Les fous littéraires* de André Blavier (París, Veyrier, 1982). Véase al respecto la relación de Pierre Popovic presentada al Coloquio Internacional «Illégitimité culturelle et marginalités littéraires (1715-1914). Modes et représentations», París, mayo de 1998.

13. *Bibliographie des fous: de quelques livres excentriques*, 1935. Ahora, París, Éditions des Cendres, 2002.

rodea a cualquier libro, ensordeciéndonos a tal punto que a menudo nos exime de leer el texto.

Saint-Hyacinthe incluso nos ofreció, con antelación, un libro, practicable solo de forma panorámica y a vuelo de águila, que permite incluso no leer ni el epitexto ni el peritexto.

Esto debería hacerlo merecedor de nuestra gratitud.

Heterotopías y falsificaciones

La peste del trapo[1]

La «peste del trapo» empezó a trastornar el mundo de los coleccionistas hacia 2080. Una bacteria de origen incierto, procedente quizá de alguna remota región asiática (la *Comestor sinensis lintei*), comenzó a difundirse en el mundo occidental y acabó afectando a todas las hojas de papel de trapos, es decir, a todos los libros producidos desde la época de Gutenberg hasta aproximadamente mediados del siglo XIX, cuando entró en uso el papel producido a partir de la celulosa. Una notable burla del destino porque, hasta entonces, era el papel producido con la madera el que se consideraba perecedero en el arco de setenta años, mientras que se consideraba imperecedero (y con razón) el papel producido a partir de trapos.

Es verdad que los editores ya llevaban tiempo produciendo libros de valor con *acid-free paper*, y el papel de madera estaba afirmándose como bastante capaz de sobrevivir al paso de los años, y competía con el papel rozagante y crujiente de los más frescos incunables. En 2080 la situación, sin embargo, se invirtió por completo: no solo el papel de madera se volvía inatacable con el tiempo, sino que el que constituía la gloria de los

1. Publicado en el *Almanacco del Bibliofilo (Corrispondenze del ventunesimo secolo)*, Milán, Edizioni Rovello, 2000.

impresores de los siglos anteriores, en las bibliotecas de todo el mundo civilizado, se estaba pulverizando literalmente por la acción funesta de la *Comestor sinensis*.

Empezaron todos los ejemplares de la *Hypnerotomachia Poliphili*: poco a poco fueron llenándose de carcoma, luego las hojas se transformaron en telarañas sutilísimas y, por último, aquellos impagables folios se disolvieron en la nada. De poco sirvieron los esfuerzos de los químicos, e incluso el miserando salvamento anastático que se intentó se puso en marcha con retraso, cuando los libros ya estaban seriamente dañados. Ya al cabo de diez años, la nueva edición Adelphi del *Polifilo*, valorada a esas alturas en mil *globols*, es decir, rayando el millón de dólares del siglo XX, mostraba páginas donde se divisaba la trama, con una pérdida de al menos la mitad de las letras.

Poco a poco las *Crónicas de Nuremberg*, los Suplementos de Foresti, las primeras ediciones de Torquato Tasso o de Ariosto, los infolios shakespearianos de 1623, las colecciones completas de la *Encyclopédie* vagaban transfigurados en nubes blanquecinas por las salas desiertas de las mayores bibliotecas del mundo, a lo largo de paredes atónitas que miraban fijamente aquel mariposeo mortífero con los grandes ojos vacíos de sus estantes despojados de todos sus tesoros.

Sin mencionar siquiera la pérdida cultural, no había que subestimar la inmediata repercusión económica de semejante desastre. Como ya sucediera en los meses más oscuros de la crisis de 1929, podía verse a los herederos de los Kraus vendiendo manzanas en la esquina de la Quinta Avenida; a Bernard Clavreuil vagando a lo largo del Sena mientras recogía corazones de manzanas en los contenedores de la basura; a lord Parmoor y a todo el equipo de Quaritch, en los ínfimos *slums* de Londres, merodeando macilentos entre la llovizna, la niebla y las ráfagas de antracita combusta, con una chistera raída y una vieja levita recosida con sórdidos parches, un niño enfermizo de la mano, que se encomendaban a la misericordia de los viandantes apresurados y distraídos igual que Scrooge la noche de Navidad. El único que se salvó dignamente del desastre fue Mario Scognamiglio, que empezó una venta al por menor de *pastiera* napolitana, que le elaboraba expresamente un pastelero de Milán Rogoredo.

Al cabo de una década, sin embargo, tanto los coleccionistas como los libreros se recobraron del golpe, impelidos por su anal necesidad de acumulación los primeros, por una razonable *auri sacra fames* los segundos. El mercado se reequilibró en torno al libro del siglo XX, desde las ediciones cartoné de Jules Verne y *Sans Famille*, hasta las obras más recientes, que se convertían en antigüedades al año de su publicación (considerando, entre otras cosas, el triunfo de internet y el libro electrónico, los libros impresos se producían ya en tiradas limitadísimas para aficionados, o para los pocos lectores alérgicos al silicio).

Una recopilación de poesías del célebre Annibale Rossi, una novela de John Smith, una antología de epigramas de Brambilla, los ensayos de Pautasso, las obras completas de Romoletto Pizzigoni o Salvatore Esposito se valoraban en muchas decenas de millones, por no hablar de un autor del movimiento caníbal de los años noventa del siglo XX, que Christie subastó por tres millones de dólares adjudicándoselo a un banco japonés.

Se trataba, naturalmente, de ejemplares no firmados por el autor. En efecto, con otro vuelco de toda antigua ley del mercado anticuario, se reputaban especialmente valiosas las *non-association copies*. Mientras que respecto a las obras de los siglos anteriores se consideraba *scarce* o *d'insigne rareté* un Kircher con la dedicatoria manuscrita *Domum Authoris* e incluso era deseado un Cordelli con la dedicatoria a Enzo Siciliano, con las nuevas antigüedades estaba sucediendo lo contrario. Es bien sabido, en efecto, que desde mediados del siglo XX, un autor no podía publicar un libro sin verse implicado en la siguiente serie de operaciones, que aquí me limito a detallar para el caso de Italia: 1) firma en las oficinas del editor de al menos cien ejemplares para prensa (para la sección «Libros recibidos»), recensores y *opinion leaders*, un ejemplar para cada miembro de la Academia Real de Suecia, para cada votante del Premio Strega, para cada miembro del jurado del Premio Viareggio, más otros centenares de ejemplares para distribuir entre torneros o barrenderos de las Tres Venecias, que podrían convertirse en jurados populares del Premio Campiello; 2) numerosas sesiones en librerías de las cien ciudades de Italia para firmar ejemplares al público presente; 3) firma de algunos millares de copias para los libreros que las vendían bajo cuerda y en sobreprecio a los clientes más fieles, asegurándoles que se trataba de un *unicum*. En resumidas cuentas, prácticamente toda la tirada del libro estaba firmada por el autor.

Aun considerando que, en general, los críticos, los periodistas, los miembros de jurados y los amigos que reciben un libro firmado lo tiran a la papelera, o lo pasan a las cárceles (donde sus páginas se usan para liarse cigarrillos de marihuana) y a los hospitales (donde acaba devorado por los ratones que prosperan en esos lugares), en cualquier caso los ejemplares en circulación de un libro firmado eran siempre lo bastante numerosos para depreciar su valor y excluirlos del mercado de libros raros.

La caza se desplazaba, pues, hacia los poquísimos ejemplares que no llevaran rastro de «asociación». Ya en 2091, Fiammetta Soave ponía en su catálogo el poemita *A Silvia*, de Oliviero

Diliberto,[2] rigurosamente no firmado por cincuenta millones. Otro poemita, *A Silvio*, del juez Antonio di Pietro, lo vendía por cien millones —pues carecía de la firma del fallo— la entidad financiera Mediolanum. La *opera omnia* de otro juez anticorrupción, Francesco Saverio Borrelli,[*] publicada por la Berlusconi Editore en su Biblioteca dell'Utopia, con un afectuoso prefacio escrito desde la cárcel por Marcello dell'Utri, monda de toda firma, aparecía en el catálogo Pregliasco por doscientos millones.

Mario Scognamiglio, abandonada la *pastiera* napolitana, rehacía su empresa y volvía triunfalmente a los mercados vendiendo por trescientos millones un ejemplar *non rogné* de *Mis prisiones*, de Giulio Andreotti (2001), que el autor envió como regalo para la boda de un monseñor amigo suyo y, para no tentar a la suerte, no le había puesto ninguna marca de identificación.

2. En la época de su composición, estaba fresca la noticia del apoyo dado por el ministro de Justicia Diliberto al traslado de la activista Silvia Baraldini desde una cárcel estadounidense a una cárcel italiana.

* Por aquel entonces eran bien conocidas las actividades estelares del equipo judicial de un famoso proceso conocido como Manos Limpias. *(N. de la T.)*

Antes de la extinción[1]

·ᘔ ꒰ᖡᴧᓬᘔ꒭ᕁᘔ

Recensión de Oaamooaa pf Uuaanoaa (Universidad de Aldebarán)

El título exacto de esta apreciable obra del estudioso marciano Taowr Shz, transliterado en nuestro alfabeto de Aldebarán, sonaría más o menos *Hg Kopyasaaz* y podríamos traducirlo, por tanto, como «El enigma del siglo XX terrestre revelado a través de documentos captados en el espacio después de la destrucción de ese planeta». Taowr Shz es un antropólogo espacial conocido no solo en toda la galaxia habitada, sino también en algunas estrellas de la Gran Nube de Magallanes, y es suya, lo recordaremos, la famosa obra en la que, hace algunos años, demostraba de forma impecable que no podía haber vida orgánica en el Sol, precisamente a causa de los procesos de fusión fría que constituyen su masa incandescente. Curiosa situación de un gran estudioso, conocido en gran parte del universo, *in albis* de su notoriedad porque, como los lectores saben perfectamente, mientras nuestras avanzadas tecnologías nos permiten captar desde hace mucho tiempo mensajes procedentes del sistema so-

---

1. Publicado en el *Almanacco del Bibliofilo (I libri dei prossimi vent'anni)*, Milán, Edizioni Rovello, 2002.

lar, la relación no es simétrica, y planetas que incluso cuentan con una avanzada civilización como Marte permanecen *in albis* sobre nuestra monitorización.

Para el conocimiento del sistema solar, la mediación de Marte es esencial, porque nuestros sistemas IEC (Intrusión Espacial Comunicativa) nos permiten captar a lo sumo señales procedentes de ese planeta, mientras que los cuerpos más internos del sistema, esto es, los más próximos al Sol, como la Tierra, Venus, Mercurio, quedan fuera de nuestra monitorización. Entre otras cosas, el mismo Marte ha logrado captar señales procedentes de la Tierra solo recientemente, y en especial en las últimas décadas, casi después de que (según afirman los marcianos) la vida en la Tierra se extinguiera. Todo lo que podemos saber sobre la Tierra procede de una compilación prácticamente casual de noticias de las que se incautaron —por decirlo de alguna manera— los científicos marcianos, y que nosotros hemos «birlado», si se nos permite la expresión, a esos estudiosos.

El trabajo de los marcianos, que ciertamente se basa en osadas conjeturas elaboradas a partir de datos muy incompletos, ha sido posible gracias a que, en sus últimos años de vida, los terrestres elaboraron un sistema de comunicación que cubría todo su globo, denominado en su lenguaje local internet. Ahora bien, al principio, ese sistema empleaba canales internos del planeta llamados «cables». Solo cuando el sistema se desarrolló por medio del aire, esto es, gracias a un sistema de captura-redistribución a través de satélites, fue posible interceptar las señales de los terrestres con los sistemas IEC marcianos. Pero justo cuando empezaba una proficua recopilación de datos, todos aún por interpretar, la vida en el planeta se extinguió, en torno a ese año que, según las cronologías terrestres, era definido como 2020.

La reconstrucción marciana se veía dificultada por el hecho de que el sistema de comunicación terrestre, denominado internet, emitía cualquier tipo de dato y se presentaba como impermeable a cualquier criterio de selección nuestro. Podían aparecer noticias e imágenes sobre el pasado de la Tierra, datos probablemente científicos de difícil descodificación (por ejemplo, todos los que procedían de las fuentes www.crucigramaen diablado.org o www.bartezzaghi.com), listas de obras de recientísima publicación (como las de un tal *Bibliopoly — the multilingual database of rare and antiquarian books and manuscripts for sale*, donde por *antiquarian books* debe entenderse probablemente «comunicaciones de inmediata actualidad»), manuales de estudios anatómicos avanzados sobre las técnicas de apareamiento terrestre en edades antiquísimas (véanse Penthouse.com y Playboy.com), mensajes encriptados propalados con toda probabilidad por servicios secretos (como, por ejemplo, «Te quiero, cabrón ☺» o «Te lo juro, algo debe de haberme sentado mal ☹, no me había pasado nunca, vuelve te lo suplico. Lalo»).

Nótese, además, que aunque fue posible captar inmediatamente mensajes alfabéticos —por lo que los descifradores marcianos elaboraron con bastante rapidez unos manuales de traducción (el primer término descifrado fue *culo*, entendido como «lugar genérico donde se va a tomar algo»)—, más laborioso resultó en cambio captar imágenes, que había que traducir mediante un protocolo especial, en cuanto (se supone) la comunicación verbal, en la Tierra, era de naturaleza analógica, mientras que la visual era de naturaleza digital.

En definitiva, por muy laboriosas e imprecisas que fueran las conjeturas marcianas, esto es lo que probablemente sucedió en la Tierra. Desde hacía unos cinco mil de nuestros años (probablemente unos millones de los suyos) había florecido en el planeta una vida inteligente, representada por seres denominados «humanos» que, como confirman muchísimas imágenes captadas de manera sucesiva, eran más o menos iguales a nosotros. Esta civilización se extendió por todo el planeta construyendo curiosos aglomerados de construcciones artificiales en las que a los terrestres les encantaba vivir, expansión que conllevó un empobrecimiento gradual de los recursos naturales. En una fase muy cercana a la extinción, se produjo un «agujero» en la atmósfera (muy parecida a la nuestra) que envolvía todo el planeta, lo que generó posteriormente una elevación de la temperatura, el derretimiento de grandes masas de H_2O en estado sólido de los casquetes del globo, una gradual elevación de una gran masa de H_2O en estado líquido y la desaparición de las tierras no cubiertas por H_2O. Los últimos mensajes captados (y todavía no completamente interpretados) hablan de una «reunión de emergencia del G8 en los fiordos de Courmayeur» y de un «encuentro urgente sobre los destinos del mundo de los presidentes Umbala Nbana, Chung Lenin González Smith y de su Santidad Platinette II en el puerto de Monte Everest». Luego, silencio.

¿Cómo eran los terrestres antes de la extinción? Este es el tema del libro de Taowr Shz que estamos reseñando, aunque no podamos hojear directamente con emoción sus hojas de amianto. Del maremágnum de internet se capturaron numerosas imágenes, que parecían antedatas con respecto a la cronología terrestre y que, por tanto, podemos asignar a varios siglos anteriores a la extinción. Una imagen denominada *Apolo de Belvedere* nos dice que sus adolescentes tenían una complexión esbelta y bellas proporciones, un *Fornarina* y un *Flora* de época más tardía nos ilustran acerca de la belleza opima de sus varones (las terminaciones en «a» indicaban nombres masculinos, como Patriarca, Centinela, mientras que las terminaciones en «o» designaban seres femeninos, como en el caso de Rosario, Soprano o Virago). Una representación denominada *Déjeuner sur l'herbe* nos muestra a mujeres púdicamente vestidas que se sientan en un prado con efebos desnudos de agradabilísimos rasgos. Los terrestres llamaban «fotografía» a esas maneras de representar del natural a otros seres, mientras que llamaban «arte» a la manera de imaginar seres inexistentes, como en el caso de una pintura de un tal Einstein, fantaseado mientras enseña la lengua, o la imagen de un guerrero musculoso y agilísimo, denominado Megan Gale, que osa trepar por los contrafuertes de una antiquísima construcción de titanio.

Pero los marcianos estaban convencidos de haber interceptado tan solo imágenes de los terrestres que se remontaban a muchos siglos antes de la extinción. Hasta que, justo pocos segundos antes de la extinción final, captaron numerosas imágenes de un sitio internet (www.moma.com) llamado *The human image in the twentieth century.* Con lo cual se dieron cuenta de que le habían echado el guante (es decir, sus antenas satelitales) al único documento que decía algo sobre los rasgos de los terrestres en el ocaso de su raza.

Evidentemente (como sugieren otras interceptaciones), antes del «agujero» en la atmósfera, los terrestres habían atentado abundantemente (por ingenuidad o malicia suicida) contra la vida de su planeta. La vida de los terrestres ya había sido puesta a dura prueba por fenómenos de incierta naturaleza denominados «radiaciones atómicas», «gases de escape», «Philip Morris», «dioxina», «vaca loca», «talidomida», «Big Mac» y «Coca-Cola». Las imágenes de *The human image* nos dicen cómo degeneró decididamente la raza mientras se acercaba a la extinción, y seguramente se deben a estudiosos de anatomía y teratología que no dudaron en representar la descomposición de la especie.

Representaciones atribuidas a no mejor identificados «Expresionistas alemanes» nos muestran el rostro humano ya desfigurado por apostemas violáceas, escamaduras, cicatrices. Un tal Bacon nos representa a mujeres (o varones) con las extremidades desarrolladas solo de manera parcial, y una tez amarillo-ocre que induciría a los médicos de Aldebarán a hospitalizar inmediatamente al individuo. Las representaciones de un tal Picasso muestran cómo la degeneración de la especie influyó en la misma disposición simétrica de los ojos y de la nariz del rostro humano. En algunas zonas, si hemos de creer a las representaciones de un tal Botero, los humanos habían desarrollado desmesuradamente una complexión deformada, con excesos de materia grasa y abultamientos en todo el cuerpo, mientras que otro tal Egon Schiele nos muestra a seres andróginos que son ya meros esqueletos. Si hemos de creer a un tal Grosz, los seres de un sexo (¿cuál?) prácticamente habían perdido el cuello, y la nuca se incrustaba directamente en los hombros, mientras que si damos crédito a un tal Modigliani el cuello se había alargado más allá de los límites de lo razonable, volviendo ciertamente difícil la estatura erecta. Que la especie estuviera abocada a multiplicarse en una serie de criaturas monstruosas ya sin regla lo demuestran las imágenes del tal Keith Haring; otras imágenes de otros tales Boccioni y Carrà nos muestran seres que, absortos en una carrera u otros movimientos, pierden el control de sus extremidades, mientras su cuerpo se desmiembra y se confunde con el ambiente. La estructura misma de los órganos de la visión debía de haber sido dañada por las «radiaciones» porque muchos de esos testigos de su tiempo, a la vez que nos representan una mesa con objetos, una ventana, un rincón de su casa, son incapaces de ver las superficies y los volúmenes en su justa relación y los perciben como descompuestos y reensamblados de forma contraria a las leyes de la gravedad, o perciben un mundo licuado. En ocasiones el bloqueo de la percepción los lleva a ver solo superficies bidimensionales confusamente coloreadas. Aparecen seres con los ojos en el lugar de los senos y la vulva en el lugar de la boca, humanos con la cabeza de animal cornudo, infantes deformes, un tal Rosai ve criaturas minúsculas y retorcidas en el fondo de una calle que alberga todavía construcciones volumétricamente sostenibles. Una representación de un tal Duchamp muestra a un varón de hermoso aspecto desfigurado por dos bigotes femeninos, señal evidente de una mutación en la práctica.

El terrestre del siglo XX aguardaba ya la muerte del planeta mientras su misma estructura corporal se arrugaba, deformaba, languidecía. El libro de Taowr Shz nos documenta de forma clara esta decadencia de una especie que había anticipado, en la deformación de su propio cuerpo, la destrucción del planeta. Leemos con ánimo perturbado y conmovido este testimonio de horror y muerte, que nos habla de seres que antaño eran como nosotros, y eligieron conscientemente su desventura.

Monólogo interior de un e-book[1]

Hasta hace poco yo no sabía qué era. He nacido vacío, si puedo expresarme de este modo. Ni siquiera era capaz de decir «yo». Luego algo ha entrado en mí, un flujo de letras, me he sentido lleno y he empezado a pensar. Naturalmente, he empezado a pensar lo que me había entrado. Una magnífica sensación, porque podía sentir en bloque lo que tenía en mi memoria, o recorrerlo línea a línea, o saltar de una página a otra.

El texto que yo era se llamaba «Del libro al e-book». Es un golpe de suerte que alguien, creo que debo llamarlo mi usuario o mi amo, me haya metido ese texto, del cual he aprendido mucho sobre qué es un texto. Si me hubiera metido cualquier otra cosa (he aprendido de mi texto que hay textos dedicados solo, es un decir, al elogio de la muerte), yo pensaría otras cosas y creería ser un moribundo, o una tumba. En cambio, sé que soy un libro y sé qué son los libros.

Soy algo maravilloso: un texto es un universo, y —por lo que he entendido— un libro se convierte en ese texto que le han impreso encima. Eso les pasa por lo menos a los libros tradicionales, cuya historia describe mi texto de forma minu-

---

1. Publicado en el *Almanacco del Bibliofilo (Confidenze di libri)*, Milán, Edizioni Rovello, 2003.

ciosa. Los libros tradicionales son uniones de muchas hojas de papel, y un libro en el que ha sido impresa, es un decir, la *Odisea* (poema griego antiguo que, sin embargo, no sé muy bien qué cuenta) piensa y vive todo lo que sucede y lo que se dice en la *Odisea*. Lo vive durante toda su vida, que puede ser larguísima, porque hay libros que tienen casi quinientos años. Naturalmente, varios usuarios de ese libro pueden escribir encima notas al margen, y el libro, me imagino, piensa también esas. No sé qué le pasa a un libro que lleva subrayados, si piensa con mayor intensidad lo subrayado o sencillamente siente que esas líneas interesaban en especial a su usuario. Me imagino también que un libro que ha vivido cuatrocientos años y cambiado de usuarios (he inferido de mi texto que los usuarios de los libros son mortales y, en cualquier caso, viven menos que un libro) sabe reconocer la mano de sus distintos lectores, y la diferencia entre su modo de leer e interpretar el texto. Quizá haya lectores que escriben en el margen «Pero ¡qué burrada!», y no sé si el libro se sentirá ofendido, o si hará examen de conciencia. Estaría bien que alguien un día hiciera escribir un texto en el que se cuenta cómo es la vida interior de un libro.

Me imagino que llevar impreso un texto terrible es, para un libro de papel, un infierno. ¿Cómo será la vida de un libro que cuenta una historia de amor infeliz? ¿Será infeliz también el libro? Y si su texto cuenta una historia de sexo, ¿se sentirá en continua excitación? ¿Es bueno no poder salir nunca del texto que uno lleva impreso en sus páginas? Quién sabe, quizá la vida de un libro de papel es buenísima, porque pasa la vida concentrado en el mundo de su texto, y vive sin dudas, sin sospechar lo que puede suceder fuera de él y, sobre todo, sin la sospecha de que existen otros textos que contradicen el suyo.

Yo no lo sé, porque por el texto que me han metido me he enterado de que soy un e-book, un libro electrónico, cuyas páginas se desplazan por una pantalla. Por lo visto, tengo una memoria superior a la de un libro de papel, porque un libro de papel puede tener diez, cien, mil páginas, pero no más. En cambio, yo podría alojar muchísimos textos, todos juntos. Lo que no sé es si sabría pensarlos todos de golpe, o de uno en uno, según cuál sea el texto que activa mi usuario. Sin embargo, además de los textos que me meterán, tengo un programa interno, una memoria mía —es un decir—. Entiendo quién soy no solo por el texto que alojo ahora, sino por la naturaleza misma de mis circuitos internos. En fin, no sé explicarme muy bien, pero es como si supiera saltar fuera del texto que estoy alojando y dijera: «¡Mira qué curioso, alojo este texto!». No creo que un libro de papel pueda hacerlo, pero quién sabe, me imagino que nunca tendré la oportunidad de dialogar con un libro de papel.

El texto que alojo es muy rico, y estoy aprendiendo muchas cosas, sobre el pasado de los libros de papel y sobre el destino de nosotros, los e-books. ¿Somos, seremos más afortunados que nuestros antepasados? No estoy muy seguro. Veremos. De momento estoy muy contento de haber nacido.

Ha sucedido algo muy extraño. Ayer (modestamente, tengo un reloj interior) me apagaron. Cuando estoy apagado no puedo vivir en el texto que llevo dentro. Pero hay una zona de mi memoria que permanece activa: aún sé quién soy, sé que llevo un texto dentro, aunque no pueda entrar en él. Sin embargo, no duermo, de otro modo se pararía también mi reloj interior, y no es así, en cuanto me reenciendo, sé decir la hora exacta, y el día y el año.

De repente me reencendieron, sentí dentro un extraño revuelo y fue como si me convirtiera en otro. Estaba en una selva oscura y me salían al encuentro tres fieras, luego me encontré con un señor que me llevó... No consigo expresar bien lo que me estaba sucediendo, pero entré en un embudo infernal y —menudo flipe— ¡qué no habré visto yo! Por suerte, me hicieron desplazarme hasta el final del texto y fue maravilloso: veía al mismo tiempo a la mujer de mi vida, a la Virgen María y al Señor Dios en persona, aunque no sé repetir bien qué veía, porque un solo instante me es mayor letargo que veinticinco siglos a la empresa que hizo a Neptuno admirar la sombra de Argo.

Como experiencia —todavía estoy viviéndola— es extraordinaria, pero siento como la nostalgia oscura del texto anterior, quiero decir que sé que yo alojaba un texto, pero es igual que si estuviera sepultado en las profundidades de mis circuitos, y en cierto sentido estoy condenado a vivir solo en el texto nuevo que...

···

Mi usuario debe de ser voraz y caprichoso. Desde luego esta mañana me ha metido no solo un texto nuevo, sino muchos, y ahora pasa del uno al otro con desenvoltura, sin darme tiempo a acostumbrarme.

Es decir, estaba realmente inmerso en la visión de una profunda y clara subsistencia de una suprema luz, y me parecía distinguir tres giros de tres colores y una continencia, cuando he sentido un olor de hollín, he oído un silbido de locomotoras y, en los fríos de una noche casi hiperbórea, ahí estaba yo arrojándome bajo un tren. Por amor, creo, y de un oficialillo de cuatro perras. Ana, ¿qué haces?, estaba preguntándome, y ya estaba experimentando el horror de las ruedas de la locomotora que me laceraban las carnes, cuando me he encontrado cerca de los Carmelitas Descalzos, junto con Athos, Porthos y Aramis, a los que acababa de desafiar en duelo, los cuatro batiéndonos contra la guardia del cardenal. Una experiencia excitante, pero luego, de golpe, he sentido de nuevo la laceración de mis carnes, y no era el acero de ese Jussac, sino las ruedas dentadas y las hojas afiladas de una máquina soltera en una misteriosísima colonia penitenciaria. Estaba a punto de gritar, en la medida en que un e-book puede hacerlo (tal vez me habría puesto en *tilt* por el horror), cuando he sentido que mi nariz se alargaba de forma desmedida por una mentirijilla que acababa de decir, sin malicia y, tras un instante —ha sido una especie de arrobamiento—, ya estaba juzgando exagerado el castigo de quien acababa de introducirme en ese momento una aguja en la nuca, y sabía que era el maldito Rocambole, a quien bien había educado yo como un hijo en el noble arte del delito...

Ha sido una mañana terrible, mi usuario parecía enloquecido, de golpe me he visto paseando por un universo no euclidiano donde las líneas paralelas se encuentran a cada instante en un atasco insoportable, e inmediatamente después me he sentido oprimido por una serie de caracteres misteriosos como ي پ گ שׁ צ.

Solo con mucho esfuerzo he notado que me había convertido en un diccionario árabe-hebreo. Es agotador convertirse en una lengua nunca aprendida, mejor dicho, en dos, y estaba aprehendiendo con esfuerzo el yo mismo en que acababa de devenir, cuando el maestro me ha preguntado algo. He contestado: «¡He sido yo!», y el maestro me ha dicho que tenía un corazón noble. Me ha llamado Garrone, mientras hasta poco antes estaba convencido de que me llamaba D'Artagnan. Se me ha acercado un chico rubio, yo creía que era Derossi, pero evidentemente había vuelto a cambiar de texto, porque me ha dicho que se llamaba Jim, y me ha presentado a lord Trelawney, al doctor Livesey y al capitán Smollett. También había un marinero con una pata de palo, pero en cuanto me he atrevido a preguntarle algo me ha dicho: «A bordo, Ismael, el *Pequod* está zarpando, esta vez esa maldita ballena no se me volverá a escapar». He entrado en el vientre de Moby Dick y me he encontrado a mi buen papá, Gepeto, que estaba comiendo una fritura de pescado a la luz de una vela. «¡Layo! —he gritado—. ¡Te juro que no sabía que esa era mi madre!», pero entonces mi mamá, que parece que se llama Medea, me ha matado, para hacerle un desplante a Orestes.

No sé si conseguiré resistir mucho. Soy un libro disociado, tener muchas vidas y muchas almas es como no tener ninguna y, además, debo estar atento a no tomarle cariño a un texto porque al día siguiente mi usuario podría borrármelo.

Quisiera de verdad ser el libro de papel que contiene la historia de ese señor que visita el infierno, el purgatorio y el paraíso. Viviría en un universo tranquilo, donde la distinción entre el bien y el mal está clara, donde sabría cómo ha de desplazarse uno para pasar del tormento a la beatitud, y donde las líneas paralelas jamás se encuentran.

Longtemps je me suis couché de bonne heure. Soy una mujer que está a punto de dormirse y le pasan por delante de los ojos de la mente (pero yo diría del útero) lo que acaba de vivir. Sufro porque no encuentro ni comas ni puntos y no sé dónde pararme. No quisiera ser lo que soy, pero me veo obligado a decir *yes yes yes...*

¿Acaso Shakespeare era Shakespeare?[1]

Desde hace mucho tiempo, bibliófilos y estudiosos del Bardo conocen perfectamente la Bacon-Shakespeare Controversy,[2] sobre todo por algunas alusiones debidas a Selenus (que al final era el duque de Brunswick), aunque en general, siguiendo la estela de numerosas especulaciones nacidas en los ambientes rosacruces, se sospechaba que el verdadero autor de las obras de Shakespeare era lord Francis Bacon. Solo en el siglo pasado y en los albores de este se ha producido una vasta bibliografía sobre el tema, de la cual me limitaré a citar tan solo los textos mayores (y nótese que participaron en esa polémica también científicos insignes como el matemático Georg Cantor):

SELENUS, GUSTAVUS
CRYPTOMENYTICES ET CRYPTOGRAPHIAE
LIBRI IX
In quibus & planissima Steganographiae a Johanne Trithemio, Abbate Spanheymensi & Herbipolensi, admirandi ingenij Viro, ma-

---

1. Publicado en el *Almanacco del Bibliofilo (Bibliofantasie di una estrosa équipe di scanzonati favolatori)*, Milán, Edizioni Rovello, 2003.
2. Cfr. Giulio Blasi, «Bakespeare. Paradoxical Operations on the Concept of Author», *Versus*, n.º 57, septiembre-diciembre de 1990, pp. 57-94.

gice & aenigmatice olim conscriptae, Enodatio traditur. Inspersis ubique Authoris ac Aliorum, non contemnendis inventis.

SI [Col.] *Lunaeburgi, Excriptum typis Johannis Henrici Fratrum, der Sternen – Biblipolarum Lunaeburgensium, Anno 1624.*

1.ª edición.

Folio pequeño (17) 493. Espléndido frontis alegórico grabado. Cinco láminas plegadas. Tablas y discos muy numerosos. Numerosas orlas y capitulares grabadas en madera. Tres grabados de Lucas Kilian, uno a plena página y dos a media página.

(Se considera la fuente de las especulaciones sobre el *affaire* Bacon-Shakespeare.)

CANTOR, GEORG

DIE RAWLEY'SCHE SAMMLUNG VON ZWEIUNDDREISSIG TRAUERGEDICHTEN AUF FRANCIS BACON

Ein Zeugniss zu Gusten Bacon-Shakespeare-Theorie mit einem Vorwort herausgegeben von Georg Cantor. [Seguido por] *Memoriae Honoratissimi Domini Francisci... Sacrum. Londini in Officina Johannis Haviland, 1636.* [Encuadernado como tercer fascículo, precedido por] *Confessio Fidei Francisci Baconi... Cum Versione Latina e Guilelmo Rawley... Anno mdciviii evulgata. Halis Saxonoum 1896. Prostat Apud Max. Niemeyer Bibliopolam. Resurrectio Divi Quirini Francisci Baconi... CCLXX annis post obitum eius in die aprili anni MDCXXVI* (Pro Manuscripto). *Cura et impensis G. C. Halis Saxonum 1896.*

Halle 1897. In Commissione bei Max Niemeyer.

1.ª edición.

16.º 31; iv, 24; (1) xxvii, 32.

(Material recopilado y publicado por Cantor para sostener la controversia Bacon-Shakespeare.)

DONNELLY, IGNATIUS
THE GREAT CRYPTOGRAM
Francis Bacon's Cipher in The So-called Shakespeare Plays, By Ignatius Donnelly, Author of «Atlantis: The Antedeluvian World» and «Ragnarok: The Age of Fire and Gravel».
London, Sampson Low, Marston, Searle & Rivington, Ltd. 1888.
1.ª edición.
8.° dos vols., vi, 998, con tablas y diagramas a dos tintas.

DURNING-LAWRENCE, SIR EDWIN
BACON IS SHAKE-SPEARE
Together with a Reprint of Bacon's Promus of Formularies and Elegancies Collated, with the original Ms. by the late F. B. Bickley and revised by F. A. Herbert, of the British Museum.
New York, The John McBride Co. 1910.
1.ª edición.
8.° xiv, 286. Láminas.

REED, EDWIN
BACON AND SHAKE-SPEARE PARALLELISMS
Boston; Charles E. Goodspeed 1902.
1.ª edición.
8.° (6) 441.

STOPES, CHARLOTTE
THE BACON-SHAKESPEARE QUESTION ANSWERED
Second Edition, Corrected and Enlarged.
London; Trübner & Co., Ludgate Hill 1889.
16.° xiv, 266, 8.

THEOBALD, BERTRAM G.

FRANCIS BACON CONCEALED AND REVEALED

[London] *Cecil Palmer Forty Nine Chandos Street 1930.*

1.ª edición.

8.° xii, 390.

THEOBALD, ROBERT M.

SHAKESPEARE STUDIES IN BACONIAN LIGHT

San Francisco; John Howell 1901.

1.ª edición.

8.° xii, 500.

WIGSTON, W. F. C.

FRANCIS BACON

Poet, Prophet and Philosopher, Versus Phantom Captain Shakespeare.
The Rosicrucian Mask.

London, Kegan Paul, Trench, Trübner & Co. 1891.

1.ª edición.

8.° xlvi, 436.

En suma: el debate nacía de la convicción de que un hombre de escasa cultura e ínfima extracción social como Shakespeare, en definitiva, un actor, no era capaz de elaborar textos con semejante valor artístico y profundidad de pensamiento. Parecía más aceptable la idea de que Shakespeare era solo un testaferro, o a lo sumo aquel que ponía en escena y recitaba las obras que se le atribuían, pero que se debían a un personaje de gran ingenio y sensibilidad. Nadie en aquellos tiempos podía exhibir tales cualidades como Francis Bacon, filósofo, hombre político, literato sutil como prueba su *New Atlantis* y profundo conocedor del ánimo humano.

La conjetura no quería ser fantasiosa: todos los textos citados en la bibliografía demuestran, a veces reimprimiendo las obras shakespearianas y subrayando o imprimiendo en rojo los pasos relevantes, que todo el *Opus* del Bardo, tal como parece en el infolio de 1623, contiene alusiones, indicios cifrados, legibilísimos criptogramas que revelan la paternidad baconiana. Es inútil citar, por último, los muchos documentos que se han sacado a la luz y que demuestran irrefutablemente esta hipótesis.

La menos conocida es la simétrica Shakespeare-Bacon Controversy. Para escribir todas las obras de Shakespeare, se decía, no solo las tragedias sino también los inmortales sonetos, era necesario el trabajo de una vida entera. ¿Cómo habría podido Bacon encontrar el tiempo de llevar a cabo esa labor titánica si no fue delegando a otros la fatiga de escribir sus obras filosóficas? Se elaboró, por tanto, la hipótesis de que Shakespeare, que con todo era hombre de no pocas habilidades, fue contratado con ese objeto por Bacon. La extracción social de Shakespeare probaría también la vena de sano sentido común con que están concebidas las obras baconianas. Por tanto, Shakespeare sería el autor de las obras que ahora se le atribuyen a Bacon.

La bibliografía al respecto ha sido tan rica como la simétrica que acabamos de citar poco más arriba, y contiene páginas enteras de la obra baconiana, subrayadas o impresas en rojo, en las que aparecen claros indicios criptográficos de la paternidad shakespeariana. Y he aquí algunos títulos que he conseguido recuperar sobre este fascinante debate:

CANTOR, GEORG

DIE RAWLEY'SCHE SAMMLUNG VON ZWEIUNDDREISSIG TRAUERGEDICHTEN AUF SHAKESPEARE

Ein Zeugniss zu Gusten Shakespeare-Bacon Theorie mit einem Vorwort herausgegeben von Georg Cantor. [Seguido por] *Ye Memories of Guillelmi Scrollalanciae. Londini In Officina Johannis Haviland, 1636.* [Encuadernado como tercer fascículo, precedido por] *Confessio Fidei Guillelmi, Cum Versione Latina a Nigra Domina... Anno mdclviii evulgata. Halis Saxonum. 1896. Prostat Apud Max. Niemeyer Biblioplam. Resurrectio Divi Stratfordini Guillemi...* (Pro Manuscripto). *Cura et impensis G. C. Halis Saxonum 1896. Halle 1899. In Commissione bei Max Niemeyer 1899.*

1.ª edición.

16.° (17 ★ 11). 31; iv, 24; (1) xxvii, 32.

DONNELLY, IGNATIUS

THE SMALL CRYPTOGRAM

William Shakespeare's Cipher in The So-called Baconian Works. By Ignatius Donnelly.

London, Sampson Low, Marston, Searle & Rivington, Ltd. 1890.

1.ª edición.

8.° x, 800, con tablas y diagramas a dos tintas.

DURNING-LAWRENCE, SIR EDWIN

SHAKE-SPEARE IS BACON

Collated, with the original Ms. by the late F.B. Bickley and revised by F.A. Herbert, of the British Museum.

New York; The John McBride Co. 1920.

1.ª edición.

8.° xv, 230. Láminas.

REED, EDWIN
SHAKE-SPEARE AND BACON PARALLELISMS
Boston; Charles E. Goodspeed 1905.
1.ª edición.
8.° v, 430.

STOPES, CHARLOTTE
THE SHAKESPEARE-BACON QUESTION ANSWERED
London; Trübner & Co., Ludgate Hill 1889.
1.ª edición.
16.° x, 210.

THEOBALD, BERTRAM G.
WILLIAM SHAKESPEARE CONCEALED AND REVEALED
[London] *Cecil Palmer Forty Nine Chandos Street 1936.*
1.ª edición.
8.° xii, 300.

THEOBALD, ROBERT M.
BACON STUDIES IN SHAKESPEAREAN LIGHT
San Francisco; John Howell 1903.
1.ª edición.
8.° xii, 500.

WIGSTON, W. F. C.
WILLIAM SHAKESPEARE
Philosopher, Versus Phantom Captain Bacon. The Templar Mask.
London, Kegan Paul, Trench, Trübner & Co. 1899.
1.ª edición.
8.° xlvi, 436.

En suma: los partidarios de la Bacon-Shakespeare y los de la Shakespeare-Bacon Controversies se pusieron de acuerdo razonablemente. Podía sostenerse que Bacon era el autor de las obras de Shakespeare y que Shakespeare era el autor de las de Bacon sin que las dos teorías entraran en contradicción. Por otro lado, los indicios textuales eran absolutamente indiscutibles en ambos casos. Las objeciones puntillosas de Julius Stapleton (*If so, Why?*, Londres, Faber & Faber, 1930) de que, si Bacon era el autor de las obras de Shakespeare y no de las suyas, no podía haber sembrado la obra de Shakespeare de indicios que se referían a las obras de Bacon, que podía ignorar perfectamente, y de que si Shakespeare era el autor de las obras de Bacon, no había razón para que introdujera remisiones a la obra de Shakespeare, de la que podía saber poquísimo; bueno, estas objeciones fueron tachadas de escepticismo positivista y rápidamente dejadas de lado.

Quedaba abierta, sin embargo, otra cuestión. Si Bacon era el autor de las obras de Shakespeare, no habría podido concebirlas sin una frecuentación cotidiana del mundo del teatro, por no decir que no habría podido escribir sus sonetos si, en lugar de frecuentar a diario el trato de la reina Isabel, no hubiera tenido tiempo de frecuentar la amistad de la Dark Lady. Al contrario, si Shakespeare era el autor de la obra de Bacon, no habría podido concebirla sin una frecuentación cotidiana tanto de la sociedad cultural de Londres como de la misma corte. Por consiguiente, había que suponer que no solo Bacon era el autor de las obras de Shakespeare, sino que se sustituyó directamente a Shakespeare en la dirección cotidiana del Globe; y viceversa por lo que concernía a la presunta obra baconiana. Por tanto, Shakespeare, esto es, aquel a quien la gente reconocía como Shakespeare, era en realidad Bacon, y Bacon era Shakespeare.

¿De quién son, entonces, los retratos que nos han llegado como retratos, respectivamente, de Shakespeare y de Bacon? Los retratos de Shakespeare retrataban evidentemente a Bacon y los de Bacon retrataban a Shakespeare.

Ahora bien, ¿cuándo se produjo la sustitución? Si sucedió en edad avanzada de ambos personajes, ambos habrían mantenido el resto de sus vidas una insostenible simulación, por lo que nos preguntamos si, en ese estado de ánimo, Bacon lograría mantener la serenidad necesaria para concebir el *Opus* shakespeariano, y Shakespeare la agudeza indispensable para concebir el *Opus* baconiano. Si, en cambio, la sustitución se produjo, digamos, en la cuna, entonces, de hecho, Shakespeare se consideraba Shakespeare y Bacon, Bacon. Lo único que habría podido iluminarlos sobre su auténtica identidad habría sido una prueba de ADN, por aquel entonces inconcebible. Así pues, a la luz de esta última hipótesis, Shakespeare era Shakespeare y Bacon era Bacon.

Por consiguiente, la obra de Shakespeare era verdaderamente de Shakespeare y la de Bacon, verdaderamente de Bacon.

Muchos de los estudiosos que habían animado la Bacon-Shakespeare Controversy (que para algunos era la Shakespeare-Bacon-Shakespeare Controversy), con el tiempo, cambiaron de opinión, como demuestra la bibliografía adjunta:

DONNELLY, IGNATIUS
THERE WAS NO CRYPTOGRAM
William Shakespeare's Cipher in The So-called Baconian Works. By Ignatius Donnelly.
London, Sampson Low, Marston, Searle & Rivington, Ltd. 1899.
1.ª edición.
8.º x, 10.

DURNING-LAWRENCE, SIR EDWIN
SHAKESPEARE WAS SHAKESPEARE
New York; The John McBride Co. 1925.
1.ª edición.
8.º xv, 100. Cien ejemplares con firma del autor.

REED, EDWIN
SHAKESPEARE AND BACON: AN INCOMPATIBILITY
Boston; Charles E. Goodspeed 1910.
1.ª edición.
8.º v, 0.

STOPES, CHARLOTTE
FUCK SHAKESPEARE (AND BACON TOO)!
London; Trübner & Co., Ludgate Hill 1890.
1.ª edición.
16.º x, 6.

THEOBALD, BERTRAM G.
BOTH SHAKESPEARE AND BACON DID NOT EXIST
[London] *Cecil Palmer Forty Nine Chandos Street 1936.*
1.ª edición.
8.º xii, 2.

THEOBALD, ROBERT M.
BACON-SHAKESPEARE STUDIES DISCOMBOBULATED
San Francisco; John Howell 1906.
1.ª edición.
8.º xii, 1200.

WIGSTON, W. F. C.

WAS SHAKESPEARE KASPAR HAUSER? THE MASONIC MASK
London, Kegan Paul, Trench, Trübner & Co. 1900.
1.ª edición.
8.° xlvi, 436.

Solo Cantor permaneció insensible al problema gracias a una teoría que había elaborado, la de la Absoluta Identidad de los Conjuntos Muy Poco Normales, aseverando que, si dos personas están locas —y locos no podían no ser, o por elección o por condena, los dos desafortunados isabelinos—, entonces ninguno de los dos podía saber ya quién era quién, y el máximo de la confusión se alcanzaría en el momento en que Shakespeare se creyera Shakespeare y Bacon, Bacon.

Está claro que, llegada a este punto, la controversia podía considerarse cerrada. Solo unas pocas alusiones a sus últimas secuelas. Hace poco, Antonio Tabucchi (*Sostiene Ulloa*, impreso a cargo de Mediaset) planteaba la hipótesis de que las obras tanto de Shakespeare como de Bacon (e incluso las de Cantor) las escribió Pessoa. Casi en la misma época, Roberto Calasso, remitiéndose a un voluminoso manuscrito de ochocientas páginas debido a la pluma de Roberto Bazlen, demostraba que ni Shakespeare ni Bacon habían escrito nada jamás (el primero, al haber sido asesinado muy jovencito en la Cripta de los Capuchinos de Viena, y el segundo, por la decisión que tomó en Praga, tras haber leído la *opera omnia* de Emanuele Severino, de que si el error de Occidente es el error de Occidente, entonces más valía callarse). Por tanto, la editorial Adelphi anunciaba la publicación inédita, en edición crítica, de todas las obras de Shakespeare y de Bacon, a cargo de Mazzino Colli, infolio con papel Fabriano y encuadernación de piel humana.

Sin embargo, Silvio Berlusconi ponía en tela de juicio el proyecto, durante una transmisión del Michele Santoro Show de la televisión de Tirana, en la que anunciaba: «Shakespeare soy yo. —Y añadía—: *Ad interim*». Luego, respondiendo a una pregunta de los periodistas: «Bacon. ¿Quién?».

Por una reforma de los catálogos

El mercado anticuario también sigue modas. Libros que hasta ayer podían obtenerse a un precio razonable, de repente alcanzan cifras imposibles, porque crece la curiosidad sobre un tema determinado. Por eso puede suceder que, una vez identificado un filón afortunado, los catálogos hagan todo lo posible para adscribir a ese filón obras que no tienen absolutamente nada que ver.

En los últimos años eso ha sucedido con el ocultismo. Cada vez se da más a menudo el caso de ver en un catálogo, precedidas por la palabra mágica «Occulta», obras que de oculto no tienen nada. Yo he encontrado incluso un san Agustín, pobrecillo, y uno de estos días me temo que encontraré, entre los *occulta*, el *Secretum* de Petrarca.

El juego puede llevar a consecuencias inaceptables, como encontrar, un día, en el sector ocultista un informe sobre *Cerraduras herméticas Yale en cifras*. Pero si hemos de jugar, hagámoslo, por lo menos, imaginando que de repente se pongan de moda algunos temas y se produzca una reorganización sustancial de las secciones de los catálogos.

Si se volvieran apetecibles las obras sobre la economía de los bancos y las organizaciones empresariales, podríamos encontrar en la lista los varios *Teatro d'imprese, Le imprese illus-*

tri, los *Discorsi sopra le imprese*, las *Empresas morales* junto a la *Tariffa Kircheriana*, el *Traité des chiffres* y la *Plutosofia*.

El gobierno de Romano Prodi, en el fondo, está de actualidad y, por tanto, por qué no asignarle a este argumento las *Institutioni Harmoniche*, el *De civitate Dei*, el *Antikrisis*, de Ireneus Agnostus, *Christianopolis*, *L'enfer demoli*, el *Opus Quadripartitum*, la *Civitas Solis*, el *Arte de navegar* y (para contentar a la oposición) el *Arca Noe* y *Stultifera Navis*. Para el ministro y exjuez Antonio Di Pietro, *In primo sententiarum*.

Un tema sobre el que se discute mucho es la reapertura de las casas de citas. Excluyendo por demasiado obvios *Il piacere*, de D'Annunzio, y la *Epístola sobre la tolerancia*, de Locke, sugiero *Diálogos de Amor*, *Aureus Vellus*, *De Fascino*, *Polygamia triumphatrix*, *Clavis convenientia linguarum*, *De secretis mulierum*, *La mirabile visione*, *La pudicitia schernita* y la *Retorica delle puttane*, de Ferrante Pallavicino (y también, ya que estamos, *La patta onorata*, de Goldoni), la *Monas Hieroglyphica*, *L'art de connaître les hommes* y, para las ciudades de mar, la *Consolatio navigantium*.

En una época de libertad sexual, mezcla de géneros, travestismo y movimientos de liberación gay, podría sugerir una sección compuesta por: *Novum Organum*, *Homo et ejus partes*, *De l'Androgyne*, *Noctes Atticae*, *Sic et non*, *L'uomo come fine*, *Uomini e no*, *Le piacevoli notti*, el *Adone*, *Coming of age in Samoa*, *Análiticos Posteriores*, *À rebours* y *Là bas*, además de las tablas anatómicas de Vesalio en sobre de plástico sellado.

Último tema: el de los poderes académicos y las oposiciones universitarias. Aquí están a disposición *De universitate*, *Les effroyables pactions*, el *Tintinnabulum sophorum*, *De regimine principum*, *Stratagematum Satanae libri otto*, *Gli arcani*

*svelati, Sur la nature de l'âme des bêtes, De lampade combi-
natoria, A true and faithful relation* (para las actas de oposiciones), *La sinagoga degli ignoranti, Kabbala desvelada, Tela
ignea Satanae.*

El código Temesvar[1]

Más de una vez en el curso de mis investigaciones he tenido que ocuparme de esa singular figura que fue Milo Temesvar. Como ya observaba en *Apocalípticos e integrados*, Temesvar (albanés, expulsado de su país por desviacionismo de izquierdas, luego exiliado en la Unión Soviética y en Estados Unidos, y por último en Argentina, donde se perdieron sus huellas) era conocido (por pocos) como autor de *Las fuentes bibliográficas de J. L. Borges, Sobre el uso de los espejos en el juego del ajedrez* y *The Pathmos Sellers*, que por aquel entonces yo reseñaba.

Tuve ocasión de mencionarlo también en la introducción a *El nombre de la rosa*, aclarando que *Del uso de los espejos en el juego del ajedrez* se publicó solo en georgiano (Tiblisi, Mamardashvili, 1934). Después de descifrar ese texto con esfuerzo (y me había ejercitado en el georgiano deletreando en su totalidad *El caballero de la piel de tigre*, de Rustaveli, en una elegante edición en 64.º de la ya desaparecida editorial Dzhugashvili), me di cuenta de que ahí estaban (más detallados y precisos) todos los acontecimientos que yo luego conté en mi novela.

1. Publicado en el *Almanacco del Bibliofilo (Antologia di racconti e saggi di bibliofilia)*, Milán, Edizioni Rovello, 2004, y posteriormente en un pequeño volumen en edición numerada, Edizioni Rovello, 2005.

Lo suficiente para convencerme de que Temesvar era un personaje singular, injustamente desconocido, cuyos textos (¿cuántos, dada su genial actividad de polígrafo?) había que ir a buscar.

En mis peregrinajes entre puestos y anticuados anticuarios de todas las ciudades, por puro azar cayó entre mis manos en Sofía (en una tiendecita de apariencia decaída donde pude encontrar por una suma irrisoria un infolio shakespeariano de 1623 y la primera edición del *Ulises* con notas autógrafas a lápiz de Sylvia Beach, parcialmente intonso, cubierta azul helénico original, un exlibris de George Brasillach y una dedicatoria manuscrita de Dolores Ibárruri al Campesino), un ejemplar (ay, ¿por qué tan estropeado?) de otra obra de Temesvar, esta vez en ruso, Тайная вечеря Леонардо да Винчи, Анекдоты, Москва, 1988, dedicada, como dice explícitamente el título, a una lectura del Cenáculo de Leonardo.

Lo más curioso es la fecha de este libro. No es necesario que un libro se publique mientras el autor sigue en vida, pero varios aspectos del texto de Temesvar inducen a considerar tal cosa, señal de que, en 1988 o inmediatamente antes, todavía vivía. De otro modo no habría podido tener en cuenta los varios libros de Gérard de Sède sobre el misterio de Rennes-le-Château, aparecidos a finales de los años sesenta y en los años setenta, como tampoco el famoso best seller de Lincoln, Baigent y Leigh, *El enigma sagrado*, que es de 1982.

Sin duda, al menos en la fecha de 1988, Temesvar no podía haber tenido noticia del muy reciente *El código Da Vinci*, de Dan Brown, pero como esta afortunada novela no hace nada más que recocer con habilidad asaz descarada todo el material tanto de Sède como de Lincoln y compañeros, no era necesario *El código Da Vinci* para empujar a Temesvar a la refutación sarcástica de lo que él consideraba una evidente impostura histórica.

Los argumentos que Temesvar emplea para desmontar todas las fantasiosas hipótesis sobre Cristo que se casa con María
Magdalena y da origen a la dinastía de los merovingios y posteriormente al mítico Priorato de Sión, no hay que referirlos
aquí, porque son los mismos que usa una sana filología y un
sano conocimiento histórico unidos a un análisis crítico de las
contradicciones que afloran a cada paso en este género, por lo
demás uniforme y bastante repetitivo, de obras de ciencia ficción históricas. Lo que llama la atención y que me lleva a proponer el redescubrimiento del texto de Temesvar es, si acaso, la
contrateoría que elabora.

Su discurso parte del Cenáculo de Leonardo da Vinci, puesto que a través de los textos de Sède o de alguno de sus innumerables repetidores le había llegado noticia de la interpretación
que constituye ahora el núcleo del libro de Brown. El Cenáculo
leonardesco (según algunos, Leonardo formaba parte con seguridad de los superiores desconocidos del Priorato) confirmaría
la hipótesis de Sède, en cuanto el san Juan representado a la
derecha de Jesús se presentaría, sin asomo de duda, como una
mujer, y la obra celebraría los esponsales, en absoluto místicos,
entre el Nazareno y María Magdalena. Además, la curiosa e
inexplicable arquitectura del cuadro, por la cual mientras entre
Jesús y los apóstoles que están a su izquierda (Tomás, Santiago
el Mayor, Felipe, Mateo, Judas Tadeo, Simón Zelote) el espacio
es mínimo, llama la atención la separación entre Jesús y el grupo constituido por Juan, Pedro y Judas (que tienen a su derecha
a Andrés, Santiago el Menor y Bartolomé), separación explica-
ble solo con el propósito de que aparezca entre Jesús y ese grupo una especie de triángulo con el vértice del revés que apunta
hacia la mano de Jesús, cabalmente una vagina (virtual), esto es,
la zona púbica de un cuerpo femenino.

Temesvar observa que, aparte de la inconsistencia de cualquier hipótesis sobre una Magdalena esposa de Cristo, aunque Leonardo por razones simbólicas hubiera querido dibujar una vagina, no se explica por qué habría debido satisfacer esa alusión esotérica con una separación inexplicable entre Juan y Jesús, separación que no tendría razón de estar tan recalcada ni si Juan hubiera sido el discípulo predilecto de Cristo ni si, por ventura, Magdalena hubiera sido su esposa. Lo que llama la atención de Temesvar es, en cambio, la naturaleza de una escena que muestra a los discípulos de la izquierda solidarios con el Maestro, o al menos (el grupo formado por Mateo, Judas Tadeo y Simón Zelote) ocupados en una alarmada conversación, mientras que el grupo de la derecha parece apartarse.

Aquí, argumenta Temesvar, más que una cena entre maestro y discípulos, o incluso una celebración nupcial, se está asistiendo a la ruptura que está produciéndose en el seno de un grupo. El Cenáculo representa una secesión, de la cual Cristo queda avisado por el dedo levantado de Tomás, así como por el aire solícito de los otros dos apóstoles que se inclinan hacia él como si quisieran ponerlo en guardia.

¿Quién está tramando algo contra Cristo? No solo Judas, como dice la *Vulgata*, el cual, antes bien, se muestra a lo sumo como deuteragonista en una historia mucho más amplia y preocupante. Leonardo no era un miembro o superior del Priorato de Sión, sino más bien un preocupado analista de las perversiones de su tiempo y (casi con espíritu de vidente) veía en el asunto de la última cena el anuncio de una conspiración histórica que aún nos toca de cerca.

Examinemos con detalle quién y qué representan los apóstoles de la izquierda, según la lectura de Temesvar. No hay duda de que Juan tiene los rasgos de una mujer, y sobre su androginia han disertado críticos de todos los países y todas las épocas. Ahora bien, andrógino no quiere decir femenino. Juan se presenta más bien como un homosexual y, por tanto, como uno a los que Jesús ya avisó, y con mucha antelación, de que en lugar de escandalizar a uno de esos pequeñitos, mejor harían en atarse al cuello una piedra de molino y arrojarse al mar; las vicisitudes sucesivas de Juan, exiliado en Patmos en una roca cortada a pico sobre el mar, y presa del evidente *delirium tremens* del Apocalipsis, autoriza a pensar que arrastró consigo durante años el remordimiento: remordimiento por sus tendencias innaturales y por la traición concebida contra el Maestro. Es posible, argumenta Temesvar, que Juan no represente la homosexualidad de forma específica, sino que represente por metonimia el pecado carnal en todas sus variedades; sin embargo, parece más verosímil que sea el símbolo del mismo pecado del que Leonardo se sentía culpable.

¿Qué representa Pedro, quien, no lo olvidemos, al cabo de poco renegaría de Jesús? No será una casualidad, aunque lo haga de mala gana, que Jesús se vea obligado a fundar sobre Pedro, es decir, sobre esa piedra, su iglesia, porque sabía que el Nuevo Testamento debía basarse en el Antiguo, por lo que la Iglesia tenía que sostenerse sobre la Sinagoga. Pedro, pues, judío de nacimiento, representa la Sinagoga, que conspira con el lobby homosexual para eliminar a Cristo. Según el proyecto judío de conquista del mundo tal como se presenta en *Los protocolos de los Sabios de Sión* (que, evidentemente, ya circulaban en los tiempos de Leonardo), Pedro se dirige al lobby homosexual a fin de que difunda en el mundo cristiano el libertinaje para así minar sus cimientos morales. Pedro tiene la fisonomía típica del Pérfido Judío tal como lo representarán la pintura, la literatura y la panfletística de los siglos siguientes. Su nariz aquilina pronunciada es un *hápax* en la iconografía del Cenáculo. En cambio, Tomás, fiel a Cristo, que sin duda preanuncia a Tomás de Aquino, tiene una nariz que definiríamos nórdica, occidental, «aria». La sonrisa de Pedro, apenas esbozada, es taimada y amenazadora, su mano se tiende hacia Juan como si le indicara lo que deberá hacer.

¿A quién representa entonces Judas? Su tez es más oscura que la de los demás y, según Temesvar, es la pre-figuración de Mahoma y del mundo árabe en general. Podrá parecer extraño, observa Temesvar, que la Sinagoga de Pedro se alíe con el islam para destruir el cristianismo. Pero hay que considerar que Leonardo no podía tener noticia del hecho de que, con la fundación del Estado de Israel, los judíos se encontrarían en conflicto directo con los musulmanes, mientras que el Cenáculo se pinta hacia 1495, cuando acaba de empezar, después de la Reconquista de 1492, la expulsión de los judíos de España, donde anteriormente eran tolerados por los árabes, a los cuales, es más, prestaban valiosísimos servicios en los ámbitos médico, comercial y financiero. En toda la tradición medieval, judíos y árabes se veían y se representaban como los enemigos tradicionales del Verbo cristiano, por lo que no había nada asombroso en verlos aliados en su complot.

En cuanto a los otros tres apóstoles a su derecha, parecen perplejos. Santiago el Menor indica a los tres traidores, Andrés se abre de brazos, en una mezcla de desolación y sensación de impotencia, Bartolomé está sorprendido y estupefacto. Es evidente que no aprueban la conspiración, pero tampoco sienten la urgencia de acercarse a Jesús (como hace Tomás) y avisarlo.

En definitiva, con *La última cena*, Leonardo quería avisar a sus contemporáneos y a la posteridad que desde el principio estaba en curso el complot descrito por los *Protocolos*, sin obviamente saber que este, aún en curso en nuestros días, adoptaría formas distintas, escindiéndose en múltiples complots independientes, el de los judíos ortodoxos, el de los árabes fundamentalistas, el de los homosexuales (y quizá en los tres subcomplots igualmente independientes de los homosexuales judíos, árabes y cristianos). O quizá, observa Temesvar, Juan, al representar la desenfrenada licencia sexual, está en lugar del complot de los medios de masas que (en la profecía leonardesca) volverían aceptable de forma espectacular la transgresión de cada uno de los diez mandamientos (hoy en día sentiríamos la tentación de decir el triple complot del Talmud, del Corán y de Mediaset).

De la lectura de la sutil interpretación de Temesvar afloran algunas preguntas. ¿Temesvar era antisemita, homófobo y antiárabe (una especie de mezcla entre Hitler, el cardenal Ratzinger y Oriana Fallaci), o quería más bien acusar a Leonardo de ser homófobo, antisemita y antiárabe? Ahora bien, ¿cómo conciliar esa supuesta homofobia de Leonardo con su (ya) fehaciente homofilia? Quizá, al contrario, Leonardo quería proclamarse celebrador y miembro de la conspiración y, por tanto, no solo homosexual, sino también judío. Quizá a este origen suyo se debe el hecho de que, aun escribiendo con caracteres latinos, él seguía estilándolos de derecha a izquierda y, por otro lado, el anagrama de Leonardo da Vinci es: *D(avid) N(oah) Arié Colon Fida*, típico nombre judío. O también, Leonardo, homófilo, ¿quería denunciar el complot árabe-judío que había intentado involucrar a los homosexuales para difamarlos? En ese caso, Juan ¿estaría tiernamente representado como víctima de la perfidia árabe-judía, su fuga a Patmos habría sido la manera de sustraerse a las seducciones de Pedro y de Judas, y el Apocalipsis, la atroz alegoría de los resultados, proféticamente vislumbrados, de las tramas de sus dos compañeros? O, por último, Leonardo ¿quería denunciar, y con antelación, las distintas teorías conspiracionistas, incluida la del *Código Da Vinci*, construyendo su Cenáculo como una burla provocadora, una parodia de las Metástasis de la Interpretación?

En cualquier caso y sin duda, *La última cena* no cuenta la historia que parece contar y que con tanta superficialidad nos han transmitido los ingenuos.

En efecto, Temesvar acaba su ensayo con una ráfaga de preguntas inquietantes basadas en seguras argumentaciones numerológicas. ¿Por qué el nombre de Leonardo Vinci tiene 13 letras, 13 son los recuadros (paneles laterales y ventanas) que aparecen en el fresco y 13 los convidados? Nótese que podríamos añadir que ya que el nombre original de la ciudad de Temesvar, en Rumanía, es Timisoara —y queda pendiente el problema de por qué el albanés Milo tenía o había adoptado un apellido rumano—, ¡también el nombre Milo Timisoara tiene 13 letras! Pero *glissons*, para no alentar paranoias interpretativas.

El hecho es que, nota Temesvar, si eliminamos a Jesús y luego a Judas (que morirían al cabo de poco), los comensales del Cenáculo son 11; 11 es el número de las letras de los dos nombres unidos de Petrus y Judas; 11 el número de las letras de la palabra *Apocalypsis*; 11 son también las letras de *Ultima Coena*; a ambos lados de Jesús aparecen dos veces un apóstol con las manos abiertas y uno con el índice tendido, para formar en ambos casos la cifra 11; 11 por 11 daría 121, ¡y nótese que este es, en efecto, un número enmascarado! Negando los diez mandamientos y restando, por consiguiente, diez de 121, obtenemos 111. Ahora, multiplicando 111 por las 6 veces en que en el Cenáculo aparece la cifra 11, obtenemos 666, ¡el número de la Bestia!

Los indicios perturbadores no se quedan ahí. Siguiendo un elemental principio cabalista, Temesvar asigna a las letras del alfabeto (26) un número progresivo. Sustituyendo cada letra con un número, el nombre Leonardo da Vinci da 12+5+15 +14+1+18+4+15+4+1+22+9+14+3+9 = 146, y la suma interna de 146 da 11. Hágase ahora la misma operación con el nombre de *Matteo*: la suma de los valores numéricos de las letras es igual a 56, cuya suma interna da 11. Procédase como en el caso anterior y se obtiene una vez más el número de la Bestia, 666.

Pero veamos ahora qué sucede con el nombre de *Johannes* y de *Giuda*. La suma de los valores numéricos de las letras de *Johannes* da 78, cuya suma interna es 15, cuya sucesiva suma interna es 6; la suma de los valores numéricos de las letras de *Giuda* da una vez más 78, cuya suma interna es 15 y cuya sucesiva suma interna da 6. Esta doble, subrayada, aparición del número 6 nos induce una vez más a multiplicar 111 por 6, y he aquí que obtenemos una vez más 666, el número de la Bestia.

Tantas coincidencias no pueden ser casuales. El Cenáculo, al denunciar la traición de Cristo, anuncia al mismo tiempo la venida del Anticristo. ¿En tono disfórico (Leonardo sería entonces un ortodoxo preocupado) o en tono eufórico (Leonardo sería entonces uno de los maestros del complot)?

Temesvar no se pronuncia, pero en cualquier caso nos avisa de que en todo mensaje (incluso en el más aparentemente inocente como «hoy llueve») hay que encontrar siempre un sentido secreto debajo de la letra.

Alguien tramó o sigue tramando algo aún en la sombra, nos dice Temesvar. Y quizá a una de esas tramas, o a la Trama Única por excelencia, se debe su desaparición. Quizá había puesto en claro un cifrado que debía permanecer oculto, o conocido solo por quienes determinan en secreto los destinos de Occidente.

Subasta de libros que pertenecieron a Ricardo Montenegro[1]

Los volúmenes quedarán expuestos durante una semana a partir del 25 de marzo de 1997, con venta pública el martes siguiente a las 10.00 h.

FLUDD, ROBERT, *Tomi Secvndi Tractatvs Secvndi Sectionis Secvndae Partis Primae Portio Secvnda De Extranatvrali et Metanatvrali Megacosmi Historia. In Portiones Tres Distributa, Avthore Roberto Flvd Alias de Flvctibvs Armigero et Medicinae Doctore Oxoniensi, In Qvo Qvasi Specvlo Politissimo E Sacro fonte radicaliter extracto non modo de Naturae Simia sed etiam de Simiae Natvra praemonstratur atq. de Adamico Pithecio Austrino origo ostenditur. Nec Non Metaphysicorum Dictis & Avthoritate ejus Decavdatio ad amussim & enucleate explicatur & comprobatvr. Vbi de Ortv Avstrino hoc est de Anvlo Irreparabiliter Perdito ante Moysaicvm Egressvm sed serendipiter post Navigationem Begelianam nouiter Invento Praenaturalis Historia narratvr Ymaginibus effabré exculptis a Theodoro de Bry. Qvasi postremum preambulum mysticum portionis tertiae secundae partis sectionis secundae tractatus secundi torni secundi Vtrivsque*

---

1. Publicado en el *Almanacco del Bibliofilo (Apologia del vocabolario)*, Milán, Edizioni Rovello, 1999.

Cosmi Historiae. Oppenheimij Impensis Gvilelmi Fitzeri, Typis excussus Caspari Rotelli Anno MDCXXXIX.

2.°: A^4 (-A^3, + U^2) B-2B^4 2C^8; pp. (2) *1-3 4-5 6-9 10 11-216 117-224* (Numerosos errores de numeración: 83 por 73, 121 por 1, 216 por 217, 224 por 33.) Portadilla y 4 frontispicios grabados, 1 mapa plegado de la Terra Incognita con la coloración original, 4 grabados a plena página, 317 grabados en madera en el texto, 1 disco móvil (que falta en todos los ejemplares conocidos) con la Rosa Zoomorphyca.

Encuadernado en piel de cerda de época con impresiones en frío, abrasión en el plano posterior, una cabeza del lomo débil. Ligeras manchas de humedad en las primeras 80 hh., taladro de carcoma marginal entre A^2-F^3. Por lo demás, ejemplar muy fresco y agradable. Magnífico exlibris «Ex Bibliotheca Magistri Michaelis de Notre Dame».

Rara y única edición de este rarísimo (e inacabado) apéndice al *Utriusque Cosmi Historia*, ausente en Mellon, Ferguson, Duveen, Hall, Caillet, Dorbon. Ningún ejemplar NUC. Guaita 23458. Thorndike xii, p. 456. «Dadas las dificultades de clasificación del *Opus* fluddiano es incierto que se trate de UCH II 2 c$_{1/2}$ (Godwin) o de UCH III 1 b$_{2/1}$.» (Gardner, según el cual UCH III 1 a, UCH III 1 b$_{1/1}$ además de UCH III 1 b$_{2/3}$ no habrían sido publicadas jamás.)

THEOPHILUS SCHWEIGHART (?) *Vervm Alchymische Clypevm. Das ist Die Ganze Kunst und Wissenschaft der Ertz Bruderschaft, Ueber Psudochymicorum Libellis Monstruosis Figuris atq. Aenigmatibus Homines Decipientibus, contra Hystriones Chaos Magnesiae & Antri Naturae und änliche Orbimeripottendificuncta undique quoversum bombitarantarantia nouissimum scutum praebens für defensionem Fratrum des löblichen Ordens Roseae Crucis. Sub umbra alarum tuarum, cave diabolum!* Sl., sf. (1617).

24.º (10 hh. s. p.) 77 pp. (1 h. blanca). Portadilla con hermoso grabado que representa la tumba de Christian Rosenkreutz. Encuadernación en pergamino de época deteriorado. Oscurecimiento constante por la calidad del papel. Notables manchas de humedad y amplia carcoma marginal con pérdida de pocas letras en las últimas hojas. Abrasión en la parte inferior del frontispicio para borrar lugar y fecha. Excepcional exlibris de Christian Knorr von Rosenroth.

Desconocido para Caillet, Guaita, Dorbon, Ouvaroff, Gardner. ¡Ausente en la Bibliotheca Hermetica de Amsterdam! Waite (*Cross and Crucible: Addenda on Early Rosicrucians*, Londres, 1923, pp. 66) lo atribuye a Schweighart y cita como editor: «Typis Rolandi Edighofferij, Armartis [*sic*], 1617». G. Arnold (*Unpartheysche Kirchen-und-Ketzer Historien*, Schaffahusen, 1743, Appendix pp. 870) no menciona al autor, pero afirma que el landgrave de Hesse habría pagado ya en su época mil ducados para adquirir el único ejemplar aún existente, probablemente este.

SCHOTT, CASPAR, P. Gasparis Schotti regiscuriani E Societate Iesv Olim in Panormitano Siciliae, nunc in Herbipolitano Franconiae Gymnasio ejusdem Societatis Iesv Matheseos Professoris. *Machina Olivetana, Sive de Technasmate Siliceo quasi Rationem Digitis Computante, singularem personam adjuvante, in quo admirandorum effectuum spectacula, inventionum miracula ad multos calculos mercationis & ad verborum processionem adhibenda, eruuntur. Ubi quomodo quilibet scribendo epistola qualibet de re, quocumque idiomate, potest alteri absenti arcanum animi sui conceptu manifestare & scripturam ab aliis eadem arte intelligere, Asperae Laminae auxilio, explicatur. Opus desideratum diu, promissum a multis, a non paucis tentatum, a Iaponicis callidissime imitatum.* Eporediae Sumptibus Haeredum Camilli. Excudebat Carolus De Benedictis jam Eporediensis Typographus, MXXIV (*sic*, probablemente 1624).

4.° (20,5 ✱ 16). (28 hh. s. p.) 488 (blanca). Hermosa portadilla de Saerial, numerosos grabados de máquinas, dieciséis discos móviles que permiten reproducir combinatoriamente todo el contenido de la obra.

Sólida encuadernación moderna en estuche. Ejemplar excepcionalmente a salvo de todo tipo de carcoma.

Cfr. para ejemplar análogo I.B.M: Israel (cat. PS 50/50). Aunque no muy rara (muchos ejemplares NUC), la obra se presenta de particular actualidad. El padre Schott anticipó muchos estudios contemporáneos sobre la inteligencia artificial. De este libro hay un facsímil (Tokio, Clone Publishers, 1990).

(ANÓNIMO), *Albedo Triumphans sive de Spermate Ceti.* Sl., sf.

(16.°) Frontispicio alegórico de P. E. Quodd que representa el Currus Leviathani, 178 pp. blancas 1 h. s. p. de fe de erratas. Encuadernado en piel blanca. Lavado, pero en su conjunto muy fresco.

Ferguson (*Books of secrets* iv, 4, 5, p. 27) lo indica como raro tratadillo alquímico dedicado a la Obra al Blanco, que debe alcanzarse a través del peregrinaje místico y no con los métodos tradicionales; cita un segundo frontispicio (ausente en nuestro ejemplar) que recitaría «Sive de Furnis Novis Philosophicus Inauditis absque flammis». Citado entre las obras de viajes a la Terra Incognita por Starbuck & Stubb (*Ismael's Forerunners*, Nantuchet, New Bedford Press, 1845). Desconocido para Caillet, Dorbon, Guaita, Duveen, Bibliotheca Magica, además de para Sabin y Du Rietz.

(RARÍSIMO INCUNABLE), Pseudo-Alberto, *De secretis mulierum*. Havantii, 1483.

F.1a tit: Albertus Magnus De Secretis Mulierum. F.2a: // Liber de admirando se//creto tampasticho sive de sudario hauriente Cum expositione Mag//gistri Tambrandi. [Al final:] Finis, Impressum Havantii, 1483//die purgationis. Registr. 4.r.ch. maj. et min. c:S. et c. in fine quaterniorum 2 col. 28 1. text. 38 1. comment. 54 ff. Espléndido ejemplar de blancura excepcional, en elegante cartoné moderno. Ligeras marcas de uso y algún florecimiento en los primeros ff.
Hain 566, Goff (A-300).

ROBSON ROBERT, *A Hooligan Guide. A Discourse occasioned by some Observations on the Inconveniences and Dangers arising from the Use of Common Spectacles, Leading the Way to know All Things, Past, Present and to Come, To Resolve all manner of questions, viz. of Pleasure, Health and Sorrow and teaching the way to cure all Diseases in all circumstances touching the Relation betwixt Spirit and Foot-Balloons*. London, At the Gascoigne corner, to be sold at the Goal Mouth.

8.º (16,5 ★ 10). (64 hh. s. p.) 1-184 y 149-226 pp. Hermosa portadilla.

Sólida encuadernación en cuero. En conjunto, deteriorado. Ejemplar de estadio.

GARZONI TOMMASO, *La Basilica degli Antiqvari Negromantici. Nouamente formato, et posto in luce da Thomaso Garzoni da Bagnocavallo, Accademico Informe di Ravenna per ancora Innominato. Diuiso in Dieci Incanti, oue si uedono i uari Prestigii del Mendacio d'Atributione, del far Cento Mappe d'un sol Portolano, et dello Scatalogar Seluatico, verbi gratia, del copiar li Frontispizi come fussero Pristini et del far parer l'Opra di S.S. Theologi come Gramatica d'Horacoli, Sogni, Sorti, Premonizioni, Prodigi, Sybille et altri Occulti Privilegi.* In Venetia: Al Portico di Sant'Anastatica.

4.º (10 ★ 6). (2 hh. s. p.) 98 pp.

Encuadernación en papel de azúcar uso monástico, deteriorada solo en cantos, charnela y planos, dorso y guardas hábilmente rehechas con páginas originales del Heraldo de san Antonio, hojas elegantemente recortadas con pérdida de pocas líneas por página, frontispicio manuscrito de Bartholomeo Garzoni, hermano del autor, hábilmente reproducido y montado, amplias manchas de agua que afectan solo a las primeras 45 hh., manchas de óxido debidas al estado de conservación, corte marmorizado con tinta China, señales de uso con recientes anotaciones manuscritas en bella caligrafía, gusano de época y termitero posterior en las cabezas del lomo (fresquísimo). En su conjunto, excelente e interesante ejemplar de esta obra singular y muy solicitada.

Galantara (*Testimonianze dell'incuria dei religiosi prima delle leggi Siccardi*, x); G. Libri (*Jolie Bibliothèque de Livres à Respecter*, 1845, xx, 6); *A WWF Catalogue of Habitats for Endangered Species*, (3659).*

DEE JOHN, *De Monade Oscillatoria. Of What Pass'd for Many Yeers at the Abbey of Saint-Martin-des-Champs as It Was Haunted by Private Conferences and Apparitions of Some Spirits, Tending to a General Alteration of most Kingdomes of the World, by Means of So-Called Horologium Oscillatorium; and shewing severall good Uses that a Sober Semathologist may take of All*. London, Printed by Valentin Boni Plani, and sold at the Templar door, 1660.

1.ª edición infolio (43*21), 450, 36 (6 hh. s. p.). Retrato de Dee junto a la Monas Oscillatoria. Portadilla con la representación de las diez Sefirot.
Encuadernado en piel de ternera de época. Espléndido y fresco ejemplar.

* Palau 1982479: «La traducción de esta célebre obra que ya corría en latín y francés se debe a Octaviano del Mozo. Después corrigió la versión de manera desgraciada D.A.P.Z.G. dejando el texto tan mal parado que nada tiene de castizo: *Historia de zorrastrones o descubrimiento interesante de la vida y diabólicas astucias de los caballeros de anticuaria industria nigromante. M. imprenta que fué de F. Símil*, 2 vols. viii 251 pp. – 222 pp. El libro consta de: 1. Arte de endilgar; 2. De un portulano cien mapas; 3. Descatalogar selvático; este a su vez comprende Trasuntar frontispicios como originales y Ofrecer la obra de los SS. Teólogos bajo especie de Gramáticas de Oráculos, Sueños, Suertes, Premoniciones, Prodigios, Sibilas y otros ocultos privilegios». (*N. de la T.*)

Meric Casaubon (*On Some Troubles occurring in Paris at the St. John's Eve*, 1894 [*sic*], xx, p. 45); G. Neuhaus, *Die frölische Foucaultschewissenschaft*, p. 88).

Finella Filippo, *De Dentorvm Phisionomia, Ubi, Quomodo ex Maxillarium, Caninorum Praecisoriumque Putredine cujuslibet Passio Animae intelligi possit, dicitur*. Eltornum Siciliae, Typis Iacobi Ciccarelli, 1648.

(Encuadernado con) Dirgby Kenelm, *Theatrum Dentarium. In quo Actio varia, singularis et admiranda Pulveris Sympathetici, & quando Ejus auxilio peniculum aspergitur et cotidiane dentes purgantur, ad eorum Extractionem vitandam, ostenditur. Opusculum lectu jucundum & utilissimum*. Durbanii, Printed by Gibbs and sold At the Coll Gate, 1633.

32.° (3*1). 32, 66 pp. Numerosas láminas.
Las dos obras en original y valiosa encuadernación de marfil, hábilmente restaurada con ceja laminada de oro. Ligeras y superficiales marcas de sarro.
Cfr. Fang & Zahn, *Books on Teeth*, «Surgeons Clarion», 5, 1986.

(Anónimo), *Il Pelago Rifiorente. O sia, dell'Algha Orientale & come per Svo Offizio il Mare diuenga Sauana Herbaria & Palvde Meotide. Oue si narra de la Fvga de le Sirene et Ondine de l'Vltima Thvle uenvte a cercar la Terra oue fioriscono i Limoni et le Caue del Svono oue si celebrauan le Piaceuoli et Sollazzeuoli Notti*. Nel Contado di Rimini, per i Tipi di Giani Fabri, Alla Porta del Paradiso, 1585.

16.º (9) 34. Portadilla de De Hooge con Venus que se hunde en la espuma del mar.

Plastificado moderno. Amplias manchas de agua. Orilla recortada. Obra curiosa y ausente de todos los catálogos turísticos.*

BOEHME JAKOB, *De Tuba Daemonum. Sive de Flatu Expulso. In quo Ima Concrepitatio, per quam interiora certamina manifestantur, fortiter tubicinat. A multis negata, a paucis confessa, ab omnibus deprecata.* Montis Catini, Impensis Falqui Haeredum, 1601.

16.º 300 hh. s. p.
Encuadernado en papel moderno uso «aseo». Hojas muy blancas con algunos florecimientos y ligeras marcas de uso. Barbas.

GAELLIUS LICIUS, *De secretis Libri vii.* Castri Fibochii, Aedibus Julij Magni Andreae, 1790.

8.º (14,5 ★),7). (16 hh. s. p.) 165 pp. El texto va de A¹ a P¹. Curiosa página de «Omissis» en P² precedida por lámina de logia. Varios sellos y tablas con criptografías en el texto.
Enc. marroquín negro. En el frontispicio sello de biblioteca eclesiástica.

---

* Palau 267789: «Historia de los Océanos florescidos. Ó de como el alga Oriental metamorphosea los amplios mares en sauana herbossa y laguna meocia. Donde se narra de la uida de las Sirenas y Ondinas de la Última Thvle llegadas en busca de la Tierra donde florescen los limones y las Grutas Sonoras en las que se celebran agradables y solazossas animaciones también llamadas mouidas. Vertida fácilmente en castellano del toscano por Pablo Herreros el Riminés (*Ebusus, donde las dos cerezas, por Ricardo el Suburense, sf.*)». *(N. de la T.)*

Jouin & Descreux (*Bibliographie Occultiste et Maçonnique et des Sociétés Secrètes*), Bruselas, 1976, p. 1480.

Foscolo Ugo, *Ultime lettere di Jacopo Ortis*, Parma, Bodoni, 1797.

Edición de aficionado con encuadernación Grolier original. Ejemplar de excepcional frescura. Se deplora solo una modesta carcoma marginal que afecta a algunos pliegos, en especial el pliego sellado del 25-3-1799.

LES DEMOISELLES. Espléndido grabado erótico de escuela aviñonesa del siglo XVI (125 ★ 270), coloreado a mano. En el margen: «Pabulus Pinxit, M.O.M.A».

El problema del umbral.
Ensayo de para-antropología

Hasta el reciente descubrimiento de la Cava Saguntina todo lo que sabíamos de aquella práctica arcaica llamada «filosofía» solo lo conocíamos gracias al fragmento del mercader griego Aristóteles (siglo II d. C.), que recita, según la lección del DK 5,00:

> Antes de que Atenas fuera conquistada por los pueblos del extremo Norte, que obedecen a los druidas, y que le llevaron el alfabeto y la convirtieron en el centro de todos los intercambios de mercancías del gran Imperio de Asurbanipal, desde las tierras del Nudo Gordiano hasta las columnas de Berbería, el centro del saber era considerado el país de los mastienos, ahora extinguidos, los cuales se decían los inventores de la filosofía. Qué era la filosofía ya no nos es dado saberlo, pero se considera que era una forma extrema de no saber que condujo a aquel pueblo a la Muerte. Por lo cual les pareció prudente a los que sobrevivieron hacer consistir el saber en el cálculo de lo que conviene o no conviene en la adquisición de la riqueza, a través de la cual se obtiene la Distracción, esto es, el Placer.

Las recientes excavaciones llevadas a cabo en la Cava Saguntina han sacado a la luz una serie de pequeñas tablillas de piedra en las que se hallaban inscritos aforismos e invocaciones, preceptos y amenazas gracias a los cuales ahora es posible reconstruir, aun de forma conjetural, qué era para los originarios habitantes de Mastienia aquello que llegaron a denominar filosofía. Esta se presenta como una forma de vida según la cual, en lugar de adquirir riquezas, los mastienos se interrogaban sobre öⱲ/ ⅏/ ⋎❀ —es decir, para usar la traducción harto oscura de Kranz— «el sentimiento inquieto de estar en el Umbral». Los mastienos no conocían la escritura, y estos testimonios son por consiguiente también vagos porque proceden de leyendas elaboradas por una civilización posterior, tras la extinción de los mastienos.

Según esos testimonios, parece claro que, antes de elaborar la filosofía, los mastienos, que vivían en esa zona que después se llamaría Celtiberia, llevaban una vida primitiva, cubiertos de pocas pieles y toscos tejidos, habitaban en cuevas y se dedicaban solo a la propia supervivencia y la reproducción. No existía la división del trabajo, el que conseguía procurarse comida la donaba a los demás después de haber consumido la cantidad que necesitaba, varones y mujeres se unían libremente entre ellos y los niños eran educados por la comunidad. No existían, pues, ni formas de intercambio ni mucho menos algo que pueda recordar nuestra noción de comercio. Entre otras cosas, una naturaleza bastante exuberante los surtía de frutos y agua en abundancia.

Es natural que, viviendo de esta forma, elaboraran formas de pensamiento muy elementales, y se vieran inducidos a considerar solo los acontecimientos materiales (como comer, defecar, copular). De los documentos que nos han llegado se deduce que eran reacios a todo tipo de abstracción. Allá donde, para nosotros los modernos, los acontecimientos de la vida deben ser subsumidos en categorías o conceptos (como la cantidad, el costo, la conveniencia y el dinero en cuanto Equivalente Universal, por lo cual tanto una fanega de trigo como dos brazadas de tela pueden verse como lo mismo, en cuanto materializan el mismo valor de intercambio), para los mastienos un hombre era alguien que «come, bebe, copula, defeca, orina y exhala el Último Aliento». En efecto, los mastienos no tenían ni siquiera un concepto de «hombre». Hablaban de ese o de aquel otro mastieno y, a lo sumo, llegaban a darse cuenta de que todos los mastienos hacían esa o aquella otra cosa.

Asimismo, los mastienos tampoco tenían una clara distinción entre el bien y el mal. El concepto que nosotros traducimos con «bueno» no solo no coincidía con el nuestro, sino que no era ni siquiera un concepto, al menos en el sentido que nosotros le damos al término, por el que son conceptos tanto la partida doble como la ganancia. Era más bien el sentimiento oscuro no de algo que debía hacerse o no hacerse, sino de algo que «solía suceder». Sin duda, los mastienos juzgaban bueno comer o copular, pero de igual modo juzgaban bueno el Último Aliento: para los mastienos, parece ser que «bueno» y «hecho» eran expresiones prácticamente sinónimas. Un mastieno que tenía hambre sentía la necesidad de moverse para buscar comida, una vez encontrada e ingerida quedaba saciado con el hecho.

No podemos afirmar que los mastienos «supieran» estas cosas. Si tuviéramos que identificar en los textos de las Cavas Saguntinas algo que sea aun vagamente traducible con «saber, o conocer algo», deberíamos recurrir no a un concepto sino a una especie de proverbio, que podríamos traducir como «Si es un hecho, ¿por qué hablar de él?».

Dentro de este marco, los mastienos no conocían ni tan siquiera lo que en otras civilizaciones arcaicas eran las divinidades. Sencillamente, entre todo lo que sucedía, fijaban su atención en

algunos fenómenos que sucedían siempre y sin cuyo acaeci-
miento ni siquiera se habría podido hablar de mastienos. Estos
«hechos» eran la Boca, por la que penetraban la comida y el aire,
indispensable para la supervivencia de un mastieno, y por la que
salía el Último Aliento; el Esfínter, por donde se evacuaban lo
que ellos llamaban «cosas» (eran cosas todo aquello que no era
un mastieno, las heces, las nubes, los animales y las piedras); el
Pene y la Vulva, no solo porque por ellos se evacuaban cosas,
sino porque de su conjunción derivaba una sensación de placer
(que para ellos era un hecho del que sentían necesidad, igual
que sentían la necesidad de la comida o la evacuación) y, por
último, porque de la Vulva salían los nuevos mastienos (parece
ser que, hasta la aparición de la filosofía, los mastienos nunca
postularon una relación de causa y efecto entre cópula y parto).

En el momento en que desde la Boca se exhalaba el Último
Aliento, es decir, el estertor final, el mastieno ya no se consideraba un mastieno. Desde ese instante en adelante se convertía
en comida (entre otras cosas, también los animales que eran
capturados exhalaban un Último Aliento y se transformaban
en comida). El cadáver era comido por los supervivientes.

En ese sentido, no puede decirse ni siquiera que los mastienos tuvieran un concepto preciso de la muerte, tal como no lo
tenían de la vida. Antes de nacer, un mastieno no existía, luego
era un hecho y luego ya no era. El Último Aliento también era
un hecho, y como tal se lo aceptaba («Si es un hecho, ¿por qué
hablar de él?»).

Así pues, la Boca, el Esfínter, el Pene, la Vulva eran considerados, por decirlo así, hechos privilegiados, objeto de una forma cultural bastante vaga, en cuanto a menudo se les practica-
ba el beso. No parece ser que el beso fuera un precepto: era
también él un hecho.

Según algunas tablillas sucedió, sin embargo, en un determinado estadio de su civilización, que por primera y última vez se produjera entre los mastienos una división del trabajo. Cuando un mastieno exhalaba el Último Aliento, el banquete que seguía era difícil de gestionar, porque alrededor del cadáver se reunía una muchedumbre impelida por la natural necesidad de devorarlo, donde los primeros se apoderaban con esfuerzo de jirones de carne y los últimos se quedaban sin nada, alterando el pacífico hábito de compartir naturalmente los bienes. Por tanto, se les delegó a algunos mastienos que habían demostrado una natural habilidad en el trabajo con cuchillos de obsidiana la disección del cadáver, su división en partes iguales y la distribución de las mismas.

A estos encargados se los llamaba con un término que, traduciendo burdamente la expresión, para nosotros sería el de *Médicos*. Parece claro que, al no considerar que existían otros medios para retrasar el Último Aliento (esto es, formas cualesquiera de curación del cuerpo), los Médicos no estaban encargados del mantenimiento de la salud, sino solo de la disección de los cadáveres. Dado que las muertes eran hechos frecuentes y que el trabajo de disección requería mucho trabajo, los Médicos eran alimentados por el resto de la comunidad y se ocupaban solo de su actividad específica. Entre una muerte y otra, sin embargo, los Médicos tenían a su disposición mucho tiempo y, por tanto (y este fue el infausto resultado de la división del trabajo), fueron inducidos lentamente a inventar la filosofía.

Al diseccionar los cadáveres, los Médicos se dieron cuenta de que entre la Boca y el Esfínter existía un recorrido interno a lo largo del cual la comida ingerida se convertía en sangre y carne, o se depositaba en los intestinos como cosas inútiles que serían expulsadas después por el Esfínter, por el Pene y por la

Vulva. Además, se descubrió la existencia de casi mastienos, es decir, de cuerpos en estado fetal, contenidos en el útero de ciertos cadáveres de sexo femenino. Por último, calculando el estadio de desarrollo de varios fetos, intentando recordar cuándo la extinta copuló por última vez, los Médicos aventuraron la idea de que el embarazo fuera efecto de la cópula.

El primer pensamiento «filosófico» fue, así pues, el de un tal Gado de Bástuli que subsumió (con un acto de abstracción desconocido en la civilización mastiena) la Vulva, el Pene, la Boca y el Esfínter bajo un concepto (aunque era justo el concepto de concepto el que hasta entonces había sido ajeno a los mastienos), el concepto de Umbral. En uno de los fragmentos que nos han llegado, Gado afirma:

> Nosotros somos mastienos en cuanto existe el Umbral. Antes de que la comida entre en ese Umbral que es la Boca, todavía no es mastiena. Cuando sale por ese Umbral que es el Esfínter, ya no es mastieno. De igual modo, antes de que un Pene penetre una Vulva no se forma una cosa que luego saldrá como mastieno completo por la Vulva, y solo después de que por la Boca se exhale el Último Aliento, pero no antes, cesa toda actividad de la Boca, del Esfínter, del Pene y de la Vulva. Es en el Umbral donde sucede que antes está lo que los mastienos todavía no son, y después lo que ya no son (TS, 777a).

Sobre estas bases, los Médicos elaboraron una idea de mastieno como «canal entre dos Umbrales». Pero fue justo al diseccionar a las víctimas de los sacrificios, según hubieran comido poco o mucho tiempo antes de su muerte, cuando se dieron cuenta de que, en algunas víctimas, asesinadas inmediatamente después de comer, la comida, como tal, seguía aún en el estómago; y en otras, la materia fecal, aún no expulsada, se manifestaba de forma ebullente en las vísceras. Nació entonces entre los Médicos el discurso de dónde habían de ponerse verdaderamente los Umbrales. No es Umbral la Boca, empezaron a decir, si después de que la comida haya pasado a través de ella, permanece todavía en el estómago, y no es Umbral el Esfínter, si la materia fecal prospera ya en el interior de un mastieno.

Puesto que los Médicos consideraban propio del mastieno su sangre, su linfa, sus humores, que se generan a través de la ingestión de comida, el problema que se plantearon fue: ¿cuándo se da que la comida, que aún no es un mastieno, pasa un Umbral y se convierte en mastieno? ¿Y cuándo se da que los desechos de la comida, aquello que no pude convertirse en ese o aquel mastieno, ya no son ese o aquel mastieno?

Algunos decían que un Umbral se situaba entre el estómago y las vísceras, otros entre el estómago y el corazón. Pero el problema que nos parece importante es otro.

Si los Médicos ponían en tela de juicio que la Boca o el Esfínter fueran Umbrales, desplazando los Umbrales del mastieno hasta su interior, allá donde perdían toda posibilidad de ser percibidos, ponían automáticamente en tela de juicio la preeminencia de la Boca, del Pene, de la Vulva y del Esfínter.

Además, una vez elaborado el Concepto de Umbral, los Médicos se dieron cuenta de que existían otros Umbrales, más allá de los de los mastienos: consideraron Umbrales las Entradas de las cavernas, los Agujeros que se creaban o eran creados en el terreno, el Acceso a ciertos conductos naturales en las vísceras de las montañas y, además, se identificaron nuevos Umbrales de los mastienos, como los pabellones de las orejas o las fosas nasales. Se dieron cuenta de este modo de que, mientras para entender los Umbrales conocidos se inventaba la idea única de Umbral, los Umbrales conocidos se multiplicaban. Remitiéndonos a otras creencias religiosas arcaicas, hoy en día diríamos que los mastienos elaboraban al mismo tiempo una forma de monoteísmo (existe un único hecho relevante, el hecho de hechos, el Umbral) y una forma de politeísmo (hay infinitos Umbrales, y cada uno es un hecho relevante).

La predicación de Gades de Bástuli generó, en efecto, la secta de los Dubitativos, quienes ponían en duda la existencia de hechos privilegiados a través de una serie de Paradojas Dubitativas (þⱦↄ⚫☙).

Paradoja del Sudado. Los Médicos habían descubierto que la comida que pasaba por la Boca salía no solo como materia fecal y orina, sino también como sudor. Si el sudor pasa desde dentro del cuerpo a su exterior, deben existir los Poros. Si los Poros son, son Umbral. Ahora bien, los Poros son imperceptibles y, por tanto, no son materia de experiencia material mientras que los hechos fundamentales, es decir, todos los demás Umbrales, son perceptibles. Dado que ser un hecho es materia de experiencia, los Poros no son hechos. Al no ser hechos, no existen. Así pues, existe un Umbral que es Umbral y aun así no existe. Pero para que un mastieno sea, es preciso que sude. Si no suda, el mastieno exhala el Último Aliento y ya no es un mastieno. Por tanto, para que el mastieno sea, es necesario que existan los Poros, que sin embargo no son.

Paradoja de la Comida. Si tú abres a un mastieno sacrificado, no localizas el Umbral antes y después del cual la comida y las heces son o no son ya tales. Pero antes de que la comida entre en la Boca todavía no es comida, y cuando sale por el Esfínter ya no lo es. Si en el mastieno no es perceptible el Umbral antes del cual algo se convierte en comida y después del cual ya no lo es, entonces no existe la comida. Pero los mastienos son solo en cuanto que ingieren comida. Si no ingieren nada, no son. Por tanto, ni mastienos, ni Vulva, ni Pene, ni Boca, ni Esfínter son.

Paradoja del Velado. Aparece una figura velada (se han encontrado en la Cava Saguntina también figuras femeninas con la cabeza cubierta por una piel disecada): ¿quién está debajo del velo? Según la Paradoja del Sudado, nadie. Pero un velo, o vela algo, o no es velo. Por tanto, el velo no es un velo. Pero hay algo peor: un velo, si vela, es Umbral entre lo que se ve y lo que no se ve. Por tanto, en un mismo momento debe postularse la existencia de otro Umbral, y afirmar que no existe.

Paradoja de la Caverna. Para entrar en la caverna tienes que superar su Umbral. Antes del Umbral de una caverna, tú estás fuera de la caverna, después estás dentro. Así pues, la caverna existe solo porque existe su Umbral. Pero si existiera el Umbral, ¿qué sucedería cuando estás en el Umbral? No estarías ni dentro ni fuera de la caverna. Pero un Umbral es tal solo si divide lo de fuera de lo de dentro. En el momento en que estás en el Umbral, por tanto, no estás ni fuera ni dentro. Pero en el momento en que no hay ni dentro ni fuera, no existe ni siquiera la caverna. Así pues, mientras tú cruzas el Umbral de una caverna, traspasas el Umbral de una caverna que no existe. Pero una caverna que no existe no puede tener ni siquiera un Umbral. Por tanto, cuando traspasas el Umbral, no traspasas nada. *Ergo*, extendiendo el razonamiento a todos los Umbrales, no puede existir Umbral alguno.

Para escapar a estas contradicciones, Eburón de Altacete osó enunciar lo que la religión y la *forma mentis* de los mastienos no podían permitir: afirmó que un Umbral en cuanto Umbral no es necesariamente una realidad material perceptible, sino algo que nosotros «pensamos», en el curso de nuestra experiencia material, cuando vemos bocas, esfínteres, anfractuosidades, agujeros, etcétera. Se ve hasta qué punto esta idea ponía en tela de juicio los principios fundamentales sobre los que se regía la cultura de los mastienos.

Ante todo, se introducía en su cultura el concepto de «pensar». Los Médicos se dieron cuenta de inmediato de que los mastienos pensaban, por ejemplo, cuando se representaban comida que todavía no habían encontrado y que deseaban encontrar. Puesto que, antes de haberla encontrado, la comida no es un hecho, sacaron la conclusión de que «lo que un mastieno piensa no es un hecho». Así pues, si el Umbral es pensado, no es un hecho. Por tanto, ningún Umbral es un hecho. Por consiguiente, no existen Umbrales.

Eburón intentó demostrar entonces que el Umbral no era algo pensado, sino algo «querido»: al querer, por ejemplo, la comida, nosotros la dirigimos hacia la Boca, que solo en ese momento, y con finalidades de alimentación, se convierte en Umbral, y en su querer llevar el Pene a su lugar natural, el varón hace de la Vulva un Umbral. Claro que de este modo se introducía la nueva idea del «querer». Olifante el Imposible intentó explicar que querer es «ir hacia cosas». Aunque, para ir hacia cosas, es necesario que alguna cosa sea un hecho; ahora, si el Umbral se presenta como efecto de un querer, eso significa que antes de quererlo todavía no hay Umbral alguno. Por tanto, querer sería «ir hacia nada». Además, alguien que quiere, antes de querer aún no quería y, en el instante en el que quiere, va ya hacia una cosa.

Así pues, hay un Umbral del querer. Pero ¿para qué sirve inventar este extraño hecho que es el querer, con la finalidad de explicar qué es el Umbral, si luego es al concepto de Umbral al que hay que recurrir para explicar el querer? Tendríamos la Paradoja de un Umbral cuya Tarea es Hacer Nacer Umbrales.

Fue probablemente a causa de estas discusiones por lo que, empezando a dudar del Umbral, los mastienos empezaron a no tomar ya comida con la Boca, a no evacuar, a no penetrar la Vulva con el Pene. A eso se debe su extinción, debida, como han concluido nuestros historiadores, a la invención de la filosofía.

Por suerte, con la extinción de los mastienos, la filosofía dejó de practicarse y se llegó a la actual Economía sobre la que se funda nuestra civilización, cuyo único hecho indiscutible es el Equivalente Universal. En este sentido, vemos con indulgencia y curiosidad la cultura de los antiguos mastienos, pero obviamente nos complacemos por haber elaborado una civilización superior.

Bibliografía

de las partes «Sobre la bibliofilia» e «Historica»

ANDREAE, J. V., *Chymische Hochzeit Christiani Rosenkreutz*, Estrasburgo, Zetzner, 1616.

—, *Mythologiae christianae, sive virtutum et vitiorum vitae humanae, imaginum libri III*, Estrasburgo, Zetzner, 1619.

ARNDT, J., *Iudicium Philosophi Anonimi Ueber die 4 Figuren dess grossen Amphitheatri D. Heinrici Khunradi* (en apéndice a Khunrath, *De igne magorum et philosophorum*).

ARNOLD, P., *Histoire des Rose-Croix et les origines de la Franc-Maçonnerie*, París, Mercure, 1955. [Hay trad. cast.: *Historia de los rosacruces y los orígenes de la francmasonería*, México, Diana, 1997.]

Bibliotheca Magica. Dalle opere a stampa della Biblioteca Casanatense, Florencia, Olschki, 1985.

Bibliotheca Philosophica, *Johann Valentin Andreae 1586-1986: Die Manifeste der Rosenkreuzerbruderschaft*, Amsterdam, Bibliotheca Philosophica Hermetica, 1986.

BRUNET, J. C., *Manuel du libraire et de l'amateur de livres*, 2.ª ed., París, Maisonneuve, 1809.

CAILLET, A. L., *Manuel bibliographique des Sciences Psychiques ou Occultes*, París, Dorbon, 1912.

Carbonarius (?), *Beytrag zur Geschichte de Höhern Chemie*, Leipzig, Hilscher, 1785.

DE BURE, G. F., *Bibliographie instructive*, París, G. F. De Bure, 1763.

Dorbon, *Bibliotheca Esoterica*, París, Dorbon-Ainé, s.f.

DUVEEN, D., *Bibliotheca Alchemica et Chemica*, 2.ª ed., Londres, Dawson, 1965.

—, «Notes on some alchemical books», *The Library*, Fifth Series, 1, 1946, p. 56.

EDIGHOFFER, R., *Rose-Croix et société idéale selon Johann Valentin Andreae*, 2 vols., Neuilly-sur-Seine, Arma Artis, 1982.

EVANS, R. J. W., *Rudolf II And His World. A Study in Intellectual History (1576-1612)*, Oxford, Clarendon, 1973.

Fama. Confessio, Kassel, Wessel, 1615.

FERGUSON, J., *Bibliotheca Chemica*, Glasgow, Maclehose, 1906.

FICTULD, H., *Probier-Stein*, Frankfurt, Leipzig, Bey Veraci Orientali Wahrheit und Ernst Lugenfeind, 1753.

FRENCH, P. J., *John Dee. The World of an Elizabethan Magus*, Londres, Routledge, 1972.

Gilhofer, *Alchemie und Chemie*, catálogo 133, Viena, Gilhofer, 1984.

GORCEIX, B., *La Bible des Rose-Croix*, París, PUF, 1970.

GRAESSE, J. G. T., *Trésor de livres rares et précieux*, Dresde, Kuntze, 1859.

Guaita, *Stanislas De Guaita et sa bibliothèque occulte*, París, Dorbon, 1899.

HALL, M., *Alchemy. A comprehensive Bibliography of the M.P. Hall Collection*, ed. de R. C. Hogart, Los Ángeles, Philosophical Research Society, 1986.

JOUIN, E., y DESCREUX, V. *Bibliographie Occultiste et Maçonnique*, París, Revue Internationale des Sociétés Secrètes, Émile-Paul Frères, 1930.

JUNG, C. G., *Mysterium Conjunctionis*, Zurich, Rascher, 1955. [Hay trad. cast.: *Mysterium Conjunctionis*, Madrid, Trotta, 2002.]

—, *Psychologie und Alchimie*, Zurich, Rascher, 1944. [Hay trad. cast.: *Psicología y alquimia*, Barcelona, Plaza y Janés, 1977.]

KHUNRATH, H., *De igne magorum philosophorumque*, Estrasburgo, Zetzner, 1608.

—, *Von hylealischen... Chaos*, Magdeburgo, Erben, 1597.

LENGLET DU FRESNOY, N., *Histoire de la philosophie hermétique*, París, Coustelier, 1742.

LENNEP, J. van, *Alchimie*, Bruselas, Crédit Communal de Belgique, 1985.

MELLON, *Alchemy and the Occult. A Catalogue of Books and Manuscripts from the Collection of Paul and Mary Mellon. Given to Yale University Library, Compiled by I. Macphail (et al.)*, New Haven, Yale U. P., 1968.

MONTGOMERY, J. W., *Cross and the Crucible. Johann Valentin Andreae*, La Haya, Nijhoff, 1973.

Rosenthal, *Bibliotheca Magica et Pneumatica*, catálogos 31-35, Munich, Rosenthal, sf.

SCHOLEM, G., *Bibliographia Kabbalistica*, Leipzig, Drugulin, 1927.

SECRET, F., *Les kabbalistes chrétiens de la Rénaissance*, París, Dunod, 1964 (2.ª ed. Milán, Arché, 1985).

SOLDNER, J. A., *Fegfeuer der Chymisten*, Amsterdam (o Hamburgo), 1702.

THORNDIKE, L., *A History of Magic and Experimental Science*, Nueva York, Columbia U. P., 1923.

VERGINELLI-VINCI, *Bibliotheca Hermetica. Catalogo alquanto ragionato della raccolta Verginelli-Rota di antichi testi ermetici (secoli XV-XVIII)*, Florencia, Nardini, 1986.

WAITE, A. E., *The Brotherhood of the Rosy-Cross*, Londres, Rider, 1924.

WEHR, G., *Rosenkreuzerische Manifeste*, Schaffausen, Novalis ed., 1980.

YATES, F., *The Rosicrucian Enlightment*, Londres, Routledge, 1972. [Hay trad. cast.: *El iluminismo rosacruz*, Madrid, Fondo de Cultura Económica de España, 1999.]

Algunos títulos imprescindibles
de Lumen de los últimos años

Flush | Virginia Woolf
Las inseparables | Simone de Beauvoir
Qué fue de los Mulvaney | Joyce Carol Oates
Léxico familiar | Natalia Ginzburg
¿Quién te crees que eres? | Alice Munro
Éramos unos niños | Patti Smith
Bitna bajo el cielo de Seúl | Jean-Marie Gustave Le Clézio
Un lugar llamado Antaño | Olga Tokarczuk
La chica | Edna O'Brien
La tierra baldía (y Prufrok y otras observaciones) | T. S. Eliot
Número cero | Umberto Eco
Poema a la duración | Peter Handke
Esa puta tan distinguida | Juan Marsé
El cuaderno dorado | Doris Lessing
La vida entera | David Grossman
Todo queda en casa | Alice Munro
La fuente de la autoestima | Toni Morrison
Rabos de lagartija | Juan Marsé
La amiga estupenda | Elena Ferrante
M Train | Patti Smith
La Semilla de la Bruja | Margaret Atwood
Gatos ilustres | Doris Lessing
La Vida Nueva | Raúl Zurita
Gran cabaret | David Grossman
El tango | Jorge Luis Borges

El año del Mono | Patti Smith
Un cuarto propio | Virginia Woolf
Eichmann en Jerusalén | Hannah Arendt
A propósito de las mujeres | Natalia Ginzburg
Las personas del verbo | Jaime Gil de Biedma
Nada se acaba | Margaret Atwood
Cuatro cuartetos | T. S. Eliot
La vida mentirosa de los adultos | Elena Ferrante
Un árbol crece en Brooklyn | Betty Smith
El mar, el mar | Iris Murdoch
Memorias de una joven católica | Mary McCarthy
El nombre de la rosa | Umberto Eco
El cuarto de las mujeres | Marilyn French
Colgando de un hilo | Dorothy Parker
Cuentos completos | Jorge Luis Borges
El chal | Cynthia Ozick
Objeto de amor | Edna O'Brien
La historia | Elsa Morante
Poesía completa | Jorge Luis Borges
Cuentos reunidos | Cynthia Ozick
La belleza del marido | Anne Carson
El pie de la letra | Jaime Gil de Biedma
Cuentos completos | Flannery O'Connor
Últimas tardes con Teresa | Juan Marsé
Paisaje con grano de arena | Wisława Szymborska
Cuentos | Ernest Hemingway
Las olas | Virginia Woolf
Si te dicen que caí | Juan Marsé
Antología poética | William Butler Yeats
Demasiada felicidad | Alice Munro
Narrativa completa | Dorothy Parker
El príncipe negro | Iris Murdoch

Este libro
acabó de imprimirse
en Barcelona
en abril de 2021